HMH SCIENCE DIMENSIONS™

Chemistry

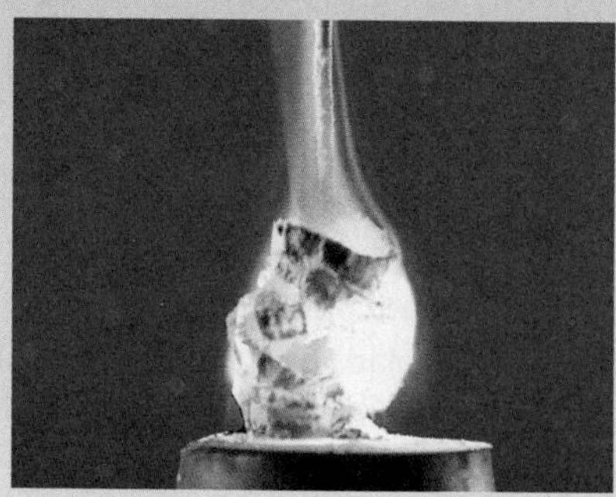

Chemistry is the study of matter and how it transforms. During chemical reactions such as the burning of magnesium, matter is transformed, releasing energy. Some reactions release so much energy that they can be used to cause changes in other matter.

Please don't write in this textbook!

The writing prompts provided throughout this textbook are designed to be answered in your Evidence Notebook. Please keep this textbook clean for all future users.

Houghton Mifflin Harcourt.
The Learning Company™

ENGINEERING CONSULTANT

Cary I. Sneider, PhD
Associate Research Professor
Portland State University
Portland, Oregon

LAB SAFETY REVIEWER

Kenneth R. Roy, PhD
Senior Lab Safety Compliance Consultant
National Safety Consultants, LLC
Vernon, Connecticut

PROGRAM ADVISORS

Doris Ingram Lewis, PhD
Professor Emerita of Chemistry
Suffolk University
Boston, Massachusetts

Reza M. Mohseni, PhD
Professor of Chemistry/
Lab Director
East Tennessee State University
Johnson City, Tennessee

Gary E. Mueller, PhD, PE
Associate Professor
Missouri University of Science
& Technology
Rolla, Missouri

CLASSROOM REVIEWERS

Max M. Bradbury
Independence High School
Independence, Kansas

Keri Breeding
Southeast of Saline High School
USD 306
Gypsum, Kansas

Steve Harrison
STEM Director
Appleton Area School District
Appleton, Wisconsin

Jennifer A. Karlen
Madison West High School
Madison, Wisconsin

Anne Markos
Holmen High School
Holmen, Wisconsin

Bhavna Rawal
Harmony School of
Excellence and Houston
Community College
Houston, Texas

Jackie Stewart
Quincy Senior High School
Quincy, Illinois

Michelle Tjugum
Madison East High School
Madison, Wisconsin

Cover Photo Credits
Cover Images: ©HMH

Interior Master Art: *connected dot pattern* ©chuckchee/Shutterstock

Printed in the U.S.A.

ISBN 978-0-358-04719-3

5 6 7 8 9 10 0690 27 26 25 24 23 22 21 20 4500803640

Michael DiSpezio

Global Educator
North Falmouth, Massachusetts

Michael DiSpezio has authored many HMH instructional programs for Science and Mathematics. He has also authored numerous trade books and multimedia programs on various topics and hosted dozens of studio and location broadcasts for various organizations in the U.S. and worldwide. Most recently, he has been working with educators to provide strategies for implementing the Next Generation Science Standards, particularly the Science and Engineering Practices, Crosscutting Concepts, and the use of Evidence Notebooks. To all his projects, he brings his extensive background in science; his expertise in classroom teaching at the elementary, middle, and high school levels; and his deep experience in producing interactive and engaging instructional materials.

Thomas O'Brien, PhD

Professor, Science Teacher Education & Educational Leadership
Department of Teaching, Learning & Educational Leadership
College of Community & Public Affairs
Binghamton University (State University of New York)
Binghamton, New York

Tom O'Brien has directed the graduate-level science teacher education programs at Binghamton since 1987. His scholarly interests include professional leadership development (e.g., co-principal investigator for NYS and national grants); science curriculum development, as related to science-technology-society themes and 5E Teaching Cycles; and K–12 science teacher education as informed by cognitive learning theory. He is the author of *Brain-Powered Science Teaching & Learning with Discrepant Events* and co-author/co-editor of *Science for the Next Generation: Preparing for the New Standards*.

Bernadine Okoro

STEM Learning Advocate and Consultant
Washington, DC

Bernadine Okoro is a chemical engineer by training and a playwright, novelist, director, and actress by nature. She went from interacting with patents and biotechnology to the K–12 classroom. A 12-year science educator and Albert Einstein Distinguished Fellow, Okoro was one of the original authors of the Next Generation Science Standards. As a member of the Diversity and Equity Team, her focus on Alternative Education, Community Schools, and now Integrating Social-Emotional Learning and Brain-Based Learning into NGSS is a pathway to support underserved groups from elementary school to adult education. An article and book reviewer for NSTA and other educational publishing companies, Okoro currently works as a STEM Learning Advocate & Consultant.

When welding with thermite, workers must wear heat-resistant protective clothing and special eye equipment.

UNIT 1

Introduction to Chemistry and Engineering 1

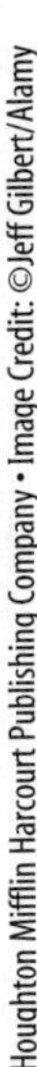

UNIT 2

Atoms and Elements 53

When some stars die, they explode as supernovas that send atoms of different elements off into space.

Various colors swirl together when you start mixing paint. Once it is all mixed up, the paint has a color unlike any of the original colors.

UNIT 3

Compounds and Mixtures 141

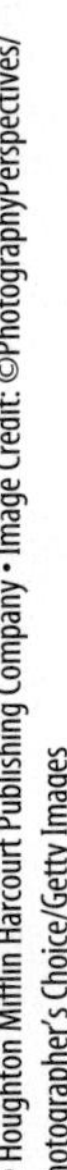

UNIT 4

Chemical Reactions 227

The reaction of copper and nitric acid produces nitric oxide gas and a solution of copper nitrate.

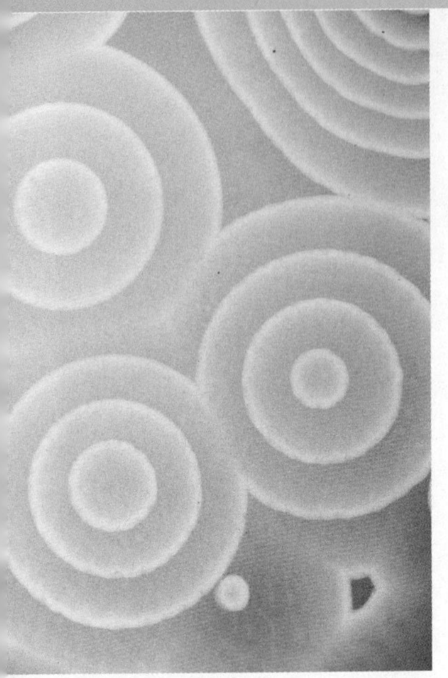

The colors of this oscillating reaction change as the amounts of products and reactants vary back and forth over time.

UNIT 5

Reaction Rates and Equilibrium 307

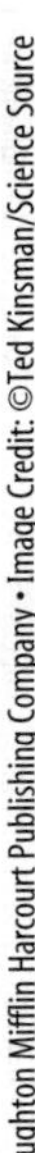

Claims, Evidence, and Reasoning

You likely use claims, evidence, and reasoning in your daily life—perhaps without even being aware of it. Suppose you leave a notebook behind in the cafeteria. When you return later, you see a number of similar notebooks on the counter. You say, "I left my notebook here earlier," and pick up one of them.

The cafeteria worker says, "Are you sure that one is yours? They all look pretty much alike."

You say, "Yes, my initials are right here on the cover." To confirm the fact, you open the notebook to show your full name inside. You also present your student ID to prove that it's your name.

This encounter is a claims-evidence-reasoning interaction. You claimed the notebook was yours, and you showed evidence to prove your point.

CLAIM

A *claim* is your position on an issue or problem. It answers the question, "What do you know?"

EVIDENCE

Evidence is any data related to your claim that answer the question, "How do you know that?" These data may be from your own experiments and observations, reports by scientists or engineers, or other reliable sources. Scientific knowledge is based on *empirical evidence*, or evidence that is derived from observation or experiment. As you read about science, perform lab activities, engage in class discussions, and write explanations, you will need to cite evidence to support your claims.

REASONING

Reasoning is the use of logical, analytical thought to form conclusions or inferences. It answers the question, "Why does your evidence support your claim?" Reasoning may involve citing a scientific law or principle that helps explain the relationship between the evidence and the claim.

Scientists use claims, evidence, and reasoning—or *argumentation*—for many purposes: to explain, to persuade, to convince, to predict, to demonstrate, and to prove things. When scientists publish the results of their investigations, they must be prepared to defend their conclusions if they are challenged by other scientists.

Here is an example of a claims-evidence-reasoning argument.

CLAIM: Ice melts faster in the sun than it does in the shade.

EVIDENCE: We placed two ice cubes of the same size in identical plastic dishes. We placed one dish on a wooden bench in the sun and placed the other on a different part of the same bench in the shade. The ice cube in the sun melted in 14 minutes and 32 seconds. The ice cube in the shade melted in 18 minutes and 15 seconds.

REASONING: We designed the investigation so that the only variable in the setup was whether the ice cubes were in the shade or in the sun. Because the ice cube in the sun melted almost 4 minutes faster, this is sufficient evidence to support the claim that ice melts faster in the sun than it does in the shade.

Construct your own argument below by recording a claim, evidence, and reasoning. With your teacher's permission, you can do an investigation to answer a question you have about how the world works, or you can construct your argument based on observations you have already made about the world.

CLAIM	
EVIDENCE	
REASONING	

For more information on claims, evidence, and reasoning, see the online **English Language Arts Handbook**.

Using Your Evidence Notebook

Throughout the units and lessons of ***HMH Science Dimensions Chemistry***, you will see notebook icons that highlight important places for you to stop and reflect. These Evidence Notebook prompts signal opportunities for you to record observations and evidence, analyze data, and make explanations for phenomena.

The Evidence Notebook is your location to gather evidence and record your thinking as you make your way through each lesson. Your teacher may determine a specific format for you to use, such as a digital or paper notebook. Whatever the format, you will record here the evidence you gather throughout the lesson to support your response to the Can You Explain the Phenomenon?/Can You Solve the Problem? challenge. You will also record significant information from the lesson to use as a study tool and to build your own study guide at the end of the lesson.

The following pages from the first lesson in the book will familiarize you with the main types of Evidence Notebook prompts you will see throughout the course.

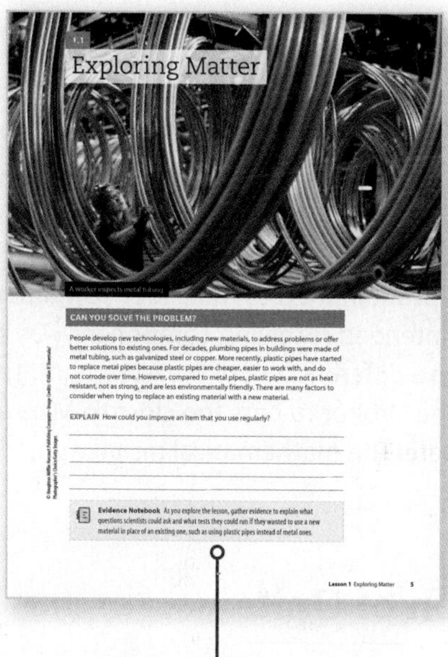

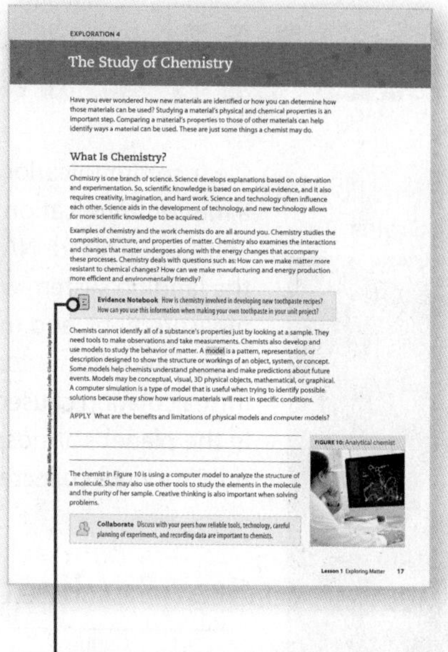

Provides general direction about the evidence to collect related to this phenomenon as you explore the lesson.

Provides a point-of-use opportunity to address the unit project or lesson phenomena.

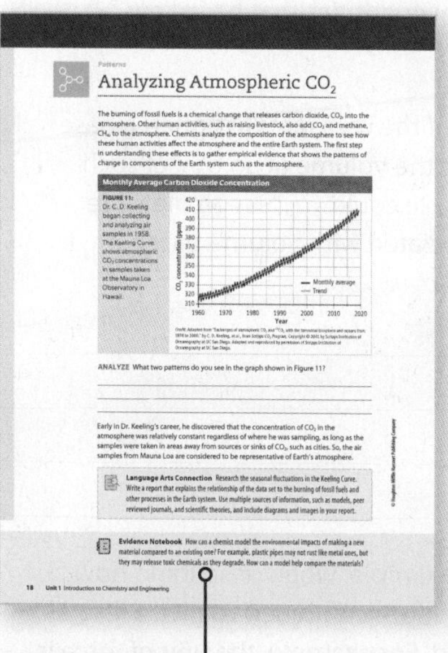

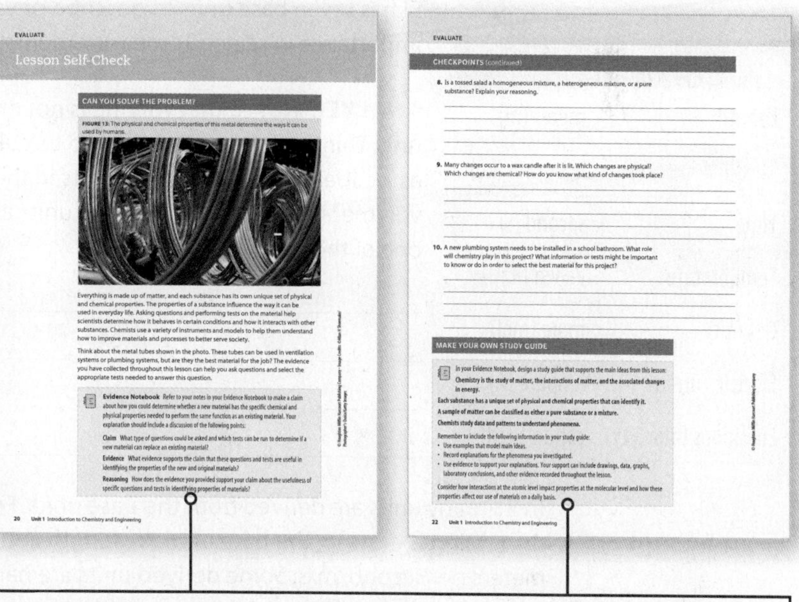

Prompts you to synthesize information from evidence, analysis, models, and other information gathered over the course of an Exploration.

At the end of each lesson, you will also be prompted to use the notes from your Evidence Notebook to construct an explanation and to make your own study guide for the main ideas from the lesson.

Working with Measurement

FIGURE 1: An artist's rendition of the Mars Climate Orbiter

Clear communication is important for scientific investigation. In 1999, a miscommunication about units of measurement had devastating consequences for NASA's Mars Climate Orbiter, shown in Figure 1. Part of the landing system was programmed to transmit information in one unit of measurement, and the intended receiving component was programmed to receive information in a different unit of measurement. The resulting miscalculation caused the Orbiter to pass too close to Mars and to disintegrate in the planet's atmosphere. The mathematical mistake cost $125 million, and no data were collected.

Standardization of Units

In 1960, scientists established a standard set of units based on the metric system called the *Système International d'Unités* (French for the International System of Units), or SI.

Derived Units and Other Accepted Units

SI has seven base units to describe physical quantities that have key importance in scientific measurements.

Measure	Base unit
Length	meter (m)
Mass	kilogram (kg)
Time	second (s)
Temperature	kelvin (K)
Quantity	mole (mol)
Electric Current	ampere (A)
Luminous Intensity	candela (cd)

ANALYZE Notice that volume is not one of the measures assigned a base unit. Think about how you would calculate the volume of an object such as a cube. Which of the base units in the table could you use to measure volume? Give an example of the units associated with volume based on one of the base units in SI.

In SI, many units are derived from the base units. For example, when describing how fast something is moving, the base units for length and time are combined to give a rate of meters per second, m/s. Some derived units are named. For example, the unit of force is called the newton (N), which is equal to 1 $kg{\cdot}m/s^2$.

Liquid volume is commonly measured in liters (L). Though not officially an SI unit, the liter is an accepted unit of measure in SI. Similarly, degree Celsius is an accepted unit to use when measuring temperature. Figure 2 shows the relationship between Kelvin, Celsius, and Fahrenheit temperature scales.

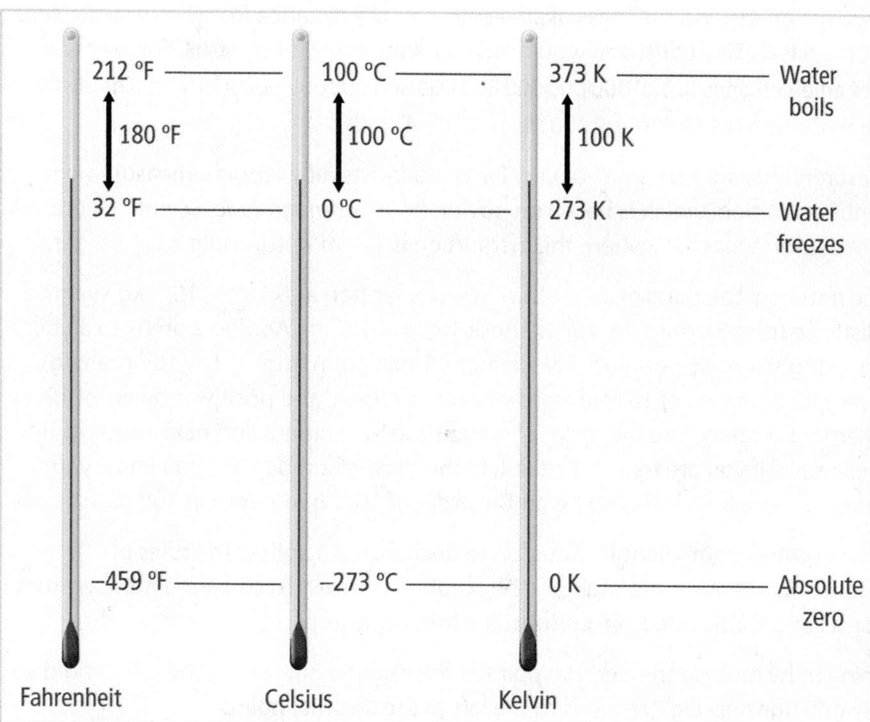

FIGURE 2: A diagram showing the relationships between the Kelvin, Celsius, and Fahrenheit temperature scales, with respect to three key temperatures. Any temperature in one of the scales can be converted to a temperature in the other scales. Though Fahrenheit is common in some parts of the world, it is not an accepted unit for scientific measurement.

Unit Prefixes

The diameter of a single atom ranges from about 0.1 to 0.3 nanometers (nm). If you measure something with a meterstick, you may report its length in centimeters (cm). The distance between two cities may be measured in kilometers (km). By appending a prefix such as kilo- or centi- onto a base unit, it is easier to report measurements for large or small quantities. SI has 20 accepted prefixes that change the magnitude of a unit by a power of 10. For example, 1 kilometer is equal to 1000 meters, and 1 millisecond is equal to 0.001 second.

Factor	Prefix (symbol)
10^{-24}	yocto (y)
10^{-21}	zepto (z)
10^{-18}	atto (a)
10^{-15}	femto (f)
10^{-12}	pico (p)
10^{-9}	nano (n)
10^{-6}	micro (μ)
10^{-3}	milli (m)
10^{-2}	centi (c)
10^{-1}	deci (d)

Factor	Prefix (symbol)
10^{1}	deka (da)
10^{2}	hecto (h)
10^{3}	kilo (k)
10^{6}	mega (M)
10^{9}	giga (G)
10^{12}	tera (T)
10^{15}	peta (P)
10^{18}	exa (E)
10^{21}	zetta (Z)
10^{24}	yotta (Y)

To convert from the original unit to the modified unit, multiply or divide by the appropriate power of 10 or simply move the decimal the corresponding number of places. For example, to convert from grams to kilograms, divide the number of grams by 1000 or move the decimal three places to the left. Fill in places with zeros if needed. Only one prefix at a time may be appended to a unit.

SOLVE Write the correct quantity for each conversion.

1. 38 000 kg = ________________ g

2. 6.5 m = ________________ mm

3. 4.3 ms = ________________ s

4. 0.02 km = ________________ cm

Magnitude and Scientific Notation

Imagine you are measuring the mass of an electron or the distance from Earth to the sun. Without some handy shortcuts, you would have to write out a lot of zeros. For example, the mass of an electron is 0. 000 000 000 000 000 000 000 000 000 000 910 9 kg. The distance from Earth to the sun is 149 600 000 000 m.

When measurements are very small or very large, scientists may report a measurement using scientific notation, which is based on powers of 10, or *magnitude*. Scientific notation is written in the form $m \times 10^n$, where the magnitude is $1 \leq m < 10$, and n is an integer.

In scientific notation, the mass of an electron may be written as 9.109×10^{-31} kg, and the average distance from Earth to the sun is about 1.496×10^{11} m. Adding a prefix to a unit is similar to using scientific notation. For example, 1 milligram (mg) $= 1 \times 10^{-3}$ gram (g). Note that negative powers of 10 represent smaller numbers, and positive powers of 10 represent larger numbers. Use the order of magnitude to estimate and help check your work. For example, if you are trying to calculate the mass of a molecule, you know your answer should be small, so it should be on the order of 10^{-23} g rather than 10^{23} g.

To convert a number from scientific notation to decimal form, follow the rules of multiplication and exponents to multiply the number as usual. To convert a number from decimal form to scientific notation, perform the following steps:

1. Determine m by moving the decimal point in the original number to the left or right so that only one nonzero digit remains to the left of the decimal point.
2. Determine n by counting the number of places you moved the decimal point in the first step. If you moved the decimal point to the right, n is negative. If you moved the decimal to the left, n is positive.

EVALUATE Use your knowledge of multiplication and exponents to rewrite the following numbers in either decimal notation or scientific notation.

Decimal notation	Scientific notation
5280	5.28×10^3
4 967 000 000 000 000	__________
__________	5.12×10^{12}
0. 000 000 000 000 159	__________
__________	9.109×10^{-31}

When it comes to very small or very large numbers, scientific notation reduces errors due to miscounting the number of digits. Numbers written in scientific notation all require approximately the same amount of space regardless of magnitude, making it easier to compare the magnitude of values by looking at the power of 10 in the number. For example, consider the distances 1.5×10^6 m, 3.4×10^6 m, and 9.5×10^{-3} m. The first two distances have the same magnitude, 10^6, and are much larger than the magnitude of the third distance, 10^{-3}. If you add these three distances, the third distance will have little effect on the final sum, even though the leading coefficient 9.5 is larger than the other two coefficients.

SOLVE A measurement may be reported in many different ways. The diameter of Earth is approximately 12 700 km. Match the quantities shown with the appropriate units to show other ways that Earth's diameter may be written.

1.27×10^4	1.27×10^7	1.27×10^{10}	12.7

________ Mm	________ km	________ m	________ mm

Many calculators and software programs can display results in scientific notation. The letter *E* is used in place of the multiplication. For example, the number 1.689×10^{-15} may be displayed as 1.689E–15 or 1.689e–15. Refer to a calculator's manual to see how to enter numbers in scientific notation and how to configure the calculator to display numbers in scientific notation.

Accuracy and Precision

The tools that scientists use to measure affect how accurately and precisely the measurement can be made. The terms *accuracy* and *precision* are often used interchangeably in everyday conversation. In science, however, these terms have different meanings. *Accuracy* is the closeness of a measurement to the correct or accepted value of the quantity measured. *Precision* is the closeness of a set of measurements of the same quantity made in the same way. Precision may also refer to the number of gradations on a measurement device.

If a balance displayed values that were two grams more than the true mass every time you used it, the balance would be precise but not accurate. Its readings are wrong, but they are consistent. Imagine you have two digital scales and a known 2 kg mass. You use the 2 kg mass to determine how accurate and precise the two scales are. You place the 2 kg mass on each scale 4 different times and record the values shown in the table.

Scale A measurements	Scale B measurements
1999 g	2005 g
2005 g	2004 g
2008 g	2005 g
1994 g	2005 g

In this example, the accuracy of each measurement on scale A varies widely, though, if averaged, the average value is close to the accepted value. The measurements are also not very precise. Scale B gives more precise measurements, but it is still inaccurate. The ideal measuring tool would be both precise and accurate.

ANALYZE Below each image, state whether the points on the target are *accurate* or *not accurate,* and whether they are *precise* or *not precise.*

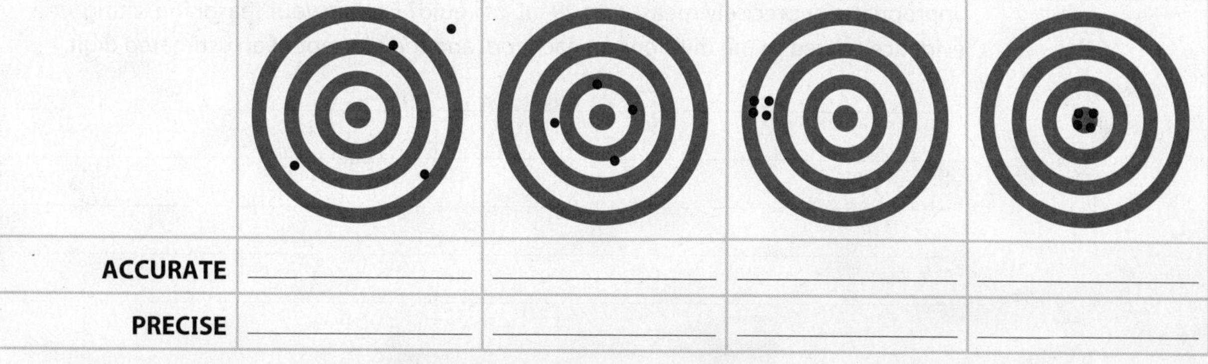

ACCURATE	________	________	________	________
PRECISE	________	________	________	________

Describing Accuracy

Consider the following two measurements: the amount of water in a swimming pool and the amount of medicine being administered to a patient. The swimming pool has a volume of 3.75×10^8 mL, and the medicine has a volume of 5.00 mL. Both measurements are 1 mL more than the true volume.

ARGUE All measurements have some error. How do you determine the acceptable level of accuracy for a measurement? Use the measurements of the swimming pool volume and medicine volume to support your claim.

Measuring Precisely

Different pieces of equipment allow for measurements with different levels of precision. Digital measuring devices may specify precision by the smallest digit presented. In the scale example earlier, the scales may be said to have a precision of 1 g, because that is the smallest increment the scales can report (though, as the example shows, that is not their true precision).

FIGURE 3: Left to right, the name and smallest increment marked on each piece of equipment: graduated cylinder (2 mL), Erlenmeyer flask (25 mL), beaker (10 mL).

For analog devices, the precision is related to how many measuring increments or graduations the device has. For example, a graduated cylinder with 0.1 mL increments allows for more-precise measurements than a graduated cylinder with 1 mL increments. The smallest division on the equipment indicates how precisely you can make a measurement using the equipment.

It is appropriate to estimate a value that is 1/10 the size of the smallest division on a measurement tool. If using equipment that clearly indicates the tenths place, you could record a value with an estimated digit in the hundredths place. For example, if a volume appeared to be between 36.2 and 36.3 mL on a graduated cylinder with 0.1 mL increments, the volume could be recorded as 36.25 mL. The 5 in the hundredths place is the estimated digit.

EXPLAIN Which of the pieces of equipment shown in Figure 3 would be the most appropriate for precisely measuring 29 mL of liquid? Explain your reasoning, citing evidence related to the divisions on each tool and the concept of an estimated digit.

Significant Figures

When manipulating and reporting measurements, it is important to know the precision with which the measurements were made. For example, you use a scale with a precision of 0.1 kg to measure the mass of an object three times. The results are 8.5 kg, 8.6 kg, and 8.5 kg. You average the three measurements and get 8.533 333 33 kg on the calculator. If you report the mass as 8.533 333 33 kg this indicates that you measured the mass much more precisely than you really did.

One way to maintain the precision of a measurement is to use significant figures. The *significant figures* in a measurement are all of the digits known with certainty, plus the first uncertain or estimated digit. Recall that the 5 in the hundredths place of the graduated cylinder measurement of 36.25 mL was an estimated digit. The measurement of 36.25 mL has 4 significant figures. The table below shows the rules for identifying significant figures in a measurement. Writing a number in scientific notation can help you see which digits are significant.

Digit	Rule	Examples
1, 2, 3, 4, 5, 6, 7, 8, or 9	Significant	275 m: three significant figures 42.35 mL: four significant figures
0 between nonzero digits (captive zeros)	Significant	40.7 °C: three significant figures 87 009 g: five significant figures
0 before nonzero digits (leading zeros)	Not significant	0.095 807 cm: five significant figures
0 at the end of a number without decimal point (trailing zeros)	Not significant	2000 kg: 1 significant figure, unless otherwise specified
0 at the end of a number with a decimal point (trailing zeros)	Significant	2000. s: four significant figures 25.00 mA: four significant figures

When a calculation is completed, you will often need to round the value to the correct number of significant figures for the problem. If the digit after the place you are rounding to is a 5 or higher, you round up. For example, 27.15 cm rounds to 27.2 cm. But 27.14 cm rounds to 27.1 cm.

SOLVE A calculator displays the number 50 238.450 124. Round this number as described for each row of the table.

Round to . . .	Rounded value
thousandths place	
tenths place	
3 significant figures	
1 significant figure, in scientific notation	
4 significant figures, in scientific notation	

Mathematical Operations and Significant Figures

Calculators do not account for significant figures, so you must properly manage the precision of reported results. The following sections describe some standard rules that should be used when calculating with measured values to ensure that significant figures are manipulated in a uniform way. If performing a multistep problem, keep track of which figures are significant as you work, but do not round until your final answer. Check with your teacher in case they have any different rules for operations with measurements.

Adding and Subtracting Significant Figures

When adding or subtracting measured values, the resulting number can have no more precision than any of the numbers used in the calculation. Perform the addition or subtraction and then round the result to the appropriate decimal place.

ANALYZE In the right column identify the decimal place, such as *tenths place*, with the most precision for each measurement and the precision of the resulting sum.

	Measured/Calculated value	Most-precise place
Length one	25.1 cm	______
Length two	2.05 cm	______
Sum	27.2 cm	______

Multiplying and Dividing Significant Figures

When multiplying or dividing measured values, the resulting number can have no more significant figures than any of the factors, divisors, or dividends. Perform the multiplication or division, and then round.

ANALYZE In the right column, write the number of significant figures for each measurement and the resulting quotient.

	Measured/Calculated value	Significant figures
Mass	3.05 g	______
Volume	8.470 mL	______
Density = mass / volume	0.360 g/mL	______

Conversion Factors and Counting Numbers

Some quantities—counted numbers, defined values and conversion factors—are considered exact numbers. These quantities have no uncertainty and therefore have infinite significant figures. These quantities do not affect the uncertainty of a calculation. For example, there are exactly 100 cm in 1 m. A measure of 460.8 cm will convert to 4.608 m. Both the original measurement and the converted measurement have 4 significant figures.

Combined Operations

When performing a multistep problem, identify the measurement with the least significant figures before you begin your calculations. The order of operations matters. If the measurement 25.1 m is subtracted from 26.1 m, the result of 1.0 m has 2 significant figures. If this result is then divided by 0.512 s, the result of 1.953125 m/s would need to be rounded to 2 significant figures, 2.0 m/s, even though the original measurements had 3 significant figures.

SOLVE To calculate the rate at which an object moves you subtract Position A, 5.20 m, from Position B, 102.10 m, and then divide by the time it took to move between positions, 4.81 s. Using the rules presented here, what should the final answer be?

○ **a.** 20 m/s ○ **b.** 20. m/s ○ **c.** 20.1 m/s ○ **d.** 20.15 m/s

Dimensional Analysis

It is common to convert units within SI or from non-SI units to SI units. Dimensional analysis is a method that helps you apply conversion factors to convert between units. *Conversion factors* are ratios relating the value of one unit of measure to another. In dimensional analysis, the conversion factors are applied such that when you multiply, all of the units except for the desired units cancel out. For example, a length of 1 foot is equivalent to 0.3048 meters.

$$1 \text{ ft} = 0.3048 \text{ m}$$

This conversion factor may be written as:

$$\frac{1 \text{ ft}}{0.3048 \text{ m}} \text{ or } \frac{0.3048 \text{ m}}{1 \text{ ft}}$$

depending on whether you want to convert from feet to meters or meters to feet. To convert a measurement of 3.1 feet to meters, you would do the following:

$$3.1 \cancel{\text{ft}} \times \left(\frac{0.3048 \text{ m}}{1 \cancel{\text{ft}}}\right) = 0.94 \text{ m}$$

Notice that the final quantity has 2 significant figures because the original measurement had 2 significant figures; significant figure rules apply during dimensional analysis.

Dimensional analysis may involve multiple conversion factors, so special care must be taken to ensure the conversion factors are placed appropriately. This may be more challenging if you are converting a ratio such as speed.

SOLVE Use the following equivalent values to convert the measurement 55 mi/h into m/s. Make sure to write each conversion factor such that units will cancel when you multiply, leaving only the desired units.

1 mi = 5280 ft 1 ft = 0.3048 m 1 h = 3600 s

____________________ m/s

Lab Safety

Before you work in the laboratory, read these safety rules. Ask your teacher to explain any rules that you do not completely understand. Refer to these rules later on if you have questions about safety in the science classroom.

Personal Protective Equipment (PPE)

- PPE includes eye protection, nitrile or nonlatex gloves, and nonlatex aprons. In all labs involving chemicals, indirectly vented chemical splash goggles are required.
- Wear the required PPE during the setup, hands-on, and takedown segments of the activity.

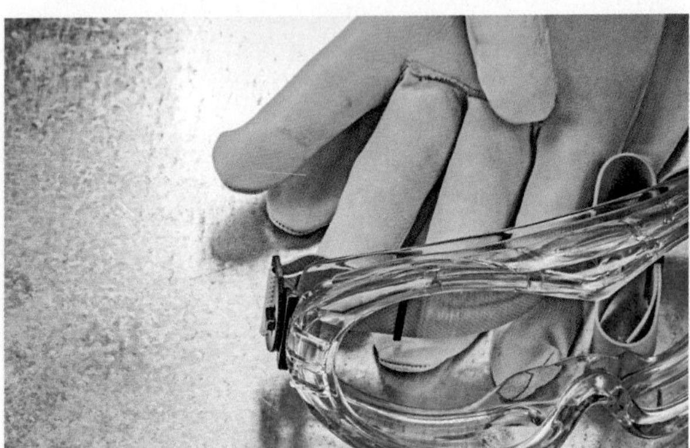

Dress Code

- Secure any article of clothing—such as a loose sweater or a scarf—that hangs down and may touch a flame, chemical, or piece of equipment.
- Wear closed-toe shoes.
- Tie back long hair or hair that hangs in front of your eyes.
- Acrylic fingernails are very flammable and should not be worn when using a flame.

Directions

- Observe all safety icons.
- Know where the fire extinguisher, fire blanket, shower, and eyewash station are located in your classroom or lab, and know how to use them in an emergency.
- Read all directions, and make sure that you understand them before starting the activity.
- Do not begin any investigation or touch any equipment until your teacher has told you to start.
- Never experiment on your own. If you want to try a procedure that the directions do not call for, ask your teacher for permission first.
- If you are hurt or injured in any way, tell your teacher immediately.

Chemical Safety

- If you get a chemical in your eye, use the eyewash station immediately. Flush the eye a minimum of 15 minutes.
- If you get a hazardous chemical on your skin or clothes, use the emergency shower for a minimum of 15 minutes.
- Never touch, taste, or sniff any chemicals in the lab. If you need to determine odor, waft. To waft, hold the chemical in its container 15 cm away from your nose, and use your fingers to bring fumes from the container to your nose.
- Take only the amount of chemical you need for the investigation. If you get too much, ask your teacher how to dispose of the excess. Do not return unused chemicals to the storage container; this can cause contamination.
- When diluting acid with water, always add acid to water. Never add water to an acid.

Heating and Fire Safety

- Keep your work area neat, clean, and free of materials.
- Never reach over a flame or heat source.
- Never heat a substance or an object in a closed container.

- Use oven mitts, clamps, tongs, or a test tube holder to hold heated items.
- Do not throw hot substances into the trash. Wait for them to cool, and dispose of them in the container provided by your teacher.

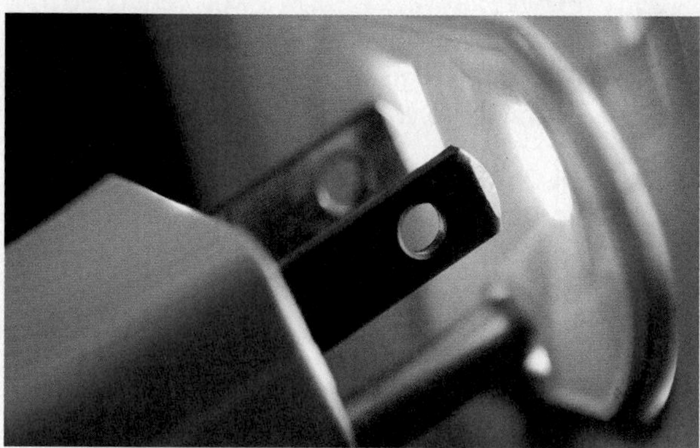

Electrical Safety

- Never use lamps or other electrical equipment with frayed cords or plugs with a missing ground prong.
- Make sure no cord is lying on the floor where someone can trip over it.
- Do not let a cord hang over the side of a counter or table so that the equipment can easily be pulled or knocked to the floor.
- Never let cords hang into sinks or other places where water can be found.
- Only use a Ground Fault Interrupter (GFI) protected circuit receptacle.

Glassware and Sharp-Object Safety

- Use only clean glassware that is free of chips and cracks.
- Use knives and other cutting instruments carefully. Always wear eye protection, and cut away from yourself.

Animal Safety

- Never hurt an animal.
- Wear gloves when handling animals or preserved specimens.
- Specimens for dissection should be properly mounted and supported.

Cleanup

- Follow your teacher's instructions for the disposal or storage of supplies.
- Clean your work area and pick up anything that has dropped to the floor.
- Wash your hands with soap and water after completing the activity.

Safety in the Field

- Be sure you understand the goal of your fieldwork and the proper way to carry out the investigation before you begin fieldwork.
- Do not approach or touch wild animals. Do not touch plants unless instructed by your teacher to do so. Leave natural areas as you found them.
- Use proper accident procedures, and let your teacher know about a hazard in the environment or an accident immediately, even if the hazard or accident seems minor.

Safety Symbols

Safety is the priority in the science classroom. In all of the activities in this textbook, safety symbols are used to alert you to materials, procedures, or situations that could be potentially hazardous if the safety guidelines are not followed. Learn what you need to do when you see these icons, and read all lab procedures before coming to the lab so you are prepared. Always ask your teacher if you have questions.

ANIMALS Never injure an animal. Follow your teacher's instructions for handling specific animals or preserved specimens. Wash your hands with soap and water after handling animals or preserved specimens.

APRON Wear a nonlatex apron at all times in the lab as directed. Stand whenever possible to avoid spilling in your lap.

BREAKAGE Use caution when handling items that may break, such as glassware and thermometers. Always store test tubes in a test tube rack.

CHEMICALS Always wear indirectly vented chemical splash goggles when working with chemicals. Stand whenever possible when working with chemicals to avoid spilling on your lap. Tell your teacher immediately if you spill chemicals on yourself, the table, or the floor. Never taste any substance or chemical in the lab. Always wash your hands with soap and water after working with chemicals.

DISPOSAL Follow your teacher's instructions for disposing of all waste materials, including chemicals, specimens, or broken glass.

ELECTRIC Keep electrical cords away from water to avoid shock. Do not use cords with frayed edges or plugs with a missing ground prong. Unplug all equipment when done. Only use GFI protected electrical receptacles.

FIRE Put on safety goggles before lighting flames. Remove loose clothing and tie back hair. Never leave a lit object unattended. Extinguish flames as soon as you finish heating.

FUMES Always work in a well-ventilated area. Do not inhale or sniff fumes; instead, use your fingers to bring fumes from the container to your nose.

GLOVES Always wear gloves to protect your skin from possible injury when working with substances that may be harmful or when working with animals.

HAND WASHING Wash your hands with soap and water after working with soil, chemicals, animals, or preserved specimens.

HEATING Wear indirectly vented chemical splash goggles, and never leave any substance while it is being heated. Use tongs or appropriate insulated holders when handling heated objects. Point any materials being heated away from you and others. Place hot objects such as test tubes in test tube racks while cooling.

PLANTS Do not eat any part of a plant. Do not pick any wild plant unless your teacher instructs you to do so. Wash your hands with soap and water after handling any plant.

SAFETY GOGGLES Always wear indirectly vented chemical splash goggles when working with chemicals, heating any substance, or using a sharp object or any material that could fly up and injure you or others.

SHARP OBJECTS Use scissors, knives, or razor tools with care. Wear goggles when cutting something. Always cut away from yourself.

SLIP HAZARD Immediately pick up any items dropped on the floor, and wipe up any spilled water or other liquid so it does not become a slip/fall hazard. Tell your teacher immediately if you spill chemicals.

UNIT 1

Introduction to Chemistry and Engineering

When welding with thermite, workers must wear heat-resistant protective clothing and special eye equipment.

FIGURE 1: When working with liquid nitrogen, scientists must wear special gloves to protect their hands from the low temperatures.

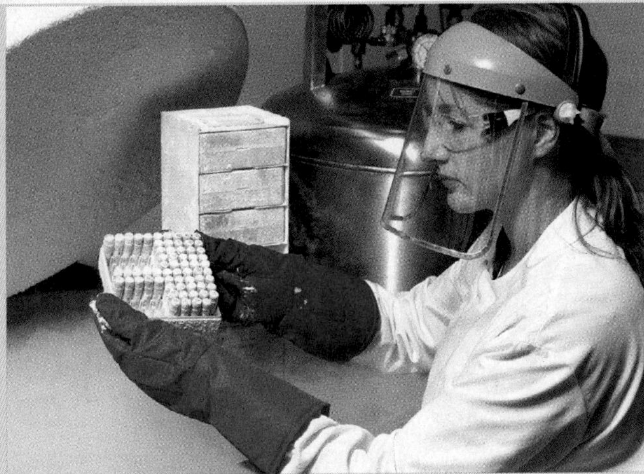

The scientist in Figure 1 is removing samples of cells from a storage container containing liquid nitrogen. She must wear protective, insulated, cryogenic gloves to protect her hands from frostbite because liquid nitrogen boils around −196 °C. Her gloves are designed to withstand extremely low temperatures. A welder, however, needs gloves that can withstand temperatures over 300 °C. When developing protective equipment for extreme conditions, scientists and engineers must consider a number of criteria. For example, if a pair of gloves can withstand extreme heat, but a welder cannot turn equipment on or off while wearing them, the material does not meet all the criteria for a good pair of welding gloves.

DESIGN What other factors do you think scientists and engineers must consider when developing protective equipment?

____

____

____

____

DRIVING QUESTIONS

As you move through the unit, gather evidence to help you answer the following questions. In your Evidence Notebook, record what you already know about these topics and any questions you have about them.

1. How do scientists study and classify matter?
2. How do chemical engineers develop optimized solutions to complex problems that balance various tradeoffs between criteria and constraints?

UNIT PROJECT

Go online to download the Unit Project Worksheet to help plan your project.

Optimizing Toothpaste

What gives a toothpaste its cleaning power? Design and produce a homemade toothpaste. Then test its cleaning capability by using it to clean a coffee-stained tile, which will serve as a model for teeth. Based on these results, optimize your design by adjusting the toothpaste ingredients.

Language Development

Use the lessons in this unit to complete the chart and expand your understanding of the science concepts.

TERM: physical property

Definition	Example

Similar Term	Phrase

TERM: chemical property

Definition	Example

Similar Term	Phrase

TERM: model

Definition	Example

Similar Term	Phrase

TERM: system

Definition	Example

Similar Term	Phrase

TERM: engineering design process

Definition	Example

Similar Term	Phrase

TERM: criterion (plural criteria)

Definition	Example

Similar Term	Phrase

TERM: constraint

Definition	Example

Similar Term	Phrase

TERM: tradeoff

Definition	Example

Similar Term	Phrase

1.1

Exploring Matter

A worker inspects metal tubing.

CAN YOU SOLVE THE PROBLEM?

People develop new technologies, including new materials, to address problems or offer better solutions to existing ones. For decades, plumbing pipes in buildings were made of metal tubing, such as galvanized steel or copper. More recently, plastic pipes have started to replace metal pipes because plastic pipes are cheaper, easier to work with, and do not corrode over time. However, compared to metal pipes, plastic pipes are not as heat resistant, not as strong, and are less environmentally friendly. There are many factors to consider when trying to replace an existing material with a new material.

EXPLAIN How could you improve an item that you use regularly?

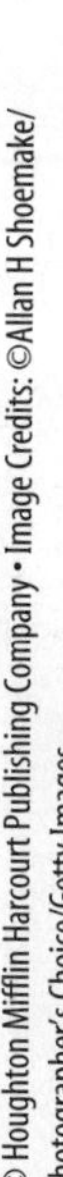

Evidence Notebook As you explore the lesson, gather evidence to explain what questions scientists could ask and what tests they could run if they wanted to use a new material in place of an existing one, such as using plastic pipes instead of metal ones.

Hands-On Lab

Exploring Physical and Chemical Changes

All substances are made of small particles known as atoms and molecules. When a property of a substance changes, its atoms and molecules have changed. The study of chemistry is the study of these changes. Some changes happen when one substance interacts with another substance. Why might we need to determine how substances interact with one another? We need to be aware of the way substances interact because some changes may be harmful and some may be beneficial.

Scientists classify changes in substances as either physical changes or chemical changes. A physical change affects the form of a substance, but its identity remains the same. In a chemical change, however, the chemical identity of a substance changes. Atoms and molecules rearrange to form new substances. In this lab, you will determine whether the changes you observe are physical or chemical changes.

RESEARCH QUESTION What are examples of physical and chemical changes that are important in your daily life?

MAKE A CLAIM

Preview each experiment you will perform. For each experiment, is the change that occurs physical, or is it chemical? How will you be able to tell what type of change took place?

MATERIALS

- indirectly vented chemical splash goggles, nonlatex apron, nitrile gloves
- chalk, calcium carbonate (5 g)
- lead nitrate solution in dropper bottle, 0.2 M
- mortar and pestle
- silver nitrate solution in dropper bottle, 0.1 M
- sodium hydroxide solution in dropper bottle, 0.5 M
- sodium iodide solution in dropper bottle, 0.5 M
- water in dropper bottle
- well plate
- vinegar (acetic acid) in dropper bottle

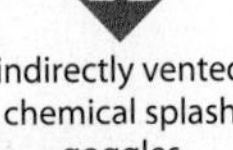

indirectly vented chemical splash goggles

SAFETY INFORMATION

- Wear indirectly vented chemical splash goggles, a nonlatex apron, and nitrile gloves during the setup, hands-on, and takedown segments of the activity.
- Never pour chemicals, either used or unused, back into their original container. Dispose of chemicals according to your teacher's instructions.
- Never touch, taste, or sniff any chemicals in the lab. If you need to determine odor, waft. To waft, hold the chemical in its container 15 cm away from your nose, and use your fingers to bring fumes from the container to your nose.

PLAN THE INVESTIGATION

In your Evidence Notebook, develop a procedure to safely combine each pair of materials listed below. Use five drops of each solution. In your procedure, consider how much of each solid you will need given this constraint. Have your teacher approve your procedure and safety plan before you start.

1. water and crushed chalk
2. vinegar and crushed chalk
3. silver nitrate solution and sodium hydroxide solution
4. silver nitrate solution and sodium iodide solution
5. lead nitrate solution and sodium iodide solution
6. sodium hydroxide solution and sodium iodide solution

Follow your teacher's instructions for disposal of the chemicals in your well plate. Wash and dry the well plate.

COLLECT DATA

In your Evidence Notebook, develop a matrix-style table to record the properties of each material before and after it was combined, as well as any evidence that a physical or chemical change took place once the materials were combined.

ANALYZE

1. Which of the changes you observed indicated a physical change, and which indicated a chemical change?

2. What are some limitations of this experiment? How could you revise your procedure to improve the results?

3. Sketch the difference between a physical change and a chemical change.

CONSTRUCT AN EXPLANATION

1. Explain the difference between a physical change and a chemical change on a molecular level.

2. Based on the materials you used and the results of your experiments, what patterns do you see? Which materials do you think have similar properties? Explain your reasoning.

DRAW CONCLUSIONS

Write a conclusion that addresses each of the points below.

Claim How were you able to determine whether a physical or chemical change occurred in each experiment?

Evidence What evidence from your investigation supports your claim?

Reasoning Explain how the evidence you gave supports your claim. Describe, in detail, the connections between the evidence you cited and the argument you are making.

Evidence Notebook Consider the differences between chemical and physical changes. How could you use physical and chemical changes to determine if a new material can be used in the same way as an existing material?

Properties of Matter

Everything around you—your desk, your chair, and even the people—are all made of matter. Even things you cannot see, such as air, are made of matter. Matter is anything that takes up space and has mass. The mass of an object is the amount of matter the object contains. Although all things are made of matter, the kind and amount of matter in each object usually varies.

FIGURE 1: A ball of clay is manipulated into different shapes in each of the images below.

ANALYZE Do the amounts of mass and matter in Figure 1 change as the size and shape of the clay ball is changed? Explain your reasoning.

The law of conservation of matter, or the law of conservation of mass, states that matter cannot be created or destroyed in either physical or chemical changes. During a chemical reaction, substances interact with each other to form new substances. The starting substances are the reactants; the new substances formed are the products. The reactant particles are rearranged to form the product particles in such a way that no atoms are lost and no atoms are added. Because no atoms are gained or lost during the chemical reaction, the total mass of the substances involved remains the same.

Now consider a spoonful of sodium chloride, also known as table salt. Sodium chloride is made when an atom of sodium bonds to an atom of chlorine. The spoonful of sodium chloride has a specific mass. You can change the total mass by adding salt to the spoon or removing salt from the spoon.

EXPLAIN You pour a spoonful of salt into a glass of water. Explain what happens to the mass of the salt and the mass of the water.

Physical Properties and Physical Changes

Every substance has physical properties that help determine its identity. Knowing the properties of a substance is important when chemists choose the best material for a specific use. A physical property is a property that can be measured or observed without changing the identity of matter. Some physical properties are shown in Figure 2.

FIGURE 2: Examples of some common physical properties of matter

Explore Online

a Density is the amount of mass per volume of a substance.

b Conductivity is a measure of the amount of electricity, heat, or sound that a substance can carry.

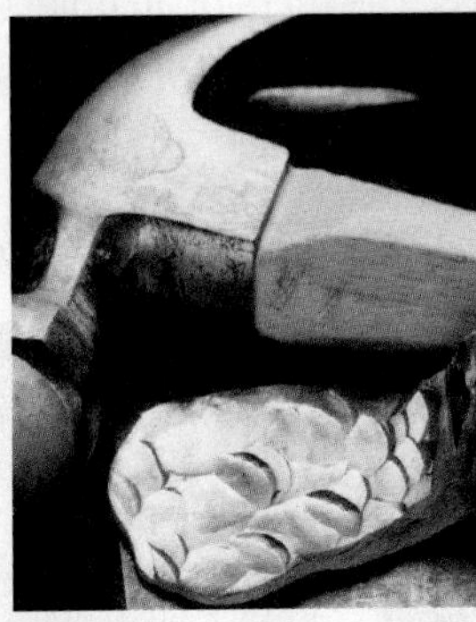

c Malleability is the ability of a substance to be flattened.

d Solubility is the amount of a substance that can dissolve in a given amount of another substance.

Collaborate With a partner, make a list of the physical properties shown in Figure 2. List questions you have about these physical properties. What other characteristics of matter do you think are physical properties?

A physical change is a change of matter from one form to another without a change in chemical properties. For example, sugar is soluble in water. When you drink the water, you can taste the sugar although you cannot see it. That is because in the water, the sugar is still sugar. Its identity has not changed.

Using Physical Properties to Identify Matter

Imagine you have two cups filled with colorless liquids. One cup contains water, and the other cup contains isopropanol, a common component of rubbing alcohol. To differentiate the liquids, you can study some of their physical properties.

Property	Water	Isopropanol
Boiling point	100 °C	82 °C
Density	1.0 g/cm^3	0.79 g/cm^3
Conductivity	poor	poor

ANALYZE Which properties would be helpful in determining the identity of the liquids, and which would not be helpful? Explain your answer.

States of Matter

States of matter—solid, liquid, gas, or plasma—are the common forms in which matter exists in the universe. When a substance goes from one state of matter to another, the process is called a *change in state*. During a change in state, the physical properties of a substance change, but the chemical composition does not. When water in the form of ice melts, it looks different on the macroscopic scale, but its chemical composition has not changed on the molecular scale.

FIGURE 3: Water changes state from solid (ice) to liquid (liquid water) to gas (water vapor).

ASK What questions could you ask about the arrangement of particles in the states of matter shown in Figure 3?

___

___

___

The particles in a solid are packed very closely together in a rigid, orderly arrangement. They are held together by the attractive forces that act between all particles of matter. Solids, therefore, have fixed volumes and shapes. In the solid state, particles cannot break away from their fixed position; they can only vibrate in place.

The particles that make up a liquid move more rapidly than those in a solid do. This causes the particles in the liquid to overcome some of the attractive forces between them, and the particles can slide freely around each other.

The particles of a gas are very far apart and move rapidly compared to particles in solids or liquids. At these distances, the attractive forces between gas particles have a lesser effect than they have on particles in liquids and solids. In general, the volume of a liquid or solid increases greatly when it forms a gas. However, the density of the gaseous state of most substances is approximately one-thousandth the density of the liquid state.

Plasma is a gas in which the particles have so much energy that they become electrically charged. Plasma is the most common state of matter in the universe, with more than 99.99% of observable matter in the universe being plasma. Most of the matter of the sun is plasma. Stars and lightning are also examples of plasma. However, this state is not experienced in the physical and chemical changes we encounter every day on Earth.

MODEL Draw a diagram of the arrangement of water molecules when water is a solid, a liquid, and a gas.

Energy and Matter

Bose-Einstein Condensate

A fifth state of matter, a Bose-Einstein condensate (BEC), was identified by scientists in 1995. In this state, extremely cold particles just above absolute zero (–273 °C or 0 K) barely move. BEC particles have so little energy that they clump and behave as a single particle. Satyendra Nath Bose and Albert Einstein predicted the BEC in the 1920s, but the technology needed to produce the matter did not exist until 1995.

Collaborate With a partner, discuss how the matter in a BEC is different from other states of matter.

Chemical Properties and Chemical Changes

A chemical property is a property that can be determined by attempting to change the identity of a substance, but it cannot be determined simply by observing the substance. Rather, a change (or lack of a change) in a substance must be observed during or after a chemical reaction.

FIGURE 4: The alkali metals lithium, sodium, and potassium react with water.

Explore Online

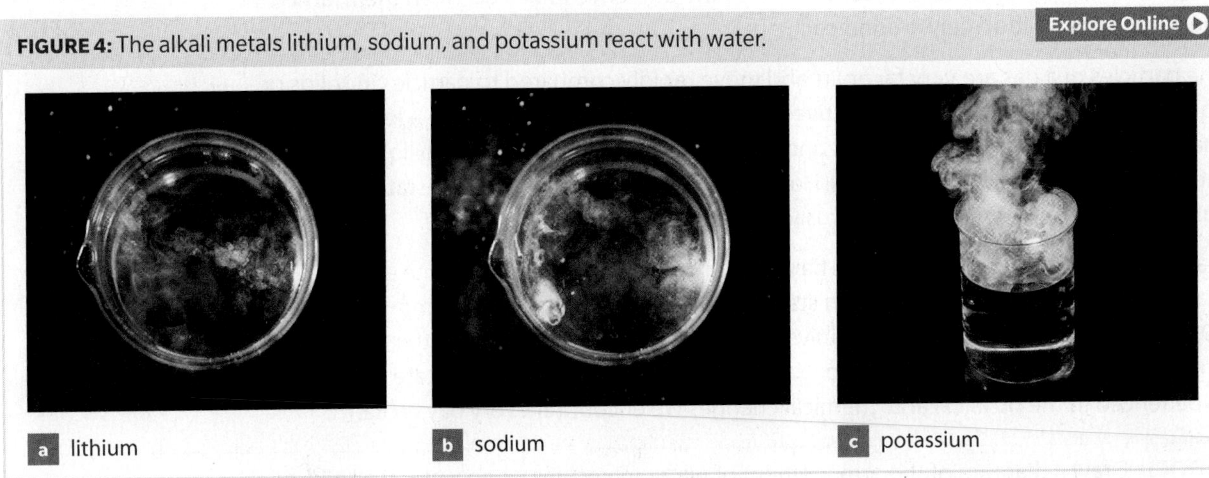

a lithium   b sodium   c potassium

In a chemical change, the particles of a substance are rearranged, resulting in a change in chemical composition. Figure 4 shows three metals—lithium, sodium, and potassium—each reacting with water. The products of the reactions include hydrogen gas, which can burn if the reactions take place in the presence of oxygen. The reactivity of alkali metals with water is a chemical property. This property cannot be observed until the metal and water react and both the metal and the water change identity in the process. Rusting is also a chemical change. Iron oxide, or rust, forms when iron is exposed to water and oxygen. Understanding the chemical properties of matter is critical for safety when using materials such as the rechargeable lithium batteries found in laptop computers.

ANALYZE Classify each statement as describing a chemical or a physical change. Explain your reasoning.

A piece of metal melts. ______________________

A piece of coal burns. ______________________

An egg cooks on a stove. ______________________

Using Chemical Properties to Identify Matter

Chemical properties can also be used to identify a substance and they determine which kinds of materials a substance will react with. An example of a chemical property is flammability, or the ability of a substance to catch on fire. Water is not flammable, but isopropanol is. Another chemical property, reactivity, describes how likely a substance is to undergo a chemical reaction. Acidity is another chemical property. Some strong acids, such as hydrochloric acid, are highly corrosive.

EVALUATE You have two samples of gray powder, both of which are flammable. Are these powders the same substance? Explain your reasoning.

____

____

____

Extensive and Intensive Properties

Scientists describe properties of matter as extensive and intensive. An **extensive property** depends directly on the amount of the substance present. An **intensive property** is one that does not depend on the amount of the substance present. For any particular substance, any amount of the substance has the same value for any intensive property.

APPLY Classify each statement as an extensive or an intensive property.

- A pot of boiling water has more energy than a cup of boiling water. extensive | intensive
- A big piece of metal melts at the same temperature as a small piece. extensive | intensive
- Copper wire conducts electricity. extensive | intensive

As seen in Figure 5, if you put a 12-ounce can of regular cola and a 12-ounce can of diet cola in a tub of water, you will notice the regular cola sinks and the diet cola floats. The sweetener in diet cola is hundreds of times sweeter per unit volume than the sugar in regular cola.

EXPLAIN Why does the can of diet cola float in water but the can of regular cola does not? Consider mass and density in your explanation.

____

____

____

____

FIGURE 5: Cans of regular cola and diet cola behave differently in water.

Collaborate With a partner, list the extensive and intensive properties described in the cola experiment. Which properties would change and which would stay the same if you ran the experiment using 7.5-ounce cans instead?

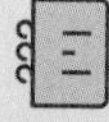

Evidence Notebook Which physical and chemical properties would allow you to determine if a new material can replace an existing material? For example, what properties must a plastic pipe have in order to perform the same function as a metal pipe?

Classifying Matter

Matter can be classified as either a mixture or a pure substance. For example, distilled water is a pure substance but salt water is a mixture. Every sample of distilled water has the same composition and the same chemical and physical properties. However, salt water may contain varying amounts of salt dissolved in water. The resulting salt water solutions have some properties that are the same and some that differ.

APPLY Is air considered a pure substance or a mixture? Explain your reasoning.

____

____

Mixtures

A mixture is a blend of two or more pure substances, each of which retains its own identity, although the mixture may have different properties than the individual components. Some mixtures are homogeneous, meaning they have a uniform composition throughout. Sugar water is an example of a homogeneous mixture. Mixtures that are not uniform throughout, such as a bowl of mixed nuts, are heterogeneous.

DESIGN You pick up a handful of soil from the ground. Design a way to separate all the components found in the soil sample.

____

____

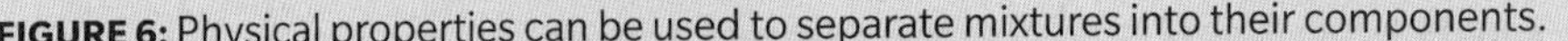

FIGURE 6: Physical properties can be used to separate mixtures into their components.

a Filtration separates based on particle size.

b Centrifugation separates based on density.

c Chromatography separates based on the nature of the pigment.

Mixtures can be separated by physical means, some of which are shown in Figure 6. These methods take advantage of different physical properties of the components. For example, filtration uses a filter to catch large particles while allowing smaller particles to pass through. Centrifugation separates particles from a mixture by spinning the mixture at a high speed. Chromatography separates mixtures based on their different relative attractions to a medium, such as paper, and a solvent, such as water.

Pure Substances

A pure substance is made up of a single element or compound so it is always homogeneous. Because a pure substance has a fixed composition it cannot be separated by physical means. The 92 naturally occurring elements cannot be broken down into simpler substances by chemical or physical means. The iron and the sulfur shown in Figure 7 are elements. Both of these elements have their own unique set of physical and chemical properties. Iron and sulfur can chemically combine, or bond, to form the compound iron(II) sulfide, which has a completely different set of characteristic physical and chemical properties compared to the elements that make it up.

FIGURE 7: Iron(II) sulfide (right) is composed of iron (left) and sulfur (center).

Collaborate Talk with a partner about the properties you observe for each substance shown in Figure 7. Do you think the formation of iron(II) sulfide is an example of a chemical or physical change? Explain your reasoning.

Pure substances that are compounds can decompose, or break down, during a chemical change. For example, water can be broken down by electrolysis. Pure water has the molecular formula H_2O. It contains two hydrogen atoms bonded to a single oxygen atom. During electrolysis, an electric current is used to split water.

Thermal decomposition is another way that some pure substances can be broken down. At extreme temperatures, the bonds holding a compound together might break, causing a compound to decompose into simpler substances.

MODEL Draw a sketch of what you think happens when water is split by electrolysis.

Table sugar, also called *sucrose*, is a carbohydrate found in sugar cane, sugar beets, and many processed foods. Sucrose is made up of two sugars, glucose and fructose, joined together. Unlike some other compounds, sucrose does not melt when exposed to extreme temperatures. As seen in Figure 8, when sucrose is heated to 186 °C, it decomposes into glucose and fructose. These sugars then undergo further reactions that cause the sugar to turn brown. The browning of sugar is also known as *caramelization*.

FIGURE 8: Sucrose can be broken down when exposed to high temperatures.

INFER Would the composition of sucrose purified from sugar cane differ from the composition of sucrose purified from sugar beets? Explain your reasoning.

When looking at a sample it can be difficult to determine if it is a mixture or a pure substance. It can be even more tricky to determine if a mixture is homogeneous or heterogeneous, or if a pure substance is an element or a compound. These classifications can be organized in a flow chart, such as the one shown in Figure 9.

FIGURE 9: This flow chart can help you classify matter.

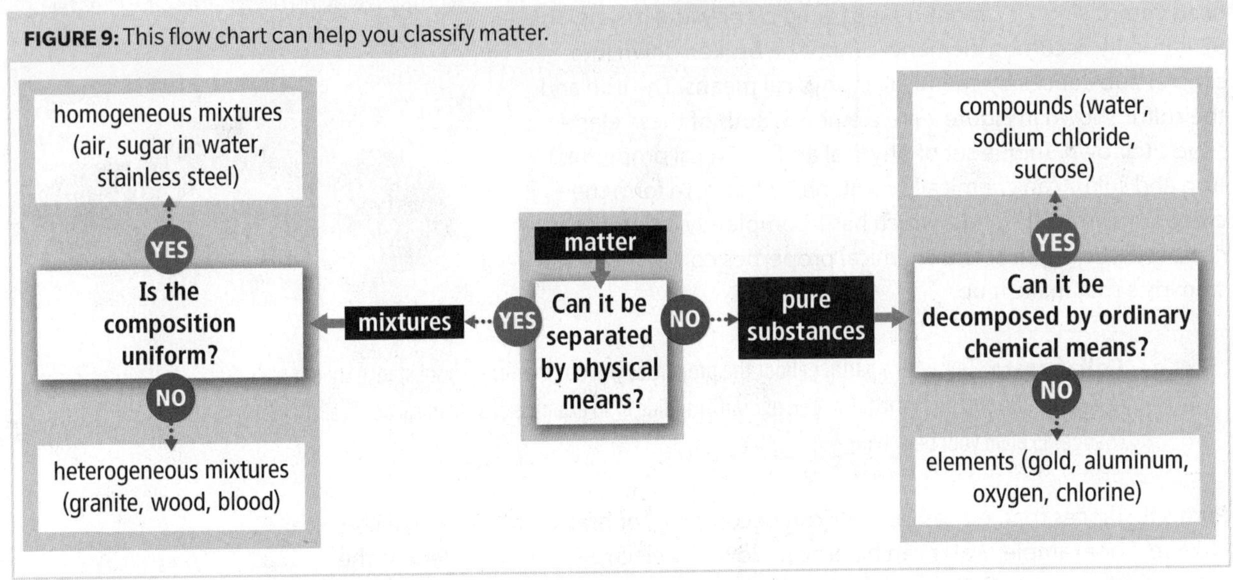

ANALYZE Use the chart in Figure 9 to categorize each material in the list below as either a homogeneous mixture, a heterogeneous mixture, a compound, or an element. Write your own examples in the final row.

salt water | fruit salad | methane (CH_4) | nitrogen (N_2)

carbon dioxide (CO_2) | juice with ice cubes | apple juice | helium (He)

Homogeneous Mixture	Heterogeneous Mixture	Compound	Element

EXPLAIN Choose three items from the table, and explain why you classified them the way you did.

Evidence Notebook Consider the differences between a sample of a pure substance and a sample of a mixture. When testing the properties of a new material, what questions should you ask and what considerations need to be made regarding the samples?

The Study of Chemistry

Have you ever wondered how new materials are identified or how you can determine how those materials can be used? Studying a material's physical and chemical properties is an important step. Comparing a material's properties to those of other materials can help identify ways a material can be used. These are just some things a chemist may do.

What Is Chemistry?

Chemistry is one branch of science. Science develops explanations based on observation and experimentation. So, scientific knowledge is based on empirical evidence, and it also requires creativity, imagination, and hard work. Science and technology often influence each other. Science aids in the development of technology, and new technology allows for more scientific knowledge to be acquired.

Examples of chemistry and the work chemists do are all around you. Chemistry studies the composition, structure, and properties of matter. Chemistry also examines the interactions and changes that matter undergoes along with the energy changes that accompany these processes. Chemistry deals with questions such as: How can we make matter more resistant to chemical changes? How can we make manufacturing and energy production more efficient and environmentally friendly?

Evidence Notebook How is chemistry involved in developing new toothpaste recipes? How can you use this information when making your own toothpaste in your unit project?

Chemists cannot identify all of a substance's properties just by looking at a sample. They need tools to make observations and take measurements. Chemists also develop and use models to study the behavior of matter. A **model** is a pattern, representation, or description designed to show the structure or workings of an object, system, or concept. Some models help chemists understand phenomena and make predictions about future events. Models may be conceptual, visual, 3D physical objects, mathematical, or graphical. A computer simulation is a type of model that is useful when trying to identify possible solutions because they show how various materials will react in specific conditions.

APPLY What are the benefits and limitations of physical models and computer models?

FIGURE 10: Analytical chemist

The chemist in Figure 10 is using a computer model to analyze the structure of a molecule. She may also use other tools to study the elements in the molecule and the purity of her sample. Creative thinking is also important when solving problems.

Collaborate Discuss with your peers how reliable tools, technology, careful planning of experiments, and recording data are important to chemists.

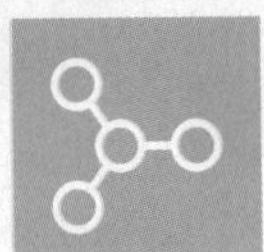

Patterns

Analyzing Atmospheric CO_2

The burning of fossil fuels is a chemical change that releases carbon dioxide, CO_2, into the atmosphere. Other human activities, such as raising livestock, also add CO_2 and methane, CH_4, to the atmosphere. Chemists analyze the composition of the atmosphere to see how these human activities affect the atmosphere and the entire Earth system. The first step in understanding these effects is to gather empirical evidence that shows the patterns of change in components of the Earth system such as the atmosphere.

Monthly Average Carbon Dioxide Concentration

FIGURE 11: Dr. C. D. Keeling began collecting and analyzing air samples in 1958. The Keeling Curve shows atmospheric CO_2 concentrations in samples taken at the Mauna Loa Observatory in Hawaii.

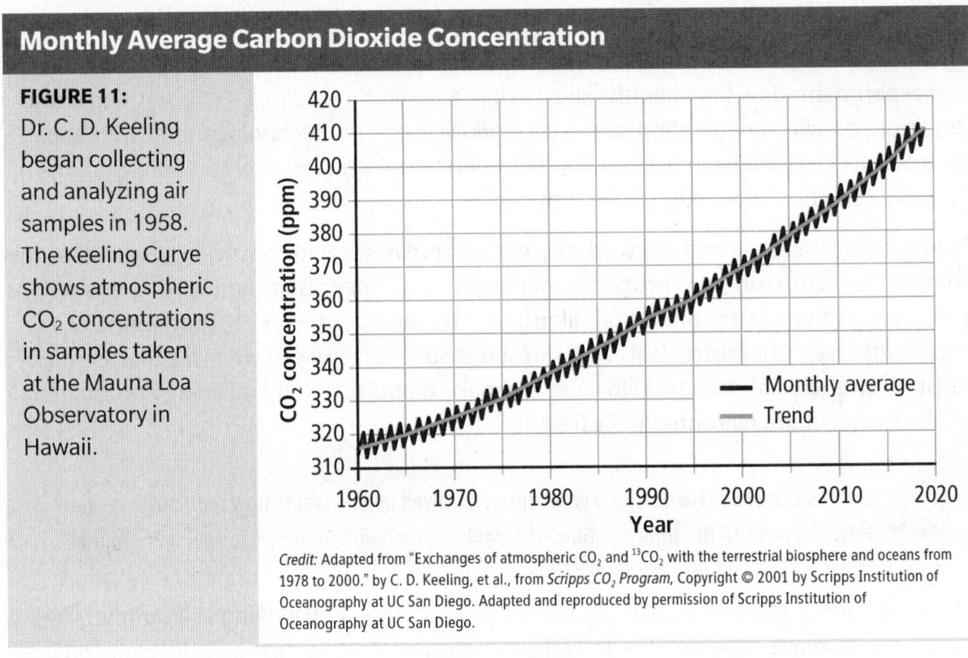

Credit: Adapted from "Exchanges of atmospheric CO_2 and $^{13}CO_2$ with the terrestrial biosphere and oceans from 1978 to 2000." by C. D. Keeling, et al., from *Scripps CO_2 Program*, Copyright © 2001 by Scripps Institution of Oceanography at UC San Diego. Adapted and reproduced by permission of Scripps Institution of Oceanography at UC San Diego.

ANALYZE What two patterns do you see in the graph shown in Figure 11?

Early in Dr. Keeling's career, he discovered that the concentration of CO_2 in the atmosphere was relatively constant regardless of where he was sampling, as long as the samples were taken in areas away from sources or sinks of CO_2, such as cities. So, the air samples from Mauna Loa are considered to be representative of Earth's atmosphere.

Language Arts Connection Research the seasonal fluctuations in the Keeling Curve. Write a report that explains the relationship of the data set to the burning of fossil fuels and other processes in the Earth system. Use multiple sources of information, such as models, peer reviewed journals, and scientific theories, and include diagrams and images in your report.

Evidence Notebook How can a chemist model the environmental impacts of making a new material compared to an existing one? For example, plastic pipes may not rust like metal ones, but they may release toxic chemicals as they degrade. How can a model help compare the materials?

Careers in Science

Crystallographer

Crystallographers study the structure and properties of crystals. A crystal is a homogeneous solid that contains a specific compound with particles in a consistent and ordered arrangement. Crystallographers explore the arrangement of atoms and the forces that hold the atoms together in a crystal. Modeling the structure of a compound helps scientists understand how it interacts with other compounds and how the compound could possibly be modified to alter its properties.

X-ray crystallography is a technique in which a crystal is placed on a platform, and an x-ray beam is directed toward it. Electrons within the crystal deflect the beam so that an image is produced on a screen. The pattern and intensity of the x-rays that hit the screen can be interpreted to reveal the structure of the crystal. The crystallographers can analyze the image to determine the size of particles within the crystal and the distances between them.

Large biomolecules, such as proteins and nucleic acids, do not normally have a crystalline structure, but crystallographers can work with highly concentrated solutions of the substances to grow small crystals. Once the crystals form, the crystallographers use x-ray diffraction to produce models of their molecular structures. The crystallographers may use other instrumentation in their investigations as well, such as robots that help grow crystals and a detector that captures and displays the diffraction image in a form that can be stored digitally.

X-ray crystallography is also used to determine the structure of viruses. An individual virus particle is so tiny that a light microscope is not powerful enough to view it. Knowing the structure of a virus is critical to figuring out how it infects organisms, and this knowledge can help in the development of treatments to prevent infection.

FIGURE 12: Crystallographers work in government agencies, universities, and industrial laboratories.

Chemistry in Your Community Research a discovery made using crystallography that has benefited your community. A community can be a group of people who live in the same region or who share similar beliefs and norms. For example, you may research a molecule whose structure helped scientists understand an important reaction within the human body or a compound that was engineered to treat a genetic disease. Consider some of the following to guide your research:

- Why was the molecule chosen for study?
- How was the molecule crystallized?
- What are important features about the molecule's structure?
- How did knowing the structure of the molecule benefit your community?

Use multiple and different types of sources to help you write a magazine article about the discovery and its importance to your community. Be sure to include a relevant image in your article that illustrates your findings.

SALTING OUT |  ESTIMATING DATA ACCURATELY | COMMUNICATING THE SIZES OF OBJECTS | Go online to choose one of these other paths.

Lesson Self-Check

CAN YOU SOLVE THE PROBLEM?

FIGURE 13: The physical and chemical properties of this metal determine the ways it can be used by humans.

Everything is made up of matter, and each substance has its own unique set of physical and chemical properties. The properties of a substance influence the way it can be used in everyday life. Asking questions and performing tests on the material help scientists determine how it behaves in certain conditions and how it interacts with other substances. Chemists use a variety of instruments and models to help them understand how to improve materials and processes to better serve society.

Think about the metal tubes shown in the photo. These tubes can be used in ventilation systems or plumbing systems, but are they the best material for the job? The evidence you have collected throughout this lesson can help you ask questions and select the appropriate tests needed to answer this question.

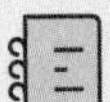

Evidence Notebook Refer to your notes in your Evidence Notebook to make a claim about how you could determine whether a new material has the specific chemical and physical properties needed to perform the same function as an existing material. Your explanation should include a discussion of the following points:

Claim What type of questions could be asked and which tests can be run to determine if a new material can replace an existing material?

Evidence What evidence supports the claim that these questions and tests are useful in identifying the properties of the new and original materials?

Reasoning How does the evidence you provided support your claim about the usefulness of specific questions and tests in identifying properties of materials?

Name

Date

CHECKPOINTS

Check Your Understanding

1. Which statement best defines matter?
   - ○ **a.** Matter is anything that is a solid at room temperature.
   - ○ **b.** Matter is anything that takes up space and has mass.
   - ○ **c.** Matter is any substance that reacts with another substance.
   - ○ **d.** Matter is any substance that contains carbon.

2. Select the correct terms to complete the statement about physical and chemical changes.

   When electricity passes through liquid water, two gases form. This is an example of a physical | chemical change because the identity of the substance changed | stayed the same.

   When liquid water loses energy, a change in state | chemical identity occurs. This is an example of a chemical | physical change.

3. Match the description of particle motion to the correct state of matter.

Description		State
Particles are packed very close together in a relatively fixed arrangement; has definite volume and shape. ○		○ liquid
Particles are close together but can move past one another; has a definite volume but an indefinite shape. ○		○ plasma
Particles are far apart and move very rapidly; has neither definite volume nor definite shape. ○		○ solid
Particles have a large amount of energy, and they become electrically charged. ○		○ gas

4. Select the correct terms to complete the statement about intensive and extensive properties.

   An intensive | extensive physical property can be used to help identify a substance because it changes | does not change with the amount of matter present. An intensive | extensive property cannot be used to help identify a substance because it changes | does not change with the amount of the substance present.

5. Choose the projects most likely to be worked on by a chemist. Select all correct answers.
   - ☐ **a.** studying the structure of an enzyme
   - ☐ **b.** analyzing the components of petroleum
   - ☐ **c.** analyzing the velocity of planets
   - ☐ **d.** observing the behavior of farm animals
   - ☐ **e.** building a computer model for producing antacids

6. Chemists have identified three new forms of alternative fuel. If the chemists want to predict how each fuel would affect the environment and change the efficiency of the car, what type of model should they use?
   - ○ **a.** 3D model
   - ○ **b.** mathematical model
   - ○ **c.** computer simulation
   - ○ **d.** visual model

7. Categorize each substance as a pure substance or a mixture.

   air | aluminum | carbon dioxide | table salt | soil | wood

Pure Substance	Mixture

CHECKPOINTS (continued)

8. Is a tossed salad a homogeneous mixture, a heterogeneous mixture, or a pure substance? Explain your reasoning.

9. Many changes occur to a wax candle after it is lit. Which changes are physical? Which changes are chemical? How do you know what kind of changes took place?

10. A new plumbing system needs to be installed in a school bathroom. What role will chemistry play in this project? What information or tests might be important to know or do in order to select the best material for this project?

MAKE YOUR OWN STUDY GUIDE

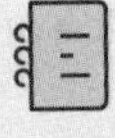

In your Evidence Notebook, design a study guide that supports the main ideas from this lesson:

Chemistry is the study of matter, the interactions of matter, and the associated changes in energy.

Each substance has a unique set of physical and chemical properties that can identify it.

A sample of matter can be classified as either a pure substance or a mixture.

Chemists study data and patterns to understand phenomena.

Remember to include the following information in your study guide:

- Use examples that model main ideas.
- Record explanations for the phenomena you investigated.
- Use evidence to support your explanations. Your support can include drawings, data, graphs, laboratory conclusions, and other evidence recorded throughout the lesson.

Consider how interactions at the atomic level impact properties at the bulk scale and how these properties affect our use of materials on a daily basis.

1.2

Chemistry and the Engineering Design Process

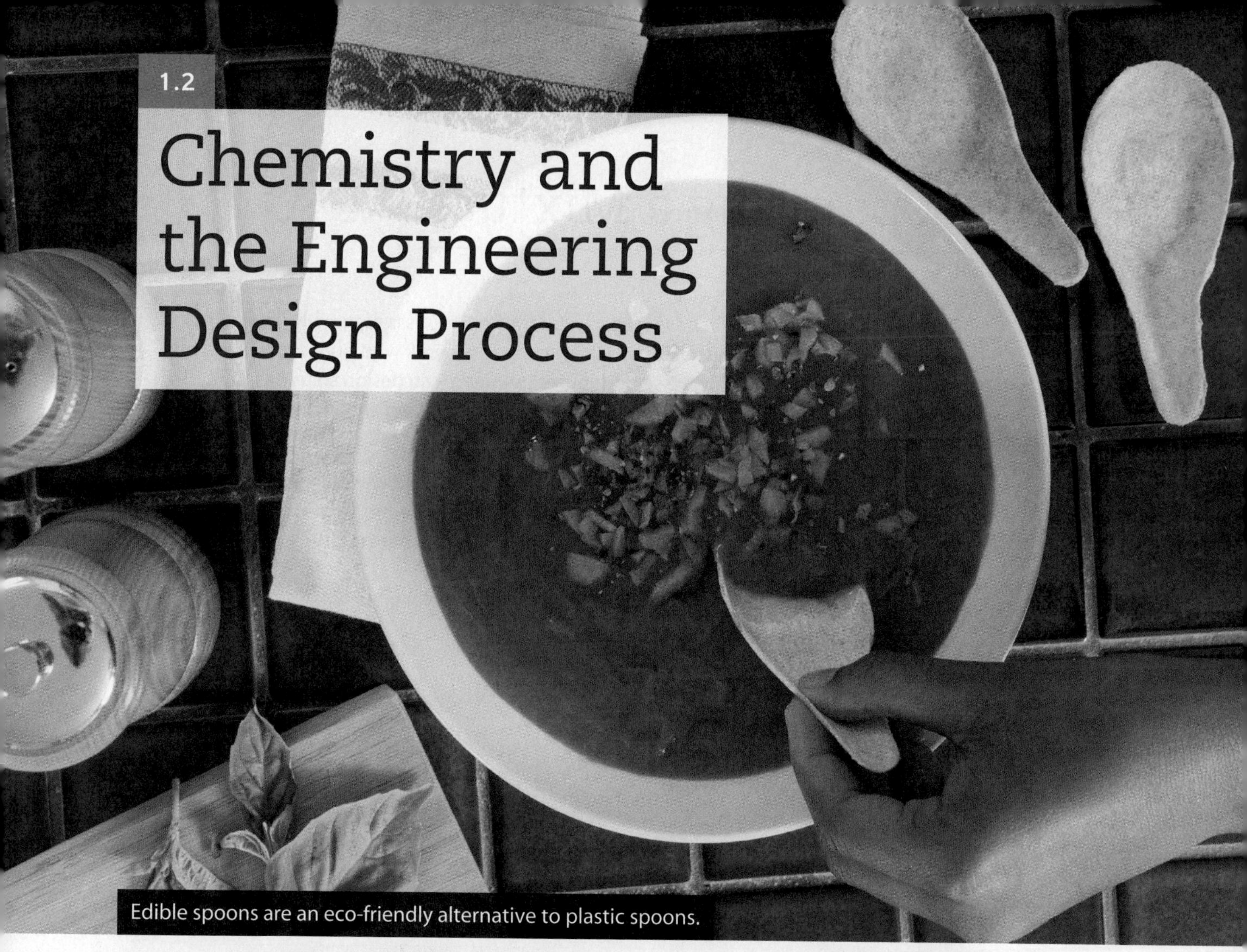

Edible spoons are an eco-friendly alternative to plastic spoons.

CAN YOU SOLVE THE PROBLEM?

You buy your lunch and pick up a plastic spoon. After lunch, you throw out the spoon. It may take hundreds of years for that spoon to decompose in a landfill. Even biodegradable plastics made from cornstarch do not break down easily. They require controlled composting facilities that aren't readily available. Edible spoons may help solve the plastic-waste problem. Such utensils are made of grains such as rice, wheat, and sorghum, with a little salt, sugar, and spice added for flavor. They taste like crackers. And if you are too full after lunch to eat your spoon, it will degrade within a few days in a landfill.

DESIGN What properties must a spoon have in order to be useful as a tool for eating? What additional properties should an edible spoon have?

Evidence Notebook As you explore the lesson, gather evidence to explain what properties an edible spoon should have—that is, what the design criteria and constraints should be.

Engineering Lab

Separating a Mixture

The ability to separate and recover substances from mixtures is extremely important in scientific research and industry. Chemists often need to work with pure substances, but naturally occurring materials are seldom pure. Engineers can design solutions to such problems. In this lab, you will use principles of engineering and chemistry to solve a similar problem—separating a mixture of common items.

DESIGN CHALLENGE Given the materials available to you, how would you design, develop, and implement a safe procedure for physically separating a mixture containing salt, sand, iron filings, and poppy seeds? All four components are in dry, granular form.

FIGURE 1: Sand, salt, poppy seeds, and iron filings have different properties that can be used to separate them from a mixture.

DEFINE THE PROBLEM

1. What physical properties do you observe or know of in salt, sand, iron filings, and poppy seeds?

2. What would be the characteristics of a successful separation? What are the limitations on any procedure you develop to separate this mixture?

POSSIBLE MATERIALS

- indirectly vented chemical splash goggles, nonlatex apron, nitrile gloves
- mixture components (salt, sand, iron filings, poppy seeds)
- distilled water
- filter funnel and paper
- forceps
- hot plate
- magnet
- mixture sample
- test tubes and rack

SAFETY INFORMATION

- Wear indirectly vented chemical splash goggles, a nonlatex apron, and nitrile gloves during the setup, hands-on, and takedown segments of the activity.
- Use caution when working with iron filings, which are hazardous if they are swallowed or inhaled, or enter the eyes, nose, or other body cavities.
- Use caution when working with hot plates, which can cause skin burns or electric shock. Use only GFI-protected circuits when using electrical equipment, and keep away from water sources to prevent shock.
- Wash your hands with soap and water immediately after completing this activity.
- Never eat any food items used in a lab activity.

indirectly vented chemical splash goggles

COLLECT DATA

1. Obtain samples of each of the four mixture components from your teacher. Use the equipment available to you to make observations about the properties of each component. Record your observations in a data table in your Evidence Notebook.
2. For each mixture component, list one or two properties that could be useful in physically separating it from the other materials in the mixture. Explain your reasoning.

TEST

1. Now that you have described the properties of each material, develop a procedure and a safety plan in your Evidence Notebook explaining how you will isolate each material in the mixture, and in what order. You may wish to include a sketch of your setup. Make sure your teacher approves your procedure and safety plan before proceeding.

2. When your procedure, safety plan, and materials are approved, begin your experiment.

OPTIMIZE

1. Summarize the results of your procedure. How well did it work for each component?

2. Describe changes you could make to improve the procedure.

3. If you have time, test the revised, optimized procedure after it is approved by your teacher. Describe the results.

ANALYZE

1. What factors did you consider when optimizing the procedure? Did your changes improve the procedure? What would you change if you were to repeat the experiment again?

2. Name the specific physical property of each component that enabled you to separate the component from the rest of the mixture, and explain how it was useful. Use evidence from your data to support your answers.

EXTEND

How could you separate each of the following two-component mixtures?

Mixture	Separation method
Aluminum filings and iron filings	
Sand and finely ground polystyrene foam	
Alcohol and water	

Evidence Notebook An edible spoon is made from a mixture of substances. What properties should the substances have so the spoon can be used to stir or consume liquids?

The Engineering Design Process

Think about the last time you had to deal with an unexpected event: maybe you were running late for school, or you had an extra chore or errand to do. How did you solve the problem? It is likely that you used a process similar to the ones engineers use, even if you were not aware of it. Humans are natural problem solvers. Engineers formalize the process of solving problems in order to work as efficiently and effectively as possible. Their work goes hand in hand with the work of scientists.

Solving Problems Step by Step

Science is the study of phenomena. Scientists ask questions and carry out investigations in order to explain phenomena. Engineering is the study of problems. Engineers use a series of steps, called the engineering design process, in order to solve problems.

FIGURE 2: The engineering design process is a set of steps that lead to designing or improving a solution to a problem.

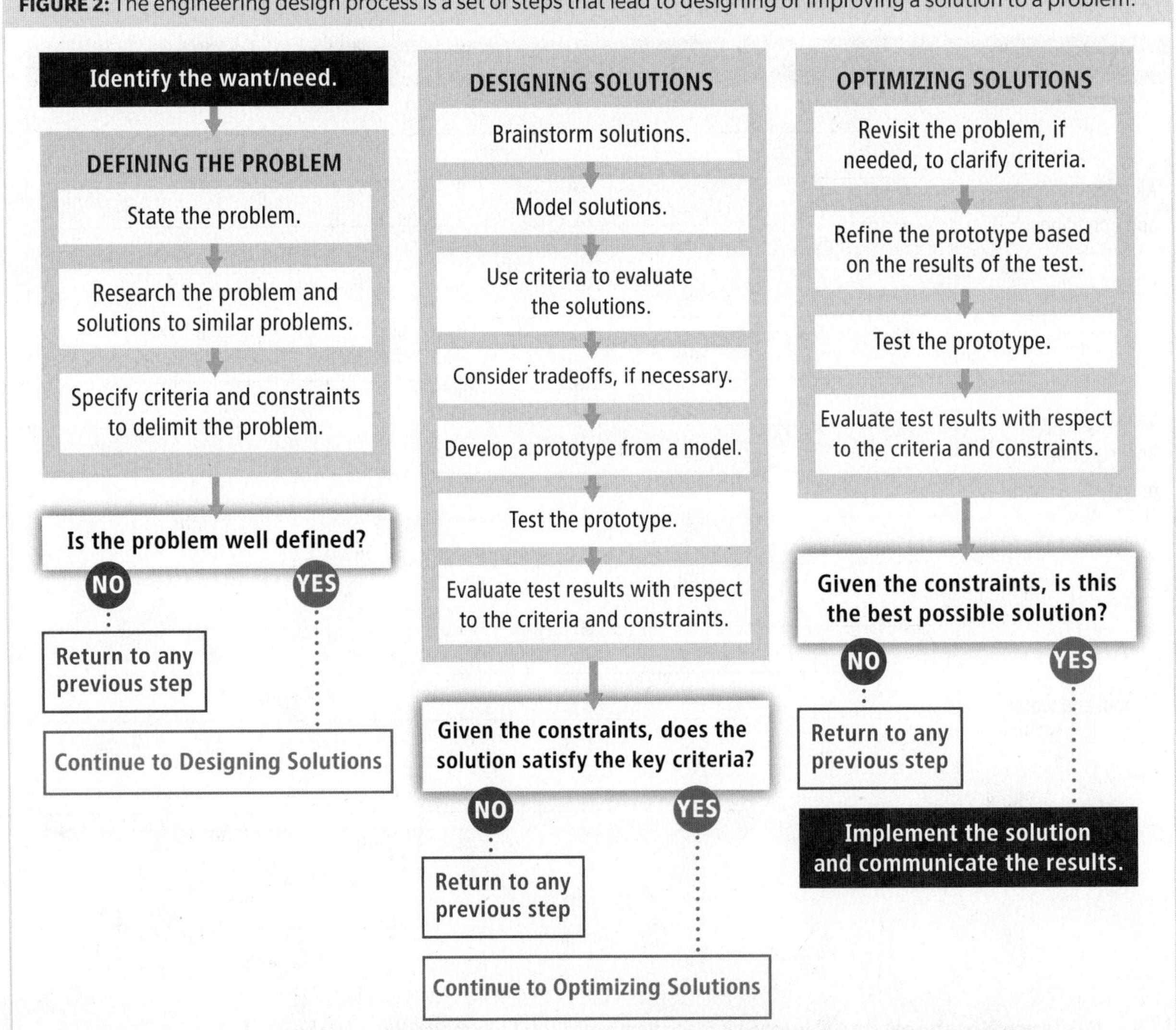

Collaborate With a partner, think of a process or tool you use at school. What need does it address? Are there other possible solutions?

The engineering design process is used to develop or improve technology to solve problems. *Technology* is any tool, machine, process, or system designed to address a problem or need. Figure 3 shows one way technology can help to model or test solutions.

APPLY How might a computer-based technology help you design a solution?

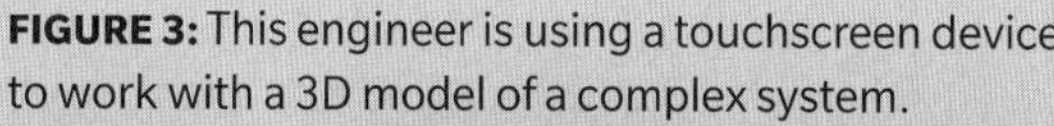

FIGURE 3: This engineer is using a touchscreen device to work with a 3D model of a complex system.

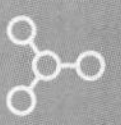

Influence of Engineering, Technology, and Science on Society and the Natural World

Chemical Engineering

Chemical engineering is the application of chemistry to solve real-world, relevant problems. Chemical engineers aim to develop products or chemical processes that are efficient, environmentally sound, safe, and cost-effective. They may develop new materials or design new equipment for a production process. Often, chemical engineers are responsible for planning, designing, and optimizing processes at plants that manufacture chemicals for use in a wide range of industries.

ASK Think of ways that technologies such as telephones, televisions, light bulbs, computers, or food packaging have changed since an adult you know was a child. What were some impacts of the changes? Were all the impacts positive?

The advancement of science and technology may provide better solutions with fewer risks to human health and environmental integrity. But today's solutions may lead to unanticipated problems tomorrow. Developing and improving products and processes is at the heart of chemical engineering.

Evidence Notebook The engineering design process is iterative, meaning some or all of its steps may be repeated. What does the iterative nature of the engineering design process tell you about your unit project goal of optimizing a toothpaste?

Defining the Problem

Imagine one of your classmates walks in one day and makes an announcement: "We need a solution!" How would you respond? To design a solution, engineers must establish what the problem is and what need or want the solution should address. Next, they identify the groups affected by the problem, relevant scientific issues, and possible impacts on the environment and society. Once this is done, they can identify the main components of the problem, including what contributes to the problem and what is affected by it.

Identifying criteria helps engineers further define the problem by giving them a set of goals for the solution. Criteria are the features that a successful solution should have—that is, criteria are the "wants" that the solution will fulfill. Criteria (or a *criterion*) can include many factors. For example, imagine a team of engineers is developing a new toothpaste that has a blue, mint-flavored stripe. They would need to consider several possible criteria.

APPLY The blue, mint-flavored stripe is an example of a design criterion for the toothpaste. What other criteria might this design have?

____

____

____

____

____

After engineers define the problem, they delimit the problem. *Delimiting* is the process of determining the constraints of the solution. Constraints are the limitations of a design. They are sometimes, but not always, provided by a client. These constraints may relate to considerations such as cost, weight, safety, available resources and technologies, and time. Any solution that does not meet the constraints of the design is generally not considered. In the toothpaste example, some constraints the client might impose include a maximum cost, a blue stripe that does not "bleed" into the white toothpaste, a specific thickness for the toothpaste, or a tube with a specific design.

ANALYZE The client told the engineering team that they want production costs for the new toothpaste (with the blue stripe) to be the same as for the old toothpaste. They want to continue to use the same design for the tube, which is made of plastic. Consider whether each of the following statements represents a criterion or a constraint for this engineering problem.

criterion constraint

The blue stripe should be a particular shade of blue. _______________

Adding the blue stripe must not exceed a certain cost. _______________

The chemicals in the blue stripe must not react with plastic. _______________

The toothpaste foam should be white or light blue. _______________

The toothpaste should taste like peppermint, not spearmint. _______________

Designing Solutions

After defining and delimiting the problem, engineers work in teams to brainstorm solutions. Potential solutions are evaluated against criteria and constraints. Teams then test the top ideas, often with the help of models or simulations. They evaluate the results of that testing, again using the criteria and constraints as a guide.

Engineering

Considering Tradeoffs

It is not always possible for a solution to fulfill every criterion within the given constraints. In such cases, engineers may need to decide which criteria are most important, and whether the drawbacks of a given design outweigh its benefits. A **tradeoff** is an exchange of one thing for another. Engineers may give up one criterion if doing so enables them to keep another or avoid a potential risk. For example, the blue, minty stripe might reduce the amount of foam the toothpaste produces when used. Engineers must then decide whether that tradeoff is worthwhile.

FIGURE 4: Even a new toothpaste design requires careful evaluation of criteria and constraints.

EVALUATE Think about some criteria that are important when developing a product such as toothpaste. What tradeoffs would you consider making to ensure that your most important criteria are met in your final design solution?

Tradeoffs may be made because of social, financial, or environmental constraints. For example, engineers may find that the dye in the blue stripe is harmful to aquatic organisms. Engineers may decide to replace the blue dye with one that is more expensive but is not harmful to aquatic organisms. Using the alternative dye might raise the price of making the toothpaste.

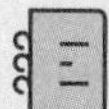

Evidence Notebook If tradeoffs are necessary, it can be helpful for engineers to rank the design criteria so they can decide which tradeoffs to make. What are the design criteria for your unit project? How important is each criterion relative to the others?

Optimizing Solutions

Optimization is the process of further evaluating a solution or design in order to improve or refine it. Scale models, prototypes, and computer simulations are often used in this step. Chemical engineers often optimize processes rather than products. Based on the test results, engineers may decide to implement a solution or return to an earlier step. Their goal may be minimizing cost, maximizing efficiency, or both. One way to optimize and test a design is through user testing. Suppose a chemical engineer develops a prototype for the toothpaste with a blue minty stripe. User tests can provide engineers with information about the flavor, the amount of foaming, and the effectiveness of the toothpaste.

Collaborate With a partner, discuss qualitative and quantitative ways of reporting user testing results for a toothpaste. Discuss other products for which each would be more useful.

Small-scale prototypes may be developed as a way to test a solution without the expense of large-scale manufacturing. Chemical engineers may develop models, conduct lab experiments, or run computer simulations to test solutions. For example, they may do lab experiments to test how fast a blue dye breaks down in different temperatures of water. They may even test two prototypes to determine how well each one meets the criteria and constraints of the design. If neither prototype fully satisfies the criteria and constraints, engineers may refine the problem definition or brainstorm new solutions.

Chemical engineers use the results of their testing to optimize their solutions. Even a finished design can be made better as new opportunities or unanticipated problems arise.

MODEL Suppose you have a lot of homework that has to be done this weekend, and an important event on Saturday. Devise a plan for how to meet all of your obligations. Make a flowchart or other model that describes the key steps of your plan.

EXPLAIN How does your model relate to the engineering design process?

Engineering

Process Design

Chemical engineers often work in process design, where they are tasked with designing or refining systems involved in large-scale production of chemicals for industrial use. Because it is not feasible to build and test multiple prototype chemical processing plants, chemical process engineers rely heavily on models such as diagrams and computer simulations. Such models enable engineers to identify unnecessary steps or other inefficiencies in a process, or to track how much product and waste is produced. Diagrams may be simple block flow diagrams, showing only a basic overview of how a starting material is converted into a final product, or they may be more complex diagrams that indicate energy flows or piping and instrumentation.

FIGURE 5: This chemical engineer is reviewing a process flow diagram.

EVALUATE Which problem would a process engineer be likely to work on?

○ **a.** developing new uses for a material in the marketplace

○ **b.** optimizing a method to increase the yield of a material

○ **c.** studying how a material behaves under different conditions

○ **d.** studying how to synthesize a material from different components

The production of methanol from syngas is an example of a chemical process. Syngas is produced by treating a starter material to yield a mixture of carbon dioxide, carbon monoxide, and hydrogen. It is often used to make methanol, an additive in fuel. Chemical engineers might use a process flow diagram to increase the yield from a given quantity of starter material such as coal, natural gas, or biomass. The process can be diagrammed with arrows showing the steps from starter material to finished product. This helps engineers analyze the process and refine it to achieve a maximum yield of methanol from a minimum amount of syngas, at the lowest cost. Constraints such as worker safety and environmental regulations may also need to be addressed.

Heat is important in syngas production, and there are many ways to produce and maintain high temperatures with minimum fuel use. Engineers use process flow diagrams along with models, computers, and sometimes prototype plants to determine whether a plant design meets temperature and fuel needs. After full-scale manufacturing begins, temperature, pressure, and input-output data are collected. Analysis of the data may reveal that changes in settings or materials could improve efficiency.

Language Arts Connection Use several sources to research process flow diagrams. Synthesize your research in a presentation that shows an example diagram, describes the system it is used for, and explains the symbols used.

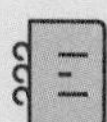

Evidence Notebook Think about how the engineering design process could be used to develop an edible utensil. In your Evidence Notebook, explain how a chemical engineer might go about defining and delimiting the problem.

Systems and Models

You have been tasked with optimizing the flow of foot traffic in a public place such as a grocery store or your school. You decide to make a scale model to test different traffic patterns and layouts. Your client gives you an information sheet that includes the dimensions of the space, the number of people who use it each day, the locations of entrances and exits, the average temperature in the area, the floor color, and the positions of obstructions such as shelves or benches.

EVALUATE Which of the factors listed on the information sheet would be useful to you in modeling the problem and testing potential solutions? Which would not? Explain.

____

____

____

____

Systems Define Scientific Problems

In choosing which features are relevant to the foot-traffic problem and which are not, you did what scientists and engineers do frequently: you defined the problem by isolating it as a system. A system is a set of interacting, interrelated, or interdependent parts that are treated as a whole for the purpose of study. Scientists or engineers define the boundaries of a system according to the question or problem they are studying.

FIGURE 6: A syngas methanol plant is a complex system. Its chemical processes use natural gas or coal as inputs to produce methanol, one of the system's outputs.

Interactions within and between Systems

A system's *inputs* are the matter, energy, or information that flow into the system. *Outputs* are the matter, energy, or information that flow out of the system.

Methanol production at the plant shown in Figure 6 involves a series of chemical reactions in which reactants, usually natural gas or coal, enter as inputs, and methanol leaves as a product, or desired output. There are many intermediate steps in this process, carried out by multiple components. Each component of the overall methanol production system can be viewed as its own system. For example, a reactor in the plant, such as the one illustrated in Figure 7, can be studied as a subsystem interacting with other subsystems inside the plant.

The components of the syngas system include controls to keep the system working properly by monitoring and managing the inputs and outputs. An important control is feedback, information from one step of a cycle that changes the behavior of a previous step. So, feedback is an output that becomes an input.

FIGURE 7: A syngas methanol plant is made of smaller subsystems, each of which can be isolated. A reactor is an example of a smaller system inside a larger system.

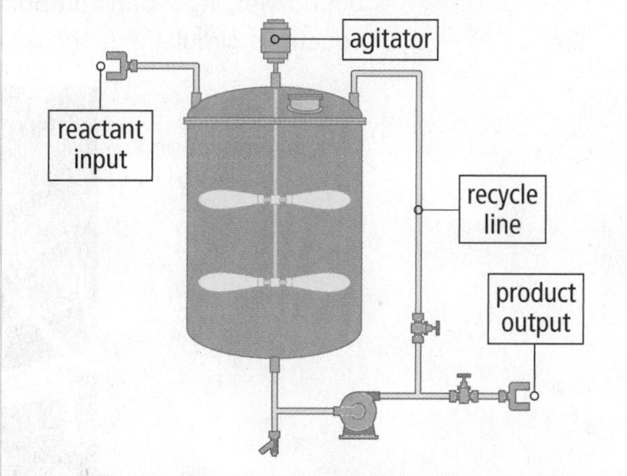

Categorizing Systems

We can use the idea of a system to study the flow of matter or energy. Energy is the capacity to change matter. Both energy and matter are conserved—that is, neither one can be created or destroyed. A system can be categorized according to whether matter or energy can move across its boundaries. In an open system, such as your body, energy and matter flow between the system and its surroundings. The boundary between the Earth system and the surrounding outer-space environment is open to energy but closed to matter. Some systems are closed to both matter and energy.

Everything inside a system's boundary is part of that system, and everything outside of the boundary is part of the surrounding environment. In a system closed to matter, or to matter and energy, the boundary often corresponds to a physical boundary, such as the glass walls of a beaker. The boundaries of an open system may or may not have a corresponding physical structure.

FIGURE 8: A hot air balloon burns fuel to heat air in the balloon, causing the balloon to float.

ANALYZE If we define the boundary of the hot air balloon system in Figure 8 as the balloon, cables, and basket, what happens to matter and energy as they flow through the system?

- ○ **a.** Both matter and energy move in and out of the system.
- ○ **b.** Energy crosses the system boundaries, but matter does not.
- ○ **c.** Neither matter nor energy can cross the system boundaries.

MODEL Draw a sketch of a hot air balloon and of a helium balloon. Define the systems by identifying the system boundaries. Show inputs and outputs of matter and energy in each.

Modeling Systems

Engineers often use models to study systems and the interactions within and among them. Think back to the hot air balloon system you sketched. You identified the system's boundaries, inputs, and outputs. This sketch is a type of model. Models can also be equations, simulations, or physical models, such as the one shown in Figure 9.

FIGURE 9: These engineers are using a physical model to study pollution.

Another way to study a system is to use a mathematical model that describes how the flow of energy or matter is affected by changes in one or more components. For example, a mathematical model might enable an engineer to figure out how hot the air inside the balloon needs to be for it to rise at a certain rate. A different mathematical model might enable the engineer to determine how much weight a balloon of a certain size can carry.

A mathematical model may include chemical or mathematical equations that represent relationships among the components of a system. Such models can be used to generate computer simulations of the system's behavior under different conditions and over different periods of time.

FIGURE 10: This computer model was generated to study how a network of tin atoms responds to changes in temperature.

APPLY An atom can be described as a subsystem that makes up part of a substance. The computer model in Figure 10 shows one way atoms can be modeled. Describe two other ways you could model atoms in a substance.

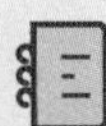

Evidence Notebook What are some different ways you could define systems involving an edible spoon? List at least two, and describe how each one could help you define the criteria and constraints of the design problem.

Case Study: Biosphere 2

Imagine you are tasked with designing a miniature version of Earth that could be used to colonize faraway planets or moons. That idea was the basis of Biosphere 2, a domed structure made of glass and concrete in Oracle, Arizona. The facility is now a tourist destination and research site, but it was originally built as a research prototype for self-sustaining space-colonization technology—a system that would contain everything needed to support human life in the hostile conditions outside the Earth system.

Collaborate With a partner, discuss the features a system would need to have in order to support human life in space. What are some criteria and constraints of the design?

Engineering an Earth-System Prototype

Biosphere 2, shown in Figure 11, contained seven biomes, including a farm area to produce food for humans living inside. The human habitat served as living quarters, and an underground technosphere housed heating, cooling, electrical, and plumbing systems. Two "lungs," connected to the structure by tunnels, regulated air pressure.

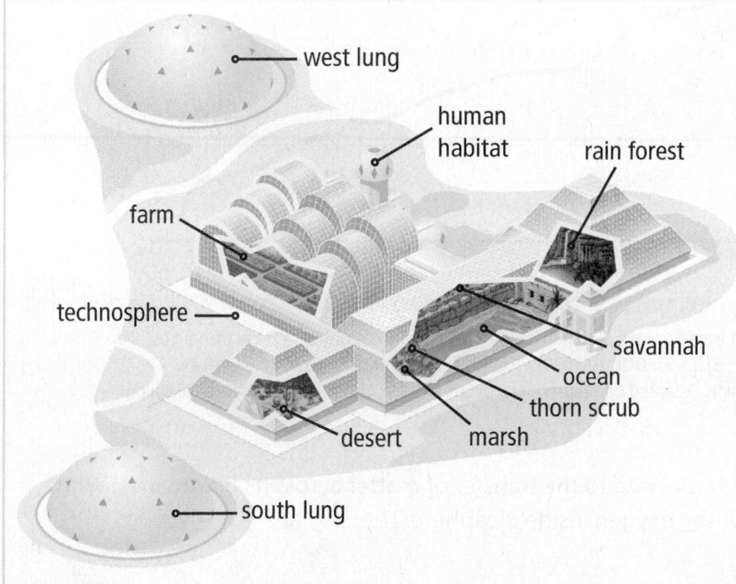

FIGURE 11: Biosphere 2 was designed to support humans and other organisms using only the sun's energy as an input from outside its boundaries.

ANALYZE The boundaries of Biosphere 2 were closed to matter but not to energy. How do you think this feature of the design helped to address its criteria and constraints?

Energy and Matter

Oxygen Loss in Biosphere 2

The first Biosphere 2 mission began in 1991, when eight scientists went into the structure and stayed for nearly two years. The scientists grew their own food, maintained the facility, and gathered data about the ecological interactions and environment inside the biosphere system over time.

The cycling of carbon and oxygen through photosynthesis and cellular respiration was crucial to the design. Plants inside provided oxygen and food for the scientists and other organisms. Cellular respiration by these organisms, in turn, provided carbon dioxide, which is necessary for photosynthesis. On Earth, these processes help keep the atmospheric oxygen concentration at about 21%. Inside Biosphere 2, however, oxygen levels began to drop soon after the experiment began, as shown in Figure 12.

Atmospheric Oxygen Concentrations in Biosphere 2

FIGURE 12: Oxygen concentrations decreased steadily over the first 500 days of the first Biosphere 2 mission.

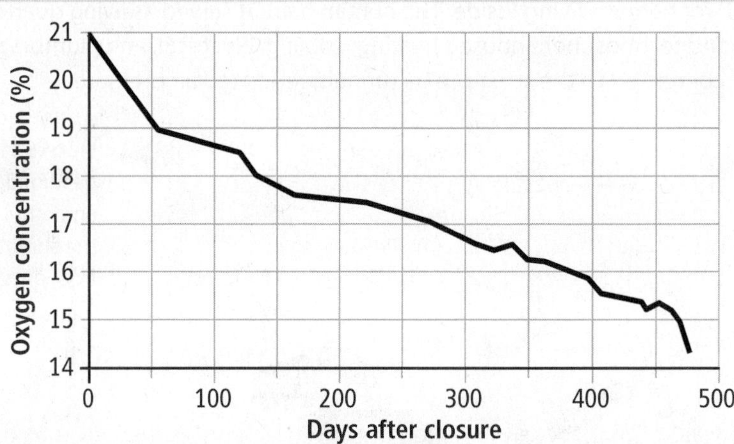

Credit: Adapted from "Oxygen Loss in Biosphere 2" by Jeff Severinghaus, et al., from *Eos, Transactions,* 75(3) 33-37. DOI: 10.1029/94EO00285. Copyright © 1994 by American Geophysical Union. Adapted and reproduced by permission of American Geophysical Union.

PREDICT Biosphere 2 was closed to the transfer of matter across its boundaries. What does that tell you about the oxygen inside Biosphere 2?

Eventually, oxygen levels decreased so much that it was not safe for the scientists to continue the experiment. Outside oxygen was pumped into the facility. The experiment to build a self-sustaining, closed system had failed, but now the researchers could continue their research safely.

Analyzing the Results

The cause of the oxygen loss in Biosphere 2 was not immediately clear, but later analysis revealed that the problem was due in part to the highly enriched farm soil. Organic matter added to the soil allowed important microbes to flourish, but the microbes' rate of respiration was faster than the plants' rate of photosynthesis.

ANALYZE Given the decrease in oxygen inside Biosphere 2, would you expect the carbon dioxide levels to have increased, decreased, or remained stable? Explain.

FIGURE 13: Despite its lush appearance and high farm productivity, the Biosphere 2 system did not provide enough atmospheric oxygen for the organisms living inside.

Carbon dioxide levels in Biosphere 2 did not increase, which pointed to a cause other than excessive respiration. That turned out to be the structure itself. Rather than being taken up by plants for photosynthesis, some of the carbon dioxide released during respiration reacted with chemicals in the concrete walls to form calcium carbonate, also known as limestone. Thus, carbon dioxide was no longer available in the atmosphere and water for photosynthetic plants and algae.

Collaborate What constraints were not met in the first Biosphere 2 experiment? Do you think engineers would respond to this result by redefining the design constraints and criteria or by modifying the design? Discuss with a partner.

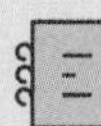

Evidence Notebook Think back to the idea of an edible spoon that will not fill up landfills. What are some potential negative impacts of designing or implementing this solution?

Engineering

Multiscale Modeling

Engineers often use models to understand problems and develop solutions. If a system problem is complex, they may use more than one model. A model is designed to represent a system at a certain scale. For example, a process flow diagram for a chemical plant shows the flow of energy and matter through the system, but it does not indicate the molecular structures of the reactants or products. The scale used for a model depends on what the engineer needs to study about the system.

Engineers who want to understand systems at different scales can use multiple-scale, or multiscale, modeling. This approach can increase the effectiveness of each model. Information obtained from a model of a system at a very small scale can be used to alter the design of a larger-scale model. Similarly, information from a larger model can reveal areas of a system that might need to be studied on a smaller scale.

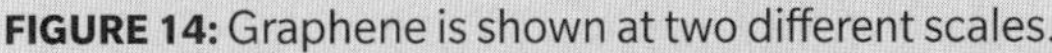

FIGURE 14: Graphene is shown at two different scales.

Explore Online

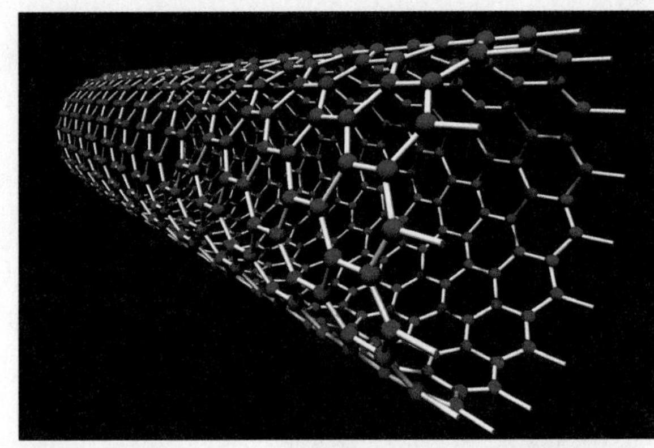

a This 3D model shows the molecular structure of cylindrical graphene, also known as a carbon nanotube.

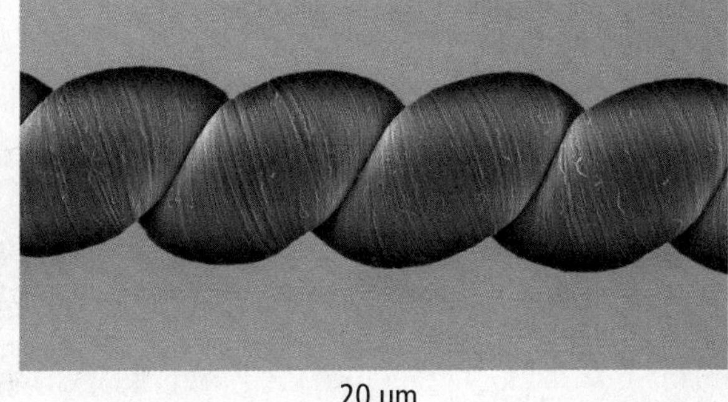

b This yarn is made up of carbon nanotubes woven together. Engineers want to use the yarn to convert mechanical energy to electrical energy.

Figure 14a is a model of a carbon nanotube (CNT) at the particle level, and Figure 14b shows a prototype for a CNT yarn that can be used to convert mechanical energy to electrical energy. CNTs are very strong, have unique electrical properties, and are good conductors of heat. Graphene molecules can be arranged in a single layer to make single-walled nanotubes, or they can be layered to form multi-walled nanotubes. The properties of CNTs vary with their structure. Because the function of a CNT is related to its molecular structure, multiscale models can be helpful to engineers and scientists studying them.

ANALYZE What unique information does each model in Figure 14 provide?

When designing a product to have a specific property, a scientist might use a physical model, such as the CNT prototype in Figure 14b, to study its physical properties. They may also use a molecular model, such as the one in Figure 14a, to understand the chemical properties of the CNT.

To better understand or solve complex problems involving many variables, scientists and engineers also often use computer simulations. Computer simulations are based on mathematical models of systems. These models enable scientists to test the effects of changing one or more variables, and to understand how a system behaves over yet another scale—time.

Use a Model Research ways that computer simulations can be used in multiscale modeling. Next, find a simulation that depicts a specific property of matter on a particle level. Ask your teacher for suggestions if you are not sure where to find a simulation.

EVALUATE What property of matter will you choose to study? How does the simulation you found model this property?

Develop a Model Now, design your own model that depicts the same property of matter as the computer simulation, but on a different scale. You may design a computer simulation, a prototype, a 3D model, or an image. Be sure to have your plan approved by your teacher before you begin development.

EXPLAIN Think about the systems that your two models work within. What are the boundaries, inputs, and outputs of each system? How does each model show the interaction of matter within and between systems at different scales?

Language Arts Connection Present your research, the computer simulation you studied, the model you designed, and the systems involved in each of your models to your class. In your presentation, explain how modeling a property of matter at two different scales helped you learn more about that property.

CORRELATION VS. CAUSATION | FOOD TECHNOLOGIST |  MODELING A SYSTEM | Go online to choose one of these other paths.

Lesson Self-Check

CAN YOU SOLVE THE PROBLEM?

FIGURE 15: Edible spoons may be a viable alternative to plastic, because they do not accumulate in landfills.

Now that you have learned about criteria and constraints in the engineering design process, you can apply them to the problem of developing an edible spoon. Like any solution, the edible spoon design should fulfill certain wants and must address certain needs. These criteria and constraints apply not just to the spoon itself but to the process by which it is manufactured. The evidence you have collected during your study of the engineering design process can be used to understand some of the criteria and constraints that might develop during the process of designing an edible spoon.

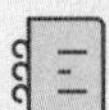

Evidence Notebook Refer to your notes in your Evidence Notebook to make a claim about the criteria of an edible spoon design. Your explanation should include a discussion of the following points:

Claims What properties should an edible spoon have—that is, what are the design criteria? What are the design constraints?

Evidence What information or evidence supports your list of criteria and constraints?

Reasoning How does the evidence you provided support your claim about the criteria and constraints for an edible spoon design?

Name

Date

CHECKPOINTS

Check Your Understanding

1. Why is it important to identify and rank criteria before designing a solution to an engineering problem?
   - ○ **a.** to establish a budget for the solution
   - ○ **b.** to identify challenges to the solution
   - ○ **c.** to avoid pursuing solutions that do not meet key goals or needs
   - ○ **d.** to determine the economic impact

2. Which step would scientists and engineers be least likely to use a model for?
   - ○ **a.** simulating interactions within or between systems
   - ○ **b.** defining and delimiting a problem
   - ○ **c.** studying systems at different scales
   - ○ **d.** demonstrating the flow of matter or energy through a system

3. An engineer is testing a new recipe for canned vegetable soup. She finds that the squash in the soup gets mushy when the soup is heat-treated to make it safe to eat. She rejects this recipe and tests a new one without squash. What does that indicate about the constraints of the soup design?
   - ○ **a.** The soup must be safe to eat.
   - ○ **b.** The soup must cost less than a certain amount to produce.
   - ○ **c.** The soup's texture is not a constraint.
   - ○ **d.** The engineer changed her mind about the constraints.

4. Complete the statement about Biosphere 2.

   The Biosphere 2 system was designed to be open | closed to the transfer of matter across its boundaries. The unexpected drop in oxygen in the Biosphere 2 atmosphere resulted from a combination of factors including soil composition and building materials. This indicates that the system boundaries | interactions were not correctly identified.

5. A chemical engineer is developing a manufacturing process for a new kind of fertilizer. Which factor would be unlikely to appear in a diagram of the process?
   - ○ **a.** amount of reactant input
   - ○ **b.** amount of product output
   - ○ **c.** boundaries between the system and the environment
   - ○ **d.** tradeoffs among different criteria

6. Which statements are true of an open system? Select all correct answers.
   - ☐ **a.** Matter enters and leaves the system but energy does not.
   - ☐ **b.** Both matter and energy leave the system.
   - ☐ **c.** Energy enters and leaves the system but matter does not.
   - ☐ **d.** Its boundaries are defined by the person studying the system.

7. You have been hired by a state government to help decide whether to retrofit a coal plant to reduce its emissions or to build a new power plant that does not rely on coal. Place these steps in the order in which you would proceed.
   - _____ **a.** Collect and evaluate data about each model.
   - _____ **b.** Design models of potential solutions to test whether they meet the criteria and constraints.
   - _____ **c.** Use the results of testing to choose a solution to use or optimize.
   - _____ **d.** Identify and define the goals of the project and any limitations such as budget, time, and community concerns.

CHECKPOINTS (continued)

8. What are some advantages to modeling a system? What are some limitations?

9. Why is it important to take into account potential environmental or social impacts when evaluating possible solutions to a problem? Give an example to support your explanation.

10. How and when does iteration occur in the engineering design process? Why is it such an important aspect of designing solutions? Use an example to explain.

MAKE YOUR OWN STUDY GUIDE

In your Evidence Notebook, design a study guide that supports the main ideas from this lesson:

Scientists and engineers define systems in order to isolate and study interactions within and between components of systems.

Chemical engineers use chemistry to define and solve problems. They use the engineering design process to find optimal solutions to these problems, and to refine solutions as new data or technologies become available.

Remember to include the following information in your study guide:

- Use examples that model main ideas.
- Record explanations for the phenomena you investigated.
- Use evidence to support your explanations. Your support can include drawings, data, graphs, laboratory conclusions, and other evidence recorded throughout the lesson.

Consider how chemical engineers use the engineering design process to find solutions to unanticipated impacts of new technologies.

Earth Science Connection

Building Stone Used for centuries to construct some of the world's most enduring structures, building stone such as granite, limestone, slate, and marble is known for its sustainability and durability. When choosing stone for countertops, roofing, or flooring, architects must consider the unique properties of each material. For example, slate can easily be split into thin sheets, making it ideal as a roofing material. Granite and marble make good countertops, because both stay cool near a hot stove.

Using a range of sources, develop a brochure on two different types of building stone and their applications. The brochure should emphasize the properties of each material that make it a good choice for a specific use. It should also include other considerations, such as price and environmental impact, which affect the decision to use one over another.

FIGURE 1: This roof is made of slate.

Music Connection

Designing Musical Instruments If you knock on metal and then knock on wood, you might hear that different materials make different types of sounds. The materials used to make a musical instrument are as important as the shape of the instrument for producing its unique sound. Sounds move through materials in different ways, and these differences affect the tone and quality of the sound the instrument produces.

Select an instrument or a family of instruments and research how the material it is made from affects the sound. Synthesize your findings into a presentation. If possible, have audio examples of sound differences or demonstrate using your own "homemade" instruments.

FIGURE 2: Some instruments are made of wood, while others are made of metal.

Technology Connection

Barnacle Glue Barnacles attach to docks, boats, and anything they come across. Their glue sets in salt water and stays set, as anyone who has cleaned the bottom of a boat can tell you. Engineers are developing ways to make similar glues that work underwater. They are also investigating using barnacle glue as a medical adhesive.

Research the properties of barnacle glue, what makes it so strong, and its ability to work underwater. How does the ability to work underwater make it useful as biomedical glue? Summarize two scientific papers or articles on the uses of barnacle glue. Do the authors come to the same conclusion? Cite specific evidence to support your analysis.

FIGURE 3: This scanning electron micrograph shows the glue threads of an acorn barnacle. These allow the barnacle to adhere to surfaces, even underwater.

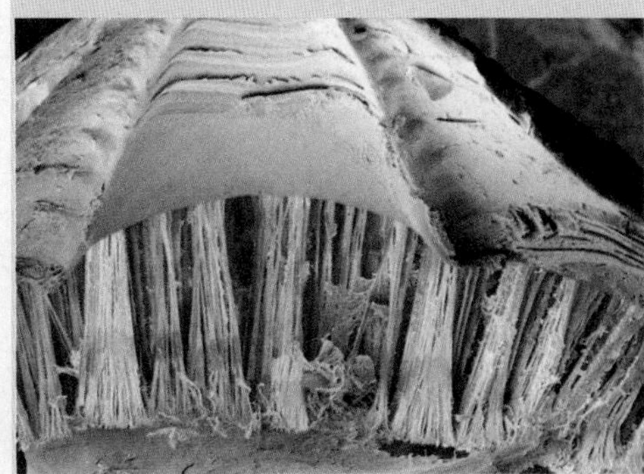

A BOOK EXPLAINING COMPLEX IDEAS USING ONLY THE 1,000 MOST COMMON WORDS

THING EXPLAINER
COMPLICATED STUFF IN SIMPLE WORDS
RANDALL MUNROE

RANDALL MUNROE
XKCD.COM

HOW TO COUNT THINGS

A counting system to help people agree with each other

You've learned that scientists all over the world have agreed on a single measurement system called SI. Here's a look at how we use SI to measure the length, velocity, temperature, and mass of things in our world.

THE STORY OF COUNTING HOW LONG, WARM, FAST, AND HEAVY

TO COUNT HOW HEAVY THINGS ARE, WE PICK A WEIGHT TO CALL "ONE." THEN, IF YOU SAY A WEIGHT IS "TEN," PEOPLE UNDERSTAND IT'S AS HEAVY AS TEN "ONES."

I THINK I LOST THREE ONES.

DO YOU FEEL THINNER?

WE DO THE SAME FOR COUNTING OTHER THINGS, LIKE HOW FAST OR HOT THINGS ARE.

I'M 37. YOU?

YOU DON'T WANT TO KNOW . . .

PEOPLE DON'T ALWAYS AGREE ON HOW MUCH "ONE" IS, WHICH CAN CAUSE A LOT OF PROBLEMS. A SPACE BOAT ONCE MISSED A WORLD BECAUSE PEOPLE GOT CONFUSED ABOUT WHICH "ONE" THEY SHOULD BE USING FOR WEIGHT.

SPACE OFFICE

I THINK IT'S TOO CLOSE!

MOST COUNTRIES HAVE AGREED TO MAKE "ONE" THE SAME THING EVERYWHERE. HERE'S WHAT NUMBERS FROM ONE TO TEN HUNDRED MEAN IN THAT COUNTING SYSTEM.

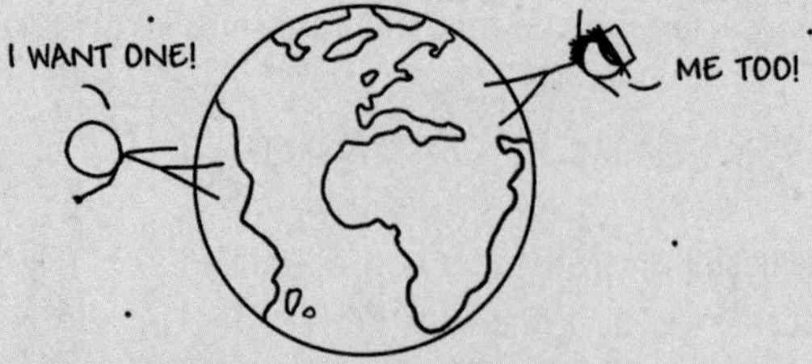

HOW LONG THINGS ARE

In this system, "one" is about half as tall as a tall person.

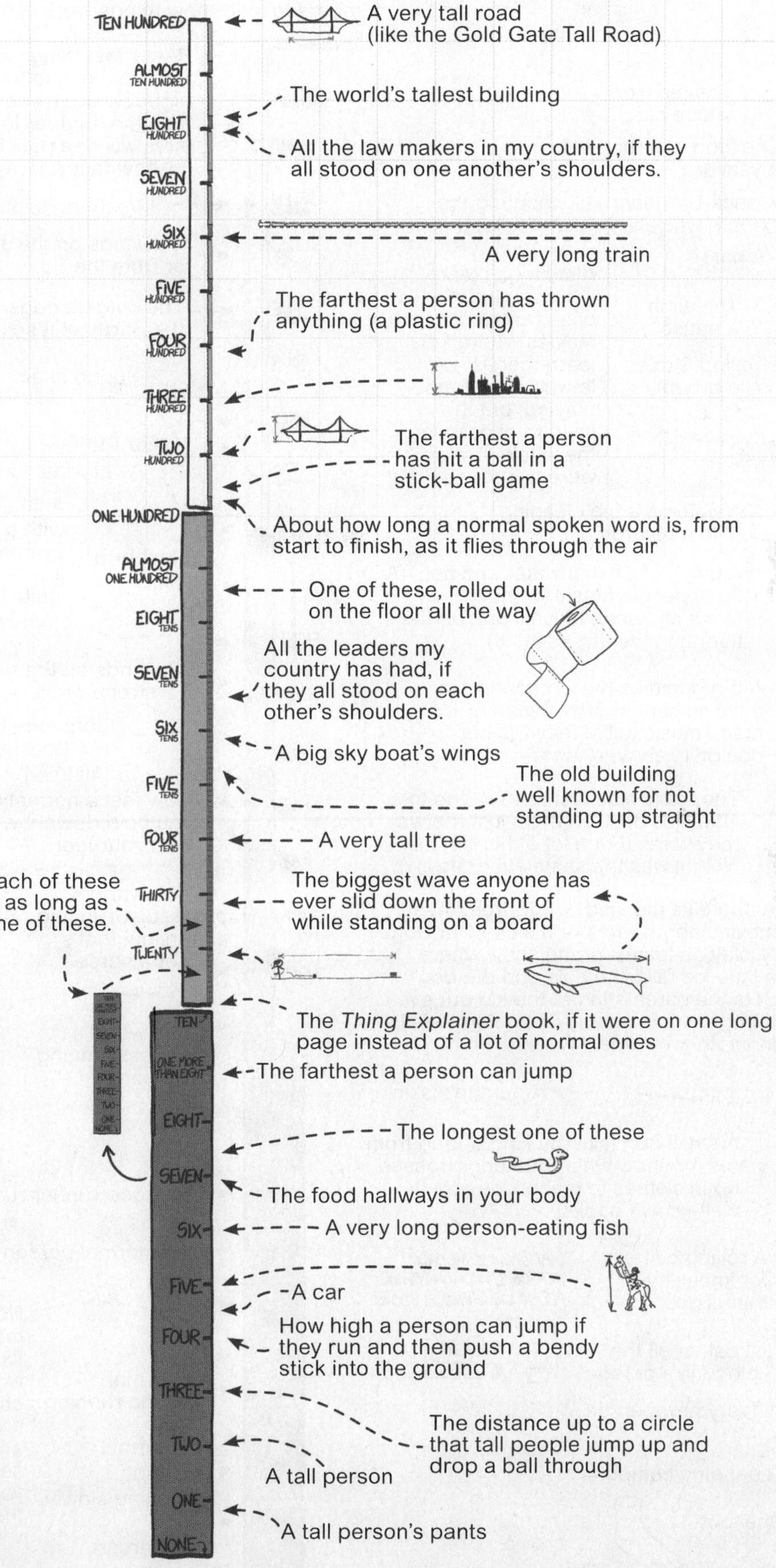

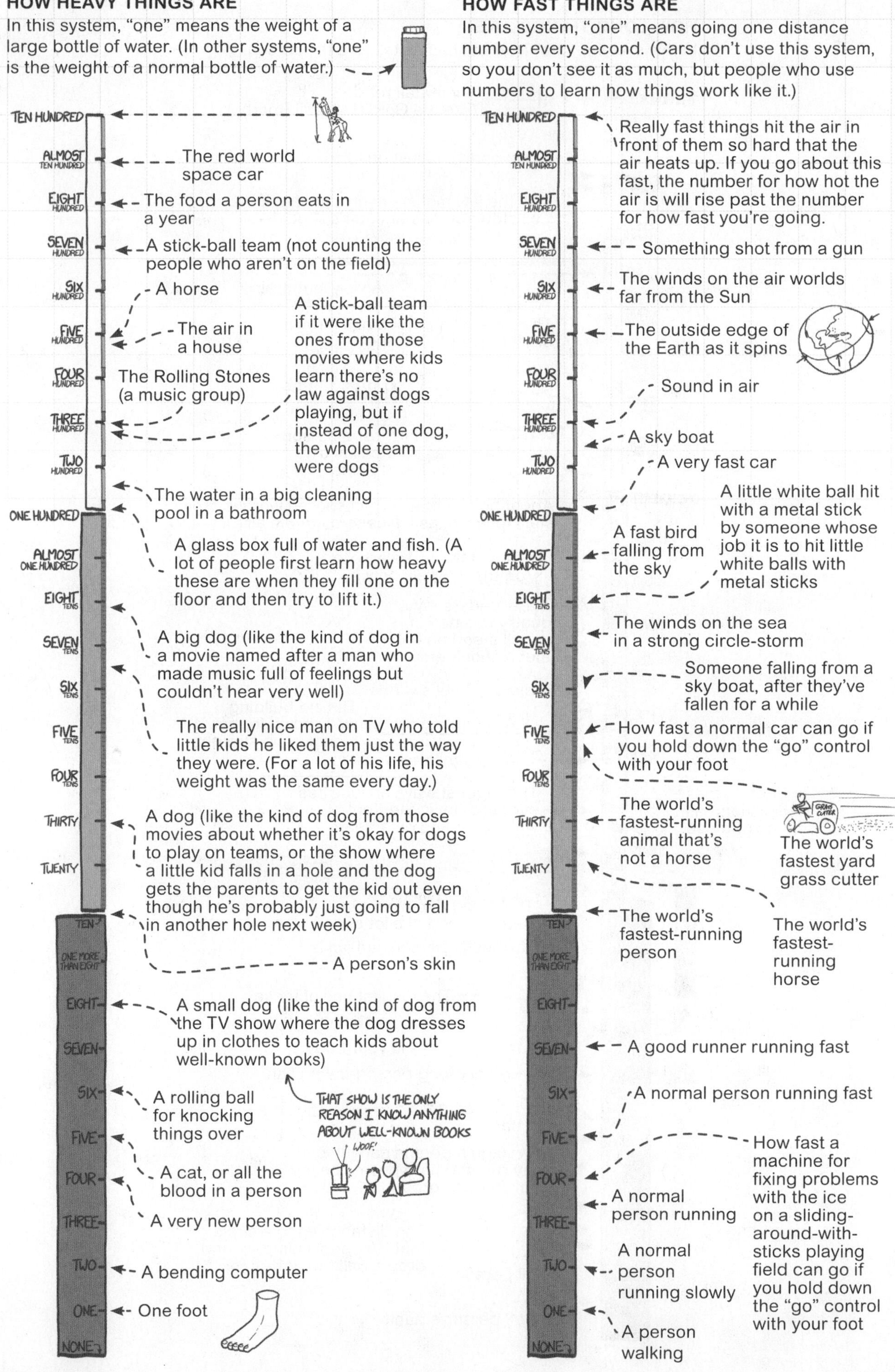
HOW HEAVY THINGS ARE
In this system, "one" means the weight of a large bottle of water. (In other systems, "one" is the weight of a normal bottle of water.)
TEN HUNDRED
ALMOST TEN HUNDRED
EIGHT HUNDRED
SEVEN HUNDRED
SIX HUNDRED
FIVE HUNDRED
FOUR HUNDRED
THREE HUNDRED
TWO HUNDRED
ONE HUNDRED
ALMOST ONE HUNDRED
EIGHT TENS
SEVEN TENS
SIX TENS
FIVE TENS
FOUR TENS
THIRTY
TWENTY
TEN
ONE MORE THAN EIGHT
EIGHT
SEVEN
SIX
FIVE
FOUR
THREE
TWO
ONE
NONE
The red world space car
The food a person eats in a year
A stick-ball team (not counting the people who aren't on the field)
A horse
The air in a house
A stick-ball team if it were like the ones from those movies where kids learn there's no law against dogs playing, but if instead of one dog, the whole team were dogs
The Rolling Stones (a music group)
The water in a big cleaning pool in a bathroom
A glass box full of water and fish. (A lot of people first learn how heavy these are when they fill one on the floor and then try to lift it.)
A big dog (like the kind of dog in a movie named after a man who made music full of feelings but couldn't hear very well)
The really nice man on TV who told little kids he liked them just the way they were. (For a lot of his life, his weight was the same every day.)
A dog (like the kind of dog from those movies about whether it's okay for dogs to play on teams, or the show where a little kid falls in a hole and the dog gets the parents to get the kid out even though he's probably just going to fall in another hole next week)
A person's skin
A small dog (like the kind of dog from the TV show where the dog dresses up in clothes to teach kids about well-known books)
THAT SHOW IS THE ONLY REASON I KNOW ANYTHING ABOUT WELL-KNOWN BOOKS
WOOF!
A rolling ball for knocking things over
A cat, or all the blood in a person
A very new person
A bending computer
One foot
HOW FAST THINGS ARE
In this system, "one" means going one distance number every second. (Cars don't use this system, so you don't see it as much, but people who use numbers to learn how things work like it.)
TEN HUNDRED
ALMOST TEN HUNDRED
EIGHT HUNDRED
SEVEN HUNDRED
SIX HUNDRED
FIVE HUNDRED
FOUR HUNDRED
THREE HUNDRED
TWO HUNDRED
ONE HUNDRED
ALMOST ONE HUNDRED
EIGHT TENS
SEVEN TENS
SIX TENS
FIVE TENS
FOUR TENS
THIRTY
TWENTY
TEN
ONE MORE THAN EIGHT
EIGHT
SEVEN
SIX
FIVE
FOUR
THREE
TWO
ONE
NONE
Really fast things hit the air in front of them so hard that the air heats up. If you go about this fast, the number for how hot the air is will rise past the number for how fast you're going.
Something shot from a gun
The winds on the air worlds far from the Sun
The outside edge of the Earth as it spins
Sound in air
A sky boat
A very fast car
A little white ball hit with a metal stick by someone whose job it is to hit little white balls with metal sticks
A fast bird falling from the sky
The winds on the sea in a strong circle-storm
Someone falling from a sky boat, after they've fallen for a while
How fast a normal car can go if you hold down the "go" control with your foot
The world's fastest-running animal that's not a horse
GRASS CUTTER
The world's fastest yard grass cutter
The world's fastest-running person
The world's fastest-running horse
A good runner running fast
A normal person running fast
How fast a machine for fixing problems with the ice on a sliding-around-with-sticks playing field can go if you hold down the "go" control with your foot
A normal person running
A normal person running slowly
A person walking

HOW WARM THINGS ARE

In this system, "none" means how cold water has to be to turn to ice, and "one hundred" means how hot it has to be to turn to air.

TEN HUNDRED — Hot rocks coming out of the ground

ALMOST TEN HUNDRED — If your kitchen table somehow got this hot, the silver eating sticks would turn to water and run off onto the floor.

A wood fire

EIGHT HUNDRED

SEVEN HUNDRED — If glass gets this hot, you can pour it like water.

SIX HUNDRED — Anything that gets this hot will start making red light

FIVE HUNDRED

The air at the surface of the hot sky world near Earth

FOUR HUNDRED

THREE HUNDRED — If food gets this hot, it will turn black and start smoking, and the box on your ceiling that yells when it gets too hot will start yelling.

TWO HUNDRED — The inside of a food-heating box

ONE HUNDRED — Water that's hot enough to turn to air

ALMOST ONE HUNDRED — Hot tea

EIGHT TENS — If you're heating food made from animals, getting the inside hotter than this will make the food bad (not everyone agrees about this).

SEVEN TENS — The wet air in those hot cloud rooms where people sit without any clothes and don't do anything

SIX TENS

The air in the world's hottest places

FIVE TENS — The inside of your body if it's having a very, very bad problem

FOUR TENS — The inside of your body

THIRTY — A warm pool people play in

TWENTY — How warm the air in a house should be. (Not everyone agrees about this.)

Cold enough that your parents will tell you that you need a coat

TEN — Cold enough that you actually do need a coat

ONE MORE THAN EIGHT

EIGHT

SEVEN

SIX — The cold box in your kitchen shouldn't get this warm. If food gets warmer than this, things can grow in it and make you sick.

FIVE

FOUR — Water deep in the sea

THREE

TWO

ONE

NONE — Ice

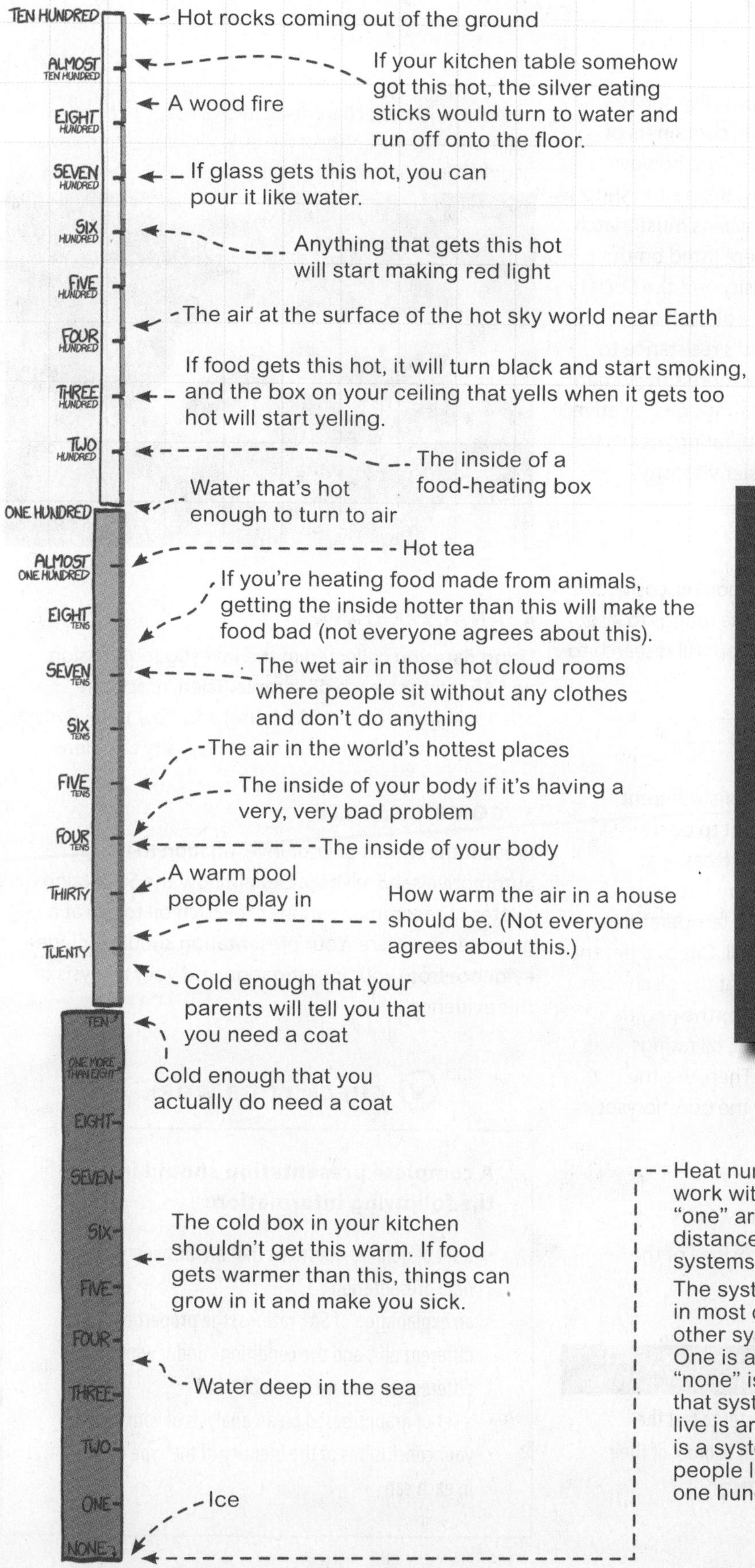

Heat numbers are a little confusing to work with, since the idea of "none" and "one" aren't as simple with heat as with distance or weight, and there are a few systems for counting it.

The system shown here is the one used in most of the world, but there are two other systems used in a lot of places. One is a system that's like this one, but "none" is the coldest anything can get. In that system, the air where most people live is around three hundred. The other is a system where the air where most people live doesn't get much hotter than one hundred or colder than none.

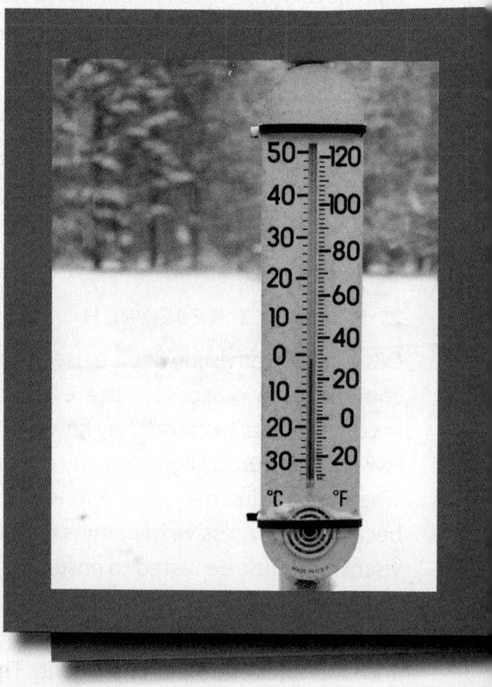

Investigating the Viscosity of Oil

You have been contacted by an automotive service shop that received a shipment of bulk containers of motor oil. Conditions during the transport, however, caused the labels to peel off the cans. Before the shop uses this oil in cars, the service technicians must match the cans with the types of oil that were listed on the shipping invoice based on the viscosity and the Society of Automotive Engineers (SAE) rating of each oil. Viscosity is a measurement of a liquid's resistance to flow. A fluid with high viscosity flows more slowly than a fluid with low viscosity does. SAE ratings give relative viscosity values for the oils. A low SAE rating means the fluid flows more readily, so it has lower viscosity.

1. ASK QUESTIONS

Develop a set of questions you have about viscosity, SAE ratings, and how you could assign these ratings to a set of oil samples. Identify all the factors you will research to answer these questions.

2. CONDUCT RESEARCH

Oils of different viscosities are used under different conditions. Low-viscosity oils are meant to be used in cold climates because they flow more easily at low temperatures. High-viscosity oils are better used when the engine may experience high temperatures because the excessive heat thins the oil. Oils of different viscosities must be tested to ensure that the oil chosen will work properly under the conditions the engine must run in. Research the different SAE oil ratings and examples of oils for each rating. Then, use the information you gathered to answer the question set you developed.

3. CARRY OUT AN INVESTIGATION

With your team, investigate the viscosities of the oil samples in the cans.

Hands-On Lab

Viscosity of Liquids Build a viscometer to test the viscosity of a set of oil samples. Rank them in order of their SAE ratings using data from your investigation.

FIGURE 4: This mechanic tests the viscosity of an oil sample. If the viscosity of the oil is too high or too low, it could cause damage to the engine.

4. ANALYZE DATA

Using data you collected in the investigation, assign an SAE rating to each oil sample. Then, graph the relationships between SAE rating and flow time, density, and viscosity, as well as between viscosity and density.

5. COMMUNICATE

Present the results of your investigation to the automotive service shop. Explain how the SAE rating relates to recommendations for which oil to use at a given temperature. Your presentation should include evidence from your investigation and your analysis of this evidence.

A complete presentation should include the following information:

- a set of guiding questions that are answered in the final presentation
- an explanation of SAE ratings, the properties of different oils, and the conditions under which different oils are meant to be used
- a set of graphs based on an analysis of your data
- your conclusions of the identity of the type of oil in each can

Name ______________________ Date ______________

SYNTHESIZE THE UNIT

In your Evidence Notebook, make a concept map, other graphic organizer, or outline using the Study Guides you made for each lesson in this unit. Be sure to use evidence to support your claims.

When synthesizing individual information, remember to follow these general steps:

- Find the central idea of each piece of information.
- Think about the relationships among the central ideas.
- Combine the ideas to come up with a new understanding.

DRIVING QUESTIONS

Look back to the Driving Questions from the opening section of this unit. In your Evidence Notebook, review and revise your previous answers to those questions. Use the evidence you gathered and other observations you made throughout the unit to support your claims.

PRACTICE AND REVIEW

1. Which of the following are chemical changes? Select all correct answers.

- ☐ **a.** table salt dissolving in water
- ☐ **b.** a liquid evaporating to form a gas
- ☐ **c.** a force causing a sheet of metal to bend
- ☐ **d.** wooden logs burning to form ash
- ☐ **e.** hydrogen and oxygen forming water

2. Select the correct terms to complete the statement.

An example of a pure substance is carbon dioxide | salt water | wood. A mixture is heterogeneous | homogeneous if it has a uniform composition. A mixture is heterogeneous | homogeneous if its composition is not uniform. A mixture | pure substance can often be separated by techniques such as evaporation or filtration.

3. A group of scientists and engineers are developing a medication to treat a disease. Which statement describes a possible constraint for the medication?

- ○ **a.** The effectiveness of the medication will be tested during production.
- ○ **b.** The cost of producing the medication will be kept as low as possible.
- ○ **c.** A process for manufacturing the medication will have to be designed.
- ○ **d.** Compounds used in the medication should be easy to obtain or produce.

4. Select the correct terms to complete the statement.

The density of a liquid substance in a container is an intensive | extensive physical property of the substance, so it can be used to help identify the substance. The volume of the substance is an intensive | extensive property, so it cannot be used in identification because it changes | does not change with the amount of the substance present.

5. A chemical engineer is modifying the formula for a window cleaner. Order the steps of the engineering design process she might follow to accomplish this.

_____ **a.** do research to identify potential solutions

_____ **b.** test a new formula to see if it meets the desired criteria and constraints

_____ **c.** identify the ways she will try to improve the formula

_____ **d.** test a revised formula and consider any tradeoffs

_____ **e.** revise the formula based on test results

6. During a laboratory experiment, a student mixes baking soda with vinegar in a water bottle. The student quickly places a balloon on top of the water bottle. As the experiment proceeds, the balloon expands. Diagram this experiment, identifying the system boundaries and components, the type of system, and the flows of matter and energy.

7. A chemical engineer is asked to modify the formula for quick-setting mold casts used in forensics so the material sets in under two minutes. How can the engineer use the engineering design process to solve this problem?

8. Two formulas for the quick-setting mold casts described in the previous question are proposed. One formula will cost slightly more to manufacture, but can be manufactured immediately. The other will cost much less to manufacture, but will require upfront costs and time to equip the factory to produce it properly. How might the engineering teams analyze tradeoffs as they decide which formula is the best solution?

UNIT PROJECT

Return to your unit project. Prepare a presentation using your research and materials, and share it with the class. In your final presentation, evaluate the strength of your claim, evidence, and conclusions.

Remember these tips while evaluating:

- Was your claim supported by your evidence?
- What are some criteria and constraints of your toothpaste design?
- Look at the evidence gathered from your experiment. Does your evidence support your claim and reasoning regarding which ingredients make a better toothpaste?
- How could you revise your setup and procedure to further test your prediction, model, or the evidence you collected?

UNIT 2

Atoms and Elements

When some stars die, they explode as supernovas that send atoms of different elements off into space.

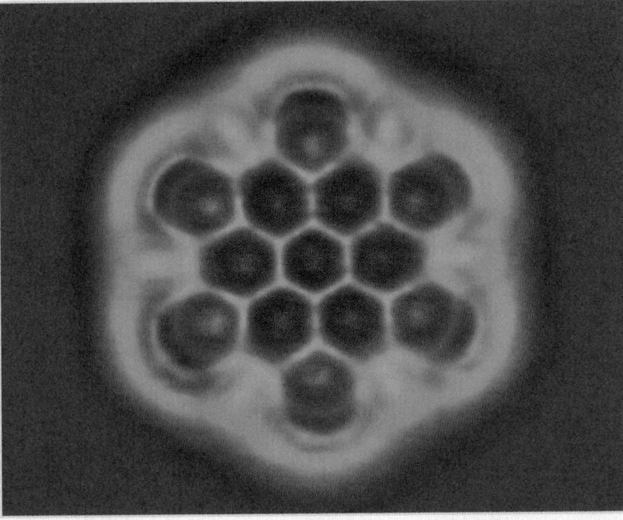

FIGURE 1: The carbon-carbon bonds of hexabenzocoronene are visible when imaged with an atomic force microscope.

Scientists study phenomena across a wide range of scales. Some scientists study tiny molecules. Hexabenzocoronene, shown in Figure 1, is only 1.4 nm in diameter and composed of even smaller molecular units. Other scientists study objects in space, such as supernova remnants, that can be thousands of light-years across. Although supernova remnants are very far away, scientists can use telescopes to determine the tiny atoms and molecules that make them up.

ANALYZE Atoms of nearly 100 elements are found on Earth. Most of these atoms formed during processes that occurred in the stars in space. What process do you think occurred in stars and supernovae to produce the atoms that make up everything on Earth?

DRIVING QUESTIONS

As you move through the unit, gather evidence to help you answer the following questions. In your Evidence Notebook, record what you already know about these topics and any questions you have about them.

1. What is the scale and basic structure of an atom?
2. How do patterns in the periodic table predict the behavior and properties of elements? How is this related to atomic structure?
3. If atoms are the building blocks of matter, can they become unstable or change their identity?

UNIT PROJECT

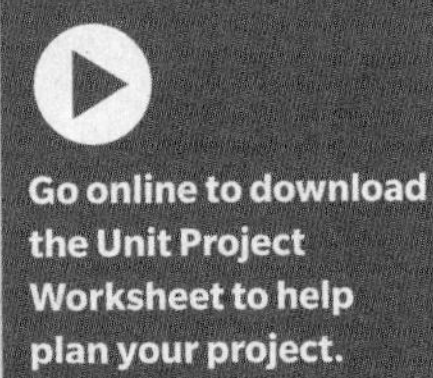

Go online to download the Unit Project Worksheet to help plan your project.

Designing an Atomic Model

Consider the benefits and drawbacks of different types of atomic models. Are some better suited to certain types of questions? Construct or research different types of atomic models and explain what could be learned from each.

Language Development

Use the lessons in this unit to complete the chart and expand your understanding of the science concepts.

TERM: nucleus

Definition	Example

Similar Term	Phrase

TERM: atomic number

Definition	Example

Similar Term	Phrase

TERM: valence electron

Definition	Example

Similar Term	Phrase

TERM: ionization energy

Definition	Example

Similar Term	Phrase

TERM: electronegativity

Definition	Example

Similar Term	Phrase

TERM: radioactive decay

Definition	Example

Similar Term	Phrase

TERM: nuclear fission

Definition	Example

Similar Term	Phrase

TERM: nuclear fusion

Definition	Example

Similar Term	Phrase

2.1

Modeling Atomic Structure

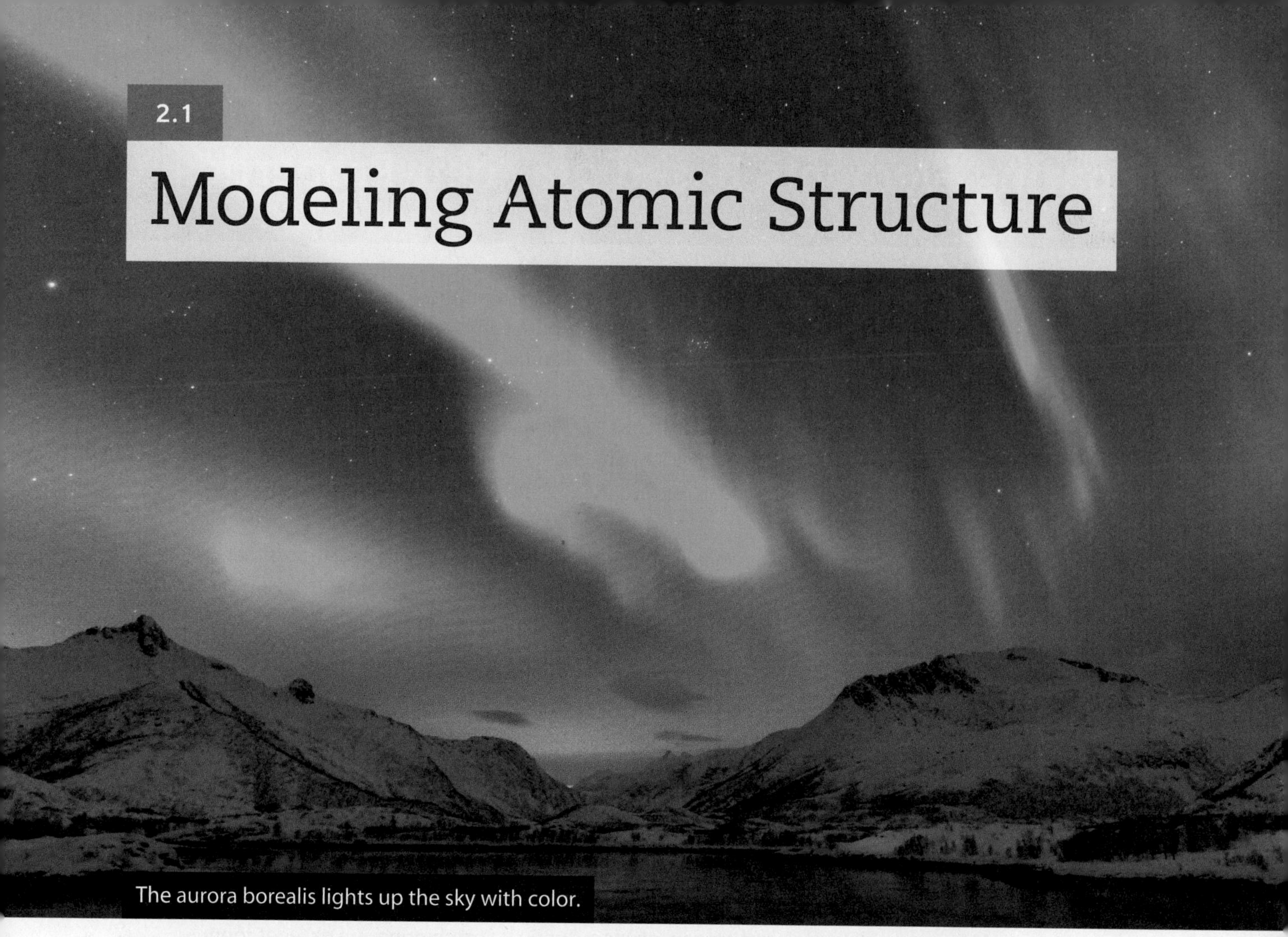

The aurora borealis lights up the sky with color.

CAN YOU EXPLAIN THE PHENOMENON?

At certain times of year, a phenomenon called the aurora polaris lights up the sky in areas near the northern and southern poles. When it occurs, different colored lights can be seen moving around in the sky. Sometimes only one color is seen, but at other times several colors appear. The lights are usually pink, green, yellow, blue, violet, red, and, less often, orange and white. They may appear as a steady glow or as constantly changing sources of light. In the northern latitudes, this phenomenon is known as the aurora borealis or northern lights. In southern latitudes, they are called aurora australis or southern lights.

APPLY How do you think matter in the atmosphere can cause a phenomenon such as the northern lights?

Evidence Notebook As you explore the lesson, gather evidence to explain how atomic structure is related to the different colors displayed as part of the aurora polaris phenomenon.

Comparing Elements Based on Their Properties

FIGURE 1: Magnesium (left), zinc (center), and copper (right) in hydrochloric acid.

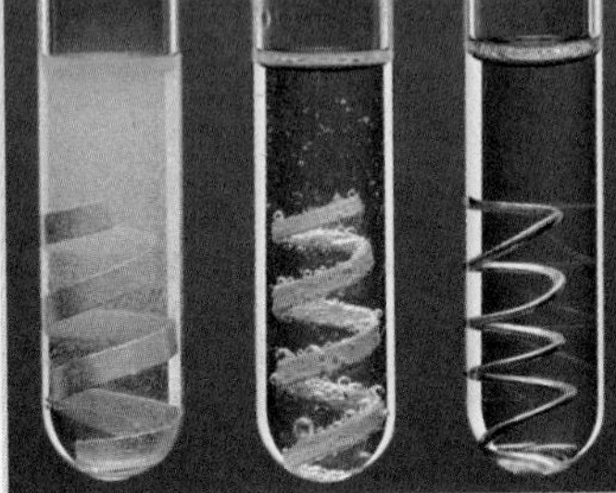

The gases in Earth's atmosphere are an example of matter in the Earth system. Matter can be classified as either a pure substance or a mixture. The metals shown in Figure 1 are all pure substances.

Collaborate Discuss the following with a partner: In Figure 1, three different metals are combined with an acid. What differences do you notice in the way these metals react? What do you think causes these differences in reactivity?

The metals shown in Figure 1 are all elements, or pure substances that cannot be broken down into simpler substances. The particles that make up these elements are called atoms. Each element contains only one type of atom.

Classifying Elements

Certain groups of elements have similar properties and can be classified together. The most general way to classify elements is as metals, nonmetals, or metalloids. *Metals* are shiny, and they are generally good conductors of electricity and heat. They can be bent or hammered into sheets easily, and almost all metals are solid at room temperature.

In contrast, *nonmetals* are generally very poor conductors of electricity and heat. Many nonmetals, such as nitrogen, oxygen, fluorine, and chlorine, are gases at room temperature. The nonmetals that are solids at room temperature, such as carbon, phosphorus, sulfur, selenium, and iodine, tend to be brittle and dull rather than shiny.

FIGURE 2: Elements are categorized into broad categories based on similar properties.

a Metals

b Nonmetals

c Metalloids

Metalloids have characteristics of metals and nonmetals. Metalloids are solids at room temperature. They are not as brittle as nonmetals. Metalloids do conduct electric current but not as well as metals. The "semiconducting" properties of metalloids, such as boron and silicon, make them useful in computer chips.

APPLY Describe some examples of metals and nonmetals from your daily life. How can you tell which type of elements are metals and which are not?

Hands-On Lab

Exploring Reactivity

Observing the behavior of an element allows chemists to draw conclusions about the properties of the atoms that form that element. Reactivity is a measure of how readily an element undergoes a chemical reaction. In this lab, you will react three metal elements with an acid and draw conclusions about the relative reactivities of the metals.

The metals you will test in this lab are aluminum, magnesium, and zinc. When these metals react with an acid, such as hydrochloric acid, hydrogen gas is given off as a product. The rate of hydrogen production can therefore be used to draw conclusions about the relative reactivities of the metals.

RESEARCH QUESTION What can observing properties such as reactivity tell us about the atoms that make up an element?

MAKE A CLAIM

Which metal do you think will react most vigorously when placed in hydrochloric acid? Explain your thinking.

MATERIALS

- indirectly vented chemical splash goggles, nonlatex apron, nitrile gloves
- aluminum, small sample
- hydrochloric acid solution, 1 M
- magnesium, small sample
- test tube rack
- test tubes (3)
- zinc, small sample

SAFETY INFORMATION

- Wear indirectly vented chemical splash goggles, a nonlatex apron, and nitrile gloves during the setup, hands-on, and takedown segments of the activity.
- The reaction between a metal and hydrochloric acid gives off hydrogen gas. Hydrogen gas and fumes from hydrochloric acid should not be inhaled, so these reactions should be completed inside a fume hood or in a well-ventilated room.
- Use caution when working with glassware, which can shatter and cut skin.
- Hydrochloric acid (HCl) is a strong acid that is highly corrosive to skin and other tissues. During a reaction with metals, inhalation of the fumes can cause irritation of the respiratory tract and shortness of breath, and the hydrogen released should be kept away from open flames.
- Tell your teacher immediately if you spill chemicals on yourself, the table, or floor.
- Follow your teacher's instructions for disposing of all waste materials.
- Wash your hands with soap and water immediately after completing this activity.

indirectly vented chemical splash goggles

PLAN THE INVESTIGATION

1. In your Evidence Notebook, write a procedure and safety plan for this investigation. For each reaction, you should combine a small piece of metal with a few drops of hydrochloric acid in a test tube. As part of your procedure, explain what variables should be kept constant and how you will ensure that this happens.

2. Draw a data table in your Evidence Notebook to record the relative reactivities of each metal element. Because hydrogen is a product of these reactions, you can use the rate of hydrogen production and the volume of hydrogen bubbles produced to infer relative reactivity. Develop a rating system to use when quantifying the relative reactivity of each metal based on hydrogen production.

3. Have your teacher approve your procedure, safety plan, and data table before you carry out your investigation.

ANALYZE

How do you think the atoms that make up the most reactive metal you tested differ from the atoms of the least reactive metal?

DRAW CONCLUSIONS

Write a conclusion that addresses each of the points below.

Claim Which of the metal elements that you tested has the highest relative reactivity when combined with hydrochloric acid? Which has the lowest?

Evidence Give specific evidence from your data and other observations you have made to support your claim.

Reasoning Explain how the evidence you gave supports your claim. Describe, in detail, the connections between the evidence you cited and the argument you are making.

Understanding Atoms

People's understanding of the atom has changed over time. The idea that matter is made up of smaller, individual units was proposed many centuries ago. Empirical evidence to support the existence of atoms did not come until much later. By the mid 1800s, most scientists agreed that each element was made up of a unique type of atom. However, they saw atoms as tiny, indivisible balls, differing only in mass.

MODEL Draw a diagram to show how a scientist in the 1800s might have modeled atoms. Include different types of atoms in your diagram and indicate how they differ in this model.

The theory that atoms were indivisible units differing only in mass did not fully explain the patterns that scientists observed in the properties of elements. For example, the metals you tested in the lab react with hydrochloric acid, but not with water. But some metals, such as sodium and potassium, are so reactive that they ignite when they are combined with water. Then there are elements, such as the gases shown in Figure 3, that almost never react with other substances. These gases are part of a group of elements known as the noble gases.

Because the noble gases appeared not to have any chemical properties that could be used to compare them, early chemists struggled to organize them into a classification scheme. Even passing an electric current through these gases did not cause a reaction. It did, however, cause the gases to produce light of different colors.

FIGURE 3: Each sign spells out the element symbol of the gas with which it is filled: helium, neon, and argon.

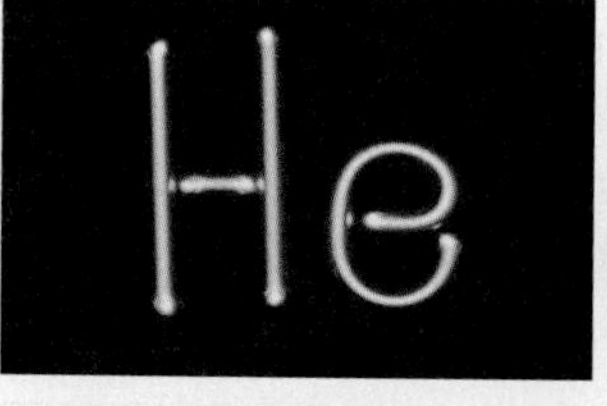

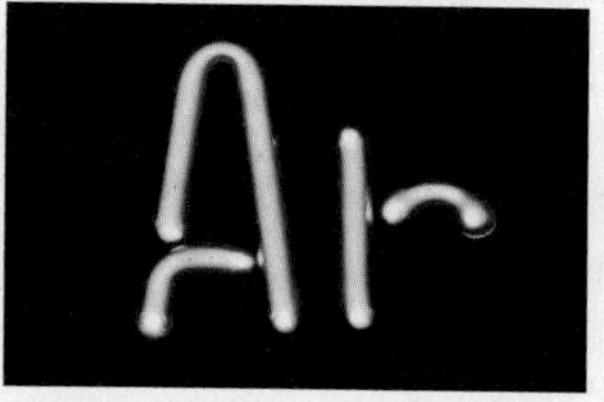

Collaborate Discuss these questions with a partner: Why do you think the elements in Figure 3 give off different colors of light when an electric current passes through them? How might the colors given off be related to the type of atom that makes up each element?

Over time, scientists concluded that something other than mass alone must be causing the patterns they observed in the properties of elements. Further experimentation would allow scientists to determine what made one type of atom different from others.

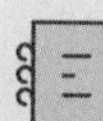

Evidence Notebook How might the properties of different elements, such as the noble gases and the metals you tested, be related to the phenomenon of the aurora polaris?

Investigating Atomic Structure

Explore Online

FIGURE 4: A negatively charged balloon attracts a stream of water.

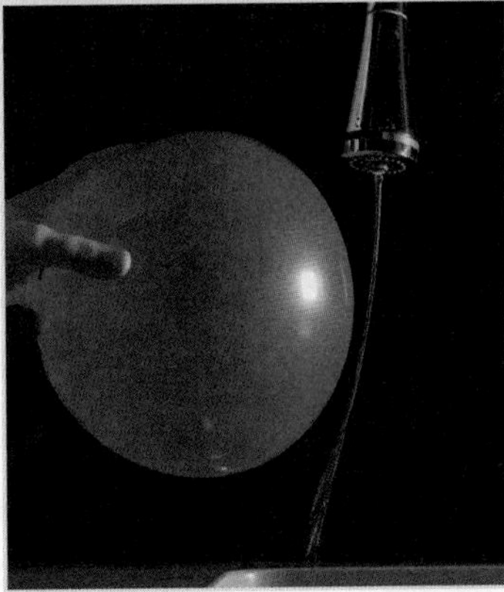

You may have experienced a shock when touching a door knob after walking across a carpeted floor. When you walk across carpet, a charge can build up on the surface of your body. When you touch a metal object, the charge is transferred with a shock. In a similar way, a balloon rubbed with a cloth builds up a negative charge. When the balloon is placed near a thin stream of water, as shown in Figure 4, the water is attracted to the balloon.

PREDICT In Figure 4, a negatively charged balloon attracts a thin stream of water. Why do you think this happens?

Identifying Electrons

Like charges repel, and opposite charges attract. Thus, the attraction between a negatively charged balloon and a stream of water is evidence that opposite charges are present. If atoms were simply tiny indivisible spheres, as scientists once theorized, how could these opposite charges form? In the late 1800s, experiments with cathode rays led to the discovery of a charged particle called the electron.

A cathode-ray tube, as shown in Figure 5, is a glass tube containing a gas at very low pressure. At one end, it has a cathode, a metal disk connected to the negative terminal of the energy source. At the other end, it has an anode, a metal disk connected to a positive terminal. When an electric current is passed through the tube, a glowing stream of particles called a cathode ray can be observed. In 1897, a scientist named J.J. Thomson noted that a magnetic or electric field could cause the cathode ray to bend. The ray bent toward a positive charge and away from a negative charge.

FIGURE 5: A cathode ray bends away from a magnet.

Explore Online

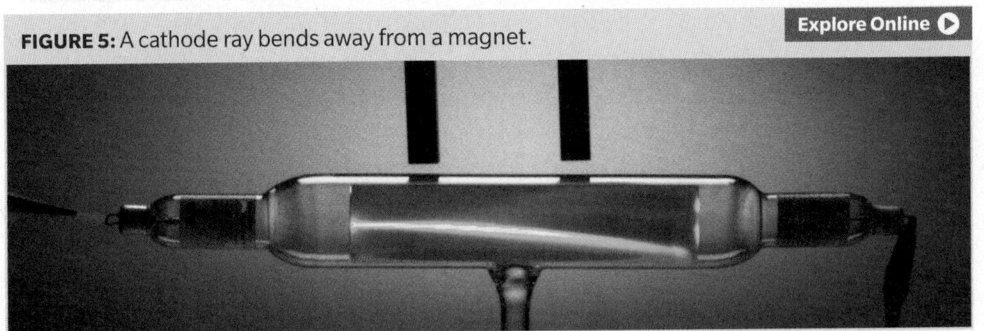

EXPLAIN Select the correct terms to complete the statement.

Opposite | like charges attract one another. So, if an electric current causes a cathode ray to bend toward a positive charge, the ray must be positively | negatively charged.

Further experimentation with cathode rays allowed J.J. Thomson to calculate the charge-to-mass-ratio of the particles that made them up. He noticed that this ratio remained constant even when different gases or metals were used in the cathode ray tube. The very small, negatively charged particles Thomson identified later became known as electrons. It was determined that electrons had a mass of 9.109×10^{-31} kg, or 1/1836 the mass of a hydrogen atom. Because electrons are so much smaller than an atom, and atoms have no overall charge, it was clear that atoms could not be made up solely of electrons.

INFER What could be inferred about atomic structure after the discovery of the electron? Select all correct answers.

- ☐ **a.** Atoms are made up of smaller "subatomic" particles.
- ☐ **b.** Atoms of different elements contain the same number of electrons.
- ☐ **c.** The electrons in an atom are attracted to each other due to their negative charge.
- ☐ **d.** Atoms must also contain a positively charged component.

FIGURE 6: A plum pudding

The discovery of the electron led scientists to develop a new atomic model. In this model, called the "plum pudding model," negatively charged electrons are evenly distributed within a mass of positively charged material. Thus, the electrons are like raisins in a cake, as shown in Figure 6. The cake itself represents the area of positive charge that surrounds the electrons.

Identifying the Nucleus

In the early 1900s, a physicist and former student of Thomson's named Ernest Rutherford devised an experiment to learn more about atomic structure. In this experiment, called the gold foil experiment, positively charged particles called alpha (α) particles were focused into a narrow beam and shot at a very thin piece of gold. Rutherford hypothesized that if the plum pudding model was correct, the area of positive charge in the gold atoms would be too spread out to repel the positively charged alpha particles. So, most of the particles should pass straight through the foil undeflected.

FIGURE 7: Gold foil experiment

Explore Online

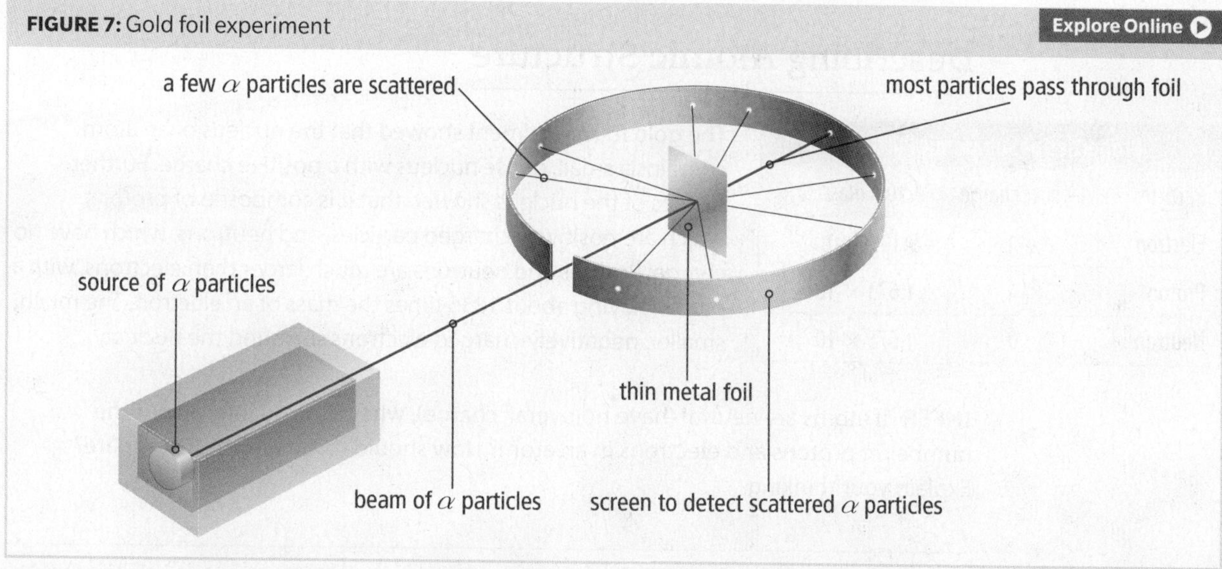

Collaborate With a partner, analyze the diagram of the gold foil experiment shown in Figure 7 and answer these questions: What happened when the alpha particles encountered the gold foil? What do you think these results indicate about atomic structure?

In the gold foil experiment, most of the alpha particles passed straight through the gold foil as expected. However, some alpha particles were deflected at large angles, as shown in Figure 8. A few alpha particles were even deflected backwards from the foil. Rutherford was very surprised by the results, later saying that it was almost as incredible as if you fired a cannonball at a piece of tissue paper and it came back to hit you.

FIGURE 8: The results of the gold foil experiment led to a new model of the atom.

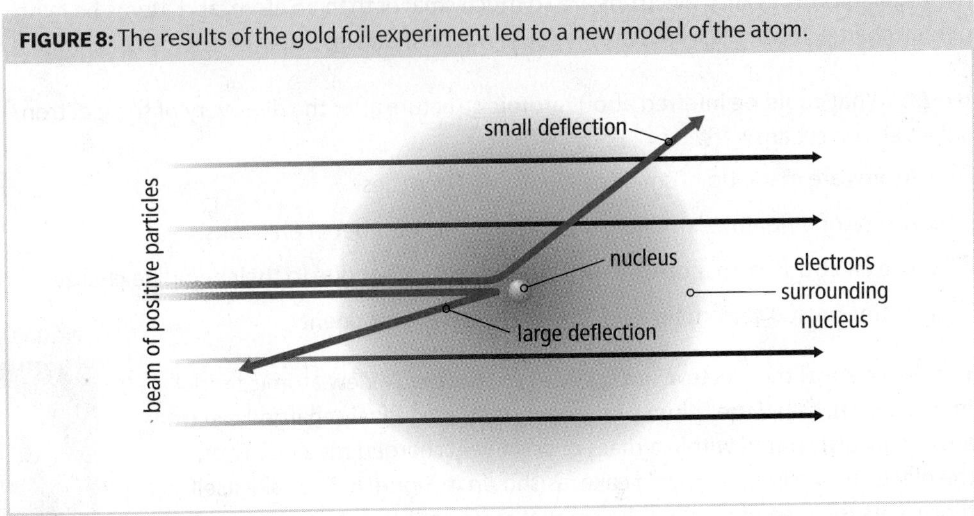

The model that Rutherford developed to explain his results depicted atoms as being made up of mostly empty space. In the center of the atom is a small, dense, positively-charged core, or nucleus, that makes up most of an atom's mass. The much lighter electrons surround the nucleus in a relatively large electron cloud.

Evidence Notebook Explain how evidence from the gold foil experiment supports each of these claims. How can you apply these ideas to the atomic model in your unit project?

- atoms have a very small, dense core
- the core of an atom has a positive charge
- atoms are made up of mostly empty space

Describing Atomic Structure

Properties of Subatomic Particles		
Particles	Electric charge	Actual mass (kg)
Electron	−1	9.109×10^{-31}
Proton	+1	1.673×10^{-27}
Neutron	0	1.675×10^{-27}

The gold foil experiment showed that the nucleus of an atom contains a small, dense nucleus with a positive charge. Further studies of the nucleus showed that it is composed of protons, which are positively charged particles, and neutrons, which have no charge. Protons and neutrons are much larger than electrons, with a proton having about 1836 times the mass of an electron. The much smaller, negatively-charged electrons surround the nucleus.

INFER If atoms are neutral (have no overall charge), what can you infer about the number of protons and electrons in an atom? How should these numbers compare? Explain your thinking.

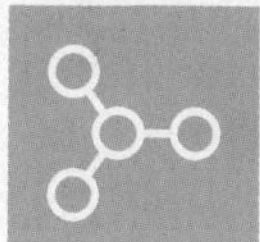

Scale, Proportion, and Quantity

Scale and Atomic Models

Atoms are too small to observe directly. So, to help scientists understand the structure of atoms, they develop models. Atomic models are useful because they allow scientists to visualize the structure of atoms. However, it can be difficult to develop a model of the atom that is to scale.

The models of atoms shown in textbooks are not to scale because it would be impossible to represent the proportions of the atom in a two-dimensional diagram. In a scale model, the electron cloud would be 100 000 times the diameter of the nucleus. To visualize this, imagine the nucleus were the size of a grain of sand. An atom with a nucleus this size would be as large around as a baseball stadium, such as the one shown in Figure 9.

FIGURE 9: An atom with a nucleus the size of a grain of sand would be the size of a baseball stadium.

In addition, atoms are three-dimensional objects, so any drawing does not show its true shape. Scientists acknowledge that their atomic models are not drawn to scale and that the distances between the nucleus and electrons are not accurate.

PREDICT What types of information do you think scientists can gain from a computational, physical, or two-dimensional atomic model that is not to scale?

Some models can be useful even when they are not to scale. For example, models of very large objects, such as the solar system, are not to scale. This is because the interplanetary distances involved are so great that it would be hard to make an accurate scale model. Consider this: If a model of the solar system were on a football field, the sun would be about the size of a dime. The planet Neptune would be 60 yards (55 m) away and about the diameter of the lead on a mechanical pencil.

Some models, however, must be made to scale. For example, blueprints for a building are a type of model. It is important that they be made to scale to make sure the rooms, plumbing, and electrical wiring are all properly constructed and fit in the required space.

Collaborate Work with a partner to develop criteria for situations that require a scale model or do not require a scale model.

Evidence Notebook Summarize what you have learned about the structure of the atom. How do you think atomic structure might be related to the aurora polaris phenomenon?

Using Numbers to Describe Atoms

You have learned that elements are made up of individual units called atoms, and that atoms are made up of smaller particles called protons, neutrons, and electrons. The differences in reactivity that you observed in the hands-on lab are related to the number of subatomic particles in the atoms of each element.

PREDICT Think back to the metals you studied in the hands-on lab. Which subatomic particles do you think most influenced reactivity? How might the numbers of subatomic particles in each type of atom explain your observations?

Atomic Number and Mass Number

One way that scientists identify atoms is by the number of protons in the nucleus. The number of protons in an atom's nucleus is called the atomic number. Each element has a certain number of protons, so this means the atomic number of an atom corresponds to a specific element. If the atomic number changes, the element has a different identity. For example, the elements you combined with acid in the hands-on lab—magnesium, aluminum, and zinc—have atomic numbers of 12, 13, and 30 respectively.

FIGURE 10: This helium nucleus has 2 protons and 2 neutrons, so it has an atomic number of 2 and a mass number of 4.

The atomic number is a handy number because it is also tells you the number of electrons in a neutral atom. Because atoms do not have a charge, the positive charges from the protons and the negative charges from the electrons must be the same. Thus, if you know the atomic number of an atom, you not only know the number of protons but also the number of electrons. So magnesium, aluminum, and zinc have 12, 13, and 30 electrons respectively.

Another way scientists describe atoms is with the mass number. The mass number is equal to the total number of protons and neutrons in an atom's nucleus. Therefore, you can find the number of neutrons in an atom by subtracting the atomic number from the mass number for that atom.

INFER Select the correct terms to complete the statement.

The element aluminum has an atomic number of 13 and a mass number of 27. The number of protons in the nucleus of an aluminum atom is 27 | 13 | 40 | 14. The number of neutrons in the nucleus is 27 | 13 | 40 | 14. The number of electrons in the atom is 27 | 13 | 40 | 14.

Evidence Notebook Summarize what you have learned about how numbers can be used to describe subatomic particles in atoms. Then write an explanation of how this information will apply to the atomic model you are developing for your unit project.

Isotopes

The mass number and atomic number are different in an important way. If two atoms have different atomic numbers, and therefore different numbers of protons, they are from different elements. But two atoms can have different numbers of neutrons and still be the same element as long as they have the same number of protons. Atoms of the same element with different numbers of neutrons are called **isotopes**. Different isotopes of the same element have the same number of protons and electrons, but each isotope has a different number of neutrons.

Scientists refer to isotopes of elements in different ways. An isotope may be identified by writing the mass number as a superscript and the atomic number as a subscript to the left of the chemical symbol, such as ${}^{14}_{7}N$ and ${}^{15}_{7}N$ for two isotopes of nitrogen. Scientists might also write the mass number after the name of the element such as uranium-235 and uranium-238 for the isotopes. In this type of notation, the atomic number is omitted because it can be assumed from the identity of the element.

FIGURE 11: The three isotopes of hydrogen have different mass numbers.

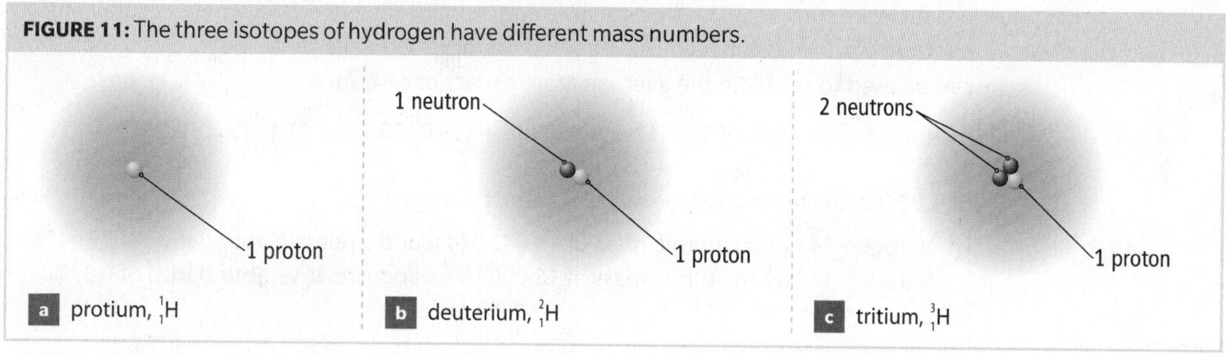

SOLVE Write the mass number for each of the isotopes of hydrogen.

protium ________ deuterium ________ tritium ________

Atomic Mass

Today, scientists measure the mass of atoms in unified atomic mass units (u). Originally, scientists defined the atomic mass unit as being the mass of a proton or neutron. So, the mass number was considered equal to the atomic mass of an element. As scientists learned more about the mass of atoms and could begin measuring the masses of atoms with more accuracy, they developed a more precise unit of measure. An atomic mass unit is defined as 1/12 of the mass of a carbon-12 isotope, or $1.660\,539\,040 \times 10^{-24}$ g.

The atomic mass unit is not the same as the mass of a proton or neutron because the mass of the carbon atom also includes the very small but necessary mass of the electrons. Carbon was chosen as the standard because a carbon atom with 6 protons, 6 neutrons, and 6 electrons was the easiest atomic mass to determine. The other common isotope of carbon, carbon-13, is relatively rare compared to carbon-12.

Language Arts Connection Conduct research to learn more about how the atomic mass unit has changed over time. Then use your findings to make a flow chart to show how and why the measurement of atomic mass has changed. Last, write an explanation for how the unit is currently quantified. Include a list of references with your final product.

Average Atomic Mass

FIGURE 12: The periodic table tile for carbon shows its average atomic mass, 12.01.

Because different isotopes of an element may be present in naturally-occurring samples, we cannot use a single atomic mass to describe a sample of an element. The atomic mass shown on the periodic table for an element is an average atomic mass that accounts for all of the isotopes of that element.

When calculating the atomic mass of a typical sample of an element, the relative abundance of each isotope must be taken into account. For example, carbon has two naturally occurring isotopes—carbon-12 and carbon-13. Carbon-12 has an atomic mass of exactly 12 u and a relative abundance of 98.89%. This means that a naturally occurring sample of carbon will be made up of 98.89% carbon-12. Carbon-13 has an atomic mass of 13.003 35 u and a relative abundance of 1.11%.

To calculate the average atomic mass of an element, the exact atomic mass for each isotope is multiplied by the isotope's relative abundance (in decimal form), and the products are summed. This gives an average atomic mass, which is a more accurate measure of the mass of a typical, real-world sample of an element. The following equation can be used to calculate the average atomic mass of carbon.

Average atomic mass of C $= (12 \text{ u} \times 0.9889) + (13.003\,35 \text{ u} \times 0.0111) = 12.0111 \text{ u}$

SOLVE Calculate the average atomic mass of nitrogen.

Nitrogen-14 has an atomic mass of 14.003 074 u and a relative abundance of 99.64%.
Nitrogen-15 has an atomic mass of 15.000 109 u and a relative abundance of 0.37%.

______________.

Math Connection

Explaining Average Atomic Mass

When using the periodic table to determine the atomic mass of an element, it is common for people to confuse average atomic mass and mass number. Imagine you wanted to determine the number of neutrons in a carbon atom. If you referenced the periodic table, you would see that the average atomic mass of carbon is 12.01 u.

You can calculate the number of neutrons in the nucleus by subtracting the atomic number from the mass number for an element. However, it would be incorrect to use the value 12.01 when performing this calculation, which would give an answer of 6.01 neutrons. Instead, you should round the average atomic mass to 12. This will give you the mass number of the most abundant isotope; in this case, carbon-12.

Collaborate With a partner, write a brief explanation that another student could reference when using the periodic table to calculate the number of neutrons in atoms of a certain element. Explain how average atomic mass differs from mass number and how this difference should be considered when using the periodic table as a reference tool.

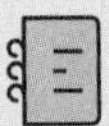

Evidence Notebook How might the fact that each element has a unique atomic number help explain the different colors in the aurora polaris? Think about what information the atomic number provides about the subatomic particles in an atom.

Hands-On Lab

Identifying Elements Using a Flame Test

The work of Rutherford and other scientists helped establish a model that depicted the atom as having a small, dense nucleus surrounded by electrons. But this model could not fully explain all the properties of elements. For example, a tube of hydrogen gas emits a pinkish glow when an electric current is passed through it, as shown in Figure 13a. Passing this light through a prism or a tool called a spectroscope separates the light into its different wavelengths. Figure 13b shows the results of this test for hydrogen, known as an emission-line spectrum.

FIGURE 13: The pinkish light emitted by hydrogen can be separated by a spectroscope.

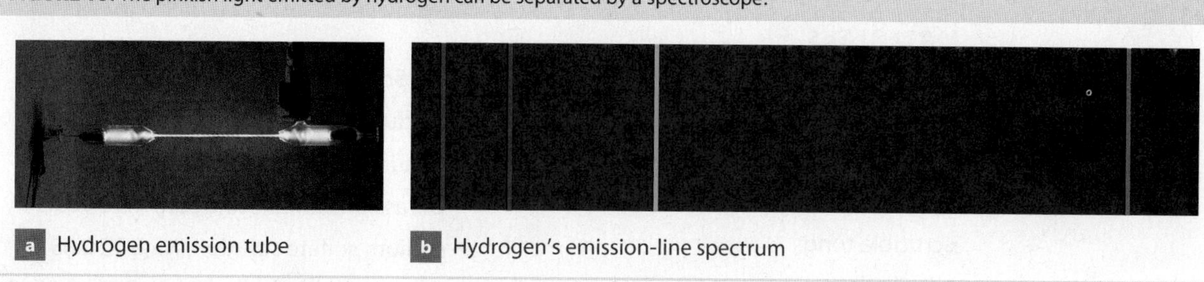

a Hydrogen emission tube

b Hydrogen's emission-line spectrum

When an electric current is passed through hydrogen gas, the hydrogen atoms absorb energy. When an atom absorbs energy, the electrons are raised to higher energy levels referred to as "excited" states. When an electron falls from a higher energy level to a lower energy level, energy in the form of light is released. This light has a specific amount of energy and so will appear as a certain color with a certain wavelength.

Collaborate With a partner, write an analogy you could use to explain what causes hydrogen gas to glow when an electric current is passed through it.

When studying hydrogen, scientists expected to observe the emission of a continuous range of frequencies, not the distinct lines shown in Figure 13b. In 1913, Danish physicist Niels Bohr developed a new model of the atom that accounted for the emission-line spectrum of hydrogen.

In Bohr's model, the electron can circle the nucleus only in allowed paths, or *orbits*, called atomic energy levels. When the electron is in one of these orbits, the atom has a definite, fixed energy. The electron is in its lowest energy state, or ground state, when it is in the orbit closest to the nucleus. The energy of the electron is higher when the electron is in orbits that are successively farther from the nucleus. Bohr used the different wavelengths of the hydrogen emission-line spectrum to calculate the allowed energy levels for the hydrogen atom. He then related the possible energy-level changes to the lines in the hydrogen emission-line spectrum.

In this lab, you will observe the colors given off by several metal salts by performing a flame test to determine the identity of an unknown substance. In a flame test, a wire or splint is coated in a solution containing a metal salt. The coated end of the wire is then placed in a flame.

FIGURE 14: Colors of light emitted when the electron in hydrogen loses energy and drops back down to its original energy level

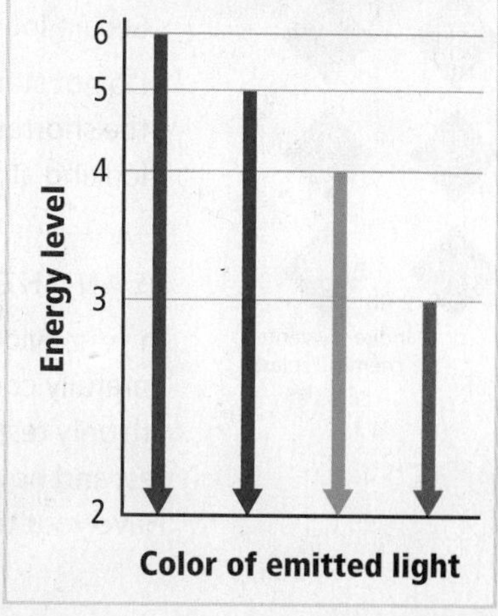

RESEARCH QUESTION How can scientists use the properties of elements to identify unknown substances?

MAKE A CLAIM

How do you think you can use the results of a flame test to identify an unknown metal?

MATERIALS

- indirectly vented chemical splash goggles, nonlatex apron, nitrile gloves
- beaker, 250 mL
- Bunsen burner
- crucible tongs
- distilled water
- flame-test wire, 5 cm
- glass test plate, or microchemistry plate with wells
- hydrochloric acid, HCl, solution, 1.0 M

Test Solutions

- calcium chloride solution, $CaCl_2$, 0.05 M
- lithium sulfate solution, Li_2SO_4, 0.05 M
- potassium sulfate solution, K_2SO_4, 0.05 M
- sodium sulfate solution, Na_2SO_4, 0.05 M
- strontium chloride solution, $SrCl_2$, 0.05 M
- unknown solution

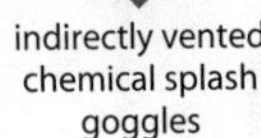
indirectly vented chemical splash goggles

SAFETY INFORMATION

- Wear indirectly vented chemical splash goggles, a nonlatex apron, and nitrile gloves during the setup, hands-on, and takedown segments of the activity.
- Do not touch any of the chemicals used in this experiment. Only touch them with the flame-test wire.
- Tell your teacher immediately if you spill chemicals on yourself, the work surface, or floor.
- If you get a chemical in your eye, use an eyewash station immediately.
- Secure loose clothing, wear closed-toe shoes, and tie back long hair.
- Do not stare directly into the flames for extended periods of time. Look at the flame for the shortest amount of time needed to determine the color. Run multiple trials to avoid looking at the flame for too long.

PLAN THE INVESTIGATION

In your Evidence Notebook, develop a procedure and safety plan for your investigation. Carefully consider the controls of your experiment, what the variables are, and that you are only testing one solution at a time. Decide how much solution you will need for each test and how many trials you will need to accurately determine the color of the flame. Have your teacher approve your procedure and safety plan before proceeding.

COLLECT DATA

In your Evidence Notebook, develop a data collection strategy. The metal ions in the salt solutions are responsible for producing the light you will observe. Consider how you will record the colors produced in each trial of the flame test. Make sure your data are clear and ordered so you can easily compare the results of the known solutions to the results of the unknown solution.

CARRY OUT THE INVESTIGATION

Before you begin testing your compounds, it is important that you clean your flame-test wire. Clean the test wire by dipping it in 1.0 M HCl solution and then holding it in the flame of the Bunsen burner. Repeat this procedure until the flame is not colored by the wire. Make sure to clean the wire between each test solution to avoid contamination.

ANALYZE

1. The images show solutions containing copper, strontium, and sodium compounds burning in Petri dishes. The colors, from left to right, are: orange, red, and green. Write a caption for each image that identifies the metal ion in each solution and briefly explains your reasoning.

2. Did you notice any differences in the individual trials for the flame tests of each metal solution? Why do you think these differences occurred?

3. How could the level of accuracy of your results for the flame test be improved?

CONSTRUCT AN EXPLANATION

Each metallic element you tested gave off a unique color when burned. What does this tell you about the energy levels in the atoms of these metallic elements? Explain your answer.

DRAW CONCLUSIONS

Write a conclusion that addresses each of the points below.

Claim Based on the data you gathered from the flame tests, what metal is present in the unknown solution?

Evidence Give specific examples from your data to support your claim.

Reasoning Explain how the evidence you gave supports your claim. Describe, in detail, the connections between the evidence you cited and the argument you are making.

EXTEND

Research the use of metal salts in fireworks. Make a visual guide explaining which metal ions are responsible for producing which colors of fireworks. Then write a brief explanation for how energy levels in atoms are related to the colors observed.

Evidence Notebook How might the different colors you observed in the flame test be related to the different colors produced in the aurora polaris?

Modeling Electron Configurations

In the Bohr model of the atom, electrons circle the nucleus only in allowed paths. The development of a new model of the atom, called the quantum mechanical model, would show that electrons are actually located in three-dimensional areas around the nucleus. The quantum mechanical model is a mathematical model that describes the areas where electrons are most likely to be found.

Electron Shells and Orbitals

Electrons, like light, have properties that describe them as both particles and waves. Because of these properties, their exact location cannot be determined. Instead, we can only consider electrons as having a high probability of being somewhere within a certain region. This region, called an energy shell, is a three-dimensional region around the atom. The lowest energy shells, closest to the nucleus, correspond to the lowest energy levels. Energy shells fill up in a specific order and are numbered 1–7.

PREDICT Hydrogen has one electron, which is located in the first energy shell. Helium has two electrons in the first energy shell. Lithium has three electrons—two in the first energy shell and one in the second. How might this pattern be related to the fact that hydrogen and lithium are both reactive, but helium is nonreactive?

Regions within each energy shell where electrons have a high probability of being found are called subshells. Each subshell contains orbitals of different shapes. An orbital can hold up to two electrons. The first subshell, called 1s, has the lowest energy and contains one orbital that is spherical in shape. This is shown in Figure 15a.

FIGURE 15: These models show the shape of orbitals in the s and p subshells.

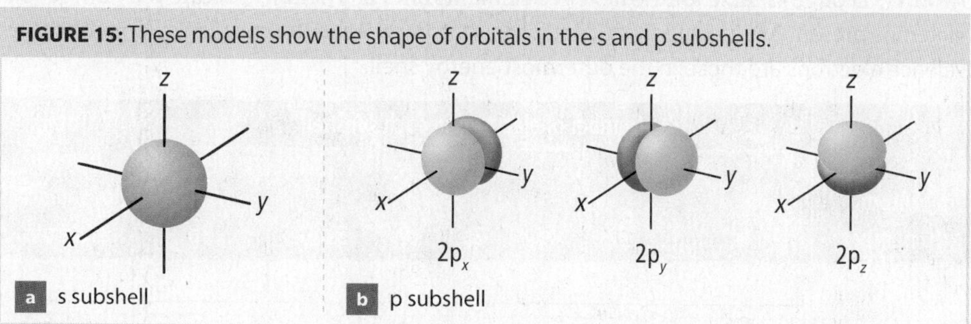

The second energy shell has two subshells, labeled s and p. The p subshell has three orbitals, as shown in Figure 15b. Each of these orbitals can hold two electrons. So, the second energy shell can hold a total of 8 electrons, with 2 in the s subshell and 6 in the p subshell. The third energy shell has three subshells, s, p, and d. The d subshell has five orbitals and can therefore hold 10 electrons. The fourth energy shell has four subshells, s, p, d, and f. The f subshell has seven orbitals and can therefore hold 14 electrons.

Figure 16 shows the subshells that electrons occupy for the elements hydrogen through helium. The 1s subshell holds 2 electrons, and is filled first. The 2s subshell is filled next, followed by 2p. Each energy shell must be full before electrons begin filling the next energy shell. For example, the second energy shell must be full, with 2 electrons in the 2s subshell and 6 electrons in 2p subshell, before electrons begin filling the third energy shell. The electrons occupying the outermost energy shell are called valence electrons. For example, oxygen has 2 electrons in the 2s subshell and 4 electrons in the 2p subshell, so it has 6 valence electrons, or 6 total electrons in the outermost energy shell.

FIGURE 16: This chart shows how the subshells of the first 13 elements are filled.

Name	Symbol	Atomic number	Number of electrons in each subshell					Total number of valence electrons
			1s	2s	2p	3s	3p	
Hydrogen	H	1	1					1
Helium	He	2	2					2
Lithium	Li	3	2	1				1
Beryllium	Be	4	2	2				2
Boron	B	5	2	2	1			3
Carbon	C	6	2	2	2			4
Nitrogen	N	7	2	2	3			5
Oxygen	O	8	2	2	4			6
Fluorine	F	9	2	2	5			7
Neon	Ne	10	2	2	6			8
Sodium	Na	11	2	2	6	1		1
Magnesium	Mg	12	2	2	6	2		2
Aluminum	Al	13	2	2	6	2	1	3

APPLY Fill out this table for the next five elements after aluminum. Indicate the number of electrons present in each subshell. If a subshell is empty, leave the cell blank. Remember that valence electrons are those in the outermost energy shell.

Name	Symbol	Atomic number	Number of electrons in each subshell					Total number of valence electrons
			1s	2s	2p	3s	3p	
Silicon	Si	14	______	______	______	______	______	______
Phosphorus	P	15	______	______	______	______	______	______
Sulfur	S	16	______	______	______	______	______	______
Chlorine	Cl	17	______	______	______	______	______	______
Argon	Ar	18	______	______	______	______	______	______

Valence electrons may take part in forming bonds in chemical reactions. So, the number of valence electrons in an atom determines the chemical properties of that element and the types of chemical reactions atoms of that element may take part in. If the outer energy shell of electrons is full, that element will typically not undergo chemical reactions. Elements that are one electron "short" from having a full outer energy shell and elements that have only one electron in the outer energy shell are typically very reactive.

EXPLAIN Revise your earlier explanation for this question based on what you now know about valence electrons, chemical reactions, and full outer shells of electrons: Hydrogen has one electron, helium has two electrons, and lithium has three electrons. Hydrogen and lithium are both reactive, but helium is nonreactive. How can electrons be used to explain this pattern of behavior?

____

____

____

____

____

Modeling Electron Configuration

The electron configuration for an element can be written using a notation that expresses numbers of electrons as superscripts following the names of the subshells they occupy. For example, the electron configuration for sulfur, which has 16 electrons, is written as: $1s^2 2s^2 2p^6 3s^2 3p^4$. Figure 17 shows another way scientists model electron configuration by logically following how electrons fill their orbitals. This method gives each element a unique configuration of electrons. Because the energy shells and subshells are typically filled in the same way, it is easy to model the electron configuration for each element.

FIGURE 17: The electron configuration for sulfur has four electrons in the 3p subshell.

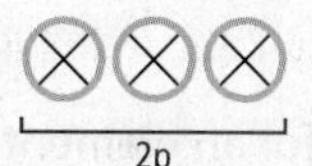
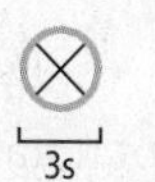
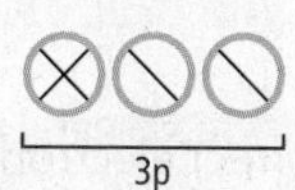

Using this model, each circle represents an orbital with two electrons. Each electron is represented by a line drawn through the circle. Each subshell must be completely filled before electrons can be placed in the next subshell. Therefore, the 1s subshell must be filled before electrons can be placed in the 2s subshell. This is represented by two lines through the circle. For the p subshell, one electron is placed in each circle before a second electron is placed in any of the circles. The p subshell must be filled before electrons can go in the next s subshell.

MODEL Using the method shown in Figure 17, draw the electron configuration of argon. Remember to fill the subshells in order.

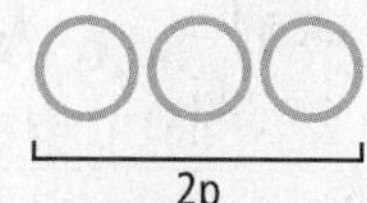
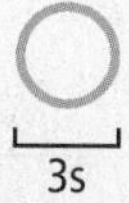
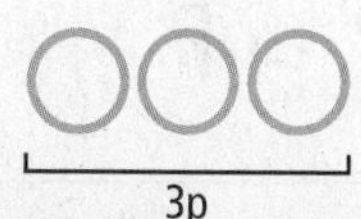

Modeling Atoms with Electron-Dot Notation

Valence electrons will most often interact with the electrons of other atoms in chemical reactions. So, when trying to predict the chemical properties of an element, it is useful to have a model for showing only valence electrons. One way to easily visualize valence electrons is by using electron-dot notation. Electron-dot notation only shows the valence electrons of a particular element. Valence electrons are indicated by dots placed around the element's symbol.

To write an element's electron-dot notation, first determine the number of valence electrons in an atom of that element. Because the periodic table, as shown in Figure 18, is organized by proton number, it also reflects patterns in numbers of valence electrons. For example, hydrogen and lithium are in the first column, or Group 1, and have 1 valence electron. Beryllium is in Group 2 and has 2 valence electrons. Boron is Group 13 and has 3 valence electrons. Carbon is in Group 14 and has 4 valence electrons, and so on. Except for helium, elements in Group 18 have 8 valence electrons, or an *octet*.

Element	Number of valence electrons	Electron-dot notation
Hydrogen	1	H·
Helium	2	He:
Lithium	1	Li·
Beryllium	2	Be· (one dot right, one dot below)
Boron	3	·B· (dots left, right, below)

Element	Number of valence electrons	Electron-dot notation
Carbon	4	·C· (dots on all four sides)
Nitrogen	5	·N: (dots on all four sides, pair on right)
Oxygen	6	·O: (pairs right and below)
Fluorine	7	:F: (pairs left, right, below)
Neon	8	:Ne: (pairs on all four sides)

To draw the correct electron-dot notation for an element, place the corresponding number of valence electrons (as dots) around the element's symbol. Each side of the element symbol gets one dot until all four sides have a dot. Dots are then added around the four sides again until all four sides have pairs of two.

MODEL Use the information above and the periodic table in Figure 18 to complete the electron-dot notations for the next eight elements after neon (sodium through argon).

Na Mg Al Si

P S Cl Ar

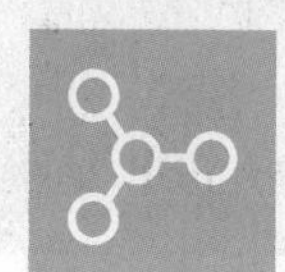

Patterns

Analyzing the Periodic Table

The periodic table shows all the elements arranged by their atomic number. Because atomic number is equal to the number of protons and electrons in atoms of an element, the periodic table can be used to predict chemical properties of different elements.

Consider the elements in Group 1. They have 1 valence electron and are very reactive. For example, hydrogen is an explosive gas, and lithium, sodium, and potassium metal all react vigorously with water. Elements in Group 17, have 7 valence electrons (one short of an octet) and are also highly reactive. The elements in Group 18, on the other hand, have a full outer energy shell with 8 electrons, and are generally nonreactive.

FIGURE 18: The periodic table lists all the elements by their atomic number in rows and columns.

6 C Carbon — Atomic number; Chemical symbol; Element name

Metals | Metalloids | Nonmetals

	1	2	3	4	5	6	7	8	9	10	11	12	13	14	15	16	17	18
1	1 H Hydrogen																	2 He Helium
2	3 Li Lithium	4 Be Beryllium											5 B Boron	6 C Carbon	7 N Nitrogen	8 O Oxygen	9 F Fluorine	10 Ne Neon
3	11 Na Sodium	12 Mg Magnesium											13 Al Aluminum	14 Si Silicon	15 P Phosphorus	16 S Sulfur	17 Cl Chlorine	18 Ar Argon
4	19 K Potassium	20 Ca Calcium	21 Sc Scandium	22 Ti Titanium	23 V Vanadium	24 Cr Chromium	25 Mn Manganese	26 Fe Iron	27 Co Cobalt	28 Ni Nickel	29 Cu Copper	30 Zn Zinc	31 Ga Gallium	32 Ge Germanium	33 As Arsenic	34 Se Selenium	35 Br Bromine	36 Kr Krypton
5	37 Rb Rubidium	38 Sr Strontium	39 Y Yttrium	40 Zr Zirconium	41 Nb Niobium	42 Mo Molybdenum	43 Tc Technetium	44 Ru Ruthenium	45 Rh Rhodium	46 Pd Palladium	47 Ag Silver	48 Cd Cadmium	49 In Indium	50 Sn Tin	51 Sb Antimony	52 Te Tellurium	53 I Iodine	54 Xe Xenon
6	55 Cs Cesium	56 Ba Barium	57–71	72 Hf Hafnium	73 Ta Tantalum	74 W Tungsten	75 Re Rhenium	76 Os Osmium	77 Ir Iridium	78 Pt Platinum	79 Au Gold	80 Hg Mercury	81 Tl Thallium	82 Pb Lead	83 Bi Bismuth	84 Po Polonium	85 At Astatine	86 Rn Radon
7	87 Fr Francium	88 Ra Radium	89–103	104 Rf Rutherfordium	105 Db Dubnium	106 Sg Seaborgium	107 Bh Bohrium	108 Hs Hassium	109 Mt Meitnerium	110 Ds Darmstadtium	111 Rg Roentgenium	112 Cn Copernicium	113 Nh Nihonium	114 Fl Flerovium	115 Mc Moscovium	116 Lv Livermorium	117 Ts Tennessine	118 Og Oganesson

Lanthanide Series	57 La Lanthanum	58 Ce Cerium	59 Pr Praseodymium	60 Nd Neodymium	61 Pm Promethium	62 Sm Samarium	63 Eu Europium	64 Gd Gadolinium	65 Tb Terbium	66 Dy Dysprosium	67 Ho Holmium	68 Er Erbium	69 Tm Thulium	70 Yb Ytterbium	71 Lu Lutetium
Actinide Series	89 Ac Actinium	90 Th Thorium	91 Pa Protactinium	92 U Uranium	93 Np Neptunium	94 Pu Plutonium	95 Am Americium	96 Cm Curium	97 Bk Berkelium	98 Cf Californium	99 Es Einsteinium	100 Fm Fermium	101 Md Mendelevium	102 No Nobelium	103 Lr Lawrencium

INFER Based on their location on the periodic table, what can you infer about the chemical properties of elements in Group 2 of the periodic table? Would you expect these elements to readily react with other substances as compared to other groups? Explain your answer.

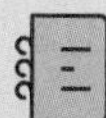

Evidence Notebook Two elements that make up gases in Earth's atmosphere are nitrogen and oxygen. Use the periodic table to explain how many valence electrons these elements have. How might differences in the electron distribution of these elements relate to the aurora polaris?

Language Arts

Mass Spectrometry

Imagine you needed to identify an unknown substance. How might you determine its identity? Scientists use a method called mass spectrometry to estimate the purity of samples, monitor complex chemical and biochemical reactions, and identify the composition of samples. Mass spectrometry can also be used to identify new compounds and organic structures quickly and easily.

In a mass spectrometer, shown in Figure 19, atoms in a sample pass through a high-energy beam of electrons. This beam knocks off one or more of the atoms' electrons, giving the atoms a positive charge. These positively charged particles are called ions. When these ions are projected through a strong magnetic field, their paths change.

The change in path, or deflection, of each particle in the sample depends on its mass. The heavier particles have the most inertia and so their path is deflected the least. The paths of the lighter particles are deflected the most. This separates the particles by mass. Finally, positions where the particles hit a detector plate are used to calculate their relative masses. Scientists can then identify the elements found in a sample by knowing their masses.

EXPLAIN Imagine you wanted to construct a physical model to demonstrate how a spectrometer works. What would your model consist of?

An important use of mass spectrometry is in the study of individual elements. For example, scientists can use mass spectrometry to determine the average atomic mass of an element. It can also be used to determine the mass of individual isotopes of an element.

Carbon has two stable isotopes, carbon-12 and carbon-13. Data from mass spectrometry shows that the ratio of the masses of carbon-12 and carbon-13 is

$$\frac{\text{mass}\,^{13}\text{C}}{\text{mass}\,^{12}\text{C}} = 1.0836$$

Because the atomic mass of carbon-12 is exactly 12 u by definition, this ratio can be used to calculate the mass of carbon-13.

$$\text{mass}\,^{13}\text{C} = 1.0836 \times 12\ \text{u} = 13.0034\ \text{u}$$

FIGURE 19: A mass spectrometer is used to determine the mass of an atom.

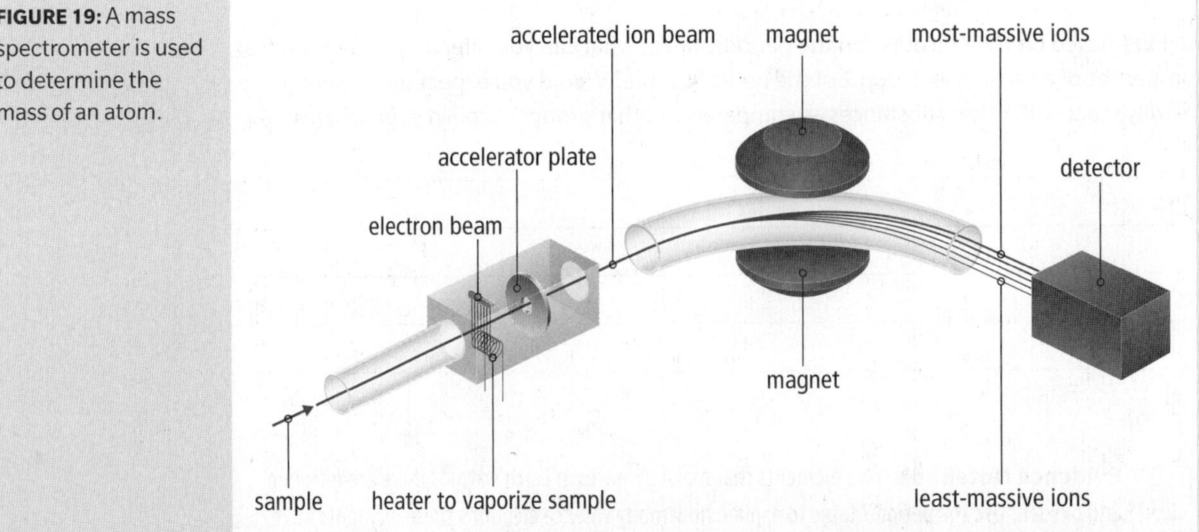

Sample Results from a Mass Spectrometer

FIGURE 20: Carbon sample

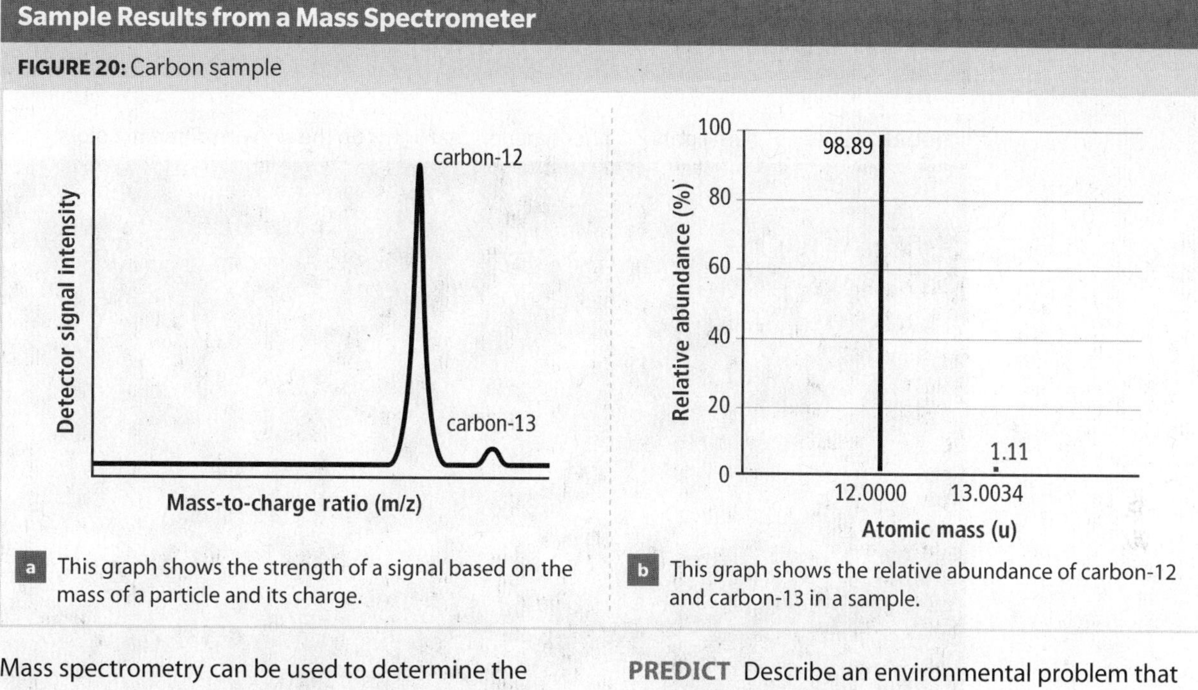

a This graph shows the strength of a signal based on the mass of a particle and its charge.

b This graph shows the relative abundance of carbon-12 and carbon-13 in a sample.

Mass spectrometry can be used to determine the percentage composition of a sample of particles of known masses. Scientists also use mass spectrometry to identify the chemical composition of a compound based on the mass-to-charge ratio of the particles.

For example, the graph in Figure 20a shows how signal intensity can be used to determine the mass-to-charge ratio of carbon-12 and carbon-13. The graph in Figure 20b shows how a mass spectrometer can be used to determine the relative abundance of these two isotopes in a sample.

Practical applications of mass spectrometry include medical applications, such as the study of different proteins. Mass spectrometry has also been used in space to identify the composition of various planets and moons.

Mass spectrometry even helps us learn about our own environment. It can be used to analyze air, soil, and water for pollutants. This technique may also be used to determine how quickly pesticides break down in the environment and identify what they break down into.

PREDICT Describe an environmental problem that could be studied using mass spectrometry. Explain how this method would help scientists learn more about the problem.

Language Arts Connection Conduct research to find an example of how mass spectrometry has helped scientists learn something about the natural world. Then, write a short blog post describing your findings. After writing the first draft, make your blog post more effective by strengthening your writing through revising, editing, and rewriting. Make sure your blog post focuses on what is most significant about the use of spectrometry by the scientists. In addition, implement revisions that make your blog post easy to read, informative, and concise.

PRACTICE WITH ELECTRON CONFIGURATIONS | EVIDENCE FOR THE ATOMIC MODEL | CRYO-ELECTRON MICROSCOPY | Go online to choose one of these other paths.

Lesson Self-Check

CAN YOU EXPLAIN THE PHENOMENON?

FIGURE 21: The northern lights is a phenomenon that lights up the sky with different colors.

The aurora polaris are multicolored lights seen in the night sky near the northern and southern poles. These lights are usually pink, green, yellow, blue, violet, red, and sometimes orange and white, and are often seen as a glow moving across the sky. These lights are not visible every night—they only occur when conditions are just right. Sometimes the colors are very faint and barely visible while other times they can provide dazzling displays. The aurora polaris may also be observed from the space station. Scientists have even observed the same phenomenon at the poles of other planets in our solar system.

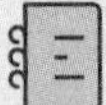

Evidence Notebook Refer to your notes in your Evidence Notebook to make a claim about how atomic structure is related to the different colors seen in the aurora polaris. Your explanation should include a discussion of the following points:

Claim How is atomic structure related to the different colors displayed as part of the aurora polaris phenomenon?

Evidence Give specific evidence to support your claim.

Reasoning Explain, in detail, how the evidence you cited supports your claim.

Name ______________________ Date ______________

CHECKPOINTS

Check Your Understanding

1. Chlorine has a total of 17 electrons and 7 valence electrons. Why are these two numbers different?
   - ○ **a.** Valence electrons are the electrons in the innermost orbital.
   - ○ **b.** Valence electrons are the electrons in the outermost energy shell.
   - ○ **c.** Some electrons are located in the nucleus of the atom.
   - ○ **d.** Some electrons are located outside the atom.

2. Why does the mass number for an element differ from the average atomic mass for that element?
   - ○ **a.** The mass number only accounts for the number of protons, while the average atomic mass only accounts for the average number of neutrons.
   - ○ **b.** The mass number accounts for the number of protons and neutrons, while the average atomic mass only accounts for the average number of protons.
   - ○ **c.** The mass number accounts for the mass of each isotope. The average atomic mass is a weighted average of the number of neutrons.
   - ○ **d.** The mass number only accounts for the mass of protons and neutrons, while the average atomic mass is a weighted average of the masses of the isotopes.

3. Select the correct terms to complete the statement.

   Electron-dot notation shows only the electrons in the innermost | outermost energy shell of an atom. These electrons are called valence | orbital electrons and are | are not involved in chemical reactions. Elements with a full outer energy shell are typically very reactive | unreactive.

4. Select from the number values below to complete the statement. A value may be used more than once or not at all.

38	50	88

   Strontium has an atomic number of 38 and an atomic mass number of 88. Therefore, it has __________ protons, __________ neutrons, and __________ electrons.

5. A scientist picks up a sample of an element. She thinks it might be a metal. Which of the following properties would support her conclusion? Select all correct answers.
   - ☐ **a.** The element is shiny.
   - ☐ **b.** The element is dull.
   - ☐ **c.** The element partially conducts electricity.
   - ☐ **d.** The element is a good conductor of electricity.
   - ☐ **e.** The element is very brittle.

6. Which of these claims are supported by the results of a flame test? Select all correct answers.
   - ☐ **a.** Different metallic elements give off different colors when they are burned in a flame.
   - ☐ **b.** Electrons absorb energy when they move from one atom to another.
   - ☐ **c.** Protons absorb light when exposed to electricity.
   - ☐ **d.** Neutrons give off energy in the form of light when they absorb energy from a source such as a flame.
   - ☐ **e.** Electrons emit energy when they move from a higher energy level to a lower energy level.

CHECKPOINTS (continued)

7. What are valence electrons, and why are they important to consider when predicting the properties of elements?

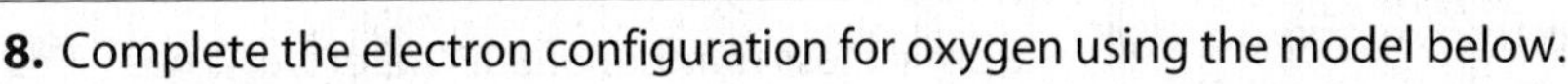

8. Complete the electron configuration for oxygen using the model below.

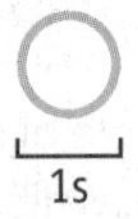

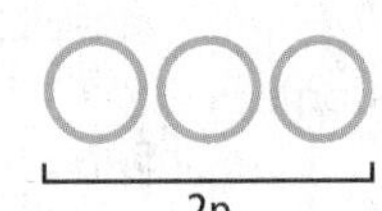

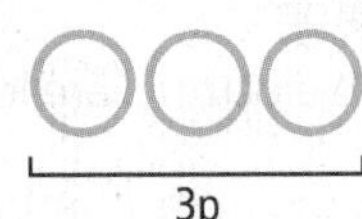

9. A chemist repeats the gold foil experiment, but she uses foil made of aluminum (atomic number 13) instead of gold (atomic number 79). How would you expect her results to compare with the experiment that used gold foil?

MAKE YOUR OWN STUDY GUIDE

In your Evidence Notebook, design a study guide that supports the main ideas from this lesson:

Chemical elements are described by their atomic mass and mass number.

Valence electrons determine the chemical properties of elements, such as how they react with other substances.

Remember to include the following information in your study guide:

- Use examples that model main ideas.
- Record explanations for the phenomena you investigated.
- Use evidence to support your explanations. Your support can include drawings, data, graphs, laboratory conclusions, and other evidence recorded throughout the lesson.

Consider how patterns observed at different scales can explain the behavior of elements.

2.2

Investigating Patterns in the Periodic Table

Silver, gold, and platinum are all metals, but they have different appearances.

CAN YOU EXPLAIN THE PHENOMENON?

For centuries, chemists have identified and studied the elements that are naturally found on Earth. Some elements, such as silver, gold, and platinum, have similar physical and chemical properties. For example, these elements do not react violently with water or oxygen. Other metals, such as potassium, do. Only about 90 elements are known to exist naturally. Other, synthetic elements can be made in a lab. Using the periodic table, scientists are able to predict some of the properties these elements should have.

PREDICT How do you think scientists can use properties of existing elements to predict the existence of synthetic elements?

Evidence Notebook As you explore the lesson, gather evidence to explain how the periodic table can be used to predict the behavior of new elements.

Hands-On Lab

Modeling Periodic Trends

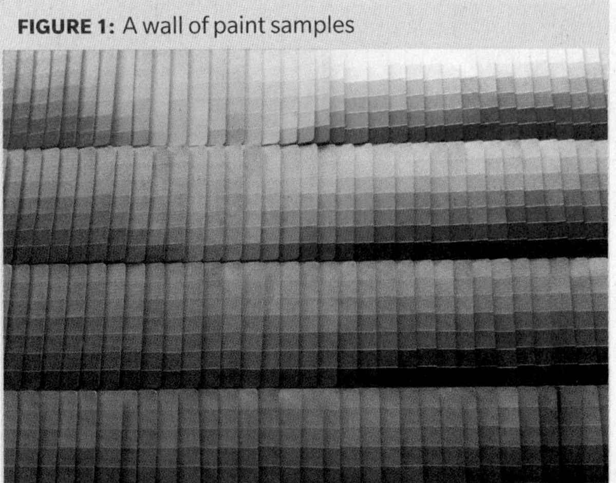

FIGURE 1: A wall of paint samples

When trying to decide what color to paint a wall, you might view paint samples to compare your choices. Samples on a palette, such as those shown in Figure 1, might have a similar color but vary by shade or intensity. For instance, samples on a palette containing different shades of red might be arranged from pink to maroon. Another palette may arrange shades of blue in a similar way. Figure 1 shows just a small selection of paint palettes a store may carry. You can also obtain paint chip cards, which are individual cards that have just one paint color on them, from stores.

Imagine that you work in a paint store and you receive a shipment of paint chip cards from your supplier. You have a box full of paint chip cards of different colors and hues, but the supplier failed to inform you how many cards there should be. You first need to determine if any cards are missing. Then, you need to find the best way to display the paint cards so your customers can easily find the colors and hues they're looking for.

RESEARCH QUESTION Recognizing patterns is an extremely important skill for scientists. How might a chemist use patterns to understand phenomena?

MAKE A CLAIM

What patterns will help you determine if any paint chip cards are missing from the set? What should you consider when determining which arrangement of paint chip cards is most beneficial to customers?

MATERIALS

- set of paint chip cards

PLAN THE INVESTIGATION

Obtain a set of paint chip cards from your teacher. Lay out all the cards so you can see the colors. Make a list of all the potential ways you can arrange your cards. For each arrangement, take notes on how the arrangement will help you find any missing cards. Also note how easily customers would be able to find the paint sample they want using each arrangement.

CARRY OUT THE INVESTIGATION

Choose the three arrangements you think will work best, and set your paint chip cards according to each plan. Develop a data table to record any missing cards. Take a picture or make a sketch of each arrangement before you set up the next one.

ANALYZE

Were any paint chip cards missing from your set? How did you determine they were or were not missing? How would you describe the missing cards to someone?

DRAW CONCLUSIONS

Write a conclusion that addresses each of the points below.

Claim What patterns helped you determine whether paint chip cards were missing? What should you consider when determining which arrangement of paint chip cards is most beneficial for customers?

Evidence Give specific examples from your data to support your claim.

Reasoning Explain how the evidence you gave supports your claim. Describe, in detail, the connections between the evidence you cited and the argument you are making.

Evidence Notebook Based on your observations in this investigation, how might observing patterns in the properties of the elements have helped scientists identify missing elements?

Predicting the Properties of Elements

In the last activity, you likely observed and used a gradually changing pattern when arranging the paint chips. In the 1800s, scientists used a similar approach when trying to organize the known elements. They began by noting patterns in the properties of elements and how these properties changed with increasing and decreasing atomic mass.

Organizing the Periodic Table

Explore Online

Hands-On Lab

The Mendeleev Lab of 1869 Use your knowledge of the periodic table to determine the identity of nine unknown elements.

Russian chemist and teacher Dmitri Mendeleev published the first periodic table in 1869 as an attempt to include all elements in one classification scheme. To do this, he began by writing element names and their characteristics on separate note cards and arranging them in various ways. This helped him compare atomic mass and other chemical and physical properties of each element. When arranging the elements by increasing atomic mass, he saw that chemical properties occurred in a repeating pattern.

FIGURE 2: Mendeleev's original periodic table

			Ti=50	Zr=90	?=180.
			V=51	Nb=94	Ta=182.
			Cr=52	Mo=96	W=186.
			Mn=55	Rh=104,4	Pt=197,4
			Fe=56	Ru=104,4	Ir=198.
			Ni=Co=59	Pl=106,6,	Os=199.
H=1			Cu=63,4	Ag=108	Hg=200.
	Be=9,4	Mg=24	Zn=65,2	Cd=112	
	B=11	Al=27,4	?=68	Ur=116	Au=197?
	C=12	Si=28	?=70	Su=118	
	N=14	P=31	As=75	Sb=122	Bi=210
	O=16	S=32	Se=79,4	Te=128?	
	F=19	Cl=35,5	Br=80	I=127	
Li=7	Na=23	K=39	Rb=85,4	Cs=133	Tl=204
		Ca=40	Sr=87,6	Ba=137	Pb=207.
		?=45	Ce=92		
		?Er=56	La=94		
		?Yt=60	Di=95		
		?In=75,6	Th=118?		

PREDICT Why do you think Mendeleev left gaps in the periodic table shown in Figure 2?

Mendeleev arranged the elements so the atomic mass increased going down a column. He arranged the columns so elements in the same row shared similar properties. Sometimes, however, he found that he needed to reverse the order of atomic masses in order to make elements with similar properties fall in the same row. Notice that iodine, I, is listed after tellurium, Te, even though iodine has a smaller atomic mass. This arrangement allowed iodine to be placed in a group of elements with which it shares similar properties.

Recognizing Periodic Patterns

Mendeleev's table of elements revealed a repeating pattern, or *periodicity*, of properties, hence the name *periodic table*. Mendeleev's ability to explain known patterns and predict unknown elements led to the acceptance of the table and the idea of periodic patterns. Scientists continue to study elements to better understand their properties.

In 1913, British chemist Henry Moseley discovered a new periodic pattern based on nuclear charge, or the number of the protons in the nucleus. Organizing the periodic table based on atomic number better fit the patterns of chemical and physical properties Mendeleev had observed. Moseley's work led to our current understanding of atomic number and the order of elements on the modern periodic table, shown in Figure 3.

FIGURE 3: The periodic table shows which elements are classified as metals, metalloids, or nonmetals.

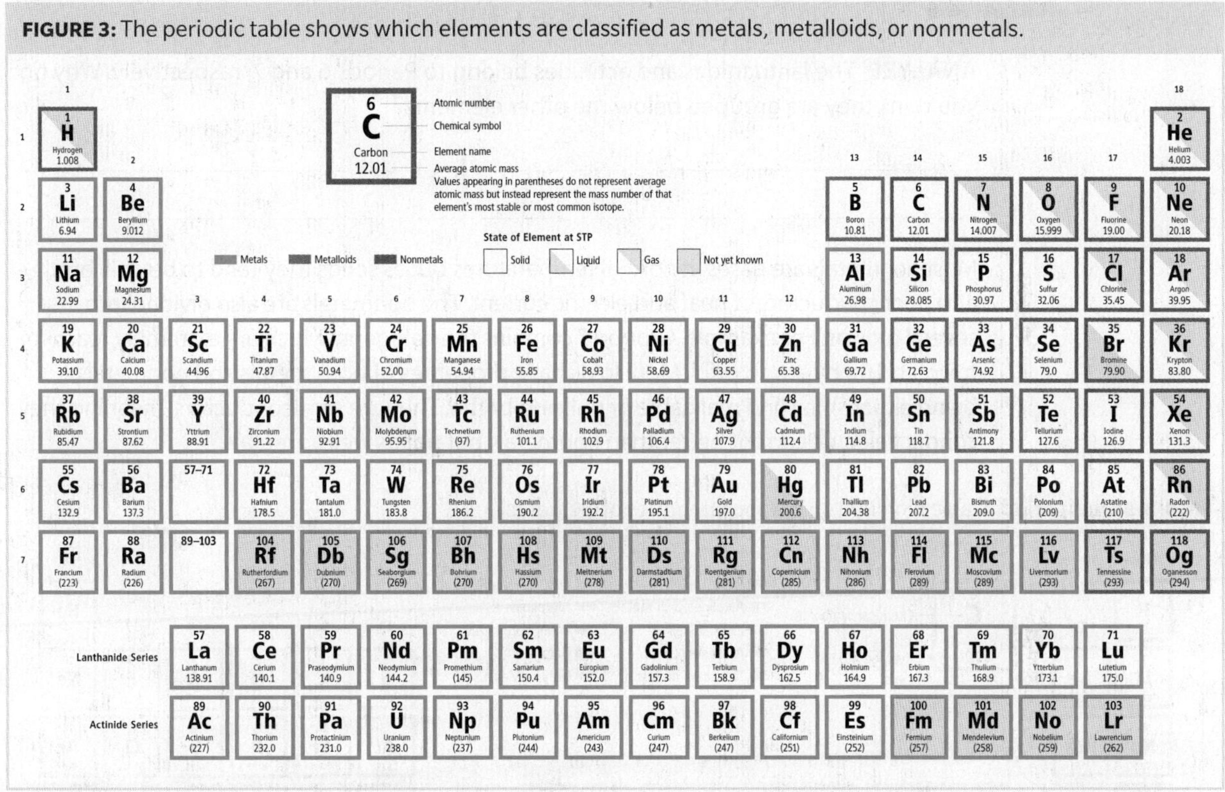

ANALYZE What patterns do you notice in the table in terms of protons, electrons, and valence electrons? How might these relate to an element being a metal or a nonmetal?

As scientists continued to study the properties of elements, they identified additional patterns that supported what would be known as the periodic law. The periodic law states that the chemical and physical properties of elements are periodic functions of the elements' atomic number. A row across the periodic table is called a *period*. A column down the periodic table is called a *group* or *family*. Adjacent elements in a period may have similar or different properties, but elements in the same group have similar properties. For example, chlorine, Cl, and argon, Ar, are adjacent in Period 3 but are in different groups, and they have very different properties. Chlorine is very reactive and easily forms compounds. Argon is nonreactive and does not readily form compounds.

Grouping Elements Using Properties

FIGURE 4: Metals and nonmetals

Elements are categorized as metals, metalloids, or nonmetals. Some examples are pictured in Figure 4. The metals are divided into several categories, which can be seen in Figure 5, based on their specific properties. Group 1 contains the alkali metals, which have low melting points and are very reactive. The alkaline-earth metals located in Group 2 are stronger, denser, and have higher melting points than alkali metals. Groups 3 through 12 are transition metals. These metals are less reactive and some exist as free elements in nature. Post-transition metals are usually more brittle and poor conductors. The lanthanides are shiny, reactive, and soft. Actinides are radioactive, and most are synthetic elements.

ANALYZE The lanthanides and actinides belong to Periods 6 and 7, respectively. Why do you think they are grouped below the other elements?

Most nonmetals are gases at normal temperatures but as solids they tend to be dull, brittle, and poor conductors of heat and electric current. The nonmetals are also divided into several groups. For example, Group 17 contains the halogens, which are extremely reactive, toxic, and many are colorful. Metalloids have properties of both metals and nonmetals, being either shiny and malleable or dull and brittle. They are semiconductors, meaning they conduct electric current better than nonmetals but not as well as metals.

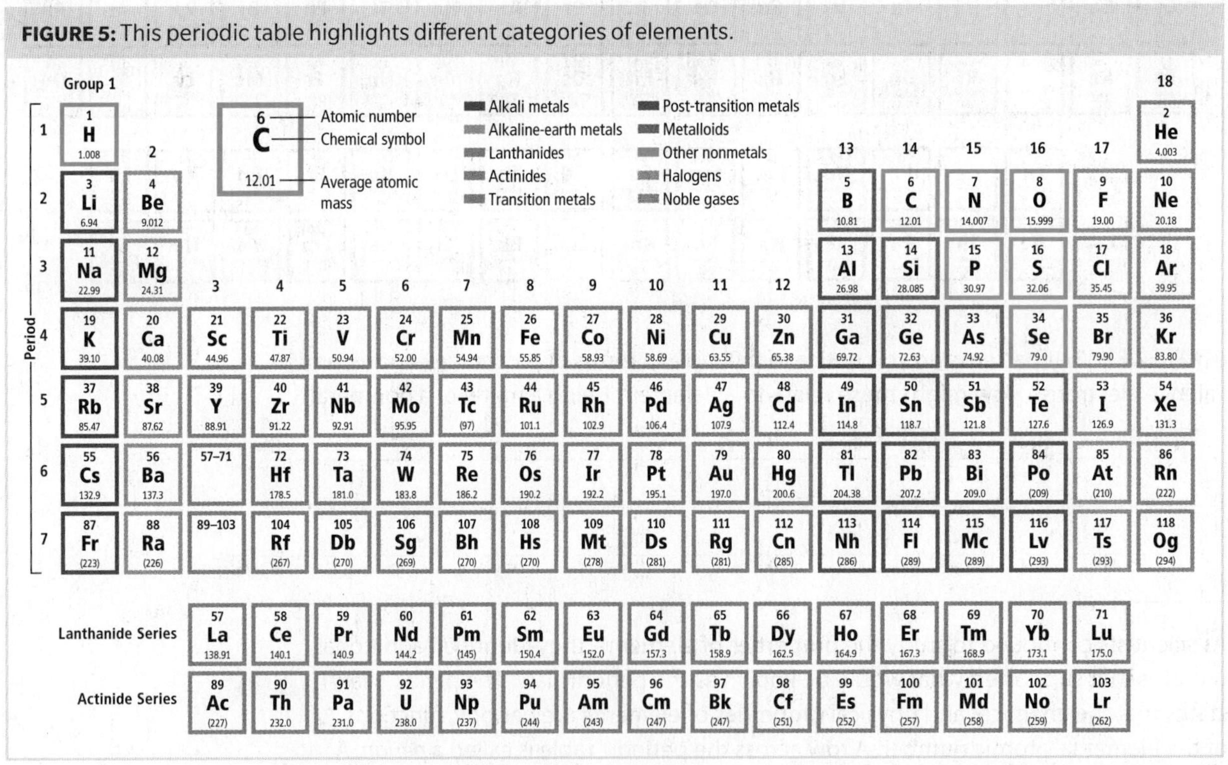

Period	Group 1	2	3	4	5	6	7	8	9	10	11	12	13	14	15	16	17	18
1	1 H 1.008																	2 He 4.003
2	3 Li 6.94	4 Be 9.012											5 B 10.81	6 C 12.01	7 N 14.007	8 O 15.999	9 F 19.00	10 Ne 20.18
3	11 Na 22.99	12 Mg 24.31											13 Al 26.98	14 Si 28.085	15 P 30.97	16 S 32.06	17 Cl 35.45	18 Ar 39.95
4	19 K 39.10	20 Ca 40.08	21 Sc 44.96	22 Ti 47.87	23 V 50.94	24 Cr 52.00	25 Mn 54.94	26 Fe 55.85	27 Co 58.93	28 Ni 58.69	29 Cu 63.55	30 Zn 65.38	31 Ga 69.72	32 Ge 72.63	33 As 74.92	34 Se 79.0	35 Br 79.90	36 Kr 83.80
5	37 Rb 85.47	38 Sr 87.62	39 Y 88.91	40 Zr 91.22	41 Nb 92.91	42 Mo 95.95	43 Tc (97)	44 Ru 101.1	45 Rh 102.9	46 Pd 106.4	47 Ag 107.9	48 Cd 112.4	49 In 114.8	50 Sn 118.7	51 Sb 121.8	52 Te 127.6	53 I 126.9	54 Xe 131.3
6	55 Cs 132.9	56 Ba 137.3	57–71	72 Hf 178.5	73 Ta 181.0	74 W 183.8	75 Re 186.2	76 Os 190.2	77 Ir 192.2	78 Pt 195.1	79 Au 197.0	80 Hg 200.6	81 Tl 204.38	82 Pb 207.2	83 Bi 209.0	84 Po (209)	85 At (210)	86 Rn (222)
7	87 Fr (223)	88 Ra (226)	89–103	104 Rf (267)	105 Db (270)	106 Sg (269)	107 Bh (270)	108 Hs (270)	109 Mt (278)	110 Ds (281)	111 Rg (281)	112 Cn (285)	113 Nh (286)	114 Fl (289)	115 Mc (289)	116 Lv (293)	117 Ts (293)	118 Og (294)

Series															
Lanthanide Series	57 La 138.91	58 Ce 140.1	59 Pr 140.9	60 Nd 144.2	61 Pm (145)	62 Sm 150.4	63 Eu 152.0	64 Gd 157.3	65 Tb 158.9	66 Dy 162.5	67 Ho 164.9	68 Er 167.3	69 Tm 168.9	70 Yb 173.1	71 Lu 175.0
Actinide Series	89 Ac (227)	90 Th 232.0	91 Pa 231.0	92 U 238.0	93 Np (237)	94 Pu (244)	95 Am (243)	96 Cm (247)	97 Bk (247)	98 Cf (251)	99 Es (252)	100 Fm (257)	101 Md (258)	102 No (259)	103 Lr (262)

FIGURE 5: This periodic table highlights different categories of elements.

Evidence Notebook Identify which period and group the elements you are modeling in your unit project belong to. Based on their location on the periodic table, what properties should these elements have?

Patterns in Chemical Properties

Recall that valence electrons are those in the outermost electron shell of an atom. They are the ones most easily gained or lost when atoms interact. Valence electrons play an important role in determining the properties of an element. As a result, an element's location on the periodic table indicates the number of valence electrons it has.

PREDICT What pattern do you think exists between the number of valence electrons an element has and its placement on the periodic table?

___

___

Engineering

The Noble Gases

The Group 18 elements are called the noble gases because these elements are all gases that are generally not reactive. The Group 18 elements are rarely found combined with other elements in compounds, so they were seen as being similar to nobility—not mixing with the "common" elements. Noble gases have extremely low reactivity because of their valence shell electron configuration.

EXPLAIN Which properties do the valence shells of every noble gas have in common? Select all correct answers.

- ☐ **a.** All electrons are paired.
- ☐ **b.** They are filled with electrons.
- ☐ **c.** All electrons are unpaired.
- ☐ **d.** They have exactly two electrons.

The unreactive nature of noble gases makes them useful in many ways. Helium is used in toy and weather balloons because it floats in air and is not flammable. Argon is used during welding to shield hot metals from reacting with oxygen and other gases in air. Argon is also used in fluorescent lighting and other gas discharge tubes.

Helium has two valence electrons, and the other noble gases have eight valence electrons. Other main-group elements can become more stable by gaining, losing, or sharing electrons so they also have full valence shells like the noble gases. The millions of unique natural and synthetic chemical compounds are due to the chemical reactivity of most of the naturally occurring elements.

APPLY Complete the statement by selecting the correct terms.

Sodium, Na, a Group 1 element, has one | two | seven | eight valence electron(s). It can easily react with chlorine, Cl, a Group 17 element, with one | two | seven | eight valence electron(s). During bonding, each sodium atom gains one | gains seven | loses one | loses seven electron(s) to become stable, and each chlorine atom gains one | gains seven | loses one | loses seven electron(s) to become stable.

Evidence Notebook How could modern scientists use the periodic table to predict the properties of newly synthesized elements? Assume the synthesized elements are stable enough for their properties to be observed.

Patterns in Atomic Size

FIGURE 6: Atomic radius

chlorine nucleus
atomic radius
99 pm
198 pm
distance between nuclei
chlorine nucleus

The exact size of an atom is difficult to define. Ideally, the size of an atom is defined by the edge of its outermost shell, but that is not easy to measure. One way to express an atom's radius is to measure the distance between the nuclei of two identical atoms that are chemically bonded, and then divide this distance by two. Therefore, the atomic radius is often expressed as half the distance between the nuclei of identical atoms that are bonded together. Figure 6 shows the atomic radius of chlorine is about 99 picometers (pm). A picometer is 1×10^{-12} meters.

Collaborate With a partner, discuss why it is challenging for scientists to measure the atomic radius of an atom.

Analyzing Trends in Atomic Radii

The atomic radius can be measured using techniques such as x-ray imaging and spectroscopy. The data from these measurements can be graphed against atomic number. Figure 7 shows the relationship between atomic radius and atomic number for elements in the same period.

Atomic Radius

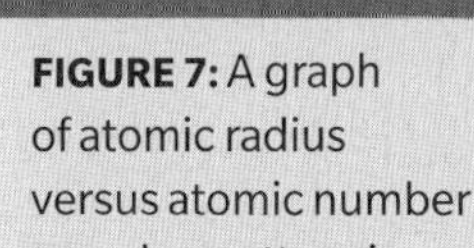

FIGURE 7: A graph of atomic radius versus atomic number reveals a pattern in the data.

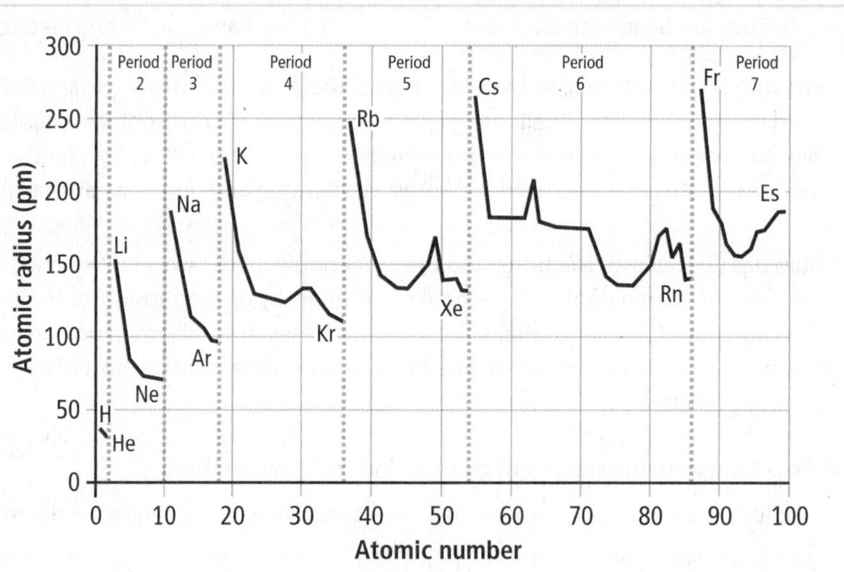

ANALYZE How does atomic radius change with atomic number? Use the elements sodium, Na; aluminum, Al; phosphorus, P; and potassium, K, to support your claim.

Explaining Trends in Atomic Radii

When the data from Figure 7 are placed on the periodic table, the patterns are even more apparent. The periodic table below shows the relative atomic radii (in picometers) of the elements. Darker colors correspond to larger atomic radii. Gray indicates atomic radii that have not been measured.

MODEL Model the pattern of atomic radii as you move across a period or down a group by drawing arrows on the periodic table.

Key: Atomic symbol — C; 6 — Atomic number; ● — Relative atomic size; 77 — Atomic radius

Period	Group 1	2	3	4	5	6	7	8	9	10	11	12	13	14	15	16	17	18
1	H 1 37																	He 2 31
2	Li 3 152	Be 4 112											B 5 85	C 6 77	N 7 75	O 8 73	F 9 72	Ne 10 71
3	Na 11 186	Mg 12 160											Al 13 143	Si 14 118	P 15 110	S 16 103	Cl 17 100	Ar 18 98
4	K 19 227	Ca 20 197	Sc 21 162	Ti 22 147	V 23 134	Cr 24 128	Mn 25 127	Fe 26 126	Co 27 125	Ni 28 124	Cu 29 128	Zn 30 134	Ga 31 135	Ge 32 122	As 33 120	Se 34 119	Br 35 114	Kr 36 112
5	Rb 37 248	Sr 38 215	Y 39 180	Zr 40 160	Nb 41 146	Mo 42 139	Tc 43 136	Ru 44 134	Rh 45 134	Pd 46 137	Ag 47 144	Cd 48 149	In 49 167	Sn 50 140	Sb 51 140	Te 52 142	I 53 133	Xe 54 131
6	Cs 55 265	Ba 56 222	57–71	Hf 72 159	Ta 73 146	W 74 139	Re 75 137	Os 76 135	Ir 77 136	Pt 78 139	Au 79 144	Hg 80 151	Tl 81 170	Pb 82 175	Bi 83 150	Po 84 168	At 85 140	Rn 86 141
7	Fr 87 270	Ra 88 220	89–103	Rf 104 —	Db 105 —	Sg 106 —	Bh 107 —	Hs 108 —	Mt 109 —	Ds 110 —	Rg 111 —	Cn 112 —	Nh 113 —	Fl 114 —	Mc 115 —	Lv 116 —	Ts 117 —	Og 118 —

APPLY Select the correct terms to complete the statement.

Moving across a period, as electrons are added to a higher | a lower | the same energy shell, they are pulled closer to the nucleus. This increased pull results in a(n) increase | decrease in atomic radius. The atomic radius increases | decreases as you move down a group because electrons occupy successively lower | higher energy shells farther from the nucleus. The farther away from the nucleus the electrons are, the more | less tightly they are held.

Trends in atomic radius data can be used to predict the reactivity of an element. For metals, as atomic radius increases, reactivity increases because the outer electrons are not held as strongly. The sodium metal in Figure 8 is highly reactive in the presence of oxygen. Nonmetals show the opposite trend—as atomic radius increases, reactivity decreases because the outer electrons are held more strongly.

FIGURE 8: Sodium metal corrodes when exposed to air.

EXPLAIN Why is fluorine, F, more reactive than bromine, Br?

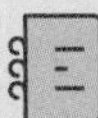

Evidence Notebook Explain how chemists could use trends in atomic radii to predict the size of a new element that has not yet been discovered.

Patterns in Ionization Energy

Neutral atoms have an equal number of protons and electrons. These oppositely charged particles are electrically attracted to each other. The energy required to remove an electron from a neutral atom is known as ionization energy. This is the energy required to overcome the attraction, remove an electron, and produce a charged atom, called an *ion*.

Analyzing Ionization Energy

As Figure 9 shows, the force needed to remove an inner electron is greater than it is to remove an outer electron. Electrons closer to the nucleus partially shield the outer electrons from the attraction of the positive charge. Also, a repulsive force exists between the inner and outer electrons, pushing outer electrons outwards. Thus, valence electrons are held more loosely than inner electrons and require less energy to remove. Ionization energy depends on the net force that keeps a valence electron in an atom.

FIGURE 9: Inner electrons partially shield outer electrons from the attraction of protons in the nucleus. They also repel the outer electrons, further weakening the nucleus's hold on them.

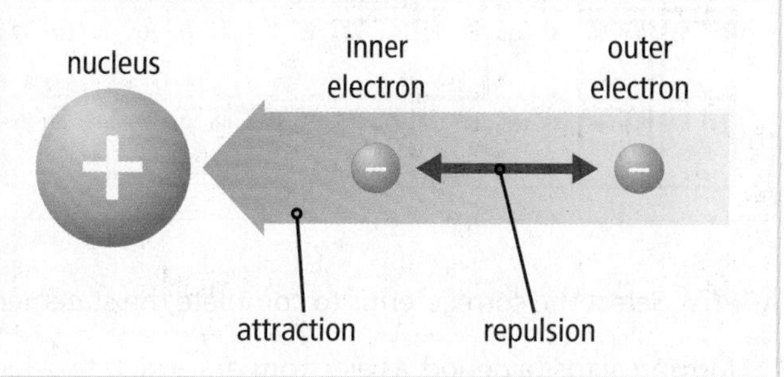

APPLY Complete the statement explaining which elements have an ionization energy greater than that of silicon, Si.

Magnesium and aluminum | Phosphorus and sulfur have a greater ionization energy because their atoms have more protons than silicon has. The additional electrons do not increase shielding because their valence shells are the same as | different from those of the outer electrons of silicon. Magnesium and aluminum | Phosphorus and sulfur have a smaller ionization energy because their atoms have fewer protons than silicon. Germanium has a smaller | larger ionization energy because the shielding effect on its outermost electron is greater than that of silicon.

Nuclei with a greater number of protons more strongly attract electrons in all energy levels. Therefore, as atomic number increases across a period, so does ionization energy. Atoms whose outermost electrons occupy higher energy shells, however, are farther from the nucleus. The increased distance and shielding from inner electrons weakens the attraction of the electrons to the nucleus causing ionization energy to decrease.

INFER How can ionization energy be used as a measure of chemical reactivity?

Patterns

Patterns in Ionization Energies

To avoid the influence of nearby atoms, measurements of ionization energies are made on isolated atoms in the gas phase. In this phase, atoms are at a much greater distance from each other than they are in the liquid or solid phase. A sample of the element is heated to produce a gas. A beam of light or a stream of electrons is used to eject an electron from the atom.

Ionization Energy

FIGURE 10: Ionization energy can be graphed as a function of an element's atomic number.

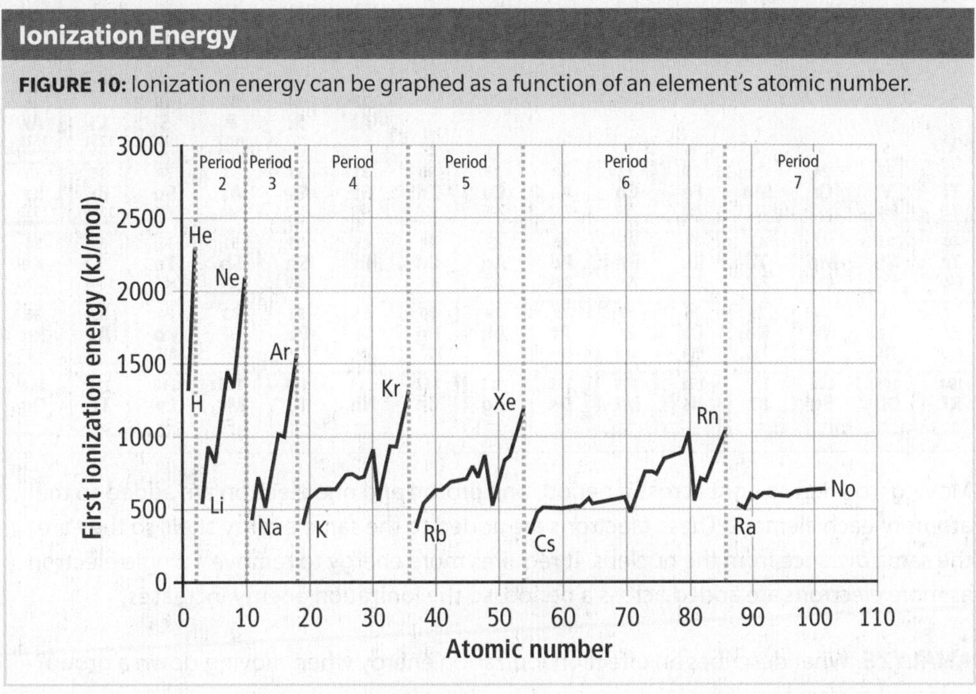

Figure 10 shows the ionization energy required to remove a single electron from a neutral atom of an element as a function of the atomic number of the element, shown on the horizontal axis. The dotted lines note the beginning of a period.

ANALYZE How does ionization energy change with atomic number? Use evidence from the graph to support your claim.

EXPLAIN How does ionization energy change across a period and down a group on the periodic table? Use evidence from the graph to support your claim.

Explaining Trends in Ionization Energy

The graphical representation of ionization energies of the elements reveals some clear patterns. These same data are mapped onto the periodic table below, and the patterns are even more apparent. Darker colors correspond to higher ionization energies. Gray indicates ionization energies that have not been measured.

MODEL Model the pattern of ionization energy as you move across a period or down a group by drawing arrows on the periodic table.

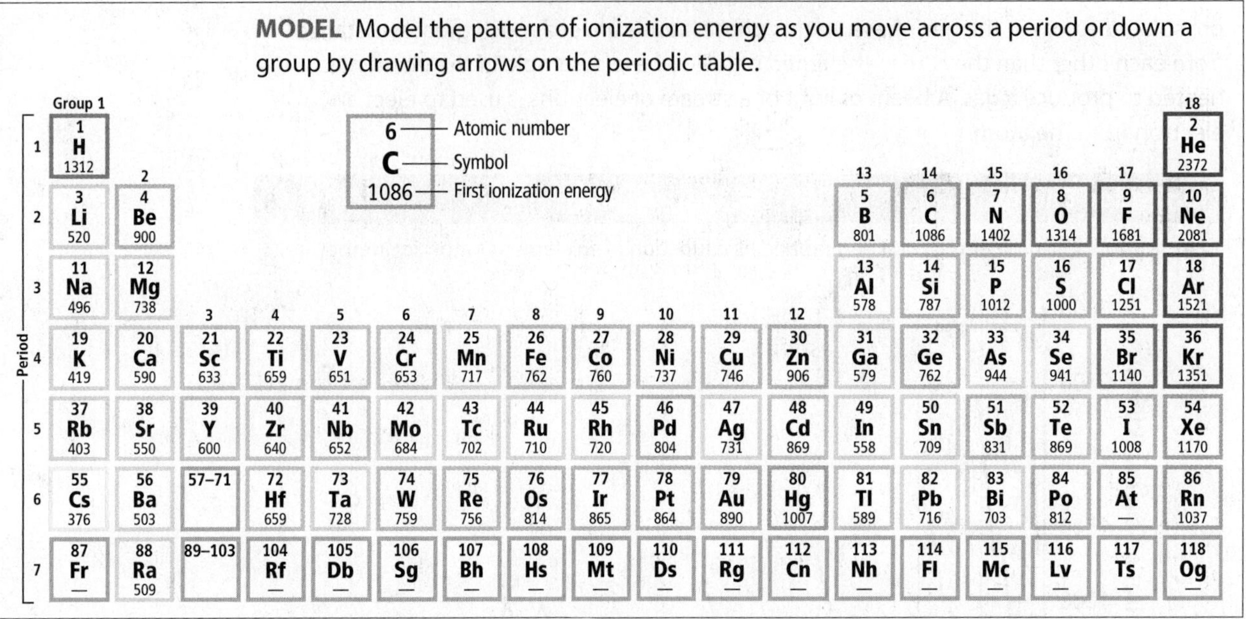

Moving from left to right across a period, one proton and one electron are added to the atoms of each element. These electrons are added to the same energy shell, so they are the same distance from the nucleus. It requires more energy to remove a single electron as more electrons are added across a period, so the ionization energy increases.

ANALYZE What describes an effect on ionization energy when moving down a group? Select all correct answers.

- ☐ **a.** the ionization energy increases down a group
- ☐ **b.** the ionization energy decreases down a group
- ☐ **c.** the valence electrons are in energy levels farther from the nucleus
- ☐ **d.** the shielding effect is less

Within each period and within some groups the individual ionization values do go up and down. In Period 2, for example, nitrogen has a higher ionization energy than oxygen. In Group 14, the ionization of lead is higher than that of tin, which is just above it. Inconsistencies in the trends remind us that all scientific models are limited approximations of nature's ultimate reality.

INFER Why do noble gases have high ionization energies? What does this pattern suggest about their chemical stability?

Evidence Notebook How can scientists use patterns in ionization energy to learn more about elements that have not been discovered yet?

EXPLORATION 5

Patterns in Electronegativity

When atoms combine to form compounds, electrons may be lost, gained, or shared between the atoms. When two identical atoms bond, electrons are shared equally. When different types of atoms bond, one atom in a compound usually attracts electrons more strongly than the other atom. You can imagine this as a sort of "tug of war" for the electrons being shared or transferred in a compound.

APPLY Write your own analogy for the sharing of electrons in a compound. With a partner, discuss how the dogs playing tug of war in Figure 11 is a good analogy for this phenomenon.

____

____

____

____

FIGURE 11: In a game of tug of war, one player may exert a stronger pull on the rope.

Analyzing Electronegativity

In Figure 11, think of the knot in the center of the rope as an electron. If the dog on the right "tugs" more strongly than the dog on the left, the dog on the right will be slightly more negative than the one on the left. This uneven concentration of charge strongly affects the physical and chemical properties of a compound. Electronegativity measures the relative attraction an atom has for the electrons it shares in a molecule.

Atoms with more protons tend to have a greater attraction for shared electrons because of their greater positive nuclear charge. Atoms with a large atomic radius tend to have a weaker attraction for shared electrons because the distance between the nucleus and the shared electrons is larger. So, electronegativity is greater for smaller atoms with a larger number of protons. It is smaller for larger atoms with a smaller number of protons.

EXPLAIN Using this information, explain how the electronegativities of the following elements compare to that of phosphorus.

higher | lower

Sulfur is to the right of phosphorus on the periodic table. It has ______________ electronegativity than phosphorus because a sulfur atom has more protons. Silicon is to the left of phosphorus on the periodic table. It has ______________ electronegativity because its atoms have fewer protons than phosphorus.

Nitrogen is above phosphorus on the periodic table. It has ______________ electronegativity than phosphorus because its atomic radius is smaller. Arsenic is below phosphorus on the periodic table. It has ______________ electronegativity because it has a larger atomic radius than phosphorus.

Patterns in Electronegativity

Electronegativity cannot be measured directly. It is calculated using the average energy required to remove an electron from an atom and the energy given off when an electron is added to an atom. Both methods express electronegativity as a quantity without units on a relative scale. The most electronegative element, fluorine, is arbitrarily assigned an electronegativity of 4.0. Other values are calculated in relation to this value. The results of the calculations are shown in Figure 12 as a function of atomic number.

Electronegativity

FIGURE 12: Electronegativity can be described as a function of an element's atomic number.

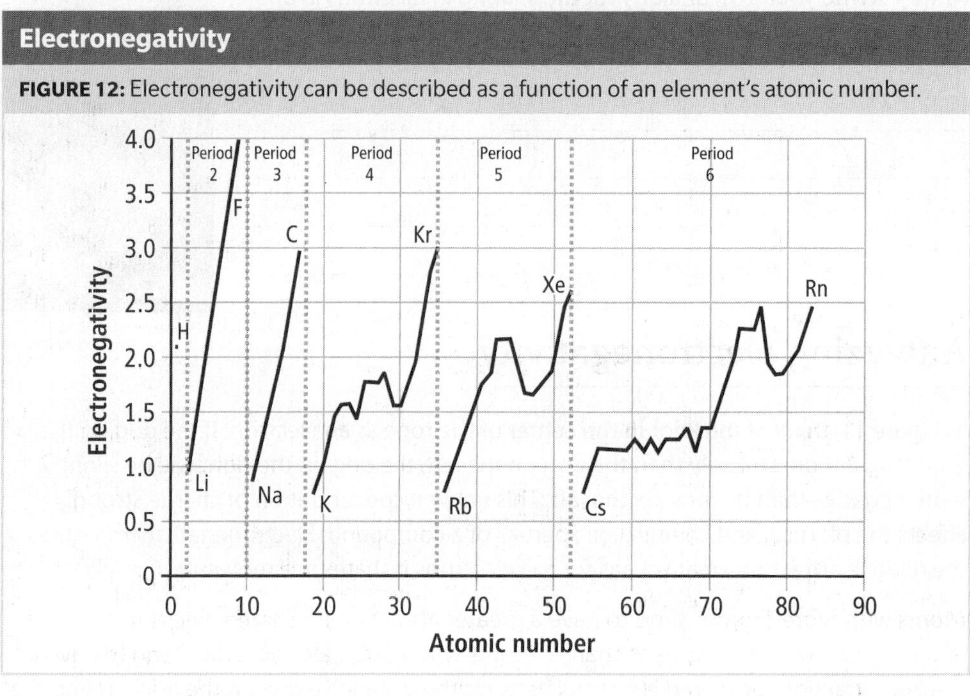

ANALYZE How would the pattern of electronegativities shown in Figure 12 appear across a period and down a group on the periodic table?

EXPLAIN How does the trend in electronegativity in the periodic table compare with the trend in atomic radii? Explain why this relationship makes sense.

EXPLAIN How does the trend in electronegativity in the periodic table compare with the trend in ionization energy? Explain why this relationship makes sense.

Explaining Trends in Electronegativity

Figure 12 shows a pattern between an element's atomic number and electronegativity. The pattern is more apparent when the data are mapped onto the periodic table below, which shows the electronegativities of the elements. Darker colors correspond to greater electronegativities. Gray indicates an undetermined electronegativity.

MODEL Model the pattern of electronegativity as you move across a period or down a group by drawing arrows on the periodic table. Circle the region of the periodic table where the most electronegative elements are located.

Key: 6 — Atomic number; C — Symbol; 2.5 — Electronegativity

Period	Group 1	2	3	4	5	6	7	8	9	10	11	12	13	14	15	16	17	18
1	1 H 2.1																	2 He —
2	3 Li 1.0	4 Be 1.5											5 B 2.0	6 C 2.5	7 N 3.0	8 O 3.5	9 F 4.0	10 Ne —
3	11 Na 0.9	12 Mg 1.2											13 Al 1.5	14 Si 1.8	15 P 2.1	16 S 2.5	17 Cl 3.0	18 Ar —
4	19 K 0.8	20 Ca 1.0	21 Sc 1.3	22 Ti 1.5	23 V 1.6	24 Cr 1.6	25 Mn 1.5	26 Fe 1.8	27 Co 1.8	28 Ni 1.8	29 Cu 1.9	30 Zn 1.6	31 Ga 1.8	32 Ge 1.8	33 As 2.0	34 Se 2.4	35 Br 2.8	36 Kr 3.0
5	37 Rb 0.8	38 Sr 1.0	39 Y 1.2	40 Zr 1.4	41 Nb 1.6	42 Mo 1.8	43 Tc 1.9	44 Ru 2.2	45 Rh 2.2	46 Pd 2.2	47 Ag 1.9	48 Cd 1.7	49 In 1.7	50 Sn 1.8	51 Sb 1.9	52 Te 2.1	53 I 2.5	54 Xe 2.6
6	55 Cs 0.7	56 Ba 0.9	57–71	72 Hf 1.3	73 Ta 1.5	74 W 1.7	75 Re 1.9	76 Os 2.2	77 Ir 2.2	78 Pt 2.2	79 Au 2.4	80 Hg 1.9	81 Tl 1.8	82 Pb 1.8	83 Bi 1.9	84 Po 2.0	85 At 2.2	86 Rn 2.4
7	87 Fr 0.7	88 Ra 0.9	89–103	104 Rf —	105 Db —	106 Sg —	107 Bh —	108 Hs —	109 Mt —	110 Ds —	111 Rg —	112 Cn —	113 Nh —	114 Fl —	115 Mc —	116 Lv —	117 Ts —	118 Og —

APPLY Select the correct terms to complete the statement.

Moving from left to right across a period, electronegativity usually increases | decreases. Because Group 1 metals have only one valence electron, they are the most | least electronegative elements. Group 17 elements are the least | most electronegative elements because they need one | seven electron(s) to fill their valence shells.

Trends in electronegativity can be used to predict reactions between elements. When elements have a large difference in electronegativity, the element with greater electronegativity has a much stronger attraction for shared electrons. These elements bond by one atom donating one or more electrons to the other atom. Elements that have similar electronegativities are more likely to share valence electrons because their attraction for the electrons is similar.

FIGURE 13: PFTE is a chemical that gives some nonstick pans their properties.

INFER Some nonstick pans, such as the pan in Figure 13, are coated with PFTE which is made of many fluorine and carbon atoms that form very strong bonds. Why do you think the bond between carbon and fluorine is so strong? How do you think this bond is related to the nonstick properties of PFTE?

Engineering

Developing Halogen Bulbs

FIGURE 14: Halogen bulb

A halogen bulb consists of a tungsten filament surrounded by halogen gas inside a clear bulb. Typical incandescent light bulbs also have a tungsten filament but they are surrounded by argon, a noble gas, that prevents oxygen in the air from corroding the metal filament and shortening the life of the bulb. In contrast, the gas in a halogen lamp is a highly reactive Group 17 element, such as bromine or iodine. As electricity begins to flow through the bulb, the tungsten filament becomes extremely hot and begins to vaporize. The halogen gas readily reacts with the tungsten vapor. A cyclic process occurs in which tungsten is redeposited onto the filament, extending the lifetime of the bulb.

The earliest halogen bulbs had a carbon filament surrounded by chlorine gas. Tungsten soon replaced carbon because it could operate at a higher temperature, emitting more light. Chlorine was replaced by iodine to avoid the blackening of the bulb that occurred with previous designs. Later, bromine was used instead of iodine to improve efficiency.

Halogen bulbs are often used in workplaces, overhead lighting, car lights, and spotlights because of their brightness. They also have a longer lifespan than other types of incandescent bulbs. A drawback, however, is that halogen bulbs are extremely hot, and the glass bulb must be kept clean to avoid breakage when the bulb reaches high temperatures.

DEFINE Engineers are designing a new car and need to decide if the headlight should use halogen bulbs or LED bulbs. What criteria might they consider?

Both standard incandescent and halogen bulbs are inefficient. They convert more electricity into energy in the form of heat than light. They are increasingly being replaced by LED bulbs that use much less energy to produce the same amount of light. An LED is a light-emitting diode, a solid state electronic device similar to the devices used in computers and calculators. When electric current passes through the LED, it emits light.

Language Arts Connection Research the benefits and drawbacks of a halogen bulb and a LED bulb that contain the same light output (measured in lumens). For a given amount of light produced, how do the halogen bulb's cost of production, lifespan, and cost of electricity needed to operate compare with those of the LED bulb? Develop a visual guide that an engineer could use to decide which type of bulb is most appropriate for a given situation.

Evidence Notebook Suppose chemists attempt to produce an element with atomic number 119. Based on its likely position on the periodic table, what would you expect its electronegativity to be? Explain how you can make this prediction.

Careers in Science

Analytical Chemist

Have you ever read a mystery novel or watched a detective show where a scientist solved a case by analyzing a sample? These movie scientists often use techniques developed by analytical chemists. The work of analytical chemists often requires "detective" work, careful analysis of samples, and the use of precise equipment. Important skills of these chemists include the ability to ask questions and identify patterns.

This drive to solve mysteries about why a product or a process is not working the way it should is part of the reason Barbara Belmont became an analytical chemist. She uses many different types of analytical methods, such as gas chromatography-mass spectrometry and gas chromatography-flame ionization, to determine if a client's products meet regulation standards. Part of this work is asking questions about what portion of the materials could be causing the product to not meet the standards, and then giving recommendations based on evidence for how to fix the problem.

Barbara Belmont identifies as a member of the LGBTQ+ community and takes on an active role increasing the visibility and inclusion of LGBTQ+ peoples in science, technology, engineering, and mathematics (STEM) programs. She performs this work through memberships in the American Chemical Society, the American Association for Advancement of Science, and the National Organization of Gay and Lesbian Scientists and Technical Professionals (NOGLSTP).

Among Barbara Belmont's most important work is her teaching career where she brings her real-life experience to the classroom. She mentors student-driven research projects and has created a safe space on campus for students to discuss LGBTQ+ issues.

She is also focusing on ways to re-design her course to be more environmentally friendly and cost-effective. This is an important task that all scientists, including analytical chemists, must consider on any project.

FIGURE 15: Barbara Belmont is an analytical chemist who works to enhance existing materials.

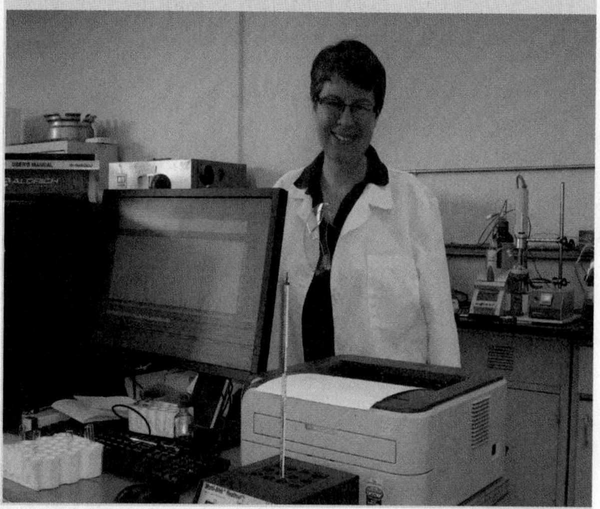

Chemistry in Your Community Research an analytical chemist, company, or government agency that performed a chemical analysis on a project in your community. For example, you may research a company that analyzed building materials for a construction project or a municipal water sanitation department. Consider the following to guide your research:

- What materials were tested by the analytical chemist, and what equipment was used to run the tests?
- What kinds of questions do you think the chemist asked before analyzing the materials?
- Did the chemist run any tests to determine the effect the materials might have on the environment or human health?

Write a magazine article or blog about the findings and contributions of the chemist. You may wish to conduct an interview with the chemist or with a group of chemists to gather this information.

PERIODIC TRENDS IN HISTORY

THE MENDELEEV LAB OF 1869

DISCOVERING NEW ELEMENTS

Go online to choose one of these other paths.

Lesson Self-Check

CAN YOU EXPLAIN THE PHENOMENON?

FIGURE 16: Certain elements, such as silver, gold, and platinum, look somewhat different but they still share some similar properties. These elements occur in nature while others are made synthetically in a lab.

The periodic table lists 118 elements. The vast majority of these are naturally occurring elements, and the rest have been produced in laboratories. With some exceptions, the arrangement of the elements on the periodic table reveals patterns in the properties of the elements. Scientists can use these patterns when searching for new elements. The newest elements on the periodic table require advanced technology to produce and they have high atomic numbers. These elements are so unstable that only tiny amounts are produced, and they may last only a few microseconds. Most of these elements have no practical or commercial use outside of research labs. Nevertheless, scientists continue the effort to develop elements with even higher atomic numbers to gain a better theoretical understanding of the nature of atoms.

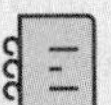

Evidence Notebook Refer to the notes in your Evidence Notebook to make a claim about how scientists are able to use the periodic table to predict the behavior of new elements. Make sure you include a discussion of periodic trends. Your explanation should include a discussion of the following points:

Claim How can scientists use the periodic table to predict the behavior of new elements?

Evidence Give specific evidence to support your claim.

Reasoning Describe, in detail, the connections between the evidence you cited and the claim you are making.

Name

Date

CHECKPOINTS

Check Your Understanding

1. In 1937, a limited supply of helium resulted in the airship Hindenburg being filled with hydrogen instead. On one trip, the Hindenburg burst into flames and was destroyed in less than one minute. Complete the statement about the Hindenburg.

Hydrogen burns easily and is more | less reactive than helium because it has a higher | lower ionization energy. Helium is unreactive because it does not lose electrons | protons easily and therefore does not have an assigned atomic radius | electronegativity.

2. Which element would you expect to have the highest electronegativity?

- ○ **a.** calcium because it has one valence electron
- ○ **b.** cesium because it has a large atomic mass
- ○ **c.** fluorine because it needs one electron to fill its valence shell
- ○ **d.** phosphorus because it is a nonmetal

3. A scientist determines that an element has a high reactivity and a large atomic radius. What other properties does the element most likely have?

- ○ **a.** high electronegativity and high ionization energy
- ○ **b.** high electronegativity and low ionization energy
- ○ **c.** low electronegativity and high ionization energy
- ○ **d.** low electronegativity and low ionization energy

4. According to periodic trends, at which position on the periodic table would an element most likely have an electronegativity higher than that of calcium? Select all correct answers.

- ☐ **a.** just above calcium
- ☐ **b.** just below calcium
- ☐ **c.** just to the left of calcium
- ☐ **d.** just to the right of calcium

5. What statement best explains why fluorine has a smaller atomic radius than oxygen?

- ○ **a.** Fluorine has fewer electrons than oxygen.
- ○ **b.** Fluorine has one more proton than oxygen.
- ○ **c.** Fluorine has low electronegativity.
- ○ **d.** Fluorine forms bonds readily with oxygen.

6. Put these elements in order of decreasing electronegativity, with the highest electronegative element as being first.

_____ **a.** tin (Sn, Group 14, Period 5)

_____ **b.** rubidium (Rb, Group 1, Period 5)

_____ **c.** bromine (Br, Group 17, Period 4)

_____ **d.** lithium (Li, Group 1, Period 2)

_____ **e.** cadmium (Cd, Group 12, Period 5)

7. Photoelectric cells produce an electric current when electromagnetic radiation shines on them. This happens only when the radiation shining on the material contains a certain amount of energy. Why is cesium often used in photoelectric cells?

- ○ **a.** Cesium has one of the largest atomic radii, so its electrons are tightly held.
- ○ **b.** Cesium has one of the highest ionization energies, so its electrons are tightly held.
- ○ **c.** Cesium has a high electronegativity, so its electrons are easily ejected.
- ○ **d.** Cesium has one of the lowest ionization energies, so its electrons are easily ejected.

8. A sample of potassium (K, found in Group 1) and a sample of iodine (I, found in Group 17) react, forming potassium iodide, KI, which is used to treat thyroid conditions. Complete the statement to describe this reaction.

The reaction that creates potassium iodide happens because electrons are pulled away from the more | less electronegative element, potassium, by the more | less electronegative element, iodine. The more electronegative element is found in Group 1 | Group 17. The less electronegative element is in Group 1 | Group 17.

CHECKPOINTS (continued)

9. Explain how the pattern in ionization energy across a period of the periodic table compares to the pattern in atomic radius size across a period.

10. Suppose you have a sample of potassium. Describe several ways you could use periodic trends and a knowledge of valence electrons to predict the element's reactivity and how the element will behave in a chemical bond.

11. Describe generally how the trends in ionization energy and atomic radius apply to the noble gases, and explain the reason for these trends.

MAKE YOUR OWN STUDY GUIDE

In your Evidence Notebook, design a study guide that supports the main idea from this lesson:

Patterns in ionization energy, atomic size, and electronegativity can be used to make predictions about the properties and interactions of elements on the periodic table.

Remember to include the following information in your study guide:

- Use examples that model main ideas.
- Record explanations for the phenomena you investigated.
- Use evidence to support your explanations. Your support can include drawings, data, graphs, laboratory conclusions, and other evidence recorded throughout the lesson.

Consider the organization of elements on the periodic table and how patterns in properties such as ionization energy and electronegativity can be used to predict the way elements bond and react in nature and in everyday applications of the elements.

2.3

Analyzing Nuclear Reactions

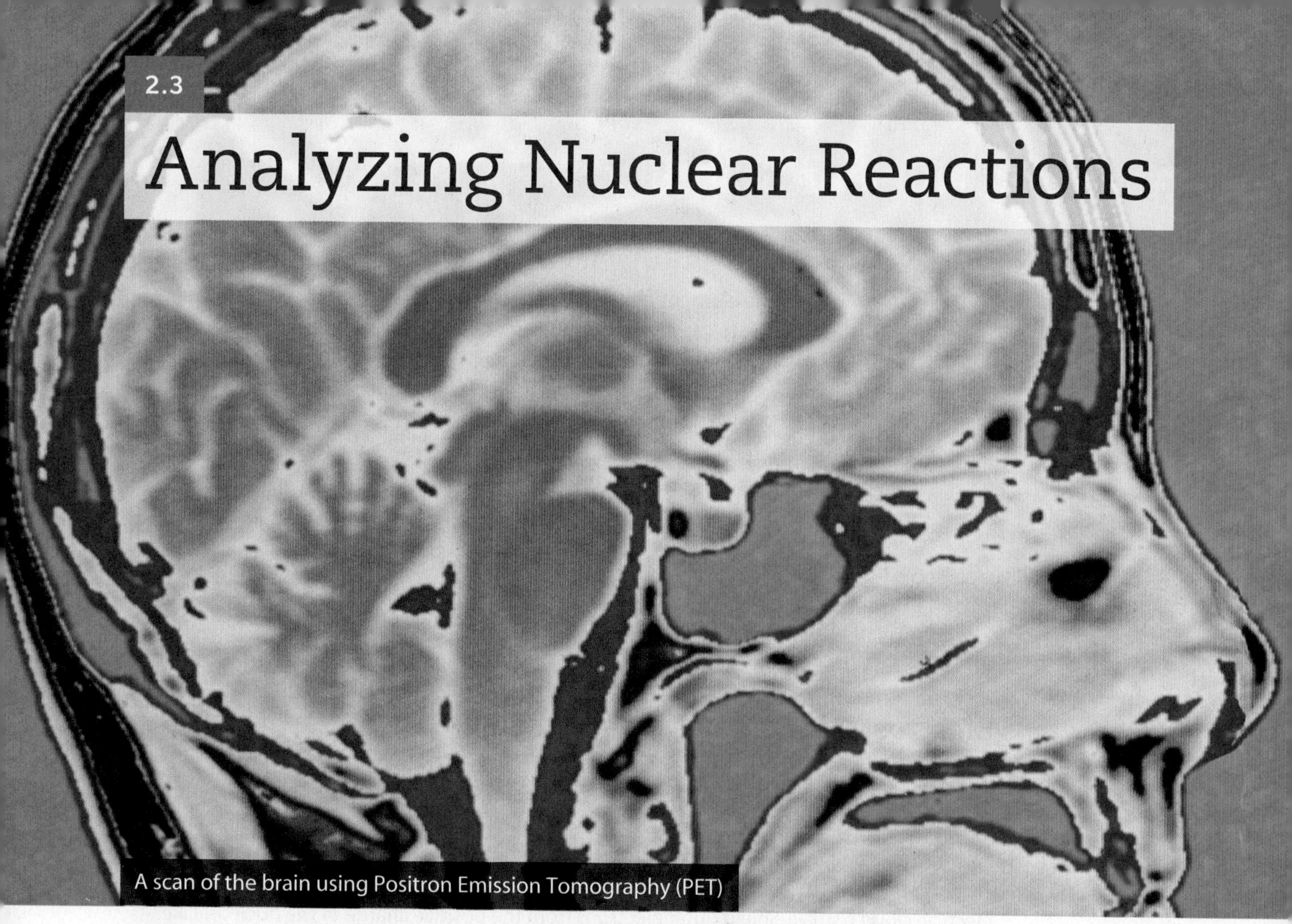

A scan of the brain using Positron Emission Tomography (PET)

CAN YOU EXPLAIN THE PHENOMENON?

Various forms of imaging can be used to diagnose and treat medical disorders. One of the most powerful imaging tools available in medicine today is Positron Emission Tomography (PET), which uses specific isotopes of certain elements, called radioisotopes. Unlike most atoms, these atoms emit radiation, which consists of high-energy subatomic particles that can penetrate tissue. When small amounts of radioisotopes are introduced into the body, they accumulate in specific areas. Devices that detect the radiation produce images of tissue and biochemical processes in the body.

EXPLAIN Before medical images are taken, radioisotopes are often injected into a vein in a patient's arm, or the patient drinks a solution containing the radioisotopes. Why do you think atoms in the body usually do not emit radiation?

Evidence Notebook As you explore the lesson, gather evidence to explain what types of nuclear reactions cause atoms to give off radiation that can be detected in a medical image, and how forces within the nuclei cause these reactions.

Explaining Nuclear Stability

FIGURE 1: A pellet of plutonium gives off energy in the form of heat and light as it emits radiation.

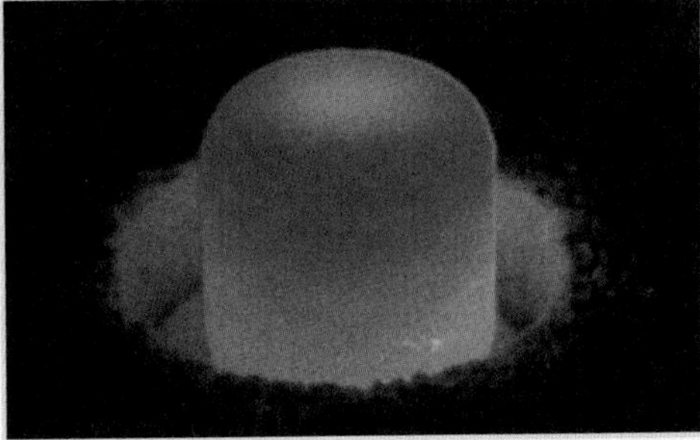

The element plutonium, shown in Figure 1, has an orange glow due to the enormous amount of energy it releases in the form of heat and light. Unlike other fuels that "burn up" quickly, plutonium releases its energy over a long period of time. This makes it an ideal fuel source for applications such as spacecraft used for interplanetary exploration because they cannot stop to refuel.

Plutonium's position on the periodic table explains why it glows. The atomic number of plutonium is 94. All elements with an atomic number greater than that of lead, 82, have nuclei that are unstable and emit radiation in the form of either particles or high-energy electromagnetic waves. As they do so, they produce other nuclei that are more stable.

Electrostatic Force and the Nucleus

To explain trends in the periodic table, you saw that the varying strengths of the attraction between the negatively charged electrons and the positively charged protons in the nucleus play an important role. Oppositely charged particles attract one another as a result of the *electrostatic force*. The electrostatic force explains why electrons closer to the nucleus in the electron cloud partially shield outer electrons from the positive charge of the nucleus. Like charges repel one another, so inner electrons repel outer electrons, partially negating the pull the nucleus has upon them. You likely have seen the electrostatic force in action when two pieces of clothing either stick to or repel one another. The cling or repulsion occurs because rubbing of the fabric surfaces together causes an imbalance in charge between them.

FIGURE 2: A helium-4 nucleus consists of two neutrons and two protons.

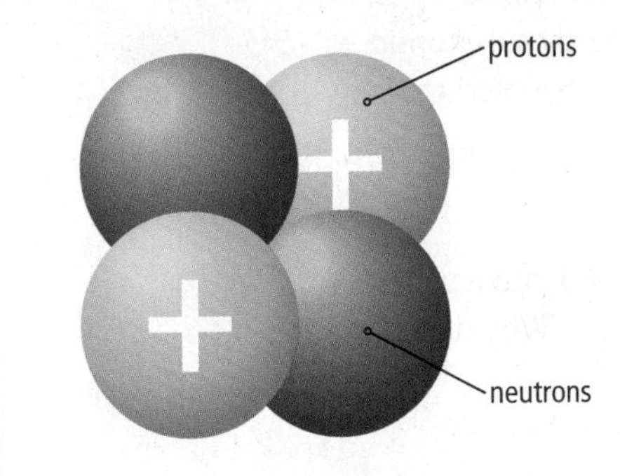

The strength of the electrostatic force between two charges depends upon both the magnitude of the charges and the distance between them. As charge increases, so does the electrostatic force. However, the force becomes weaker as the distance between charges increases.

Now, consider a helium-4 nucleus such as the one shown in Figure 2. The nucleus stays intact despite the two positively charged protons being so close together. All stable atomic nuclei contain protons and neutrons, and the electrostatic force exists between all charges. Many even larger nuclei are quite stable despite having many protons.

INFER What is the most probable explanation for how two positively charged protons could be held together within the incredibly small and dense nucleus?

○ **a.** The charge on the protons is so small that the repulsion is very weak.

○ **b.** Neutrons provide enough distance between protons to make the repulsion weak.

○ **c.** There is another force at work in the nucleus holding protons and neutrons together.

○ **d.** Electrons surrounding the nucleus keep it from breaking apart.

Nuclear Forces

If only the electrostatic force existed, atomic nuclei would not remain intact. But the elements and compounds surrounding us are evidence that nuclei are, in general, stable. Scientists concluded, therefore, that there must be another force at work in the nucleus. This force had to be opposite to the electrostatic force and sufficiently strong enough to counteract it. Scientists called this force the *strong nuclear force*, and found that it acted between all particles in the nucleus. Figure 3 shows how the strong nuclear force and electrostatic force increase as two protons come together.

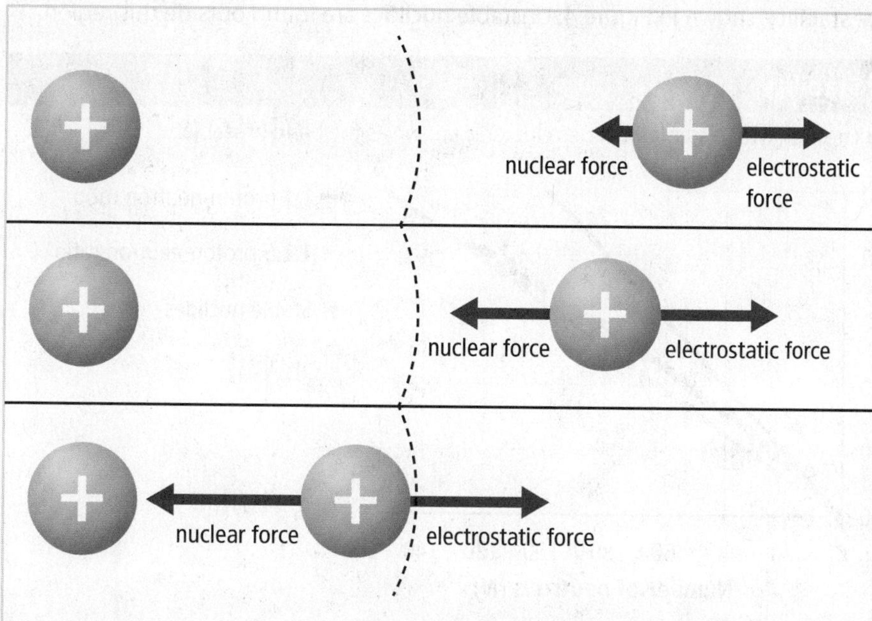

FIGURE 3: As two protons move toward each other, electrostatic repulsion increases, but the strong nuclear force attracting them increases even more.

EXPLAIN Using the diagram in Figure 3, describe how the relative influences of the electrostatic force and the strong nuclear force compare as two protons approach one another. How does the nuclear strong force keep nuclei together?

As two protons move closer together, the electrostatic force increases. When the protons get sufficiently close, however, the strong nuclear force takes hold to keep protons together. Notice that the attraction of the strong nuclear force becomes stronger than the repulsion of the electrostatic force, but the electrostatic force does not stop acting on the nucleus. A stable nucleus, therefore, is influenced by both the electrostatic force and the strong nuclear force.

ANALYZE Select the correct terms to complete the statement about stable nuclei.

Stable nuclei are stable because the repulsion of the electrostatic | strong nuclear force is overcome by the attraction of the electrostatic | strong nuclear force at very short distances. Because the electrostatic force is always present, a nucleus might be unstable if protons and neutrons are too far apart from | close to each other. This would most likely affect larger | smaller nuclei.

Nuclear Stability

Nuclear forces affect both protons and neutrons. It is convenient, therefore, to speak of these particles collectively. A **nucleon** is either a proton or a neutron. A **nuclide** is a nucleus with a specific number of protons and neutrons. Unlike isotopes, nuclides can be compared without reference to which elements are involved. These terms help scientists emphasize nuclear composition rather than the chemical identity of the element.

Scientists found that when the number of protons (Z) in a nuclide is plotted against the number of neutrons (N), stable nuclides cluster in a limited area. This area is referred to as the band of stability, shown in Figure 4. Unstable nuclides are found outside this region.

Band of Stability

FIGURE 4: The area where stable nuclides cluster is known as the band of stability.

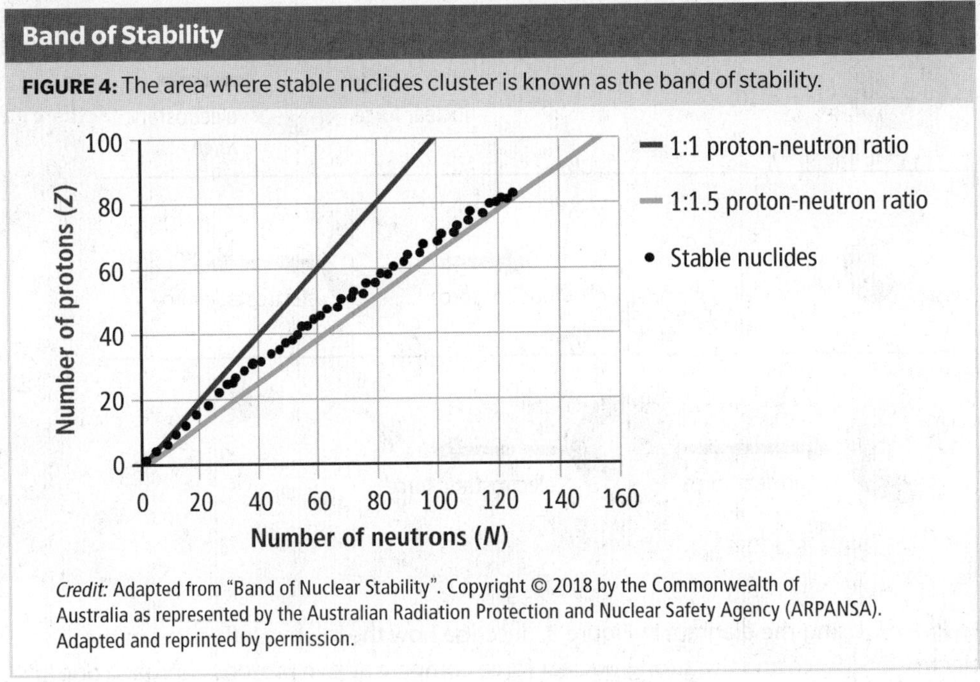

Credit: Adapted from "Band of Nuclear Stability". Copyright © 2018 by the Commonwealth of Australia as represented by the Australian Radiation Protection and Nuclear Safety Agency (ARPANSA). Adapted and reprinted by permission.

SOLVE Calculate the ratio of protons to neutrons in stable and unstable nuclides. Round values to the nearest tenth place.

Stable Nuclides		Unstable Nuclides	
$^{12}_{6}C$	________	$^{14}_{6}C$	________
$^{40}_{20}Ca$	________	$^{45}_{20}Ca$	________
$^{192}_{76}Os$	________	$^{182}_{76}Os$	________

EXPLAIN Using Figure 4 and the ratios you calculated, explain why the ratio of stable nuclides is different for nuclides with 1 to 20 protons compared to larger nuclides.

When the number of nucleons is high enough that the nucleus is too large for the strong nuclear force to hold it together, the electrostatic force pushes the protons apart. This is why elements that are heavier than lead, atomic number 82, are always unstable.

Energy and Matter

Mass Defect

To understand how atomic nuclei can be stable, observe what occurs when nucleons form a nucleus. A proton has a mass of 1.007 276 u. A neutron's mass is 1.008 665 u. Logically, the mass of a nucleus should equal the sum of the masses of its nucleons.

ANALYZE For each nuclide, use the masses of the proton and neutron to calculate the expected mass, and the difference between the measured and expected masses.

Nuclide	Expected	Measured	Difference
$^{2}_{1}H$	______	2.014 102 u	______
$^{3}_{1}H$	______	3.016 049 u	______
$^{4}_{2}He$	______	4.002 603 u	______
$^{7}_{3}Li$	______	7.016 004 u	______

FIGURE 5: A helium-4 nucleus and one neutron (right) has less mass than a hydrogen-2 nucleus and a hydrogen-3 nucleus (left), even though the total number of nucleons is the same in both cases.

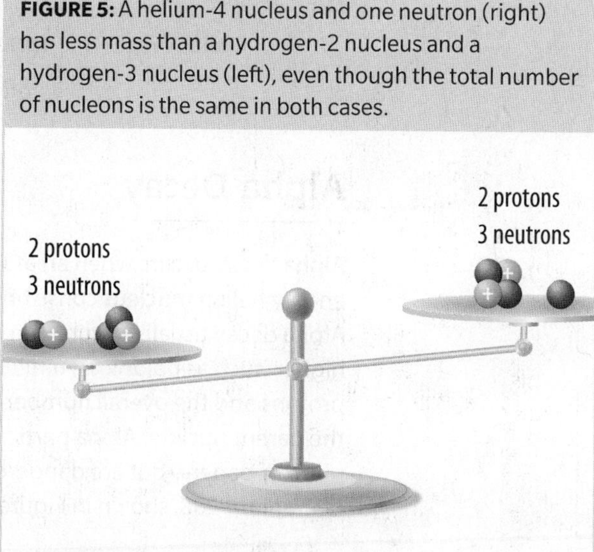

A nucleus actually has less mass than the sum of the nucleons that compose it. The difference between the mass of a nucleus and the sum of the masses of its nucleons is known as the *mass defect*. Where did the mass go? You may have heard of Albert Einstein's famous equation $E = mc^2$. With this equation, Einstein proposed that mass and energy are related. Energy is equal to mass, measured in kilograms, times the speed of light (3.00×10^8 m/s) squared. In other words, mass can be converted to energy and energy can be converted to mass.

INFER Describe how mass defect relates to what you know about the conservation of matter and energy. Can the law of conservation of matter still be true?

______

______

______

Mass defect corresponds to the amount of energy released when nucleons come together. This is also known as *nuclear binding energy*. The larger the nucleus, the larger the binding energy, but also the larger the number of nucleons this energy needs to hold together. Thus, nuclides with low and intermediate numbers of nucleons are most stable.

As you can calculate with the equation $E = mc^2$, the amount of energy released when one helium-4 nucleus forms is only about 4.5×10^{-12} J. This is a very small amount, but it adds up quickly when you consider how unimaginably tiny atoms are.

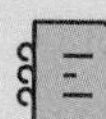

Evidence Notebook Do you think the nuclei of the atoms used in medical imaging are stable or unstable? Use evidence to support your claim.

Investigating Radioactive Decay

Nuclei are unstable when the forces among their nucleons are unbalanced because of an excess of either protons or neutrons. Unstable nuclei will spontaneously break apart. This spontaneous transformation of an unstable nucleus into a more stable form is called radioactive decay. When a nucleus undergoes radioactive decay, it releases nuclear radiation in the form of energy, subatomic particles, and, in many cases, one or more new nuclei. The original nuclide is called the parent nuclide, and the resulting nuclide is called the daughter nuclide. If a daughter nuclide is unstable, it will also decay.

Collaborate With a partner, identify the following nuclides and give the number of protons and neutrons in each: $^{238}_{92}U$, $^{14}_{6}C$, $^{40}_{19}K$, and $^{30}_{18}Ar$.

Alpha Decay

Alpha decay occurs when an atomic nucleus emits an alpha (α) particle, which is a high-energy helium nucleus consisting of two neutrons and two protons bound together. Alpha decay usually occurs in very heavy nuclei of elements with atomic numbers of 83 or higher, such as polonium, uranium, and radium. Alpha decay reduces both the number of protons and the overall number of nucleons, so the daughter nuclide is more stable than the parent nuclide. Alpha particles are not very penetrating—they can be stopped by a piece of paper—but are dangerous if ingested or inhaled. An example is the alpha decay of uranium-238, shown in Figure 6.

FIGURE 6: Uranium-238 is a large, unstable nuclide that decays into thorium-234.

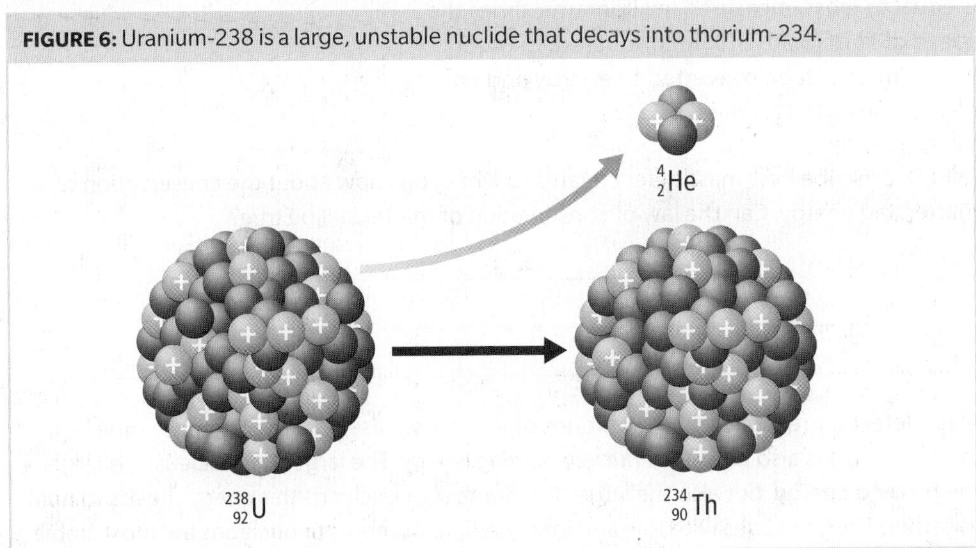

EXPLAIN Using uranium-238 as an example, explain whether alpha decay conserves the number and type of atoms and nucleons during the process.

Writing nuclear equations is one way to model radioactive decay. The parent nuclide is shown on the left of a reaction arrow, and the daughter nuclide and the emitted particles are on the right. The nuclear equation for the decay of uranium-238 is $^{238}_{92}U \rightarrow\ ^{234}_{90}Th +\ ^{4}_{2}He$.

MODEL Model the alpha decay of americium-241, a radioisotope used in smoke detectors. Then write a nuclear equation that models the alpha decay of americium-241.

Beta Decay

In beta (β) decay, an unstable nuclide produces a more-stable daughter nuclide by transforming a neutron into a proton, or vice versa. Because the number of protons changes, the daughter nuclide is of a different element than the parent nuclide. Beta decay is observed as a natural process in the heavier isotopes of some elements, which have too many neutrons to be stable. In this type of decay, a neutron changes into a proton by emitting a high-energy electron ($^{0}_{-1}e$).

APPLY Fill in the missing text to complete the model of the beta decay of carbon-14.

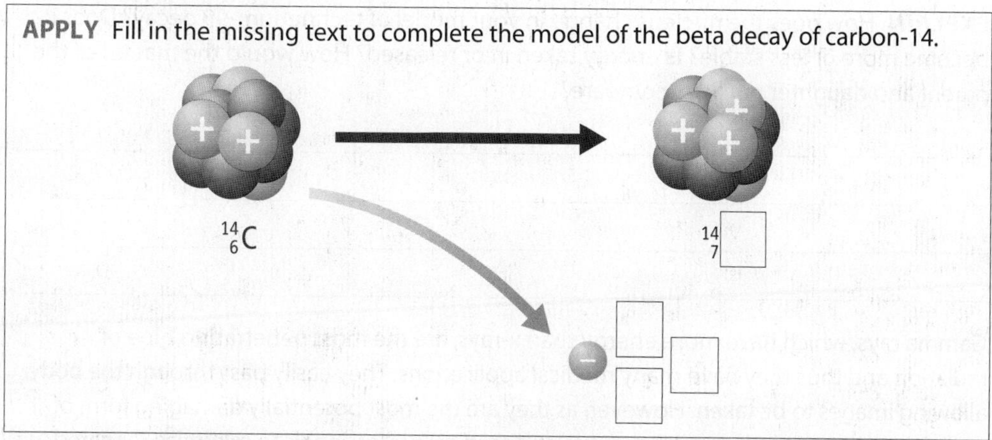

Because the subscripts in nuclear symbols represent protons, which have a positive charge, it makes sense to think of the subscripts as representing charge. In beta decay, the total charge and number of nucleons remain the same—are conserved—but the ratio of protons to neutrons changes.

EVALUATE Consider the decay of carbon-14. Between the parent and the daughter nuclide, what changes, and what remains the same? Which nuclide is more stable?

Alternately in isotopes of an element that have too few neutrons to be stable, a proton can decay into a neutron by emitting a *positron* ($^{0}_{+1}e$), a particle with the same mass as the electron but the opposite charge. An example is the decay of carbon-11, represented by the equation $^{11}_{6}C \rightarrow\ ^{11}_{5}B +\ ^{0}_{+1}e$. In Positron Emission Tomography (PET) scans, the radioactive substance injected into a patient's body might be a lighter isotope of carbon, oxygen, nitrogen, or fluorine. Beta radiation can be damaging to tissues. Therefore, doctors and patients must consider the tradeoffs involved in repeated use of PET scans and other medical imaging procedures that use radiation.

Gamma Decay

Gamma (γ) rays are high-energy photons, a form of electromagnetic radiation, emitted from a nucleus. Gamma decay usually occurs immediately following other types of decay. A high-energy nucleus releases excess energy by emitting gamma rays and returning to its ground energy state. An example is the gamma decay of technetium-99: ${}^{240}_{94}Tc \rightarrow {}^{240}_{94}Tc + \gamma$.

MODEL Draw the gamma decay of technetium-99. Make sure your model includes the numbers of nucleons in the parent and daughter nuclide.

EXPLAIN How does the nucleus change in your model of technetium-99 decay? Does it become more or less stable? Is energy taken in or released? How would the masses of the parent and daughter nuclides compare?

Gamma rays, which have more energy than x-rays, are the most penetrating type of radiation and thus they have many medical applications. They easily pass through the body, allowing images to be taken. However, as they are the most potentially damaging form of radiation, care must be taken by patients and medical professionals to minimize repeated exposure. Gamma rays can be stopped by a heavy lead shield, such as a lead apron.

SOLVE Complete the table of types of radioactive decay by selecting the correct term for each row.

increases by 1 | decreases by 1 | decreases by 2 | unchanged

Type	Symbol	Charge	Neutron/proton ratio	Atomic number of the nucleus
Alpha particle	${}^{4}_{2}He$	2+	decreases	
Electron	${}^{0}_{-1}\beta$	1−	decreases	
Positron	${}^{0}_{+1}\beta$	1+	increases	
Gamma ray	${}^{99}_{43}\gamma$	0	unchanged	

Evidence Notebook Is the atomic model from your unit project able to model the release of radiation, either in the form of particles or gamma rays? Explain.

Analyzing Rates of Decay

Each radioactive nuclide has a specific rate at which it decays, defined by its half-life. One half-life is the time it takes for half of the radioactive nuclei in a sample to decay. After one half-life, half of the original nuclei will remain in the sample and half will have decayed into other nuclides. After two half-lives, one-fourth of the original nuclei will remain and three-fourths will have decayed to other nuclides, and the process continues.

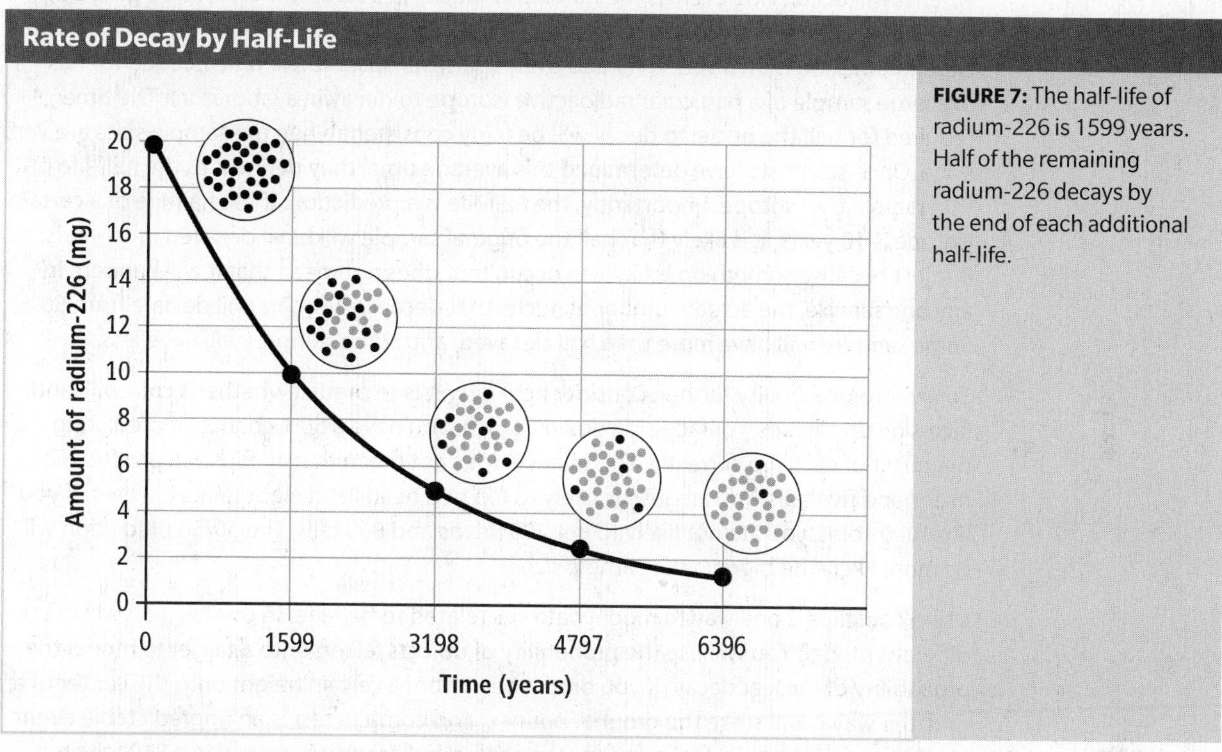

FIGURE 7: The half-life of radium-226 is 1599 years. Half of the remaining radium-226 decays by the end of each additional half-life.

The half-lives of radioactive nuclides vary widely. Some nuclides found in nature have half-lives of billions of years, while others have half-lives of only seconds. The heaviest synthetic nuclides are very unstable, having half-lives of just a fraction of a second. Such a short existence can only be detected with special equipment. Regardless of its duration, the half-life of each nuclide is constant over time.

Some Radioactive Nuclides and Their Half-Lives

Nuclide	Half-life	Nuclide	Half-life
$^{3}_{1}H$	12.32 years	$^{214}_{84}Po$	1.64×10^{-4} seconds
$^{14}_{6}C$	5700 years	$^{218}_{84}Po$	3.1 minutes
$^{32}_{15}P$	14.268 days	$^{218}_{85}At$	1.5 seconds
$^{40}_{19}K$	1.248×10^{9} years	$^{238}_{92}U$	4.469×10^{9} years

Collaborate Radioactive nuclides have many uses in industry and medicine. With a partner, discuss how the half-life of a radioactive nuclide might influence the way it is used. What could be the advantage of using radioactive nuclides with shorter or longer half-lives?

Hands-On Lab

Modeling Radioactive Half-Lives

The decay of any single radioactive nucleus is a random event. You cannot predict when it will occur. However, as the number of nuclei in a sample increases, so does our ability to predict the time required for a certain percentage (half) of the nuclei to decay. Experimentation is involved. Over and over, scientists observe the time needed for half of a large sample of a particular radioactive isotope to decay in a laboratory. The time required for half the nuclei to decay will be fairly consistent when the sample sizes are very large. Once scientists have determined this average time, they define it as the half-life of that radioactive isotope. Importantly, the half-life is a prediction. If the half-life of a certain isotope is 10 years, it is likely that half the original sample will have decayed in 10 years. But just because something is likely to occur, that does not mean that it will happen. In any one sample, the actual number of nuclei that decay in 10 years will deviate from 50%. Some samples will have more than half decayed, and some samples will have less.

To explore probability further, consider how easy it is to predict whether a coin will land face-side up ("heads") or face-side down ("tails"). You have a 50% chance of predicting the result of each flip correctly. This chance does not mean that 10 flips will produce five heads and five tails. You are just as likely to flip two heads and eight tails. However, if you flip 1000 coins, you are not likely to get 200 heads and 800 tails. The 50/50 prediction will be more likely the bigger your sample size is.

Using coin flips is one way to model patterns related to half-life. In this lab, you will use a different model. You will use the probability of objects falling onto a target to model the probability of nuclear decay. If you drop a bean from a certain height onto the center of a grid, the way it will strike the ground, bounce, and come to rest is an unpredictable event. Most beans will land and remain near the center, but many will spread in a 360° circle around the center in a predictable pattern.

RESEARCH QUESTION How do scientists use the known half-life of a radioactive nuclide to determine how long ago a sample of it formed?

MAKE A CLAIM

How do you think dropping beans on a target could be used to model radioactive decay?

MATERIALS

- indirectly vented chemical splash goggles
- beans, color 1 (100)
- beans, color 2 (100)
- box or self-sealing bag

SAFETY INFORMATION

- Wear indirectly vented chemical splash goggles during the setup, hands-on, and takedown segments of the activity.
- Immediately pick up any items dropped on the floor so they do not become a slip/fall hazard.

indirectly vented chemical splash goggles

PLAN THE INVESTIGATION

In your Evidence Notebook, describe a procedure to safely model radioactive decay. Include the data you plan to collect in your description. As you plan, consider the following questions:

- Assume all beans are radioactive nuclei of a substance. What would each drop represent? What would show successive decrease in radioactive nuclei in the bean-and-grid model?
- How does the use of a grid as a target provide you with an opportunity to collect quantitative data related to the research question?
- How will half-life relate to what data you will collect?

Make a table and graph in your Evidence Notebook to record your data. Your data table and graph should reflect your investigational choices. For example, if you used each bean type to represent a different isotope, include columns in your table to record numbers for each isotope.

Have your teacher approve your procedure and safety plan before you begin. Your safety plan should also include steps you will take to keep all beans in a contained area.

COLLECT DATA

Follow your procedure, and record your data in the table that you constructed. Then use your data to construct a graph to help you identify the pattern in your results. Label the x-axis "Trials," and label the y-axis "Parent Isotopes Remaining." If you gathered data on two isotopes, remember to plot data for each isotope type.

ANALYZE

1. What happens to the starting number of beans after each trial?

2. What variable in this lab represents one half-life? Is this a valid representation? Explain your answer.

3. What individual events were predictable when you dropped the beans? What individual events were unpredictable?

4. How do scientists use numbers to describe predictable events? How do scientists use numbers to describe unpredictable events?

5. **Interpret Data** While individual events may be unpredictable, trends may emerge when sample sizes are large. Does your graph reveal any trends related to unpredictable events? Explain your answer.

CONSTRUCT AN EXPLANATION

1. **Use Mathematics** Suppose that a radioactive sample included 200 nuclei. How would you graph the change in the number of undecayed nuclei over time if the half-life of the isotope is 50 000 years? Sketch a graph of the decay of the isotope on the grid provided. Label each axis with a descriptive title.

2. **Argue from Evidence** Suppose you only used 10 beans in your model. Would your model still accurately represent nuclear decay? Why or why not? Use evidence from your investigation to justify your claims and explain your reasoning.

DRAW CONCLUSIONS

Write a conclusion that addresses each of the points below.

Claim How did your experiment model half-life in the process of radioactive decay?

Evidence What evidence from your investigation supports your claim?

Reasoning Explain how the evidence you gave supports your claim. Describe in detail the connections between the evidence you cited and the argument you are making.

EXTEND

Suppose you have 500 grams of a radioactive substance with a half-life of 15 000 years. How many grams of the undecayed sample would remain after 45 000 years? Do you think you would have exactly that mass of parent nuclide? Why or why not?

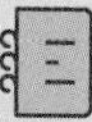

Evidence Notebook How does half-life relate to radioactive decay? Why might radioactive nuclides with short half-lives be used in medical imaging?

Analyzing Nuclear Fission and Fusion

Nuclear reactions can change atomic nuclei in different ways, and various particles can be emitted. Radioactive decay can emit alpha particles, beta particles, or gamma rays. Large nuclei can also break apart into smaller nuclei, and small nuclei can join to produce a larger nucleus. Energy is emitted in a variety of forms during each of these reactions.

Nuclear Fission

In nuclear fission, a large nucleus splits into two smaller, more stable fragments, releasing energy. When a nucleus undergoes fission, it may also undergo decay.

INFER Which type of radioactive decay is also a type of fission?

○ **a.** alpha decay ○ **b.** beta decay ○ **c.** gamma decay

Fission can be induced by bombarding certain large, unstable nuclei with neutrons, which are not repelled by the electrostatic force of the protons in the nucleus. The nucleus briefly captures the neutron ($^{1}_{0}n$) and becomes more unstable. Then, this nucleus splits into two smaller nuclei. In Figure 8, a uranium-235 nucleus is struck with a neutron and splits into barium-141 and krypton-92 nuclei, releasing three more neutrons in the process:

$$^{1}_{0}n + ^{235}_{92}U \rightarrow ^{141}_{56}Ba + ^{92}_{36}Kr + 3^{1}_{0}n$$

FIGURE 8: A neutron is briefly captured by a uranium-235 nucleus, initiating fission.

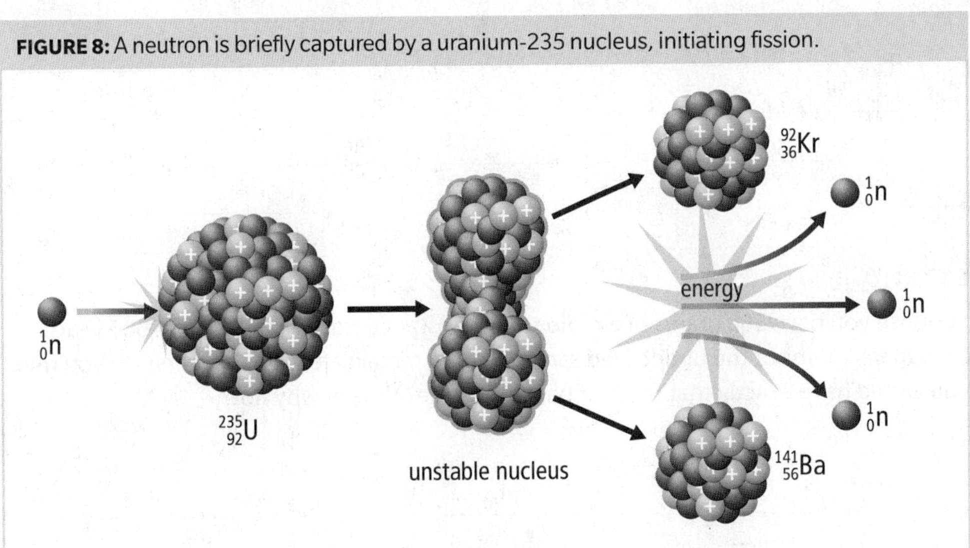

ANALYZE Consider the decay of uranium-235 shown in Figure 8. How do the masses of the particles in the ending materials compare to the mass of the starting material? How does this relate to the energy released?

The fission of uranium-235 produces neutrons that can induce the fission of other uranium-235 nuclei. If, on average, one of the three released neutrons causes another fission reaction, a chain reaction can occur. A chain reaction is a self-sustaining reaction in which the material that starts the reaction is also one of the products and so can start other reactions. In the chain reaction shown in Figure 9, the uranium-235 will continue to undergo fission until the uranium-235 is used up.

Collaborate With a partner, come up with an analogy that describes nuclear fission. What aspects of fission does the analogy capture? What aspects are not captured by the analogy?

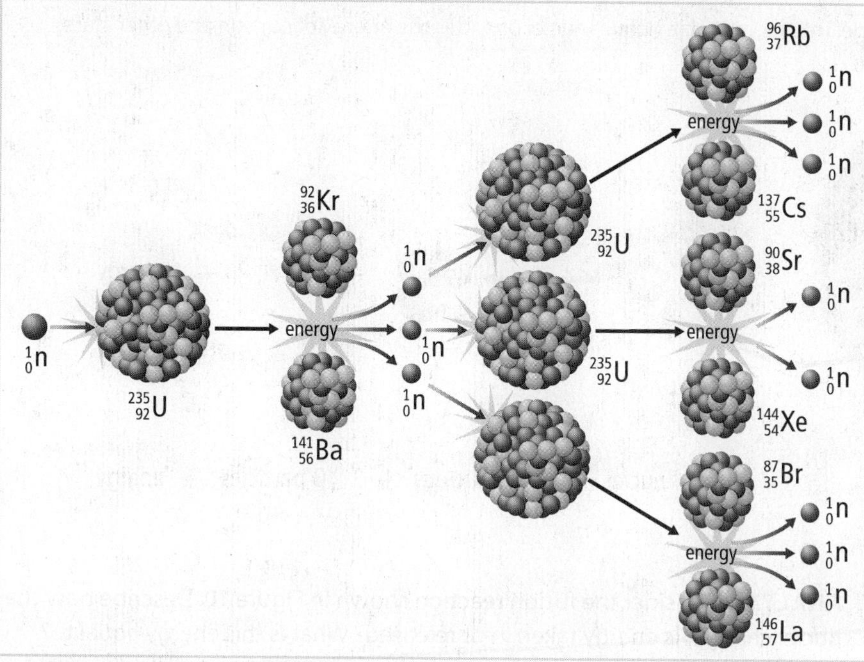

FIGURE 9: A slow-moving neutron is briefly bound to a uranium-235 nucleus, destabilizing it and causing it to undergo fission into two smaller nuclei and three free neutrons. Each free neutron collides with another uranium-235 nucleus, starting a chain reaction.

MODEL Draw the next step in the chain reaction in Figure 9.

The minimum amount of a radioactive substance needed to sustain a chain reaction is called the *critical mass*. If the starting mass of uranium-235 is lower than this critical mass, many neutrons will escape the sample rather than bind to other uranium-235 nuclei. As a result, the chain reaction is subcritical, and the rate will decrease. If the starting mass is greater than this critical mass, more than one neutron from each fission event causes another event. The chain reaction is supercritical, and the rate will increase uncontrollably.

Language Arts Connection One of the first nuclear bombs was developed by using a supercritical chain reaction to trigger fission in plutonium-239. Research this reaction and the energy it releases relative to explosives based on chemical reactions. Prepare a report that synthesizes your research and includes images.

Nuclear Fusion

In nuclear fusion, small nuclei combine to form larger nuclei. To overcome electrostatic repulsion, the nuclei must be moving at high speed or subject to high temperature or high pressure, such as within an artificial fusion reactor or a star, which is a natural fusion reactor. Large amounts of energy are released in the fusion of light nuclei such as hydrogen. An example of nuclear fusion that is constantly occurring in the sun is the reaction $^{1}_{1}H + ^{1}_{1}H \rightarrow ^{2}_{1}H + ^{0}_{+1}e$, in which two protons fuse to form deuterium and a positron. Another reaction that also occurs in the sun is $^{2}_{1}H + ^{3}_{1}H \rightarrow ^{4}_{2}He + ^{1}_{0}n$, in which deuterium and tritium form a helium nucleus, emitting a high-energy neutron.

FIGURE 10: Fusion of hydrogen nuclei into more-stable helium nuclei provides the energy of our sun and other stars.

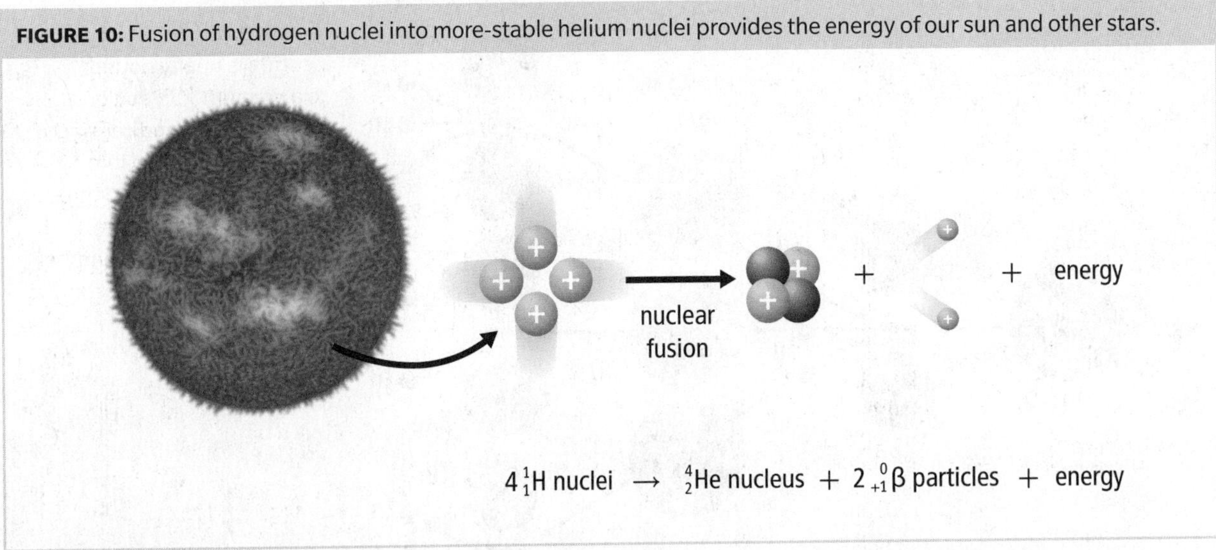

Explore Online

Hands-On Lab

Modeling Fusion
Model the fusion of hydrogen and helium nuclei.

ANALYZE Consider the fusion reaction shown in Figure 10. Describe how the nuclei change. Is energy taken in or released? What is this energy equal to?

The binding energy per nucleon in a nucleus varies with the atomic mass, with a maximum at a mass of around 56, the atomic mass of iron. Energy is released by the fusion of elements lighter than iron and by the fission of elements heavier than iron.

When two light nuclei combine and the new mass is lighter than the mass of iron, the nucleons will be more tightly bound than they were in the lighter nuclei. This tighter bond corresponds to a decrease in mass, and this decrease in mass corresponds to a release of energy.

When a heavy nuclide breaks apart, its daughter nuclides are closer to the mass of iron. The daughter nuclides are more tightly bound together than the large parent nuclide, and these tighter bonds are reflected in a decrease in mass and release of energy.

Evidence Notebook What changes occur in atomic nuclei, and what particles are emitted during nuclear fission and nuclear fusion? How do these processes compare to radioactive decay?

Case Study: Exploring Nuclear Energy

The binding energy of the nucleus is orders of magnitude greater than the energy in chemical bonds that is released in chemical reactions. Energy released in nuclear reactions is therefore orders of magnitude greater than that released in chemical reactions, such as combustion. Ever since scientists discovered that huge amounts of energy are released in nuclear fission, they have tried to develop methods to harness this energy in useful ways, especially in generating electricity. Some have thought that nuclear power held the promise of meeting all of the world's growing energy needs as an alternative to fossil fuels such as coal, which are in limited supply and produce air pollution. But evaluating nuclear power as an energy solution requires carefully weighing its costs and benefits.

Nuclear Fuel

One way in which energy from fission and radioactive decay can be harnessed is in thermoelectric batteries such as those used in space probes. This engineering design harnesses the thermoelectric effect, in which a change in temperature generates electricity. One benefit of nuclear power for thermoelectric batteries is a long lifetime. Radiation from the decay of plutonium used in thermoelectric batteries, such as in the Mars rover Curiosity shown in Figure 11, generates continuous heat at a reliable level for many years. Such nuclear-powered batteries also have the advantage over solar power in that they can be used in areas with little sunlight. Another benefit of thermoelectric batteries is that they use no moving parts, which wear down over time and require maintenance and replacement.

FIGURE 11: The robot Mars rover Curiosity runs on a thermoelectric battery powered by plutonium.

EVALUATE Why would nuclear fuel be appropriate for thermoelectric batteries in space probes but less appropriate for thermoelectric batteries on Earth?

In nuclear power plants that generate electricity, a uranium fuel pellet such as the one shown in Figure 12 can produce the same amount of thermal energy as the combustion of about 900 kg of coal. Unlike combustion of fossil fuels, nuclear fission produces no air pollutants or greenhouse gases such as carbon dioxide. If these are the only facts taken into account, then nuclear power would seem to be an ideal replacement for fossil fuels as an energy source. However, a fair comparison of sources of energy requires taking into account their fuel life cycles—the entire process of harvesting the fuel and using it. When the cost in energy of a fuel life cycle is subtracted from that produced by the actual generation of electricity, it yields the *net energy*—the balance of energy that the fuel source provides.

FIGURE 12: A fuel pellet of uranium dioxide, the source of energy for a common type of fission reactor

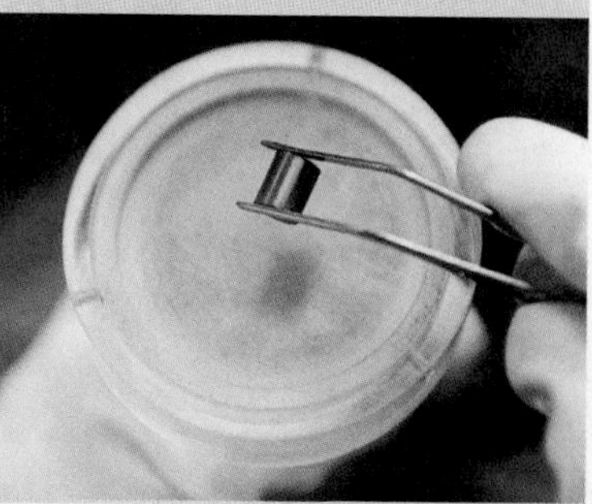

Extraction and Enrichment of Uranium

FIGURE 13: Workers at uranium mines have to take special precautions to limit their exposure to radiation.

The fuel cycle of uranium is a process with several stages, most of which involve significant use of fossil fuels. The first step is extraction of ore at mines such as the one shown in Figure 13. Uranium ore is found naturally in Earth's crust and can therefore be mined in areas where a relatively high concentration is present. Uranium is radioactive, as is the noble gas radon, a natural decay product of uranium that is always present where uranium is found. Therefore, uranium mining poses unique hazards. The entire process of mining the ore and separating of uranium oxide (UO_2) from it is heavily dependent on fossil fuels.

The isotope of uranium that undergoes fission is uranium-235, but more than 99% of natural uranium consists of the isotope uranium-238. To be used for nuclear fuel, uranium must be enriched to increase the concentration of uranium-235. After uranium is converted to gaseous form, chains of centrifuges such as those shown in Figure 14 use the slight difference in mass between the two isotopes to increase the concentration of uranium-235. Each centrifuge spins at an extremely high speed. The centrifugal force draws heavier isotopes of uranium toward the walls of the cylinder, while uranium-235 becomes more concentrated near the center. The process is repeated through a number of columns, leaving more and more of the heavier isotopes behind until the concentration of uranium-235 is 3–5%. This enriched uranium is made into fuel pellets.

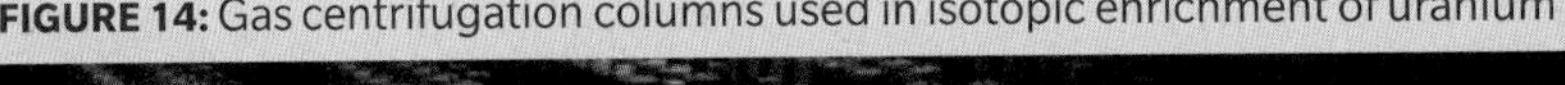

FIGURE 14: Gas centrifugation columns used in isotopic enrichment of uranium

ANALYZE What aspects of the total process required to produce uranium fuel pellets do you think have significant impact on the net energy of nuclear power?

Nuclear Fission Power Plants

Nuclear power plants are a type of thermoelectric power plant, which uses a heat source to turn water into steam. The expansion of the steam spins a turbine, which generates electricity by the spin of a magnet near a wire coil. For nuclear power plants, the source of the heat is the energy produced by the fission of nuclear fuel in a nuclear reactor. A nuclear reactor is a device that can initiate and control a sustained fission chain reaction. Nuclear reactors are used for research; to produce radioactive isotopes, such as those used in nuclear medicine; to propel some ships and submarines; and, most commonly, in nuclear power plants.

The fuel pellets are arranged into fuel rods. Between the fuel rods are movable control rods containing a neutron-absorbing substance such as boron. When the control rods are lowered between the fuel rods, the control rods absorb neutrons, and thus prevent an uncontrolled, runaway nuclear reaction that could cause a reactor meltdown. Fully inserting the control rods will shut down the fission reaction. The nuclear reactor is housed inside a containment structure of concrete and steel designed to prevent the escape of radioactive material if a meltdown occurs.

Water continuously circulates, both acting as a coolant and transferring heat to another water system, which is heated into steam. A third water system takes in cool water from a nearby source, such as a lake or ocean, and condenses the steam back into water. Heated water is returned to the water source or is released as steam from cooling towers.

ANNOTATE On the diagram, trace the path of the energy released as heat from its source through the nuclear power plant.

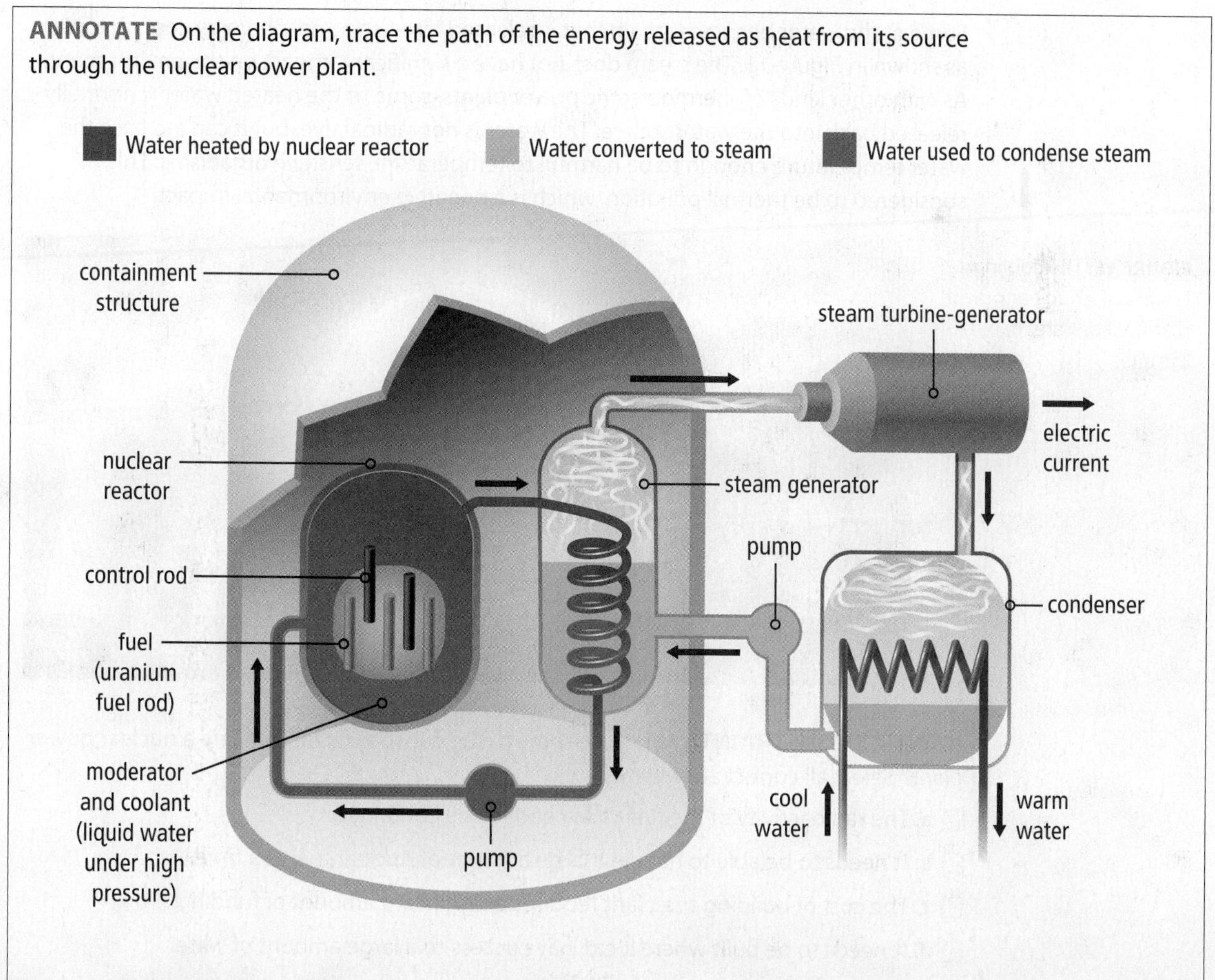

Analyzing Tradeoffs in Nuclear Power

The concept of the total fuel cycle and its energy demands provides a model that can be used to evaluate the net energy of an energy resource. Likewise, the use of any energy resource has an effect on social, cultural, and environmental systems that must be critically evaluated when considering tradeoffs.

Because of the enormous amount of energy that is released by nuclear fission, nuclear energy is very reliable and has a very high power output compared to other sources of energy. Because of the dangers of radioactivity that go along with its high energy output, however, the power of nuclear fission also poses unique safety challenges. This tradeoff is the single largest issue that must be considered in regard to nuclear power. Uranium is a radioactive element, and it remains radioactive throughout its fuel cycle. This makes it far more hazardous to obtain, process, and use than other energy sources. Nuclear power plants are also more expensive to build than other types of power plants, in part because safety constraints require a number of systems to be put in place to prevent disasters.

Thermal Pollution

A large amount of energy is given off by a nuclear reactor, but not all of it is converted into electricity. Any machine converts some energy into heat that is not used. Large amounts of water are required to absorb heat in a nuclear power plant, which is why most nuclear power plants are built near bodies of water such as lakes or oceans.

Some of the water becomes steam that is released into the atmosphere by cooling towers, as shown in Figure 15. The steam does not have a significant impact on the environment. As with other kinds of thermoelectric power plants, some of the heated water is normally released back into the water source. The water is not radioactive, but it can increase the water temperature enough to be harmful to temperature-sensitive organisms. This is considered to be thermal pollution, which is a negative environmental impact.

FIGURE 15: The cooling towers of a nuclear power plant release steam into the air.

IDENTIFY CONSTRAINTS What are some of the constraints for building a nuclear power plant? Select all correct answers.

- ☐ **a.** The radioactivity of the fuel rods needs to be contained.
- ☐ **b.** It needs to be able to handle a large amount of nuclear fuel at a time.
- ☐ **c.** The cost of building the plant requires a significant amount of funding.
- ☐ **d.** It needs to be built where it can have access to a large amount of water.
- ☐ **e.** It needs to be prevented from releasing pollutants into the atmosphere.

Radioactive Waste

One of the biggest concerns about nuclear power is the production of nuclear waste in the form of spent fuel rods, which still contain radioactive products. In many cases, the first step in processing the rods is to submerge them in large water tanks, such as the one shown in Figure 16, to be cooled. Then, they must be permanently stored in special containment facilities because radioactive products in spent fuel rods have half-lives of many thousands of years. This constraint has a large social impact because communities generally do not want radioactive waste to be stored near them. More than 60 000 tons of spent nuclear fuel is currently stored at facilities near U.S. nuclear power plants.

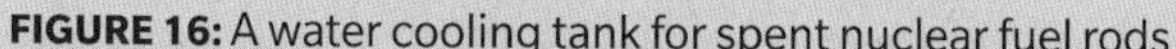

FIGURE 16: A water cooling tank for spent nuclear fuel rods

ANALYZE Suppose you are voting on a decision on whether to build a nuclear power plant near your town. Describe two pairs of tradeoffs you would consider that would inform your vote.

____

____

____

____

____

Energy Production and Energy Demands

The potential of producing plentiful energy for electricity is perhaps the main factor that has made nuclear power an attractive energy solution. For this to be an important benefit assumes that energy demands will remain high or keep increasing. But many new ways have been developed to reduce energy use in society. For example, LED light bulbs use 75% less energy than traditional incandescent bulbs.

When the goal of energy conservation is taken into account, nuclear power's energy benefits may be evaluated as less worth its costs than if energy demands are considered to be a factor that society cannot change. With energy conservation measures put into practice, other forms of energy production that produce less power but involve less cost and environmental impact, such as wind and solar energy, become more attractive.

The Possibility of Nuclear Disasters

Most of all, the possibility of an accident that releases radiation into the environment is always a significant concern wherever there are nuclear power plants. Such accidents can be caused by human error or by natural disasters. For example, the Fukushima Daiichi nuclear disaster in 2011 was caused by a tsunami from a powerful offshore earthquake. The reactors automatically shut down when the earthquake struck, but water from the tsunami that followed knocked out the backup generators that kept the coolant water circulating in the reactor. As a result, the uncontrolled heat of the reactors caused meltdowns, explosions, and the release of radioactive material into the environment.

FIGURE 17: An aerial view shows the aftermath of the reactor explosions at the Fukushima Daiichi power plant.

The Fukushima accident was the most significant nuclear disaster since the 1986 reactor meltdown in Chernobyl, Ukraine (then part of the Soviet Union). There, a flawed reactor design coupled with poor safety practices led to a meltdown that caused a steam explosion. A significant amount of radioactive material was released and spread over a large area. Over a period of weeks, many people died from acute radiation exposure, and many more suffered ill health effects from the radioactive material spread over the area.

Language Arts Connection Research a nuclear disaster and determine what caused the accident, as well as its social and environmental impacts. Write a report in which you critically analyze the accident to illustrate how nuclear power plants had impacts that were not anticipated.

Nuclear accidents such as the one in Chernobyl may be considered to have been avoidable. But it is impossible to completely prevent the possibility of human error, which raises the concern about what could be done to ensure that such accidents never happen again. Such concerns still loom large in the public view, and although the possibility of such accidents is very slight, the fact that they have happened has had a major impact on society. The huge social and environmental impacts of nuclear accidents when they do happen highlight the risks that nuclear power always carries with it.

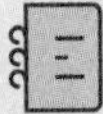

Evidence Notebook Compare the benefits and risks involved in the use of radioactive nuclides in nuclear power with those involved in their use in medical imaging.

Careers in Engineering

Environmental Engineer

Environmental engineers research efficient and cost-effective ways to clean up toxic material in the environment. Some environmental engineers research ways to remove radioactive waste from the environment.

In Figure 18, toxic waste is poured into a biomagnetic separator. The waste contains uranyl ions, a type of waste produced at sites where uranium ore was mined. A chemical is mixed into the separator and bacteria are added. The bacteria carry out chemical reactions that cause the uranyl ions to form a coating on the bacteria. This coating is magnetic, and so the uranyl coating can be separated from the rest of the sample with a magnetic field, decontaminating the sample.

In bioremediation processes, special strains of common bacteria such as *E. coli* that are resistant to radiation are added to hazardous waste to transform contaminants into forms that can be easily removed. These bacteria incorporate radioactive atoms of elements such as uranium or thorium dissolved in water into compounds that are not soluble in water, which can then be easily removed from the water. Such bacteria are very useful because they perform chemical reactions that would otherwise be expensive and time-consuming to carry out artificially.

Once radioactive material has been removed from the environment, it still needs to be sealed off for a long period of time while it is still radioactive. One approach to doing this is glass vitrification. In this process, radioactive waste is combined with glass powder, and the mixture is heated to a high enough temperature to melt it. The liquid glass is cooled, producing a solid, glassy material with the radioactive material locked within it. The glass material can then be stored underground. Environmental engineers are working to determine glass compositions that will best hold different types of radioactive waste. They also need to address concerns about the glass becoming cracked over time.

FIGURE 18: In this device, bacteria are used to remove nuclear waste ions from a biological sample.

Chemistry in Your Community Scientists from diverse backgrounds are responsible for many of the advances in the field of environmental science, such as remediation of radioactive waste. Research an environmental engineer whose work has benefited your community. These may include, but are not limited to, the jobs of health and safety engineer, chemical engineer, microbiologist, and mining engineer. Integrate multiple sources to write a blog post that describes how this person's work has improved the environment in your area and assesses their solution.

NUCLEAR DISASTERS | HALF-LIFE AND RADIOMETRIC DATING | NUCLEAR MEDICINE | Go online to choose one of these other paths.

Lesson Self-Check

CAN YOU EXPLAIN THE PHENOMENON?

FIGURE 19: In a PET scan, small amounts of radioactive nuclides are injected into the bloodstream to produce images of the body.

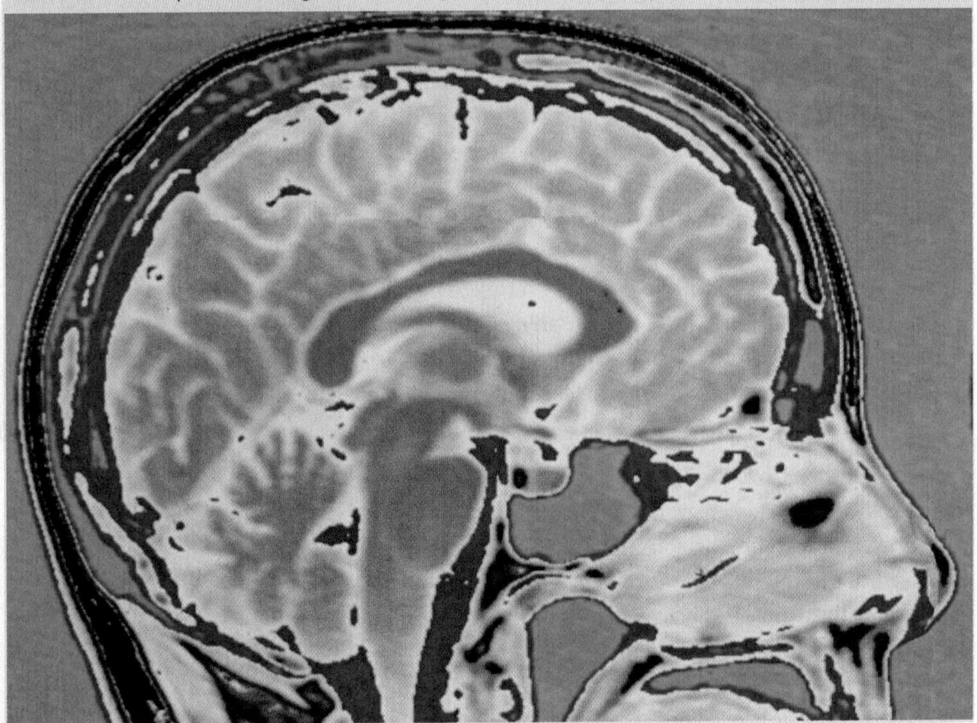

Medical images can be produced using a variety of techniques and processes. In one process, x-ray radiation moves through the body, and a detector on the opposite side of the body produces an image. In a PET scan, however, a medical image is generated from instruments that detect radiation emitted from within the body. Radioactive nuclides are introduced into the body either by injection or by having the patient drink a solution containing the nuclides.

Evidence Notebook Refer to your notes in your Evidence Notebook to make a claim about why some atoms give off radiation that can be detected in a medical image. Your explanation should include a discussion of the following points:

Claim What types of nuclear reactions would cause atoms to give off radiation that can be detected in a medical image, and how do forces within the nuclei cause these reactions?

Evidence What evidence supports a claim of whether the nuclear reactions are a form of radioactive decay, fission, or fusion? What evidence supports a claim of the types of forces within the nuclei that cause the reactions?

Reasoning Explain how the evidence you cited supports your claim.

Name Date

CHECKPOINTS

Check Your Understanding

1. Select the correct terms to complete the statement.

   In fission, nuclei break apart | join. This reaction is found spontaneously in nuclides with few | many nucleons.

   In fusion, nuclei break apart | join. This reaction is possible when energy is added to | released from nuclei with few | many nucleons.

2. Which force repels like charges from each other?
   - ○ **a.** gravitational
   - ○ **b.** electrostatic
   - ○ **c.** strong
   - ○ **d.** weak

3. Which of the following are conserved in all nuclear reactions? Select all correct answers.
   - ☐ **a.** mass
   - ☐ **b.** charge
   - ☐ **c.** number of protons
   - ☐ **d.** number of neutrons
   - ☐ **e.** number of nucleons

4. Select the correct terms to complete the statement.

   When nucleons come together to form a nucleus, they gain | lose mass and gain | lose energy. This difference in energy is absorbed | released if the nucleus comes apart.

5. How would you expect the nuclide $^{17}_{7}N$ to decay to result in a more stable nuclide?
   - ○ **a.** alpha decay
   - ○ **b.** beta decay of an electron
   - ○ **c.** beta decay of a positron
   - ○ **d.** gamma decay

6. Which properties might a nuclide on the band of nuclear stability have?
   - ○ **a.** atomic number 10 and 15 neutrons
   - ○ **b.** atomic number 30 and 30 neutrons
   - ○ **c.** atomic number 52 and 78 neutrons
   - ○ **d.** atomic number 86 and 128 neutrons

7. Match each type of radioactive decay with the decay particle it produces.

Decay	Particle
alpha decay ○	○ γ
beta decay ○	○ $^{4}_{2}He$
gamma emission ○	○ $^{0}_{+1}e$

8. When uranium-235 undergoes fission in nuclear power plants, thorium-231 is produced, which soon decays to protactinium-231. Protactinium-231 has a half-life of 32 760 years. Complete the sentences to describe the decay of a 5.00-g sample of protactinium-231 over time.

   After 32 760 years, the sample will contain about ________ grams of the radioactive nuclide.

   After 65 520 years, the sample will contain about ________ grams of the radioactive nuclide.

   After 98 280 years, the sample will contain about ________ grams of the radioactive nuclide.

9. What are some disadvantages of using nuclear energy to produce electricity compared to a coal-fired power plant? Select all correct answers.
   - ☐ **a.** It has a lower power output.
   - ☐ **b.** It requires larger amounts of fuel.
   - ☐ **c.** It requires more water.
   - ☐ **d.** It produces waste products that require long-term storage.
   - ☐ **e.** It requires mining operations and processing that are more costly.

CHECKPOINTS (continued)

10. Explain how the conservation of energy applies to nuclear reactions.

11. Nuclear submarines use a process similar to the process used in thermoelectric power plants, using the heat of fission to generate steam from water and spin turbines. Explain why nuclear energy might be a practical power source for a submarine.

MAKE YOUR OWN STUDY GUIDE

In your Evidence Notebook, design a study guide that supports the main ideas from this lesson:

A stable atomic nucleus is held together primarily by the strong nuclear force.

Unstable nuclei spontaneously decay, releasing radiation in the form of energy and particles.

Large nuclei may undergo nuclear fission, and small nuclei may undergo nuclear fusion.

Nuclear energy can be harnessed for practical applications.

Remember to include the following information to your study guide:

- Use examples that model main ideas.
- Record explanations for the phenomena you investigated.
- Use evidence to support your explanations. Your support can include drawings, data, graphs, laboratory conclusions, and other evidence recorded throughout the lesson.

Consider the costs and benefits that nuclear technology has for society and the environment.

Physical Science Connection

FIGURE 1: The CMS detector at CERN

Subatomic Particles The properties of subatomic particles smaller than protons, neutrons, and electrons are studied by observing high-energy interactions of particle beams at large accelerator facilities such as CERN, the European Organization for Nuclear Research. Institutes from many countries use the equipment at CERN to run studies. CERN employs over 2500 people to build and maintain equipment, run experiments, and interpret data.

Research recent discoveries about subatomic particles and the scientists and engineers that work at facilities such as CERN. Write a news article explaining how one discovery was made, the importance of that discovery, and the team responsible for making the discovery.

Literature Connection

FIGURE 2: Chernobyl nuclear power station after the accident in 1986.

Nuclear Reactions in Literature After atomic bombs saw use in World War II, books and films began exploring story lines about the new nuclear age. Villains and superheroes alike were depicted as creations of nuclear radiation's effect on the human body. Nuclear disasters, such as the accidents at Chernobyl in 1986 or Fukushima Daiichi in 2011, have been the basis for fiction and nonfiction works on the possible dangers of nuclear energy.

Select a piece of literature influenced by nuclear energy, nuclear weapons, or nuclear disasters. Research how the author was influenced by the perceptions of nuclear energy at the time. Synthesize your findings in a book report, including a plot synopsis of your selection.

Technology Connection

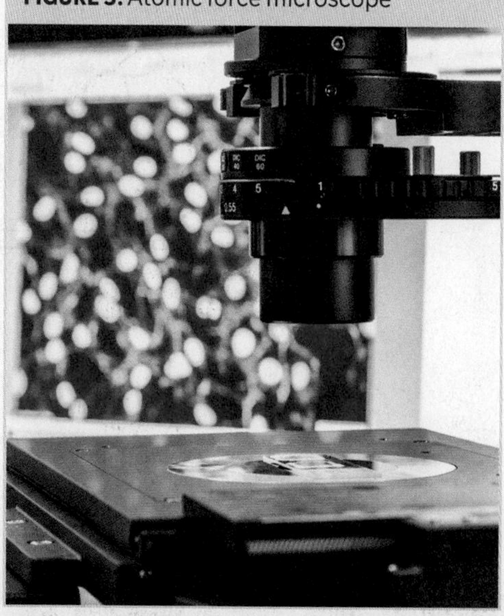
FIGURE 3: Atomic force microscope

Imaging Molecules Light microscopes allow scientists to research cells that range in size from 10^3–10^5 nanometers and therefore can reflect visible light. But molecular structures ranging in size from 0.1 to 10 nanometers are so much smaller that new imaging techniques had to be developed to render them visible. Today, scientists have a variety of techniques for imaging molecules. For example, the atomic force microscope can produce a three-dimensional image with a resolution less than one nanometer by measuring the force between a probe and the sample surface.

Make a multimedia presentation about a molecule that was imaged using a molecular imaging technique. Explain how the molecule was imaged, and what scientists and engineers learned from being able to image the molecule you researched.

THE PIECES EVERYTHING IS MADE OF

A table for putting small pieces in order

You know that the periodic table is an arrangement of the elements in order of their atomic numbers so that elements with similar properties fall in the same column. Here's a look at how this arrangement of elements helps us understand the world on an atomic scale.

A BOOK EXPLAINING COMPLEX IDEAS USING ONLY THE 1,000 MOST COMMON WORDS

RANDALL MUNROE
XKCD.COM

THE STORY OF PUTTING THINGS IN ORDER

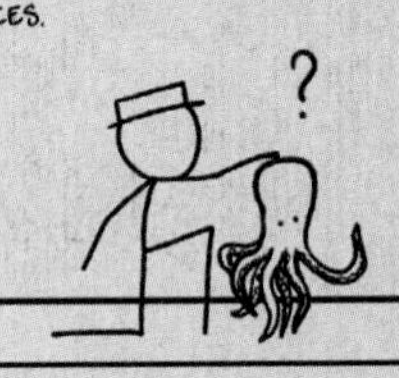

PIECES OF PIECES

These pieces are made of even smaller pieces. Different kinds of pieces have different numbers of those smaller parts. There are three main kinds of these smaller parts—two heavy ones and a light one.

Over the past hundred years, we've learned that the idea of "where" doesn't always work well for very small things.

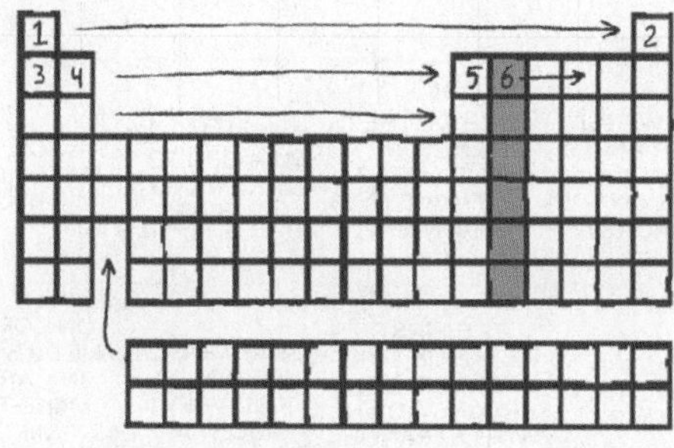

TABLE SHAPE

The boxes in this table are in order from left to right and top to bottom. It has this strange shape because pieces are in groups with other pieces that are a lot like them.

(The reason those groups are like each other has to do with the number of light parts around the outside of the piece—which is mostly the same as the piece's center number—and the way different numbers of light parts sort themselves around the outside of the piece.)

CENTER NUMBER

We number the pieces by counting how many of one kind of heavy part they have in their center, and use that number to put pieces in boxes in the table. The other heavy part doesn't matter to the count, so pieces with different numbers of that part may share the same box in the table.

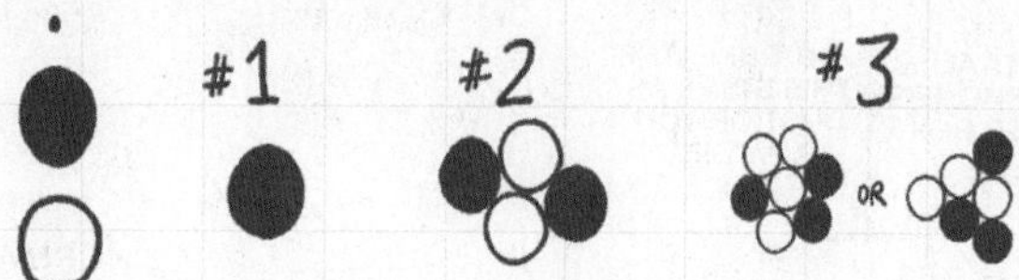

SHORT LIVES, STRANGE HEAT

Some kinds of pieces don't last very long, slowly breaking down into other pieces over time by throwing away bits of their centers in all directions, which makes them give off a kind of strange heat.

We count how long a kind of piece lasts by timing how long it takes for half of it to break down. We call this the piece's "half-life."

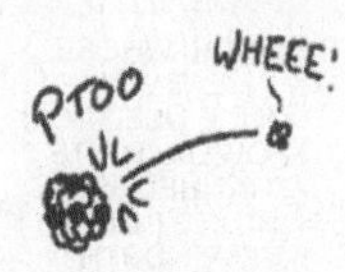

NAMES

Some of the things on this table have had names for a long time (like gold) but some of them were only found in the last few hundred years.

Many of the pieces in this table are named after people or places—and especially for people who helped to learn about them or the places where those people worked.

Here are a few of the things these pieces are named after.

THE PIECES EVERYTHING IS MADE OF

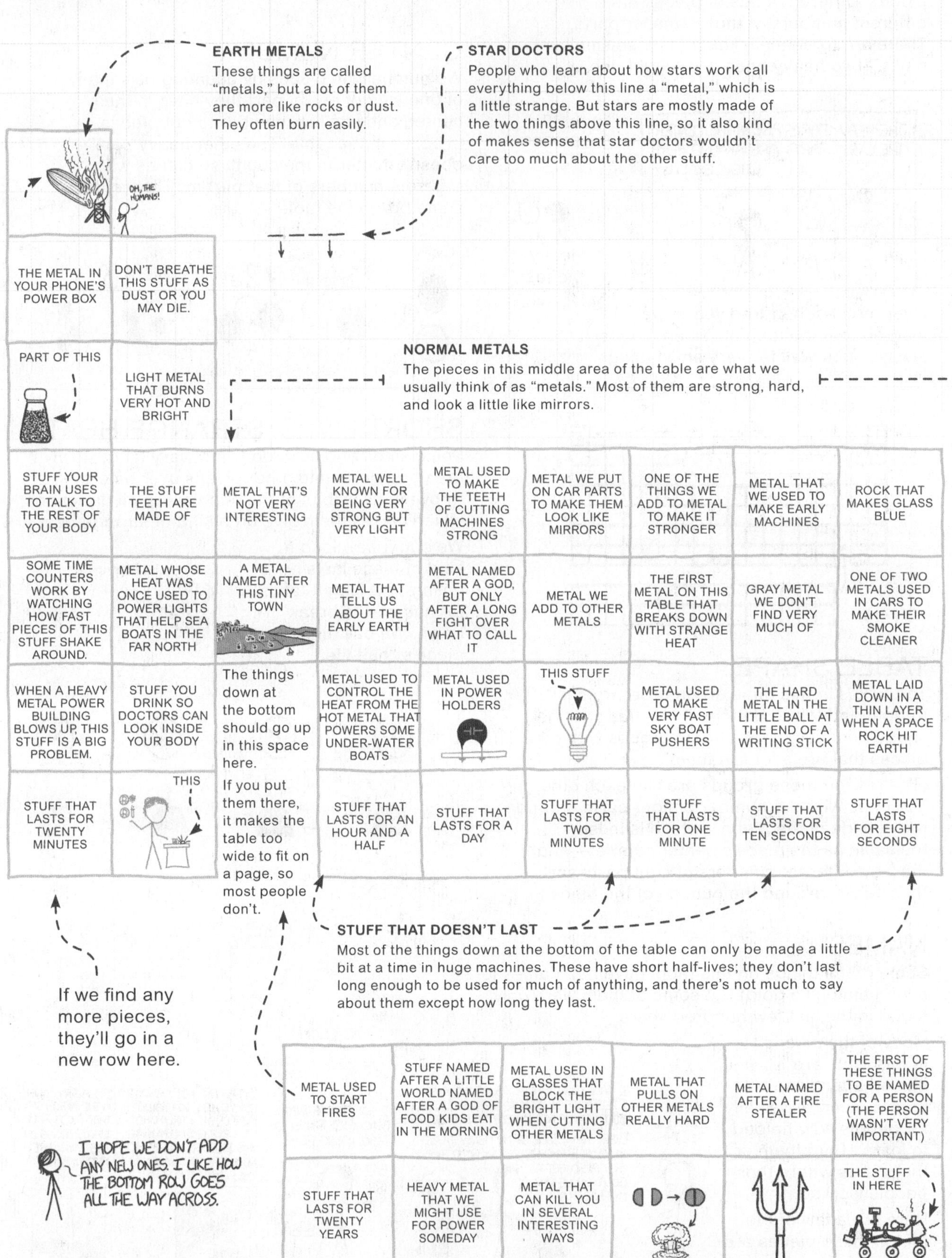

Go online for more about *Thing Explainer*.

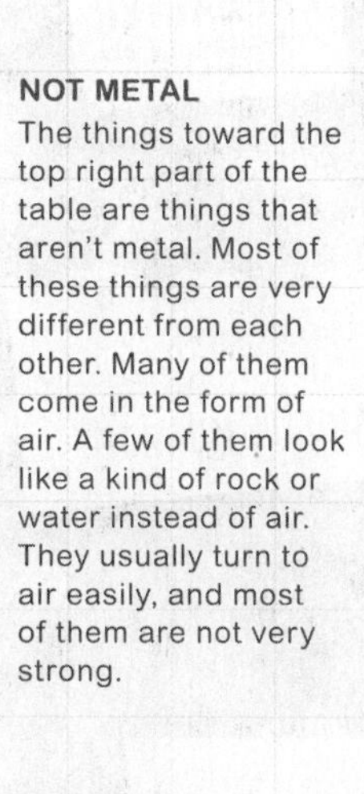

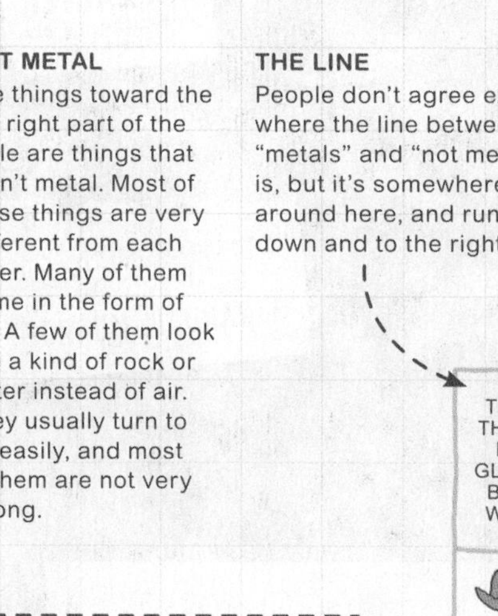

NOT METAL
The things toward the top right part of the table are things that aren't metal. Most of these things are very different from each other. Many of them come in the form of air. A few of them look like a kind of rock or water instead of air. They usually turn to air easily, and most of them are not very strong.

THE LINE
People don't agree exactly where the line between "metals" and "not metals" is, but it's somewhere around here, and runs down and to the right.

AIR, WATER, AND FIRE
The things in this area of the table do a lot of things. When you put them near things from the other end of the table, they can turn to different kinds of water, start fires, or make everything blow up.

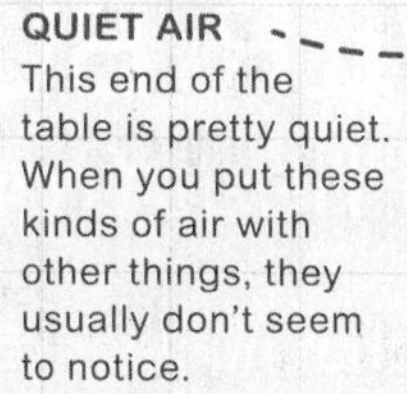

QUIET AIR
This end of the table is pretty quiet. When you put these kinds of air with other things, they usually don't seem to notice.

			THE STUFF THAT KEEPS KITCHEN GLASS FROM BREAKING WHEN HOT	THE STUFF ALL KNOWN LIFE IS MADE FROM	THE PART OF AIR WE DON'T NEED TO BREATHE TO STAY ALIVE	THE PART OF AIR WE DO NEED TO BREATHE TO STAY ALIVE	GREEN BURNING AIR THAT KILLS	AIR IN BRIGHT SIGNS MADE FROM COLORED LIGHT
			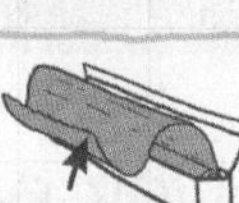 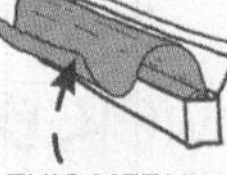 THIS METAL	THE ROCK THAT MAKES UP BEACHES, GLASS, AND COMPUTER BRAINS	BURNING WHITE ROCKS	SMELLY YELLOW ROCKS LIKE THIS	THE STUFF THEY PUT IN POOLS SO NOTHING BAD CAN GROW IN THEM	AIR THAT DOESN'T DO MUCH OF ANYTHING
THE GRAY METAL AT THE CENTER OF THE EARTH	BROWN METAL WE USE TO CARRY POWER AND VOICES	METAL USED TO MAKE THE BROWN METAL STRONGER (NOW USED FOR MANY OTHER THINGS)	WATERY METAL THAT MAKES DRINK CANS TEAR LIKE PAPER	METAL NAMED AFTER THIS PLACE	THE ROCK MOST WELL KNOWN FOR KILLING YOU IF YOU EAT IT	A ROCK THAT CAN CHANGE ONE KIND OF POWER INTO ANOTHER	RED WATER	AIR USED BY DOCTORS TO MAKE THIN BRIGHT LIGHTS FOR CUTTING EYES
ONE OF TWO METALS USED IN CARS TO MAKE THEIR SMOKE CLEANER		METAL USED IN PAINT UNTIL WE REALIZED IT MADE PEOPLE SICK	PART OF THE SILVER METAL YOU CAN HEAT UP AT HOME TO STICK PARTS TOGETHER	METAL PUT ON FOOD CANS TO KEEP WATER FROM MAKING HOLES IN THEM	METAL PUT IN THINGS TO KEEP THEM FROM BURNING	METAL THAT CAN BE FOUND IN LOTS OF PLACES, BUT MOST OF THEM AREN'T EARTH	STUFF THEY ADD TO THIS SO YOUR BRAIN GROWS RIGHT	AIR USED IN CAMERA FLASHES
A ROCK THAT PEOPLE WILL PAY AS MUCH FOR AS GOLD	GOLD	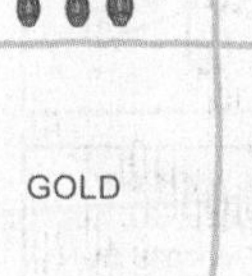 THIS	METAL WE USED FOR KILLING ANIMALS BUT STOPPED USING BECAUSE IT WAS TOO GOOD AT IT	METAL WELL KNOWN FOR BEING HEAVY	ROCK THAT LOOKS LIKE A COOL TINY CITY	THIS 	STUFF NO ONE HAS SEEN CLEARLY BECAUSE IT BURNS UP TOO FAST	AIR THAT COMES FROM ROCKS UNDER HOUSES AND CAN MAKE YOU SICK
STUFF THAT LASTS FOR TEN SECONDS	STUFF THAT LASTS FOR HALF A MINUTE		STUFF THAT LASTS FOR A THIRD OF A MINUTE	STUFF THAT LASTS THREE SECONDS	STUFF THAT LASTS FOR LESS THAN A THIRD OF A SECOND	STUFF THAT LASTS FOR THE TIME IT TAKES YOU TO CLOSE AND OPEN YOUR EYES		STUFF THAT LASTS FOR THE TIME IT TAKES SOUND TO TRAVEL ONE FOOT

MONEY METAL
We use a lot of the things in this group as money—although not the bottom one, since it disappears very fast.

(Some people who know a lot about money actually think that having money that disappears over time could be good, but they probably don't mean quite this quickly.)

FEEL BETTER
This stuff is made from the rock that looks like a tiny city. If you feel like food is going to come out of your mouth, you can eat or drink some of this, and it might help you feel better.

SO MANY DIFFERENT PARTS OF THE WORLD!

METAL NAMED AFTER THIS PLACE 	METAL THAT PULLS ON OTHER METALS WHEN IT GETS JUST A LITTLE COLDER THAN NORMAL AIR	ANOTHER METAL NAMED AFTER THIS TINY TOWN 	METAL WHOSE NAME MEANS "HARD TO GET"	METAL NAMED AFTER THIS PLACE 	ANOTHER METAL NAMED AFTER THIS TINY TOWN	THE NAME PEOPLE HERE USED FOR PEOPLE HERE 	I'M SURE THIS IS A NICE TOWN, BUT COME ON. 	METAL NAMED AFTER THIS PLACE
STUFF IN THE BOXES THAT TELL YOU WHEN YOUR HOUSE IS ON FIRE 	METAL NAMED FOR HER 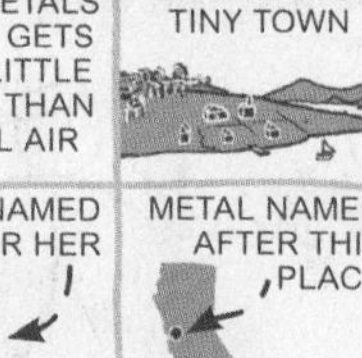	METAL NAMED AFTER THIS PLACE 	METAL NAMED AFTER THIS PLACE 	METAL NAMED FOR HIM	METAL NAMED FOR A MAN WHO HELPED BUILD THE FIRST HEAVY METAL POWER BUILDING 	METAL NAMED FOR HIM THIS WAS MY IDEA. 	METAL NAMED FOR HIM 	METAL THAT LASTS FOR FOUR MINUTES

NAMED FOR THIS PLACE

A BOOK EXPLAINING COMPLEX IDEAS USING ONLY THE 1,000 MOST COMMON WORDS

RANDALL MUNROE
XKCD.COM

HEAVY METAL POWER BUILDING

Making heat from heavy metals

You know that nuclear reactors use controlled-fission chain reactions to produce energy and radioactive nuclides—and that nuclear power plants use heat from nuclear reactors to produce electrical energy. Here's a look at the process that turns nuclear fission into electric current.

THE STORY OF THE HEAVY METAL POWER BUILDING

THESE BUILDINGS USE SPECIAL KINDS OF HARD-TO-FIND HEAVY METAL TO MAKE POWER. SOME OF THE METALS THEY USE CAN BE FOUND IN THE GROUND, BUT ONLY IN A FEW PLACES. OTHER KINDS CAN BE MADE BY PEOPLE—BUT ONLY WITH THE HELP OF A POWER BUILDING THAT'S ALREADY RUNNING.

THESE METALS MAKE HEAT ALL THE TIME, EVEN WHEN THEY'RE JUST SITTING. THEY MAKE TWO KINDS OF HEAT: NORMAL HEAT—LIKE HEAT FROM A FIRE—AND A DIFFERENT, SPECIAL KIND OF HEAT. THIS SPECIAL HEAT IS LIKE LIGHT THAT YOU CAN'T SEE. (AT LEAST, YOU CAN'T SEE IT MOST OF THE TIME. IF THERE'S A WHOLE LOT OF IT, ENOUGH TO KILL YOU QUICKLY, YOU CAN SEE IT. IT LOOKS BLUE.)

NORMAL HEAT CAN BURN YOU, BUT THE SPECIAL HEAT FROM THESE METALS CAN BURN YOU IN A DIFFERENT WAY.

IF YOU SPEND TOO MUCH TIME NEAR THIS HEAT, YOUR BODY CAN START GROWING WRONG. SOME OF THE FIRST PEOPLE WHO TRIED TO LEARN ABOUT THESE METALS DIED THAT WAY.

THE SPECIAL HEAT IS MADE WHEN TINY PIECES OF THE METAL BREAK DOWN. THIS LETS OUT A LOT OF HEAT, FAR MORE THAN ANY NORMAL FIRE COULD. BUT FOR MANY KINDS OF METAL, IT HAPPENS VERY SLOWLY. A PIECE OF METAL AS OLD AS THE EARTH MIGHT BE ONLY HALF BROKEN DOWN BY NOW.

WITHIN THE LAST HUNDRED YEARS, WE LEARNED SOMETHING VERY STRANGE: WHEN SOME OF THESE METALS FEEL SPECIAL HEAT, THEY BREAK DOWN FASTER. IF YOU PUT A PIECE OF THIS METAL CLOSE TO ANOTHER PIECE, IT WILL MAKE HEAT, WHICH WILL MAKE THE OTHER PIECE BREAK DOWN FASTER AND MAKE MORE HEAT.

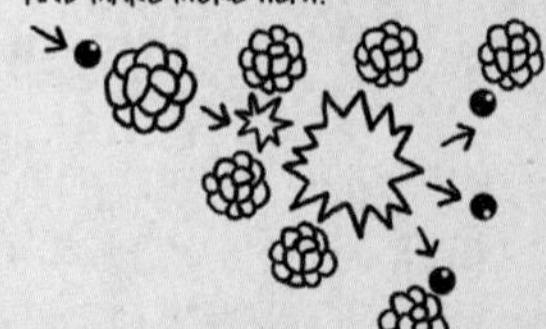

IF YOU PUT TOO MUCH OF THE METAL TOGETHER LIKE THIS, IT GETS HOTTER AND HOTTER SO FAST THAT IT CAN ALL BREAK DOWN AT ONCE, LETTING OUT ALL ITS HEAT IN LESS THAN A SECOND. THIS IS HOW A SMALL MACHINE CAN BURN AN ENTIRE CITY.

TO MAKE POWER, PEOPLE TRY TO PUT PIECES OF THIS METAL CLOSE ENOUGH TOGETHER THAT THEY MAKE HEAT FAST, BUT NOT SO CLOSE THAT THEY GO OUT OF CONTROL AND BLOW UP. THIS IS VERY HARD, BUT THERE IS SO MUCH HEAT AND POWER STORED IN THIS METAL THAT SOME PEOPLE HAVE WANTED TO TRY ANYWAY.

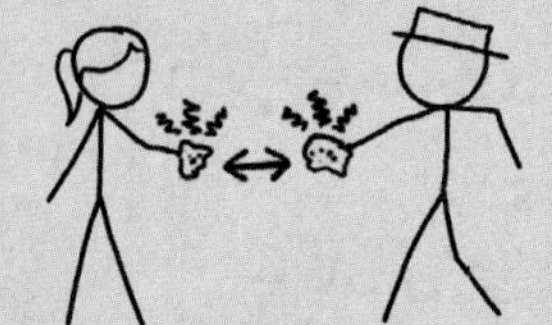

OUTSIDE POWER LINE
Even though the building makes power, without outside power it will stop running.

This is important, because it means that if there's a very big problem, you can stop things from the outside by turning off the power.

COOLING BUILDING
After they're done with it, the sea water is very hot. They put it in this building to let it cool down a little so it's not too hot when they put it back in the sea.

They pour the water out into the air, where it falls like rain. As it falls, the air cools it down. This warms up the air, which makes it rise, and new cold air moves in from the outside to take its place.

POWER BUILDING
This building holds the metal and makes power. Water comes in, and it uses the metal to heat the water, then makes power from the hot water. (There's a bigger picture of it on the next page.)

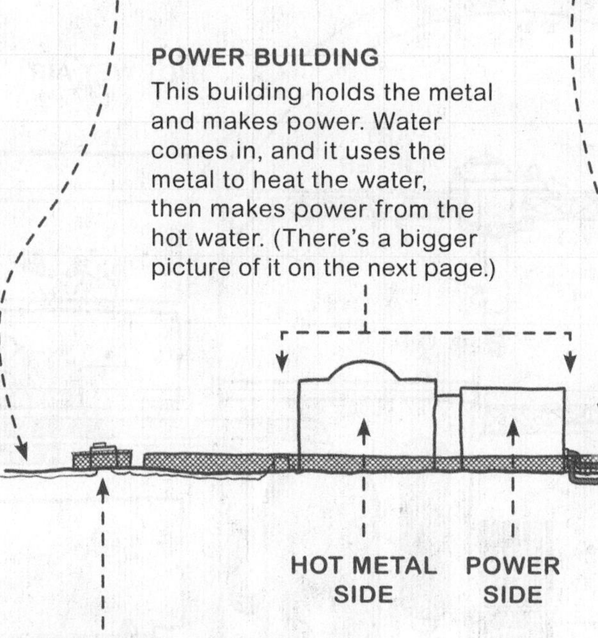

Used water comes out here. The used water is clean, but it's still warm. Animals like to hang around here when it's cold out.

POWER LINE BOX
Sometimes animals get in here and break something, and it makes the entire building stop working.

Cold water gets pulled in here. Sometimes fish get stuck in it and they have to turn off the power building to figure out what's wrong.

MAKING POWER WITH WATER
The building makes power by heating water. This means they need lots of cold water, which is why they're usually built near the sea or a big river.

They don't let the water from the sea touch the water that goes near the hot metal itself. Instead, they let the metal heat up water that runs through metal lines. Then the heat from those lines heats water in another water carrier, which goes over to the other part of the building. Then *that* water heats the water from the sea.

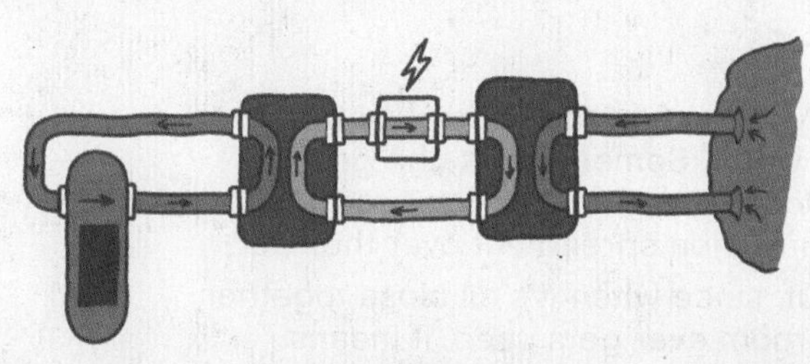

HEAVY METAL POWER BUILDING

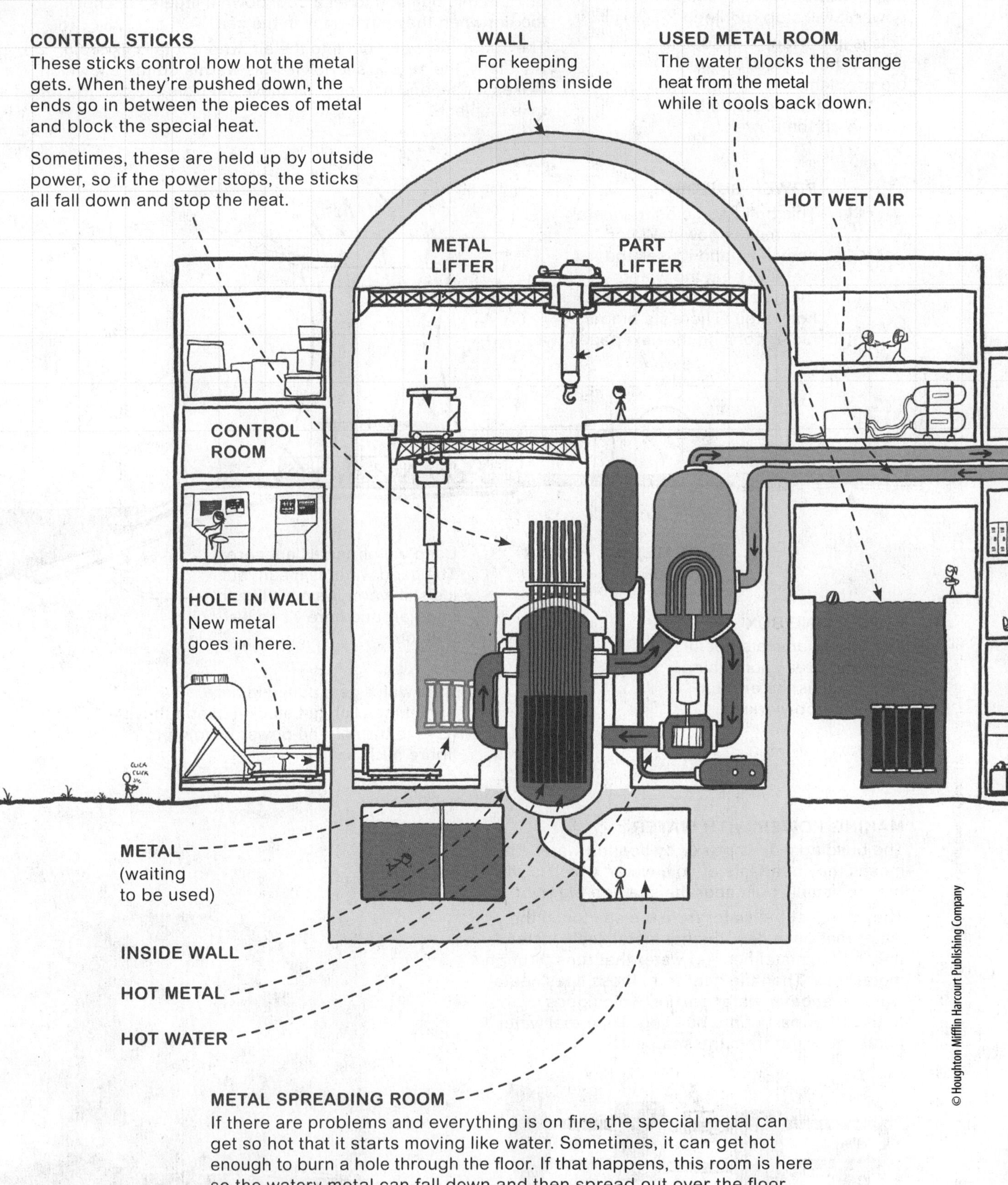

Go online for more about *Thing Explainer*.

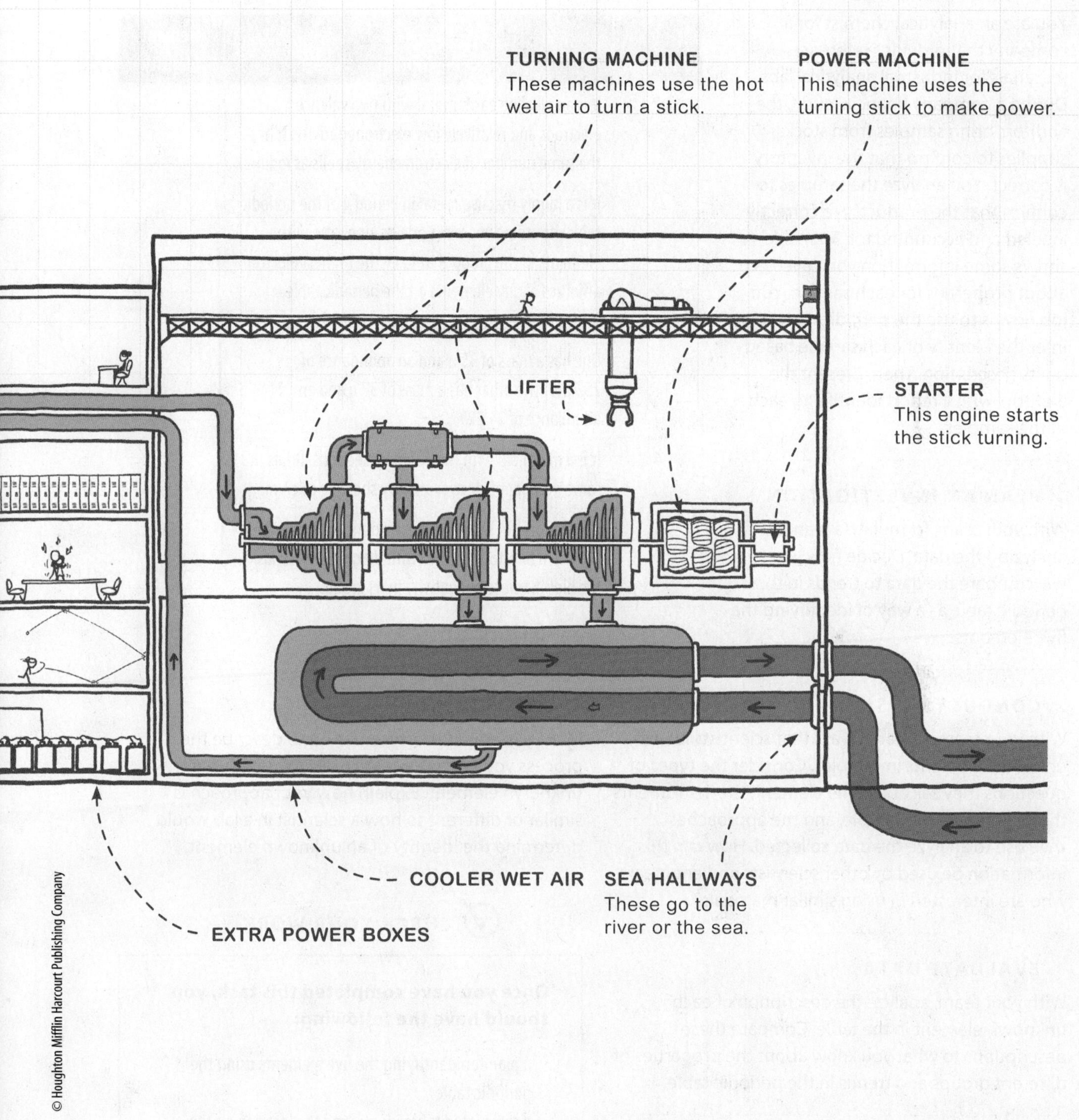

Identifying Elements Using Patterns

You are an analytical chemist for a company that provides reference materials for industrial analytical labs. During a company financial audit, the auditors bring samples from stock supplies to confirm that the inventory is correct. You analyze the samples to confirm that the products are correctly labeled and accounted for. The table shows some information you collected about properties for each sample. Your job now is to use the periodic table to infer the identity of each sample based on its description. Then, present the auditors with a report identifying each of the samples.

Unknown	Description	Element Identity
1	It is an alkaline earth metal with two valence electrons and relatively low electronegativity. It has the same number of electron energy shells as iodine.	______
2	It is a highly reactive metal in Period 4 of the periodic table. Its atoms bond in a one-to-one ratio with elements in the group that have the highest electron affinities of any elements on the periodic table.	______
3	It is a highly reactive nonmetal with two isotopes. One has a mass of 35 u and an abundance of 75.78%. The other has a mass of 37 u and an abundance of 24.22%.	______
4	It is a metalloid with five valence electrons. It has the same number of electron energy shells as calcium.	______
5	Its electron-dot structure has six dots, and its atoms bond in a one-to-one ratio with magnesium. It has the highest electronegativity in its group.	______

1. PLAN AN INVESTIGATION

With your team, formulate a plan for analyzing the data. Decide how you will compare the data to trends in the periodic table as a way of identifying the five elements.

2. CONDUCT RESEARCH

With your team, research ways that scientists identify unknown elements in samples. Consider the types of questions they ask about the element, the instruments they use to test the sample, and the approaches they use to analyze the data collected. How can this information be used by other scientists and engineers who are interested in using similar materials?

3. EVALUATE DATA

With your team, analyze the description of each unknown element in the table. Compare these descriptions to what you know about the properties of different groups and trends in the periodic table.

4. CONSTRUCT AN EXPLANATION

Describe the location of each unknown element on the periodic table. Explain how you inferred the identity of each element. Then, record the identity of each element in the table.

5. COMMUNICATE

Make a multimedia presentation to describe the process you and your team used to identify each unknown element. Explain how your approach is similar or different to how a scientist in a lab would determine the identity of an unknown element.

Once you have completed this task, you should have the following:

- a plan for identifying the five elements using the periodic table
- a completed table identifying the location on the periodic table of the five unknown elements
- a presentation explaining the process used to determine the unknown elements
- images and data that further support your explanation

Name Date

SYNTHESIZE THE UNIT

In your Evidence Notebook, make a concept map, other graphic organizer, or outline using the Study Guides you made for each lesson in this unit. Be sure to use evidence to support your claims.

When synthesizing individual information, remember to follow these general steps:

- Find the central idea of each piece of information.
- Think about the relationships among the central ideas.
- Combine the ideas to come up with a new understanding.

DRIVING QUESTIONS

Look back to the Driving Questions from the opening section of this unit. In your Evidence Notebook, review and revise your previous answers to those questions. Use the evidence you gathered and other observations you made throughout the unit to support your claims.

PRACTICE AND REVIEW

1. Select the correct terms to complete the statement about chlorine.

Chlorine is often used as an oxidizing agent and disinfectant in large pools. It is very reactive because it has a small | large electronegativity value. The atomic number for chlorine is 17. This means it has 17 electrons and protons | electrons and neutrons | protons and neutrons. There are two stable isotopes of chlorine, and both are used to study environmental pollution. Chlorine-35 has seventeen | eighteen | nineteen | twenty neutrons, and chlorine-37 has seventeen | eighteen | nineteen | twenty neutrons.

2. If numbered consecutively, what describes the relationship of group number to valence electrons? Select all correct answers.

- ☐ **a.** For Groups 1 and 2, the number of valence electrons is equal to the group number.
- ☐ **b.** For Groups 1 and 2, the number of valence electrons is twice the group number.
- ☐ **c.** For Groups 13–18, the number of valence electrons is the group number minus 5.
- ☐ **d.** For Groups 13–18, the number of valence electrons is the group number minus 10.

3. Complete these statements about trends in ionization energy on the periodic table.

As you move from left to right across a period, the ionization energy tends to increase | decrease. As you move down a group, the ionization energy tends to increase | decrease.

For example, lithium is in Group 1, Period 2, and boron is in Group 13, Period 2. Based on these locations, you would expect boron | lithium to have a higher ionization energy.

4. Which of the following are true of stable nuclei? Select all correct answers.

- ☐ **a.** The electromagnetic force between nucleons is stronger than the strong force.
- ☐ **b.** The nucleus has a low binding energy.
- ☐ **c.** For a midsize nucleus, the nucleus contains slightly more neutrons than protons.
- ☐ **d.** For a small nucleus, the nucleus has equal numbers of protons and neutrons.

5. Carbon has 6 protons, and nitrogen has 7 protons. Fill in the following information about the decay of carbon-14 to nitrogen-14.

a. The charge of the particle emitted: __________

b. The final number of neutrons: __________

c. The total number of nucleons: __________

6. Visual atomic models do not represent the relative scale of the atom. Explain why they are still useful, even though they may be inaccurate.

7. Explain how patterns in electronegativity on the periodic table can be used to predict bond formation.

8. Discuss two benefits and two drawbacks of nuclear-fueled electric power plants compared to conventional fossil fuel power plants. How and why have the relative tradeoffs of these two sources of electricity changed in the last fifty years?

UNIT PROJECT

Return to your unit project. Prepare a presentation using your research and materials, and share it with the class. In your final presentation, evaluate the strength of your hypothesis, data, analysis, and conclusions.

Remember these tips while evaluating:

- What atomic properties were best illustrated by your models?
- How did you incorporate the patterns of the periodic table into your models?
- Were you able to demonstrate radioactive decay, fission, and fusion with your models?

UNIT 3

Compounds and Mixtures

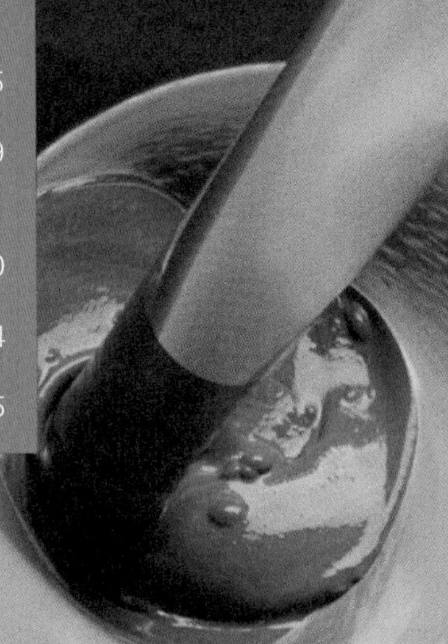

YOU SOLVE IT

Which Planetary-Rover Materials Are Suitable?

How Can You Change the Properties of a Substance?

To begin exploring this unit's concepts, go online to investigate ways to solve a real-world problem.

Various colors swirl together when you start mixing paint. Once it is all mixed up, the paint has a color unlike any of the original colors.

FIGURE 1: The cutting edge of this drill bit is coated with diamonds to protect it from wearing out too quickly when it is used to cut into hard metals.

Diamond is a form of pure, elemental carbon and is one of the hardest substances found in nature. Because it is so hard, it can scratch or cut most other substances and is used in a variety of industries. For example, tools that are used to cut, shape, or smooth metal, rock, or other hard substances are sometimes coated with diamonds. Natural diamonds are not easy to mine from Earth. Diamond mining techniques include digging large pits and drilling into the ocean floor. Because of diamond's industrial importance, engineers developed methods of producing synthetic diamonds. One method of making diamonds involves subjecting graphite, which is another form of elemental carbon, to extremely high pressures and temperatures. A second method of producing synthetic diamonds involves growing diamond crystals in a chamber filled with carbon-rich gases. Both processes are reliable, cost less than mining, and have been used to make industrial-quality diamonds. However, the second method has advantages: very high pressures are not needed and diamonds can be grown on larger surfaces.

PREDICT Diamond is not the only naturally-occurring substance that scientists and engineers have made in laboratories. For example, scientists have made a synthetic form of indigo, which is the dye used to color jeans. What information do you think scientists need in order to make a substance in a laboratory?

DRIVING QUESTIONS

As you move through the unit, gather evidence to help you answer the following questions. In your Evidence Notebook, record what you already know about these topics and any questions you have about them.

1. How can different kinds of bonding affect the properties of substances?
2. How can you use the periodic table to predict the types of bonds atoms will form?
3. How can interactions between particles be modeled?
4. How do forces between particles affect the properties of materials?

UNIT PROJECT

Go online to download the Unit Project Worksheet to help plan your project.

Designing Detergents

A detergent is a cleansing agent that cleans materials by bonding with dirt and oil so that they can be dissolved and washed away. Investigate properties of soaps and detergents. What is the difference between the two and does it affect how they work? Develop a plan to optimize the effectiveness of a homemade detergent mixture.

Language Development

Use the lessons in this unit to complete the chart and expand your understanding of the science concepts.

TERM: ionic bond

Definition	Example

Similar Term	Phrase

TERM: covalent bond

Definition	Example

Similar Term	Phrase

TERM: metallic bond

Definition	Example

Similar Term	Phrase

TERM: polarity

Definition	Example

Similar Term	Phrase

TERM: hydrogen bond

Definition	Example

Similar Term	Phrase

TERM: solution

Definition	Example

Similar Term	Phrase

TERM: solubility

Definition	Example

Similar Term	Phrase

TERM: composite

Definition	Example

Similar Term	Phrase

3.1

Investigating Chemical Compounds

A fiery reaction occurs when sodium metal is exposed to chlorine gas.

CAN YOU EXPLAIN THE PHENOMENON?

Sodium is an essential element required by the human body to function. In the United States, about 11% of a person's daily sodium intake comes from adding table salt to food. Table salt is a perfectly safe material made from two elements that can be highly hazardous by themselves: sodium and chlorine. Sodium metal is toxic, corrosive, and reacts vigorously with water to produce hydrogen, a flammable gas. Exposure to elemental chlorine gas can result in poisoning and health complications. Chlorine was weaponized during World War I. Today, chlorine is a commonly manufactured chemical in the United States and is a key component of bleach.

FIGURE 1: Sodium chloride (left) is the product of the reaction of sodium metal (center) and chlorine gas (right).

PREDICT How do you think the properties of sodium and chlorine change when they are combined to make sodium chloride?

Evidence Notebook As you explore the lesson, gather evidence to explain why the properties of sodium chloride are so different from the properties of sodium and chlorine.

Hands-On Lab

Analyzing the Properties of Compounds

Differences in the structures of compounds at the atomic level cause the differences that are observed at the macroscopic scale. One physical property that varies widely among different materials is melting point. As such, melting point is an example of a physical property that scientists can use to identify an unknown compound. Other physical properties, such as density, boiling point, and electrical conductivity, can also be analyzed to help verify the identity of the compound.

Knowing physical properties of compounds also allows scientists to identify possible uses of the compound. Additionally, knowing these properties allows scientists to properly store and handle compounds and can help determine how to clean up or dispose of the material in the event of a spill.

RESEARCH QUESTION How does a compound's atomic-level structure influence its use in natural or human-designed systems?

MAKE A CLAIM

In this lab you will compare the melting points of three common substances: citric acid, $C_6H_8O_7$; paraffin wax, $C_{31}H_{64}$; and table salt, NaCl. Which one do you think will have the highest melting point? Which one will have the lowest? Explain.

MATERIALS

- indirectly vented chemical splash goggles, nonlatex apron, nitrile gloves
- aluminum foil
- Bunsen burner
- citric acid, small amount
- paraffin wax, small amount
- permanent marker
- ring stand, ring, and clamp
- salt, small amount
- spatula or scoop
- striker
- wire gauze

SAFETY INFORMATION

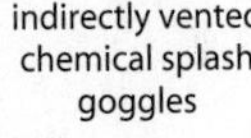

indirectly vented chemical splash goggles

- Wear indirectly vented chemical splash goggles, a nonlatex apron, and nitrile gloves during the setup, hands-on, and takedown segments of the activity.
- Secure loose clothing, wear closed-toe shoes, and tie back long hair.
- Never eat any food items used in a lab activity.
- If you get a chemical in your eye, use an eyewash station immediately.
- Never pour chemicals, either used or unused, back into their original containers. Dispose of chemicals according to your teacher's instructions.

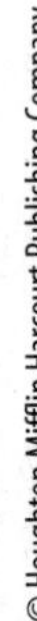

COLLECT DATA

Construct a data table in your Evidence Notebook to record the findings from your investigation. Your data table will record the melting order of the three substances. It should do so with both qualitative and quantitative data. Consider how you will determine when a substance begins to melt and whether or not it matters how long it takes to melt completely. Have your teacher approve your data table and data-collection plans.

FIGURE 2: Experimental setup

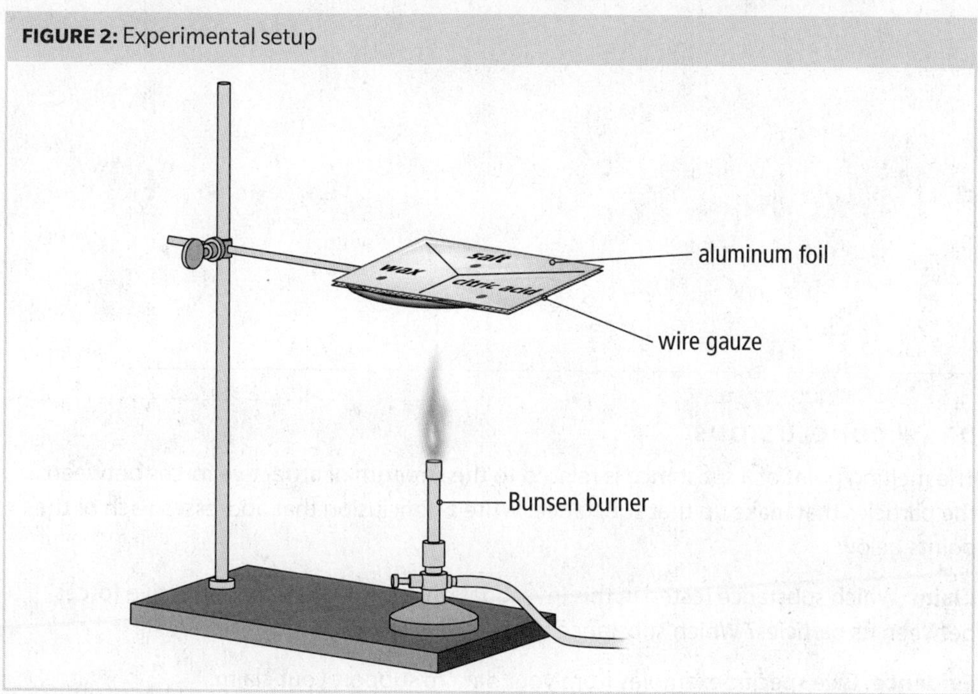

CARRY OUT THE INVESTIGATION

1. Use a marker to divide a square piece of aluminum foil into three sections. Label the sections *salt, wax,* and *citric acid.* Fold the edges up to keep melted wax from spilling.
2. Use a spatula to transfer a very small (pea-sized) amount of each substance onto the foil. Be sure to clean and dry the spatula between each substance.
3. Set up a ring stand as shown in Figure 2. Adjust the ring's height so that the Bunsen burner can fit under it.
4. Place a piece of wire gauze on top of the ring, and carefully place the aluminum foil on top of the gauze.
5. Secure loose clothing and tie back hair. Light the Bunsen burner, and carefully place it under the wire gauze. Observe the order in which the substances melt. Record the melting order in the data table.
6. Turn off the Bunsen burner when the substances have melted. Dispose of your materials as instructed by your teacher.

ANALYZE

Choose one of the substances tested in the lab, and sketch the particles in the substance before, during, and after being heated.

DRAW CONCLUSIONS

The melting point of a substance is related to the strength of attractive forces between the particles that make up that substance. Write a conclusion that addresses each of the points below.

Claim Which substance tested in this investigation has the strongest attractive forces between its particles? Which substance has the weakest?

Evidence Give specific examples from your data to support your claim.

Reasoning Explain how the evidence you gave supports your claim. Describe, in detail, the connections between the evidence you cited and the argument you are making.

Evidence Notebook As you have seen, sodium metal, chlorine gas, and sodium chloride have different properties. What conclusion can you make about the forces holding the atoms of these substances together? What tests could you run to learn more about each substance?

Describing Chemical Bonds

The electron arrangement of most atoms causes them to have a high potential energy. Recall that a chemical bond forms when atoms gain, lose, or share valence electrons and end up with a full outer shell, or octet. A full outer shell has lower potential energy than a partially filled shell, so the full shell is a more stable arrangement. Therefore, when atoms form chemical bonds, the compound formed typically has a lower potential energy than the total potential energy of the individual atoms.

Collaborate Like a ball rolling down a hill, systems tend to naturally change toward lower, more stable energy states. The ball at the top of the hill represents a large amount of stored, or potential, energy. That potential energy is converted to kinetic energy as the ball rolls down the hill to a more energetically stable position. With a partner, make your own analogy to explain how chemical bond formation leads to more stable energy states.

Making Predictions about Bonding

Electronegativity is a measure of the tendency of an atom to attract electrons. Differences in electronegativity can be used to predict the types of chemical bonds atoms will form.

FIGURE 3: Patterns in electronegativity can be observed on the periodic table.

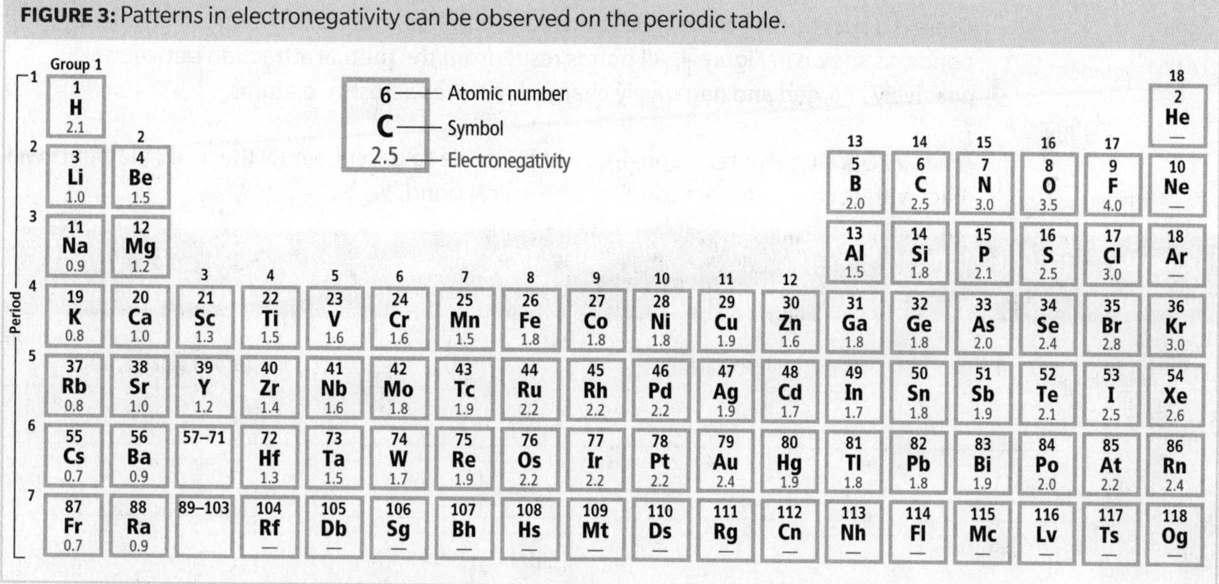

EXPLAIN Using Figure 3, select the correct terms to complete the statement.

As you move from left to right across a row in the periodic table, the electronegativity of the elements increases | decreases | does not show a pattern. As you move down a column, the electronegativity of the elements increases | decreases | does not show a pattern. The more electronegative elements can be found in the upper right | upper left | lower right | lower left of the periodic table.

When there is a large electronegativity difference between two atoms—between about 1.7 and about 3.3—their bonding pattern is best explained as a transfer of electrons from the less electronegative atom to the more electronegative atom. An ionic bond is formed by the transfer of one or more electrons. A greater difference in electronegativity corresponds to a more complete transfer of electrons from one atom to the other.

FIGURE 4: Bond types fit into a continuous range that is related to the difference in electronegativities of the two atoms that form the bond.

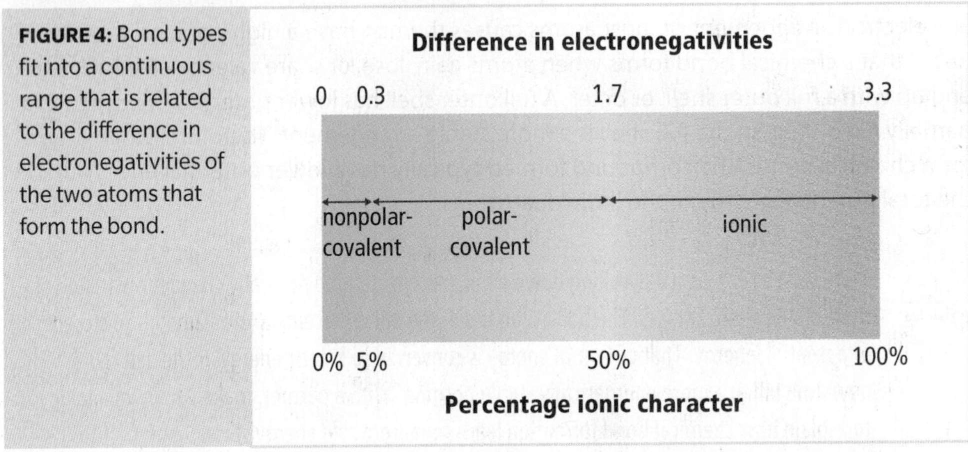

As the electronegativity difference decreases, so does the tendency of either atom to attract or "let go" of valence electrons. The two atoms share their valence electrons, forming what is called a covalent bond. If there is a small difference in electronegativity, atoms share electrons unevenly, forming a *polar covalent bond*. If two atoms are from the same element, their electronegativity difference is 0, and they form a *nonpolar covalent bond*. The diatomic elements of hydrogen, nitrogen, oxygen, and the halogens are examples of this type of bond, and the electrons are shared equally between the atoms.

There is a spectrum of bond types between completely ionic and nonpolar covalent bonds, as shown in Figure 4. All bonds result from the mutual attraction between positively charged and negatively charged particles across two atoms.

ANALYZE Using Figures 3 and 4, fill out the table to describe how the listed elements will react with each other when forming a chemical bond.

Elements Bonded	Electronegativity Difference	Bond Type	More Electronegative Atom	Example Compound
C and O	1	polar covalent	O	carbon dioxide, CO_2
C and S				
O and H				
Na and Cl				
Mg and O				

A difference in electronegativity between two bonding atoms indicates how much, if any, sharing of electrons will occur. As this difference increases, the sharing of electrons becomes more uneven. If the electronegativity difference becomes great enough, the unequal pull on valence electrons will result in the transfer of electrons to the more electronegative element, forming an ionic bond. For this reason, we can discuss bonds as having a percentage ionic character.

Patterns

Patterns in Bonding

You can find patterns in the ways some categories of elements form compounds. In general, metallic elements do not attract electrons, and they have low electronegativities. Nonmetals have higher electronegativities that increase toward the top right of the periodic table. The noble gases are an exception, as they do not attract electrons.

INFER Complete the statement about how different elements bond.

Metals tend to have relatively high | low electronegativities, and nonmetals have relatively high | low electronegativities. When a metal bonds with a nonmetal, electrons will most likely be transferred, and a covalent | an ionic bond will form. When a nonmetal bonds with a nonmetal, the difference in electronegativity values is relatively low. Therefore, electrons will be shared between the two nonmetals, and a covalent | an ionic bond will form.

Explore Online

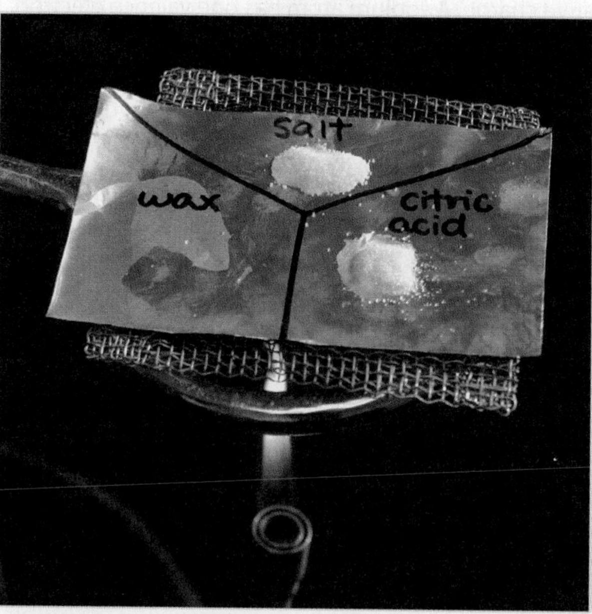

FIGURE 5: Melting point can be used to determine the relative strength of interactions between particles in various compounds in the solid state.

APPLY The chemical formulas for salt, citric acid, and paraffin wax are NaCl, $C_6H_8O_7$, and $C_{31}H_{64}$, respectively. Use this information and data you collected earlier in this lesson to determine which statements below are true. Select all that apply.

- ☐ **a.** Salt has a high melting point and there is a high electronegativity difference between sodium and chlorine, so, salt contains ionic bonds.
- ☐ **b.** Salt and citric acid both have high melting points, and there are high electronegativity differences between the atoms, so, both contain ionic bonds.
- ☐ **c.** Citric acid and wax both have relatively low melting points, and there are low electronegativity differences between the atoms, so, both contain covalent bonds.

Notice that none of the examples above involve bonds between metal atoms. Metal atoms do not interact with one another to form ionic or covalent bonds. The interactions between metals will be discussed in another section.

Describing Ionic Bonding

Elements with very different electronegativity values generally form ionic bonds. Sodium chloride is an example of an ionically bonded compound. Recall that a mixture of sodium metal and chlorine gas reacts to form sodium chloride. Each sodium atom loses an electron, and each chlorine atom gains an electron. The attraction between positive and negative ions holds the ions together in an ionic bond. The ionization of the atoms and the formation of the ionic bond increase the stability of the system. The reaction releases energy as light and heat, resulting in a much lower energy state for the compound as compared to the sum of the energy states of the individual atoms.

Evidence Notebook When soaps are used in hard water, ions such as calcium or magnesium in the water form soap scum, which is made up of insoluble compounds such as magnesium stearate, $Mg(C_{18}H_{35}O_2)_2$. What bond types are present in this compound? How might bond type explain the properties of the soap you are investigating in your unit project?

When an atom loses one or more electrons, it becomes a positive ion, or *cation*. Cations have more protons than electrons and so have an overall positive charge. When an atom gains electrons, it becomes a negative ion, or *anion*. Anions have more electrons than protons and so have an overall negative charge. A sodium atom has one valence electron, and chlorine has seven valence electrons.

ANALYZE Sodium transfers an electron to chlorine when forming sodium chloride. Write either a positive sign or a negative sign as a superscript by each ion formed in this bond. Then, label each as either a *cation* or an *anion* below the chemical symbol.

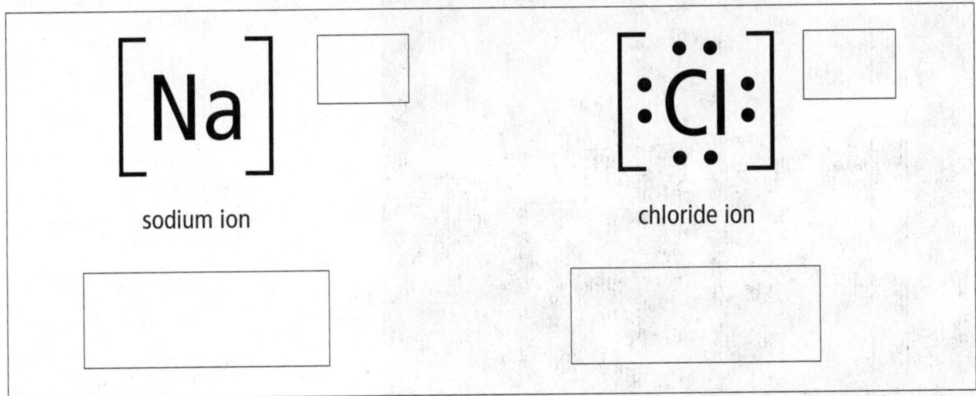

FIGURE 6: The regular arrangement of ions in salt creates a pattern seen in the crystals.

When sodium donates one electron to chlorine, both the negative chloride ion and the positive sodium ion end up with stable octet configurations. Thus, this ionic compound is more stable than either of its highly reactive elements.

An ionic compound consists of many bonds between positive and negative ions, which form repeating patterns in the solid state of the compound. This gives the compound a regular, geometric shape, as shown in Figure 6. As solids, ionic compounds do not conduct electric current, but they do conduct electric current when dissolved in water. They are also very hard and brittle, and they have high melting and boiling points.

The structure formed by atoms in a solid ionic compound like the one in Figure 6 is called a *crystal*. The repeating, symmetrical arrangement of atoms in a crystal is called a *crystal lattice*. In the model of a sodium chloride crystal lattice shown in Figure 7, attractions between ions are represented with solid lines.

FIGURE 7: Sodium ions and chloride ions arrange to form a network.

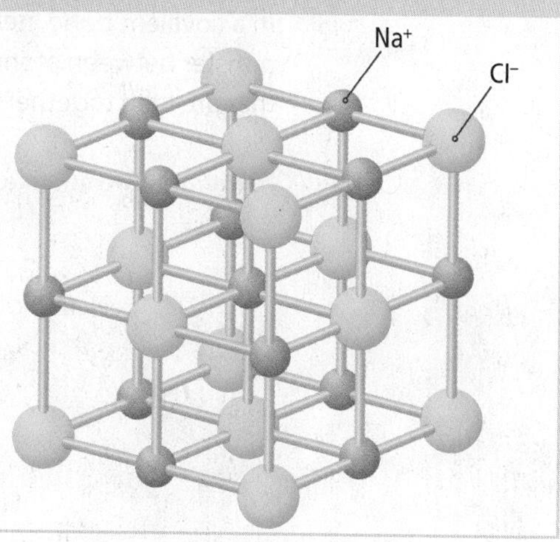

Notice that each ion is attracted to more than one ion of opposite charge. The chemical formula of an ionic compound represents the simplest ratio of its ions in an electrically neutral crystal. A neutral compound has equal amounts of positive and negative charge.

GATHER EVIDENCE Observe sodium chloride with a hand lens. How is the relatively high melting point of sodium chloride related to its structure at the atomic scale? Use your observations and the model in Figure 7 to support your claim.

Engineering

Producing Salts

Salts are ionic compounds made of metal and nonmetal ions. They are important for human life and activities. Salts can be mined from deposits left by natural evaporation of ancient oceans. As the water evaporated, the ions in solution formed new ionic bonds, producing a crystalline ionic compound. Salts can also be produced by evaporating water from seawater. For example, some of the lithium metal used in batteries comes from lithium salts harvested by evaporation of brine deposits, as shown in Figure 8.

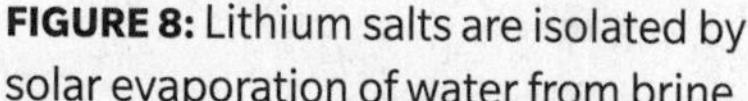

FIGURE 8: Lithium salts are isolated by solar evaporation of water from brine.

Long-lasting, recyclable lithium batteries are essential to many consumer products. They are also used to store renewable energy from sources such as solar and wind power. Chemical engineers must weigh tradeoffs to minimize the economic and environmental costs of producing lithium salts and maximize the benefits. As current lithium deposits become exhausted and demand for lithium continues to increase, costs and environmental concerns will continue to be considerations for engineers searching for and mining new deposits of lithium.

Language Arts Connection Research the development of lithium batteries, the increased demand for lithium, and how and where this demand is currently being met. Make a news article or presentation explaining how the need for lithium is related to modern technologies.

Describing Covalent Bonding

In a covalent bond, neither atom exerts sufficient attractive force to cause an electron to transfer between atoms, so electrons are shared. A molecule is a neutral group of atoms that are held together by covalent bonds. A fluorine molecule is shown in Figure 9.

FIGURE 9: Two fluorine atoms share a pair of electrons equally.

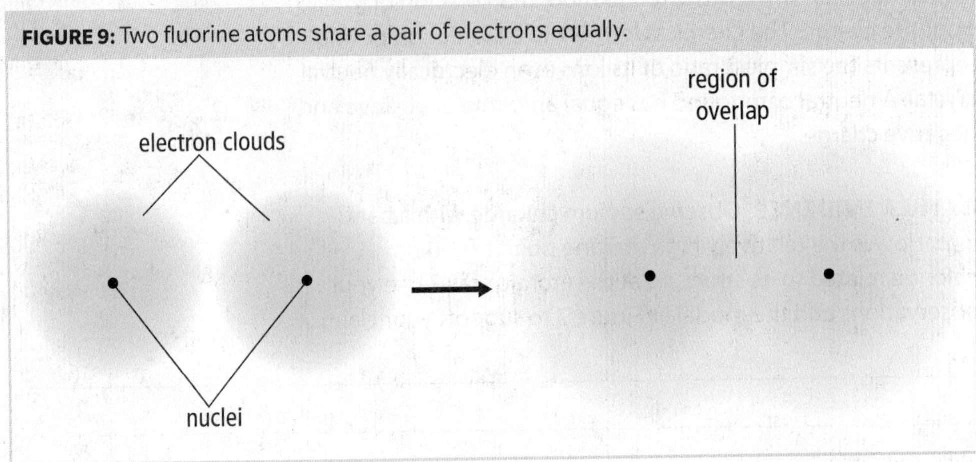

A single molecule of a chemical compound is an individual unit that functions, in many ways, as a single particle. A molecule consists of two or more atoms bonded together by covalent bonds. Some molecules, such as diatomic oxygen, shown in Figure 10a, are made up of atoms of only one element. Other molecules, such as water and sugar, shown in Figure 10b and Figure 10c, are made of atoms of two or more elements. A chemical compound in which the simplest units are molecules is called a *molecular compound*. Molecular compounds have different properties from ionic compounds.

FIGURE 10: Molecules consist of two or more covalently bonded atoms.

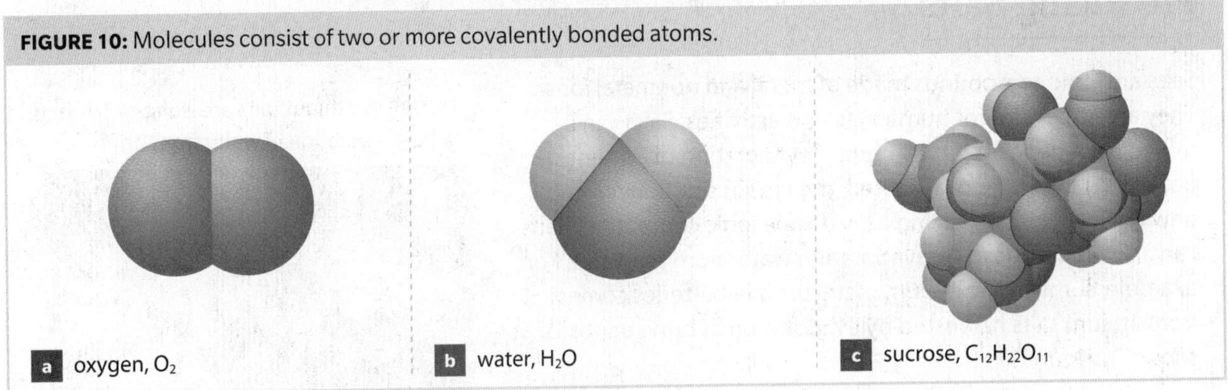

a oxygen, O_2 b water, H_2O c sucrose, $C_{12}H_{22}O_{11}$

EXPLAIN In general, the melting and boiling points of molecular compounds are much lower than those of ionic compounds. What can explain this difference?

Molecular compounds such as those in Figure 10 are formed when one or more atoms transfer | share | release electrons to form molecules. The covalent bonds *within* a molecule are very strong | weak. However, it requires more | less energy to melt a molecular compound than an ionic compound such as the one in Figure 7. This is because the attractive forces *between* individual molecules are weaker | stronger than the forces between ions in an ionic compound.

In general, properties of molecular compounds result from their structure as molecules. In addition to having lower melting and boiling points than ionic compounds, some of them are gases at room temperature. Because molecules are neutral, covalently bonded compounds do not conduct electric current in either their solid or liquid state.

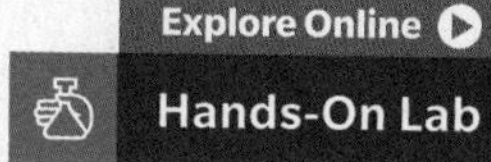

Hands-On Lab

Types of Bonding in Solids
Analyze conductivity, solubility, and melting point to determine the bonding type present in solids.

Describing Metallic Bonding

Metal atoms have low electronegativity values. They do not attract additional electrons, and their own outer electrons are loosely held. Inside a sample of metal, the positive metal ions are surrounded by delocalized valence shell electrons. Delocalized electrons are not tightly held by any one atom, so they can move about within the sample. The chemical bonding that results from the attraction between metal atoms and the surrounding sea of electrons is called metallic bonding.

ANALYZE Mercury is a liquid at room temperature, gallium will melt if held in your hand, and aluminum is a solid that has a high melting point. All three are metals. How can you explain these observations using information about the strength of metallic bonds?

FIGURE 11: Electrons are able to move freely within a metal substance.

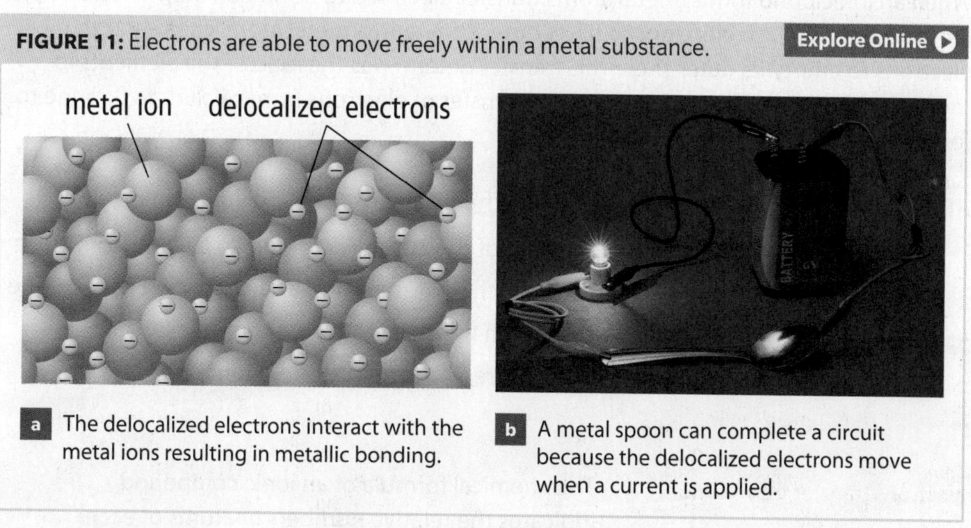

a The delocalized electrons interact with the metal ions resulting in metallic bonding.

b A metal spoon can complete a circuit because the delocalized electrons move when a current is applied.

As with all substances, the properties of metals are related to the bonds they form. Metals are malleable, or easily hammered into sheets. The delocalized electrons around the positive ions form relatively weak links within the substance, making it easy to bend and shape metal. The mobile electrons moving easily throughout the substance allow metals to conduct electric current and contribute to their ability to conduct energy as heat. Gold is used in solid-state electronic devices due to the low voltage and currents that these devices operate under, which might cause other metals to oxidize or corrode. However, copper is still the choice for wiring in a home, as it is more cost effective. In both cases, delocalized electrons allow an electric current to flow through the circuits.

Evidence Notebook What types of bonds form within a sample of sodium metal, chlorine gas, and sodium chloride crystals? How does the electron structure of each substance affect the properties of compounds that it forms?

Predicting the Structure of Compounds

Every molecule of a covalently bonded substance has the same number and type of atoms in the same arrangement as other molecules of the substance. Ionic compounds have a fixed ratio of ions, and this ratio determines their three-dimensional arrangement within the substance. For example, calcium and fluorine always combine in a ratio of one calcium ion to two fluoride ions. Calcium fluoride occurs naturally as the mineral fluorite. Calcium fluoride is used to make hydrofluoric acid, which is used to produce pharmaceuticals and other materials.

Collaborate With a partner, research other compounds formed when Group 2 and Group 17 atoms combine. What do you notice about the ratio of atoms in the compound? How many bonds form, and what types of bonds? Do other groups, such as Group 1 and Group 16, show a pattern when their atoms combine?

Analyzing Chemical Formulas for Ionic Compounds

When an ionic bond forms, metal atoms transfer electrons to nonmetal atoms. A nonmetal atom accepts enough electrons to fill its outer shell, and a metal atom loses enough electrons to empty its outer shell. This transfer determines the ratio of the elements in the ionic compound. Figure 12 shows the transfer of electrons from calcium to fluorine to form calcium fluoride.

APPLY Complete the statement about the chemical formula of calcium fluoride.

Calcium is located in the second column of the periodic table, so a calcium atom has one | two | three valence electron(s), which it loses to form a calcium ion. Each fluorine atom has seven valence electrons, so each fluorine atom accepts one | two | three electron(s) to form a fluoride ion. Therefore, the formula for calcium fluoride is CaF | CaF_2 | Ca_2F.

FIGURE 12: Two valence electrons transfer from calcium to fluorine.

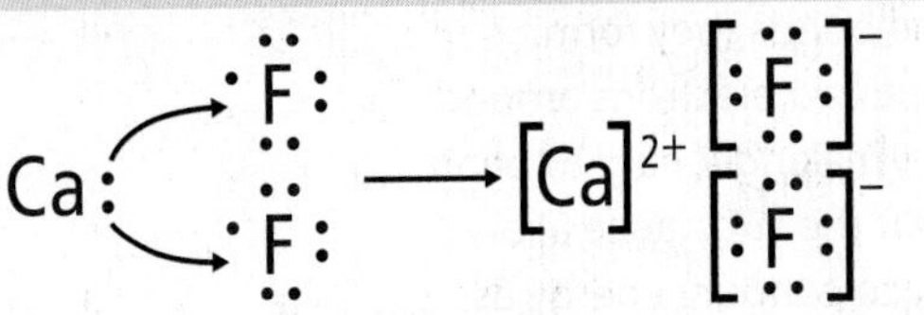

The chemical formula of an ionic compound indicates the relative numbers of atoms of each element in the compound, using atomic symbols and subscript numerals. The formula for calcium fluoride indicates that the simplest unit of the compound contains a ratio of two fluoride ions to one calcium ion.

EXPLAIN Calcium chloride, $CaCl_2$, and potassium chloride, KCl, are also ionic compounds. Which of the following statements is likely to be true based on this information?

- ◯ **a.** Calcium and potassium ions require the same relative number of chloride ions to empty their outer electron shells.
- ◯ **b.** Ionic compounds never contain more than two ions of an atom.
- ◯ **c.** $CaCl_2$ has three atoms in its simplest unit, and KCl has two atoms in its simplest unit.

Patterns

Ionic Formulas

The table below shows some chemical formulas for binary ionic compounds, which are compounds containing one metal and one nonmetal element. The elements are all found in Period 3 of the periodic table.

Compounds containing sodium	Na_3P	Na_2S	NaCl
Compounds containing magnesium	Mg_3P_2	MgS	$MgCl_2$
Compounds containing aluminum	AlP	Al_2S_3	$AlCl_3$

Collaborate With a partner, discuss the patterns you see in the chemical formulas. How does the placement of the elements on the periodic table appear to relate to the numbers in the chemical formula?

Describing Patterns in Ionic Bonding

In order to determine the formula for an ionic compound, the number of valence electrons for each atom in the compound must be known. Previously, you learned to determine the number of valence electrons using an element's electron configuration. You can also use the periodic table to determine the number of valence electrons of any main group element.

MODEL Draw the dot diagrams for the elements in each group. When you see a pattern, draw an electron-dot diagram around the X that represents the entire group.

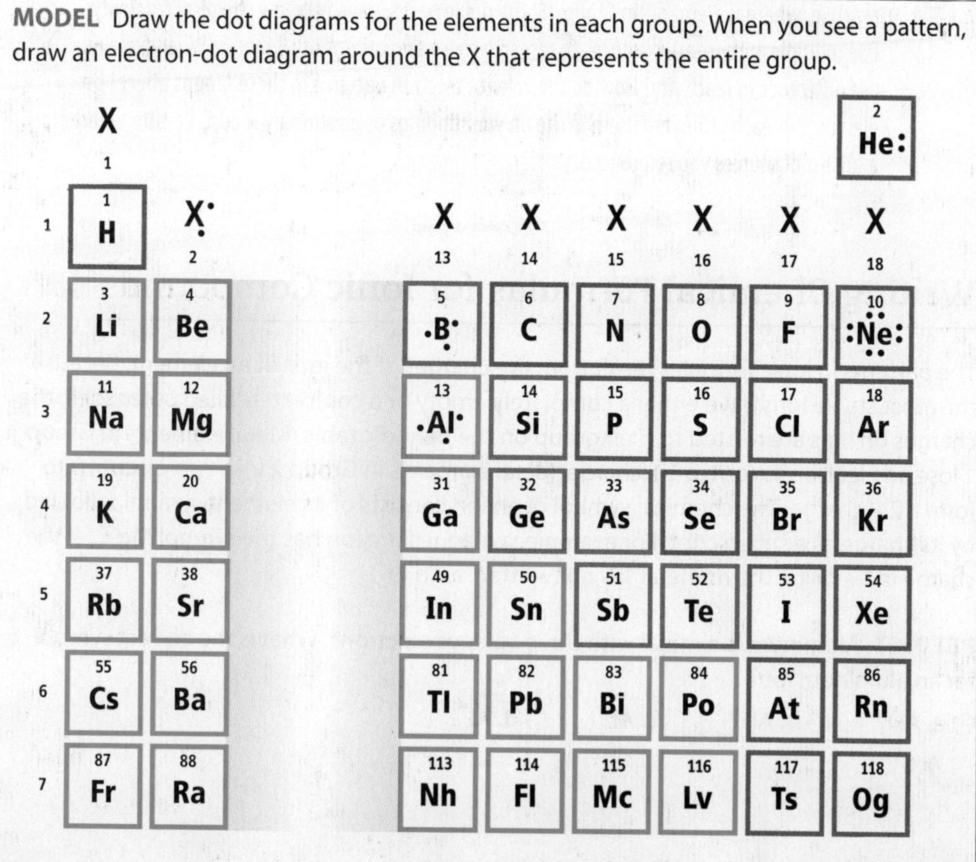

All of the elements found in Group 1 have one valence electron, those in Group 2 have two valence electrons, those in Group 13 have 3 valence electrons, and so on through Group 18. Based on this pattern, scientists know that the ratio of atoms will be the same when an element from Group 1 bonds with an element from Group 17, regardless of which elements bond.

EXPLAIN Use the valence electron pattern you found in the periodic table to determine the pattern between group numbers in the chemical formula for each example.

Group 1	Group 13	Group 16	MX	MX_2	$CaCl_2$	Li_2O	B_2O_3

Group Number	Group Number	Chemical Formula	Example
__________	Group 16	M_2X	__________
Group 2	__________	__________	MgO
__________	__________	M_2X_3	__________
__________	Group 17	__________	KCl
Group 2	Group 17	__________	__________
__________	Group 17	MX_3	$AlCl_3$

The locations of elements on the periodic table allows their compound formulas to be determined. For example, aluminum is in Group 13 and oxygen is in Group 16. Based on the patterns you observed, the resulting compound has the formula Al_2O_3.

Language Arts Connection Elements in Group 17, known as the halogens, are highly reactive, whereas elements in Group 18, the noble gases, have very low chemical reactivity. Use multiple authoritative sources to research these two groups of elements. What explains the difference in reactivity? How do the valence electron patterns in these groups affect how elements in each group are used? Write up your findings as a summary report. Be sure to include a full list of sources you referenced.

Writing Chemical Formulas for Ionic Compounds

The patterns in ionic formulas result from the charges of the ions of an element. Because the most stable ions have either a completely empty or a completely filled outer shell, the charges on ions are related to their group on the periodic table. Metal elements in Group 1 lose an electron to form a 1+ charge. Metal elements in Group 2 lose two electrons to form a 2+ charge. The chemical symbol of an ion consists of its element symbol followed by its charge as a superscript. For example, a magnesium ion has the symbol Mg^{2+}. If the charge is 1+ or 1–, the numeral 1 is not written, as in Cl^-.

PREDICT Aluminum is a metal with three valence electrons. What is the correct symbol for an aluminum ion?

○ **a.** Al^{5+} ○ **b.** Al^{3+} ○ **c.** Al^{3-} ○ **d.** Al^{5-}

Nonmetals typically have 5, 6, 7, or 8 valence electrons, and nonmetals have higher electronegativities than metals. The most stable arrangement occurs when these elements gain electrons when forming ionic bonds. Noble gases in Group 18 beyond helium, such as neon and argon, do not typically bond with other elements because they already possess a full outer shell.

ANALYZE Write in the charges you would expect elements in each group to form. Then, choose an example element from that group, and write its ion symbol in the next row.

Group	1	2	13	14	15	16	17	18
Charge		2+		4+/4−		2−		0
Example ion			Al^{3+}	Si^{4+}	N^{3-}			N/A

The transition metals, Groups 3–12 of the periodic table, do not follow the same predictable pattern of ion formation as do the main group elements. The valence electron structure of transition metals is more complex than those of the metals in the main groups. Many of the transition metal elements can form several different stable cations, depending on the number of electrons lost.

For example, an iron atom can lose two electrons to form Fe^{2+}, or it can lose three electrons to form Fe^{3+}. The ratio of iron ions to nonmetal ions in an ionic iron compound depends on which iron ion is present. For example, iron and oxygen form iron oxide in two different forms, FeO and Fe_2O_3, shown in Figure 13. When you write the name of a compound of a metal that can form more than one ion, the charge on the metal is indicated by a roman numeral in parentheses. The reddish-brown compound, which you may recognize as rust, is designated as Fe_2O_3, or iron(III) oxide, because the iron ion has a 3+ charge.

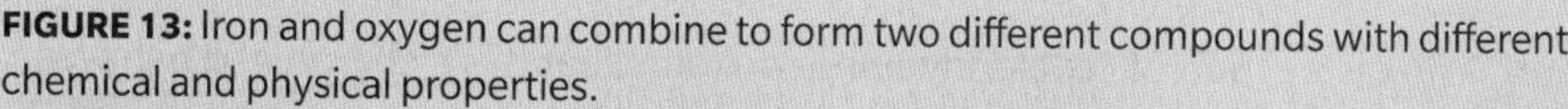

FIGURE 13: Iron and oxygen can combine to form two different compounds with different chemical and physical properties.

a Iron(II) oxide, FeO, is used as a pigment.

b Iron(III) oxide, Fe_2O_3, is the rust that forms when iron is exposed to air.

APPLY What differences do you notice between iron(II) oxide and iron(III) oxide in Figure 13? How does the charge of the iron ions result in different chemical formulas?

Math Connection

Writing Ionic Formulas

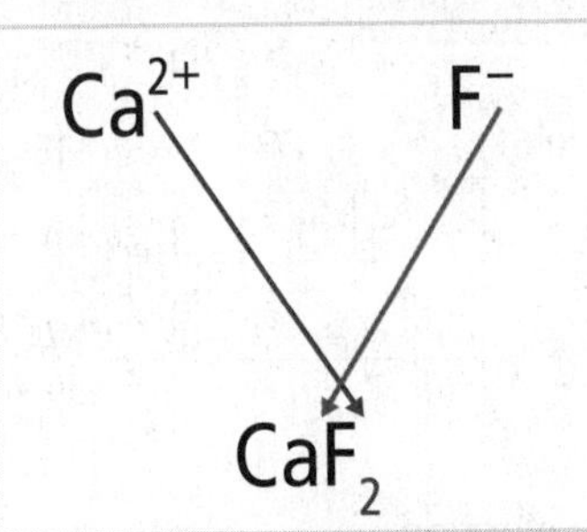

FIGURE 14: Crisscross method

The crisscross method, shown in Figure 14, is a shortcut for determining the formula of an ionic compound. Using this method, the charge for each ion becomes the subscript for the other ion in the formula. For example, to write the formula for calcium fluoride, first determine the charges on each ion. Calcium has a 2+ charge, and fluorine has a 1− charge. Using this method, calcium has a subscript of 1, which is not written, and fluorine has a subscript of 2. This shortcut is useful, but the chemical formula might need to be reduced to its simplest ratio. For example, the formula for iron(II) oxide obtained by the shortcut is Fe_2O_2, which can be reduced to FeO.

ANALYZE Write the ion of each element in the combination. Then use the crisscross method to determine the chemical formula.

Elements	Positive ion	Negative ion	Chemical formula	Chemical name
Magnesium and chlorine	Mg^{2+}	Cl^-	$MgCl_2$	magnesium chloride
Lithium and phosphorus				lithium phosphide
Calcium and sulfur				calcium sulfide
Aluminum and oxygen				aluminum oxide
Aluminum and nitrogen				aluminum nitride

A polyatomic ion is a group of covalently bonded atoms that has a charge and behaves as an ion. To determine the chemical formula for compounds containing a polyatomic ion, follow the same rules about making the compound neutral as with a single-atom ion. For example, when ammonium, NH_4^+, bonds with sulfate, SO_4^{2-}, the resulting compound is ammonium sulfate, $(NH_4)_2SO_4$, a common ingredient in fertilizers.

Analyzing Covalent Compounds

Working with formulas for covalent compounds is more complex than it is for ionic compounds. Many covalent compounds have large and complex molecules, and the arrangement of atoms affects the properties of the molecules. We start our formula work by considering how many electrons atoms must share in order to obtain full energy levels.

FIGURE 15: These models show that four pairs of electrons are shared in a methane molecule.

H· ·C· ·H → H:C:H → H—C—H

As in ionic bonding, each atom in a covalent molecule obtains a stable outer shell, usually in the form of an octet. For example, the carbon atom in Figure 15 shares its four valence electrons with four hydrogen atoms, which each contribute one electron. Each pair of electrons forms a single covalent bond, represented by two dots or a line. This way, the carbon atom obtains an octet. Hydrogen is an exception to the octet rule because a hydrogen atom only needs two electrons to fill its outer shell.

FIGURE 16: Each oxygen atom obtains an octet by forming a double covalent bond.

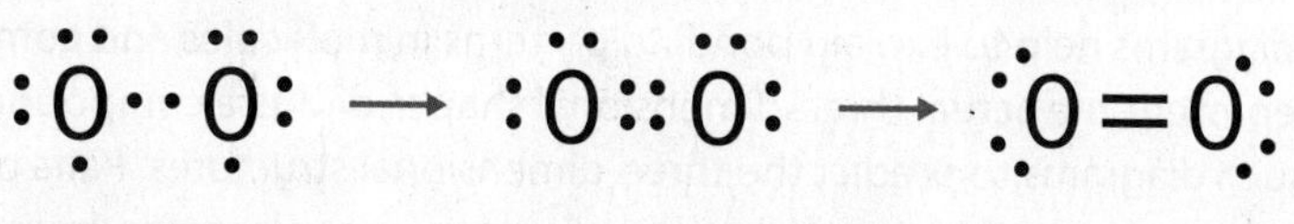

$$:\ddot{O}\cdot\cdot\ddot{O}: \rightarrow :\ddot{O}::\ddot{O}: \rightarrow \ddot{O}=\ddot{O}$$

In some cases, covalent bonds occur as double or triple bonds. A double bond represents four shared electrons, and a triple bond represents six shared electrons. Figure 16 shows an electron-dot diagram of the covalent bond formed between two oxygen atoms. Each oxygen atom has six valence electrons. In order to obtain an octet, the atoms must share four electrons. This results in a double covalent bond, represented by two lines between the atoms. A triple bond is represented by three lines. Triple bonds are the strongest and shortest type of covalent bond, while single bonds are the weakest and longest.

MODEL Model the structure of carbon tetrafluoride, a low-temperature refrigerant and greenhouse gas. It contains one carbon atom and four fluorine atoms.

EXPLAIN How many valence electrons are present in carbon and fluorine, and how are they shared in carbon tetrafluoride? How many bonds are present? Why are the bonds considered covalent?

______

______

______

All models have advantages and limitations. This type of model does not show the actual three-dimensional shape of the carbon tetrafluoride molecule, and real bonds are not made of dots or lines. A more accurate model would consider the size of the atoms and the dynamic structure of the molecule.

Evidence Notebook Determine the chemical formulas for sodium metal, chlorine gas, and sodium chloride. How can you use the electron-dot structures of chlorine gas and sodium metal to predict their reactivity levels and the compound they form when they react?

Hands-On Lab

Modeling the Shapes of Molecules

Electron-dot diagrams help to explain bonding patterns in molecules and compounds, but they do not represent the actual three-dimensional shapes of these compounds. However, you can use such diagrams to predict the three-dimensional structures. Pairs of valence electrons of an atom in a molecule repel other pairs of valence electrons, because like charges repel. Therefore, the three-dimensional structure of a molecule results from the electron pairs arranging themselves as far apart as possible.

FIGURE 17: Ammonia can be modeled using an electron-dot diagram or VSEPR theory.

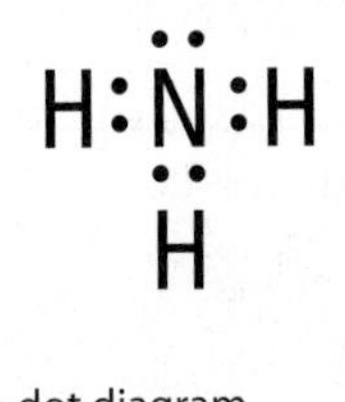

a electron-dot diagram

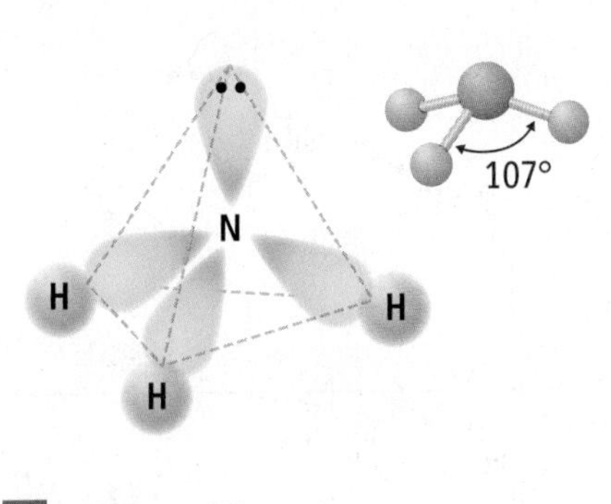

b VSEPR model

This idea is known as valence-shell electron-pair repulsion, or VSEPR. In this lab, you will use electron-dot structures and the VSEPR theory to predict the three-dimensional structures of several covalently bonded molecules.

Consider the example of ammonia shown in Figure 17. The electron-dot diagram shows that ammonia consists of a nitrogen atom bonded to three hydrogen atoms, with one pair of lone electrons. VSEPR theory predicts that the four pairs of electrons surrounding the nitrogen atom will arrange themselves as far apart as possible. Because of the lone pair, there is no atom at one apex of the resulting arrangement of electron pairs. The shape of the molecule is a pyramid with three hydrogen atoms spread apart on one side of the nitrogen atom.

There are a number of shapes that molecules can have, such as linear, pyramidal, or tetrahedral. You will explore some of these shapes in this lab.

The first step in determining molecular shape using VSEPR is to draw an electron-dot diagram of the molecule. Use the periodic table to find the number of valence electrons for each atom. Then, draw a structure that shows the pairs of shared electrons, how many bonds form, and any unshared electrons. The unshared electrons should be indicated in pairs.

RESEARCH QUESTION What shapes can molecules take on, and why is this important in understanding the behavior of substances?

MAKE A CLAIM

How can you determine the shape of a molecule?

POSSIBLE MATERIALS

- indirectly vented chemical splash goggles, nonlatex apron
- foam spheres
- modeling clay, various colors
- molecular modeling kit
- pompoms, various colors
- sticks, craft
- toothpicks

SAFETY INFORMATION

indirectly vented chemical splash goggles

- Wear indirectly vented chemical splash goggles and a nonlatex apron during the setup, hands-on, and takedown segments of the activity.
- Use caution when using sharp materials, which can cut or puncture skin.
- Wash your hands with soap and water immediately after completing this activity.

PLAN THE INVESTIGATION

In this activity, you will model the molecular shapes of six substances: carbon tetrachloride, oxygen difluoride, carbon disulfide, phosphorus tribromide, methanal, and silicon dioxide. You will need to plan how you will build your models, including the materials that you will use to model the atoms, the bonds, and the lone electron pairs. Write your procedure and a safety plan in your Evidence Notebook. Be sure to include enough detail that someone reading your procedure would be able to replicate your models. Have your teacher approve your procedure and your safety plan.

COLLECT DATA

Once your teacher has approved your plans, construct a data table to record the following information for each molecule you model: chemical formula, electron-dot diagram, and a drawing of the model showing its molecular shape. Any other types of information that will aid in your understanding of the models you build should also be included in the data table. Now, build your models.

CONDUCT RESEARCH

Research each molecule in this investigation to find out its applications and whether the shape of the molecule is an important factor in these applications. Be sure to research the safety data sheet (SDS) for each molecule and record any safety implications or other important concerns for storage, handling, and disposal for each substance.

ANALYZE

1. Research the shape of each of the six molecules. How close were your models to the actual shapes?

2. How could you revise your models to be more accurate based on your research?

3. How might the shape of the compound influence how it behaves?

DRAW CONCLUSIONS

Write a conclusion that addresses each of the points below.

Claim How can you determine the shape of a molecule?

Evidence What evidence from your investigation supports your claim?

Reasoning How does your evidence support or refute your claim?

EXTEND

Based on your results, what should the shape of a molecule be that consists of one atom of a Group 15 element and three atoms of a Group 17 element? Explain your answer.

Evidence Notebook How do valence electrons in sodium chloride determine its structure as an ionic compound? How does that compare to the valence electrons in the molecular structures you investigated in this lab?

Guided Research

Asking Questions about Minerals

If you pick up a rock and look at it closely using a hand lens, you can often detect crystal shapes in its structure. Occasionally, you might even find a rock that is itself a single crystal. Rocks are made up of one or more minerals. Minerals are naturally occurring solid materials with a definite chemical composition and a crystalline structure.

What kind of chemical compounds would you expect minerals to be composed of? In general, minerals are composed of ionic compounds. Most minerals consist of compounds of one or more metallic elements bonded to nonmetallic elements or polyatomic ions composed of nonmetallic elements.

A familiar use of minerals is for decoration. Gems are minerals that are especially popular in jewelry. A key part of the attractiveness of many gems is their color. The color is caused by the ways different minerals reflect or absorb light. In many cases, the color of a mineral is determined by the metal atoms it contains. The addition of a small amount of different metal atoms in the crystal lattice can change the appearance of the mineral. This occurs because the electrons of each element interact with other atoms in specific ways. Differences in electron interactions affect how the mineral interacts with light, as shown in Figure 18.

Quartz, for example, is an ionic compound of silicon and oxygen that is colorless and transparent. However, the addition of a small amount of iron to the quartz forms amethyst, a mineral with a violet color.

Transition metals generally produce minerals with strong colors. Minerals containing copper ions are blue or green. Chromium causes red and green colors, depending on other components. For example, red rubies consist mostly of aluminum oxide, but their color comes from the presence of chromium compounds in the crystal. Small amounts of iron and titanium in sapphires give them a rich blue color. In other minerals, iron imparts a reddish color.

Language Arts Connection Research minerals that are found in your area. Consider the following when conducting your research:

- What features about different minerals stand out to you?
- How are the features related to the chemical composition of the mineral?
- How have people manipulated mineral structure for their own needs?

Present your information as a slide show, photo gallery, or live presentation. Prepare a list of sources used in your research.

FIGURE 18: The color of a mineral is often determined by metal ions in the crystal.

a Amethyst gets its purple color from iron.

b Copper causes the green bands in malachite.

c The transition metal vanadium makes vanadinite red.

MORE PRACTICE WITH FORMULAS

TYPES OF BONDING IN SOLIDS

TEACHING TYPES OF BONDING

Go online to choose one of these other paths.

Lesson Self-Check

CAN YOU EXPLAIN THE PHENOMENON?

FIGURE 19: The reaction between sodium metal and chlorine gas produces sodium chloride.

a Sodium reacting in a beaker of chlorine gas

b Samples of sodium chloride, sodium metal, and chlorine gas

Chlorine is a versatile element. It is used as a disinfectant and to make many household products, and it has even been developed as a chemical weapon. Sodium metal is used as a coolant in nuclear reactors, but sodium salts are used more commonly than the metal itself. Sodium salts are used in a variety of applications, including deicing roads and softening water. One of the most common sodium salts is sodium chloride, also known as table salt. Unlike its individual components, sodium chloride is extremely stable and does not readily react with other substances.

Evidence Notebook Refer to your notes in your Evidence Notebook to explain why sodium metal and chlorine gas are dangerous and reactive on their own but combine to form the stable compound sodium chloride. Your explanation should include a discussion of the electrical forces within and between atoms in each substance. Using this information, address the following:

Claim Make a claim about why the compound sodium chloride has properties that are so different from the properties of sodium and chlorine.

Evidence What evidence supports your claim? For example, what differences in chemical structure could explain the differences in reactivity among the three substances?

Reasoning Explain how the evidence you gave supports your claim about why sodium chloride is different from sodium metal and chlorine gas.

Name ______________________ Date ______________

CHECKPOINTS

Check Your Understanding

1. Which of the following best explains why ionic crystals are brittle?

- ○ **a.** They have low melting points.
- ○ **b.** They have high melting points.
- ○ **c.** The strong ionic bonds do not allow flexibility within the structures.
- ○ **d.** The forces of attraction between positive and negative ions are weak, so they break easily.

2. Categorize each compound as exhibiting ionic bonding or covalent bonding.

a. LiF ______________

b. Cl_2 ______________

c. NH_3 ______________

d. $CaCl_2$ ______________

e. NaOH ______________

f. FeO ______________

g. NO_2 ______________

h. H_2O ______________

3. A student tests a solid sample of a compound and determines that it does not conduct an electric current. When the compound is dissolved in water, the solution does conduct an electric current. What type of bonding does the compound have?

- ○ **a.** covalent
- ○ **b.** ionic
- ○ **c.** metallic

4. A long, thin sample of a substance bends easily. When the substance is placed in an electric circuit and the switch is closed, an LED light turns on. What type of bonding holds the particles of the substance together?

- ○ **a.** covalent
- ○ **b.** ionic
- ○ **c.** metallic

5. Select the correct terms to complete the statement about bonding.

A nitrogen molecule, N_2, has less | more potential energy than two separate nitrogen atoms, so the molecule is less | more stable. Each nitrogen atom has five valence electrons, so a nitrogen atom needs one | two | three electron(s) to reach maximum stability. Therefore, the diatomic nitrogen molecule has three | six electrons that are shared between the atoms, forming a triple covalent bond.

6. Use the crisscross method and the periodic table to determine the values of x and y in the formula for aluminum sulfide, Al_xS_y.

x = ______________

y = ______________

7. Which statements correctly describe the compound potassium bromide? Select all correct answers.

- ☐ **a.** The compound is considered a salt.
- ☐ **b.** It contains potassium and bromide ions in a one-to-one ratio.
- ☐ **c.** Potassium bromide likely has a higher melting point than does candle wax.
- ☐ **d.** The electronegativities of the two component atoms are very similar.

8. The electronegativities of carbon and sulfur are almost the same. Both elements form covalently bonded compounds with oxygen. Why are the molecular shapes of carbon dioxide, CO_2, and sulfur dioxide, SO_2, different?

- ○ **a.** Carbon has a smaller atomic radius than sulfur.
- ○ **b.** A molecule of SO_2 has a lone pair of electrons, but CO_2 does not.
- ○ **c.** A molecule of CO_2 has one single and one double bond, but SO_2 does not.
- ○ **d.** A molecule that contains carbon cannot have a linear shape.

CHECKPOINTS (continued)

9. Which compound likely has a higher melting point—aluminum trichloride, $AlCl_3$, or phosphorus trichloride, PCl_3? Use the periodic table to support your claim, and explain your reasoning.

10. Water, H_2O, consists of a central oxygen atom bound to two hydrogen atoms. Draw an electron-dot structure of water. Below, explain how you determined the number of bonds and unpaired electrons, the types of bonds, and, if applicable, where the unpaired electrons are located.

11. Potassium metal is mixed with argon gas in one flask and with chlorine gas in another flask. Use the periodic table to explain what happens in each flask. If you predict that a reaction will occur, describe the type of compound that forms.

MAKE YOUR OWN STUDY GUIDE

In your Evidence Notebook, design a study guide that supports the main ideas from this lesson:

Patterns in the periodic table can be used to predict the types of bonds that will form between atoms.

The properties of substances are related to the atomic structures of the substances.

Patterns in valence electrons can be used to predict the structure of substances.

Remember to include the following information in your study guide:

- Use examples that model main ideas.
- Record explanations for the phenomena you investigated.
- Use evidence to support your explanations. Your support can include drawings, data, graphs, laboratory conclusions, and other evidence recorded throughout the lesson.

Consider how patterns of atomic structure, as shown in the periodic table, can provide evidence for explanations of properties of chemical compounds at the bulk scale.

3.2

Analyzing the Properties of Compounds and Solutions

Undersea organisms depend on substances that are dissolved in ocean water.

CAN YOU EXPLAIN THE PHENOMENON?

There is more than just salt (sodium chloride) in the ocean. There are many different salts, minerals, and gas molecules dissolved in ocean water that undersea organisms of all kinds require for life. You know that oxygen is a gas, but fish do not get oxygen from bubbles of oxygen in the water. Rather, individual oxygen molecules are mixed together with, and dissolved in, the water molecules. Water molecules have unique properties that allow it to dissolve many different substances. In particular, attractive forces between water molecules, and also between water molecules and dissolved substances, allow them all to mix freely with one another.

EXPLAIN How is water important in the Earth system?

Evidence Notebook As you explore the lesson, gather evidence to explain why water has unique properties and provide examples of how these properties are important in the Earth system.

Hands-On Lab

Exploring Intermolecular Forces in Liquids

Patterns in how liquids behave can be explained in terms of patterns in the intermolecular forces between their molecules. Intermolecular forces are the forces of attraction between molecules. When a substance has strong intermolecular forces, that substance requires more energy than a substance with weaker intermolecular forces requires to go from the solid state to the liquid state, or from the liquid state to the gas state. Intermolecular forces also affect surface tension, which is a force that tends to pull adjacent parts of a liquid's surface together.

In this lab, you will design a procedure to analyze intermolecular forces in four common household chemicals—water, acetone, isopropyl alcohol, and glycerol. Figure 1 shows the structures of these substances. You will collect data on the evaporation rates and surface tensions of these compounds.

RESEARCH QUESTION How do intermolecular forces determine the uses of commonly-used molecular compounds?

FIGURE 1: The molecular structures of water, acetone, isopropyl alcohol, and glycerol

Water	Acetone	Isopropyl Alcohol	Glycerol
O H H	H O H H—C—C—C—H H H	H OH H H—C—C—C—H H H H	OH OH OH H—C—C—C—H H H H

MAKE A CLAIM

Which substance do you think will have the strongest intermolecular forces, and which the weakest? Explain your reasoning.

MATERIALS

- indirectly vented chemical splash goggles, nonlatex apron, and nitrile gloves
- acetone in dropper bottle
- flasks with stoppers (4), each containing water, acetone, isopropyl alcohol, or glycerol
- glycerol in dropper bottle
- isopropyl alcohol in dropper bottle
- marker
- stopwatch or clock with second hand
- water in dropper bottle
- wax paper (1 sheet)

SAFETY INFORMATION

- Wear indirectly vented chemical splash goggles, a nonlatex apron, and nitrile gloves during the setup, hands-on, and takedown segments of the activity.
- All operations in which noxious or poisonous gases or flammable vapors are used or produced must be carried out in the fume hood.

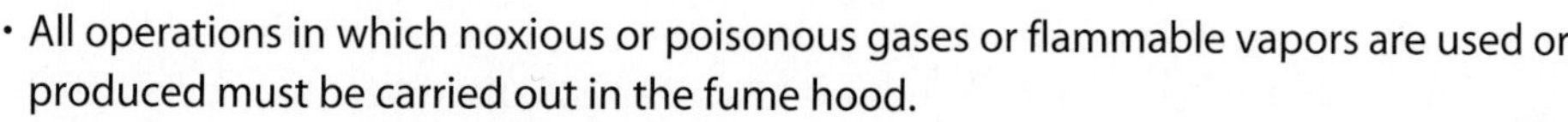

- Never pour chemicals, either used or unused, back into their original container. Dispose of chemicals according to your teacher's instructions.
- Use caution when working with glassware, which can shatter and cut skin.
- Wash your hands with soap and water immediately after completing this activity.

indirectly vented chemical splash goggles

PLAN THE INVESTIGATION

1. In your Evidence Notebook, develop a procedure and safety plan to test the surface tension and the rate of evaporation of water, acetone, isopropyl alcohol, and glycerol.
2. Draw a data table in your Evidence Notebook for recording your observations and data. When designing your data table, consider what types of data would be appropriate for analyzing surface tension and rate of evaporation.
3. Have your teacher approve your plans before you begin your work. If you need additional materials to complete your procedure, discuss these with your teacher.
4. Clean up your lab area and dispose of your lab materials as instructed by your teacher.

DRAW CONCLUSIONS

Write a conclusion that addresses each of the points below.

Claim Based on the patterns you observed in the surface tension and evaporation rate of the compounds, how would you rank the strength of the intermolecular forces in the compounds from strongest to weakest?

Evidence Give specific examples from your data to support your claim.

Reasoning Explain how the evidence you gave supports your claim. Describe, in detail, the connections between the evidence you cited and the argument you are making.

Evidence Notebook What did you discover from this investigation about the properties of water that make it different from the other substances?

Explaining Intermolecular Forces

FIGURE 2: Static charges on a balloon affect water molecules.

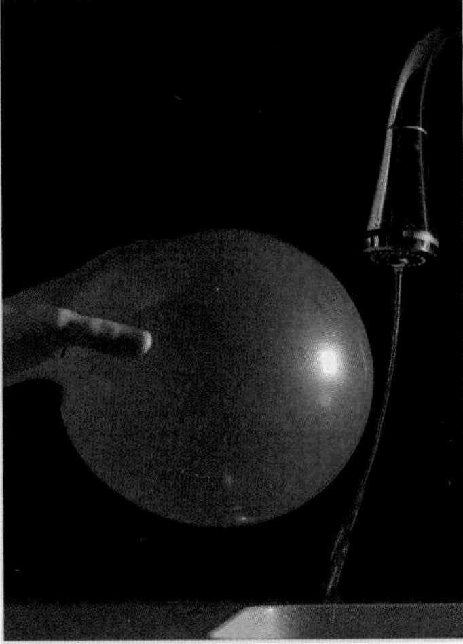

Rubbing a balloon with a cloth generates "static" that attracts certain substances, such as the stream of water shown in Figure 2. Similarly, you may have noticed that when clothes are first taken out of a dryer, they stick to each other, a phenomenon known as "static cling."

INFER What do you think is happening at the atomic scale that causes the water in Figure 2 to bend toward the balloon?

____

____

Forces between Particles

FIGURE 3: Charged particles may attract or repel each other.

opposite charges attract

like charges repel

Most materials have no overall charge because they have equal numbers of protons and electrons. When you rub a balloon with a cloth, however, electrons are transferred from the cloth to the balloon. This transfer makes some atoms in the cloth positively charged and some atoms in the balloon negatively charged. Because opposite charges attract, positively charged particles will stick to the negatively charged balloon. Phenomena related to static electricity are caused by forces between electric charges that attract or repel each other, as seen in Figure 3. Repulsions and attractions due to electric charge are known as electric forces. Another name for electric force is the Coulomb force.

The attractive forces that exist between the particles of a substance affect the physical and chemical properties of that substance. Ionic compounds have strong attractive forces that hold ions tightly together. Thus, these compounds typically have relatively high melting points.

Math Connection

Calculating Force

Coulomb's law describes how to calculate electric force. This law states that the magnitude of the electric force ($F_{electric}$) between two point charges (q_1 and q_2) is directly related to the product of the charges and inversely related to the square of the distance (d) between them. The Coulomb constant (k_C) is a constant used in the calculation of electric force. The equation for Coulomb's law is:

$$F_{electric} = k_C\frac{q_1q_2}{d^2}$$

Collaborate As charge increases, electric force increases. However, if the distance between two charges doubles, electric force decreases by a factor of four. With a partner, discuss how the equation for this law demonstrates these relationships between charge, distance, and force.

Uneven Molecular Charges

Why do different molecular compounds exhibit different intermolecular forces? The answer has to do with the type of atoms in a molecule and how they are arranged in the 3-dimensional space of the molecule relative to each other. Recall that electronegativity is the tendency of an atom to pull electrons toward itself. As Figure 4 shows, a *nonpolar covalent bond* forms when the bonding electrons are evenly shared between two atoms. On the other hand, if one of the atoms has a higher electronegativity than the other atom, the more electronegative atom attracts the bonding electrons more strongly than does the other atom. This results in the formation of a *polar covalent bond*. This uneven distribution of charges in a molecule is known as polarity.

FIGURE 4: In a nonpolar covalent bond, the electron cloud is evenly dispersed. In a polar covalent bond, it is not.

nonpolar covalent bond

polar covalent bond

The ball-and-stick model shown in Figure 5 represents the polar molecule iodine monochloride, ICl. The chlorine end of the molecule has a partial negative charge, and the iodine end has a partial positive charge. These two ends are called poles, and a molecule with two poles is said to have a *dipole*. Its dipole is represented by an arrow with a head that points toward the negative pole and a crossed tail near the positive pole. Partial charges are represented by the lowercase Greek letter delta, δ. A partial positive charge is shown as δ+, and a partial negative charge is shown as δ−.

FIGURE 5: Iodine monochloride has a dipole.

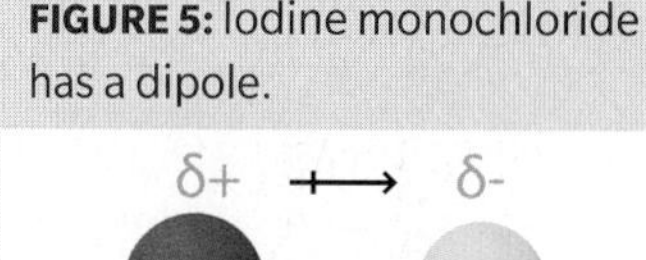

EXPLAIN Select the correct terms to complete the statement.

Water is a polar molecule. The oxygen atom is more | less electronegative than the hydrogen atom, so the oxygen atom has a partial negative | positive charge, and each hydrogen atom has a partial negative | positive charge. The oxygen atom of a water molecule is attracted to a hydrogen | an oxygen atom of another water molecule.

The polarity of diatomic molecules such as ICl is determined by just one bond. For molecules that contain more than two atoms, polarity is determined by both the polarity of the individual bonds and the three-dimensional arrangement of the molecule. The ball-and-stick models in Figure 6 show how the three-dimensional arrangement of bonds in a molecule affects the overall polarity of the molecule.

FIGURE 6: The three-dimensional arrangement of a molecule affects the overall polarity of the molecule.

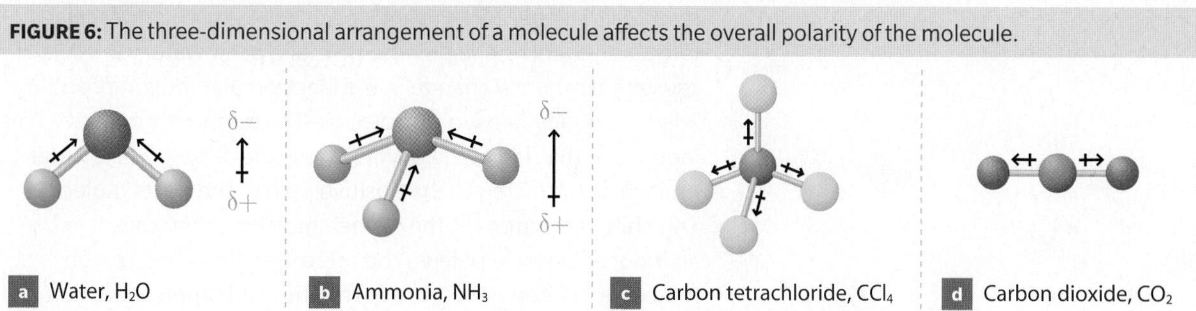

a Water, H_2O b Ammonia, NH_3 c Carbon tetrachloride, CCl_4 d Carbon dioxide, CO_2

Since H_2O and NH_3 have a bent shape, the bond polarities in each molecule combine to give one end of the molecule a partial positive charge and the other end a partial negative charge. Thus, these molecules are polar. Carbon dioxide, by contrast, is nonpolar, even though it has two polar bonds. The carbon dioxide molecule is linear, so polarities of the two bonds cancel each other out, and there is no net dipole in the molecule.

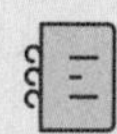

Evidence Notebook How can understanding the polarity of water help you design detergents in your unit project?

Dipole-Dipole Forces

In the molecule iodine monochloride, the highly electronegative chlorine atom has a partial negative charge, and the iodine atom has a partial positive charge. As Figure 7 shows, the partially negative and partially positive ends of neighboring iodine monochloride molecules attract each other.

FIGURE 7: The arrows show the dipole-dipole forces between the positive and negative ends of neighboring ICl molecules.

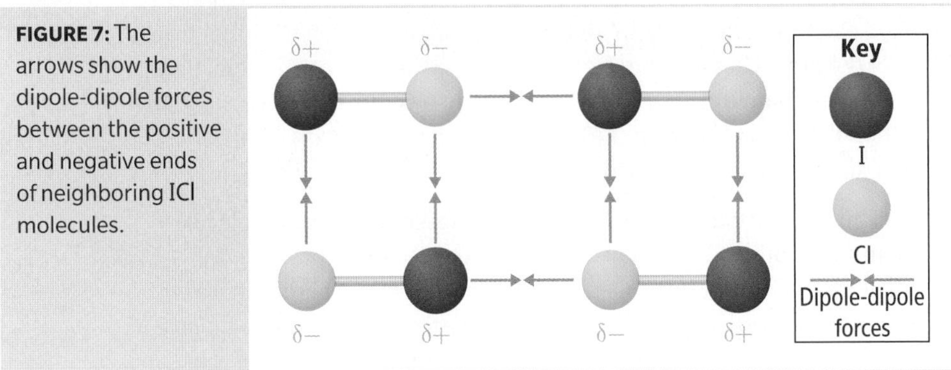

When a liquid is heated, energy is added to the system. The kinetic energy of the liquid's molecules increase, and they move faster. As the temperature approaches the boiling point, the molecules move fast enough to overcome the attractive forces between molecules. They pull away from each other and enter the gaseous state. The stronger the forces are between molecules, the higher the boiling point will be. Boiling point is a good measure of the attractive forces between molecules of a liquid.

APPLY Select the correct terms to complete the statement.

ICl is a polar | nonpolar molecule, whereas Br_2 is polar | nonpolar. The boiling point of ICl is likely to be higher | lower than the boiling point of Br_2. This is due to dipole-dipole intermolecular interactions between two positive | two negative | positive and negative portions of polar molecules.

FIGURE 8: Dipole-induced dipole interaction

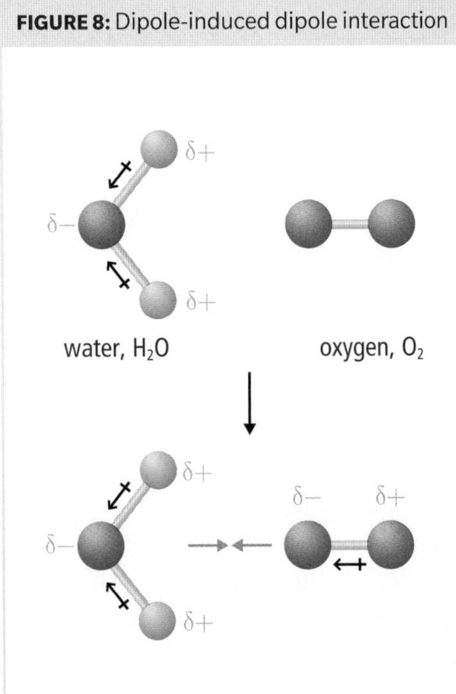

A polar molecule also can induce the formation of a dipole in a nonpolar molecule by temporarily attracting the electrons in the nonpolar molecule. This results in a short-term intermolecular force. For example, the positive pole of a polar water molecule causes a temporary change in the electron distribution of an adjacent nonpolar oxygen molecule. The temporary negative pole induced in the side of the oxygen molecule closest to the water molecule is attracted to the positive pole of the water molecule. This shift of electrons in the oxygen molecule then causes an induced positive pole on the opposite side of the oxygen molecule, as shown in Figure 8. This induced dipole attraction allows oxygen to be dissolved in water, which is important for sustaining life in aquatic environments.

EXPLAIN Do you think a dipole-induced dipole interaction is stronger or weaker than a dipole-dipole interaction? Explain your answer.

Hydrogen Bonding

Some dipole-dipole interactions can be especially strong. For example, in some hydrogen-containing compounds such as hydrogen fluoride, HF; water, H_2O; and ammonia, NH_3; a special kind of dipole-dipole interaction exists.

Molecules that contain a hydrogen atom bonded to the highly electronegative atoms fluorine, oxygen, or nitrogen are strongly polar. Particularly strong dipole-dipole intermolecular forces, called hydrogen bonds, exist between molecules of these compounds. The highly electronegative atom attracts the electrons in the bond away from the hydrogen atom and toward itself. Consequently, the highly electronegative atom has a partial negative charge and the hydrogen atom has a partial positive charge. The partial positive charge on one molecule is attracted to a partial negative charge on a nearby molecule.

MODEL Label the partial negative and partial positive charges on the water molecules. Red spheres indicate oxygen atoms, blue spheres hydrogen atoms. Then, draw dotted lines to represent hydrogen bonds.

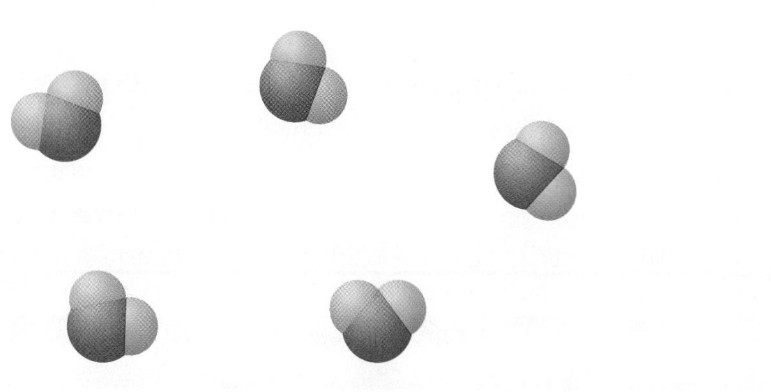

Surface Tension

FIGURE 9: Droplets of mercury, water, dimethyl sulfoxide, and acetone have different amounts of surface tension.

The attraction between molecules of the same substance is known as cohesion. Cohesion between neighboring water molecules is especially noticeable at the surface of water. These water molecules form many hydrogen bonds with the water molecules beneath them and beside them, but not with the molecules in the air above them. This causes the surface water molecules to be drawn together, forming a spherical shape. This cohesion at the surface of a liquid is known as surface tension. Figure 9 shows liquids that have different amounts of surface tension. The stronger the intermolecular forces in a liquid are, the greater its surface tension will be.

Surface tension explains how some small insects such as water striders can stand on water's surface even though they have greater density than water. The surface tension of water also lowers its rate of evaporation. In general, a substance with strong intermolecular forces will have high surface tension and require more energy to disrupt those interactions. Therefore, substances with high surface tension also have a high boiling point.

Collaborate With a partner, explain how hydrogen bonding at the molecular scale explains surface tension in water.

The Low Density of Ice

If you have ever frozen a full container of water you have discovered that, unlike most other substances, water expands when it freezes. Like many of water's unusual properties, this is related to the formation of hydrogen bonds. When water freezes, the molecules lose kinetic energy and slow down, so more hydrogen bonds form between them. The water molecules form a network structure in which each water molecule is held away from nearby molecules at a fixed distance.

FIGURE 10: Water molecules are arranged differently in solid water than in liquid water.

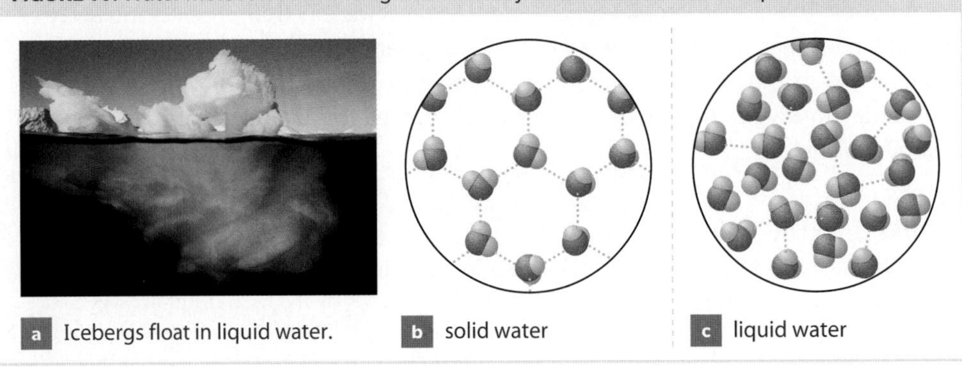

a Icebergs float in liquid water. b solid water c liquid water

INFER Complete the statement to explain why icebergs float in liquid water.

The amount of space between molecules in solid water is less | greater than that in liquid water. As a result, the density of solid water is less | greater than that of liquid water. Because substances with lower density float | sink in substances with higher density, ice floats in liquid water. This explains why icebergs float, instead of sink, in liquid water.

Patterns

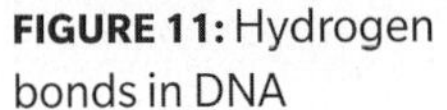

Living Systems

FIGURE 11: Hydrogen bonds in DNA

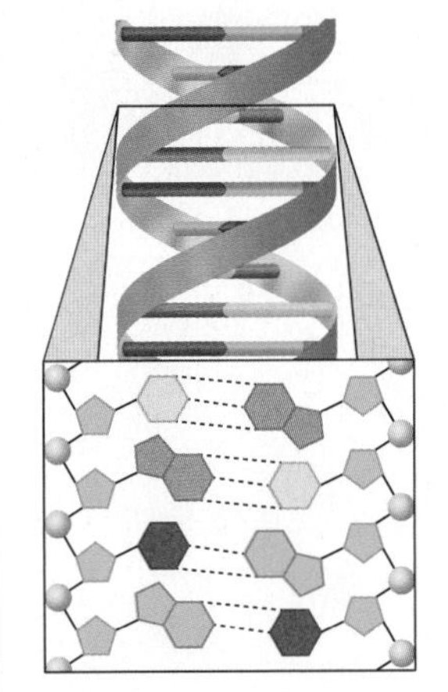

Hydrogen bonds play an important role in living organisms. For example, DNA molecules are held together by hydrogen bonds. Patterns of DNA at the molecular scale determine the traits of an organism. A DNA molecule looks like a long twisted ladder, with two chains of sugar molecules and phosphate groups making up the sides of the ladder and nitrogen bases sticking into the center like steps of the ladder. DNA is stabilized by millions of pairs of nitrogen bases that are held together by hydrogen bonds. Because individual hydrogen bonds are relatively weak, they can break to allow the chains to separate during DNA replication and protein synthesis.

Language Arts Connection Research the structure of DNA. Why is it important that hydrogen bonds, not ionic or covalent bonds, hold the two strands of DNA together? Develop a presentation answering this question, citing specific textual evidence.

Evidence Notebook How do the intermolecular forces between water molecules explain the unique properties of water, and how do they make water important in the Earth system?

Describing Solutions

If you've ever looked at a bottle of oil and vinegar, you probably noticed that the oil settles in a layer above the vinegar, which is a mixture of acetic acid and water. You can mix the oil and vinegar by shaking the bottle, but they quickly separate into layers again. This is what people mean when they say that "oil and water don't mix." Figure 12 shows what happens when you try to mix oil and water.

FIGURE 12: Cooking oil being poured into water

There are many substances that do mix easily. For example, both salt and sugar readily dissolve in water. Heating or cooling the water can also have a strong effect on whether a substance will dissolve in water and the speed at which it dissolves.

Collaborate Discuss with a partner why some compounds dissolve in water while others do not. What properties of water do you think contribute to its ability to dissolve some compounds?

Vinegar, salt water, and sugar water are examples of solutions. A solution is a homogeneous mixture, which means that two or more substances are uniformly dispersed at the molecular level. Solutions contain both a solvent and a solute. The solvent is the substance in which the solute dissolves. The solvent usually makes up the greatest amount of the solution. Solute particles may be atoms, molecules, or ions. They are so small that they maintain their even distribution without settling. One substance is *soluble* in another if it can dissolve in that substance.

A solution that contains the maximum amount of dissolved solute is *saturated*. If you increase the amount of solvent in a saturated solution, the solution becomes *unsaturated* and you can dissolve more solute. For any given solution, there is a maximum ratio of solute to solvent that the solution can contain at a given temperature.

The Dissolving Process

Table salt, NaCl, is made of tiny, cubic-shaped crystals. When stirred into water, however, salt does not keep this crystal shape. The crystals quickly begin to break apart into separate sodium and chloride ions. When a substance dissolves and becomes a solute, it breaks into smaller and smaller pieces until it is thoroughly mixed with the solvent at the particle level.

PREDICT Why do you think stirring, shaking, or heating a mixture help a solute dissolve more quickly?

FIGURE 13: Dissolution occurs in a system when the particles of a solute move away from each other and become mixed in with the solvent particles.

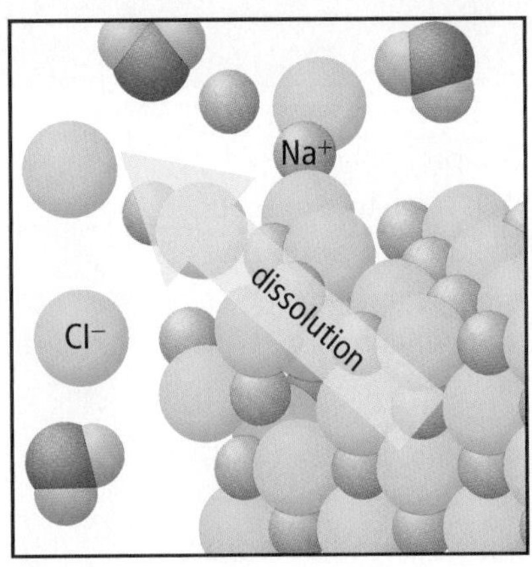

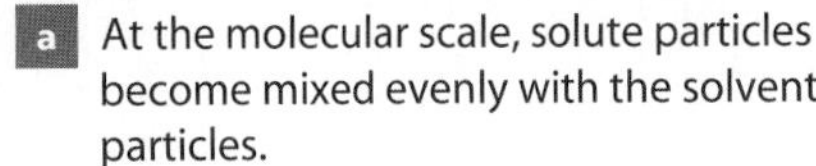

a At the molecular scale, solute particles become mixed evenly with the solvent particles.

b At the observable scale, the solute will seem to disappear after it is thoroughly mixed with the solvent.

Figure 13a shows what happens at a particle scale when sodium chloride dissolves in water. For any soluble compound, there is a limit to how much of it can dissolve in the solvent. The amount of solute that can dissolve depends on the volume of the solvent and on the temperature of the solution. For gases, it also depends on pressure. Solubility is the extent to which a solute can dissolve in a solvent at a given temperature and pressure. Increasing the temperature of a solution generally increases the solubility of a solute in the solvent. Decreasing the temperature generally decreases the solubility, which might cause some of the dissolved solute to come out of solution and form a crystalline solid again.

Because dissolution happens at the interface between the dissolving substance and the solvent, the surface area of the solute affects how fast dissolution happens. Think about what happens to a single crystal of salt when it is placed into water. As the salt dissolves, only the particles on the surface of the crystal touch the water. The rate of dissolving depends on the surface area of the crystal. If you were to break the single salt crystal into smaller crystals before mixing, the salt would dissolve faster. The separate crystals have a greater surface area that can interact with the water.

MODEL Draw a model on the particle scale showing how patterns in the interaction of solvent particles with a large block of solute are different from patterns in the interaction of solvent particles with finely powdered solute.

The solvent of a solution can be either a solid, a liquid, or a gas. The same is true for the solute. The table gives examples of solute and solvent combinations in various solutions.

Collaborate Examine the table showing different kinds of solutions. With a partner, discuss other common examples of solutions you can think of.

Examples of Solutions		
Example	**Solute State**	**Solvent State**
oxygen in nitrogen	gas	gas
carbon dioxide in water	gas	liquid
alcohol in water	liquid	liquid
mercury in silver and tin	liquid	solid
sugar in water	solid	liquid
copper in nickel	solid	solid

Factors Affecting Solubility

Many solutions used in chemistry have liquid solvents. A solution in which the solvent is water is called an *aqueous solution*. Chemical formulas of solutes in water are sometimes labeled (*aq*) to identify them as solutes in an aqueous solution.

Solubility and Polarity

Recall that water molecules are polar. Oxygen atoms have a slightly stronger attraction for electrons than hydrogen atoms do. When crystals of an ionic solid, such as sodium chloride, NaCl, dissolve in water, the electrical forces in the positive and negative ends of water molecules separate the sodium and chloride ions. The negatively-charged parts of water molecules attract and surround the positive ions of the ionic solid. The positively-charged parts of water molecules attract and surround the negative ions of the ionic solid. This process, called *hydration,* is how ionic compounds dissolve in water.

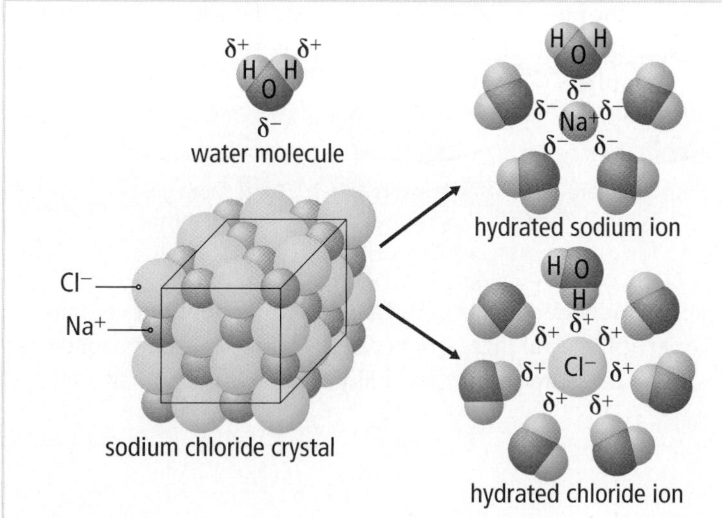

FIGURE 14: Water's polarity allows it to hydrate the positive and negative ions of an ionic solid. This conceptual model shows that the partial negative charge of water is attracted to the positive ion. The partial positive charge of water is attracted to the negative ion.

Although not all substances dissolve in water, water is sometimes referred to as "the universal solvent." The ability to dissolve many different covalent and ionic compounds is unique to polar solvents such as water.

INFER Complete the statement about the behavior of nonpolar solvents.

Ionic compounds would generally be soluble | not soluble in nonpolar solvents. Nonpolar solvents have | do not have the charges necessary to draw the ions out of the crystal and into solution.

Explore Online

Hands-On Lab

Temperature and Solubility
Investigate how temperature affects the solubility of a substance.

Nonpolar substances, such as fats, oils, and greases, do not easily dissolve in polar liquids because the forces between the polar molecules are stronger than the forces between polar and nonpolar molecules. This is why oil and water form layers instead of mixing. Liquids that are not soluble in each other are called *immiscible*. Nonpolar substances generally do dissolve in nonpolar liquids, such as gasoline and carbon tetrachloride. The intermolecular forces are weak in nonpolar solvents, so solvent and solute particles can mix freely. Liquids that dissolve freely in one another in any proportion are called *miscible*.

Collaborate A common way to remember the relationship between polarity and solubility is the phrase "like dissolves like." With a partner, explain how this description is useful for determining the solubility of substances.

Solubility and Pressure

Because the particles in liquids and solids are already very close together, pressure has little effect on the solubility of substances in these states. Changes in pressure, however, do affect the solubility of gases. Imagine you have a closed container containing a liquid and a gas, as shown in Figure 15. The liquid is the solvent and the gas above it is the solute. When the pressure on the system is increased, the gas and liquid particles collide more often than they did at the original pressure. As a result, more gas dissolves in the liquid.

FIGURE 15: A change in pressure affects the rate at which gas particles encounter the liquid's surface.

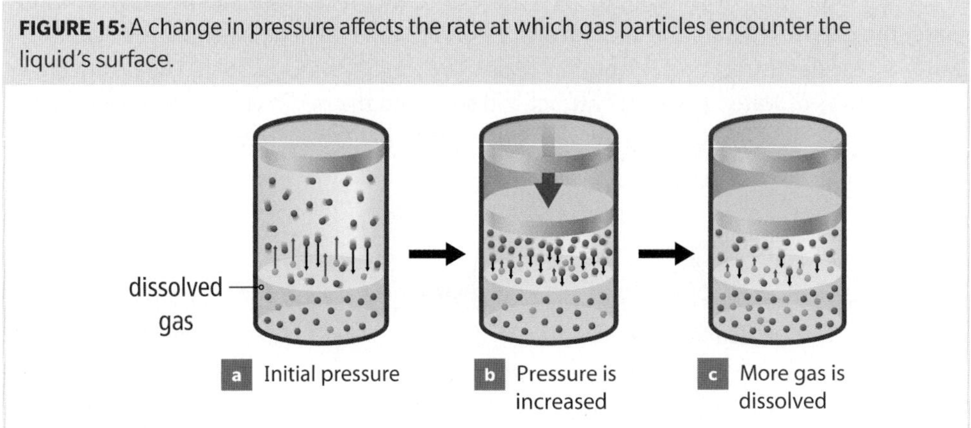

APPLY It may appear that an unopened bottle of carbonated water does not contain any gases, but when you open it the water fizzes. How can the large-scale behavior of this system be explained in terms of pressure and the solubility of particles at a small scale?

Carbonated beverages, those with dissolved carbon dioxide gas, CO_2, demonstrate how pressure affects the solubility of a gas. During production of the beverage, CO_2 gas is forced into the liquid under high pressures. When the bottle is opened, the pressure of the gas suddenly decreases. The CO_2 can now escape from the liquid, causing the drink to fizz.

Solubility and Temperature

Temperature has a different effect on the solubility of gases in water from its effect on the solubility of solids in water. Figures 16 and 17 show how the solubility of different solids and gases change when the temperature is increased.

ANALYZE Based on the patterns in Figure 16, what effect does temperature have on the solubility of a solid in water?

- ○ **a.** Solubility always increases with an increase in temperature.
- ○ **b.** Solubility always decreases with an increase in temperature.
- ○ **c.** Solubility generally increases with an increase in temperature, but sometimes decreases.
- ○ **d.** Solubility generally decreases with an increase in temperature, but sometimes increases.

Solubility of Solids in Water

FIGURE 16: Effect of temperature on the solubility of a solid in water

Solubility of Gases in Water

FIGURE 17: Effect of temperature on the solubility of a gas in water

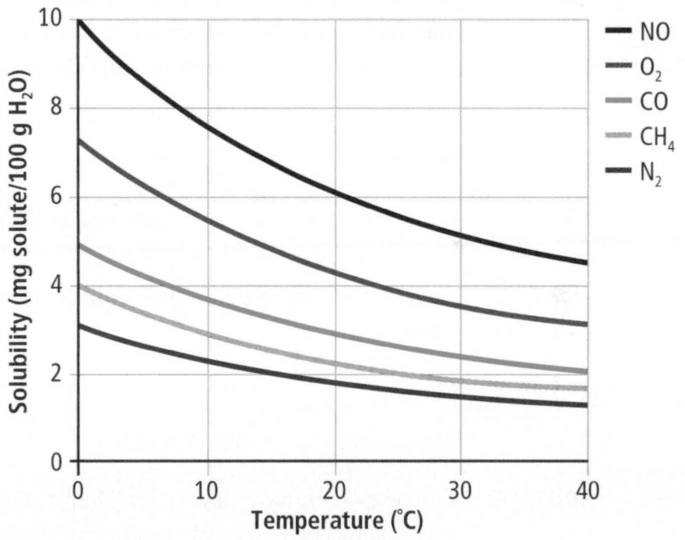

For a solid dissolved in a liquid, increasing the temperature generally increases its solubility. The effects shown in Figure 16 on an observable scale can be explained on the scale of particles. When the temperature is increased, the particles of the solution have more kinetic energy. The increased movement allows the solvent particles to surround and dissolve the solute particles more effectively.

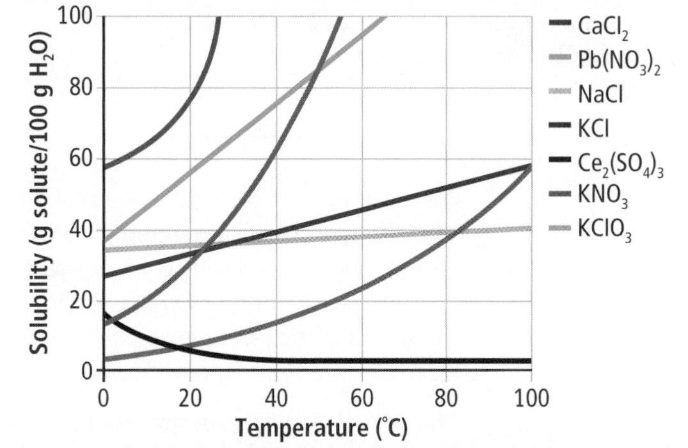

The effect of temperature on solubility is different for a gas dissolved in a liquid. As shown in Figure 17, as temperature increases, the gas particles have more kinetic energy and are better able to escape from the liquid solvent. For all gases, increasing temperature decreases the solubility of the gas. As with liquids and solids, polarity also affects the solubility of the gas particles.

INFER Would you expect an opened can of carbonated water to go "flat" more quickly if it was cold or warm? Use evidence from the graph to support your claim.

Problem Solving

Measuring Solution Concentration

Just as objects are sometimes counted in dozens, chemical amounts are expressed in units of *moles* (mol). Given the incredibly small size of atoms, the number of atoms in a sample large enough to be visible is very large. A mole is 6.02×10^{23}, and represents the number of particles, whether they are atoms, ions, or molecules. It is used to convert mass to number of particles. For example, because an atom of potassium has greater mass than an atom of sodium, one gram of potassium has fewer atoms than one gram of sodium.

The periodic table shows the atomic mass of each element, which is the mass of one mole of atoms of that element. For example, using the periodic table, you will find that one mole of oxygen atoms has a mass of 15.999 grams, whereas one mole of iron atoms has a mass of 55.85 grams.

The molar mass of a compound is the mass of one mole of molecules or formula units of that compound. To find the molar mass of a compound, you add up the molar masses of the atoms of each element in the compound.

If you know the mass of a sample and its molar mass, you can use the following equation to find the amount in moles.

$$\text{amount (mol)} = \frac{\text{mass (g)}}{\text{molar mass (g/mol)}}$$

SAMPLE PROBLEM Suppose you have a 5.00-g sample of calcium chloride, $CaCl_2$. How many moles of calcium chloride is this?

ANALYZE

Known: mass = 5.00 g $CaCl_2$

Unknown: moles of $CaCl_2$

SOLVE Obtain the atomic masses of calcium and chlorine from the periodic table. Calcium chloride has one atom of calcium and two atoms of chlorine per formula unit, so the molar mass of calcium chloride is 40.08 g/mol + (2 × 35.45 g/mol) = 110.98 g/mol.

To find the amount of calcium chloride in your sample in moles, divide the mass by calcium chloride's molar mass.

$$\frac{5.00\ \cancel{g}}{110.98\ \cancel{g}/\text{mol}} = 0.0451\ \text{mol } CaCl_2$$

PRACTICE PROBLEM **SOLVE** One gallon is about 3.785 liters, and this volume of water has a mass of about 3785 grams. Use the space below to calculate how many moles of water are in one gallon. Report your final answer using the correct number of significant figures.

__________ mol H_2O

The concentration of a solution is the amount of solute in a given amount of solution. The concentration of a solution is usually expressed by the molarity of the solution. *Molarity* (*M*) is the number of moles of solute in one liter of solution, as shown in the following equation.

$$\text{Molarity (M)} = \frac{\text{amount of solute (mol)}}{\text{volume of solution (L)}}$$

For example, a one-molar solution of sodium hydroxide, NaOH, contains one mole of NaOH in every liter of solution. The concentration of a one-molar solution of sodium hydroxide is written as 1 M NaOH.

SAMPLE PROBLEM An IV saline solution commonly found in hospitals contains 9.00 grams of NaCl dissolved in enough solvent to form a solution with a volume of 1.00 L. What is the molarity of the saline solution?

ANALYZE

Known: solute mass = 9.00 g NaCl

solution volume = 1.00 L

Unknown: molarity of NaCl solution

SOLVE Use the periodic table to compute the molar mass of NaCl as 58.44 g/mol. Calculate the molarity using the molar mass of NaCl as a conversion factor.

$$\frac{9.00\ \cancel{\text{g NaCl}}}{1.00\ \text{L solution}} \times \frac{1\ \text{mol NaCl}}{58.44\ \cancel{\text{g NaCl}}} = 0.154\ \text{M NaCl}$$

PRACTICE PROBLEM **SOLVE** A scientist wants to test the effects of different potassium chloride, KCl, solution concentrations. Potassium chloride is sometimes used to treat conditions that result from potassium depletion, such as cardiac or kidney disease. The scientist dissolves 255 g KCl to make a 3.20 L solution. Use the space provided to calculate the molarity of the potassium chloride solution. Report your final answer using the correct number of significant figures.

__________ M KCl

Evidence Notebook How does water's ability to dissolve substances make it important in the Earth system?

Hands-On Lab

Measuring the Electrical Conductivity of Solutions

Conductivity is a measure of how well a solution can carry an electric current. The presence of anions, cations, and pollutants can alter the conductivity of water. Thus, water quality can be determined by measuring its conductivity. You will explore the electrical conductivity of solutions containing various covalent and ionic compounds as solutes.

RESEARCH QUESTION Why might some solutions be better conductors of electrical charge than others?

MAKE A CLAIM

Which of the test solutions will conduct electricity well and which will not? How might the physical and chemical properties of each solution affect their conductivity?

____

____

____

MATERIALS

- indirectly vented chemical splash goggles, nonlatex apron, nitrile gloves
- beaker, 100 mL (8)
- conductivity tester
- paper towels
- wash bottle

Test Solutions

- aluminum chloride, $AlCl_3$, solution, 0.05 M (50 mL)
- calcium chloride, $CaCl_2$, solution, 0.05 M (50 mL)
- distilled water (300 mL)
- ethanol, C_2H_5OH, (50 mL)
- sodium chloride, NaCl, solution, 0.05 M (50 mL)
- sugar water (50 mL)
- tap water (50 mL)

indirectly vented chemical splash goggles

SAFETY INFORMATION

- Wear indirectly vented chemical splash goggles, a nonlatex apron, and nitrile gloves during the setup, hands-on, and takedown segments of the activity.
- Never pour chemicals, either used or unused, back into their original container. Dispose of chemicals according to your teacher's instructions.

PLAN THE INVESTIGATION

In your Evidence Notebook, write a procedure to test the electrical conductivity of the seven test solutions. Consider the accuracy you could achieve based on the limitations of your materials. Your procedure should also include safety considerations and any additional materials you may need. Have your procedure and safety plan checked by your teacher before you begin.

COLLECT DATA

Decide what data to record, the conditions for the measurements, and how many trials you will need to complete. Develop a data table in your Evidence Notebook.

ANALYZE

1. Did the result you found for distilled water match your result for tap water? Explain why the results do or do not make sense.

2. Compare the results you found for NaCl solution and sugar water. Considering the intermolecular forces that exist between the atoms of these molecules, why do you think the results were the same or different?

3. Compare your results for $AlCl_3$, $CaCl_2$, and NaCl. How do you think the intermolecular forces associated with these compounds affect their conductivity?

DRAW CONCLUSIONS

Write a conclusion that addresses each of the points below.

Claim Compare how well each of the solutions you tested conducted electricity. What about their physical or chemical properties could influence this ability?

Evidence Give specific examples from your data to support your claim.

Reasoning Explain how the evidence you gave supports your claim. Describe, in detail, the connections between the evidence you cited and the argument you are making.

Evidence Notebook What did you learn from this experiment about the unique properties of water?

Analyzing the Behavior of Solutions

You have learned how the formation of solutions is affected by the electric forces between solute and solvent particles. Properties of solutions at the observable scale, such as electrical conductivity, product formation, and changes in freezing point and boiling point, can often be explained by describing the effects of electric forces between particles.

Strong and Weak Electrolytes

You previously tested the conductivity of different solutions. An electrolyte is a substance that conducts an electric current when dissolved in solution because it yields ions. A *nonelectrolyte* is a substance that does not conduct an electric current when dissolved in solution because it does not yield ions. As shown in Figure 18, the strength with which substances conduct an electric current is related to their ability to form ions in solution.

FIGURE 18: Sugar is a nonelectrolyte, while sodium chloride and hydrochloric acid are electrolytes.

a Sucrose (sugar) solution

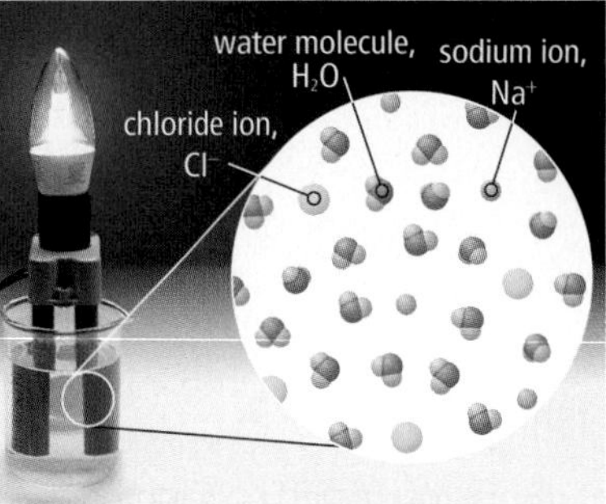

b Sodium chloride (salt) solution

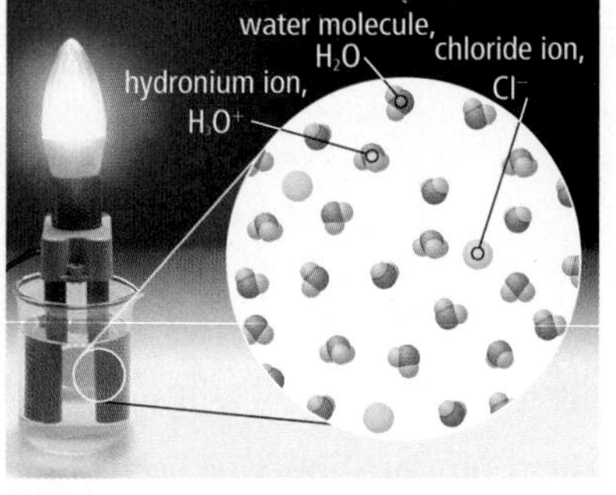

c Hydrochloric acid solution

All soluble ionic compounds are considered *strong electrolytes*, whose dilute aqueous solutions conduct electricity well. A few molecular compounds, such as HCl, also yield only ions when they dissolve and are therefore strong electrolytes. A *weak electrolyte* forms only a few ions in water, so it is not a good conductor of electric current. Ammonia, NH_3, is an example of a weak electrolyte. When ammonia is dissolved in water, only about one out of every hundred ammonia molecules interacts with water molecules to produce ions.

APPLY Classify each substance you tested in the conductivity lab according to its ability to conduct electric current.

aluminum chloride, $AlCl_3$ | calcium chloride, $CaCl_2$ | distilled water
ethanol, CH_3CH_2OH | sodium chloride, NaCl | sugar | tap water

Strong electrolyte	Weak electrolyte	Nonelectrolyte

Modeling the Dissociation of Ionic Compounds

Explore Online

Hands-On Lab

Testing Water for Ions
Investigate the ion content of various substances.

Ionic and covalent substances often behave differently when dissolved in an aqueous solution. Suppose you dissolve an ionic substance, such as sodium chloride, in a polar solvent, such as water. Sodium chloride contains ionic bonds, which means sodium ions and chlorine ions already exist before the substance is added to the water.

Similarly, a solution of manganese bromide, $MnBr_2$, contains the ions Mn^{2+} and Br^-. A chemical equation can be used to model the fact that a total of three moles of ions are produced for each mole of $MnBr_2$.

$MnBr_2(s)$	$\rightarrow$	$Mn^{2+}(aq)$	$+$	$2Br^-(aq)$
1 mole		1 mole		2 moles

The "(*s*)" indicates that manganese bromide is solid, and "(*aq*)" is placed next to the ions to indicate that they are dissolved in aqueous solution. The "2" before "Br^-" means that for every 1 mole of manganese bromide dissolved, there are 2 moles of bromide ions in solution.

When dissolved in a solvent, ionic compounds dissociate completely into their separate ions. For example, if you dissolve silver nitrate, $AgNO_3$, in water, the solution does not actually contain $AgNO_3$. It contains only Ag^+ and NO_3^- ions. For each mole of $AgNO_3$ that you dissolve, the solution will contain a total of two moles of ions, one mole of Ag^+ ions and one mole of NO_3^- ions.

$AgNO_3(s)$	$\rightarrow$	$Ag^+(aq)$	$+$	$NO_3^-(aq)$
1 mole		1 mole		1 mole

PREDICT Sodium nitrate and ammonium chloride are soluble in water. Sodium chloride and ammonium nitrate are also soluble in water. What ions will be present in a solution that results when solutions of sodium nitrate and ammonium chloride are mixed?

____

____

Ionic compounds dissociate completely up to their solubility limit. But if the amount of compound exceeds its solubility in the solution, some of the compound will not dissociate and so will remain undissolved. Some ionic compounds' solubilities are so low that they are considered *insoluble*.

If the mixing of two solutions results in a combination of ions that forms an insoluble compound, a precipitation reaction will occur. Precipitation occurs when the attraction between the ions is greater than the attraction between the ions and surrounding water molecules. Precipitation reactions can be used for making pigments, for removing salts from water in water treatment, and in chemical analysis to measure the amounts of substances in solution.

For example, potassium iodide and lead nitrate are each soluble in water, and form colorless solutions. But when you mix them, a bright yellow solid forms, as shown in Figure 19. The yellow precipitate is lead iodide, PbI_2, which is not soluble.

FIGURE 19: A precipitation reaction of aqueous lead nitrate and aqueous potassium iodide

Collaborate With a partner, discuss which ions are present in solution after potassium iodide and lead nitrate are mixed.

Scientific Knowledge Assumes an Order and Consistency in Natural Systems

Recycling Palladium

FIGURE 20: Palladium can be recovered from dental scraps.

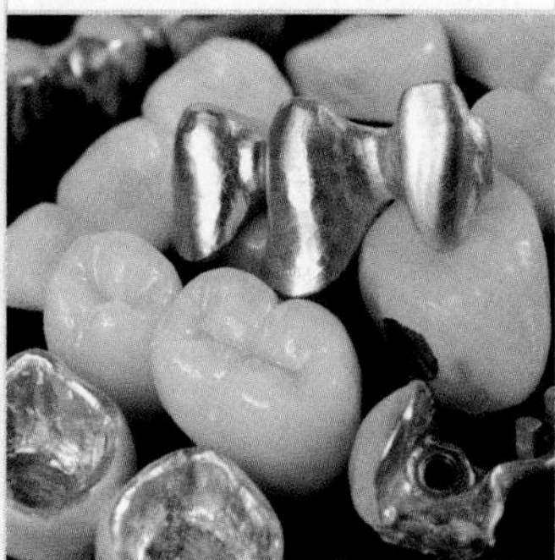

Dental fixtures often include precious metals because of their low reactivity. If the fixtures are removed, the metal can be recovered by dissolving the scrap in a carefully chosen solvent in which the metal precipitates. Palladium in dental scrap can be retrieved by dissolving the scrap in hydrochloric acid and adding a compound to precipitate out the palladium from the solution. This kind of recycling saves energy compared to mining and processing new raw palladium ore. It also conserves a limited valuable resource from going to a landfill.

Language Arts Connection Using multiple sources, research other precipitation reactions used to recycle rare materials. How do these reactions offset the impacts of mining? Write a newspaper article describing your findings.

Modeling the Ionization of Molecular Compounds

FIGURE 21: HCl completely ionizes in water. $HC_2H_3O_2$ partially ionizes in water.

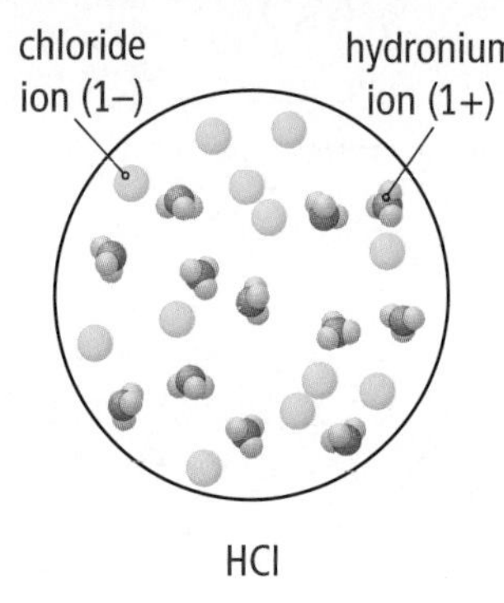

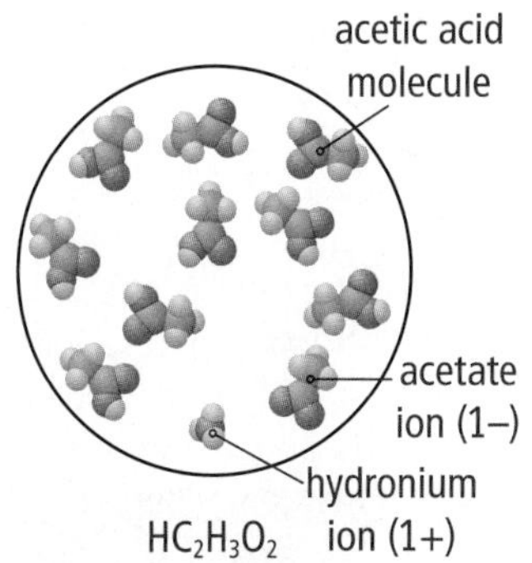

Some molecular compounds, such as sugar, dissolve in water but do not form ions. But when the polar covalent compound hydrogen chloride is dissolved in water, it forms an ionic solution called hydrochloric acid. The process by which polar covalent solute molecules form ions in solution is called *ionization*. Hydrogen chloride completely ionizes in water, so it is a strong electrolyte. The attraction of the hydrogen atom to the water molecules breaks the H—Cl bond, forming a hydrogen ion, H^+, and a chloride ion, Cl^-. This ionization can be modeled by a chemical equation:

$$HCl(aq) \xrightarrow{H_2O} H^+(aq) + Cl^-(aq)$$

Molecular compounds such as HCl that have a hydrogen atom covalently bonded to a highly electronegative atom can release H^+ ions in an aqueous solution. An H^+ ion, however, is so strongly attracted to other charged particles that it bonds covalently with a water molecule to form a *hydronium ion*, H_3O^+. The presence of hydronium ions is what makes a solution acidic at the bulk scale.

$$H_2O(l) + H^+(aq) + Cl^-(aq) \rightarrow H_3O^+(aq) + Cl^-(aq)$$

Some molecular compounds have stronger bonds to their hydrogen atoms. Acetic acid, $HC_2H_3O_2$, is a weak electrolyte. It ionizes less readily than hydrochloric acid because hydrogen is bonded more strongly to the $HC_2H_3O_2$ molecule. A small proportion of acetic acid molecules ionize in water, but most remain un-ionized.

EXPLAIN What determines whether a molecular compound will ionize in water?

Colligative Properties

A solution made by dissolving a solute in a liquid will have different physical and chemical properties than those of the solvent alone. Pure water cannot conduct electricity, freezes at 0 °C, and boils at 100 °C. Salt water does conduct electricity, freezes at a slightly lower temperature than pure water, and boils at a slightly higher temperature than pure water.

Some of the properties of solutions are affected by the presence of solutes (either molecules or ions) regardless of whether they are electrolytes or not. Such properties are referred to as colligative properties, which are dependent only on the concentration of solute particles, not on the identity of the solute particles. The greater the concentration of solute particles in a certain mass of solvent, the greater the change in the colligative property of the substance.

APPLY Select the correct terms to complete the statement about the colligative properties of sodium chloride, NaCl, and calcium chloride, $CaCl_2$, solutions.

One mole of NaCl dissolves to give one | two | three dissolved particles per formula unit. One mole of $CaCl_2$ dissolves to give one | two | three dissolved particles per formula unit. Therefore, NaCl will have a lesser | greater effect than $CaCl_2$ when added to water.

Changing Freezing Point and Boiling Point

Two important colligative properties are the changes in freezing point and boiling point of a liquid when substances are dissolved in the liquid. The boiling point and freezing point of a solution differ from those of the pure solvent. For example, ethylene glycol, also known as antifreeze, is miscible in water. Adding antifreeze to a car's radiator forms a solution that has a freezing point that is lower than the freezing point of water, preventing freezing in cold weather. This change is called *freezing-point depression*. Antifreeze also increases the boiling point of water in the radiator, which prevents overheating. This change is called *boiling-point elevation*.

FIGURE 22: Ocean water remains liquid at lower temperatures than pure water does.

Another example of freezing point depression is seen when salt is added to icy sidewalks or roads to melt the ice. The salt lowers the freezing point of the water so that ice melts at a lower temperature than it normally would. Freezing point depression also plays an important role in ocean water, as shown in Figure 22.

ANALYZE Imagine what would happen if ocean water froze each time the temperature reached the freezing point of pure water, 0 °C. The constant movement of the water partly explains why the ocean water remains liquid. How does freezing-point depression also explain the behavior of ocean water?

Freezing point depression and boiling point elevation are explained by changes in vapor pressure, the pressure caused by solvent molecules in the gas phase directly above the solution. Increasing the concentration of solute particles means fewer solvent particles are able to escape from the liquid to enter the gas phase. This lowers the vapor pressure, which keeps the solution in a liquid state over a larger temperature range.

Explore Online

Hands-On Lab

Diffusion and Cell Membranes
Investigate osmosis across a semipermeable membrane.

Osmotic Pressure

Figure 23 shows a U-tube containing sucrose solutions of different concentrations. The solutions are separated by a semipermeable membrane that blocks the passage of certain particles but allows others to pass through. In this case, the larger sucrose molecules are blocked, but the smaller water molecules can pass through freely.

Collaborate With a partner, discuss what is happening in the U-tube that would cause the levels of the solutions to change. Why did the level of the more highly concentrated solution rise? Use evidence from Figure 23 to support your ideas.

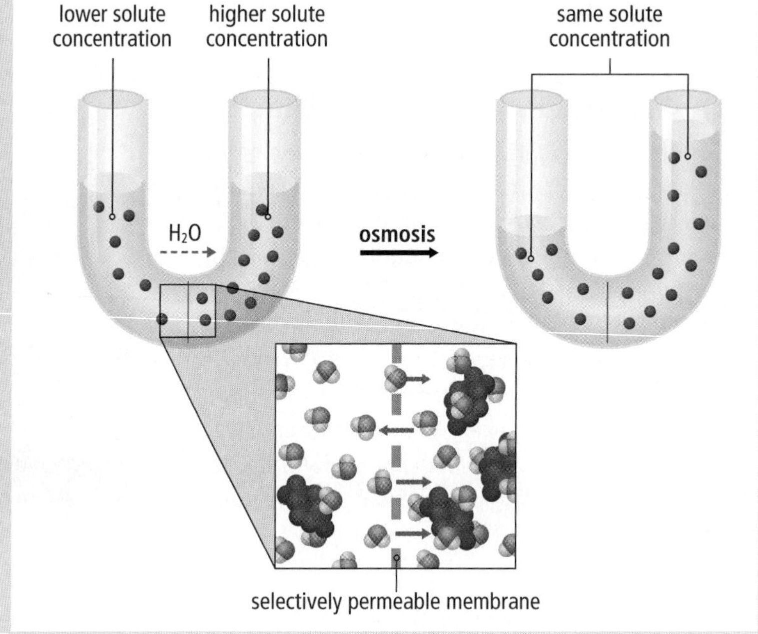

FIGURE 23: Osmosis is the movement of solvent molecules from the solution with lower solute concentration to the solution with higher solute concentration.

A higher concentration of solute particles in the solution allows fewer water molecules to strike the membrane than on the side with the lower solute concentration. So, the rate of water molecules moving into the higher concentration solution is greater than the rate moving in the opposite direction. *Osmosis* is the diffusion of a solvent through a semipermeable membrane to the side of higher solute concentration. As the difference in the heights of the solutions increases, an increasing pressure difference will develop. Eventually, the rate of solvent molecules moving each way across the membrane will become equal. *Osmotic pressure* is the external pressure that must be applied to stop osmosis. Osmotic pressure is dependent on the concentration of solute particles, not on the type of solute particles, so it is also a colligative property.

Evidence Notebook How are the properties of pure water different from the properties of water when dissolved solutes are present in it? How do you think this affects the importance of water in the Earth system?

Careers in Engineering

Water Supply Engineer

When you turn on a faucet, you expect a flow of clean, drinkable water. If you are confident in the purity of your water supply, you can thank a water supply engineer. Water supply engineers identify and develop water sources, produce and maintain water purification systems, and develop water distribution systems.

The water you drink may originate in a lake or a river, or it may come from groundwater. Groundwater is usually pumped to the surface from drilled wells that are sometimes hundreds or thousands of feet deep. Regardless of its source, the water must be cleaned and purified before it can be sent to homes, schools, and businesses.

A water supply engineer develops the water purification processes, designs the equipment, and plans the methods for testing the water to make sure it is fit for consumption. Screening is the first step in the purification process. During screening, water passes through a screen to remove larger objects such as trash, leaves, and twigs.

The water then flows into large sedimentation pools where residual solid material settles. To remove any remaining small particles, chemicals such as aluminum sulfate, $Al_2(SO_4)_3$, or soluble iron salts are added. This causes small particles, unwanted ions, and residual chemicals to clump together. These precipitates are removed through different filtration processes.

Typically, the last step in water purification is to disinfect the water. Chlorine gas is the cheapest and most common substance used to disinfect water on a large scale. However, an unanticipated result of this method is that chlorine can react to form chlorine-containing organic byproducts that may cause cancer. As a result, engineers modified the process to minimize chlorine treatment and supplement it with chloramine, NH_2Cl. Chloramine is also an effective disinfectant, and it does not form harmful byproducts.

FIGURE 24: A water supply engineer collecting a sample

Chemistry in Your Community Imagine you are a water supply engineer. Develop a plan for a water treatment plant for a community that is located away from developed areas. After researching this issue, write a report describing criteria and constraints for the task of identifying and developing a suitable source of water for this community. Define the components and the boundaries of the system. When writing your report, consider how the diverse needs of the community might be met by the water treatment system you develop, and what costs and benefits you would anticipate. How will you address their demand for water while keeping the stress on the water resource low? In addition, analyze the need for drinking water as a major global challenge.

SEPARATING SALT MIXTURES | PAPER CHROMATOGRAPHY | REVERSE OSMOSIS | Go online to choose one of these other paths.

Lesson Self-Check

CAN YOU EXPLAIN THE PHENOMENON?

FIGURE 25: Ocean water contains a number of dissolved solutes that are important for living organisms.

Not every interaction of substances is a chemical reaction. In some interactions, changes take place, but the identity of the substances involved remains the same. One example of this type of interaction is the dissolution of a solute into a solvent as a solution forms. An understanding of intermolecular forces makes it possible to predict which interactions will take place and to explain what happens during these interactions. The interactions that take place in ocean water affect many parts of the Earth system, including the organisms that live in and near the ocean. Understanding these interactions starts with a consideration of how intermolecular forces affect interactions between water and the ionic and molecular compounds that are dissolved in the ocean.

Evidence Notebook Refer to your notes in your Evidence Notebook to make a claim about water. Your explanation should include a discussion of the following points:

Claim Why does water have unique properties and what are some examples of how these properties are important in the Earth system?

Evidence Give specific evidence to support your claim.

Reasoning Describe, in detail, the connections between the evidence you cited and the claim you are making.

Name Date

CHECKPOINTS

Check Your Understanding

1. Water, H_2O, and hydrogen sulfide, H_2S, are both molecules with a bent structure, but the melting point of H_2O is much higher than the melting point of H_2S. Why is this?
   - ○ **a.** The intermolecular forces in H_2S are much greater than those in H_2O.
   - ○ **b.** H_2O molecules have hydrogen bonds between them.
   - ○ **c.** The three-dimensional arrangement of H_2O makes it a nonpolar molecule.
   - ○ **d.** H_2S has a lower molar mass than H_2O.

2. Select the correct terms to complete the statement about charged particles.

   The pattern that electrical forces show is that like charges attract | repel and opposite charges attract | repel. According to Coulomb's law, as the distance between two charged particles decreases, the force between the particles decreases | increases. As the magnitude of the charges decreases, the force decreases | increases.

3. If solutions are produced from each of these compounds, which solutions would most likely conduct an electrical current? Select all correct answers.
   - ☐ **a.** aluminum chloride, $AlCl_3$
   - ☐ **b.** chromium trioxide, CrO_3
   - ☐ **c.** ethanol, C_2H_5OH
   - ☐ **d.** glucose, $C_6H_{12}O_6$
   - ☐ **e.** sodium azide, NaN_3

4. Which statement correctly describes the effect of an increase in temperature on the solubility of gases dissolved in a liquid?
   - ○ **a.** Solubility increases for all gases.
   - ○ **b.** Solubility decreases for all gases.
   - ○ **c.** Solubility increases for most gases but decreases for some.
   - ○ **d.** Solubility decreases for most gases but increases for some.

5. Which statement best explains why oil and water do not mix?
   - ○ **a.** Water molecules are polar and oil molecules are nonpolar.
   - ○ **b.** Oil molecules are polar and water molecules are nonpolar.
   - ○ **c.** Water molecules are carbon-based and oil molecules are not.
   - ○ **d.** Oil and water both have covalent bonds and repel one another.

6. Which of the following types of compounds is most likely to be a strong electrolyte?
   - ○ **a.** a polar compound
   - ○ **b.** a nonpolar compound
   - ○ **c.** a covalent compound
   - ○ **d.** an ionic compound

7. Select the correct terms to complete the statement.

   The freezing point of water when a solute is dissolved in the water is higher | lower than the freezing point of pure water. The change in the freezing point occurs because the vapor pressure of the solution is higher | lower than that of the pure water. This change in vapor pressure also causes the boiling point of the solution to be higher | lower than the boiling point of pure water. The change in boiling point is directly proportional to the number of | identity of the solute particles.

8. A 3.25 L solution is prepared by dissolving 285 g of $BaBr_2$ in water. Use the space provided to determine the molarity. Report your final answer using the correct number of significant figures.

   ________ M $BaBr_2$

CHECKPOINTS (continued)

9. Explain whether HCl or HF shows the stronger intermolecular forces and how this is related to trends in the periodic table. Then, explain which of these compounds would have a higher boiling point based on differences in intermolecular forces.

10. A student makes a solution by dissolving $CaBr_2$ in water. Describe what happens at the bulk scale and at the particle level as the $CaBr_2$ dissolves.

MAKE YOUR OWN STUDY GUIDE

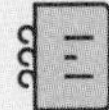

In your Evidence Notebook, design a study guide that supports the main ideas from this lesson:

Intermolecular forces between molecules explain how a liquid behaves.

Polarity results when there is an uneven distribution of charges in a molecule.

The solubility of a substance depends on the forces that exist between the solute particles and the solvent particles.

Solutions of charged particles can conduct electric current.

Remember to include the following information in your study guide:

- Use examples that model main ideas.
- Record explanations for the phenomena you investigated.
- Use evidence to support your explanations. Your support can include drawings, data, graphs, laboratory conclusions, and other evidence recorded throughout the lesson.

Consider how patterns may be observed in the intermolecular forces that exist between compounds.

3.3

Engineering Materials

Cars are made from many types of materials, including metal, glass, plastic, and rubber.

CAN YOU SOLVE THE PROBLEM?

A car is a complex system with many parts, which have macro- and microscopic structures designed to serve specific functions. Engineers decide what materials to use for each part of a car using defined criteria and constraints. For example, the car frame provides basic structure and strength and absorbs energy during a collision. Frame materials must be strong but not too brittle. Windows let people see out. The windows must be able to withstand weather and flying pebbles and absorb the energy of a minor collision. The dashboard separates the passengers from the wiring and engine of the car. It must be easy to clean and tough enough to withstand daily life but as lightweight as possible to help increase fuel efficiency. Modern vehicles have on-board computers that control many functions. The materials for these systems are chosen for their electrical properties.

EXPLAIN How would understanding the properties of different materials be useful for selecting the best material for each part of a car?

Evidence Notebook As you explore the lesson, gather evidence to determine what the best material (ceramic, metal, polymer, or semiconductor) would be for each car component: dashboard, frame, on-board computer, and windshield.

EXPLORATION 1

Exploring Materials Science and Design

FIGURE 1: This apparatus is testing the flexibility of screen glass.

Have you ever wondered how smartphone glass was developed? To start, engineers had to understand the function that the part required, such as being resistant to cracks, as well as the properties that could help fulfill that function, such as being able to flex without breaking. To identify glass with this property, engineers can test the flexibility of glass samples, as shown in Figure 1. Engineers also had to find an efficient way to deliver the glass to manufacturers. To solve this problem, flexible glass is delivered in rolls and then cut into pieces. Materials science is the scientific study of the properties and applications of materials.

PLAN Consider a material that you use in your daily life. If you could improve it to make it function better, what would you change about it?

The Engineering Design Process

FIGURE 2: The engineering design process includes many iterations or cycles.

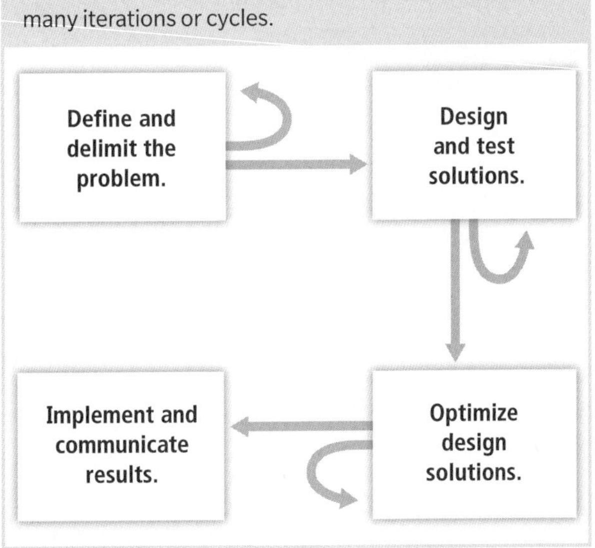

The engineering design process is used to develop and optimize solutions to problems. The process is iterative and can cycle through different parts of the process in various ways. Figure 2 shows a brief overview of the engineering design process.

The process begins by defining a problem that the solution will address. This includes listing criteria and constraints. At any stage in the process, engineers may discover new aspects of the problem and return to the initial definition to modify it. For example, an engineer working on a better cell phone cover might define the problem as the need to strengthen the glass face of the phone. If testing indicates that the glass is likely to crack when the phone lands on its edge, the problem might be redefined to include the need to protect the sides of the phone. Then, the criteria and constraints of the problem may need to be reevaluated as well.

When a potential solution to the defined problem is identified, the process is not over. Testing and evaluation of prototypes often lead to ideas for optimizing the design.

Explore Online

YOU SOLVE IT

How Can You Change the Properties of a Substance?
Investigate the properties of five chemical additives that will be used to optimize an adhesive.

Collaborate With a partner, discuss what types of testing phone glass would undergo. Consider everything a phone might go through on a daily basis to help brainstorm ideas.

Engineering

Collecting Water from Fog

In some areas, it is common to see fog even though rain is rare and water is scarce. Engineers are developing ways to efficiently "harvest" water from the fog using engineered materials that collect water from the air.

Defining and Delimiting the Problem

Water needs vary greatly between communities and applications. Understanding how much water must be produced will determine whether fog harvesting can meet the water needs of an area. For example, a person in the United States might use 300 liters of water per day, while a person in Asia or Africa may use one-third or even one-sixth this much fresh water. In addition, fog is seasonal in many places and may not be a year-round solution for water needs. The social, cultural, and environmental impacts of a potential solution should be evaluated throughout this process. For example, many plants and animals depend on fog for water. Reducing the amount of water in the air may harm these organisms. Also, removing moisture from the air decreases the humidity. This may have unintended consequences that should be considered even if they cannot be fully predicted.

DEFINE Imagine you are designing a system to supply fog-harvested water to seedlings. Define the problem and break it down into smaller, more manageable sub-problems.

____

____

____

ANALYZE Consider the sub-problem of designing a material that can harvest water from fog. Identify criteria and constraints for this problem.

____

____

____

____

Designing and Testing Solutions

Potential solutions can be brainstormed, modeled, and evaluated after the problem is defined. Engineers often research natural or human-designed solutions to similar problems as part of this step.

FIGURE 3: The Namib desert beetle can harvest water from the air.

One group of engineers took inspiration from living things as they designed water-collecting materials. The Namib desert is one of the driest environments on Earth. The Namib desert beetle, shown in Figure 3, survives in its desert home in southern Africa by drinking water that condenses on its hard, bumpy wing covers in early morning fog. A microscopic examination of the beetle's wings shows that they are covered with tiny bumps and grooves that are composed of different materials. The bumps are made of a material that attracts water from the air, and the material that makes up the grooves repels the water. Thus, the water flows along the grooves and is channeled into the beetle's mouth.

Engineers used observations from the Namib desert beetle to develop new materials that mimic the way the beetle's water-gathering system works. One material attracts and collects water from the air. Another material repels the collected water.

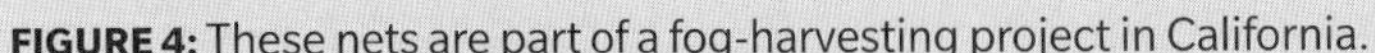

FIGURE 4: These nets are part of a fog-harvesting project in California.

Mesh nets that collect fog are usually nylon, polyethylene, or polypropylene. The density of the mesh can be varied to capture more or less water. Droplets that collect on the mesh may drip to the ground, providing water for plants, or they may flow into a gutter that channels the water into a storage tank. Dust, debris, and algae must be regularly removed from nets, and tanks must be maintained to prevent algal and bacterial growth.

EVALUATE Does the design in Figure 4 meet your criteria and constraints? How would you analyze the performance of this material? What tests would you run, and how would you evaluate the design?

Optimizing Design Solutions

After developing a new material, such as a water-collecting fabric, engineers test and analyze the material to make sure it has the properties to perform the desired function. A decision matrix can help determine how well a design meets important criteria. In a decision matrix, each criterion is given a number, or weight, based on its importance. Proposed designs are rated on how well they meet the identified criteria. The designs in the decision matrix on the next page are rated on a scale of 0–5. The score for each criterion in a decision matrix is multiplied by its respective weight, and the score for that design is the sum of those products. Engineers may choose to make additional prototypes of the design with the highest score, or they may choose to brainstorm new ideas if no designs meet the requirements satisfactorily.

Decision Matrix for Fog-Collecting Material				
Design criteria	**Weight**	**Design 1**	**Design 2**	**Design 3**
Durability	4	5	1	4
Water collected	3	2	3	4
Cost	2	1	2	1
Resists algae growth	1	1	4	0
Total Points		29	21	30

ANALYZE Select the correct terms to complete the statement.

According to the decision matrix, the most important criterion is durability | water collected | cost | algae growth, which has a large effect on the total score. If engineers decided to test only two of the designs further, they would likely eliminate Design 1 | Design 2 | Design 3 from further consideration. Although it is not the most durable, Design 3 scores better than the others in water collected | cost | algae growth.

A decision matrix also helps engineers consider tradeoffs, or the relative cost-benefit ratio of different design solutions. If having a more durable product is more important than minimizing costs, then durability can be given a higher weight in a decision matrix than cost. This indicates which tradeoffs are acceptable for a particular problem. If a material, product, or manufacturing process is inefficient or too costly, a new process may be developed. The optimization process considers these tradeoffs.

Implementing the Solution and Communicating Results

Engineers are getting better at designing computer simulations and prototypes that are more accurate models of how particular solutions will work at full-scale implementation. As particular solutions are implemented, unanticipated outcomes, new technologies, or new constraints may require further optimization or a new solution.

Fog collectors could provide an alternative source of fresh water in dry areas. This technology works best in areas with frequent foggy periods, including areas in California, Chile, Peru, and Guatemala. Prototypes have been tested in some areas as part of solution optimization. Data from the evaluation of prototypes or fully implemented solutions can be communicated to clients or the public through reports or scientific articles. These data are valuable for further design optimization and for solving related problems in the future.

Often the final decision about whether a new device or process will be produced or implemented is not made by the engineering team. There may be economic, political, or cultural considerations unrelated to the technical performance of the design that must be considered. For example, the environmental impacts of harvesting water from fog in particular areas must be considered.

Evidence Notebook What are the environmental impacts of detergents? How might these impacts compare to those of the homemade detergent from your unit project?

Life Cycle of Engineered Materials

Everything that we make or use requires materials. Because Earth is essentially a closed system with a finite supply of materials available, decisions about resource use should be carefully evaluated. For example, some resources, such as aluminum, are easily recycled and become materials for other products. Other resources, such as gasoline, exist in limited supply that cannot be reused. It takes many steps to manufacture and dispose of a consumer product, and each step has different impacts on society and the environment.

Collaborate With a partner, discuss why the entire life cycle of a material should be considered when analyzing costs and benefits.

FIGURE 5: The life cycle of a cell phone

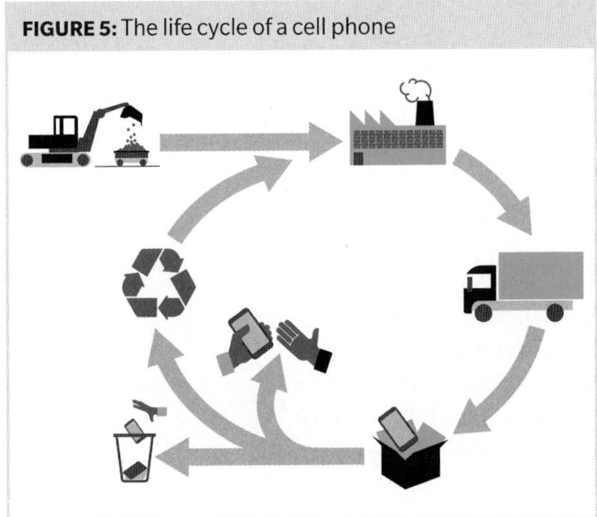

Figure 5 shows an example life cycle of a consumer product. Manufacturing begins with obtaining resources. These can be natural resources obtained by mining ores for metal, harvesting trees for lumber, or extracting fossil fuels from underground reservoirs. Resources may also come from recycled materials.

Raw resources are shaped into parts, assembled into a product, or manufactured into synthetic materials using chemical processes. Distribution of a consumer product may involve several transportation steps, such as moving the product to a warehouse then delivering to a retail outlet. Each input, such as worker time, fuel, or water usage, adds to the price of the product.

Some products may only be used once, such as food or a newspaper. Other products, such as a microwave or clothes, may be used many times. Eventually, consumers dispose of most products, which begins the final stage of the life cycle. This could consist of discarding the product as trash, reusing the product in a different way, or recycling it to use the materials in a new product.

EVALUATE Engineers reduce the impact of a product by optimizing various processes at different stages of its life cycle. Match the criteria engineers might optimize with the stage.

obtaining resources | production | distribution | consumer use | disposal

Engineering criteria	Life cycle stage
reduce the energy consumption of an appliance	____________
develop more efficient natural gas drilling techniques	____________
design a material that can be easily separated into recyclable components	____________
automate the assembly process for putting car parts together	____________
develop software systems to improve warehouse operations	____________

Evidence Notebook The dashboard, frame, on-board computer, and windshield in a car all serve different functions. How could you determine the best material from which to build each car component? Define this complex problem and divide it into multiple sub-problems using a diagram or flowchart.

Engineering Lab

Experimenting with Polymers

You are a materials scientist who has been hired by a toy company to develop a toy made of a bouncy material. You will make an initial version of the material with a reaction of polyvinyl alcohol (PVA) and sodium tetraborate, also known as sodium borate or borax. In this reaction, borate ions link chains of PVA together, as shown in Figure 6. Then, you will test the properties of the material and optimize your design.

FIGURE 6: PVA and borate ions react to form a cross-linked polymer and water.

PVA polymer + borate ion → cross-linked polymer + $4\ H_2O$ (water)

DESIGN CHALLENGE

The company wants a colorful toy that is fun to look at and will bounce at least 15 cm high when dropped from a height of 30 cm onto a tile floor at room temperature. The toy should retain a spherical shape for several bounces and be stretchy and moldable by hand.

CONDUCT RESEARCH

Research the material you will be making from PVA and sodium tetraborate. This material is composed of very large molecules, called polymers, that are made up of repeating units, known as *monomers*. How do the monomers combine to form the polymer? How do the properties of the polymer influence the properties of the final material? As part of your research, look for information that could help you meet the criteria for a successful solution and maximize the bounciness of a toy made with this polymer.

DEFINE THE PROBLEM

Define the engineering problem you must solve and identify the criteria and constraints for the problem. Break the problem and criteria into smaller pieces as necessary.

FIGURE 7: Polyvinyl alcohol, sodium tetraborate, and food coloring can be mixed together to make a colorful new material.

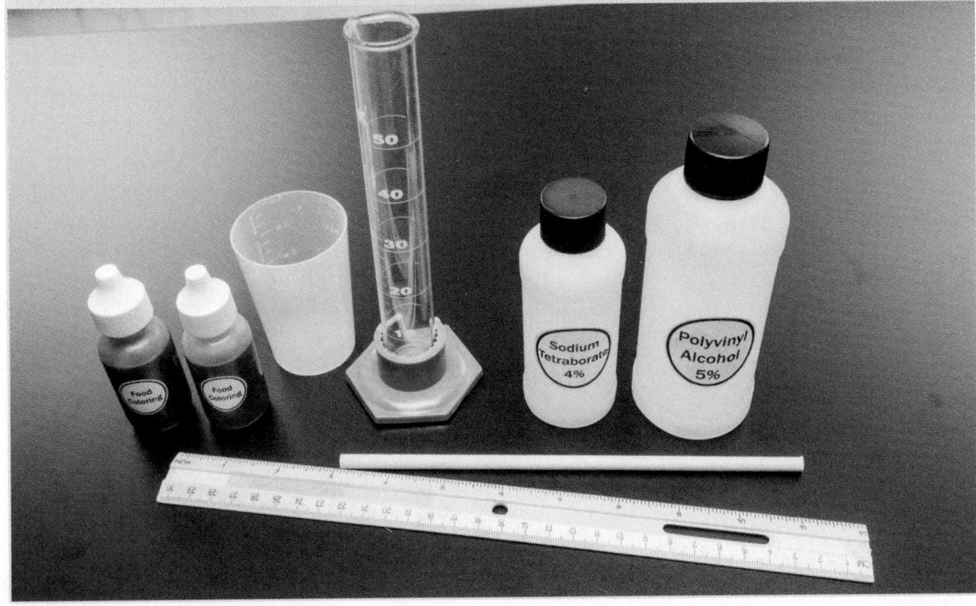

POSSIBLE MATERIALS

- indirectly vented chemical splash goggles, nonlatex apron, nitrile gloves
- food coloring, assorted colors
- graduated cylinder, 50 mL
- plastic cup, 4 oz
- polyvinyl alcohol (PVA), 5% solution
- ruler, 30 cm
- sodium tetraborate, 4% solution
- wooden dowel, ¼-in. diameter, 8 in. long

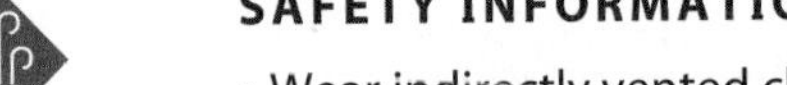

SAFETY INFORMATION

indirectly vented chemical splash goggles

- Wear indirectly vented chemical splash goggles, a nonlatex apron, and nitrile gloves during the setup, hands-on, and takedown segments of the activity.
- If you get a chemical in your eye, use an eyewash station immediately.
- Never pour chemicals, either used or unused, back into their original container. Dispose of chemicals according to your teacher's instructions.
- Wash your hands with soap and water immediately after completing this activity.

DESIGN SOLUTIONS

Your first step is to make a polymer and determine whether it is a suitable solution. In your Evidence Notebook, develop a procedure and safety plan and get your teacher's approval before proceeding. Include a plan for recording your initial observations. You will decide how much of each chemical to use. The total volume of reactants should be 35 mL.

TEST

In your Evidence Notebook, develop a procedure and safety plan for testing how well the polymer meets the criteria and constraints of the problem. Get your teacher's approval before proceeding. Include a table to record your data and quantitative measurements, and decide on an appropriate level of accuracy. Then, test your polymer in a safe area.

1. How accurate and precise are the data you collected? What could increase your accuracy and precision?

2. Which criteria were met by the current toy design? Which criteria were not met?

3. What are the limitations of your investigation? Are the data you gathered enough to accurately assess your design?

4. Describe changes that will improve your testing procedure and investigation. Get approval from your teacher, and test your polymer again using the new procedure.

OPTIMIZE

1. How do you think the recipe should change to optimize the polymer? Support your answer using information about how patterns in the polymer at the atomic scale cause changes to the properties of the polymer at the bulk scale.

2. You now need to optimize the design solution. You will need to consider certain tradeoffs. For example, if you try to optimize how high the toy can bounce, it might not be as stretchy and moldable. Rank the criteria in order of importance and explain the tradeoffs that you expect to make.

3. Make a decision matrix and indicate the relative weight of each criterion. Evaluate your first design using the matrix. Then, make your optimized polymer and test it. As you test new designs, use your decision matrix to compare each iteration.

ANALYZE

Based on your research and observations, what is happening at the atomic scale to explain the function of your materials at the bulk scale?

COMMUNICATE

Develop a presentation that evaluates how well your final material worked, how you tested the design, and how you determined if the solution was suitable for the intended function. Include information about the structure and properties of the material based on your observations and research, and a mathematical display of your quantitative data.

EXTEND

List potential environmental impacts of your bouncy toy. Make sure to consider the entire life cycle of the product. Do you think minimizing environmental impacts should be prioritized over other criteria, such as cost or aesthetics? In your Evidence Notebook, write an argument supporting your position.

Evidence Notebook For the problem of material selection for automobile parts, identify criteria and constraints for each component (dashboard, frame, on-board computer, and windshield) based on its function.

Analyzing Types of Materials

Most complex objects consist of many parts made of different materials. Each part has a specific function and must be composed of materials that have the best properties for its function. An example of a very complex object is the space shuttle, shown in Figure 8. The space shuttle was used to ferry people and supplies to the International Space Station, carry repair crews to the Hubble telescope, and conduct many other missions. Shuttle engineers designed a vehicle that could travel into orbit using as little fuel as possible because fuel is heavy and expensive. To solve this problem, the shuttle body was built with aluminum, which is relatively light. To withstand the high temperatures caused by friction with the atmosphere upon the shuttle's return to Earth, the skin of the shuttle was covered with ceramic tiles. As the shuttle entered the atmosphere, these tiles became red hot, but the interior remained cool.

Explore Online

FIGURE 8: The layers of the space shuttle give it strength and the ability to withstand high temperatures.

Collaborate Space vehicles operate in extreme conditions with limited ability for repairs. With a partner, discuss how safety and reliability considerations might affect cost-benefit analyses during the engineering design process for shuttle materials.

Metals: Applications and Properties

People first used the metal copper in a relatively pure form more than 10 000 years ago for ornaments and jewelry. Later, the development of bronze, which is a mixture of copper and tin, led to the invention of harder, more durable metal tools and weapons. Metal has been a part of human activities for thousands of years, and we continue to explore new ways to make and use metal products.

The properties of metals allow them to be used in numerous applications. Bridges and large buildings incorporate steel beams as structural support. In the form of nails, bolts, or screws, metal is an ideal fastener to hold other materials together. Metals are good conductors of electric current, so metal wires are common in electrical systems. Smooth metal surfaces are easy to clean, tolerate high temperatures, and are antimicrobial, making them ideal for medical uses, such as the titanium hip shown in Figure 9.

Explore Online

FIGURE 9: Titanium metal is used for artificial hips.

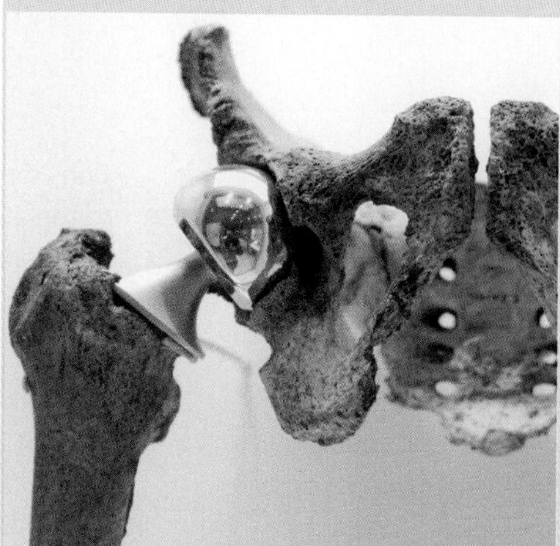

EXPLAIN What characteristics at the atomic scale determine the properties of metals at the bulk scale? Select all correct answers.

☐ **a.** ionic bonds

☐ **b.** sea of electrons

☐ **c.** low electronegativity

☐ **d.** interaction of cations and anions

Although a few metals, such as copper and gold, are found in small amounts in their pure form, almost all metal production begins with mining rock, known as an ore, that contains metal compounds. The extraction of metal from ore is an energy-intensive and expensive process. In general, it is much less expensive to recycle metal than to mine new metal. Thus, recycling is typically a positive for costs and the environment.

INFER Select the correct terms to complete the statement.

Due to the low | high electronegativity of metal atoms, the valence electrons form a "sea" of electrons that results in weak | strong metallic bonds. Copper is used for electrical wiring because the nuclei | protons | electrons are free to move, giving copper a low boiling point | high conductivity | high brittleness. Aluminum is brittle and soft | ductile and malleable and can be shaped into thin, flexible sheets through pressure. A lot of energy is needed to break metallic bonds, which makes many metals hard | soft.

Metals can be mixed with one another, and in some cases with nonmetals such as carbon, to form alloys. These alloys, such as bronze and steel, have different properties from the metals of which they are composed. Many alloys are, in fact, stronger and harder than the individual metals. That is why the development of bronze had a much greater effect on civilization than did the use of copper.

MODEL Draw the structure of a pure metal and an alloy at the atomic scale. Use your model to support an explanation of why alloys are typically stronger than pure metals.

Explore Online

YOU SOLVE IT

Which Planetary-Rover Materials Are Suitable?
Investigate the effects of the extreme Venus environment on the metals and metal alloys used to build planetary rovers.

Consider how you use metals every day and how their useful properties relate to the atomic level arrangement of particles. For example, most tools are made of metal. The strong, delocalized bonds in metals make these tools hard and strong.

Many bicycle frames are made of steel or aluminum. These metals are strong and durable. The frame lasts for many years because the materials are hard but not brittle. Within a piece of metal, atoms can move a bit without breaking bonds because the electrons flow among the nuclei. This property keeps the frame from shattering when the bike runs over a bump or large pothole.

Ceramics: Applications and Properties

If you need a strong, durable material for a retaining wall, driveway, or building, concrete is a great choice. Concrete is made of cement, stone or sand, and water. When these components are mixed together, they form a solid material that is as hard and strong as rock. Concrete is a ceramic material. Ceramics are very stable and have been used for thousands of years. Roman concrete structures, such as the Colosseum, still stand today.

Ceramics are usually made up of bonded metal and nonmetal atoms and are typically inorganic, or not made mostly of carbon. They are produced by mixing earth materials, usually in the form of powder. For concrete, water is added to the earth materials to begin a reaction that forms the chemical bonds. In other ceramics, the chemical reaction occurs when the mixture is heated in an oven or kiln.

FIGURE 10: The ceramic magnesia is a network of magnesium and oxygen.

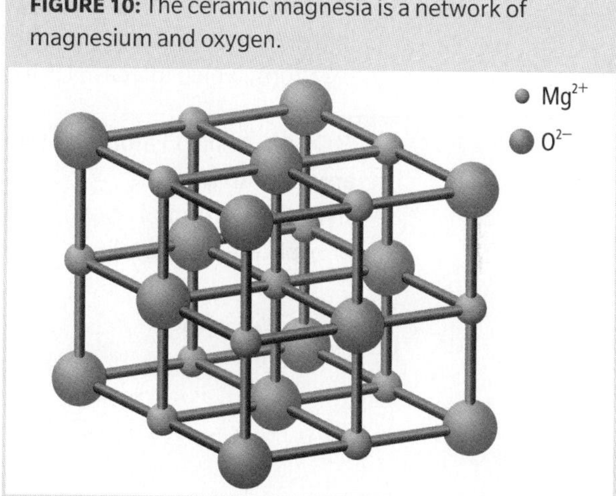

Ceramic materials have ionic or covalent bonds. Ionic bonds form between metal and nonmetal atoms. Covalent bonds form between nonmetal atoms. The atoms are linked by these bonds in a regular structure that is more complex than that of metals. Atoms in a ceramic may form a three-dimensional network with a rigid structure similar to the magnesia network in Figure 10. The bonds in ceramics are formed by the transfer or sharing of electrons between atoms, which is different from metallic bonding. As a result, the properties and applications of ceramics are different from those of metals.

ANALYZE Select the correct terms to complete the statement.

In general, ceramics are hard and strong, but they are also brittle. If you drop a pottery vase and a metal vase on a hard surface, the metal | pottery is likely to bend while the metal | pottery shatters. Most ceramics are good | poor conductors of electric current because the electrons are locked into the chemical bonds and are free | unable to flow. Ceramics are good conductors | insulators of energy as heat because the atoms are held in place, so energy does not flow readily from one atom to another. For example, heat-resistant ceramic tiles protected the space shuttle during flight.

Ceramic often refers to pottery, but there are many other ceramic materials, including bricks, tiles, and glass. Glass consists mostly of silicon and oxygen atoms. When sand is melted and cooled, it forms glass. Like other ceramics, glass is hard, although brittle. Glass is often transparent to visible light, so glass has been used to make windows for many centuries.

EXPLAIN Why are insulators made of ceramics and not metals?

FIGURE 11: Porcelain or glass insulators may protect utility poles from high voltages.

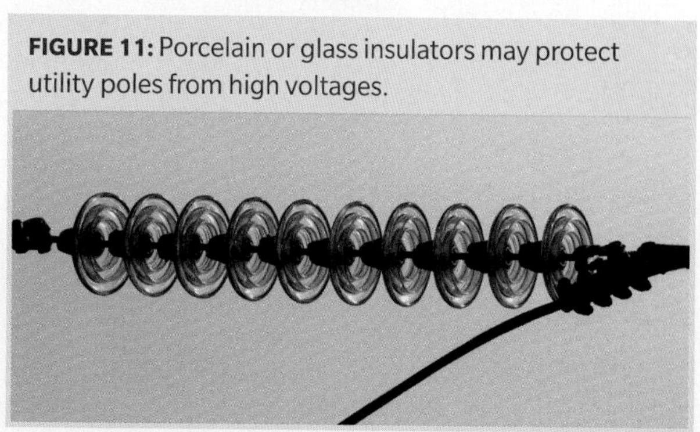

Semiconductors: Applications and Properties

Semiconductors are materials that have electrical conductivity values between that of a conductor, such as copper, and that of an insulator, such as glass. Their conductivity increases as their temperature increases. Thus, they are not effective conductors at low temperatures, but they do conduct electrical current at temperatures above room temperature. The metalloid elements in pure form are semiconductors. They form crystals with covalent bonds. Electrons in metalloids do not flow as freely as they do in metals, but they are more mobile than the electrons are in ceramics.

The electrical properties of semiconducting elements, such as silicon, change when impurities are added to the crystal in a process called *doping*. These impurities are atoms of other elements, such as boron or phosphorus, that can take the place of silicon atoms in the crystal structure. Impurities affect the crystal by either donating or accepting electrons, which increases the conductivity of the semiconductor.

MODEL A silicon atom has four valence electrons and bonds with four other silicon atoms. With a partner, explain using claims, evidence, and reasoning why adding small amounts of phosphorus to silicon makes it a conductor. Draw the structure of phosphorus-doped silicon to support your explanation.

FIGURE 12: Clean room precautions at a computer-chip production facility

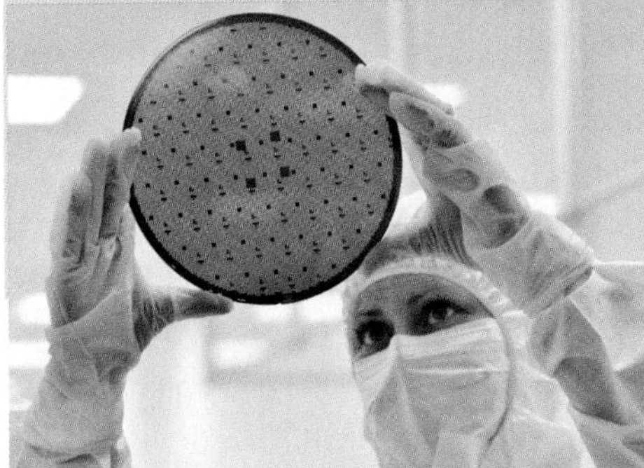

Silicon is the most widely-used semiconductor. Pure silicon makes up chips in virtually all electrical devices. Because impurities affect semiconductors at extremely low concentrations, chip production must be done in clean rooms with low concentrations of impurities. Figure 12 shows clean room conditions.

Semiconductor devices have had revolutionary effects on people's lives. Computers, which many people use on a daily basis, contain chips made of semiconductors. Semiconductors have many other applications, including solar cells, lasers, and LEDs. Modern LED light bulbs use a fraction of the power of incandescent light bulbs, which produce much more waste heat and emit much less light.

Language Arts Connection Semiconductors are a good example of the influence of society on science and engineering. Research the development and application of semiconductors. Analyze the costs and benefits of semiconductors and explain how this technology has affected society and the environment. Write a summary of your findings, drawing evidence from your research to support your analysis.

Polymers: Applications and Properties

Synthetic polymers are everywhere—from storage containers to contact lenses. DNA, spider silk, and proteins are natural polymers built by living organisms.

Plastic materials are manufactured polymers, mostly consisting of chains or networks of hydrocarbons that come from fossil fuels. Hydrocarbons are compounds that contain only carbon and hydrogen. Polymers have different structures, as shown in Figure 13. Structural patterns at the molecular scale cause polymers to have different properties.

FIGURE 13: Polymer structures

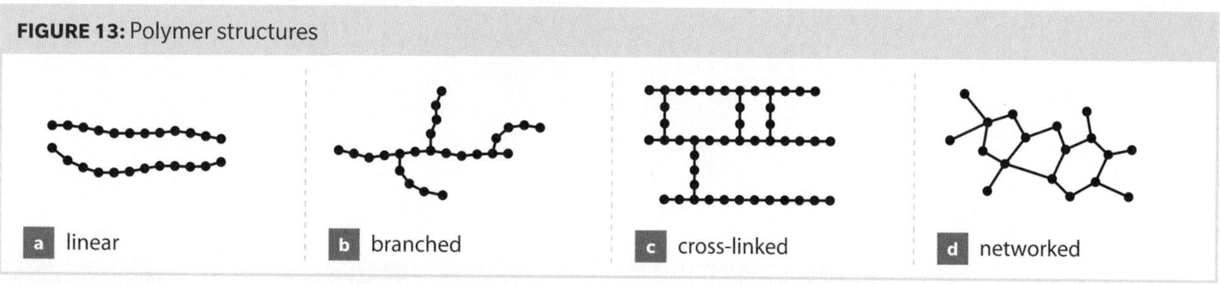

ANALYZE Match each polymer description with the most likely structure from Figure 13.

Low-density polyethylene (LDPE) is a flexible polymer with many subunits as side chains. ____________

Epoxy adhesives are strong and heat resistant. These polymers have so many connections between chains, an entire sample may be one molecule.

____

Synthetic rubber is strong and stable. This polymer forms long chains with strong covalent bonds between the polymer chains. ____________

Nylon is strong with high density and a high melting point. It is made of long polymer chains stacked closely together. ____________

Thermoplastics are polymer materials that melt when heated. The covalent bonds within the polymer chains are very strong. There are no covalent bonds between chains. Instead, they are held together by weak attractive forces. The length of the chains can be controlled to influence properties, such as toughness. Density and the temperature at which it melts determine how easily a thermoplastic material can be recycled.

FIGURE 14: Thermoplastic

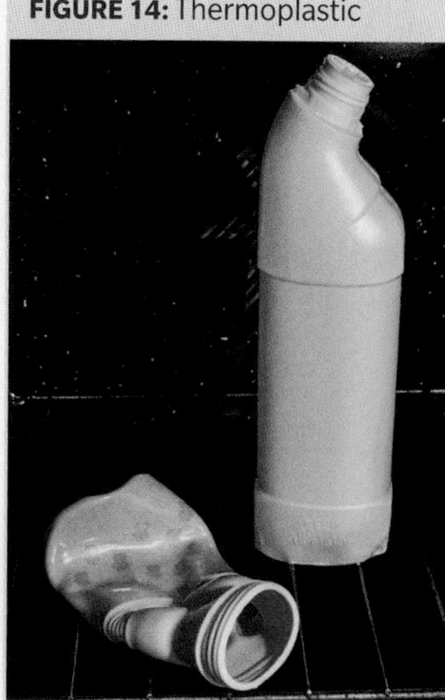

EXPLAIN Select the correct terms to complete the statement.

The greater the attractive forces are between molecules in a thermoplastic, the more flexible | tougher the material will be. Greater intermolecular forces between chains also means the plastic will melt at a lower | higher temperature. In Figure 14, the bottle with stronger intermolecular forces between its molecules is most likely the intact | melted bottle. The bottle that would be easier to recycle is most likely the intact | melted bottle. Recycling increases | reduces pollution and the need for raw materials and is typically less | more energy efficient than manufacturing new materials from scratch.

Petrochemical-based, human-designed plastics did not exist on Earth until the 1920s. Unfortunately, these plastics do not decompose readily in nature. In recent years, engineers have designed processes to recycle many types of plastics. Practical problems still remain, though, and overall plastic recycling rates are not yet optimized.

EVALUATE Some plastic objects, such as drinking straws or plastic bags, are designed to be used one time and then discarded. Describe the environmental and societal impacts of a single-use plastic. Should the production of single-use plastics be limited?

Structure and Function

Composite Materials in Prosthetic Limbs

FIGURE 15: Carbon fiber is a composite material that makes prosthetic limbs lightweight and durable.

In a composite, different materials are combined to form a new material with unique properties. One component of a composite typically surrounds and binds the other component. The original materials and the new material all exist separately in the final structure. Fiberglass is made of glass fibers and plastic. Glass is strong but brittle. The plastic holds glass fibers together to form a light, strong, and flexible fiberglass composite. Other composites include wood laminates, reinforced concrete, and waterproof clothing.

Composite materials have revolutionized prosthetic limbs. For example, "blade legs," such as the one shown in Figure 15, typically contain carbon fiber. This composite material was originally developed for use in aerospace technologies, but its use has expanded quickly due to its desirable properties. The advantages of using carbon fiber over more traditional materials include increased flexibility, greater durability and strength, and reduced weight.

Language Arts Connection Research composite materials used in prosthetic limbs. Write a blog post explaining the costs and benefits of these materials in terms of affordability, durability, and environmental impact. Use evidence from your research to analyze how the properties of these materials at the larger scale are related to their properties at the atomic scale.

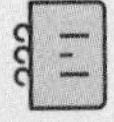

Evidence Notebook For the automobile design problem, consider how the identified criteria and constraints and material limitations affect the choice of materials for each component (dashboard, frame, on-board computer, and windshield). Decide which criteria should have the highest priority, and propose two or more materials that could be considered as a solution for each component.

Case Study: Shape Memory Alloys

Eyeglass frames must be shaped just right to hold the lenses where they belong. Imagine wearing glasses with a metal frame and dropping them in gym class—where someone steps on them and bends the frame. Although you can adjust the shape of the metal to some degree, it is hard to get the frames back to the original shape.

APPLY What criteria would eyeglass frames need to meet to be able to bend but return to their original shape?

Shape Memory Alloys

Plasticity is the ability of an object to change shape permanently without breaking when a force is applied. Elasticity refers to the ability of an object to return to its original shape when a force is applied and then removed. Many objects have either elasticity or plasticity. Shape memory alloys (SMAs) are metal alloys that exhibit both properties.

When an SMA object is bent, it can take a new shape. However, it returns to its original shape when heated. The temperature change causes the alloy to become elastic. The eyeglass frames shown in Figure 16 are made from an SMA. While stepping on the frame might permanently bend or break eyeglass frames made from plastic or a different metal, frames made from an SMA will return to their original shape.

Shape memory alloys were first produced in the mid-20th century. Initial applications were in switches responsible for opening and closing valves or turning things on or off in response to applied forces and temperature changes.

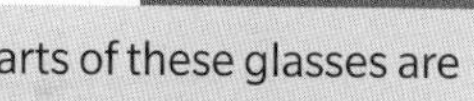

FIGURE 16: The metal parts of these glasses are made of a shape memory alloy. They return to their original shape after being bent.

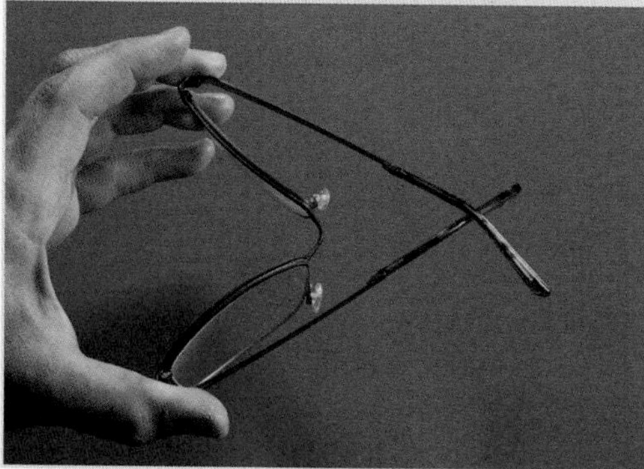

ANALYZE Based on the properties discussed, which type of device would be the best use of a shape memory alloy?

- ○ **a.** a device that can be bent into shape and then remain in position
- ○ **b.** a device that remains in the same shape during all operating conditions
- ○ **c.** a device that immediately returns to its original shape after being bent
- ○ **d.** a device that is easier to put into place in one shape but is used in another shape

SMAs are composed of two or three metal elements. The atoms are held together by metallic bonds in which valence electrons move freely among positively charged metal ions. These ions have a crystalline arrangement that can exist in different phases.

Molecular Structure Leads to Macroscopic Function

The key to shape memory is the arrangement of atoms in the alloy. The austenite phase of an SMA, shown in Figure 17, occurs above a transition temperature, which varies among SMAs. In this phase, the atoms are tightly packed, and the metal is hard and rigid.

FIGURE 17: Austenite structure

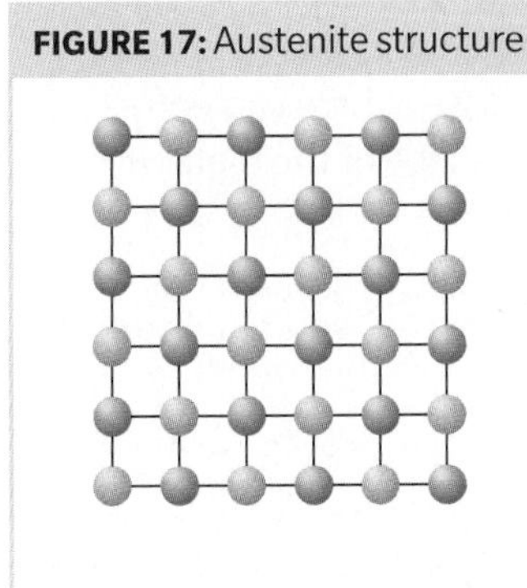

FIGURE 18: Martensite structures

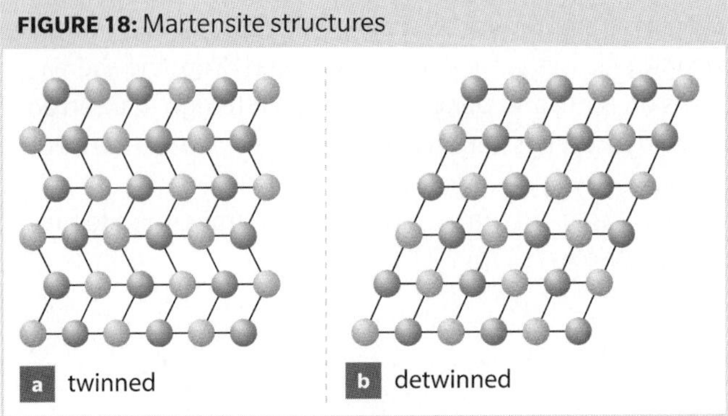

a twinned

b detwinned

At lower temperatures, a phase change occurs. The layers in the crystal rearrange and form the martensite phase, shown in Figure 18. The twinned martensite phase has the same bulk shape as the austenite material, but the layers are not locked into place. When a force is applied, the layers shift and the material deforms. The deformed phase is detwinned martensite. Because the material in this phase is plastic, the object holds the new shape.

APPLY Select the correct terms to complete the statement.

Shape memory alloys exist in different phases, depending on the temperature. A wire formed of material in the austenite | martensite phase keeps its shape, even when heated. When the wire is cooled below the transition temperature, it enters the austenite | martensite phase. Applying a force to the wire at this point can | cannot change the shape of the wire. When the wire is heated after being deformed, it returns to the austenite | martensite phase and takes on the original | deformed shape.

Collaborate As a group, discuss patterns in SMAs at the molecular scale that affect their properties at the macroscopic scale. How do the three phases affect the function of the metal?

Another property of SMAs that can be useful is superelasticity above the transition temperature. When a large force is applied to material in the austenite phase, the stressed area changes into the martensite phase, and the object bends. When the force is removed, the object returns to the austenite phase and the original shape. SMA eyeglass frames that spring back into shape after you step on them take advantage of this property.

MODEL Develop a diagram that shows how an SMA device could expand and contract. What problems might this function help solve?

Applications of Shape Memory Alloys

After the shape memory effect was discovered, engineers began looking for problems that SMAs could solve. One issue is that SMAs are more expensive than many other metals, so the applications of SMAs have to provide benefits that justify their higher price.

EVALUATE Propose a problem that could be solved through the phase change of an SMA that would provide a benefit that is worth the price of the SMA.

____

____

____

____

Consider the criteria and constraints for a medical device implanted in the human body. The device should have long-term stability and provide health benefits that outweigh its price. One constraint is size. In addition, the device must be compatible with the tissues that it touches. Based on this analysis, SMAs may be a good choice for biomedical devices. For example, arterial stents can be made of SMAs, as shown in Figure 19. A stent is implanted into a narrow artery to hold it open, restoring blood flow. A stent with shape memory can be manufactured and then cooled below the transition temperature to the martensite phase. In this phase, it is collapsed to a much thinner shape that is easier to slide into position in the artery. Once in place, the stent is warmed by the body and expands into its original austenite shape.

FIGURE 19: This stent can be collapsed in the martensite phase and will return to its original shape when warmed by the body.

EXPLAIN Place the steps of making and using a shape memory alloy as a medical stent in the correct order.

____ **a.** Stent is compressed in its martensite form.

____ **b.** Stent is cooled to below transition temperature.

____ **c.** Stent is formed into its final shape in its austenite form.

____ **d.** Stent is placed into the patient's artery.

____ **e.** Stent undergoes transition from detwinned martensite form.

Applications of shape memory alloys can also be found in space. A common constraint is size, as room inside a space vehicle is very limited. For space telescopes, the arms that hold the solar panels can be manufactured with SMAs, cooled, and bent inward to fit inside the vehicle for launch. Once the telescope is in space and absorbing energy from the sun, the arms become warm enough to change phase. They expand and straighten to the original shape, effectively deploying the solar panels.

Other applications take advantage of the unusual properties of SMAs. For example, because the size and shape of an SMA device can change as temperature changes, it may be able to expand and contract. That motion could drive a generator to produce electrical energy. Although it is not yet commercially feasible, engineers have designed a prototype SMA device that generates electrical energy from waste heat in industrial processes.

Limitations of Shape Memory Alloys

A major limitation of shape memory alloys is metal fatigue due to repeated cycling between phases. Imagine what would happen if you bent the end of a paper clip back and forth repeatedly. The end would eventually break off due to metal fatigue. This is similar to fatigue in shape memory alloys. When an SMA is fatigued, its ability to change between phases decreases, and it may break or bend permanently.

Some applications, such as the arms that open solar panels in space, require only one phase change cycle. In other cases, a device may be required to undergo many phase changes. Currently, SMAs are not suitable solutions to these problems because they are limited by how many deformations they can undergo before breaking.

Explore Online

FIGURE 20: NASA engineers conduct tests on the durability of shape memory alloy tires.

ARGUE The tire in Figure 20 is made of a shape memory alloy formed into many chains. Describe how the SMA in the tire will change as the tire is tested. Would you expect metal fatigue to be an issue in this situation? Use evidence to support your argument.

Materials scientists and engineers work to optimize the function of materials, including shape memory alloys. Scientists have developed a new alloy formula that is not limited by fatigue, even after many cycles between phases. Like most SMAs that have been used in commercial and medical applications, the new material consists mostly of titanium and nickel, but it also contains some copper and cobalt as well.

Although the research is not finished, scientists think that the copper atoms form tiny chunks within the alloy that act like bricks in a wall. The bricks bond with the surrounding atoms in both phases and function like a guide during transitions. This configuration helps the atoms jump back into place more reliably, avoiding the possibility of the bonds breaking and forming in ways that cause instability in the crystal. As scientists and engineers study this new shape memory alloy, they are looking for ways to produce it as a bulk material. Possible applications could include heart valve replacements that would need to open and close thousands of times each day. This application is currently not feasible due to metal fatigue in shape memory alloys.

Evidence Notebook Each material used to build a car has particular properties that add or detract from its usefulness for a particular purpose. Cost and availability of materials also vary. For each component, consider the tradeoffs that must be made when selecting a material type. Then use a decision matrix to evaluate your proposed materials for each component.

Careers in Science

Organic Chemist

Could you use your knowledge of intermolecular forces to help develop a cure for a disease? One person who is doing just that is James Nowick, a professor and organic chemist. Organic chemistry is the field of study that focuses on the chemistry of carbon-based molecules, especially those in living things. An organic chemist may study the structure and function of proteins, carbohydrates, DNA, or lipids. A person in this field might want to learn how these molecules are produced in the body, how they interact with other molecules, or how they affect a person's health.

Understanding the structure and function of proteins is an important part of finding cures for diseases such as Alzheimer's disease. Professor Nowick studies proteins involved in Alzheimer's and other neurodegenerative diseases. His research group is developing synthetic molecules that are similar in structure and function to these proteins. The purpose of developing these synthetic proteins is to model interactions between different parts of molecules. For example, a beta-pleated sheet is a zig-zag-shaped structure found in some proteins. When two beta-pleated sheets are near each other, hydrogen bonds form between the polar carbon-oxygen and nitrogen-hydrogen groups on the two sheets.

By using synthetic proteins as models, Nowick and his team are able to learn more about the forces that hold these molecules together and how changes in these interactions might lead to disease. The techniques his team uses include molecular modeling, spectroscopy, and x-ray crystallography. These tools allow the team to understand how the building blocks of proteins interact and how the team could possibly manipulate those interactions. The general process Nowick's team uses typically involves making new molecules that they think will interact through hydrogen bonding and other intermolecular forces. They can then analyze how the proteins fold and interact with other molecules and how they might operate in the human body.

FIGURE 21: Professor Nowick studies a model of an organic molecule.

James Nowick has been honored many times for his teaching, mentorship, and contributions to his community. He identifies as part of the LGBTQ+ community and has worked with organizations such as the Gay and Transgender Chemists and Allies subdivision of the American Chemical Society. This group works to promote inclusion, advocacy, and collaboration among LGBTQ+ chemists. Nowick's contributions to science and his community are numerous. His work will likely continue to drive important discoveries in this field and inspire others to pursue careers in science.

Chemistry in Your Community Using multiple sources, research a scientist who works in the field of organic chemistry or biochemistry. Develop a profile for this person that explains the topics they study, what questions they hope to answer through their research, and how they collaborate with others in their field. Discuss the real-world applications of their research, and, if applicable, explain how intermolecular forces are related to their area of study.

APPLICATIONS OF MATERIALS SCIENCE

EVAPORATION AND INK SOLVENTS

CAREER: BIOMEDICAL ENGINEER

Go online to choose one of these other paths.

Lesson Self-Check

CAN YOU SOLVE THE PROBLEM?

FIGURE 22: Materials for car parts are designed and chosen based on the properties of the material, the function of the part, and defined criteria and constraints.

The choice of a material for a specific function depends on the properties of the material and how well it meets the defined criteria and constraints. Engineers decide what materials to use for each part of a car by analyzing the role of that part in the operation of the car and matching materials to the criteria determined for that role. The structural elements that give strength and bind together the rest of the vehicle have very different functions from the panels that provide the outer covering. Every material has specific properties that are based on its structure at the molecular level. Therefore, some materials are suitable for a particular function, but others are not.

Evidence Notebook What are the best materials to use for manufacturing different parts of a car? Refer to notes in your Evidence Notebook to propose a solution using a claim, evidence, and reasoning. Your solution should address the following points:

Claim What is the best material type (ceramic, metal, polymer, or semiconductor) for each car component: dashboard, frame, on-board computer, and windshield?

Evidence Summarize the evidence you have gathered to support your claim. Include information about the relationship between the molecular structure and properties of the material, and the function of each car component.

Reasoning Explain how the evidence you cited supports your claim.

Name Date

CHECKPOINTS

Check Your Understanding

1. Why are metals generally ductile, or able to be pulled into wires?
   - a. Metal ions form strong, rigid three-dimensional networks.
   - b. Ions within the metal structure easily slide past one another.
   - c. The bonds between metal atoms are very strong and they stick tightly together.
   - d. Valence electrons can flow freely through the material when there is an electric potential.

2. How does the addition of an element that can donate electrons, such as phosphorus, into a silicon crystal change the electrical properties of the crystal?
   - a. Conductivity is not affected by an increase in electrons.
   - b. The donor atoms bond with all free electrons, increasing conductivity.
   - c. The unbonded electrons from the donor atoms are mobile, increasing conductivity.
   - d. Conductivity is lower at high concentrations of the donor atoms than at low concentrations of the donor atoms.

3. Select the correct terms to complete the statement about thermoplastic polymers.

   The strength of intermolecular forces between polymer chains affects the properties of the material. The greater the intermolecular forces between adjacent molecules, the more | less rigid one would expect the material to be. As the strength of attractive forces between molecules increases, more | less energy is required to melt the material. Therefore, it would be easier to recycle a plastic with relatively strong | weak intermolecular forces between its molecules as compared to other types of plastics.

4. Which statements best describe a composite material? Select all correct answers.
   - a. Composites all contain carbon, which makes them lightweight.
   - b. A composite may have more desirable properties than its components.
   - c. Composites form hydrogen bonds, which makes them stronger than their components.
   - d. A brick made of mud and straw is an example of a composite; a brick made of mud is not.

5. Select the correct terms to complete the statement about how molecular patterns affect a shape memory alloy valve.

   A temperature-sensitive valve is manufactured from a shape memory alloy in its austenite | twinned martensite | detwinned martensite phase. When the device is cooled, a phase change occurs, and the material's plasticity decreases | increases | remains stable. After being deformed, the material holds its new shape until it is bent | cooled | heated | stressed, which causes another phase change. The phase change from the deformed state to the original state is an example of the conductivity | elasticity | plasticity of shape memory alloys.

6. Given the constraint of metal fatigue, for which of these problems might SMA materials be a suitable solution? Select all correct answers.
   - a. wires that hold teeth in place for a long time during orthodontic procedures
   - b. automated pistons that move up and down in an automobile engine
   - c. connectors between bones in a replacement knee joint
   - d. sensors to open a sprinkler head during a fire
   - e. landing gear on a robotic Mars lander

CHECKPOINTS (continued)

7. How does defining an engineering problem and identifying criteria and constraints help engineers determine the types of materials that are likely to be suitable for use in a device?

8. How do the electrical interactions of attraction and repulsion determine the properties of a material and how it can be applied to an engineering solution?

9. Describe a material that has had unintended consequences on society or the environment. What constraints could be considered when evaluating solutions that use this material?

MAKE YOUR OWN STUDY GUIDE

In your Evidence Notebook, design a study guide that supports the main ideas from this lesson:

The engineering design process is a way to determine the best material for a solution.

The properties of materials are determined by structure at the molecular level.

Different materials are used based on the required function of the part or product.

Remember to include the following information in your study guide:

- Use examples that model main ideas.
- Record explanations for the phenomena you investigated.
- Use evidence to support your explanations. Your support can include drawings, data, graphs, laboratory conclusions, and other evidence recorded throughout the lesson.

Consider how the structure and function of a system or product can be explained by examining how its components are connected and determining the molecular structure of materials used.

Engineering Connection

Studying Volcanoes Scientists have limited, but ever-growing, knowledge about the conditions inside active volcano craters. These are places filled with toxic and corrosive gases, extreme heat, and unpredictable shifts of matter—not easy laboratories in which to work. Because scientists cannot enter a volcano themselves, they send in robots to collect data for them. The challenge for engineers is to design a robot or drone that can withstand those inhospitable conditions that keep humans out of volcano craters.

Using a range of sources, prepare a poster presentation describing the processes used to engineer robots for extreme tasks, such as collecting data in an active volcano. Pay attention to the properties of the materials engineers use to build robots for these extreme tasks.

FIGURE 1: Conditions inside an active volcano crater are not suitable for humans, so research relies on robots and drones.

Social Studies Connection

Pigments Pigments are substances used for coloring. They have the ability to absorb and emit light at certain wavelengths, giving them distinct colors. Pigments derived from natural sources, such as plants or minerals, often have special significance for cultures where the natural source is located.

Research ways that pigments are used in various cultures around the world. Write a report explaining how the pigments are used, how they are derived, and ways in which their production may have become more environmentally friendly or safe over time.

FIGURE 2: An array of different pigments

Life Science Connection

Cell Chemistry Cells in the nervous system called *neurons* rely on the charges of sodium and potassium ions in order to send signals through the nervous system. When a neuron receives a signal, sodium ions are quickly pumped into the inner membrane of the cell while potassium ions are slowly pumped out. This begins a chain reaction that moves the signal through the neuron. Eventually, the neuron releases neurotransmitters which then signal a different neuron to begin the cycle again.

Choose another type of cell to investigate. Research the roles of ions, molecules, and chemical reactions in the cell. Using multiple sources as references, develop a comic strip or short animation that shows how the cell uses chemistry to function. Along with your comic strip or animation, provide a short description that briefly explains the process.

FIGURE 3: A false color scanning electron micrograph of a neuron (green) grown on cultured cells (orange).

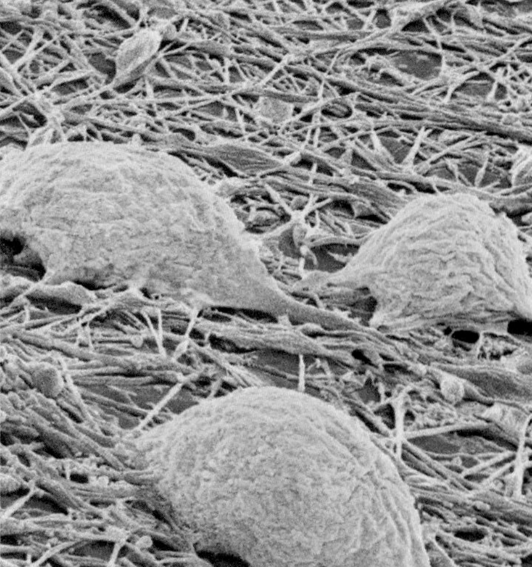

THING EXPLAINER BY RANDALL MUNROE

THE WATER IN OUR BODIES

Blood and other kinds of watery stuff inside us

Plasma, the liquid part of blood, is made up of water, salts, and protein. Blood also contains some solids, such as red blood cells, white blood cells, and platelets. What makes up the other watery substances our bodies produce?

A BOOK EXPLAINING COMPLEX IDEAS USING ONLY THE 1,000 MOST COMMON WORDS

RANDALL MUNROE
XKCD.COM

THE STORY OF WATERY STUFF INSIDE OUR BODIES

OUR BLOOD, AND MOST OF THE WATER IN OUR BODIES, HAS THIS STUFF IN IT:

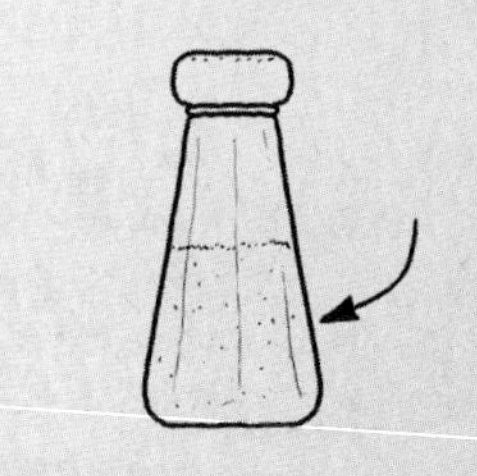

SO DOES THE SEA.

A WORLD LEADER ONCE SAID THAT THERE'S EXACTLY AS MUCH OF THAT STUFF IN OUR BLOOD AS THERE IS IN THE SEA, BECAUSE ALL LIFE CAME FROM THE SEA.

HE WAS RIGHT THAT LIFE COMES FROM THE SEA, BUT WRONG ABOUT OUR BLOOD. THERE'S MORE OF THAT WHITE STUFF IN THE SEAS THAN IN OUR BLOOD.

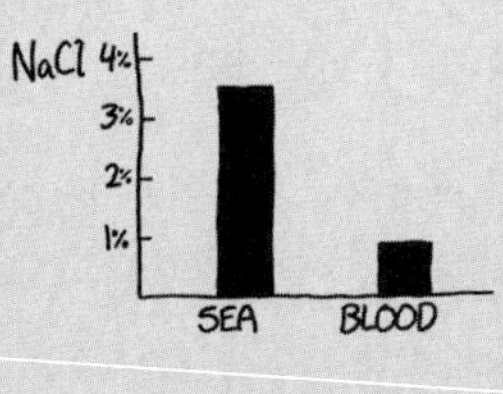

THANKS TO THE STUFF IN IT, THE WATER IN OUR BODIES CAN CARRY POWER. POWER MOVES THROUGH THE BODY BY PUSHING AND PULLING ON THE STUFF IN THE WATER.

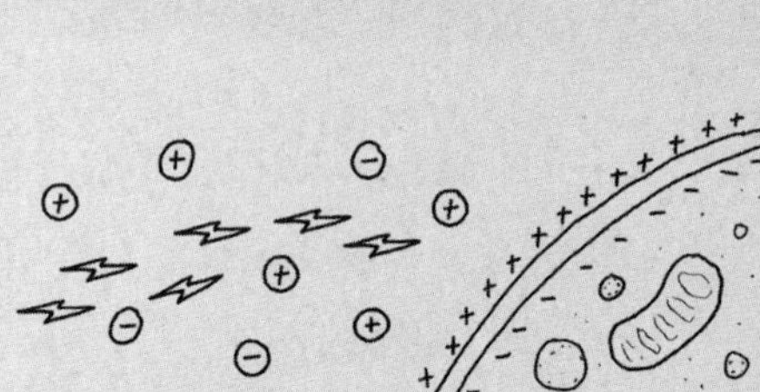

THIS WATER CAN CARRY MESSAGES IN OUR BODY THE WAY PHONE LINES CARRY VOICES, AND LETS OUR BODIES USE POWER TO PUSH AND PULL THINGS IN AND OUT OF OUR BLOOD.

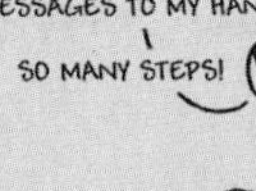

IT MAY NOT BE EXACTLY THE SAME AS THE SEAS THAT LIFE CAME FROM, BUT THE WATER IN OUR BODIES IS LIKE A LITTLE SEA OF OUR OWN, FULL OF HIDDEN POOLS AND TINY WONDERS.

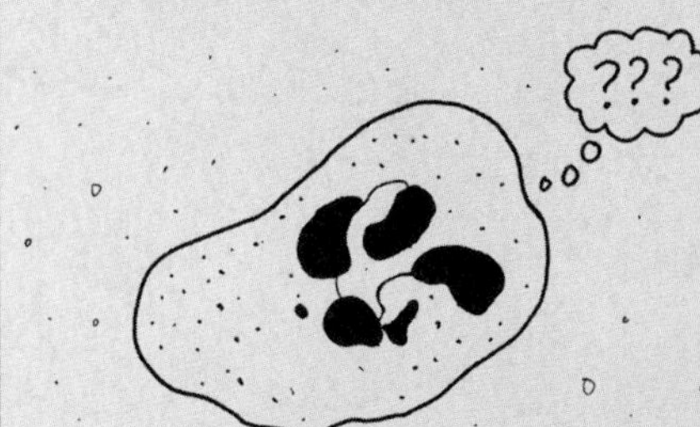

MOSTLY WATER

People often say that our bodies are mostly water, which is true. By weight, our bodies are about three parts water to two parts everything else. This water has all kinds of other things added to it. Your blood, the wet stuff in your mouth, the stuff that comes out of your eyes when you cry, and the stuff in your nose are almost all water; there's just a little other stuff in there too, and that stuff makes those kinds of water different from the normal clear water that you drink.

Since so much of our bodies are made of water, you might think that if you got a hole in your body, all your water would run out. It's true that your blood could come out—which is why people try not to get holes in them—but blood makes up only a small part of a human body's water. Most of the water is locked up in other parts of our body. Almost all the pieces we're made of have water in them—even our bones!

Most of our body parts, like all living things, are made of very tiny bags. Some of these bags hang around in our blood, while others stick together to make body parts like our hearts and skin. These bags are full of all kinds of things, but they're also full of water. If you get a hole in your body, a lot of the water is stuck in those bags—or in small spaces in between them—and won't go anywhere unless all the tiny bags break up.

WHERE IS ALL THE WATERY STUFF?

Here's what the different kinds of water in your bodies would look like if you put it in large bottles. (These are the size of bottles that people bring to parties to fill lots of people's cups from. They're often full of colorful drinks that make young people stay up all night.)

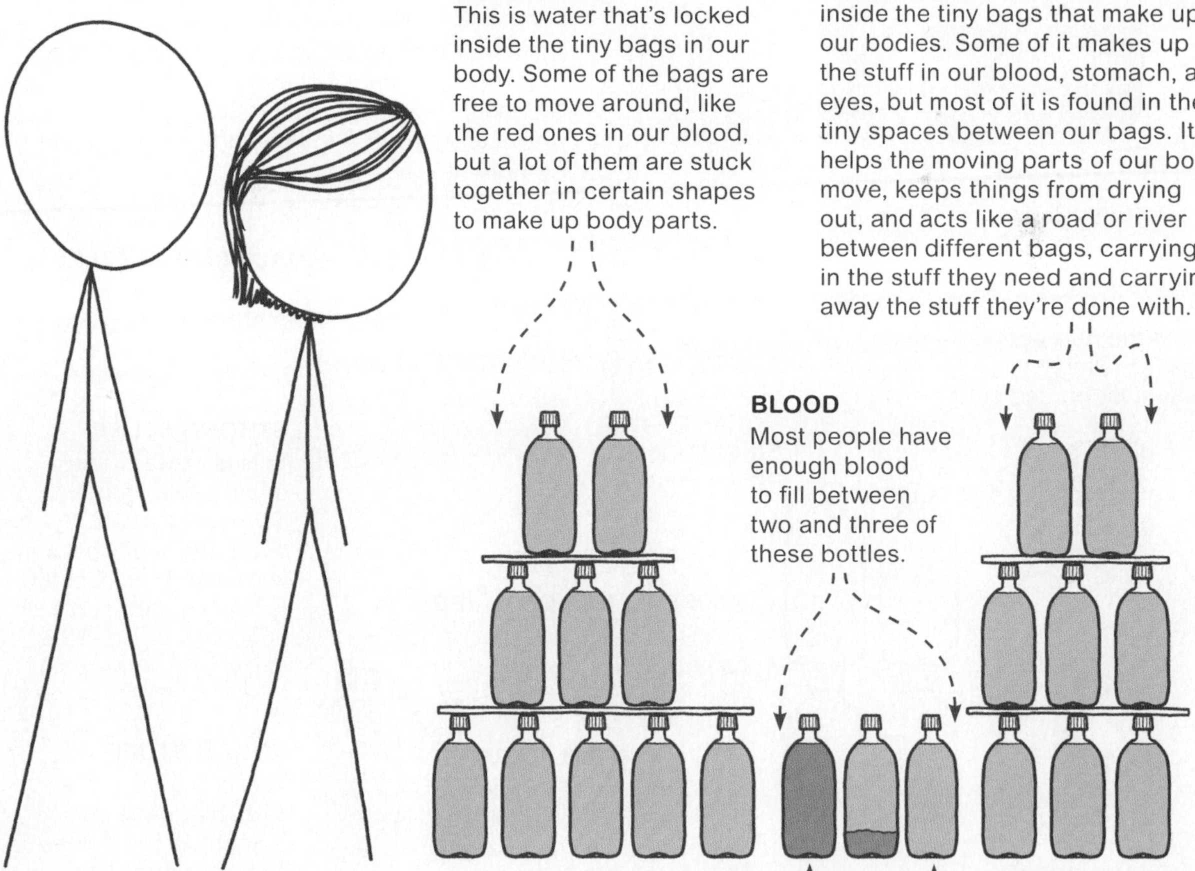

BLOOD

WATER INSIDE OUR BAGS

This is the water that's inside the red bags in our blood. These bags are red because they have a lot of metal in them.

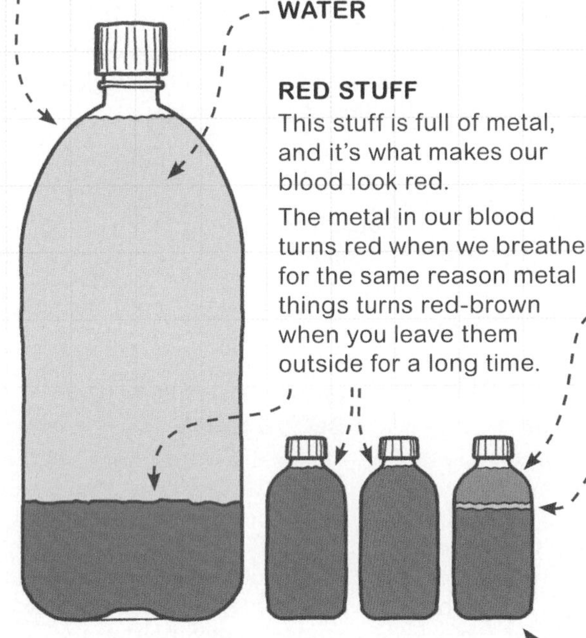

STUFF THAT STICKS TOGETHER TO COVER HOLES

If something makes a hole in your body, all your blood can fall out, which is bad. This stuff tries to fill those holes before you lose too much blood.

The hole-filling stuff is made of tiny flat circle-shaped bags. When they get near a hole, they stick together, making a thick layer that's strong enough to hold in your blood while your skin grows back over the hole.

BODY GUARDS

Some of the bags in your blood are there to keep you safe from attacks by tiny living things. Things that get into your body can make you sick. To stop them, these guards are always traveling around your body, looking for anything that's not supposed to be there. When they find something they don't like, they have all kinds of ways to mark it, attack it, and get rid of it.

SMALL-SIZE BOTTLES

These bottles are the largest size that you're allowed to carry on a flight in the US.

WATER OUTSIDE OF OUR BAGS

This is the part of our blood that's not locked up in the red bags. It's almost all water, and is kind of yellow in color if you take out all the red stuff.

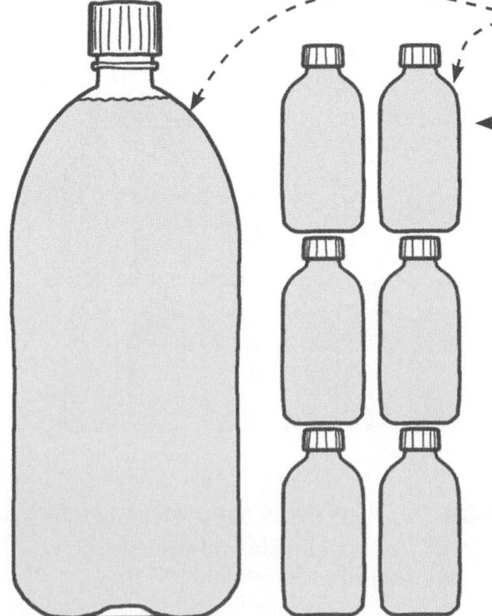

STUFF TO PUT ON CHIPS

This part of blood has the same stuff as on chips or in the sea.

METAL CARRIER

This stuff carries red metal in the blood. It can pick up metal and carry it into a bag.

WHITE STUFF

This is like the stuff in egg whites. Lots of things stick to it, and it carries them around the body.

STRONG STUFF

This is made of lots of long, thin pieces shaped like hairs. When the sticky bags in your blood are coming together to stop up a hole, these hairs help make them strong.

ROUND STUFF

This is like the white stuff, but made of bigger pieces. It does a lot of things , like carrying stuff around the body and sticking to things that shouldn't be there so your body guards can find and get rid of them.

OTHER WATERY STUFF

SKIN WATER

This is the water that comes out of your skin when you get too hot. As your skin dries, the water carries away heat. This water comes from the clear part of your blood.

A normal person might make this much of it in a day, but they might make a lot more if they spend time in the heat.

KINDS OF SKIN WATER

One kind of skin water keeps you cool. It comes out of your skin all over your body, and it doesn't smell like much. It's mostly water, with just a little bit of stuff in it that makes it like the sea.

Another kind of water only comes out of certain parts of the body with hair on them, like under your arms. Your body makes it when you're worried or afraid, and it's thicker and less watery than the other kind. And after it's been there for a while, it starts to smell.

A drink bottle for one person

A tiny glass, the kind that holds drinks that you drink all at once

YELLOW WATER

This stuff holds all the watery things your body is getting rid of.

It's mostly water. The main other thing in it—which got its name because it's found in yellow water—carries stuff out of the body. It's full of the kind of stuff that makes trees and grass grow.

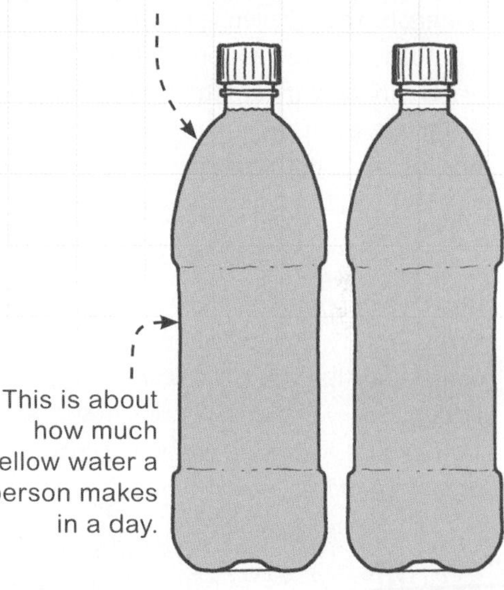

This is about how much yellow water a person makes in a day.

BRAIN WATER

This is the layer of water that goes around the brain. It's very much like the yellow stuff in your blood, but it's more clean and clear, so nothing gets in the brain and hurts it.

When you hit your head, this water holds your brain in place and tries to keep it from running into the bone around it.

MOUTH WATER

The water in your mouth helps food slide down your throat. It's also full of stuff that starts breaking down food as you eat it.

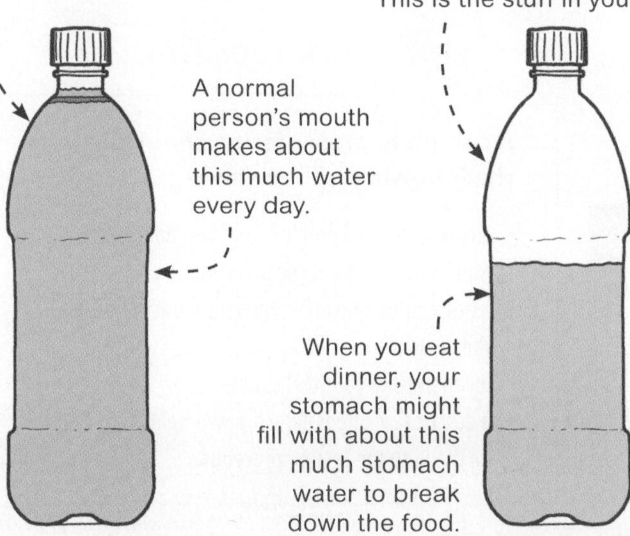

A normal person's mouth makes about this much water every day.

STOMACH WATER

This is the stuff in your stomach.

When you eat dinner, your stomach might fill with about this much stomach water to break down the food.

If you have a cold, this is how much of this stuff can fit in your nose.

NOSE STUFF

This is the stuff that comes out of your nose sometimes. It's mostly water and is a lot like the stuff that lines your throat and stomach. It helps keep the layers under it from drying out and breaking open, and catches and stops dust and things that you breathe in.

THE STUFF INSIDE YOUR EYE

This is almost completely water, but it's full of thin hairlike stuff, too small to see, which makes it thicker than water and helps the eye keep its shape.

Testing Water-Repellent Fabrics

You are working for a company that makes water-repellent materials. Water-repellent fabrics are often used in tents, garments such as coats and shoes, and tarps that protect valuable materials. Your challenge is to develop a procedure to test a fabric that repels water. Not only should the material keep water out, but it should be breathable, or allow air to flow through.

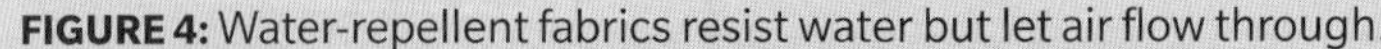
FIGURE 4: Water-repellent fabrics resist water but let air flow through.

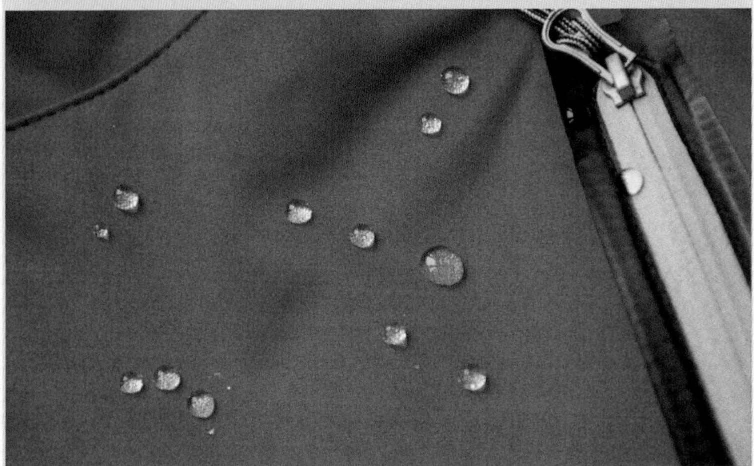

1. DEFINE THE PROBLEM

Describe the problem you will address in this activity. Include criteria and any constraints that you will consider in your design. How will you determine how well your design repels water and how breathable it is?

2. CONDUCT RESEARCH

Research water-repellent fabrics and methods used for testing them. What is meant by the term *water-repellent*, and how is this different from waterproof? How do the adhesive and cohesive properties of water influence the way water-repellent fabrics are designed? Consider examples of plants that can also repel water and how these have influenced human-made designs.

3. CARRY OUT AN INVESTIGATION

Develop a plan for testing water-repellent fabric. Consider what materials and technology you will need, how you will safely collect and analyze data, and how you will properly dispose of waste materials.

Explore Online

Engineering Lab

Design Water-Repellent Fabrics Plan an investigation to design and test a water-repellent fabric. Develop a procedure to test how well the fabric repels water, as well as its breathability.

4. EVALUATE DATA

Explain which parts of your testing procedure worked well and which could be improved. How might the testing procedure differ if the tests were conducted in a facility with more advanced equipment? How would you use the results of your tests to suggest further improvements to water-repellent fabrics?

5. COMMUNICATE

With your team, develop a presentation including the problem you defined, your research on water-repellent fabrics, and the results of your tests. Explain how intermolecular forces are related to the results you obtained, and suggest areas for further research.

CHECK YOUR WORK

A complete presentation should include the following information:

- a clearly defined problem that was addressed during the course of the investigation
- a description of water-repellent fabrics and how they work
- an analysis of your test results
- a description of possible improvements that could be made to the testing procedure

Name ______________________ Date ______________

SYNTHESIZE THE UNIT

In your Evidence Notebook, make a concept map, other graphic organizer, or outline using the Study Guides you made for each lesson in this unit. Be sure to use evidence to support your claims.

When synthesizing individual information, remember to follow these general steps:

- Find the central idea of each piece of information.
- Think about the relationships among the central ideas.
- Combine the ideas to come up with a new understanding.

DRIVING QUESTIONS

Look back to the Driving Questions from the opening section of this unit. In your Evidence Notebook, review and revise your previous answers to those questions. Use the evidence you gathered and other observations you made throughout the unit to support your claims.

PRACTICE AND REVIEW

1. Which of these compounds would likely conduct an electrical current if dissolved in water? Select all correct answers.

- ☐ **a.** dioxygen, O_2
- ☐ **b.** magnesium bromide, $MgBr_2$
- ☐ **c.** gallium(III) nitrite, $Ga(NO_2)_3$
- ☐ **d.** carbon tetrabromide, CBr_4
- ☐ **e.** dinitrogen tetroxide, N_2O_4

2. A company wants to develop a plastic that can be used to hold food while it cooks in an oven. Complete the statement comparing different types of polymers the company could use.

Linear polymers stack together neatly, whereas branched polymers do not. Linear polymers are held together less | more tightly by intermolecular forces. As a result, linear polymers typically have melting points that are lower than | higher than | the same as branched polymers. Therefore, a linear | branched polymer is best because the product will be used at high temperatures.

3. Which of these is a correctly written formula for the compound? Select all correct answers.

- ☐ **a.** aluminum bromide, $AlBr_3$
- ☐ **b.** strontium iodide, Sr_2I
- ☐ **c.** sodium fluoride, NaF
- ☐ **d.** barium phosphide, Ba_3P_2
- ☐ **e.** magnesium selenide, Mg_2Se

4. Scientists are conducting an experiment to determine the melting point of a substance. They find that the melting point is about 90 °C higher than they expected based on the size and molecular mass of the compound. What would explain their results? Select all correct answers.

- ☐ **a.** Dipole-induced dipole attractions strongly hold the molecules together.
- ☐ **b.** Temporary dipole-induced attractions form in the solid when it melts.
- ☐ **c.** The substance is strongly polar, so dipole-dipole attractions exist.
- ☐ **d.** Hydrogen bonding strongly holds the molecules together in the solid state.

5. A substance is dissolved in pure water, and both the freezing point and the boiling point of the liquid change. Which of these statements are true? Select all correct answers.

- ☐ **a.** The change in boiling point is directly proportional to the molarity of the solution.
- ☐ **b.** The freezing point of the pure water is higher than the freezing point of the solution.
- ☐ **c.** The change in the freezing point occurs because the vapor pressure of the solution is higher than that of the pure water.
- ☐ **d.** The change in vapor pressure causes the boiling point of the solution to be higher than the boiling point of the pure water.

6. A 3.28 L solution is prepared by dissolving 535 g $CaCl_2$ in water. What is the molarity of the solution? Though more expensive than NaCl, $CaCl_2$ can prevent water from freezing and melt ice at lower temperatures than standard road salt. Explain why this happens.

7. Explain how hydrogen bonding is related to the properties of materials, such as water. Why is hydrogen bonding so important to biochemistry?

8. A water molecule, H_2O, has a bent shape. Explain how the valence electrons of the atoms cause the molecule to have this shape.

UNIT PROJECT

Return to your unit project. Prepare a presentation using your research and materials, and share it with the class. In your final presentation, evaluate the strength of your hypothesis, data, analysis, and conclusions.

Remember these tips while evaluating:

- What structural features are common to all detergents, and how do they affect the properties of detergents?
- How can you model detergent and soap structures to help illustrate their functions?
- Why might different detergents be used for different applications?
- How do intermolecular forces facilitate the usefulness of detergents?

UNIT 4

Chemical Reactions

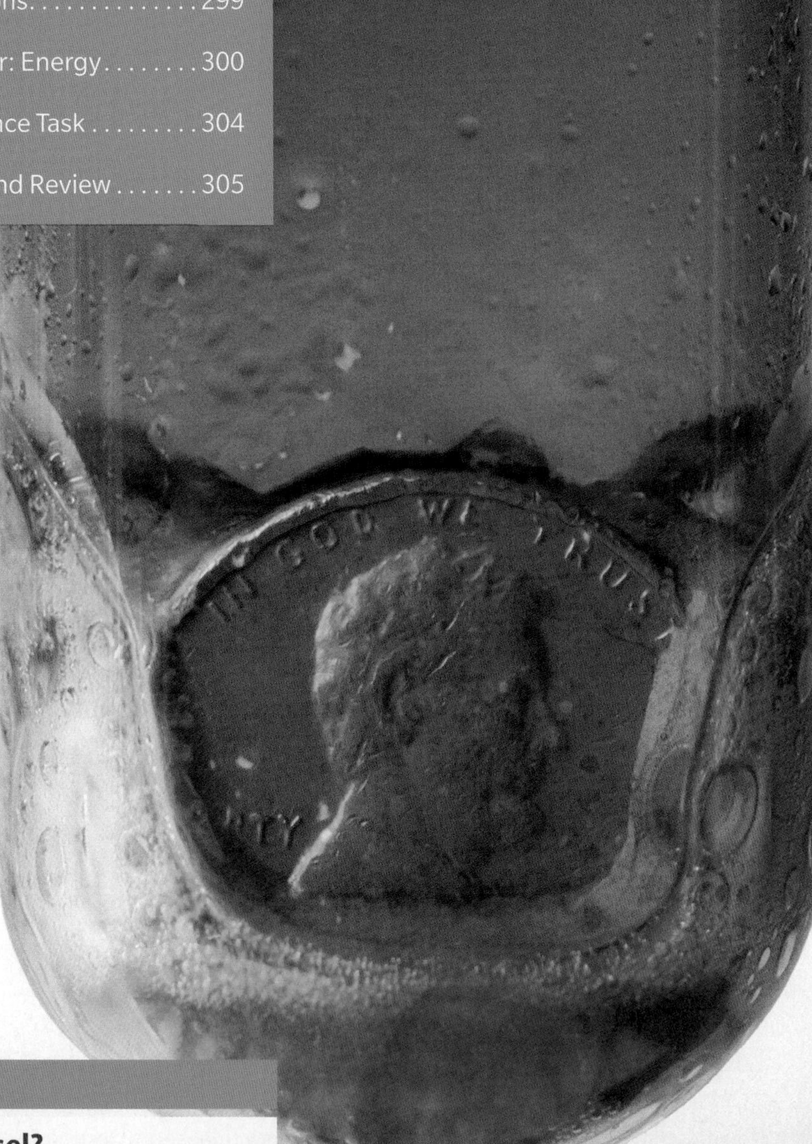

The reaction of copper and nitric acid produces nitric oxide gas and a solution of copper nitrate.

YOU SOLVE IT

Why Use Diesel?

To begin exploring this unit's concepts, go online to investigate ways to solve a real-world problem.

FIGURE 1: The Statue of Liberty is green due to the formation of patina.

If you've ever visited the Statue of Liberty, you likely noticed the unusual blue-green color of its metal exterior. The metal, however, is copper. When the statue was dedicated in 1886, it was the color of a shiny copper penny. In time, the exposure of the statue's outer surface to compounds in the air changed it first to a dull brown and then, finally, to the blue-green color it is today. This color change occurred due to the formation of compounds on the statue's surface, forming what is called a patina. The statue will stay this color for a long time, as the patina protects it from further reactions. You might have seen similar changes in the color of copper pipes or tools left out in the rain.

PREDICT How might a chemical reaction be related to the change in color of the statue? Why might the statue gain or lose mass?

DRIVING QUESTIONS

As you move through the unit, gather evidence to help you answer the following questions. In your Evidence Notebook, record what you already know about these topics and any questions you have about them.

1. How does the law of conservation of mass apply to chemical reactions at both the macroscopic and atomic scales?
2. In what ways can the changes in chemical reactions be quantified in terms of reactants and products?
3. What are the sources of energy in chemical systems and processes?
4. How can we model the patterns of energy flow in a chemical reaction?

UNIT PROJECT

Go online to download the Unit Project Worksheet to help plan your project.

Modeling Heating Efficiency

Develop a model demonstrating how the energy released by burning fuel in a furnace is distributed throughout a building. Use your model to test where heat loss occurs in the building and refine your model to minimize that heat loss. Determine possible tradeoffs in using different types of fuels to heat buildings, such as cost and potentially harmful emissions.

Language Development

Use the lessons in this unit to complete the chart and expand your understanding of the science concepts.

TERM: chemical reaction

Definition	Example

Similar Term	Phrase

TERM: chemical equation

Definition	Example

Similar Term	Phrase

TERM: law of conservation of mass

Definition	Example

Similar Term	Phrase

TERM: mole

Definition	Example

Similar Term	Phrase

TERM: specific heat capacity

Definition	Example

Similar Term	Phrase

TERM: law of conservation of energy

Definition	Example

Similar Term	Phrase

TERM: exothermic reaction

Definition	Example

Similar Term	Phrase

TERM: endothermic reaction

Definition	Example

Similar Term	Phrase

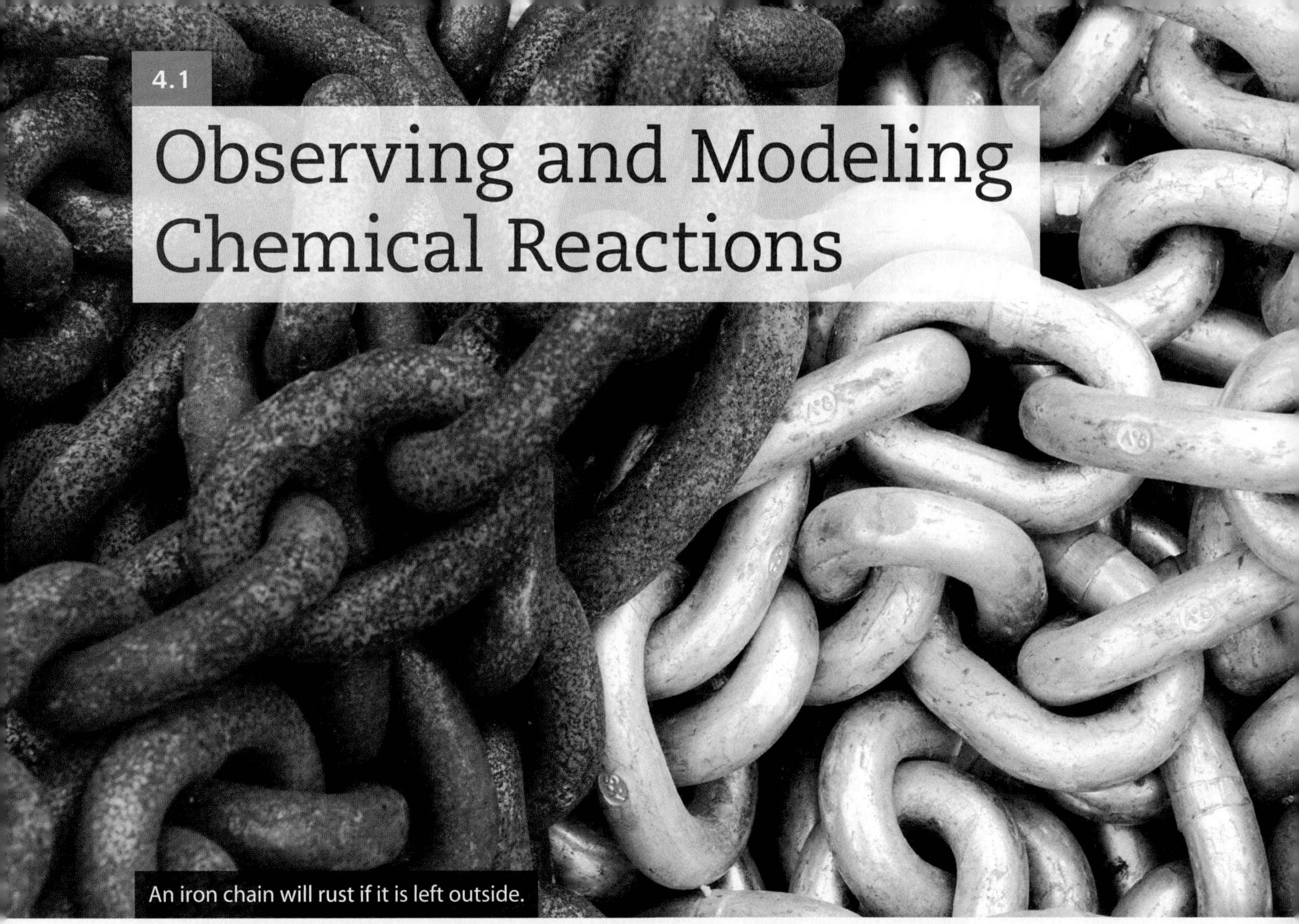

4.1

Observing and Modeling Chemical Reactions

An iron chain will rust if it is left outside.

CAN YOU EXPLAIN THE PHENOMENON?

Some metal objects, such as this iron chain, will corrode within a few months if left outdoors. Other objects, such as something made of gold, probably will not. C*orrosion* is the reaction of metals with substances in their environment. Many metals are prone to corrosion. In humid or wet climates, the corrosion of metals is common. In dry climates, however, corrosion is much less prevalent, which explains why automobiles and metal structures in dry areas last longer. Not all corrosion is bad. The green hue on the Statue of Liberty is corrosion that protects the underlying copper from further damage.

INFER Rusting is the corrosion of iron that appears as a reddish-brown deposit. Why might iron corrode more quickly than other metals? Why do you think rusting is more pronounced in some environments than others?

Evidence Notebook As you explore the lesson, gather evidence to explain why rust forms and how it can be prevented.

Hands-On Lab

Evaluating Systems in Chemical Reactions

In your everyday life, you have seen many examples of chemical reactions. Chemical reactions involve the change of one or more substances—the reactants—into one or more different substances—the products. Burning wood is an example of a chemical reaction. The wood and oxygen from the air change into carbon dioxide, water, and ash.

Observable evidence that a chemical change has occurred includes a color change, the formation of a new solid or gas, and the release of energy in the form of light, sound, or heat. Chemical reactions may also absorb energy, leaving the reaction vessel feeling cold to the touch. But how do you quantify the amount of matter consumed and produced by a chemical reaction?

In this lab, you will perform two reactions, each occurring in a different type of system. For each reaction, you should record both qualitative and quantitative data, including evidence that a chemical reaction has occurred and the masses of the reactants and products.

RESEARCH QUESTION How does the flow of energy and matter in chemical reactions in open and closed systems differ? Develop a visual model to explain your findings.

POSSIBLE MATERIALS

- indirectly vented chemical splash goggles, nonlatex apron, nitrile gloves
- balance
- balloon, nonlatex
- Bunsen burner
- calcium chloride, $CaCl_2$, (5–10 g)
- crucible
- Erlenmeyer flask, 250 mL
- funnel
- graduated cylinder, 25 mL
- magnesium, Mg, ribbon, (5 cm)
- resealable plastic bag
- sodium bicarbonate, $NaHCO_3$, (5–10 g)
- spoons or spatulas (2)
- tongs
- water, 25 mL
- weighing boats or weighing paper (4)

SAFETY INFORMATION

indirectly vented chemical splash goggles

- Wear indirectly vented chemical splash goggles, a nonlatex apron, and nitrile gloves during the setup, hands-on, and takedown segments of the activity.
- Use caution when working with Bunsen burners, because this heat source can seriously burn skin and clothing.
- Secure loose clothing, wear closed-toe shoes, and tie back long hair.
- Use tongs to handle magnesium. Never look directly at magnesium when it is burning.
- Never pour chemicals, either used or unused, back into their original container. Dispose of chemicals according to your teacher's instructions.
- Use caution when working with glassware, which can shatter and cut skin.
- Wash your hands with soap and water immediately after completing this activity.

Part I: Burning Magnesium in an Open System

FIGURE 1: Magnesium is ignited in an open system.

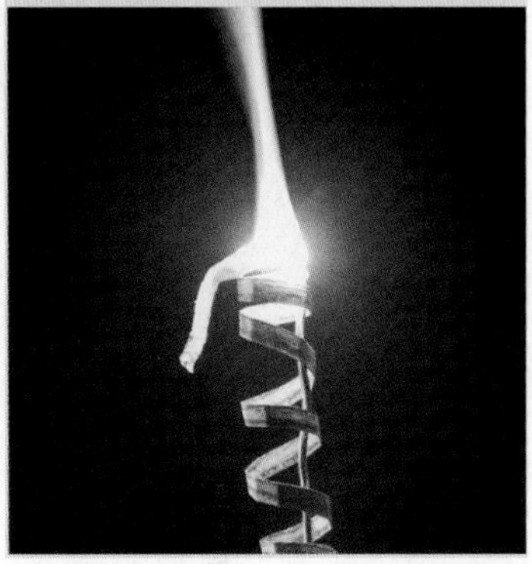

MAKE A CLAIM

In Part I, you will burn magnesium in a crucible. Magnesium emits a bright light when burning, as shown in Figure 1, so do not look directly at the burning magnesium. A crucible is an open system. How will the mass of the reactants compare to the mass of the products in an open system?

PLAN THE INVESTIGATION

Describe the experimental setup for this investigation. What do you think will happen, and how will you collect and measure any products that form?

In your Evidence Notebook, develop a procedure and a safety plan for your investigation. Have your teacher approve your plans before proceeding.

COLLECT DATA

Collect both quantitative and qualitative data before and after the reaction. Choose an appropriate level of accuracy, and record your data in a table.

ANALYZE

1. What evidence is there that a chemical reaction occurred in Part I?

2. Use your data to compare the reactants and products. Is this what you expected to observe? How would you explain any changes in mass between the reactants and the products?

DRAW CONCLUSIONS

Write a conclusion that addresses each of the points below.

Claim When magnesium metal burns, it reacts with oxygen gas in the air to form a compound called magnesium oxide. How did performing this reaction in an open system affect measurements of mass for the reactants and products?

Evidence Describe evidence from your experiment to support your claim.

Reasoning Explain how the evidence you cited supports your claim. How does your evidence show the effects the open system had on your measurements?

Part II: Capturing Carbon Dioxide Produced in a Closed System

MAKE A CLAIM

In Part II, you will design a closed system that will capture all of the products of the chemical reaction, including carbon dioxide gas. How will the mass of the reactants compare to the mass of the products in a closed system?

PLAN THE INVESTIGATION

To perform this experiment, you will combine water, calcium chloride, and sodium bicarbonate in a plastic bag. The closed system should include only these substances. The water you add is not a reactant, but it is necessary for the reaction to proceed because calcium chloride and sodium bicarbonate only react in solution. The products are calcium carbonate, sodium chloride, water, and carbon dioxide. The mass of water can be calculated indirectly by measuring its volume because the density of water is 1.00 g/mL. For example, 30.0 mL of water has a mass of 30.0 g.

1. Your task is to determine how the mass of the reactants compares to the mass of the products in a closed system. Describe what you think will happen and how you will collect and measure products that form.

2. Draw a diagram that shows your experimental setup to carry out the reaction in a closed system using a plastic bag.

In your Evidence Notebook, develop a procedure and a safety plan for your investigation. Ask your teacher to approve your plans before proceeding.

COLLECT DATA

Collect both quantitative and qualitative data before and after the reaction. Choose an appropriate level of accuracy, and record your data in a table. Consider how you will account for the mass of the container when analyzing your data.

ANALYZE

1. What evidence is there that a chemical reaction occurred in Part II of this lab?

2. Use your data to compare the reactants and products in Part II. Is this what you expected to observe?

3. With precise and accurate measurements, do you think the measured mass of reactants will always equal the measured mass of products in a chemical reaction that occurs in a closed system? Use evidence to support your answer.

DRAW CONCLUSIONS

Write a conclusion that addresses each of the points below.

Claim How did performing this reaction in a closed system affect measurements of mass for the reactants and products?

Evidence Describe evidence from your experiment to support your claim.

Reasoning Explain how the evidence you cited supports your claim. How does your evidence show the effects the closed system had on your measurements?

EXTEND

Air is 78% nitrogen gas and 21% oxygen gas by volume. Which gas is more reactive, and what causes the difference in reactivity? Why must air be considered when determining reactants and products in a chemical reaction?

Evidence Notebook Compare rusting to your experiment burning magnesium. List similarities and differences between the two reactions, and predict what might be happening in the formation of rust. Do you think a rusty iron chain has more or less mass than the original chain?

Exploring the Conservation of Mass

Chemists have long observed patterns in the way matter changes when undergoing chemical reactions. In the late 1700s, Antoine Lavoisier, often called the first "modern chemist," hypothesized that matter was never created or destroyed during a chemical reaction. To test this hypothesis, Lavoisier needed to take accurate and precise measurements while performing experiments under controlled conditions. He designed apparatus for his experiments that would prevent gases from escaping. This allowed Lavoisier to carefully weigh the materials before and after his experiments.

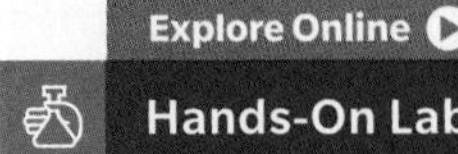

The Composition of Hydrates
Analyze how much water is released when varying amounts of copper sulfate pentahydrate are heated.

Collaborate As a class, discuss why it was important for Lavoisier to measure his experiments accurately and precisely. How might the production of gases have frustrated earlier attempts to understand conservation of mass?

Mass Is Conserved

Through further experimentation, scientists confirmed that when a chemical reaction occurs, the total amount of matter present in a system before the reaction always equals the total amount of matter present after the reaction. So, the total mass of the reactants, or starting materials, equals the total mass of the products, or ending materials. This is known as the law of conservation of mass, and it is illustrated in Figure 2.

FIGURE 2: Hydrogen and oxygen react to form water. Count the number of atoms of hydrogen and oxygen in the reactants and the product. Mass has been conserved.

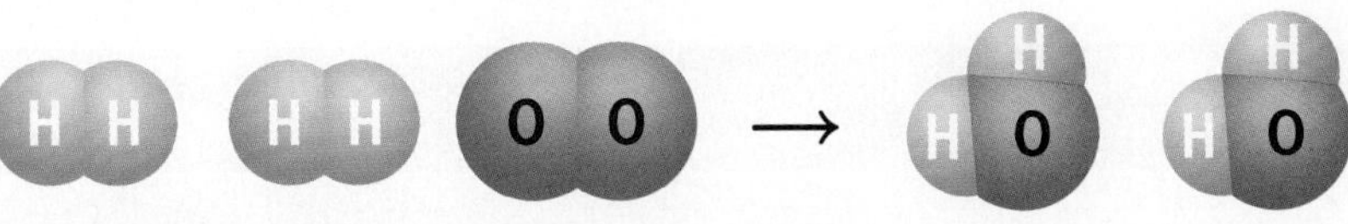

ANALYZE How does this representation of the formation of water, H_2O, from hydrogen gas, H_2, and oxygen gas, O_2, demonstrate the law of conservation of mass? What is the relationship between atoms and mass?

You can also observe conservation of mass in the formation of lead sulfide from the elements lead and sulfur. Lead sulfide, also known as galena, forms black, metallic crystals and is an important naturally occurring compound of lead. Lead sulfide is used in infrared detectors and humidity sensors and as a semiconductor in solar cells. Figure 3 shows different amounts of lead and sulfur that react to form lead sulfide.

FIGURE 3: Three different combinations of lead and sulfur, which react to form lead sulfide

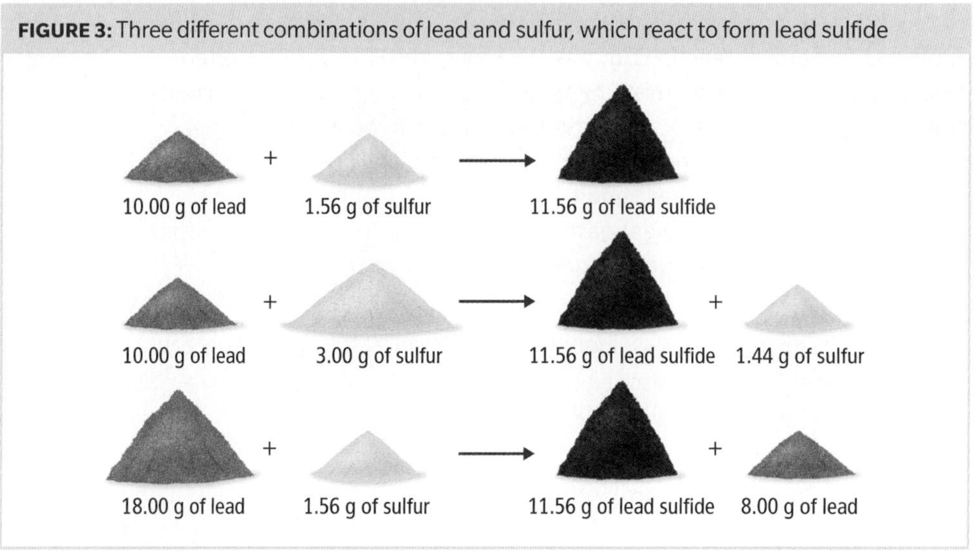

GATHER EVIDENCE How do the data shown in Figure 3 support the law of conservation of mass? What other patterns do you notice in the data?

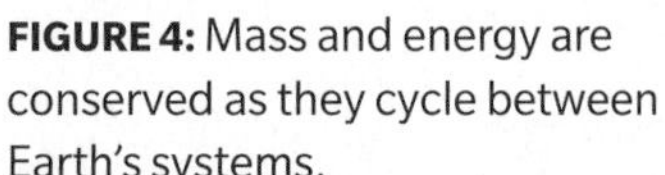

Patterns

FIGURE 4: Mass and energy are conserved as they cycle between Earth's systems.

Cycles in Nature

Mass and energy are conserved in the Earth system. Plants use light energy from the sun along with water and carbon dioxide to produce sugar and oxygen. When animals, such as the bison in Figure 4, eat plants they take in the matter that was in the plants. Animals use oxygen and these food sources to build DNA, proteins, and carbohydrates. When animals die, their tissues decompose and are cycled again.

Language Arts Connection Research different ecological pyramids. How can patterns at the macroscopic scale of a pyramid be explained by interactions at the atomic scale? Write a paper that explains how these pyramids demonstrate the conservation of mass and energy. Ask a classmate to review your paper. Then, revise your explanation based on the feedback.

Elements React in Predictable Proportions

You may have noticed patterns in the data for the formation of lead sulfide from lead and sulfur. The amount of lead sulfide produced was the same, even when a portion of one reactant remained. Observations such as this led scientists to conclude that when elements combine to form compounds, they do so in predictable proportions. The table shows the composition of water by mass as an example.

Composition of Water by Mass

Mass of water (g)	Mass of oxygen (g)	Mass of hydrogen (g)
18	16	2
36	32	4
54	48	6
72	64	8

EXPLAIN Select the correct terms to complete the statement.

According to the data in the table, the simplest ratio by mass of hydrogen to oxygen in a water molecule is 1 | 2 | 8 | 16 to 1 | 2 | 8 | 16. These data show this ratio to be true in every example given. This means that exactly 10 g | 80 g | 160 g of hydrogen would combine with 10 g | 80 g | 160 g of oxygen to form water with no reactant left over. The proportion of hydrogen to oxygen always remains the same.

Scientists also noticed that when metals were burned in air, the metals always combined with a proportional amount of oxygen. If potassium burned in oxygen, every 39.1 g of potassium combined with 8.00 g of oxygen. If calcium burned, every 40.1 g of calcium combined with 16.0 g of oxygen. These observations became known as the *law of definite proportions*. This law states that chemical compounds contain fixed, constant proportions of their constituent elements.

MODEL An unknown mass of hydrogen gas and oxygen gas react in a closed system, producing 108.0 g of water. An oxygen atom is 16 times more massive than a hydrogen atom. Using the space provided, develop a mathematical equation demonstrating that mass is conserved and that elements react in definite proportions. Use your equation to determine the mass of hydrogen and oxygen gas that reacted in the closed system. Recall that oxygen and hydrogen are both diatomic molecules.

FIGURE 5: Models of carbon monoxide, CO, and carbon dioxide, CO_2, molecules

As more chemical compounds were identified, chemists realized that while a specific compound always had the same proportions of elements, the same elements sometimes could form different compounds, each with its own specific proportions. In each compound, the ratio of elements reduced to small, whole-number ratios unique to the compound. This is known as the *law of multiple proportions*. For example, carbon monoxide contains a different proportion of carbon and oxygen atoms than does carbon dioxide, as shown in Figure 5. However, both compounds have ratios of carbon to oxygen that are reducible to small, whole-number ratios. Scientists concluded that in chemical reactions atoms do not break apart. Rather, combinations of atoms simply rearrange. This phenomenon is evident in the data tables below.

Composition of Carbon Monoxide by Mass

Mass of carbon monoxide (g)	Mass of carbon (g)	Mass of oxygen (g)
28	12	16
56	24	32
84	36	48

EVALUATE Complete the remaining rows of the table to show the pattern of composition of carbon dioxide.

Composition of Carbon Dioxide by Mass

Mass of carbon dioxide (g)	Mass of carbon (g)	Mass of oxygen (g)
44	12	32
88	________	________
132	________	________

APPLY Hydrogen and oxygen can form water, H_2O, or hydrogen peroxide, H_2O_2. A chemist determined that a sample contains 20 g of hydrogen and 320 g of oxygen. Is this sample water, or is it hydrogen peroxide? Include evidence to support your claim.

Evidence Notebook Iron reacts readily with oxygen in the presence of water to form iron oxides, also known as rust. Rust can be yellow, black, red, or brown, but each type of rust is made of the same elements. Explain how atoms and mass are conserved in these reactions and why iron and oxygen can combine to form differently colored compounds.

Modeling Chemical Reactions

If you are able to use patterns to predict chemical reactions, you can perform a reaction more efficiently and minimize waste. Imagine you own a company that makes ready-to-eat foods. You want to buy exactly the right amounts of ingredients to make a certain number of turkey and cheese sandwiches. For the most efficient process, you would have to know the proportions in which the ingredients combine, and, to do this, you would need to model the recipe.

2 pieces of bread + 4 slices of turkey + 1 piece of cheese → 1 sandwich

Collaborate If you needed to make 1350 sandwiches, how many slices of turkey would you need? Explain to a partner how you determined your answer.

FIGURE 6: Making sandwiches with exact proportions of ingredients

Writing Chemical Equations

Chemical reactions can also be modeled in order to make predictions about how much product is expected to form. Consider the burning of magnesium. Magnesium is an element, so it can be represented by its chemical symbol from the periodic table, Mg. Oxygen is one of several diatomic elements. These elements exist in nature as molecules made up of two atoms of that element. Therefore, the chemical formula for a molecule of oxygen is O_2. Mg and O_2 combine to yield a product called magnesium oxide, MgO.

In a chemical equation, the reactants are separated with plus signs, as are the products. The production of a new substance is shown with an arrow. The ratio of magnesium atoms to oxygen atoms in magnesium oxide is 1:1 because a magnesium atom loses two electrons to form a 2+ charge, and an oxygen atom gains two electrons to form a 2− charge.

$$Mg + O_2 \rightarrow MgO$$

Explore Online

Hands-On Lab

Modeling the Conservation of Mass Model the relationships between the masses of reactants and products in a chemical reaction.

MODEL Draw a model illustrating this reaction at the atomic level. Use labels to show whether the reaction, as shown in the equation, obeys the law of conservation of mass.

Chemical equations also may indicate the reactant's or product's physical state. This is shown as a lowercase letter in parentheses, such as (*g*) for gas, (*l*) for liquid, (*s*) for solid, and (*aq*) for aqueous. For this magnesium reaction, the physical states are indicated as

$$Mg(s) + O_2(g) \rightarrow MgO(s)$$

Problem Solving

Balancing Chemical Equations

SAMPLE PROBLEM The chemical equation you saw for the burning of magnesium is unbalanced. There are two oxygen atoms in the reactants and only one in the product. But, the law of conservation of mass states that matter cannot be destroyed. The equation must be balanced to show the true ratios in which the reactants combine. All chemical reactions are represented by balanced equations that follow the conservation of mass.

PLAN To balance a chemical equation, first list the number of atoms of each element on both sides of the equation. Figure 7 shows there are 1 Mg atom and 2 O atoms on the reactants side, and 1 Mg atom and 1 O atom on the products side.

FIGURE 7: Count the atoms in the equation.

Mg + O_2	→	MgO
Mg: 1		Mg: 1
O: 2		O: 1

ANALYZE Next, identify any element that does not have the same number of atoms on both sides of the equation. The number of atoms of each element needs to be the same for the reactants and the products for the equation to be balanced. Figure 8 shows that for this equation, the oxygen is not balanced because there are 2 O atoms on the left and only 1 O atom on the right.

FIGURE 8: Compare the number of atoms.

Mg + O_2	→	MgO
Mg: 1		Mg: 1
(O: 2)		(O: 1)

SOLVE Then, use coefficients to balance the equation. Coefficients are numbers that are placed in front of a reactant or product to indicate the number of units of the substance. When a coefficient is placed in front of a chemical formula with subscripts, you multiply each subscript by the coefficient to determine the number of atoms for each element in the chemical formula. Remember that subscripts represent the ratio of atoms in a chemical formula. You cannot change the subscripts in a chemical formula when balancing a chemical equation because this would change the identity of the substance. When no coefficient or subscript is shown, it is assumed to be 1.

FIGURE 9: Add coefficients.

Mg + O_2	→	2MgO
(Mg: 1)		(Mg: ~~1~~ 2)
O: 2		O: ~~1~~ 2

As shown in Figure 9, a coefficient of 2 is added to MgO, bringing the product to 2 Mg atoms and 2 O atoms. This balances the number of O atoms, but it also disrupts the balance of the Mg atoms. Figure 10 shows that a coefficient of 2 is added to Mg, bringing the total number of atoms in the reactants to 2 atoms of Mg and 2 atoms of O. This matches the number of atoms on the products side. The equation is now balanced. The ratio of coefficients for this equation is 2:1:2. You can translate this as 2 parts magnesium react with 1 part oxygen to produce 2 parts magnesium oxide.

FIGURE 10: Balanced equation

2Mg + O_2	→	2MgO
Mg: ~~1~~ 2		Mg: ~~1~~ 2
O: 2		O: ~~1~~ 2

CHECK YOUR WORK Check your work by multiplying the coefficient by the subscript for each element or compound. The number and type of atoms or ions should be equal on both sides.

PRACTICE PROBLEMS

1. Sodium phosphate, Na_3PO_4, is a compound that makes cake batter thicken and baked goods rise. Sodium phosphate reacts with calcium chloride, $CaCl_2$, to form sodium chloride, NaCl, and calcium phosphate, $Ca_3(PO_4)_2$. Calcium phosphate is the main mineral in human bones and teeth. The unbalanced equation for this reaction is:

$$Na_3PO_4(aq) + CaCl_2(aq) \rightarrow NaCl(aq) + Ca_3(PO_4)_2(s)$$

PLAN List the number of atoms of each element or ions on each side of the equation. Polyatomic ions such as PO_4^{3-} can be treated as a single unit if they are found on both sides of the equation.

Reactants		Products
	Ca	
	Cl	
	Na	
	PO_4^{3-}	

ANALYZE In your list above, circle the elements and ions that are not balanced. Add coefficients to begin balancing the equation. Repeat the Plan and Analyze steps as needed until all elements are balanced.

SOLVE Use coefficients to write the balanced chemical equation. Verify that the number and type of atoms and ions on both sides of your equation are equal.

2. Aluminum oxide, Al_2O_3, is a major component of the mineral bauxite and is known as corundum. The hardness of aluminum oxide makes it useful as an abrasive in sandpaper and toothpaste. Rubies and sapphires are large crystals of Al_2O_3 that contain metal ion impurities, which give them their color. In a chemical reaction, aluminum oxide breaks apart into aluminum atoms and oxygen molecules.

SOLVE Follow the Plan and Analyze steps to write the balanced chemical equation. Verify that the number and type of atoms on both sides of your equation are equal.

Patterns in Types of Reactions

There are millions of possible chemical reactions. Analyzing the reactants helps chemists predict the products. These predictions are used to classify reactions into recognizable patterns based on how the reactants break apart, combine, or rearrange.

Collaborate With a partner, list information you can determine about reactants and products in a chemical reaction. Consider how the arrangement of and patterns within the periodic table can help you determine characteristics of elements. How could this information be used to identify or predict the outcome of a chemical reaction?

Synthesis

In a synthesis reaction, two or more reactants combine to form one product. The reactants may be elements or compounds. The product is always a compound.

EXPLAIN Select the correct terms to describe the synthesis of sodium chloride.

Sodium, Na, has 1 | 2 | 7 valence electron(s), and the chlorine atoms in diatomic chlorine, Cl_2, have 5 | 7 | 8 valence electrons. In this reaction, Na atoms gain | lose one electron and Cl atoms gain | lose one electron, forming full and stable outer energy shells. When Na and Cl_2 combine, ionic | covalent | metallic bonds are formed because of the large difference in atomic sizes | electronegativities | ionization energies.

APPLY Write a balanced chemical equation for the synthesis of sodium chloride, NaCl.

Evidence Notebook Write a balanced chemical equation for rusting, a synthesis reaction between iron, Fe, and oxygen gas, O_2. Analyze valence electrons, chemical properties, and bond types to predict the outcome. Assume that iron loses 3 electrons in the reaction.

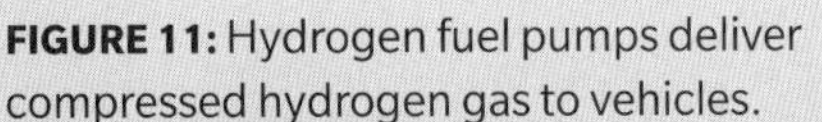

FIGURE 11: Hydrogen fuel pumps deliver compressed hydrogen gas to vehicles.

Decomposition

Due to its low density and chemical reactivity, hydrogen gas does not naturally occur on Earth; it must be produced by the decomposition of substances that contain hydrogen atoms, such as water molecules. In a decomposition reaction, one reactant breaks down to form two or more simpler products. The formation of hydrogen through the decomposition of water is still relatively expensive, which makes clean-burning hydrogen fuel expensive. However, scientists are working to optimize a reaction that would make hydrogen fuel cheaper to make and use in vehicles.

$$2H_2O(l) \longrightarrow 2H_2(g) + O_2(g)$$

APPLY Write a balanced chemical equation for the decomposition of hydrogen peroxide, H_2O_2, into water and oxygen molecules.

Single Displacement

Copper, Cu, is a ductile, highly conductive metal that is used in electrical systems, as a building material, and in jewelry. Silver nitrate, $AgNO_3$, has antiseptic properties and is used to prepare silver compounds used in photographic film. When a copper wire is added to a solution of silver nitrate, a single displacement reaction occurs in which one element replaces another element or ion in a compound.

APPLY Write a balanced chemical equation for the single displacement reaction of copper with silver nitrate.

FIGURE 12: A copper wire is placed in a solution of silver nitrate. The products are solid silver and aqueous copper(II) nitrate.

In an aqueous solution, silver nitrate exists as a combination of Ag^+ ions and NO_3^- ions. When a copper wire is added to aqueous silver nitrate, the copper atoms lose electrons and become Cu^{2+} ions. The Ag^+ ions gain electrons and become solid, elemental silver, which is deposited on the copper wire, as shown in Figure 12. This reaction occurs because copper is more reactive than silver and so forms compounds more readily. If enough copper is used, all of the silver will come out of solution. The Cu^{2+} ions in the aqueous copper(II) nitrate give the solution a blue tint.

Double Displacement

In a double displacement reaction, ions of two compounds switch places. This type of reaction occurs when solutions of potassium iodide, KI, and lead(II) nitrate, $Pb(NO_3)_2$, both soluble ionic compounds, are mixed together. The lead and potassium ions essentially switch places.

APPLY Write a balanced chemical equation for the double displacement reaction of potassium iodide and lead(II) nitrate.

FIGURE 13: When solutions of lead(II) nitrate and potassium iodide are combined, solid lead(II) iodide and aqueous potassium nitrate are produced.

The Pb^{2+} ions bond with the I^- ions to form lead(II) iodide. Lead(II) iodide is insoluble in water at room temperature and precipitates as a yellow solid, shown in Figure 13. Lead(II) iodide was once used as a yellow pigment in lead paint, but this was discontinued due to the dangers of lead poisoning.

Potassium nitrate is the other product of this reaction. It is an ionic compound only moderately soluble in water and is often not seen due to the yellow lead(II) iodide precipitate. Potassium nitrate is used as a fertilizer, a food preservative, and a major component in gun powder and fireworks.

Combustion Reactions

Explore Online

FIGURE 14: A balloon filled with hydrogen gas explodes when ignited.

Combustion reactions are often used to provide heat and light, as they do in fireplaces and bonfires. These reactions often release large amounts of energy. Figure 14 shows the results of this energy after a balloon filled with hydrogen gas is ignited and explodes.

Most automobiles, buses, and airplanes have internal combustion engines, in which a fuel containing hydrocarbons burns in oxygen to produce carbon dioxide, water, and energy. An internal combustion engine is an inefficient system because much of the energy it produces is lost to the environment.

EXPLAIN Select the correct terms to describe combustion reactions.

In a combustion reaction with carbon-based fuels, thermal energy | chemical energy in the reactants is converted to thermal energy | chemical energy when the fuel is ignited. Carbon dioxide is a greenhouse gas, so using combustion engines leads to a decrease | an increase in the amount of energy stored in Earth's atmosphere and hydrosphere.

As a result of these increased carbon dioxide emissions, scientists are looking for alternative energy sources that do not contain carbon. Hydrogen fuel might be an alternative because the end product of the combustion of hydrogen is water, not carbon dioxide. One of the challenges with hydrogen fuel is that elemental hydrogen is not found in nature as the hydrocarbons of petroleum and natural gas are.

Evidence Notebook Identify the type of reaction you are modeling for your unit project and write a balanced chemical equation. Use your reaction equation to show how matter is conserved during the reaction.

Predicting the Outcomes of Chemical Reactions

The periodic table can be a useful tool for predicting the outcomes of chemical reactions or even whether or not a reaction will occur. For example, from an element's position on the periodic table, you can determine the number of outermost electrons it has. This tells how likely the element is to gain or lose electrons when forming bonds. In addition, periodic trends in electronegativity, ionization energy, and atomic size also influence the types of chemical bonds two elements will form. The relative significance of each trend also can be determined from an element's position on the periodic table. Examining a reaction will help show how this might work.

Thermite is a mixture of aluminum, Al, and iron(III) oxide, Fe_2O_3. When thermite is exposed to high temperatures, an exothermic reaction occurs, shown in Figure 15. The two metals in this reaction, aluminum and iron, can be ranked by their tendency to lose electrons and form cations.

FIGURE 15: Thermite reaction

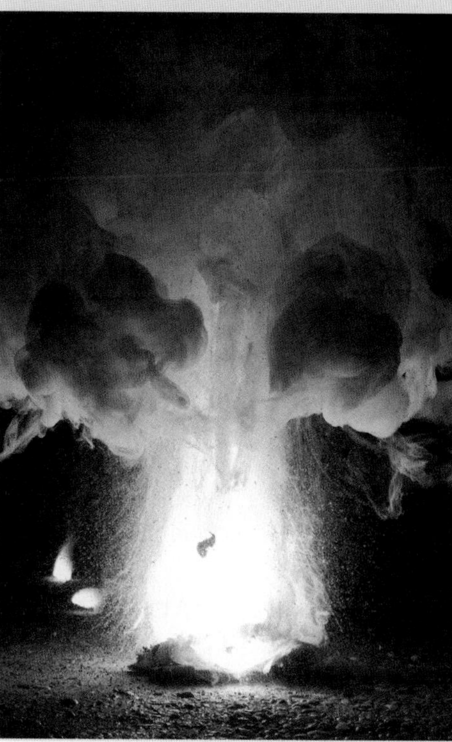

ANALYZE Which metal in this reaction is more reactive? How might you determine this?

○ **a.** Al is more reactive because it has a lower ionization energy than Fe.

○ **b.** Al is more reactive because it has a higher ionization energy than Fe.

○ **c.** Fe is more reactive because it has a lower ionization energy than Al.

○ **d.** Fe is more reactive because it has a higher ionization energy than Al.

The difference in electronegativities between oxygen and iron is 1.7. This means the iron(III) oxide bond is slightly ionic. Oxygen holds the shared electrons more strongly than does iron, but the electrons are not fully transferred. The energy added to start the thermite reaction makes it easier to break the bonds in iron(III) oxide. If a more reactive metal is present, it will take the place of iron, producing a different oxide and different elemental metal.

PREDICT Write the balanced chemical equation for the thermite reaction. Think about how many valence electrons aluminum and oxygen have when writing the formulas for the products. What type of reaction is this?

A reaction of thermite releases a large amount of energy and reaches temperatures high enough to melt iron. This makes thermite useful for welding, or joining, large pieces of metal such as railroad rails. An outside energy source begins the reaction. Once started, the thermite reaction produces enough energy to continue. The molten iron produced fills the weld joint, and the energy produced from the exothermic reaction joins the ends to be welded together with the new joint.

In the thermite reaction, aluminum is more reactive than iron. Therefore, when the reaction begins, iron is displaced by aluminum. The products of this reaction are aluminum oxide and elemental iron. The iron is what is useful in welding applications. It is heavier and sinks to the bottom of the weld, and the aluminum oxide, called *slag* in this case, rises to the top.

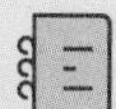

Evidence Notebook Rust often flakes away, exposing more iron underneath. Explain why this makes rust particularly destructive for iron or iron alloys. Why is the prevention of rust an important problem to solve? Use your knowledge of rust to suggest a solution. As you consider solutions, think about the materials and conditions that are necessary for rust to form.

Hands-On Lab

Modeling the Conservation of Mass

There are many types of models, including conceptual, physical, mathematical, and computer models. Some models are better at demonstrating certain characteristics of a system than others. Make a model to demonstrate conservation of mass in a chemical reaction. Then, use your model to determine how much product is made when different amounts of reactant are available.

RESEARCH QUESTION Explore different types of atomic models. Which model type would allow you to demonstrate a connection between number of atoms and mass in a chemical reaction?

MAKE A CLAIM

How can a model of a chemical reaction be used to demonstrate conservation of mass?

POSSIBLE MATERIALS

- indirectly vented chemical splash goggles, nonlatex apron
- balance
- beads, assorted sizes and colors
- chemical modeling kit
- computer
- glue
- nuts and bolts
- paper clips, assorted sizes and colors
- paper, white and assorted colors
- polystyrene-foam balls, assorted sizes and colors
- scissors
- snap-together blocks
- string
- tape
- toothpicks
- trays, plastic (2)

SAFETY INFORMATION

indirectly vented chemical splash goggles

- Wear indirectly vented chemical splash goggles and a nonlatex apron during the setup, hands-on, and takedown segments of the activity.
- Use caution when using sharp tools, which can cut or puncture skin.

PLAN THE INVESTIGATION

1. Consider the reaction in which propane, C_3H_8, is burned in oxygen to produce carbon dioxide and water. Propane is a flammable gas at room temperature and pressure. It can easily change from a liquid to a gaseous state with changes in pressure. This property makes it a suitable fuel to heat homes that are not served by natural gas lines. Write a balanced chemical equation for the combustion of propane.

2. Write a procedure describing the type of model you will use to show the conservation of mass in this reaction. If you need additional materials, discuss these with your teacher. Write a safety plan for making and using your model. Have your teacher approve your balanced chemical equation and plans before you start.

3. How will your model demonstrate that atoms combine in definite proportions to form compounds and that subscripts in a chemical formula show these proportions?

CARRY OUT THE INVESTIGATION

Construct your model according to your plan. Then, use your model to investigate and record what happens when different amounts of reactants are available.

DRAW CONCLUSIONS

Write a conclusion that addresses each of the points below.

Claim How did your model demonstrate conservation of mass?

Evidence Describe evidence from your experiment to support your claim.

Reasoning Explain how the evidence you cited supports your claim. How did different amounts of reactants affect your model?

COMMUNICATE

Present your model to your classmates. Explain how it demonstrates conservation of mass, and use it to show how changing the amount of available reactants affects the amount of carbon dioxide and water produced.

MORE PRACTICE WITH BALANCING EQUATIONS | FLUORIDE AND YOUR TEETH |  THE COMPOSITION OF HYDRATES | Go online to choose one of these other paths.

Lesson Self-Check

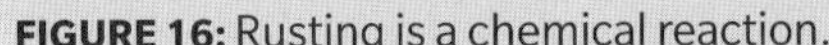

CAN YOU EXPLAIN THE PHENOMENON?

FIGURE 16: Rusting is a chemical reaction.

Rusting is the corrosion of iron. The reddish-brown signs of rust can be seen in everyday life, such as on a rusty can or rooftop. The rusting process tells you how iron interacts with its environment. When a chemical reaction such as rusting occurs, mass is conserved. You can use your knowledge of chemical properties and periodic trends to predict and describe the outcomes of chemical reactions, including the formation of rust.

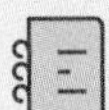

Evidence Notebook Refer to your notes in your Evidence Notebook to make a claim about why rust forms and how it can be prevented. Your explanation should include a discussion of the following points:

Claim Make a claim that explains how rust forms, why rusting occurs more readily in some climates, and how rust can be prevented.

Evidence Give specific evidence to support your claim. Include a balanced chemical equation for the formation of rust.

Reasoning Describe, in detail, the connections between the evidence you cited and the claim you are making.

Name Date

CHECKPOINTS

Check Your Understanding

1. How is the law of conservation of mass met in a balanced chemical equation? Select all correct answers.
   - ☐ **a.** The same number of atoms of each element appears on both sides of the equation.
   - ☐ **b.** Subscripts are added to balance the number of atoms of each element.
   - ☐ **c.** Formulas of reactants are changed to ensure that the mass of elements is conserved.
   - ☐ **d.** Coefficients are added to balance the number of atoms of each element.
   - ☐ **e.** Formulas of products are changed to ensure that the mass of elements is conserved.

2. Write the coefficients necessary to balance the equation for the reaction between aluminum and hydrochloric acid.

   ___ $Al(s)$ + ___ $HCl(aq)$ → ___ $AlCl_3(aq)$ + ___ $H_2(g)$

3. Match the description of the reaction type with the correct chemical reaction.

Description		Reaction
Simpler substances are made from a complex substance. ○		○ Magnesium and hydrochloric acid react to form magnesium chloride and hydrogen gas.
A new compound is the only product. ○		○ Iron(II) sulfide reacts with hydrochloric acid to form hydrogen sulfide and iron(II) chloride.
One element replaces another. ○		○ Calcium carbonate is heated until calcium oxide and carbon dioxide form.
Two elements are exchanged. ○		○ Aluminum and bromine react to form aluminum bromide.

4. The atmosphere is 21% oxygen gas. How would a combustion reaction change if it were carried out in a closed system with 80% oxygen instead of an open system with 21% oxygen? Assume all other variables remain the same.
   - ○ **a.** The products of the reaction would change because more oxygen is present.
   - ○ **b.** The reaction would proceed slower because there would not be enough fuel for the oxygen to react with.
   - ○ **c.** The equation representing the combustion reaction would need to be rebalanced because more oxygen is present.
   - ○ **d.** The reaction would proceed faster because more oxygen atoms would react with the fuel in a shorter amount of time.

5. Write the chemical equation for the complete combustion of methane, CH_4.

6. Ammonia, NH_3, has a nitrogen-to-hydrogen ratio by mass of 14:3. What is the mass of a sample of ammonia if there are 25.0 g of nitrogen?
   - ○ **a.** 3.00 g
   - ○ **b.** 5.36 g
   - ○ **c.** 30.4 g
   - ○ **d.** 75.0 g

7. Which of the following is an accurate description of the decomposition of water in a closed system?
   - ○ **a.** 36 g of water decomposes to 2 g of hydrogen gas and 32 g of oxygen gas.
   - ○ **b.** 36 g of water decomposes to 4 g of hydrogen gas and 32 g of oxygen gas.
   - ○ **c.** 4 g of hydrogen gas and 32 g of oxygen decompose to 36 g of water.
   - ○ **d.** 36 g of water decomposes to 36 g of oxygen gas.

CHECKPOINTS (continued)

8. In one trial, scientists find that a 200-g sample of chalk, $CaCO_3$, contains 80 g of calcium. In a second trial, the scientists find that a 100-g sample of chalk contains 40 g of calcium. Explain how the data demonstrate the law of definite proportions.

9. How can the setup of a system—that is, whether matter can enter or leave the system—affect the outcome of a chemical reaction in which one of the two reactants is a gas?

10. A double displacement reaction between two reactants produces $PbCrO_4$ and KNO_3. What must have been the two reactants? Be sure to write the correct formulas and a balanced equation for the reaction, and explain how you determined the answer.

MAKE YOUR OWN STUDY GUIDE

In your Evidence Notebook, design a study guide that supports the main ideas from this lesson:

The law of conservation of mass and the law of definite proportions are the basis for writing balanced equations and apply to all chemical reactions.

The outcome of a reaction can be predicted using patterns in chemical properties.

Remember to include the following information in your study guide:

- Use examples that model main ideas.
- Record explanations for the phenomena you investigated.
- Use evidence to support your explanations. Your support can include drawings, data, graphs, laboratory conclusions, and other evidence recorded throughout the lesson.

Consider how the methods you developed in this lesson can be used to model patterns in chemical reactions and show that the total mass in all closed systems is conserved.

4.2

Analyzing Chemical Reactions

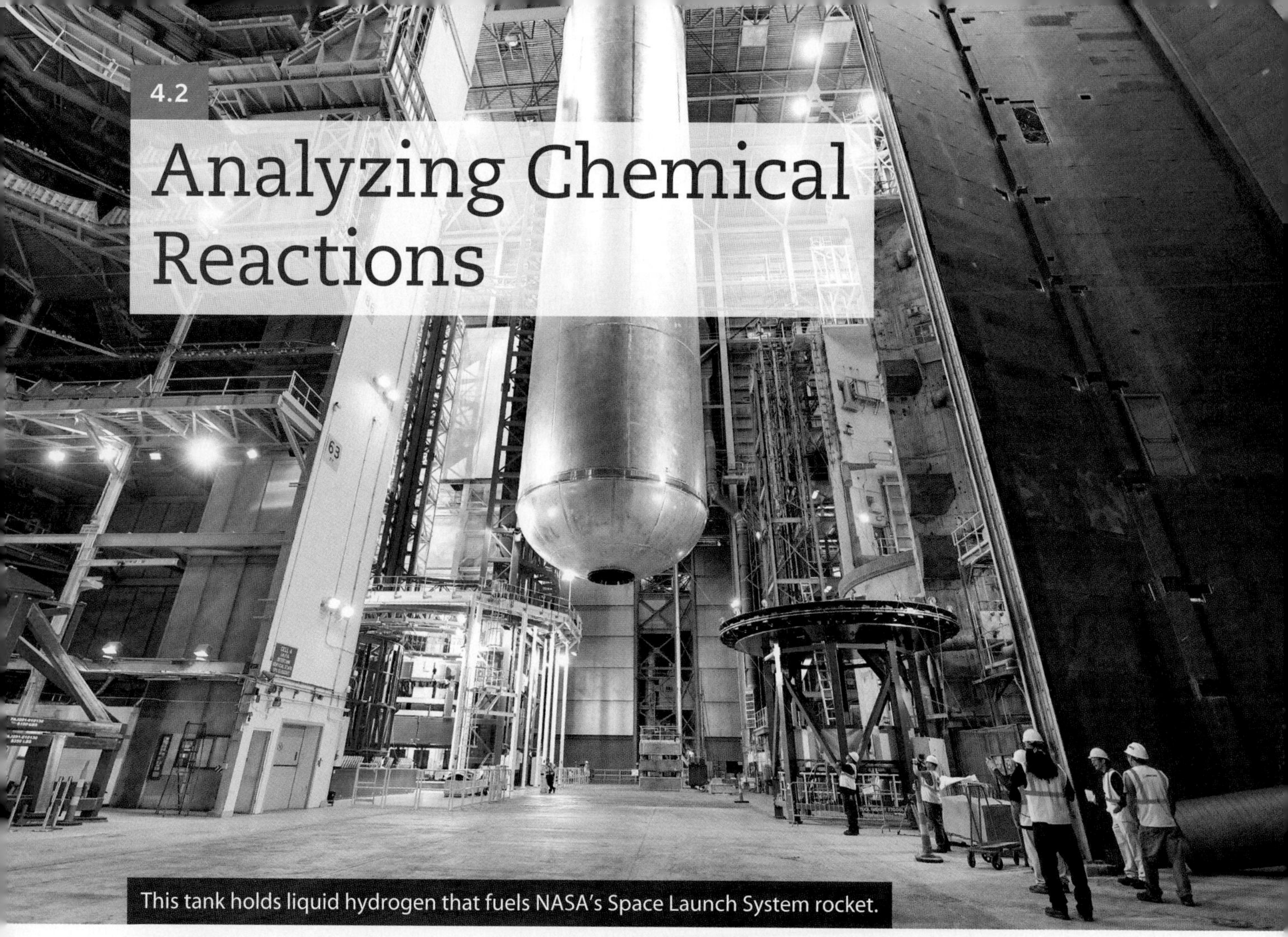

This tank holds liquid hydrogen that fuels NASA's Space Launch System rocket.

CAN YOU SOLVE THE PROBLEM?

Chemical reactions occur at all scales, from those that occur in living cells to those that occur in incredibly large rocket fuel tanks. Rockets, unlike most vehicles, use liquid hydrogen as fuel. Hydrogen is lightweight, burns at a very high temperature, and provides more thrust per unit of volume than other fuel. Liquid oxygen is required to make the hydrogen burn. When these two reactants combine explosively inside a rocket engine, water is formed. A water molecule, H_2O, contains twice as many hydrogen atoms as oxygen atoms. Scientists must consider the exact proportions of substances involved in this reaction to calculate the amount of fuel that is required for a mission.

ASK Suppose you wanted to optimize the fuel mixture used for a space flight in order to avoid the presence of excess fuel. What questions would you ask to get started?

Evidence Notebook As you explore the lesson, gather evidence to explain how, given a certain quantity of oxygen, you could determine the exact amount of hydrogen needed for a space flight.

Quantifying Matter in Chemical Reactions

A balanced chemical equation demonstrates the conservation of matter. So, you can use an equation to make predictions about the amounts of matter a reaction should produce.

Quantifying Moles in Chemical Reactions

FIGURE 1: One mole of several substances

Atoms and molecules are too small to be measured individually, so chemists use a unit of measurement called the mole to quantify matter in chemical reactions. Figure 1 shows exactly one mole of five substances. From left to right, they are: sugar, salt, carbon, oxygen (in a balloon), and copper.

Collaborate The table below shows the number of particles in one mole of each substance in the photo. Discuss the patterns you see with a partner. Does the chemical formula affect the number of particles in one mole of each substance? What is similar about one mole of each substance, and what is different?

Substance	Table sugar ($C_{12}H_{22}O_{11}$)	Salt (NaCl)	Carbon (C)	Oxygen (O_2)	Copper (Cu)
Particles in one mole	6.02×10^{23} molecules	6.02×10^{23} formula units	6.02×10^{23} atoms	6.02×10^{23} diatomic molecules	6.02×10^{23} atoms

The mole is referred to as "the chemist's dozen" because it can be used to compare different substances by count. But atoms and molecules are much, much smaller than everyday items, such as eggs, so the number of particles in one mole of a substance is incredibly large. This number, which is approximately 6.02×10^{23}, is also called Avogadro's number. It was originally defined as the number of atoms in 12 g of carbon-12.

In order to understand how moles are used to quantify matter in chemical reactions, think back to the ingredients needed to make sandwiches.

$$2 \text{ slices of bread} + 4 \text{ slices of turkey} + 1 \text{ piece of cheese} \rightarrow 1 \text{ sandwich}$$

If you had 288 slices of turkey, how many sandwiches could you make? You could use a technique called dimensional analysis to find out. Start by writing the known amount, 288 slices of turkey. Then, multiply this amount by a fraction that compares sandwiches to slices of turkey. The unit "slices of turkey" cancels out, leaving 72 sandwiches.

$$288 \cancel{\text{ slices of turkey}} \times \frac{1 \text{ sandwich}}{4 \cancel{\text{ slices of turkey}}} = 72 \text{ sandwiches}$$

APPLY Use dimensional analysis to complete the problems.

How many sandwiches could you make with 452 slices of bread and plenty of other ingredients? __________ sandwiches

Using a fraction comparing Avogadro's number and 1 mole, determine how many atoms are in 15.0 moles of carbon. __________ atoms

You can also use dimensional analysis to predict how much matter a chemical reaction should produce. Consider the following reaction, in which magnesium burns in oxygen. This reaction produces a bright white light, so it is often used in fireworks and road flares.

$$2Mg + O_2 \rightarrow 2MgO$$

You can use the coefficients in this equation to make predictions about amounts of reactants and products. To do this, you must use a conversion factor that shows the coefficients as mole quantities. A conversion factor is a ratio between two quantities that is written as a fraction. By definition, a conversion factor always equals one, so either quantity can be written as the numerator. Below are some conversion factors that could be used to solve problems related to this chemical equation.

Comparing magnesium to magnesium oxide:

$$\frac{2 \text{ mol Mg}}{2 \text{ mol MgO}} \quad \text{or} \quad \frac{2 \text{ mol MgO}}{2 \text{ mol Mg}}$$

Comparing oxygen to magnesium oxide:

$$\frac{1 \text{ mol } O_2}{2 \text{ mol MgO}} \quad \text{or} \quad \frac{2 \text{ mol MgO}}{1 \text{ mol } O_2}$$

MODEL Use the balanced equation for the synthesis of magnesium oxide to write the conversion factors you could use to compare moles of oxygen to moles of magnesium.

[ ] or [ ]

Problem Solving

Calculating Molar Amounts

SAMPLE PROBLEM If 45.3 moles of magnesium burn in excess oxygen, how many moles of magnesium oxide should be produced?

$$2Mg + O_2 \rightarrow 2MgO$$

ANALYZE Start with the given amount. Then, set up a conversion factor that will allow you to cancel the given unit and convert to the requested unit.

$$45.3 \text{ mol Mg} \times \frac{\text{mol ?}}{\text{mol ?}} = \text{mol MgO}$$

SOLVE Use the balanced equation to complete the conversion factor and solve.

$$45.3 \cancel{\text{mol Mg}} \times \frac{2 \text{ mol MgO}}{2 \cancel{\text{mol Mg}}} = 45.3 \text{ mol MgO}$$

PRACTICE PROBLEMS **SOLVE** Use the balanced equation to complete these problems. Report your final answers using the correct number of significant figures.

1. How many moles of MgO are produced if 0.37 moles of O_2 react with excess Mg?

2. If 8.2 moles of Mg are burned, how many moles of O_2 are consumed?

Quantifying Mass in Chemical Reactions

Using a balanced chemical equation to calculate quantities of matter, such as moles, volumes, or masses, is called *stoichiometry*. Stoichiometry allows you to convert from a quantity that is difficult to measure, such as the number of atoms in a substance, to a quantity that is easy to measure, such as the mass in grams. So how can you convert from moles to mass? Think back to the sandwich-making scenario. If you had to order sandwich supplies by mass, you would need to know the mass of the ingredient you were working with. For example, if you purchased 1000.0 grams of turkey and wanted to calculate how many sandwiches you could make, you would need to know the mass of one slice of turkey. If you knew that one slice of turkey had a mass of 15.0 grams, you could use dimensional analysis to determine how many sandwiches are possible.

$$1000.0\ \cancel{\text{g turkey}} \times \frac{1\ \cancel{\text{slice of turkey}}}{15.0\ \cancel{\text{g turkey}}} \times \frac{1\ \text{sandwich}}{4\ \cancel{\text{slices of turkey}}} = 16.7\ \text{sandwiches}$$

In the same way that you must know the mass of each item when ordering food by mass, you must consider the mass of different particles to make predictions about the mass of product made in a chemical reaction. You can measure mass by putting a substance on a balance, but how do you determine the mass of one mole?

The following table shows the mass in grams of one mole of each substance.

Substance	Table sugar ($C_{12}H_{22}O_{11}$)	Salt (NaCl)	Carbon (C)	Oxygen (O_2)	Copper (Cu)
Mass of one mole in grams	342.3 g	58.44 g	12.01 g	32.00 g	63.55 g

EXPLAIN Complete the statement based on the data shown in the table.

One mole of sugar has the same | a different mass than one mole of salt. This indicates that the mass of one mole of a substance depends | does not depend on the chemical makeup of the substance. However, the number of particles in one mole depends | does not depend on the identity of the substance.

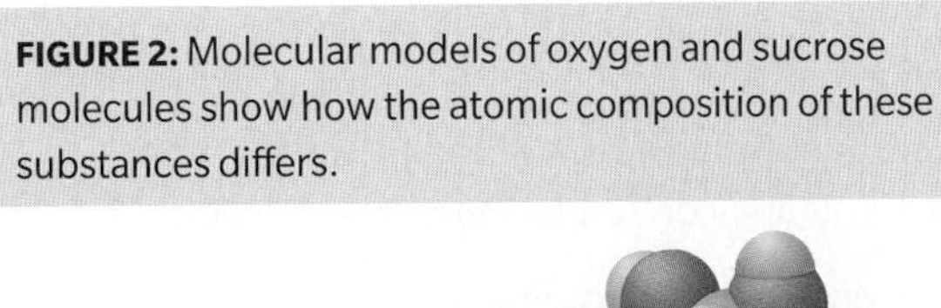

FIGURE 2: Molecular models of oxygen and sucrose molecules show how the atomic composition of these substances differs.

oxygen, O_2

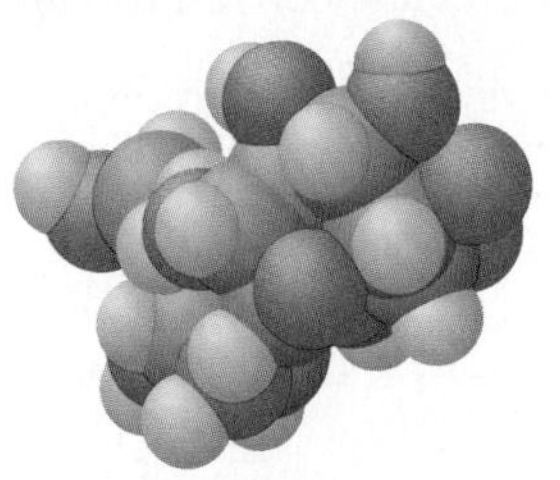

sucrose, $C_{12}H_{22}O_{11}$

Why does the mass of one mole differ from one substance to another, but the number of particles in one mole does not? Consider the atomic composition of each of the substances presented in the table. Figure 2 shows models of two of these substances—a diatomic oxygen molecule and a sucrose (sugar) molecule.

PREDICT What differences do you notice when looking at the models of an oxygen molecule and a sucrose molecule? How do you think the mass of one mole of these substances is related to their atomic composition?

The mass in grams of one mole of an element or compound is called its molar mass. The molar mass of a single monatomic element, such as carbon, is equivalent to its atomic mass, as listed on the periodic table, expressed in grams. So, the mole is a unit that allows you to convert from grams, which you can measure on a balance, to individual molecules or atoms. The molar mass of a substance is expressed in grams per mole, or g/mol.

$$\text{molar mass in grams} = 1 \text{ mole} = 6.02 \times 10^{23} \text{ particles}$$

The molar mass of a compound depends on the atomic masses of the elements that make it up and how many atoms of each element are present. For example, a copper atom has a higher molar mass than an oxygen molecule, even though an oxygen molecule is made up of two atoms. This is because copper has a much higher atomic mass than oxygen. Large molecules, such as sucrose, have high molar masses because so many atoms are present in one particle. In the case of sucrose, one molecule contains 45 atoms!

To calculate molar mass, use the periodic table to find the atomic masses of the elements. (Unified atomic mass units, u, are equivalent to grams per mole.) Multiply each atomic mass by the number of atoms indicated by the subscripts, and add the values you obtain. For example, the molar mass of sucrose, $C_{12}H_{22}O_{11}$, is calculated as follows:

C: 12.01 u (g/mol) $\times$ 12 atoms

H: 1.008 u (g/mol) $\times$ 22 atoms

O: 15.999 u (g/mol) $\times$ 11 atoms

So, the molar mass is: $(12.01 \times 12) + (1.008 \times 22) + (15.999 \times 11) = 342.3$ g/mol

SOLVE Use a periodic table to calculate the following molar masses.

1. The molar mass of $CaCl_2$ is __________ g/mol.

2. The molar mass of $Mg_3(PO_4)_2$ is __________ g/mol.

Suppose you wanted to obtain the molar mass of a substance to use in a chemical reaction. You would have to measure out that mass in grams on a balance. The precision of your balance can make a big difference in your final outcome.

Scale, Proportion, and Quantity

Molar Mass at an Industrial Scale

Correctly calculating the molar mass of a substance and correctly measuring that mass on a balance are two requirements for large-scale industrial processes. Imagine, for example, a chemical process for manufacturing a product such as aspirin tablets on an industrial scale. If a chemical engineer either miscalculated the molar mass of the ingredients or they made an error in measuring their mass on a balance, the entire product batch would be affected. Too little reactant would produce a smaller product yield. Too much of a reactant might show up as an impurity in the finished product, with dangerous health effects.

Language Arts Connection Research the production of aspirin. Then write an explanation for how a small calculation or measurement error might affect the production of this medicine at an industrial scale. Explain how the error might occur and why it would affect the final product in the way you claimed.

FIGURE 3: Even on an industrial scale, precise measurement is crucial to obtaining the desired amount of product.

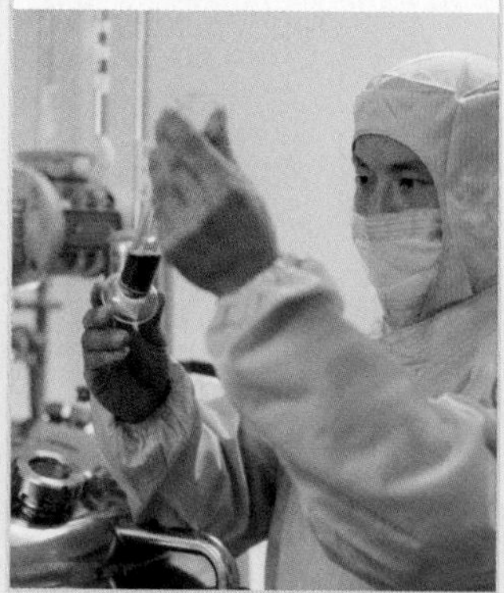

Problem Solving

Calculating Mass

SAMPLE PROBLEM Consider again the reaction between magnesium and oxygen. Imagine you wanted to know how much MgO would be produced if you burned 3.06 g of Mg. You would again reference the balanced chemical equation, which demonstrates conservation of matter.

$$2Mg + O_2 \rightarrow 2MgO$$

ANALYZE To convert from grams of magnesium to grams of magnesium oxide, you need to know the molar masses of both substances. Do not include the coefficients when calculating molar mass. They will be included in another step of the solving process.

Mg: 24.31 g/mol

MgO: (24.31 g/mol × 1) + (15.999 g/mol × 1) = 40.309 g/mol

SOLVE Now, you start with the given quantity and set up conversion factors in a way that allows all the units to cancel except for the unit on your final answer.

$$3.06\ \cancel{g\ Mg} \times \frac{1\ \cancel{mol\ Mg}}{24.31\ \cancel{g\ Mg}} \times \frac{2\ \cancel{mol\ MgO}}{2\ \cancel{mol\ Mg}} \times \frac{40.309\ g\ MgO}{1\ \cancel{mol\ MgO}} = 5.07\ g\ MgO$$

Notice that the mole-to-mole ratio, shown in the middle of the three conversion factors, is always present in a stoichiometry problem. Other conversion factors can be placed before and after it, but the comparison of moles of one substance to moles of another based on the balanced chemical reaction is vital to any stoichiometry problem.

PRACTICE PROBLEM How many grams of aluminum are produced in this reaction if 100.4 grams of aluminum oxide are supplied? Report your answer using the correct number of significant figures.

$$2Al_2O_3 \rightarrow 4Al + 3O_2$$

ANALYZE Calculate the molar masses of aluminum and aluminum oxide.

SOLVE Start with the given from the question, and set up the conversion factors in a way that will allow units to cancel out, leaving only the unit required for the final answer.

Collaborate With a partner, show how you could determine the number of oxygen molecules produced if 36.9 grams of aluminum are consumed in this reaction.

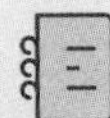

Evidence Notebook The unbalanced equation for the burning of hydrogen in a rocket engine is:

$$H_2 + O_2 \rightarrow H_2O$$

Balance this equation and calculate how many grams of water are produced if 3.45×10^8 grams of oxygen are burned in excess hydrogen. Then, calculate how many water molecules are produced by burning the same amount of oxygen. Last, write an explanation for how you solved these problems.

Limiting and Excess Matter

Consider again the reaction between magnesium and oxygen. Only now, imagine two different scenarios. In one, the reaction between the magnesium ribbon and oxygen takes place in the open air. In the second, the reaction occurs in a glass chamber that prevents the magnesium from reacting with any more oxygen than what is present in the chamber.

FIGURE 4: Magnesium is ignited in an open system and a closed system.

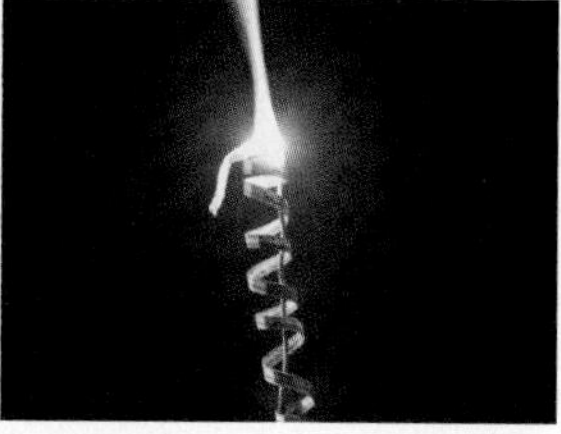

a Magnesium is ignited in the open air.

b Magnesium is ignited inside a glass chamber.

PREDICT The mass of magnesium oxide produced in the open system in Figure 4a differs from the mass produced in the closed system in Figure 4b. Why do you think this is? How might this relate to the amount of reactants available in each scenario?

____

____

____

____

____

Quantifying Limiting and Excess Matter

When following a recipe, it may be the case that you have more than enough of one ingredient or a limited amount of another. Think about making sandwiches using this recipe.

$$2 \text{ slices of bread} + 4 \text{ slices of turkey} + 1 \text{ piece of cheese} \rightarrow 1 \text{ sandwich}$$

If you had 20 slices of bread, 10 pieces of cheese, and 39 slices of turkey, you would run out of turkey first and could only make 9 sandwiches. In chemistry, having too much or too little reactant also occurs. If there is too little of one reactant compared to another, the reactant that runs out first is called the limiting reactant. The reactant that has extra left over after the reaction ends is called the excess reactant.

ANALYZE Select the correct terms to complete the statement.

Imagine you had 75 slices of bread, 200 slices of turkey, and plenty of cheese to make sandwiches with. You would run out of turkey | bread first, so it is the limiting | excess ingredient. There would be cheese and turkey | bread left over when all the sandwiches are made, so these are the limiting | excess ingredients.

Problem Solving

Determining Limiting and Excess Reactants

SAMPLE PROBLEM To determine the limiting and excess reactant for a reaction, you must first know the quantity of each reactant that is available. Consider this problem:

If you burn 48.6 grams of magnesium in 39.0 grams of oxygen:

1. How much magnesium oxide is produced?
2. Which reactant is the limiting reactant?
3. Which is the excess reactant?

$$2Mg + O_2 \rightarrow 2MgO$$

ANALYZE To determine how much product will actually be made, we must determine how much product each amount of reactant would produce if the other reactant was in excess. This means we will calculate two quantities.

$$48.6\ \cancel{g\ Mg} \times \frac{1\ \cancel{mol\ Mg}}{24.31\ \cancel{g\ Mg}} \times \frac{2\ \cancel{mol\ MgO}}{2\ \cancel{mol\ Mg}} \times \frac{40.309\ g\ MgO}{1\ \cancel{mol\ MgO}} = \boxed{80.6\ g\ MgO}$$

$$39.0\ \cancel{g\ O_2} \times \frac{1\ \cancel{mol\ O_2}}{31.998\ \cancel{g\ O_2}} \times \frac{2\ \cancel{mol\ MgO}}{1\ \cancel{mol\ O_2}} \times \frac{40.309\ g\ MgO}{1\ \cancel{mol\ MgO}} = 98.3\ g\ MgO$$

SOLVE The amount of product that can be made is equal to the lesser amount from the two calculations because the limiting reactant runs out when this amount is made. Therefore:

1. The amount of product made is equal to 80.6 g MgO.
2. Magnesium is the limiting reactant.
3. Oxygen is the excess reactant.

PRACTICE PROBLEM **ANALYZE** If a sample of magnesium with a mass of 35.0 grams reacts with 35.0 grams of oxygen, how much magnesium oxide will be produced? Show your work, and circle your final answer.

SOLVE In this reaction, the limiting reactant is ______________ and the excess reactant is ______________.

Evidence Notebook In the sample problem, the reactant that was present in a greater amount was actually the limiting reactant. Explain why this is, citing evidence from the balanced chemical equation to support your claim. Last, explain how you could apply this concept to the chemical reaction you are modeling as part of your unit project.

Determining Percent Yield

In the real world, chemical reactions do not always produce the expected amount of a product. Often, unpredictable side reactions take place. For example, if you ignite 0.972 g of Mg metal in the open air, you may get only 0.988 g of MgO, not the expected 1.61 g. The possible reasons for this include the fact that some hot Mg metal will react with nitrogen in the air to produce magnesium nitride, Mg_3N_2. Also, the hot magnesium can react with any water vapor that might be present to yield magnesium hydroxide, $Mg(OH)_2$. The products of these side reactions are called byproducts and may be difficult to predict.

The amount of product that should be produced from given amounts of reactants is called the theoretical yield of a reaction. The amount of product that actually results from a reaction is called the actual yield. If the actual yield of a reaction is the same as the theoretical yield, the reaction is said to be 100% efficient. With some exceptions, reactions are not 100% efficient. The efficiency of a reaction is measured by calculating percent yield. The percent yield is the ratio of the actual yield to the theoretical yield, multiplied by 100.

$$\text{Percent yield} = \frac{\text{actual yield}}{\text{theoretical yield}} \times 100$$

EXPLAIN If the percent yield for a chemical reaction is below 100%, are atoms still conserved? Explain your thinking.

____

____

____

____

____

____

Percent yield is important when trying to determine how much product will actually be produced in a chemical reaction. When a chemist is considering a reaction, he or she needs to know whether the expectations about the amount of product formed is realistic.

SOLVE Suppose you burn magnesium in a limiting amount of oxygen in a closed system, expecting to get 1.61 g MgO. You measure only 0.988 g MgO after the reaction. Show how you would calculate the percent yield for this reaction.

The percent yield of this reaction is ________%

The theoretical yield of a reaction reflects an idealized situation. In real situations, however, there are a number of factors that reduce the actual yield of a chemical reaction, so the actual yield of a reaction is never quite equal to the theoretical yield. The factors that reduce actual yield include side reactions, reactions of a product with other substances in the surroundings, and impurities in the reactants. Even inaccurate measurements can affect the percent yield of a reaction. Although 100% yields are almost never possible, chemists and chemical engineers try to run reactions under conditions that will maximize the percent yield. This lowers the cost of chemical production and reduces waste.

Engineering

Maximizing Percent Yield

FIGURE 5: Hydrogen can be made from wood chips.

Hydrogen is a clean-burning fuel, producing only water vapor when it is burned. This fuel is used to power a small number of buses and automobiles as well as rocket engines. But it is not widely used at this time because hydrogen does not occur in any significant concentrations as a pure element on Earth. If hydrogen-fueled vehicles become more numerous, a large amount of hydrogen fuel will be needed.

Hydrogen can be chemically removed from a wide variety of abundant, naturally occurring hydrogen-containing compounds. One solution to producing low-cost hydrogen in quantity is to stockpile and distribute biomass, converting it to hydrogen as needed. The wood chips in Figure 5 are one such example of biomass.

Unlike fossil fuels, plant material such as wood, leaves, and stalks are renewable. Chemists and chemical engineers are collaborating to develop a process that produces hydrogen from sugars in wood. Enzymes convert the sugars to hydrogen gas with a yield of two hydrogen molecules per carbon atom, the maximum possible yield. The hydrogen can then be easily separated from aqueous substances in the reaction chamber. Wood that would have normally been discarded can be used for this process.

PREDICT Describe some of the solutions that engineers might propose for maximizing the percent yield of hydrogen from discarded wood.

ANALYZE What types of criteria and constraints might engineers consider when evaluating competing solutions for maximizing the percent yield for this process? Discuss issues related to technology, science, affordability, and environmental impacts.

Evidence Notebook Explain how the concepts of limiting reactant, excess reactant, and percent yield apply to the question of how NASA calculates the necessary amount of hydrogen fuel for a space flight.

Case Study: Greenhouse Gas Emissions

Many of our daily activities are possible because of combustion reactions. The thermal energy released by the combustion of fossil fuels, such as coal, petroleum, and natural gas, can be converted to electricity or used to power vehicles. When a carbon-based fuel reacts with oxygen in a combustion reaction, carbon dioxide and water are released. The amount of carbon in Earth's atmosphere has increased significantly since the Industrial Revolution due to human activities involving combustion reactions. Because carbon dioxide is a greenhouse gas, an increasing concentration of this gas in Earth's atmosphere has led to an increase in average global temperatures.

ASK Imagine you are a researcher calculating the amount of carbon dioxide emitted by your family, class, or other local group. Write some questions you would ask to get started.

____

____

____

____

____

Sources of Greenhouse Gases

Greenhouse gases are emitted as the result of many different types of human activities. While carbon dioxide makes up the great majority (over 80%) of the greenhouse gases emitted by human activities, other greenhouse gases such as methane, nitrous oxide, and fluorinated gases are also released.

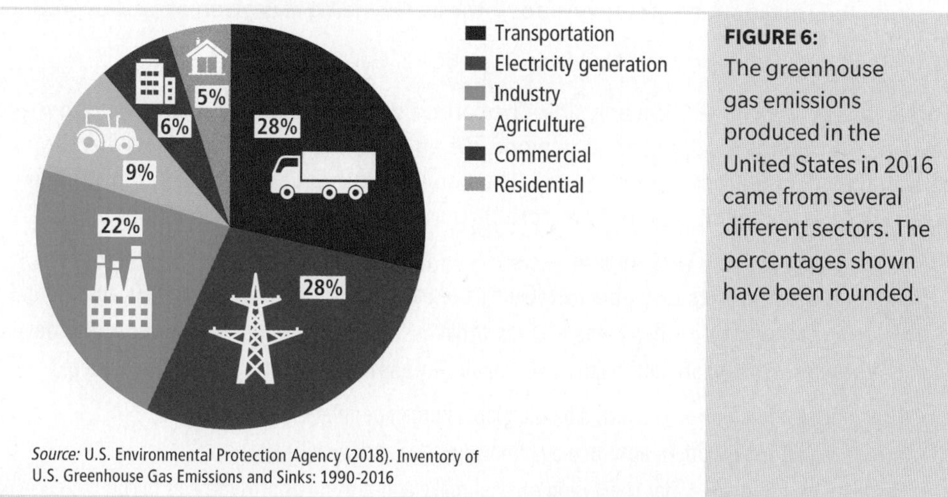

FIGURE 6: The greenhouse gas emissions produced in the United States in 2016 came from several different sectors. The percentages shown have been rounded.

SOLVE Use the graph in Figure 6 to answer the following question.

The total greenhouse gas emissions in the United States in 2016 was the equivalent of 6511 million metric tons (MMT) of CO_2. Use the graph to calculate how much of this total was emitted by the transportation sector. ____________

Almost all of the fossil fuel that is burned by the transportation sector comes from the burning of petroleum—gasoline, jet fuel, and diesel—in internal combustion engines.

ANALYZE Use this information to calculate the answers to the following questions. Gasoline is the main fuel used for transportation. It is composed mainly of octane, C_8H_{18}. The balanced chemical equation for the combustion of octane is shown below.

$$2C_8H_{18} + 25O_2 \rightarrow 16CO_2 + 18H_2O$$

Assume a gallon of gasoline contains 2370.0 grams of octane. How many grams of carbon dioxide would be produced by the complete combustion of the octane in this gallon of gasoline? ___________ g CO_2

In 2017, people in the United States used about 143 billion gallons of gasoline. How many grams of carbon dioxide were generated by the combustion of this gasoline, assuming the value you calculated in the first question was accurate?

___________ g CO_2

About 68% of the electricity generated in the United States in 2016 came from the combustion of coal and natural gas. The industry sector uses various fossil fuels both as an energy source and as reactants in the chemical reactions that make products such as plastics. The commercial and residential sectors also use various fossil fuels, mainly for heating, so the amount of emissions depends on weather conditions. Emissions from agriculture come from farming and livestock. Because each sector uses different fossil fuels with different chemical components, solutions for reducing greenhouse gas emissions will vary.

Absorbing Greenhouse Gases

Carbon dioxide can also be absorbed and stored. Anything that absorbs and stores carbon is called a *carbon sink*. One major carbon sink is photosynthetic organisms. Plants and algae take in carbon dioxide from the atmosphere and water from the soil. Using energy from sunlight, they make sugars during photosynthesis. Oxygen gas is given off as a byproduct.

$$6H_2O + 6CO_2 \rightarrow 6O_2 + C_6H_{12}O_6$$

Forests are a major natural carbon sink. The carbon dioxide forests absorb is used to make carbon compounds that are stored in wood. When trees and other organisms die, the carbon they contain moves into the soil. Thus, soil is another carbon sink. A third sink is water. Oceans and rivers absorb and store carbon dioxide from the atmosphere.

Language Arts Connection Conduct research about CO_2 emissions and CO_2 absorption via photosynthesis. Then prepare a report that answers the questions below. Cite specific text evidence to support your claims, and explain any gaps or inconsistencies you encountered.

- How much carbon dioxide is emitted by the global human population each year?
- How much carbon dioxide is absorbed by photosynthesis each year?
- Based on your findings, what conclusion can you make about using photosynthesis to completely offset human carbon emissions? Is this a viable solution? Why or why not?

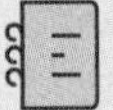

Evidence Notebook Think back to the chemical reaction between hydrogen and oxygen in rocket engines. How is this reaction related to the chemical reaction that results in carbon dioxide emissions? How are the two reactions similar? How are they different?

Hands-On Lab

Gravimetric Analysis

Hard water is water that has a high mineral content. Hard water causes problems because the minerals in the water can clog plumbing and make soaps less effective. One way to "soften" hard water is to use a water-softening agent, such as sodium chloride or potassium chloride, to help remove the ions that cause the water to be hard.

You are working for a company that makes water-softening agents for homes that have hard water. Recently, there was a mix-up on the factory floor. Sodium carbonate, Na_2CO_3, spilled into a 575-L tub of distilled water, and the company needs you to determine the amount of Na_2CO_3 in the tub.

When chemists are faced with problems that require them to determine the quantity of a substance by mass, they often use a technique called *gravimetric analysis*. In this technique, a small sample of the material undergoes a reaction with an excess of another reactant. For example, you can combine excess strontium chloride, $SrCl_2$, with the spilled sodium carbonate to form sodium chloride, NaCl, and solid strontium carbonate, $SrCO_3$. The unbalanced chemical equation for this reaction is shown below.

$$SrCl_2(aq) + Na_2CO_3(aq) \rightarrow NaCl(aq) + SrCO_3(s)$$

This double-displacement reaction produces a precipitate, which forms when one of the products is insoluble (does not dissolve) in water. The (*s*) in the chemical equation indicates that strontium carbonate, $SrCO_3$, is the precipitate in this reaction. Because the precipitate is not dissolved, it is easy to separate, dry, and weigh the solid. This provides the mass for one of the products.

RESEARCH QUESTION How can you use the results of a reaction that produces a precipitate to determine how much reactant was present in an aqueous solution?

MAKE A CLAIM

How do you think you can use the results of this chemical reaction to determine how much sodium carbonate was spilled into the tub of water?

MATERIALS

- indirectly vented chemical splash goggles, a nonlatex apron, and nitrile gloves
- beaker tongs
- beakers, 250 mL (3)
- distilled water
- drying oven
- electronic balance
- filter paper
- glass funnel or Büchner funnel
- glass stirring rod
- graduated cylinder, 100 mL
- paper towel
- ring and ring stand
- rubber policeman
- sodium carbonate, Na_2CO_3, solution
- spatula
- strontium chloride, $SrCl_2$, solution, 0.30 M
- wash bottle

indirectly vented chemical splash goggles

SAFETY INFORMATION

- Wear indirectly vented chemical splash goggles, a nonlatex apron, and nitrile gloves during the setup, hands-on, and takedown segments of the activity.
- The substances used in this lab are toxic and should only be disposed of in the chemical waste container provided by your teacher. Never place these substances in the trash or sink.
- Secure loose clothing, wear closed-toe shoes, and tie back long hair.
- Follow your teacher's instructions for disposing of waste materials.
- Use caution when working with glassware, which can shatter and cut skin if dropped.
- Wash your hands with soap and water when you are finished handling chemicals.

CARRY OUT THE INVESTIGATION

1. Wash all of the necessary lab equipment with soap and water. Rinse each piece of equipment with distilled water.
2. Measure the masses of the following to the nearest 0.01 g, and record each mass in a data table in your Evidence Notebook:
   - a piece of filter paper
   - a paper towel (labeled with your name and the date) inside a clean, dry beaker
3. Measure 15 mL of the Na_2CO_3 solution into the graduated cylinder. Record this volume in your data table. Pour the Na_2CO_3 solution into a clean, empty 250-mL beaker. Wash and rinse the graduated cylinder.
4. Measure 25 mL of the $SrCl_2$ solution into the graduated cylinder. Record this volume in your data table. Pour the $SrCl_2$ solution into the beaker with the Na_2CO_3 solution. Gently stir the solution with a glass rod.
5. Repeat Step 4 with 10 mL of $SrCl_2$. Repeat this step until no more precipitate (solid) forms. Record the volume of $SrCl_2$ each time you repeat Step 4.
6. Once the precipitate has settled, slowly pour the mixture into the funnel. Use the rubber policeman to transfer as much of the precipitate into the funnel as possible. Rinse the rubber policeman once into the beaker. Pour the rinse water into the funnel, then rinse the beaker several times, pouring the rinse water into the funnel each time.
7. After all of the solution and rinses have drained through the funnel, use the wash bottle to slowly rinse the precipitate on the filter paper in the funnel with distilled water to remove any soluble impurities.
8. Carefully remove the filter paper from the funnel, and place it on your paper towel. Unfold the filter paper, and place the paper towel and filter paper in the rinsed beaker. Then place the beaker in the drying oven, if available. For best results, allow the precipitate to dry overnight.
9. Using beaker tongs, remove your sample from the drying oven, and allow it to cool. Measure and record the mass of the beaker with paper towel, filter paper, and precipitate to the nearest 0.01 g.
10. Clean up the lab and all equipment after use, and dispose of substances according to your teacher's instructions. Wash your hands thoroughly after all lab work is finished and before you leave the lab.

CALCULATE

1. Write a balanced equation for the reaction between strontium chloride and sodium carbonate. Which product is the precipitate? Are atoms of each element conserved in this reaction?

2. Calculate the mass of the dry precipitate. Use this mass to calculate the moles of $SrCO_3$ produced in this reaction.

3. According to your results from Question 2 and the balanced chemical equation, how many moles of Na_2CO_3 were present in the starting sample of 15 mL?

4. According to your results from Question 3, how many grams of Na_2CO_3 were present in the starting sample?

5. How many grams of Na_2CO_3 were present in the factory's 575-L tub? (Hint: Use conversion factors to convert from the sample size to the tub size.)

ANALYZE

1. Why was the precipitate rinsed in Step 7? What soluble impurities could have been on the filter paper along with the precipitate? How would the calculated results vary if the precipitate had not been completely dry? Explain your answer.

2. Based on the concentration of the Na_2CO_3 solution you used, the theoretical mass of Na_2CO_3 is 0.795 g for every 15 mL of sample. Calculate your percentage error.

$$\text{Percentage error} = \frac{\text{value}_{\text{experimental}} - \text{value}_{\text{accepted}}}{\text{value}_{\text{accepted}}} \times 100$$

3. Was your percentage error value positive or negative? What does this tell you about how your final value compares with the theoretical value? How might errors have contributed to this result?

DRAW CONCLUSIONS

Write a conclusion that addresses each of the points below.

Claim To help this company address this problem in the future, summarize the method you used. How can you use the results of a reaction that produces a precipitate to determine how much reactant is present in an aqueous solution?

Evidence Give specific examples from your investigation that support your claim.

Reasoning Explain how the evidence you gave supports your claim. Describe, in detail, the connections between the evidence you cited and the arguments you are making.

Evidence Notebook Could rocket engineers use gravimetric analysis to determine how much liquid hydrogen was present in a fuel tank before the reaction with liquid oxygen took place? Explain your answer.

Guided Research

Redefining the Mole

When is a kilogram not a kilogram? Are all kilograms equal? These riddles don't seem to make sense until you learn that the definitions of the kilogram, the mole, and some other units of measurement have recently changed.

Since 1889, the kilogram had been officially defined as the mass of a small metal cylinder that is kept inside three glass jars within an underground locked vault in France. But, scientists observed that whenever this prototype kilogram was weighed, its mass was a tiny bit less than the mass of its six official replicas. They hypothesized that a few atoms of the metal rubbed off when the prototype was handled. In addition, the prototype got dirty and had to be cleaned to remove tiny specks of dust and dirt. Cleaning rubbed off a few atoms, too. As a result, the prototype kilogram lost 50 micrograms of mass over its 129 years. But because the mass of the kilogram was defined as the mass of the prototype, this meant that when the prototype changed, the amount of mass in one kilogram also changed! By definition, the mass of the prototype could not be different from one kilogram. Instead, all of the replicas were now too massive by 50 micrograms.

Scientists from 58 countries decided to change the definitions of several SI units, including the kilogram, to give them more precision. They proposed to define these units in terms of calculations based on universal constants of nature rather than on physical objects. The scientists met in November 2018 and voted unanimously for the changes.

The definition of a mole was also changed. Previously, a mole was defined as the amount of a substance that contains as many elementary particles as there are atoms in 0.012 kilograms of carbon-12. These particles could be electrons, atoms, ions, or molecules. But this definition of a mole had drawbacks. It was tied to the old definition of a kilogram, which, as you have just read, had difficulties. The Avogadro's constant that defines the mole is now defined as precisely $6.022\,140\,76 \times 10^{23}$.

FIGURE 7: This silicon sphere in a measuring machine was used as part of the International Avogadro Project.

The silicon sphere shown in Figure 7 is a uniform crystal of silicon-28, which was carefully shaped into a sphere. Using the mass and dimensions of the sphere, the structure of silicon's crystal lattice, and the atomic mass of silicon, scientists can calculate the total number of atoms in the sphere. Scientists in many different countries worked together in this effort, titled the International Avogadro Project, and performed measurements on several different silicon spheres. The redefinition of these units will allow the work of scientists to be more precise in the future.

Language Arts Connection Conduct research to learn more about the techniques scientists used to originally define and then redefine the mole and the kilogram. Then write a blog post that answers the following questions.

- How are the mole and the kilogram related?
- What specific techniques and experiments did scientists use to redefine the mole as part of the International Avogadro Project?
- How will this project affect future scientific work?

MORE PRACTICE WITH STOICHIOMETRY | CAREER: ATMOSPHERIC SCIENTIST | EXPLAINING STOICHIOMETRY | Go online to choose one of these other paths.

Lesson Self-Check

CAN YOU SOLVE THE PROBLEM?

FIGURE 8: Tanks aboard NASA's Space Launch System rocket hold liquid hydrogen fuel and liquid oxygen oxidizer.

How did engineers know how large to make the tanks that hold the liquid hydrogen and oxygen in the rocket, and how much fuel they would need? A thorough knowledge of the chemical reaction that will boost the rocket into space was needed. Carrying excess reactant would result in extra weight without extra thrust, decreasing efficiency and increasing cost. In this lesson, you learned that hydrogen burns in the presence of oxygen to produce water.

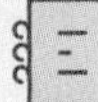

Evidence Notebook Refer to your notes in your Evidence Notebook to make a claim about how you could determine the amount of hydrogen needed for a space flight. Your explanation should include a discussion of the following points:

Claim Explain how, given a certain quantity of oxygen, you could determine the exact amount of hydrogen needed for a space flight.

Evidence Use evidence and examples to support your claim. Show the balanced equation for this reaction and include example calculations to illustrate your thinking.

Reasoning Explain how the evidence you cited supports your claim.

Name

Date

CHECKPOINTS

Check Your Understanding

1. A chemist wants to calculate the amount of product that will be formed in a chemical reaction. Which of the following steps ensures that the chemist's calculations are in alignment with the law of conservation of mass?

- ○ **a.** writing the states of matter for each reactant and product
- ○ **b.** looking up the atomic numbers for each element involved in the reaction
- ○ **c.** correctly balancing the chemical equation
- ○ **d.** determining whether one product is a precipitate or not

Silicon dioxide, or sand, reacts with finely ground carbon at high temperatures to produce silicon carbide and carbon monoxide gas. Use this chemical equation to answer Questions 2 and 3:

$$SiO_2(s) + 3C(s) \rightarrow SiC(s) + 2CO(g)$$

2. Select the correct terms to complete the statement.

When 50.0 grams of silicon dioxide reacts with excess carbon, carbon monoxide gas is formed. This amount of silicon dioxide is equal to 83.2 | 0.832 | 1.66 moles. As a result, 83.2 | 1.66 | 0.416 moles of carbon monoxide are formed. This amount of carbon monoxide is equal to 46.6 | 25.7 | 11.6 grams.

3. Suppose 50.0 grams of silicon dioxide reacts with excess carbon. How many grams of silicon carbide should be produced? ________

4. Select the correct terms to complete the statement.

A chemist has two bottles of gas. One bottle contains 2.6 moles of O_2, and the other bottle contains 2.6 moles of Cl_2. The two bottles contain equal | different numbers of particles and equal | different amounts of mass.

5. Which of the following are sources of carbon dioxide emissions? Select all correct answers.

- ☐ **a.** internal combustion engines
- ☐ **b.** generation of electricity in fossil-fueled power plants
- ☐ **c.** solar energy panels on roofs of homes
- ☐ **d.** photosynthesis by green plants and algae

Sodium and chlorine can be isolated from sodium chloride, which is a natural source of these two valuable elements. Use this chemical equation to answer Questions 6 and 7:

$$2NaCl(s) \rightarrow 2Na(s) + Cl_2(g)$$

6. What mass of sodium should be produced from 25.0 mol of sodium chloride?

- ○ **a.** 288 g Na
- ○ **b.** 575 g Na
- ○ **c.** 1150 g Na
- ○ **d.** 1460 g Na

7. What mass of chlorine should be made from 25.0 mol of sodium chloride?

- ○ **a.** 222 g Cl_2
- ○ **b.** 443 g Cl_2
- ○ **c.** 886 g Cl_2
- ○ **d.** 1772 g Cl_2

8. A chemist mixed sodium sulfide and cadmium nitrate solutions in a test tube. The equation is

$$Na_2S(aq) + Cd(NO_3)_2(aq) \rightarrow 2NaNO_3(aq) + CdS(s)$$

Sodium sulfide is the limiting reactant. Which substances are found in the test tube after the reaction has ended? Select all correct answers.

- ☐ **a.** Na_2S
- ☐ **b.** $Cd(NO_3)_2$
- ☐ **c.** $NaNO_3$
- ☐ **d.** CdS

CHECKPOINTS (continued)

9. Explain why, when performing stoichiometric calculations, it is important to use a balanced equation with correct chemical formulas and to consider the coefficients in the equation when converting from one quantity to another.

10. Nitric acid has a wide variety of industrial uses, including as an oxidizer in liquid-fueled rockets. The first step in the industrial manufacture of nitric acid is the catalytic oxidation of ammonia.

$$4NH_3(g) + 5O_2(g) \rightarrow 4NO(g) + 6H_2O(g)$$

The reaction is run using 824 g NH_3 and excess oxygen. Show how you could determine how many moles of NO and how many moles of H_2O are formed.

11. Explain what happens to the mass that appears to be "lost" when the percent yield of a reaction is less than 100%. According to the law of conservation of mass, what happens to the atoms that did not become part of the product?

MAKE YOUR OWN STUDY GUIDE

In your Evidence Notebook, design a study guide that supports the main ideas from this lesson:

The mole is the basic unit for all calculations used to determine the expected amount of product or reactant for a chemical reaction.

Stoichiometric calculations must be based on a balanced chemical equation in order to be in alignment with the law of conservation of mass.

Reactants might be limiting or in excess.

Remember to include the following information in your study guide:

- Use examples that model main ideas.
- Record explanations for the phenomena you investigated.
- Use evidence to support your explanations. Your support can include drawings, data, graphs, laboratory conclusions, and other evidence recorded throughout the lesson.

Consider how the methods you have developed in this lesson can be used to show that the total amount of matter in all closed systems is conserved.

4.3

Investigating Energy in Chemical Reactions

A sparkler gives off energy in the form of light that can be seen and heat that can be felt.

CAN YOU EXPLAIN THE PHENOMENON?

The brilliant flashes of light produced by a sparkler make it popular in many different celebrations around the world. A sparkler is a small, handheld firework that consists of a thin metal rod coated at one end with a combustible paste. The paste contains a fuel source such as carbon or sulfur, and an oxidizing compound. When the sparkler is lit, chemical reactions occur that release energy in the form of light and heat. Bits of metal embedded in the paste, such as iron, aluminum, and titanium, make the sparks that you see when a sparkler burns. Other metals present in the sparkler may make sparks of different colors.

INFER What do you think is the source of the energy in a chemical reaction, such as the reaction that occurs when you light a sparkler?

Evidence Notebook As you explore the lesson, gather evidence to explain how energy in the form of heat is transferred in processes such as the chemical reactions that light up a sparkler.

Investigating Thermal Energy and Heat

Energy comes in many different forms. It may take the form of stored energy, such as energy stored in a chemical bond, or it may take the form of movement, such as the energy associated with the movement of individual particles. Energy may also change form or be transferred from one place to another. Scientists and engineers study energy transformations so that they can control natural and designed systems.

FIGURE 1: Examples of materials that store chemical energy include foods, such as carbohydrates, and fuels, such as propane.

Energy Transformations

Potential energy is stored energy associated with the position, shape, or condition of an object. One form of potential energy is chemical energy, which is the energy stored in the bonds of chemical compounds, such as the examples shown in Figure 1. Energy stored in the chemical bonds of food is transformed into other forms that your body can use. Energy in the chemical bonds of a fuel such as propane is released as heat when the fuel is burned. Other forms of potential energy include gravitational potential energy, elastic potential energy, and nuclear energy. Recall that nuclear energy is released when the nucleus of an atom breaks apart or when the nuclei of two smaller atoms fuse.

Kinetic energy is the energy associated with the motion of an object. Many processes transform potential energy to kinetic energy, or vice versa. When you throw a baseball, you transfer potential energy from your muscles to the ball, which then has kinetic energy while it is moving. Molecules and atoms also have kinetic energy. Sound energy is a form of kinetic energy because it is caused by the vibration of molecules in a medium such as air.

Electromagnetic energy is a type of kinetic energy carried by electromagnetic waves, which are types of radiation that include visible light, x-rays, and microwaves. Electromagnetic energy can be transferred to an object, increasing the kinetic energy of its particles.

Any form of energy can transform into any other. In particular, when chemical reactions and other processes transfer energy as heat, there are always transformations between potential energy and kinetic energy.

EXPLAIN Which of the following are examples of kinetic energy? Select all correct answers.

☐ **a.** the energy in a sports drink

☐ **b.** the energy given off by the sun

☐ **c.** the energy of molecules in motion

☐ **d.** the energy of a book on a tall shelf

☐ **e.** the energy that holds together ions in a crystal

Temperature and Thermal Energy

Thermal energy is the total kinetic energy of the particles in a substance. Temperature is a measure of the average kinetic energy of the particles of a substance. When there is a temperature difference between two systems that are nearby or in contact with each other, thermal energy will transfer from the higher temperature system to the lower temperature system. This transfer of energy is the result of collisions between individual particles that make up the two substances. The mechanism by which thermal energy is transferred is called *heat transfer*.

When you feel hot, the temperature of your body has risen, either because thermal energy is transferring to your body, or because your body is generating too much thermal energy. When you feel cold, thermal energy is being transferred from your body to the surrounding system. If a system and its surroundings have the same temperature, they are in *thermal equilibrium*, and no net energy transfer occurs.

The pressure cooker in Figure 2 is an example of a closed system in which heat transfer is taking place. When the pressure cooker is sealed, thermal energy from the stovetop is transferred to the pressure cooker and is trapped there. This allows food within it to be cooked rapidly.

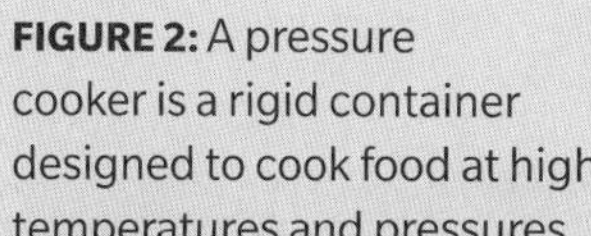

FIGURE 2: A pressure cooker is a rigid container designed to cook food at high temperatures and pressures.

APPLY Select the correct terms to complete the statement about the pressure cooker. Some terms may be used once or not at all.

kinetic energy | thermal energy | thermal equilibrium

Heat transfer from the stove increases the ____________________ of the particles of the pressure cooker system, which increases its ____________________. The pressure cooker's temperature reflects the average ____________________ of the particles in it.

Math Connection

Temperature Scales

You are probably familiar with the Celsius and Fahrenheit temperature scales. The Fahrenheit scale was one of the earliest widely adopted temperature scales, and it is still commonly used in the United States. In this scale, water freezes at 32 °F and boils at 212 °F. In the Celsius scale, which is more commonly used worldwide, water freezes at 0 °C and boils at 100 °C. The degrees in the Celsius scale are 100 equal divisions between these two arbitrarily assigned values.

Having to carry out calculations with negative temperature values can complicate a scientist's work. So, they often use the Kelvin temperature scale, which has its zero point at *absolute zero*, a theoretical temperature at which all particle motion stops. Thus, a kelvin temperature will never be negative. Because the Kelvin scale is absolute, temperatures on it are measured in *kelvins* rather than degrees.

Language Arts Connection Research the types of analyses that are typically carried out using kelvins. Then make a claim for why the Kelvin scale is necessary for a certain type of analysis. Cite specific text evidence from scientific sources to support your claim.

Conservation of Energy

When a system loses energy, that energy does not simply disappear. Rather, it is transferred to the system's surroundings. Similarly, if a system gains energy, the energy it gains must come from the system's surroundings. The law of conservation of energy states that energy cannot be created or destroyed, which means the total amount of energy in the universe remains constant.

Figure 3 shows an example of how the law of conservation of energy applies to a system made up of water in a beaker. The initial temperature of the water is due to its average thermal energy at the start. After a hot piece of metal is added to the system, thermal energy from the piece of metal is transferred to the water. An increase in the water's temperature provides evidence for this transfer. The temperature of the metal continues to drop until the metal and water are at thermal equilibrium—that is, when they are at the same temperature. Systems always evolve toward more stable states. In other words, the distribution of thermal energy in the system becomes more uniform over time.

FIGURE 3: Thermal energy is transferred when a hot piece of metal is submerged in cool water.

Explore Online 

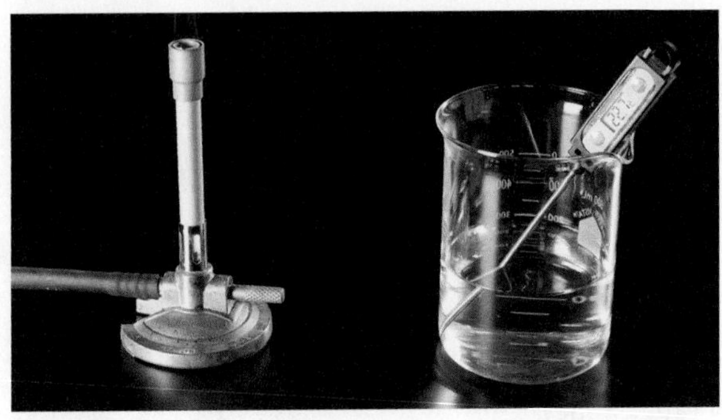

a Before the hot metal piece is added, the temperature of the water is 22.6 °C.

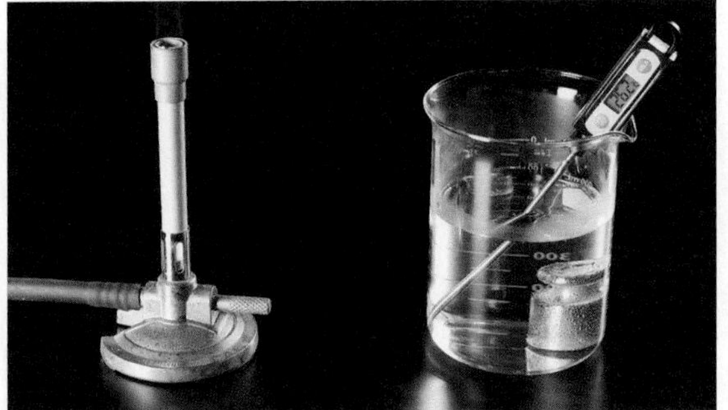

b After the hot metal piece is added, and the water and the metal reach thermal equilibrium. The temperature of the water is 26.2 °C.

ANALYZE Select the correct terms to complete the statement.

In the system shown in Figure 3, the amount of energy gained by the water is greater than | less than | equal to the amount of energy lost by the metal. Energy is conserved because the energy gained by the water was transferred from | to the water from | to the metal. Over time, stability in the system decreases | increases as thermal equilibrium is reached.

The First Law of Thermodynamics

In thermodynamics, the conservation of energy is described by the *first law of thermodynamics*. If you apply the law of conservation of energy to a system in which energy does not leave or enter the system, it means that the energy of the system does not change. Energy can be transformed or transferred within the system, but the total amount of energy in the system remains constant.

In an open or closed system, the first law of thermodynamics implies that the change in energy in the system is equivalent to the energy that passes through the system's boundaries. For example, in Figure 3, the amount of energy gained by the water is equal to the amount of energy that is lost by the hot piece of metal. Energy was not created, but rather transferred from one location to another.

The Second Law of Thermodynamics

The second law of thermodynamics states that thermal energy spontaneously flows from a substance at a higher temperature to a substance at a lower temperature. Heating a pot of water on a stove provides a good example of the direction of energy transfer. Thermal energy is transferred from the burning fuel or hot surface of a stove to the cooler pot of water. Thermal energy never moves from the cooler water back toward the stove. Once the stove is turned off, energy from the hot pan is transferred to the air until thermal equilibrium is reached, and the pan is the same temperature as the air.

FIGURE 4: Thermal energy spontaneously transfers from the flame on the stove to the cooler pan.

Collaborate With a partner, write an explanation of how the first and second laws of thermodynamics apply to the system shown in Figure 4. As part of your explanation, describe the system boundaries, the direction of energy transfer, and the conservation of energy. Include diagrams as needed.

Particle Behavior and Energy Transfer

Imagine what would happen if you placed a cold metal object in the hot water in the pan in Figure 4. As you have seen, the system would eventually reach thermal equilibrium. But how would interactions between the water molecules and metal atoms account for your observations at the larger scale? At the particle level, thermal energy takes the form of kinetic energy. The particles of a substance with a higher temperature move faster on average because they have a higher kinetic energy.

MODEL Draw a model showing how interactions between water molecules and metal atoms could cause a closed system to reach thermal equilibrium when a cold metal object is placed in hot water. Illustrate at least two points in time. Include components that help show how kinetic energy and collisions between particles are related to this phenomenon.

Hands-On Lab

Exploring Thermal Energy and Temperature

The amount of thermal energy in a substance is related to both the temperature and the amount of substance. In this lab, you will plan and carry out an investigation to explore how thermal energy changes when water of different temperatures is combined into a single system.

MAKE A CLAIM

How can you use temperature to measure the change in thermal energy of a system?

______

______

______

MATERIALS

- indirectly vented chemical splash goggles, nonlatex apron
- beaker, 500 mL (3)
- thermometer (3)
- water

SAFETY INFORMATION

indirectly vented chemical splash goggles

- Wear indirectly vented chemical splash goggles and a nonlatex apron during the setup, hands-on, and takedown segments of the activity.
- Immediately wipe up any spilled water on the floor so it does not become a slip/fall hazard.

CARRY OUT THE INVESTIGATION

In your Evidence Notebook, write a procedure and safety plan to test your claim. What are the variables of your investigation, and what qualitative and quantitative data will you collect to determine the change in the thermal energy of the system?

DRAW CONCLUSIONS

In your Evidence Notebook, write a conclusion that addresses each of the points below.

Claim How did thermal energy change when water of different temperatures was combined into a single system?

Evidence What evidence from your investigation supports your claim?

Reasoning Explain how the evidence you gave supports your claim. Describe, in detail, the connections between the evidence you cited and the argument you are making.

EXTEND

How do you think the transfer of thermal energy and the final temperature of the system would change if you used insulated bowls with lids instead of glass beakers? In your Evidence Notebook, write a procedure to investigate this question. If time allows, have your teacher approve your plan, and carry out your procedure.

Analyzing Specific Heat Capacity

The amount of thermal energy needed to change the temperature of a system by one degree is the system's *heat capacity*. The heat capacity of a system depends on the type of material from which it is made and its mass. Therefore, heat capacity is an extensive property.

PREDICT Select the correct terms to complete the statement.

To change the temperature of a large tub of water and a small glass of water by the same amount, less | more energy must be added to the large tub of water than to the small glass of water. This is because the water in the glass has a lower | higher mass than the water in the tub.

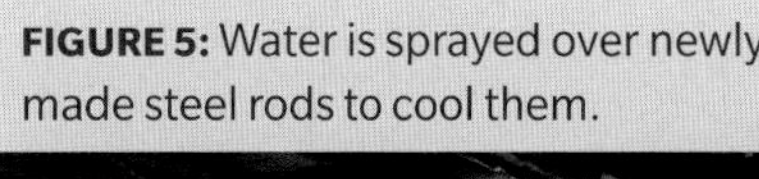

Experimenting with Calorimetry Build a calorimeter and test it to determine the specific heat capacity of a known sample.

In order to compare the heat capacities of different materials, scientists compare heat capacity per unit of mass. This is known as the specific heat capacity of the material. Specific heat capacity (c_p) is an intensive property defined as the amount of energy (q) required to raise the temperature of one gram of a substance by one kelvin. (The subscript p refers to standard pressure.) Specific heat capacity relates heat to a substance's temperature change by the following equation.

$$q = mc_p\Delta T$$

The SI unit for energy is joules (J), and values of specific heat capacity are often expressed in units of joules per gram per kelvin (J/(g•K).

Specific Heat Capacities of Some Common Substances (at 298.15 K and atmospheric pressure)

Substance	Specific heat (J/(g•K))	Substance	Specific heat (J/(g•K))
Water (*l*)	4.18	Iron (*s*)	0.449
Water (*s*)	2.06	Copper (*s*)	0.385
Aluminum (*s*)	0.897	Gold (*s*)	0.129

Materials with a low specific heat capacity undergo a larger increase in temperature as thermal energy is transferred to them than materials with a high specific heat capacity. These differences make certain materials more appropriate for different purposes. For example, as shown in Figure 5, the relatively high specific heat capacity of liquid water makes it useful as a coolant in industrial processes.

FIGURE 5: Water is sprayed over newly made steel rods to cool them.

INFER Suppose you had three pans with the same mass, but made of different materials: iron, aluminum, and copper. Based on the values in the table above and the definition of specific heat capacity, which pan would cook food the fastest?

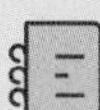

Evidence Notebook Explain how conservation of energy and the laws of thermodynamics apply to the sparkler system you saw at the beginning of this lesson. What forms of energy are present in this example? How does this system demonstrate the principles of energy conservation?

Hands-On Lab

Measuring the Energy in Food

We get the energy we need by eating food. The energy comes from the chemical energy stored in the food that gets released during digestion. This energy is described on food labels with the unit Calorie (always with a capital C). One Calorie is equivalent to 4.184 kJ. How do food makers determine how many Calories a food has? They burn the food in a device called a calorimeter. In this lab, you will build a calorimeter to measure the energy released when two different snack foods are burned.

RESEARCH QUESTION How can the specific heat capacity of water be used to determine the amount of energy stored in another substance?

MAKE A CLAIM

Predict how well your energy values will compare to those on the food labels. What must you consider when designing your calorimeter to ensure that it measures the energy released as precisely and accurately as possible? Explain your thinking.

MATERIALS

- indirectly vented chemical splash goggles, nonlatex apron, nitrile gloves
- aluminum foil, 30 cm × 30 cm sheet
- balance
- beaker tongs
- evaporating dish
- graduated cylinder, 100 mL
- matches or propane lighter
- ring and clamp
- ring stand
- snack foods with nutrition labels, 2 types (cheese puff, marshmallow, dry cereal, etc.)
- soda can
- spatula
- thermometer
- thermometer clamp
- three-finger clamp
- water
- weighing boat or weighing paper (2)
- wire gauze

SAFETY INFORMATION

indirectly vented chemical splash goggles

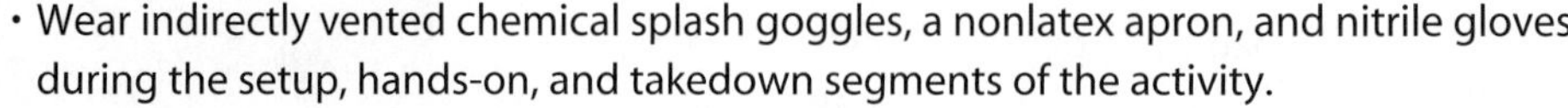

- Wear indirectly vented chemical splash goggles, a nonlatex apron, and nitrile gloves during the setup, hands-on, and takedown segments of the activity.
- Secure loose clothing, wear closed-toe shoes, and tie back long hair.
- Never eat any food items used in a lab activity.

PLAN THE INVESTIGATION

Write a procedure and safety plan in your Evidence Notebook explaining how you will measure the amount of energy contained in the snack foods using the calorimeter. Use Figure 6 and the materials list to develop your plan. Decide what substances you will test, and how many trials you will need to conduct. Ask your teacher to approve your procedure and safety plan before you begin.

COLLECT DATA

Make a data table in your Evidence Notebook. Use the specific heat equation below to determine the data you should collect for each food sample. Consider your experimental setup when deciding how much data to collect and how to ensure the data are as accurate as possible.

- When measuring the temperature of water in a container, the thermometer should only contact the water, not the container.
- Because the density of water is 1.00 g/mL, the volume of water can be used to infer its mass. A 50.0 mL sample of water is 50.0 g.

FIGURE 6: Energy from the burning snack food sample warms the water in the soda can calorimeter.

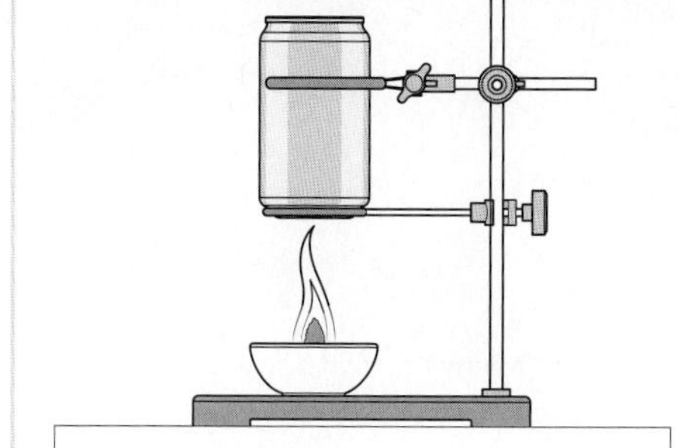

ANALYZE

1. Use the following equation to calculate the number of Calories per gram for each food:

$$q = mc_p\Delta T$$

How do your values compare to the Calories per gram shown on the nutrition label?

2. Sketch your calorimeter. Label the system and the surroundings. Use arrows to show the flow of energy into and out of the system.

3. Discuss the limitations of the data you collected. How do these limitations correlate to the design of your calorimeter? Describe how you would redesign your calorimeter to minimize energy loss.

4. The calorimeter you used is an open system. Sketch how you could determine the energy content of a snack food using a closed system. Label the system in your sketch.

DRAW CONCLUSIONS

Write a conclusion that addresses each of these points.

Claim How do your findings compare with the values shown on the food labels for these foods? How did the design of the calorimeter affect the data you collected?

Evidence Use evidence from your data and calculations to support your claim.

Reasoning Explain how the evidence you cited supports your claim. In addition, discuss possible reasons for differences between your measurements and the Calorie values shown on the nutrition label for each food.

EXTEND

How do you think the results of your investigation would have been different if you had used a liquid with a different heat capacity, such as salt water? If time allows, write a procedure in your Evidence Notebook describing how you could investigate this question. With your teacher's permission, carry out your procedure, and analyze your results.

Evidence Notebook Discuss why you do not get burned if a few sparks from a sparkler touch your skin. Consider how the mass of the spark and its thermal energy affect this phenomenon.

Exploring Reaction Energy

Some chemical reactions release thermal energy, while others absorb it. These phenomena are explained in terms of the chemical energy stored in the bonds between the atoms that make up a compound. During a chemical reaction, energy must be absorbed by a reactant in order to break these chemical bonds, and energy is released when the chemical bonds of the products form. The difference in energy stored in the reactant bonds and the product bonds determines whether there is an overall absorption or release of thermal energy by the reaction.

Analyzing Changes in Energy

Observe the transformations that result from the three chemical reactions shown in Figure 7. Along with new substances being produced in the reactions, a significant amount of thermal energy is either absorbed or released to the surroundings.

FIGURE 7: Energy changes can happen in different ways during chemical reactions.

Explore Online

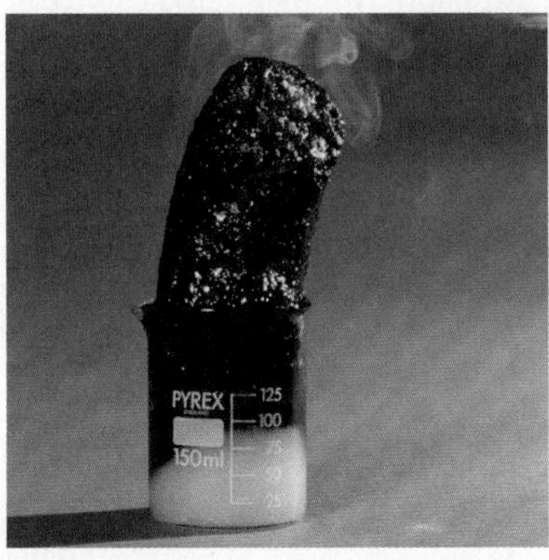

a **Reaction 1** Sugar is combined with sulfuric acid, producing black carbon and water vapor. The water is vaporized due to the increase in temperature.

b **Reaction 2** When barium hydroxide reacts with ammonium chloride, the temperature in the flask decreases, and the flask freezes to the wood.

c **Reaction 3** When glycerin is added to a sample of potassium permanganate, the energy released by the reaction ignites the glycerin.

MODEL Draw the system and surroundings for each of the reactions in Figure 7. Identify the system boundaries and use arrows to model the movement of energy.

Exothermic and Endothermic Reactions

Explore Online

Hands-On Lab 

Investigating Energy in Chemical Processes Carry out an investigation to explore which chemicals make the best hot and cold packs.

A reaction that releases thermal energy is called an exothermic reaction. Other than an increase in temperature, the formation of light or sound can also indicate the release of energy in a chemical reaction. In these reactions, bond energy changes into kinetic energy that leaves the reaction system and enters the surroundings. This transfer of energy increases the temperature of the surroundings. A reaction that absorbs thermal energy is called an endothermic reaction. In an endothermic reaction, the temperature of the surroundings decreases because kinetic energy leaves the surroundings and enters the system. When kinetic energy is absorbed in an endothermic reaction, that energy becomes chemical potential energy in the products of the reaction.

Energy and Matter

Using Reaction Energy

FIGURE 8: MREs rely on chemical reactions to warm food.

Chemical hand warmers are used to warm up your hands and feet. These warmers contain finely powdered iron in a porous envelope inside a sealed pouch. When the pouch is opened, the iron reacts with atmospheric oxygen to form iron(III) oxide, releasing energy in the form of heat.

$$4Fe + 3O_2 \rightarrow 2Fe_2O_3$$

A similar reaction can also be used to produce higher temperatures, such as in MREs ("meals-ready-to-eat") used by the military. MREs contain iron and magnesium, both of which react with oxygen. Water is added to the MRE, which reacts with the magnesium, releasing energy in the form of heat. This allows military personnel to have hot meals without requiring heating equipment such as stoves.

An exothermic reaction such as this can gently warm your hands, or potentially produce enough heat to burn your skin. Thus, it is important that the MRE be a closed system. Once water is added to the MRE, it is sealed to prevent heat transfer from inside the system to the surroundings.

APPLY Is the chemical reaction between iron and oxygen endothermic or exothermic? In your explanation, discuss how energy is transformed in the MRE.

Collaborate With a partner, make a model of a system that shows how the potential energy in the chemical bonds in the MRE is transformed into kinetic energy in the surroundings through molecular collisions. Your model should show how energy is conserved in the system.

We can infer information about the properties of the substances involved in a reaction from the energy changes in the reaction. Consider the combustion of carbon.

$$C(s) + O_2(g) \rightarrow CO_2(g)$$

In this reaction, carbon dioxide is more stable than carbon or diatomic oxygen molecules due to the reactants having more potential energy than the products. The reaction is exothermic because energy is released into the surroundings as thermal energy.

FIGURE 9: Some reactions give off energy, and others absorb energy.

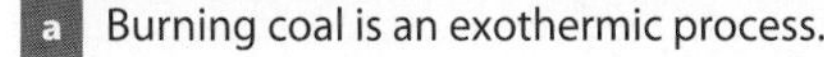

a Burning coal is an exothermic process.

b Nitric oxide, which contributes to smog, forms in an endothermic process.

The synthesis of nitric oxide, NO, is endothermic, so it requires energy:

$$N_2(g) + O_2(g) \rightarrow 2NO(g)$$

This reaction does not occur spontaneously at typical air temperatures. When fossil fuels are burned, the nitrogen and oxygen in the surrounding air can react to form nitric oxide. Nitric oxide is a major contributor to acid rain, ozone depletion, and smog. In the atmosphere, NO undergoes an exothermic reaction to form another pollutant, nitrogen dioxide, NO_2, which is an irritant to the respiratory system. The formation of NO is endothermic because much more energy is needed to break the chemical bonds of NO_2 than is used to form the chemical bonds of NO.

ANALYZE Select the correct terms to complete the statement.

For a chemical reaction to occur, particles must collide. Chemical bonds contain potential | kinetic energy. During the combustion of carbon, the reactant molecules must have enough potential | kinetic energy that their bonds will break when they collide. When new bonds form, the surroundings absorb potential | kinetic energy, and the temperature of the surroundings will increase | decrease.

Modeling Changes in Energy

Modeling energy changes can help clarify interactions that occur during chemical reactions. Examples include diagrams, graphs, and chemical equations. Reactions can first be classified in terms of whether the overall reaction absorbs energy or releases energy. Then, a model can be used to represent the flow of energy over the course of the reaction.

Collaborate With a partner, brainstorm examples of temperature changes caused by chemical reactions. For each example, model the chemical system and show how matter flows within it. Using your model, explain why these chemical reactions are accompanied by a transfer of thermal energy. How does the energy in the system change?

Energy Diagrams

Graphs are a useful way to model the difference in energy between the reactants and products of a reaction. Time is represented on the horizontal axis, indicating how the reaction proceeds from reactants to products. The relative energy of reactants and products is represented on the vertical axis. The shape of the graph shows whether the reaction involves an overall absorption or release of energy.

FIGURE 10: Energy diagrams represent changes in energy as chemical reactions proceed from reactants to products.

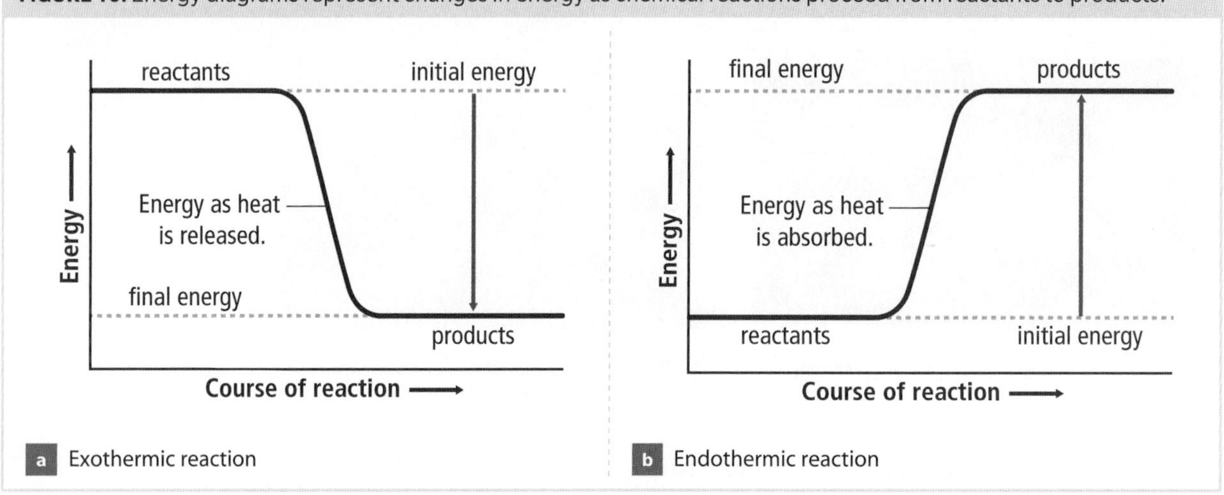

a Exothermic reaction

b Endothermic reaction

On the graph of an exothermic reaction, the potential energy of the reactants is higher than that of the products. On the graph of an endothermic reaction, the potential energy of the products is higher than that of the reactants. In both cases, the difference in energy between reactants and products represents the change in energy of the reaction.

INFER Write generic chemical equations that include energy for the exothermic and endothermic reactions shown in Figure 10. Would energy be on the reactant or product side of the equations? Explain your reasoning.

Modeling Energy as a Reactant or a Product

The change in energy in a reaction can also be modeled as a reactant or a product. For example, because energy is released during the formation of CO_2, it can be represented as a product of the reaction, as shown below. This equation shows that 393.5 kJ of energy are released in the reaction per mole of CO_2 formed. Given the law of conservation of energy, this also means that 393.5 kJ of energy are needed to break down 1 mole of CO_2.

$$C(s) + O_2(g) \rightarrow CO_2(g) + 393.5 \text{ kJ}$$

For an endothermic reaction such as the formation of nitric oxide, energy from the surroundings is absorbed and becomes part of the chemical energy of the products. Therefore, energy can be represented as one of the reactants in the chemical equation.

$$\frac{1}{2}N_2(g) + \frac{1}{2}O_2(g) + 90.29 \text{ kJ} \rightarrow NO(g)$$

Normally, a balanced chemical equation for the formation of NO would have no coefficients for the reactants and a coefficient of 2 for the product. But to compare the amounts of energy released or absorbed, the chemical equations must each represent 1 mole of product formed, so the coefficients must all be divided by 2. The equation above does not indicate that half a molecule each of N_2 and O_2 can react to form NO.

In an exothermic reaction such as the one in which carbon dioxide is formed, energy is released from the system into the surroundings. Therefore, the final potential energy of the system is lower than the initial potential energy. In an endothermic reaction such as the one in which nitric oxide is formed, energy enters the system from the surroundings, so the system has higher potential energy after the reaction.

MODEL Draw two energy diagrams, one representing the reaction in which CO_2 is formed and another representing the reaction in which NO is formed. Label each graph with the amount of energy released or absorbed. Consider the origin and an appropriate scale when making your diagrams.

Systems and System Models

Energy and Reaction Systems

When an energy diagram of an exothermic reaction shows the products having lower energy than the reactants, where does that energy go? The law of conservation of energy says that energy cannot be created or destroyed. So, to understand and control processes, scientists and engineers must keep track of energy. A useful way of doing this is to model thermodynamic changes in terms of a system and its surroundings. The compounds involved in a chemical reaction can be modeled as a system that absorbs energy from the surroundings or releases energy to the surroundings of the system.

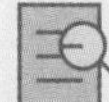

Language Arts Connection Research changes in energy that occur during endothermic and exothermic reactions. Develop a presentation in which you describe a specific endothermic and exothermic reaction. Use various forms of digital media to model the energy changes that occur in each reaction.

Reaction Energy and Bond Energy

FIGURE 11: These models show the formation of CO_2 and NO from their elements.

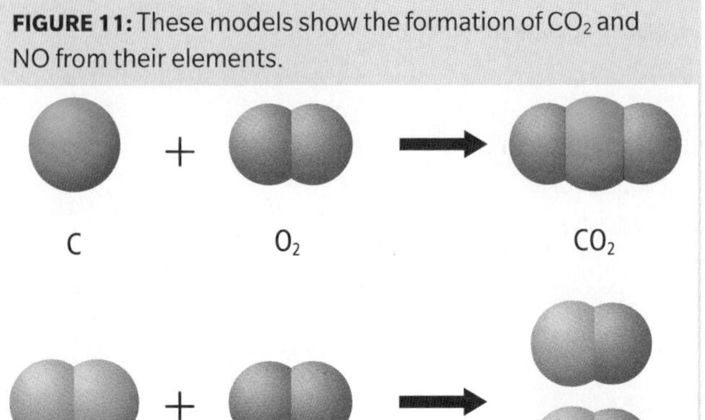

All chemical reactions, even those that release energy, must first absorb enough energy for the reactant bonds to be broken. The energy required to break the bonds of a chemical compound is the bond energy. The difference in the energy required to break bonds in the reactants and the energy released when new bonds are formed in the products determines the overall reaction energy. Bond energies therefore determine the stability of the products of a reaction. Stable compounds have more bond energy than less stable compounds. CO_2 has a higher bond energy than O_2, so it is more stable, and its formation is exothermic. But NO has a lower bond energy than N_2 and O_2, so NO is less stable, and its formation is endothermic.

APPLY Select the correct terms to complete the statement.

In an exothermic reaction, the total bond energy of the products | reactants is greater than the total bond energy of the products | reactants, so the products are more | less stable than the reactants.

As chemical reactions occur, a change in the total bond energy is accompanied by changes in kinetic energy. Energy released during exothermic reactions is converted to kinetic energy, which increases the temperature of the surroundings. Endothermic reactions absorb energy from the surroundings, which decreases the kinetic energy and the temperature of the surroundings.

Explore Online

FIGURE 12: The detonation of nitrogen triiodide

The solid compound nitrogen triiodide, NI_3, has high potential energy due to the low bond energy of its very weak chemical bonds. NI_3 easily undergoes a decomposition reaction forming nitrogen gas, N_2, and iodine gas, I_2. This reaction releases a great deal of energy, as can be seen in Figure 12.

INFER What can you conclude about the bond energies of nitrogen and iodine molecules compared to those of nitrogen triiodide?

Similarly to nitrogen triiodide, many commonly-used explosives are nitrogen-containing compounds that release stable, diatomic nitrogen as well as large amounts of energy. An example is nitroglycerine, $C_3H_5N_3O_9$, a component of dynamite. The decomposition of sodium azide, NaN_3, is used to inflate automobile air bags in as few as 40 milliseconds. Many fertilizers contain ammonium nitrate, NH_4NO_3. This compound is a cost-effective way to increase the amount of nitrogen in the fertilizer, but it is also extremely explosive. Manufacturers must use extreme care to keep any source of ignition away from ammonium nitrate.

Evidence Notebook What do you think an energy diagram would look like for the reaction that occurs when a sparkler is lit? Would energy be treated as a reactant or a product in the chemical equation of the reaction? What evidence supports your answer?

Case Study: Energy in Fuels

A combustion fuel is any substance that releases energy in the form of heat when it is burned. These fuels can be solids, liquids, or gases. Wood, for example, can be used as a fuel because it releases heat when it burns. The most common fuels for energy production are fossil fuels, including coal, petroleum, and natural gas. Fossil fuels are primarily hydrocarbons, which are compounds composed of only carbon and hydrogen atoms.

FIGURE 13: Gasoline is a mixture of liquid fossil fuels that releases energy in engines.

PREDICT If you were selecting a fuel for a new type of vehicle you were developing, what are three criteria and two constraints you might consider? Which would be most important to you?

Combustion of Fuels

Hydrocarbon fuels release large amounts of energy during combustion because the carbon-hydrogen bond in the fuel has a lower bond energy than the carbon-oxygen double bond in carbon dioxide. The following chemical equations show the combustion reactions of methane, CH_4, and propane, C_3H_8.

$$CH_4(g) + 2O_2(g) \rightarrow CO_2(g) + 2H_2O(g) + 891 \text{ kJ}$$

$$C_3H_8(g) + 5O_2(g) \rightarrow 3CO_2(g) + 4H_2O(g) + 2200 \text{ kJ}$$

The table shows the amounts of energy released per mole by various hydrocarbon fuels.

Energy Released by Combustion of Carbon-Based Fuels

Name	Chemical formula	Energy released (kJ/mol fuel)
Methane (natural gas)	CH_4	891
Ethane	C_2H_6	1561
Propane	C_3H_8	2200
Butane	C_4H_{10}	2878
Octane	C_8H_{18}	5430

EXPLAIN Select the correct terms to complete the statement.

When a fuel such as octane combusts, atoms are rearranged to form new molecules. This reaction is endothermic | exothermic, so the bond energy of the products is greater than | less than the bond energy of the reactants. In this reaction, chemical energy, a form of potential | kinetic energy, is transformed into thermal energy, which is related to the potential | kinetic energy of particles.

FIGURE 14: An oil refinery breaks down crude oil to produce petroleum products in different forms for various uses.

Petroleum is a liquid fossil fuel extracted from underground rock formations. Unrefined petroleum is called crude oil. At oil refineries such as the one shown in Figure 14, crude oil is processed to produce a variety of petroleum products, such as kerosene, lubricants, and waxes. The main product of refineries is gasoline. Gasoline is a mixture of hydrocarbons, primarily octane (C_8H_{18}).

An environmental concern with petroleum refining is that refineries produce pollutants in areas where they are located. These include air pollutants such as benzene, nitrogen oxides, carbon monoxide, and sulfur dioxide. Benzene is a carcinogen, or cancer-causing agent. In addition, some of these pollutants cause developmental problems in children and exacerbate respiratory conditions such as asthma. Air pollution from refineries comes from a variety of sources. These include equipment leaks, the heating of steam and fluids, and high-temperature combustion processes.

DEFINE Write a problem statement that an engineer could use to develop a solution to an environmental problem associated with petroleum refining. Then write some criteria and constraints that might be associated with a successful solution.

Efficiency

Some of the energy released in the combustion of gasoline is always lost as thermal energy that dissipates into the surroundings rather than powering an engine. Fuels and engines that maximize the amount of useful energy output are said to be more *efficient,* and thus reduce cost as well as pollution and carbon emissions.

The efficiency of a fuel can be expressed as the ratio of energy output to the energy released by the combustion reaction. The efficiency is often expressed as a percentage by multiplying this ratio by 100. The efficiency of gasoline engines is typically less than 50%.

$$\text{efficiency} = \frac{\text{power output}}{\text{power input}} \times 100$$

SOLVE Calculate the solution to the following question about efficiency.

A car engine produces 750 kJ of mechanical energy from a fuel capable of producing 2550 kJ of energy. Calculate the efficiency of this engine. ____________

In an effort to increase fuel efficiency while decreasing pollution and carbon emissions, many governments around the world have set fuel efficiency and emissions standards for vehicles. Because these types of regulations vary from place to place, vehicle makers must consider a wide range of factors when developing new designs for international markets.

Collaborate With a partner, write a list of information you would gather to compare tradeoffs when developing a more fuel efficient vehicle for a certain country. What would you want to know about the country's laws, infrastructure, economy, and people?

Criteria and Constraints

Fuels that have a higher efficiency can be designed, but the changes often require tradeoffs in other criteria for the fuel. Fuel dispensers at gas stations, for example, often have fuels with different octane levels available. Higher-octane fuels are more efficient, but they are also more expensive, and require engines that are specially designed to take advantage of them. So for the typical vehicle, higher-octane fuel does not offer enough benefit to make the added cost worthwhile.

Fuels that have a higher energy output may release more carbon dioxide or pollutants into the atmosphere, contributing to climate change and atmospheric pollution. Combustion fuel emissions include pollutants such as sulfur dioxide and nitrogen oxides, which can combine with water vapor and oxygen in the air to form smog and acid rain. Reducing these emissions is therefore also an important criterion in managing fuel use.

Designing combustion fuels that have low emissions of harmful gases can be difficult because of the associated costs. Reducing carbon dioxide emissions of liquid fuels decreases the energy output of the fuel, but other harmful emissions may be produced instead. Methods have been developed to reduce the sulfur dioxide output of coal, either before or after combustion, but the processes are expensive and have had limited success.

EVALUATE Consider the new type of fuel that you previously defined in terms of its criteria and constraints. How well does high-octane fuel meet the criteria and conform to the constraints that you specified?

Tradeoffs

Ethanol, C_2H_5OH, is commonly added to gasoline to reduce the amount of carbon monoxide produced when the fuel is burned. The combustion of ethanol releases 1337 kJ of energy per mole of ethanol burned. The chemical equation for this combustion is:

$$C_2H_5OH(g) + 3O_2(g) \rightarrow 2CO_2(g) + 3H_2O(g) + 1337 \text{ kJ}$$

While this more efficient combustion is better for the environment, the combustion of ethanol produces less energy per gram than the combustion of gasoline.

Language Arts Connection Research the global challenge of inefficient fuel combustion. Write a position statement in which you give a rationale for why inefficient fuel combustion is a major global challenge, describing the extent of the problem and its consequences to society on the local and global scales if it remains unsolved. Finally, make a claim about whether adding ethanol to gasoline is a worthwhile solution to the problem. Cite evidence from reliable scientific journals as part of your statement.

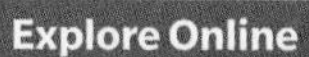

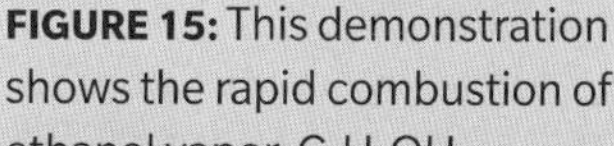

FIGURE 15: This demonstration shows the rapid combustion of ethanol vapor, C_2H_5OH.

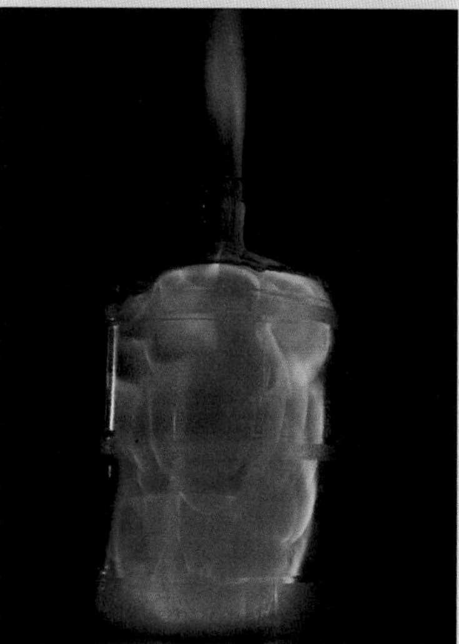

Carbon Emissions

A major concern with fossil fuels and other carbon-based combustion fuels is that they produce carbon dioxide. As the concentrations of carbon dioxide and other greenhouse gases increase in Earth's atmosphere, the flow of energy in Earth's atmosphere also changes. This leads to observable changes, such as increased average global temperatures, altered patterns of extreme weather events, and higher average ocean levels. In order to address the challenges associated with global climate change, scientists and engineers have begun working together to develop evidence-based solutions.

Figure 16 shows the carbon dioxide concentration in Earth's atmosphere over the last 400 000 years. The concentration of carbon dioxide is expressed in parts per million.

Historical Carbon Dioxide Levels

FIGURE 16: Atmospheric carbon dioxide levels fluctuated in the past, but have increased significantly in recent years.

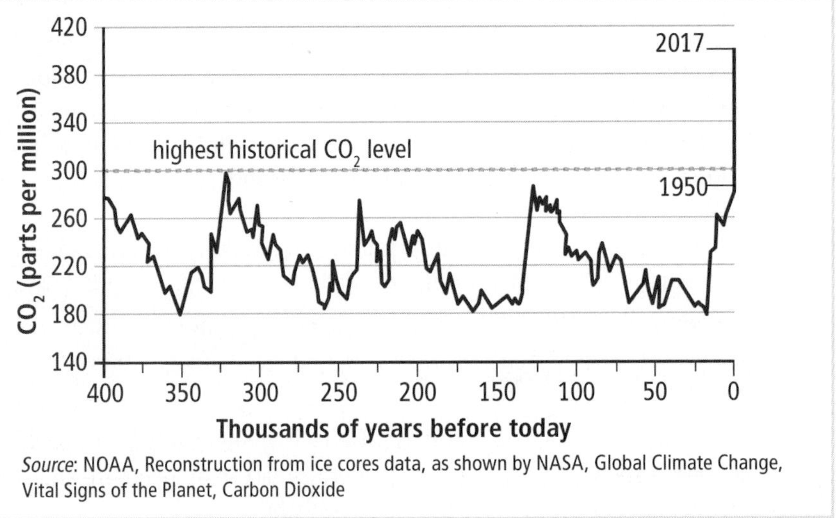

Source: NOAA, Reconstruction from ice cores data, as shown by NASA, Global Climate Change, Vital Signs of the Planet, Carbon Dioxide

ANALYZE Describe the patterns you see in the graph. How do you think carbon emissions from burning fuels have contributed to the increase in carbon dioxide concentration shown in Figure 16?

Because increased carbon emissions cause changes in Earth's climate, many countries have begun developing solutions that will minimize the use of fossil fuels and maximize the use of renewable energy sources. Some countries have put in place regulations that require all new vehicles purchased after a certain date to use electrical energy. Hydrogen fuel-cell vehicles are another solution that has been proposed. Each of these technologies has impacts on people and the environment. Some of these effects can be predicted, and some cannot. As a result, the impacts of a given solution must be carefully considered before it is implemented.

PREDICT How do you think regulatory agencies weigh important factors such as societal, economic, and environmental impacts when considering a new law or regulation related to fuel sources, fuel efficiency, or emissions levels for vehicles?

Engineering Lab

Fuel Alternatives

Increasing concerns about climate change have led to an urgency in the need to develop alternatives to fossil fuels used to power automobiles and produce electricity. The environmental impact of drilling for and refining fossil fuels is also a concern. In addition, fossil fuels are a nonrenewable resource, so over time supplies will become increasingly limited. Fuel mixtures have been developed that reduce harmful emissions, but clean-burning fuels are needed.

Most vehicles on the road today still use gasoline or diesel fuel, but alternatives are becoming common. Ethanol is an example of an alternative fuel that reduces the reliance on fossil fuels. Other examples of alternative fuels include biodiesel and hydrogen fuel.

FIGURE 17: Corn can be used as a biofuel, as ethanol can be produced from it.

DESIGN CHALLENGE Use a simulation to model large-scale societal reliance on different types of fuel for transportation, including alternative fuels. Your model should allow for comparison of tradeoffs and identify the criteria and constraints involved in fuel choices.

CONDUCT RESEARCH

To learn more about the large-scale factors involved in fuel choices, research a range of sources and simulations. Based on your results, identify an appropriate computational model that will allow you to simulate your own system.

1. Describe the simulation you will use to investigate optimal fuel choices. What are the limitations of the simulation?

2. What factors involved in alternative fuel choices do you think can be modeled effectively through this simulation? Explain your answer.

3. How can you use the simulation to predict trends related to economic costs, societal considerations, and environmental impacts? Explain your answer.

DEFINE THE PROBLEM

Identify a long-term problem that you can solve in a sustainable way using the simulation you have chosen. Identify the criteria and constraints for a successful solution and rank them based on importance. Examples might include fuel cost, marketing considerations, emissions levels required by law, and tradeoffs measured as part of the simulation.

DESIGN SOLUTIONS

Brainstorm solutions that would help you fulfill the criteria and constraints of a successful solution. Your simulation should help you model the boundaries, inputs, and outputs of the system under study.

TEST

Use your model to simulate at least three solutions to your problem, and collect data on the consequences of the choices modeled in the system. Record your main findings here in the form of a decision matrix.

OPTIMIZE

Use your decision matrix to evaluate your criteria and constraints. Prioritize the criteria you outlined. Then adjust the inputs of your model and run your simulation again.

COMMUNICATE

Prepare a report for a specific client in which you synthesize and communicate the results of your research and tests. Explain your reasoning in the choices you made, and communicate clearly what you have concluded based on the results of your test using the model. Be prepared to defend your choices of tradeoffs, and use multiple forms of media in your presentation.

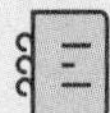

Evidence Notebook Explain how the type of fuel used in the paste part of a sparkler affects the amount of energy that is released when the sparkler is lit.

Careers in Science

Computational Chemist

Suppose scientists want to study the thermodynamics of a volcanic eruption. They might want to know how the sulfur, sulfur dioxide, and sulfur trioxide spewed into the atmosphere combine with water to form acid rain. A great many reactions involving sulfur and oxygen take place. These reactions cannot be duplicated in such a large scale in a lab, but they can be simulated in a computer model. The chemists must break down the overall reactions into subcomponents of the system to build their model.

FIGURE 18: Computational chemists use computers to develop models and interpret data.

Computational chemists use computer simulations to help solve chemical problems by building mathematical models. In 1995, three computational chemists won the Nobel Prize in chemistry for explaining how ozone forms and decomposes in the atmosphere. Their work involved little lab experimentation. Instead, they constructed models using known thermodynamic and chemical laws. The prize-winning chemists constructed their model by examining the relationships among chemical reactions involving chlorine and bromine atoms in the atmosphere. They used this model to study how these atoms interact with reactant concentrations, wind, air temperatures, and seasonal changes in sunlight.

Computational chemists may study atoms or molecules at a sub-microscopic level. Or, they may model the properties of larger systems, such as large volumes of gases, solutions, or solids. They may try to find a starting point for a new laboratory synthesis, such as to help develop new drugs. Computational chemists can also improve the productivity and efficiency of industrial processes using computer models to predict how reacting molecules combine under different conditions. Many chemical problems cannot be solved analytically or experimentally, so mathematical models are often necessary.

For example, much about ozone depletion in the atmosphere could not be studied experimentally. Computational chemists may use supercomputers and computing clusters that require massive amounts of data. Statistical analysis is often involved.

Chemistry in Your Community Research a computational chemist whose contributions to the field were influenced by his or her community. How did his or her diverse background influence the decision to become a computational chemist? Imagine that you are such a chemist, and you have been asked to give a presentation using digital media for career night at your school. Make a presentation for your class that explains the following:

- the daily tasks of a computation chemist
- the research a computational chemist performs
- the educational background required for the position

EXPLAINING ENDOTHERMIC AND EXOTHERMIC PROCESSES | PHOTOSYNTHESIS AND RESPIRATION | ALTERNATIVES IN FUEL SOURCES | Go online to choose one of these other paths.

Lesson Self-Check

CAN YOU EXPLAIN THE PHENOMENON?

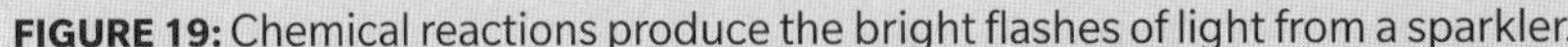

FIGURE 19: Chemical reactions produce the bright flashes of light from a sparkler.

Lighting a sparkler provides a small input of energy that starts a chemical reaction. The chemical system then emits intense flashes of light and burns at a temperature of about 650 °C, although it may burn at temperatures as high as 1000 °C. According to the second law of thermodynamics, energy moves from a warmer area to a cooler area. The release of light and heat energy from the sparkler system therefore shows that the sparkler is warmer than its surroundings. An energy diagram used to describe this reaction would show the chemical components of the sparkler having a high energy level, and the various gases that are products of the combustion reaction at a much lower energy.

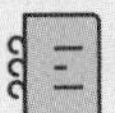

Evidence Notebook Refer to your notes in your Evidence Notebook to make a claim about how energy is transferred in the form of heat in processes such as chemical reactions. Your explanation should include a discussion of the following points:

Claim What do you think is the source of the energy in a chemical reaction, such as the reaction that occurs when you light a sparkler?

Evidence Give specific evidence to support your claim.

Reasoning Describe, in detail, the connections between the evidence you cited and the claim you are making.

Name Date

CHECKPOINTS

Check Your Understanding

1. You have two flasks of water. You place a thermometer in the first flask and leave it until the temperature no longer changes. The temperature reads 25 °C. When you move the thermometer to the second flask and again leave it, it also reads 25 °C. Select all correct answers for this scenario.

- ☐ **a.** The thermometer begins at thermal equilibrium with the first flask of water.
- ☐ **b.** The thermometer ends up at thermal equilibrium with the second flask of water.
- ☐ **c.** The two flasks of water are in thermal equilibrium with each other.
- ☐ **d.** The thermometer can be in thermal equilibrium only with the first flask.

2. Select the correct terms to complete the statement about energy transfer.

When a hot piece of metal is placed in cool water, thermal energy is transferred from the metal to the water | water to the metal. The average kinetic energy of the particles in the metal increases | decreases | stays the same, while the average kinetic energy of the water molecules increases | decreases | stays the same. This results in an increase | a decrease | no change in the temperature of the metal.

3. Determine whether each description is characteristic of an endothermic reaction or an exothermic reaction.

Reaction Description	Reaction Type
absorbs heat	endothermic | exothermic
releases heat	endothermic | exothermic
warms the surroundings	endothermic | exothermic
cools the surroundings	endothermic | exothermic
product energy > reactant energy	endothermic | exothermic
product energy < reactant energy	endothermic | exothermic

4. In which reactions are the products more stable than the reactants? Select all correct answers.

- ☐ **a.** a reaction in which energy is absorbed
- ☐ **b.** a reaction in which energy is released
- ☐ **c.** a reaction in which energy is represented as a product
- ☐ **d.** a reaction in which the products have less bond energy than the reactants.

5. A scientist mixes two substances in a beaker and then notices that the outside of the beaker feels colder. Which of the following can the scientist infer about this reaction? Select all correct answers.

- ☐ **a.** The reaction absorbs thermal energy.
- ☐ **b.** The reaction releases thermal energy.
- ☐ **c.** The products are more stable than the reactants.
- ☐ **d.** Energy can be represented as a product of the reaction.
- ☐ **e.** Energy can be represented as a reactant of the reaction.
- ☐ **f.** The products have more potential energy than the reactants.

6. Select the correct terms to complete the statement about bond energy.

In an exothermic | endothermic reaction, the bond energy of the reactants is greater than that of the products of the reaction. Therefore, energy must be absorbed from | released into the surroundings. This decreases the potential | kinetic energy of the surroundings, which increases | decreases the temperature.

7. Which of these are among the tradeoffs that should be considered when attempting to increase fuel efficiency? Select all correct answers.

- ☐ **a.** environmental impacts
- ☐ **b.** economic impacts
- ☐ **c.** local regulations
- ☐ **d.** the chemical formula of the fuel

CHECKPOINTS (continued)

8. Sketch a diagram of a lit sparkler and illustrate how energy flows from one location to another and how energy changes form in this system.

9. Describe some of the tradeoffs in efficiency and emissions that must be considered when choosing fuels for automobiles.

MAKE YOUR OWN STUDY GUIDE

In your Evidence Notebook, design a study guide that supports the main ideas from this lesson:

Thermal energy moves from warmer areas to cooler areas.

A reaction releases thermal energy in an exothermic reaction and absorbs thermal energy in an endothermic reaction.

The energy absorbed or released during a reaction is the difference in bond energy between the reactants and the products.

Hydrocarbons are used as fuels because they release energy during combustion reactions.

Remember to include the following information in your study guide:

- Use examples that model main ideas.
- Record explanations for the phenomena you investigated.
- Use evidence to support your explanations. Your support can include drawings, data, graphs, laboratory conclusions, and other evidence recorded throughout the lesson.

Consider how changes in energy and matter during an exothermic or endothermic reaction affect the stability of the products of the reaction.

Earth Science Connection

Cycling Matter The law of conservation of mass implies that atoms on Earth are continually recycled. Carbon, nitrogen, and other elements and compounds cycle through Earth's biosphere, geosphere, atmosphere, and hydrosphere. Because chemical changes are involved in the cycling of matter, an element can be transferred between different compounds throughout a cycle.

Develop a model describing the cycling of one type of matter, such as carbon, through Earth's systems. Use your model to describe the chemical reactions that are involved in the cycle and explain whether the total amount of matter in the system is conserved. Research the ways large-scale chemical manufacturing and consumer habits can negatively impact the natural recycling systems and efforts to restore this balance.

FIGURE 1: Changes in the carbon cycle occur from the interaction of chemical, geological, and biological processes.

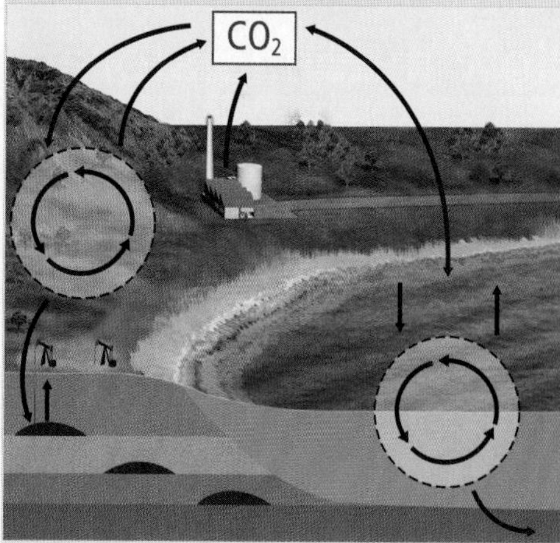

Art Connection

Restoration Physical and chemical changes can degrade the original quality of artwork. A person trained in preserving and restoring paintings is called a conservator. Conservators evaluate paints and the surfaces on which they are applied. They must understand how paints age and how exposure to various chemicals and light affect them. Conservators must ensure that materials used in preserving and restoring paintings do not cause unintended reactions with the original artwork.

Use multiple authoritative sources to make a brochure explaining how conservators use chemistry to restore and preserve paintings. Evaluate the strengths and limitations of each source and cite each one.

FIGURE 2: A conservator examines a painting for restoration.

Technology Connection

Smelting Most metals exist in nature as ores, which are rocks containing compounds of the metal mixed with other elements, such as oxygen. The smelting process extracts the metal from the ore. During smelting, ores are heated to provide energy for the chemical reactions that separate the metal from oxygen. The amount of energy needed to separate metal atoms varies with the metal and the type of ore. The most important advances in ancient metallurgy involved ways to make hotter fires to refine metals.

Write a short report about the history of smelting in ancient cultures as well as modern smelting processes. When did different metals come into production? How has the necessary temperature for smelting been achieved, both historically and in modern industry?

FIGURE 3: The process of making pure metals, such as iron, from ores is an important industrial process.

A BOOK EXPLAINING COMPLEX IDEAS USING ONLY THE 1,000 MOST COMMON WORDS

RANDALL MUNROE
XKCD.COM

ENERGY

How much is stored in things and how much it takes to do stuff

It is a fundamental law of science that the total amount of energy remains the same before and after a change. Energy cannot be destroyed or created. Take a look at some ways of measuring all that energy.

THE STORY OF HOW ENERGY HELPS US KEEP TRACK OF THINGS

ENERGY ISN'T A REAL THING. THAT IS, IT'S NOT A THING YOU CAN HOLD OR TOUCH. IT'S MORE LIKE A WAY OF KEEPING TRACK OF THINGS. IT'S KIND OF LIKE MONEY.

YOU CAN CHANGE YOUR MONEY FROM PAPER TO PIECES OF METAL TO NUMBERS ON A COMPUTER, BUT IT DOESN'T CHANGE HOW MUCH YOU HAVE.

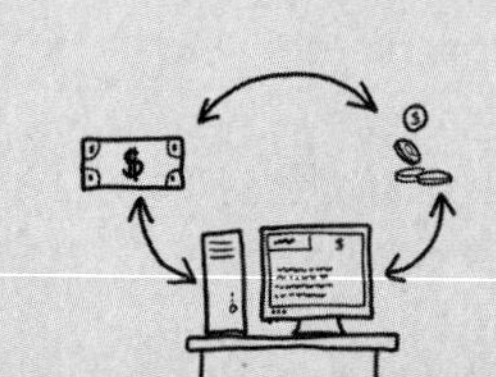

EVEN THOUGH YOU DON'T HOLD ON TO ANY OF THE SAME STUFF, HOW MUCH YOU HAVE STAYS THE SAME.

ENERGY IS LIKE THAT. IT'S NOTHING BUT A NUMBER THAT HELPS US KEEP TRACK OF THINGS. IT ALWAYS STAYS THE SAME — IT JUST MOVES FROM ONE THING TO ANOTHER. AND KNOWING HOW MUCH ENERGY SOMETHING HAS TELLS US ABOUT HOW MUCH IT CAN DO.

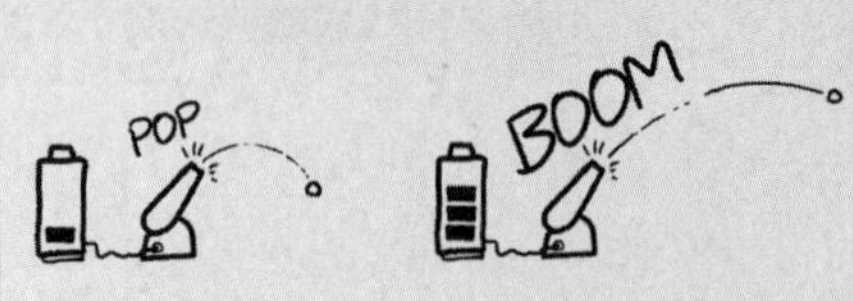

KEEPING TRACK OF ENERGY HELPS US KNOW HOW FAR WE CAN DRIVE A CAR, HOW HIGH WE CAN LIFT SOMETHING, AND HOW LONG YOUR PHONE WILL LAST BEFORE IT TURNS OFF.

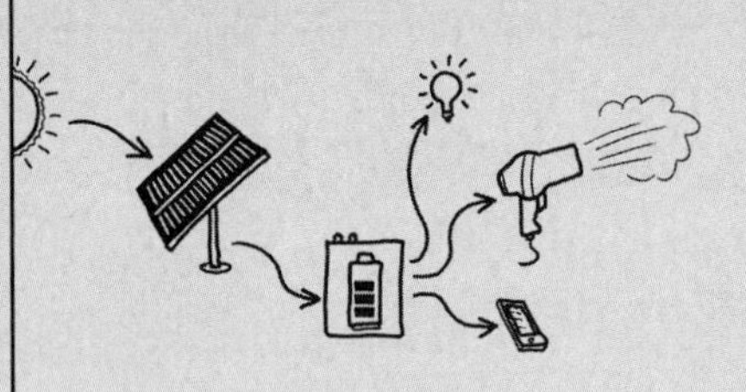

KEEPING TRACK OF ENERGY CAN ALSO HELP US LEARN NEW THINGS. IF WE COUNT HOW MUCH ENERGY IS GOING INTO SOMETHING, AND HOW MUCH IS COMING OUT, SOMETIMES THOSE NUMBERS DON'T MATCH UP. THAT TELLS US THAT WE'RE MISSING SOMETHING, AND WE SHOULD LOOK AT EVERYTHING MORE CAREFULLY. THERE MIGHT BE SOMETHING BIG TO DISCOVER.

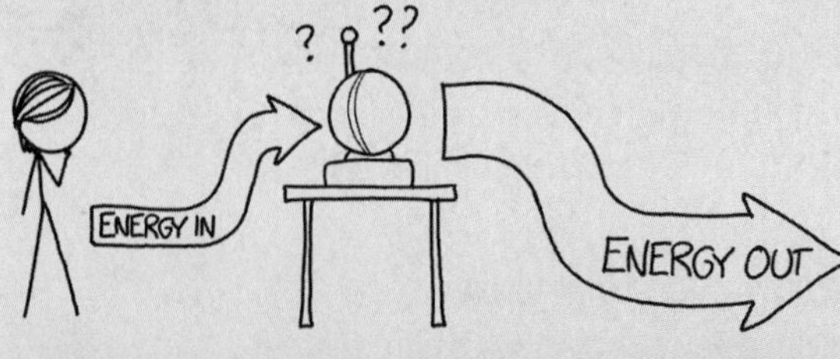

HOW MUCH ENERGY THINGS TAKE

These pictures show how much energy is stored in things and how much energy it takes to do things.

1 PIECE OF ENERGY

You can use different kinds of numbers to talk about how much energy is stored in something, just like how you can use different kinds of numbers to say how tall you are. Lots of countries got together and agreed to use one size of number for energy to make things less confusing. Each of these squares is "1" using that size.

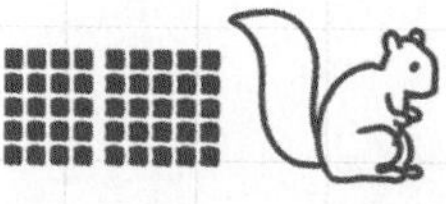

CLIMBING A TREE

This is how much energy a small animal uses to climb a tree.

WHITE FOOD

This is how much energy is in one tiny piece of white food.

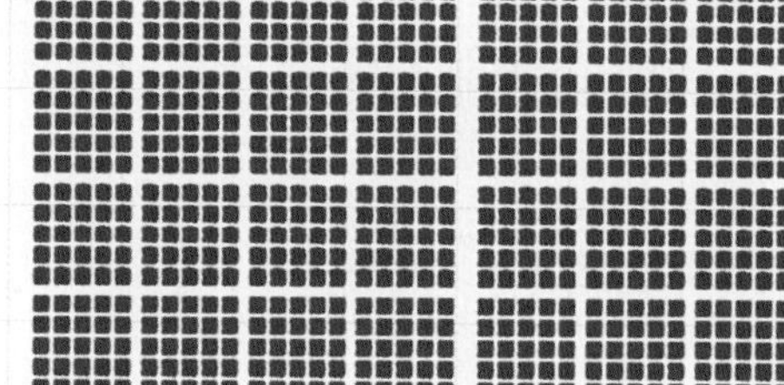

WATCH

This is how much energy is held in those silver circles that make small things like old watches run.

BIGGER BOXES

To show things with more stored energy, let's add a new kind of box that's as big as ten hundred of the old ones.

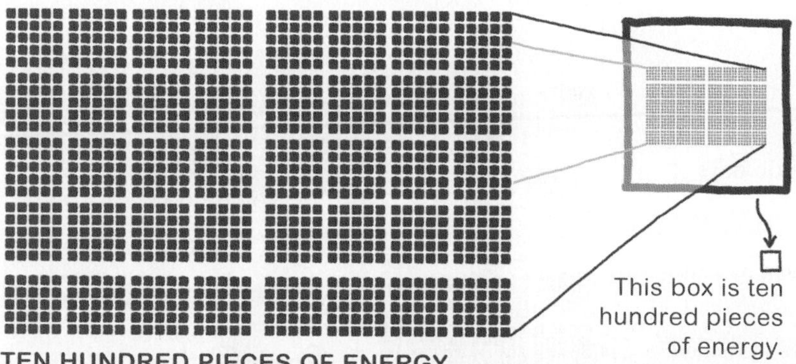

This box is ten hundred pieces of energy.

TEN HUNDRED PIECES OF ENERGY

GOING UP A FEW STAIRS

One of these bigger boxes is as much energy as it takes for a person to climb a short set of stairs.

GOING UP A FLOOR

Climbing enough stairs to go up one floor in a building takes about two of these boxes.

(That's only six of those pieces of white food!)

1 FOOD-ENERGY

On the sides of food boxes in the US, they tell you how much energy is in the food. "1" using their numbers is the same as three of these boxes.

"AA" POWER BOX

A PHONE

The energy stored in a small phone or hand computer

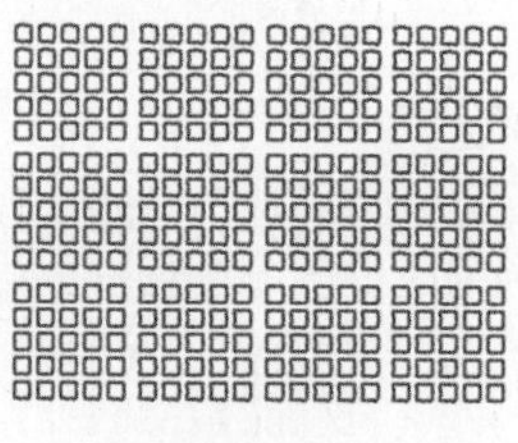

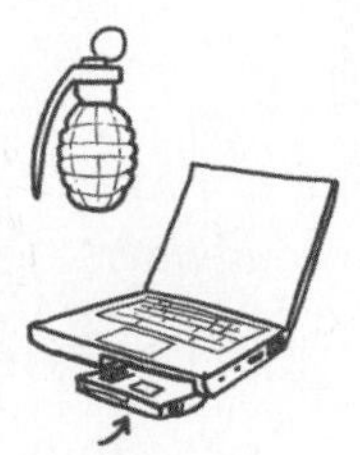

THE ENERGY STORED IN A SMALL COMPUTER

These hold about as much energy as those things people throw at each other during wars.

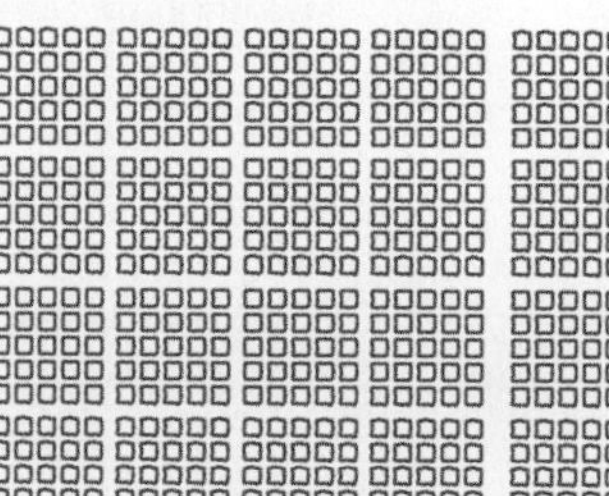

THE ENERGY STORED IN THESE THINGS YOU STAND ON AND RIDE AROUND

These things have a name that makes it sound like they can fly, but they can't.

They're fun to ride around on, but they need so much energy that sometimes, if their power boxes aren't very well made, they catch fire.

MORE ENERGY

EVEN BIGGER BOXES

To show things that carry more energy, each of the boxes in this part of the page hold as much energy as ten hundred of the boxes on the page before this one.

Here's how you write this much energy: 10^6J.

HAIR DRYER (10 MINUTES)
The energy used by a hair dryer in ten minutes

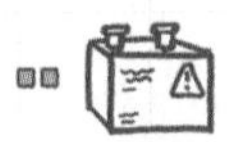

CAR STARTER
The energy in the power box that starts a car

OLD LIGHT (1 DAY)
The energy used by an old light in one day

NEW LIGHT (1 DAY)
The energy used by a new light in one day

FOOD (NORMAL PERSON)
The energy in the food a normal person eats in one day

FOOD (THE ROCK)
The energy in the food The Rock eats in a day. ("The Rock" is the name of a very strong man who acts in movies.)

$1 OF POWER
The energy you would get from your wall if you paid $1 to the power company

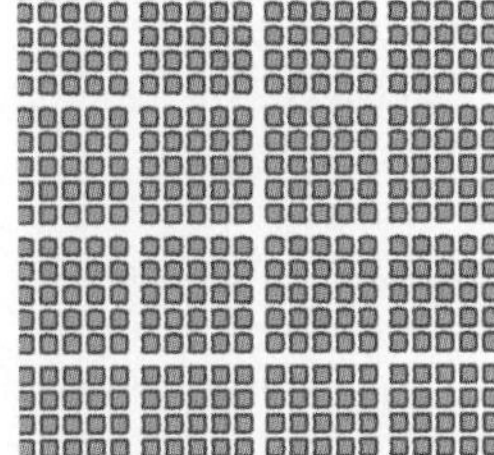

CAR THAT USES WALL POWER
This is how much energy is stored in the power box used by the kind of new car that doesn't burn anything.

STORM FLASH HITTING SAND
The energy that goes into the ground and turns sand to rock and air when the ground is hit by a flash of light from a big storm

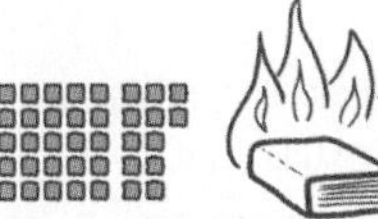

ONE LARGE BOOK
If you burned a big book for its heat, this is how much energy you'd get.

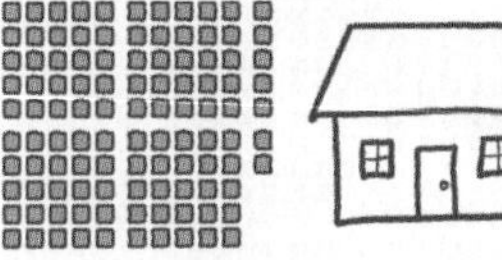

A HOUSE FOR A DAY
The energy used by a normal house in the US in one day

A CAR FOR A DAY
The energy used by a normal car in the US in one day

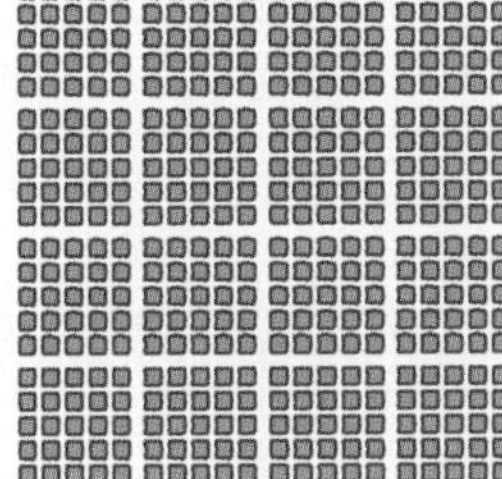
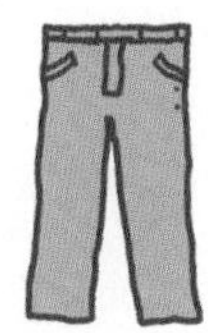

THE ENERGY USED TO MAKE A PAIR OF BLUE PANTS
This is how much energy is used by one pair of blue pants during its life. This counts the sun's light needed to grow the stuff the pants are made of and the energy to run the machines that keep the pants clean.

WAY MORE ENERGY

Go online for more about *Thing Explainer*.

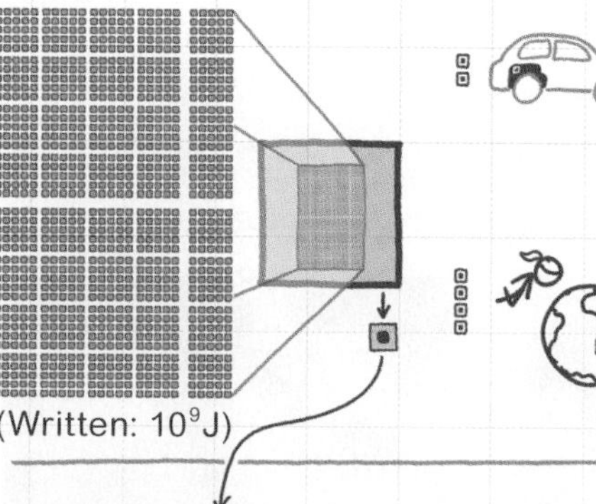

(Written: 10^9J)

ENERGY IN A CAR
The energy in a normal car when you fill it up before a long drive

GOING TO SPACE
This is how much energy it takes to lift a person to space (if you don't throw away energy on extra stuff along the way like a rocket does).

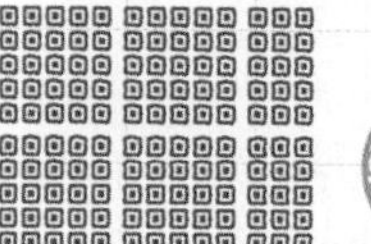

THE ENERGY IT WOULD TAKE TO DRIVE A CAR AROUND THE WORLD
(if there were a road running around the middle of the Earth)

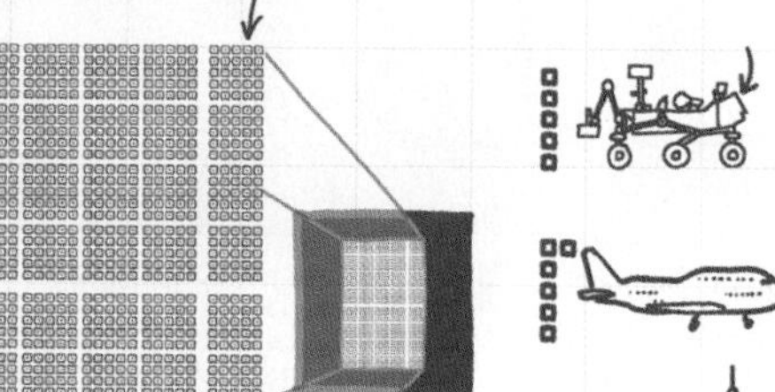

(Written: 10^{12}J)

BOX OF HEAVY METAL
The energy in a box of heavy metal powering a space car.

SKY BOAT
The energy in a sky boat that carries people across the sea

MOON BOAT
The energy in one of the space boats we flew in to visit the moon

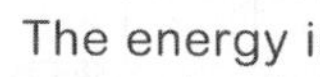

A BIG OCEAN-CROSSING BOAT
The energy a big boat uses when carrying stuff across our biggest body of water

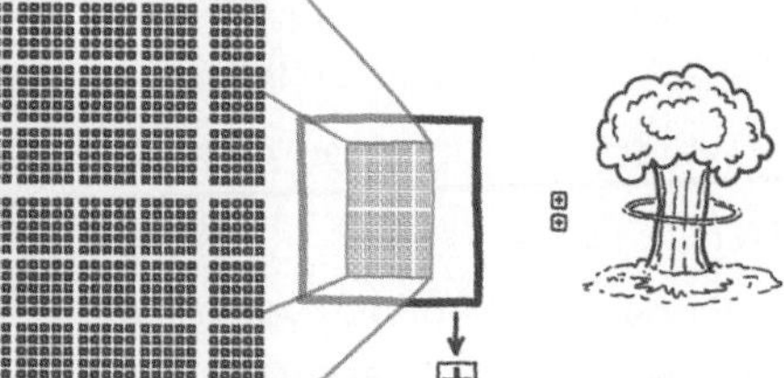

(Written: 10^{15}J)

CITY-BURNING MACHINE
The energy that would come out if we set off one of our war machines—the kind that flies around the world, blows up, and burns a city

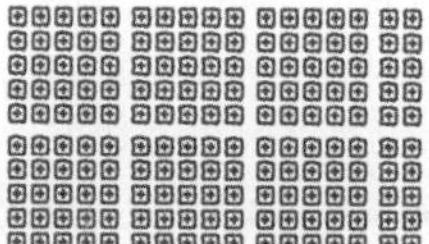

ONE SECOND OF SUN
The energy from all the sun's light that hits the Earth in one second

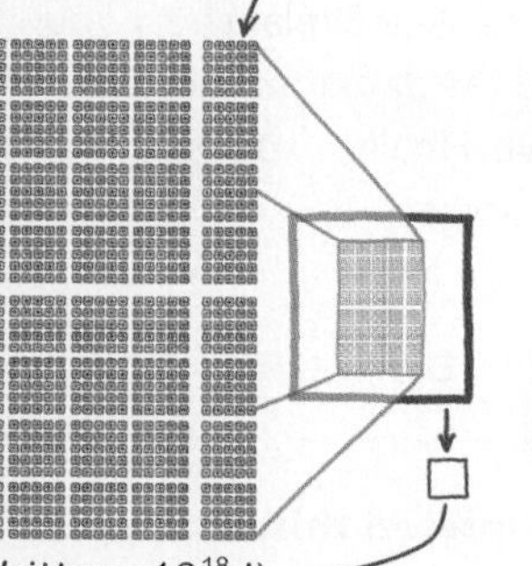

(Written: 10^{18}J)

A BIG CIRCLE STORM
The energy from all the winds, from start to end, in the kind of big circle storm that forms over warm seas

US WALL POWER
The energy all the people in the US use in a year (only counting the kind of power carried by power lines)

US ENERGY USE (ALL KINDS)
The energy used by the US in a year, adding together all the stuff we get power from

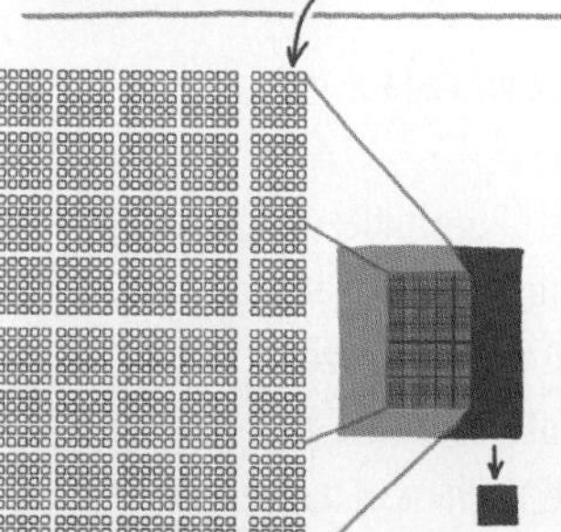
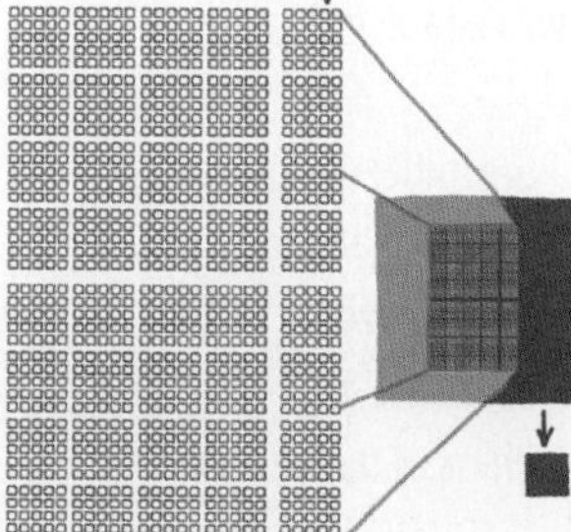

(Written: 10^{21}J)

ONE DAY OF SUN
The energy in the sun's light that hits Earth every day

ENERGY IN THE GROUND
The energy we could get if we dug up all the stuff in the ground we can burn for power

SPACE ROCK OF DEATH
Long ago, one of these hit Earth and killed most of the animals in the family birds are from. This is how much energy it let out when it hit.

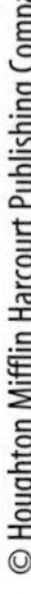

Optimizing Heat Packs

There are many different types of heat packs available, but what are the differences between them? Research heat packs and the different ways they release energy in the form of heat. Your engineering challenge is to build a heat pack and optimize it by increasing the temperature or making it last longer.

1. DEFINE THE PROBLEM

Decide which engineering challenge to investigate. What criteria and constraints need to be considered in your final design? Are there any tradeoffs to consider when developing a solution to this problem?

2. CONDUCT RESEARCH

Investigate three to four different kinds of heat packs that use a chemical reaction to release energy in the form of heat, and develop a decision matrix to help you weigh the pros and cons of each. Determine the type of chemical reaction that occurs in each heat pack and the amount of energy released by each reaction. Consider what situations or environments each kind of heat pack is designed to work within. How did these considerations influence each design?

3. CARRY OUT AN INVESTIGATION

With a small group, build a homemade heat pack.

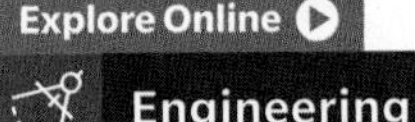

Engineering Lab

Design a Heat Pack Many heat packs rely on simple chemical reactions to produce heat. Develop a homemade heat pack, then optimize your design.

4. PLAN AN INVESTIGATION

With your team, optimize your heat pack to either produce more heat or to last longer. Consider which materials in the heat pack are most important. Then, write a plan about how you will adjust your heat pack to build a successful solution. Consider what data you will collect and how you will measure success.

FIGURE 4: Heat packs can use physical or chemical changes to release energy in the form of heat.

a A reversible physical change releases energy when the disc in this heat pack is pressed.

b An irreversible chemical reaction releases energy when this heat pack is exposed to air.

5. EVALUATE DATA

Evaluate the data you collected for your heat pack. Was your design successful? How can you tell?

6. COMMUNICATE

Make a research poster that outlines your team's findings on heat packs and the design challenge you investigated. Your poster should display data on your initial heat pack, including the chemical reaction and the amount of energy it releases. Explain how you optimized the design and the data that shows whether your solution was effective. Finally, explain how you evaluated your design process.

Once you have completed this task, you should have the following:

- a problem statement that was addressed in the final presentation
- data on the performance of the initial design
- a presentation explaining how the heat pack works and the process used to optimize it
- data on the performance of the final design
- an evaluation of the effectiveness of the design solution process

Name

Date

SYNTHESIZE THE UNIT

In your Evidence Notebook, make a concept map, other graphic organizer, or outline using the Study Guides you made for each lesson in this unit. Be sure to use evidence to support your claims.

When synthesizing individual information, remember to follow these general steps:

- Find the central idea of each piece of information.
- Think about the relationships among the central ideas.
- Combine the ideas to come up with a new understanding.

DRIVING QUESTIONS

Look back to the Driving Questions from the opening section of this unit. In your Evidence Notebook, review and revise your previous answers to those questions. Use the evidence you gathered and other observations you made throughout the unit to support your claims.

PRACTICE AND REVIEW

1. Consider the following unbalanced chemical equation:

$$Al + C \rightarrow Al_4C_3$$

What mass of aluminum is required to produce 125 g Al_4C_3?

- **a.** 12.6 g
- **b.** 23.4 g
- **c.** 46.9 g
- **d.** 93.7 g

2. Complete the statement.

When predicting the outcome of a chemical reaction, the periodic table is useful because it shows elements with similar chemical properties in the same column | row. The number of protons | valence electrons that elements have indicates how many bonds they can form. The number of moles of particles can | cannot change during a chemical reaction.

3. Using the unbalanced equation below, predict what happens if 1.5 moles of Na react with excess Cl_2.

$$Na + Cl_2 \rightarrow NaCl$$

If 1.5 moles of Na reacts with excess Cl_2, then ________ moles of NaCl are produced, which equals ________ grams of NaCl.

4. Which statements describe the reactants and products of an endothermic reaction? Select all correct answers.

- **a.** The products are more stable.
- **b.** The reactants are more stable.
- **c.** The products have greater bond energy.
- **d.** The reactants have greater bond energy.
- **e.** The reactants must have energy input to start reacting.

5. Complete the statement.

The first law of thermodynamics describes conservation of energy in a system. Energy is transferred within | removed from a system as faster | slower particles collide with faster | slower particles within that system.

6. Which statement describes the atoms and mass in a chemical reaction?

- **a.** The mass and the number of each type of atom can change.
- **b.** The mass and the number of each type of atom cannot change.
- **c.** The mass can change, but the number of each type of atom cannot.
- **d.** The mass cannot change, but the number of each type of atom can.

7. Use the concept of a mole to explain why a chemical reaction may not consume all of the reactants. Why is this idea so important in chemical manufacturing?

8. Explain why chemical equations must be balanced and how this relates to the law of conservation of mass.

9. Fuels used in automobiles release different amounts of energy when burned. Explain some tradeoffs that must be considered when deciding whether to use fuels that release greater amounts of energy.

UNIT PROJECT

Return to your unit project. Prepare your research and materials into a presentation to share with the class. In your final presentation, evaluate the strength of your hypothesis, data, analysis, and conclusions.

Remember these tips while evaluating:

- How well did your model convey the energy released in a combustion reaction?
- In the United States, what percentage of greenhouse emissions are from heating buildings?
- How does your model demonstrate how heat is transferred through a building?
- Explain how tradeoffs between different fuel types and the energy they release add to gas emissions.
- What are some "green energy" alternatives to the combustion of fossil fuels for heating buildings?

UNIT 5

Reaction Rates and Equilibrium

YOU SOLVE IT

How Can You Increase Ammonia Production?

How Can You Design a Battery?

To begin exploring this unit's concepts, go online to investigate ways to solve a real-world problem.

The colors of this oscillating reaction change as the amounts of products and reactants vary back and forth over time.

FIGURE 1: The longfin squid can use bioluminescence from chemical reactions in its body to distract prey.

Even on the brightest day, sunlight is absorbed before it reaches the bottom of the deep ocean. When scientists began exploring the deepest parts of the ocean, however, they were surprised to find eerie lights far below the surface. The environment is not all dark after all. Many deep ocean organisms produce their own light. This light, called bioluminescence, comes from chemical reactions that release energy as light. The organisms can turn the light on or off and even change its color. The intensity of the light emitted by the organisms depends on the rate of the chemical reaction that produces the bioluminescence. Many organisms in the ocean and on land use bioluminescent signals to communicate, to hunt for prey, to attract mates, and to scare off predators.

PREDICT How do you think a bioluminescent organism is able to change the rate of a chemical reaction to control the intensity of the light it emits?

DRIVING QUESTIONS

As you move through the unit, gather evidence to help you answer the following questions. In your Evidence Notebook, record what you already know about these topics and any questions you have about them.

1. How can energy be used to control chemical reactions?
2. What cause and effect mechanisms explain how a reaction proceeds?
3. What predictable patterns are observed when chemical equilibrium is disturbed?
4. How can the cycles of matter and the flows of energy in chemical equilibrium processes be used to address ecological and economic concerns?

UNIT PROJECT

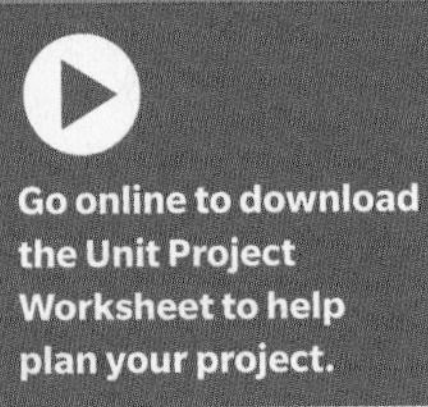
Go online to download the Unit Project Worksheet to help plan your project.

Investigating the Solvay Process

The Solvay process produces sodium carbonate, which is used in a variety of applications, including to soften water, as a food additive, and to make glass. Research the Solvay process and how it is used in manufacturing. Then, prepare a presentation that explains how controlling and optimizing equilibrium reactions are essential parts of this process.

Language Development

Use the lessons in this unit to complete the chart and expand your understanding of the science concepts.

TERM: collision theory

Definition	Example

Similar Term	Phrase

TERM: activation energy, E_a

Definition	Example

Similar Term	Phrase

TERM: reaction rate

Definition	Example

Similar Term	Phrase

TERM: chemical equilibrium

Definition	Example

Similar Term	Phrase

TERM: Le Châtelier's principle

Definition	Example

Similar Term	Phrase

TERM: acid

Definition	Example

Similar Term	Phrase

TERM: base

Definition	Example

Similar Term	Phrase

TERM: pH

Definition	Example

Similar Term	Phrase

5.1

Investigating Reaction Rates

Light sticks glow brighter in warm water than they do in cold water.

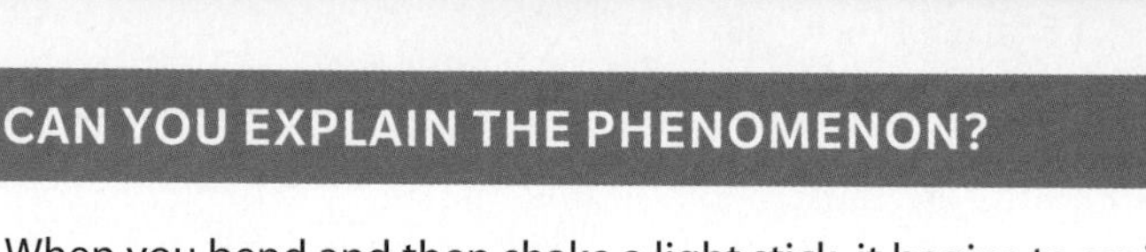

CAN YOU EXPLAIN THE PHENOMENON?

When you bend and then shake a light stick, it begins to emit light. The light is evidence that a chemical reaction is occurring inside the tube. This reaction is similar to the reaction that occurs in fireflies and other bioluminescent organisms. Light sticks are common decorations often used in festive settings. They can also serve as emergency light sources or distress signals in both military and civilian settings. Notice the difference in the light intensity emitted by the light sticks in the photograph. The light stick in the beaker of warm water on the left shines more brightly than the light stick in the beaker of ice water on the right does.

PREDICT Why do you think the light stick in the warm water glows more brightly than the light stick in the cold water does?

____

____

____

____

____

____

Evidence Notebook As you explore the lesson, gather evidence to explain at the particle level why changing the temperature of a light stick affects the intensity of the light it emits.

Hands-On Lab

Observing Reaction Rates

Some reactions occur very rapidly, and others occur much more slowly. When oxygen and hydrogen are mixed in a rocket engine, they explode instantaneously. But when you leave your bike outside in the rain, it rusts very slowly. The rates of the two reactions are quite different. A rate is a measure of change over time. There are several factors that can affect the rate of a reaction. Temperature, the surface area of the reactants, concentration, and the nature of the reacting substances can all have an effect.

The usefulness of a chemical reaction often depends on controlling the reaction so that it is not too fast or too slow for a particular application. Chemists often speed up or slow down reactions to optimize each reaction for a variety of safety, economic, and environmental reasons.

RESEARCH QUESTION How can scientists use knowledge of patterns in reaction rates to control the reactions that make useful products?

MAKE A CLAIM

Review the experiments you will be conducting. How do you think the factor being tested in each part will affect the reaction rate?

MATERIALS

- indirectly vented chemical splash goggles, nonlatex apron, nitrile gloves
- beaker, 250 mL (3)
- Bunsen burner
- copper foil strip
- effervescent antacid tablet (3)
- graduated cylinder, 10 mL
- HCl solution, 0.1 M
- hot plate
- ice
- magnesium ribbon
- matches
- sandpaper
- steel wool
- test tube, 16 × 150 mm (6)
- tongs
- vinegar
- water
- zinc strip

SAFETY INFORMATION

indirectly vented chemical splash goggles

- Wear indirectly vented chemical splash goggles, a nonlatex apron, and nitrile gloves during the setup, hands-on, and takedown segments of the activity.
- Use caution when working with Bunsen burners because this heat source can seriously burn skin and clothing. Secure loose clothing, wear closed-toe shoes, and tie back hair.
- Use caution when working with hot plates, which can cause skin burns or electric shock.
- Use caution when working with glassware, which can shatter and cut skin.
- Never pour chemicals, either used or unused, back into their original containers. Dispose of chemicals according to your teacher's instructions.

PLAN THE INVESTIGATION

In your Evidence Notebook, develop procedures for the following four experiments. Identify the independent and dependent variables for each experiment. In addition, consider which variables should be held constant to ensure reliable results. Have your teacher approve your procedures and safety plans before proceeding.

Part 1 Test how magnesium, zinc, and copper react when each is placed in 0.1 M HCl. In these reactions, the metal combines with acid to produce hydrogen gas and an aqueous solution of the metal chloride. Compare the reaction rates for these reactions by observing hydrogen gas production. This indicates the rate of the reaction.

Part 2 Test how fast a small, tightly balled sample of steel wool burns in a flame compared to a loosely balled sample of steel wool. The amount and size of the flame indicate the rate of the reaction.

Part 3 Test how a strip of magnesium reacts in different concentrations of vinegar. Vinegar contains acetic acid. You can make different concentrations of vinegar by adding water to the vinegar solution. Compare the reaction rates for these reactions by observing hydrogen gas production.

Part 4 Test how water temperature affects the rate at which an effervescent antacid tablet reacts with water. The time it takes for the reaction to go to completion (when the tablet completely disappears) indicates the rate of the reaction.

COLLECT DATA

Develop a plan for collecting and organizing data. The data you record should provide evidence to support claims about how different factors affect reaction rate. Consider limitations such as time and the availability of materials when developing your plan. Draw data tables in your Evidence Notebook before carrying out your procedures.

ANALYZE

1. What factor that affected the reaction rate did you test in each of the four experiments?

2. In this investigation, there were limitations on the precision of the data you could obtain. How could the procedures you used be revised to obtain more precise data?

DRAW CONCLUSIONS

Write a conclusion that addresses each of these points.

Claim For each experiment, explain how the factor you tested affected the reaction rate.

Evidence Give specific examples from your data to support your claim.

Reasoning Explain how the evidence you gave supports your claim. Describe, in detail, the connections between the evidence you cited and the argument you are making.

EXTEND

1. Choose one factor you tested. Make a drawing to show how you think changing that factor affected the reaction rate at the scale of atoms, ions, or molecules.

2. What are the limitations of a two-dimensional model? What benefits would a computer simulation have when modeling the effect of a certain factor on reaction rate?

Evidence Notebook In the light stick example, what factor was changed to cause the light sticks to glow with different intensities?

Collision Theory

When you burn charcoal in a grill, it burns slowly, often without a noticeable flame, as shown in the charcoal sample in Figure 1a. As it burns, the charcoal reacts with oxygen in the air in the cylinder. Air also contains other gases, such as nitrogen, argon, and carbon dioxide. The cylinder in Figure 1b shows charcoal burning in pure oxygen. In pure oxygen, the reaction is much faster and burns with a bright glow.

FIGURE 1: Charcoal burns differently in air than it does in pure oxygen.

a Charcoal in air

b Charcoal in pure oxygen

PREDICT Why do you think charcoal burns more slowly in air than it does in pure oxygen? How might this be related to interactions between the particles that make up the charcoal samples and those that make up the gas particles around them?

If cylinders containing pure oxygen are exposed to a flame or other heat source, they can explode and cause serious bodily harm. As a result, the use, storage, and transportation of pure oxygen must be closely monitored. So, why does air, which is about 21% oxygen, not react in the same way? The answer has to do with collisions between particles.

Chemical Reactions and Collisions

Chemical reactions involve the breaking of bonds in the reactants, which absorbs energy, and the forming of new bonds in the products, which releases energy. How does this happen at the level of individual particles? During a chemical reaction, reactant particles are constantly colliding. In some of these collisions, products are formed, and in some collisions, the reactant particles remain unchanged. When a collision has sufficient energy and proper orientation, a reaction is likely to occur between the colliding particles. These requirements are explained in collision theory.

Collision theory states that in order for a chemical reaction to occur, particles must collide with sufficient energy and in the correct orientation for bonds in the reactants to be broken and new bonds to form in the products. If a collision does not have enough energy, or if the colliding particles are not correctly oriented to cause a change, a collision will not result in a chemical reaction.

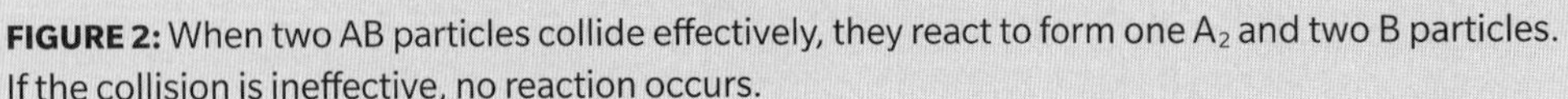

FIGURE 2: When two AB particles collide effectively, they react to form one A_2 and two B particles. If the collision is ineffective, no reaction occurs.

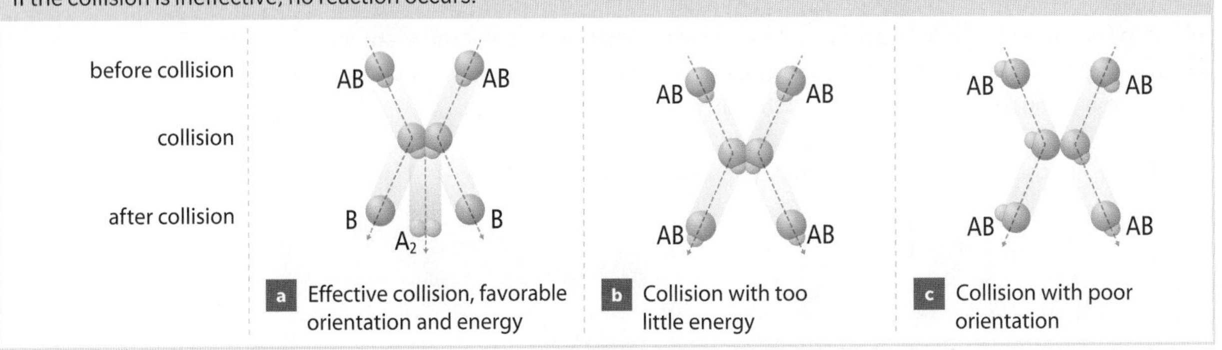

a Effective collision, favorable orientation and energy

b Collision with too little energy

c Collision with poor orientation

ANALYZE Review the diagrams in Figure 2. Which of these collisions will result in a new product, and which will not? Explain your thinking.

____

____

____

____

Reaction Rate Factors

FIGURE 3: Reaction rate changes with concentration

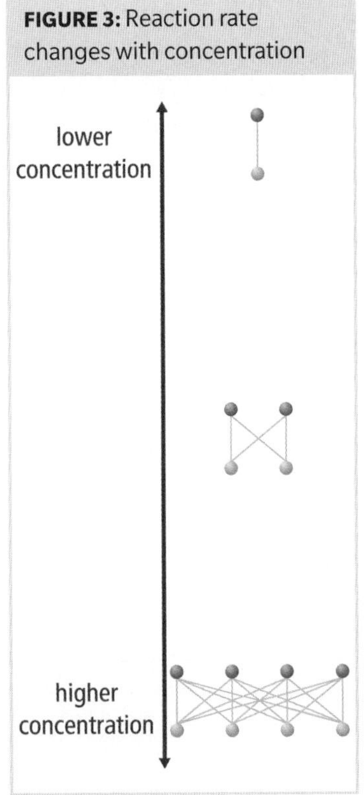

The reaction rate of a chemical reaction is measured as the change in concentration of reactants per unit of time as the reaction proceeds. As the number of effective collisions per unit of time increases, reaction rate also increases. Changing a variable such as temperature, surface area, or concentration affects the rate of effective collisions and therefore changes the rate of the reaction.

Concentration

Though there are exceptions, almost all reactions increase in rate when the concentrations of the reactants are increased. Figure 3 is a simple model showing that, as the concentrations of the reactants increase, the number of total collisions between particles, represented by gray lines, also increases.

EXPLAIN Select the correct terms to complete the statement about why charcoal burns more quickly in pure oxygen than it does in air.

The concentration of oxygen in a cylinder filled with air is higher | lower than that in a cylinder filled with pure oxygen. So, the rate of collisions between reactant particles is higher in the cylinder of pure oxygen | air. Higher concentration causes an increase in effective | ineffective | all collisions between reactants, but an increase in effective | ineffective | all collisions is what leads to an increase in the rate of reaction.

You can observe patterns in reaction rates when cleaning with vinegar. Because vinegar contains acetic acid, it can remove hard water stains caused by the buildup of minerals. The type of vinegar used for cleaning is often more concentrated than the type used in foods. The higher the concentration of acetic acid, the more particles there are to collide with stain-causing particles.

MODEL Draw a diagram illustrating why, in the hands-on lab, the most concentrated vinegar solution reacted most vigorously with magnesium metal. In your diagram, include components that describe the connections among concentration, total collisions, effective collisions, and reaction rate.

Temperature

Temperature is a measure of the average kinetic energy of the particles in a substance. As temperature increases, particles move faster and have more energy. In the hands-on lab, you tested the effect of temperature on reaction rate by placing effervescent tablets in warm and cold water. This test is also shown in Figure 4.

FIGURE 4: Effervescent antacid tablets react with hot water (left) and cold water (right).

INFER Use data from the hands-on lab to complete the statement.

In the reactions between the antacid tablet and water, the molecules in the warmer water have less | more kinetic energy than those in the cooler water have. This energy difference leads to a higher frequency of collisions between molecules. Also, a greater percentage of the collisions have the energy | orientation to be effective. So, the reaction rate is greater when the tablets are placed in the cooler | warmer water.

Think about how you could control the temperature of an oven to manipulate the rates of reactions that occur when baking bread. As the temperature inside the oven increases, the kinetic energy of the particles in the ingredients increases, and they collide more frequently. This leads to an increase in reaction rates. To decrease the rates of these reactions, you could set the oven to a lower temperature, thereby decreasing the kinetic energy of the reactant particles and the rate of collisions between particles.

Evidence Notebook In your Evidence Notebook, write two claims for how changes in temperature and concentration lead to changes in reaction rate. For each claim, provide evidence from the reactions you observed in this lesson and explain how chemical bonds, particle collisions, and kinetic energy are related to your observations. Last, explain how the concepts you described are related to the solutions you are evaluating as part of your unit project on the Solvay Process.

Surface Area

In chemical reactions involving two phases, such as a liquid and a solid reactant, collisions can only occur where the phases come together. In this type of reaction, known as a heterogeneous reaction, the reaction rate partly depends on surface area—the area of contact between the two phases. In Figure 5, equal masses of crushed marble and solid marble react with hydrochloric acid. The crushed marble has a greater surface area, so more particle collisions occur per unit of time. In the solid marble piece, only the particles on the outside surface are available to collide.

FIGURE 5: Crushed marble (left) reacts more vigorously in hydrochloric acid than a solid piece of marble (right) does.

EXPLAIN Explain why, in the hands-on lab, the loosely balled steel wool reacted at a higher rate than the tightly balled steel wool did. Use evidence from your data to support your claim, and relate your observations to interactions at the particle level.

____

____

____

____

Nature of Reactants

Different substances can vary greatly in their tendencies to react. As you observed in the lab, different metals react differently with the same acid. In this case, the reaction rate is determined by the metal's reactivity. Reactivity in this example is the ease with which the metal atoms give up their valence electrons to hydrogen ions in acid to form metal ions.

ANALYZE Based on the results you obtained in the hands-on lab, which type of metal most easily lost valence electrons?

○ **a.** magnesium ○ **b.** zinc ○ **c.** copper

 Patterns

Simulating Reaction Rate

Computer models can simulate the effects of different factors on particle collisions and reaction rates. Many simulations report inputs and outputs in the form of data tables and graphs that show proportions of reactants and products. They may also allow the user to examine the effectiveness of collisions between individual particles.

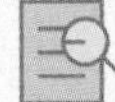

Language Arts Connection Find a simulation that will allow you to alter one of the factors that affects particle collisions and reaction rate. Using the patterns you have learned about, predict how changing a certain variable will affect the rate of a reaction. Then use the simulation to gather data related to your claim. Last, write an explanation that tells whether your prediction was correct and how you might revise your prediction based on the results you obtained.

Evidence Notebook What is happening at the particle level that causes the difference in the amount of light produced when light sticks are submerged in cold and in warm water?

Energy Flow in Chemical Reactions

For a chemical reaction to occur, particles must collide with enough energy to break the bonds in the reactants. Breaking bonds always requires energy, and forming bonds always releases it. Why, then, do some reactions release energy while others absorb it?

Collaborate Describe to a partner why you think only some reactions give off energy.

Investigating Reaction Energy

Many chemical reactions do not occur spontaneously. The magnesium in Figure 6, for example, is quite stable when exposed to air. Adding thermal energy from a lighted match, however, causes it to burn rapidly, releasing heat and bright light. For a chemical reaction to occur, the kinetic energy of the reactant particles must be great enough to break the bonds of reactants. In Figure 6, the heat from the match provides that energy. The minimum kinetic energy required for the collision of reactant particles to result in a reaction, or the "hill" in Figure 7, is called the activation energy, E_a. For a collision to be effective, two particles must collide with adequate kinetic energy to get "over the hill." Once started, the reaction proceeds spontaneously.

FIGURE 6: Once started, the reaction between magnesium and oxygen continues.

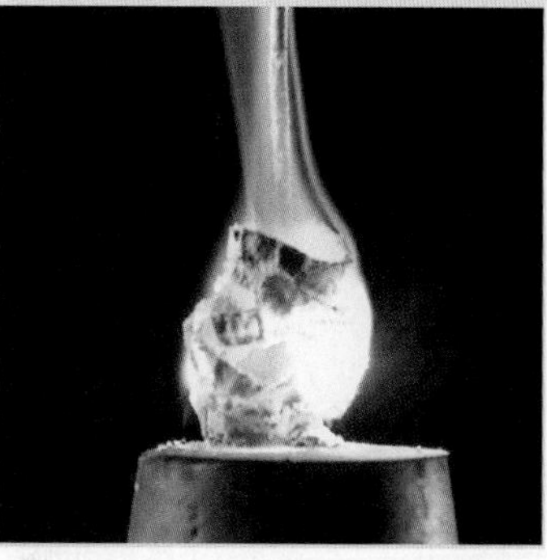

Exothermic Reactions

In an exothermic reaction, as shown in Figures 6 and 7, chemical potential energy in the reactants is converted to kinetic energy. This energy may be released in the form of heat, light, or sound. The potential energy of the products is lower than that of the reactants, so the energy change for the reaction, or ΔE, is negative. ΔE is equal to the energy of the products minus the energy of the reactants and represents the energy released.

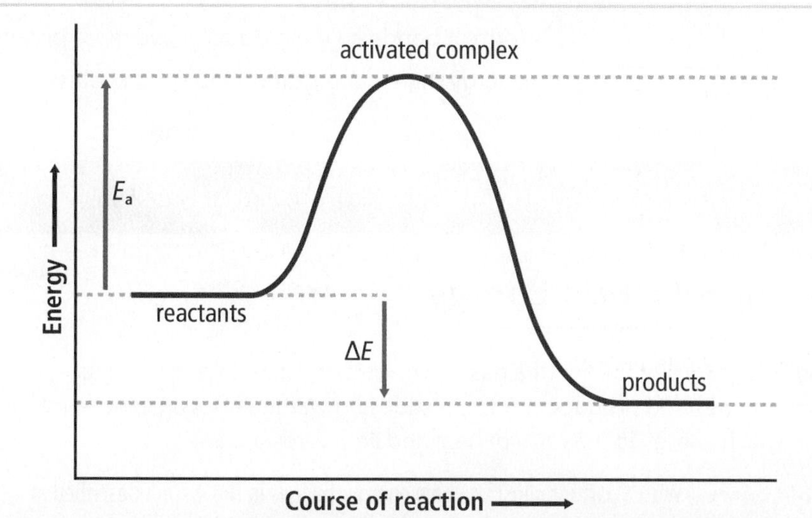

FIGURE 7: In an exothermic reaction, the reactants have more potential energy than the products, and energy is released into the surrounding system. The overall change in energy between the reactants and products is calculated as the energy of the products minus the energy of the reactants, so the change in energy, ΔE, is negative.

Evidence Notebook In your Evidence Notebook, explain how energy changes form in the light stick reaction. Cite evidence to support your claim, and explain your reasoning.

At the peak of the graph in Figure 7, a transitional structure called the *activated complex* forms as the reactant bonds are broken and the product bonds are formed. The activated complex may go on to form products, or it may return to the original reactants. Increasing the temperature of the reaction causes more particles to have sufficient energy to form the activated complex on collision. This is why reaction rate increases as temperature increases. Increasing temperature increases the opportunities for products to form.

APPLY According to what you have learned about concentration, how does increasing the concentration of one or more reactants affect the formation of the activated complex?

____

____

____

____

Endothermic Reactions

In an endothermic reaction, kinetic energy is converted to chemical potential energy. As shown in Figure 8, the products of an endothermic reaction have more chemical potential energy than the reactants do. So, ΔE is positive for endothermic reactions and represents the energy that endothermic reactions absorb from the environment. These reactions typically feel cold to the touch because thermal energy is converted to chemical potential energy in the form of chemical bonds in the products.

FIGURE 8: In an endothermic reaction, the products have more chemical potential energy than the reactants.

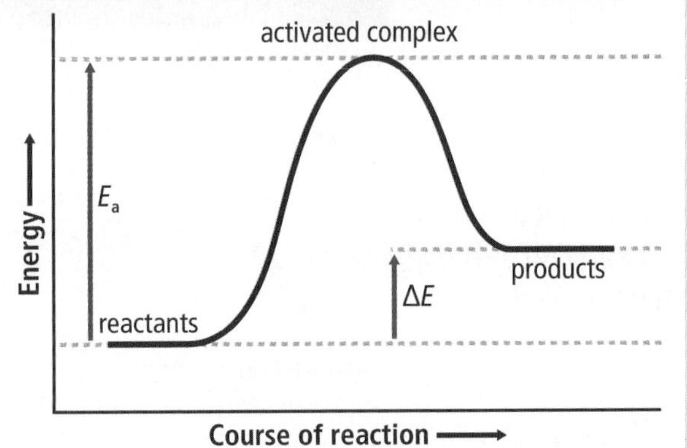

EXPLAIN Select the correct terms to compare the way energy flows in exothermic and endothermic reactions.

In exothermic reactions, potential | kinetic energy is converted to potential | kinetic energy, so the products have less potential energy than the reactants, and ΔE is negative. The energy released may take the form of heat, light, or sound. In endothermic reactions, potential | kinetic energy is converted to potential | kinetic energy in the form of bonds, so the products have more potential energy than the reactants, and ΔE is positive.

Systems and System Models

Analyzing Reaction Energy

When you light a Bunsen burner or a gas stove, methane in natural gas reacts with oxygen in the air to produce carbon dioxide and water. This is an exothermic reaction in which energy in the form of heat and light is released.

Collaborate With a partner, illustrate how energy changes in the system described in this scenario. First, draw a diagram that defines the boundaries of the system you would like to use and show the general direction of energy flow. Next, draw a graph showing the relationship between energy in the reactants and energy in the products.

Problem Solving

Calculating Energy Requirements

SAMPLE PROBLEM Figure 9 shows an energy diagram for a hypothetical chemical reaction. The energy level of the reactants is shown to the left, and that of the products is shown to the right. The total energy change, ΔE, is the difference between these two levels. Activation energy, E_a, is the minimum energy for an effective collision. E_a is the difference between the reactant energy level and the peak.

FIGURE 9: Energy diagram

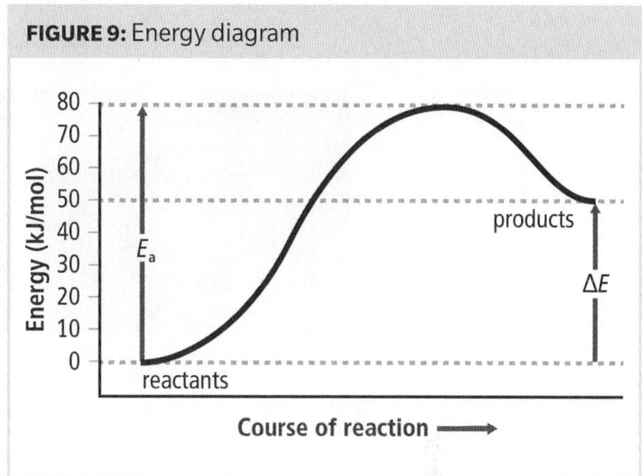

Use the graph to calculate the value of ΔE and E_a. Then, use your calculations to determine whether this reaction is endothermic or exothermic.

SOLVE **1.** To calculate ΔE, subtract the energy of the reactants from that of the products.

ΔE = energy of products − energy of reactants
$\Delta E = 50$ kJ/mol − 0 kJ/mol = 50 kJ/mol

2. To calculate E_a, subtract the energy of the reactants from that of the activated complex.

E_a = energy of activated complex − energy of reactants
$E_a = 80$ kJ/mol − 0 kJ/mol = 80 kJ/mol

3. To determine whether the reaction is endothermic or exothermic, analyze the relationship between the energy of the products and the energy of the reactants. In this case, the energy of the products is higher than the energy of the reactants, so energy was absorbed, and the reaction is endothermic.

PRACTICE PROBLEM **SOLVE** Use the energy diagram in Figure 10 to calculate each of the following values:

1. ΔE ____________

2. E_a ____________

3. Is this reaction endothermic or exothermic? Use evidence to support your claim.

FIGURE 10: This energy diagram shows how energy changes in a hypothetical reaction.

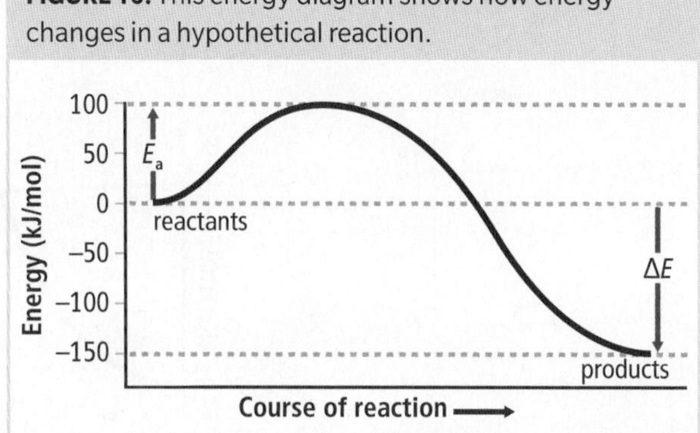

Lowering Activation Energy

Hydrogen peroxide decomposes to form water and oxygen gas in a very slow chemical reaction. When soap is added, the reaction causes bubbles to form. In Figure 11, a small amount of sodium iodide, NaI, is added to the mixture, and bubbles form rapidly.

FIGURE 11: When sodium iodide is added to a hydrogen peroxide and dish soap solution, the reaction occurs very quickly.

Explore Online

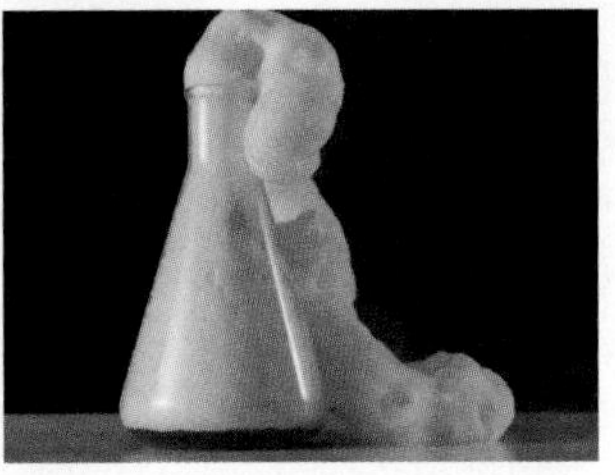

ASK What questions do you have about the role of sodium iodide in this reaction?

In this reaction, the sodium iodide acted as a catalyst. A catalyst is a substance that increases the rate of a chemical reaction without being consumed during the reaction. As a result, catalysts are written above the arrow in a chemical equation.

$$2H_2O_2 \xrightarrow{\text{NaI}} O_2 + 2H_2O$$

Catalysts help lower the activation energy required to form the activated complex in a chemical reaction. So, a lower activation energy is required to start the reaction. Many reactions inside living things are catalyzed by proteins called enzymes so they can proceed rapidly at relatively low temperatures.

ANALYZE The energy diagram for the decomposition of hydrogen peroxide is shown. Label the graph with the chemical formulas of the reactants and products. Then, draw a line representing the energy of this reaction when the sodium iodide catalyst is added.

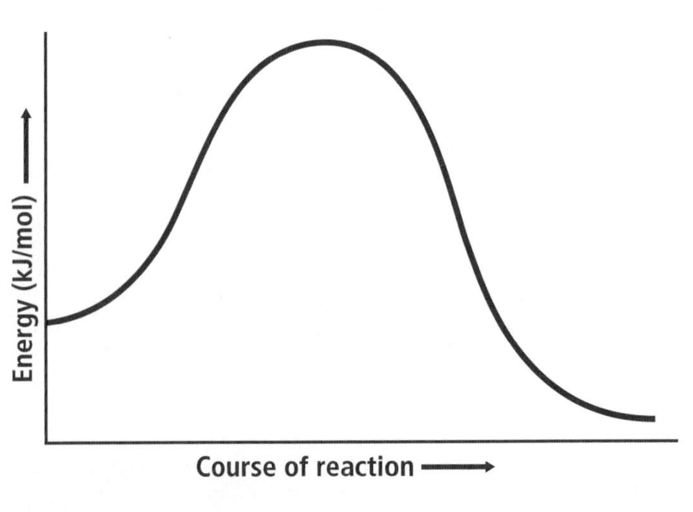

Engineering

Catalyzing Changes

Think about all of the things you use that are made of plastic: shopping bags, packaging materials, bottles, plastic wrap, and many others. Plastic is convenient, but it can also be a big problem. Plastic materials, such as polyethylene bottles, do not break down in the environment for a very long time. As a result, plastic accumulates in landfills.

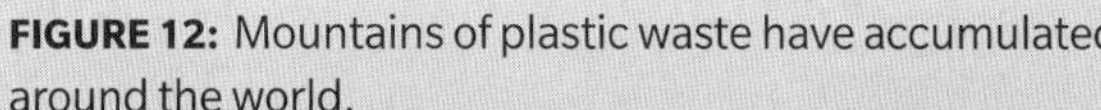

FIGURE 12: Mountains of plastic waste have accumulated around the world.

PREDICT What are some criteria and constraints engineers might consider when developing materials that could serve as alternatives to plastics?

Scientists are now studying a process that uses two catalysts to convert waste plastic into diesel fuel. The conversion is a two-step process using polyethylene, the most common plastic material in use. Polyethylene, $(C_2H_4)_n$, is commonly produced from the catalytic polymerization of ethylene, which comes from crude oil. Polyethylene is made up of a long chain of carbon atoms, each attached to two hydrogen atoms. The first catalyst speeds up a reaction that removes the hydrogen atoms from these long chains. As the hydrogen is removed, double bonds form between carbon atoms of the giant polyethylene molecules. This reaction is useful because carbon chains with double bonds react much more readily with other compounds than do chains with only single bonds.

Although the double bonds provide sites for reactions that break apart the chain, those reactions are not fast enough to be practical for handling large volumes of plastic. This is where a second catalyst comes into play. This catalyst reduces the activation energy and helps break apart the plastic at the double bonds. The result is a mixture of hydrocarbon chains of various lengths. The reactions that are sped up by the catalysts continue to break apart the long hydrocarbon chains until they are short enough to be recycled for other purposes, such as fuel.

The catalyst molecules for this process are expensive to produce. They contain expensive metals, such as iridium and rhenium. To make the process cost-effective, the catalysts are recovered and reused. Each molecule of catalyst can promote the conversion of polyethylene molecules over and over again.

Language Arts Connection Research this method of converting plastic into fuel, and write a news article explaining its benefits and drawbacks. Cite specific text evidence to support your analysis, and discuss possible unanticipated effects of using this method.

Evidence Notebook Draw an energy diagram for the light stick reaction, and label the reactants, products, and the activation energy of the reaction. Then explain your reasoning for drawing the energy diagram the way you did.

The Rate Law

FIGURE 13: A series of controlled explosions breaks apart rock at a quarry.

An explosion at a quarry is an impressive example of a chemical reaction. Explosive materials such as nitroglycerin, trinitrotoluene (TNT), and dynamite are primarily organic substances. They contain mostly carbon, hydrogen, oxygen, and nitrogen atoms held together by relatively weak bonds.

These materials undergo rapid decomposition. The released elements immediately react to form gaseous N_2, CO, CO_2, and NO_2. These molecules are much more stable than those in the original explosive material, so an enormous amount of energy is released. In addition, the sudden formation of gaseous material causes a tremendous increase in pressure that provides the force to demolish an unwanted building or break apart rock for building roads.

PREDICT How do you think scientists determine the reaction rate of an explosive reaction?

Relating Concentration and Reaction Rate

We can experimentally determine the rate of a reaction by measuring the rate at which reactants are consumed or products are formed. It is often important to know and control the rate of a chemical reaction. For example, in an industrial process, equipment must be designed to handle a certain rate of production. If the reaction rate is too slow, then more time is required to make a product, and the product may cost too much as a result. If the reaction rate is too fast, gaseous products and energy may be produced too rapidly. This can damage equipment or even cause a dangerous explosion.

The relationship between reaction rate and concentration is determined by keeping the temperature of the system constant and varying the concentration of a single reactant at a time. By running a series of such experiments, changing the concentration of one reactant at a time, a chemist can determine how the concentration of each reactant affects the reaction rate.

For example, nitrogen monoxide gas reacts with hydrogen gas to produce nitrogen gas and water vapor as shown in the equation:

$$2NO(g) + 2H_2(g) \rightarrow N_2(g) + 2H_2O(g)$$

A series of experiments was performed to measure the rate of this reaction. First, scientists measured how changing the H_2 concentration affected the reaction rate when the NO concentration was held constant. Then, the scientists ran another series of experiments to measure the effect of the NO concentration while the H_2 concentration was held constant. When determining the rate of a reaction, it is important to change the concentration of only one reactant at a time. Otherwise, scientists would not be able to determine the effect of each reactant on the rate.

Experimental Reaction Rates Data		
Concentration of NO	Concentration of H_2	Rate
Initial	Initial	R
Initial	Doubled	$2R$
Initial	Tripled	$3R$
Doubled	Initial	$4R$
Tripled	Initial	$9R$

Math Connection

Identifying Rate Relationships

To calculate the relationship of rate to concentration for a reaction, you can analyze patterns in data. For example, the Experimental Reaction Rates Data table shows how the rate of this reaction changes as the concentration of each reactant changes.

ANALYZE Select the correct terms to complete the statement.

According to the data in the table, doubling the concentration of H_2 causes the reaction rate to double | triple | quadruple. So, the reaction rate is inversely | directly proportional to the concentration of H_2. Doubling the concentration of NO causes the reaction rate to double | triple | quadruple. Thus, the reaction rate is directly proportional to the square | cube of the concentration of NO.

A rate law is an equation that expresses the dependence of reaction rate on the concentrations of the reactants. The general form of a rate law is

$$R = k[A]^n[B]^m$$

where R represents the reaction rate, k is the specific rate constant, and [A] and [B] represent the molar concentrations of reactants A and B. The powers to which the concentrations are raised in calculating the rate law are represented by n and m. The rate law is applicable for a specific reaction at a given set of conditions. The value of k must be determined experimentally after the exponents have been determined experimentally.

In the example of the hydrogen gas and nitrogen monoxide gas reaction, we can use patterns in the concentration and reaction rate data to determine the rate law. Based on the experiment, you can determine that the rate is directly proportional to the concentration of hydrogen gas. So, the n in this rate law is 1, which is not written. The rate is also directly proportional to the square of the nitrogen monoxide concentration. So, the m in this rate law is 2. Thus, the concentration of NO is squared in the rate law equation.

$$R = k[H_2][NO]^2$$

The specific rate constant does not change over the course of the reaction if conditions other than concentration of reactants and products are constant. A change in the temperature of the reaction mixture, however, does change the value of k.

Problem Solving

Determining the Rate Law

SAMPLE PROBLEM Fluorine gas reacts with chlorine dioxide gas according to the following equation:

$$F_2(g) + 2ClO_2(g) \rightarrow 2FClO_2(g)$$

Use the following experimental data to write a rate law for this reaction.

Experiment	Concentration of F_2	Concentration of ClO_2	Rate (mol/L•s)
1	0.10 M	0.10 M	1.1×10^{-3}
2	0.20 M	0.10 M	2.2×10^{-3}
3	0.10 M	0.20 M	2.2×10^{-3}
4	0.20 M	0.20 M	4.4×10^{-3}

ANALYZE To write the rate law, first examine the data to see how the rate of reaction changes as the concentrations of the reactants change.

When $[F_2]$ doubles and $[ClO_2]$ remains constant, the rate of reaction doubles. So, the reaction rate is directly proportional to $[F_2]$.

When $[ClO_2]$ doubles and $[F_2]$ remains constant, the rate of reaction also doubles. So, the rate is directly proportional to $[ClO_2]$.

SOLVE Because the reaction rate is proportional to both $[F_2]$ and $[ClO_2]$, you can write the rate law $R = k[F_2][ClO_2]$. The data from Trial 4 help confirm the rate law because when both $[F_2]$ and $[ClO_2]$ double, the rate increases by a factor of four, from 1.1×10^{-3} mol/L•s to 4.4×10^{-3} mol/L•s.

PRACTICE PROBLEM **SOLVE** Nitrogen monoxide forms in combustion engines and can subsequently react with oxygen in the air to produce nitrogen dioxide, which is an air pollutant:

$$O_2(g) + 2NO(g) \rightarrow 2NO_2(g)$$

Experiment	Concentration of O_2	Concentration of NO	Rate (mol/L•s)
1	1.20×10^{-2} M	1.40×10^{-2} M	3.30×10^{-3}
2	2.40×10^{-2} M	1.40×10^{-2} M	6.60×10^{-3}
3	1.20×10^{-2} M	2.80×10^{-2} M	1.32×10^{-2}

Use this data to briefly explain how the rate changes as the concentration of each reactant changes. Then use your explanation to write the rate law for this reaction.

Evidence Notebook Consider the rate law for the reaction occurring in a light stick. What information would you need in order to set up an experiment to determine the rate law?

Engineering

Chemical Kinetics

Industrial explosives are used to break apart rock, clear paths for new roads, and even demolish buildings. During the explosion of these materials, matter moves very rapidly—several kilometers per second—and with a lot of force. In order to design explosives that are both safe and effective, chemists must apply their knowledge of reaction rates, also called chemical kinetics. Because these reactions occur at such high rates and give off so much energy, it can be difficult to study exactly how these chemical changes occur.

FIGURE 14: A detonation test for a mining explosive

There are many forms of explosives used in mining, each with unique properties and reactions. Mining explosives are designed to be stable and safe to handle for long periods of time, but they also need to provide as much energy as possible when they are used. Because they provide so much energy, engineers must understand how they will react in order to prevent accidental explosions.

Scientists and engineers process data from test explosions to model exactly what is occurring during the reaction. By calculating the rate of reaction under different conditions and the amount of energy released, they can determine the best design for an explosive system that performs the task safely.

Understanding chemical kinetics also helps in the design of safer materials. For example, a simple mechanical impact on an explosive device can result in localized heating. This effect can cause mechanical deformation and possibly fracturing or fragmenting of the material. One section may ignite, and as the ignition spreads, the energy released could lead to anything from slow combustion of the material to violent detonation of the whole explosive device. Chemists, materials scientists, and engineers work together to predict explosive sensitivity and design new materials that do not accidentally detonate.

The behavior of explosives is a challenging topic because the reactions themselves are very complex, and they occur extremely rapidly. Modern technology allows engineers to determine reaction rates with more precision than in the past. This advancement allows them to design explosive materials and direct forces in a way that maximizes productivity and safety.

Language Arts Connection Conduct research to learn more about how engineers use knowledge of chemical kinetics to optimize processes in another field, such as pharmaceutical production or food storage. Then, write a blog post that explains your findings and addresses the following questions. Focus on the most important aspects of the information, and explain any inconsistencies you find.

- How do engineers use knowledge of chemical kinetics to optimize this process?
- How are the data and results from chemical kinetics experiments and tests used in this field?
- Why is an understanding of reaction rates important when optimizing this process?

CONTROLLING REACTION RATES

REACTION MECHANISMS

CLOCK REACTIONS
Go online to choose one of these other paths.

Lesson Self-Check

CAN YOU EXPLAIN THE PHENOMENON?

FIGURE 15: Temperature affects the rate of the reaction in the light sticks.

Light sticks consist of two nested tubes. The tough, plastic, outer tube is filled with a solution of a reactant and a dissolved dye. A thin, inner tube made of glass or brittle plastic holds a solution of a second reactant. When the tube inside a light stick is broken, the two reactants mix and start reacting. The reaction releases energy that is absorbed by the dye. Energy released by the reaction causes the dye to glow. As the reactants are used up and their concentration decreases, the light stick gradually becomes dimmer.

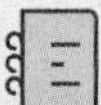

Evidence Notebook Refer to your notes in your Evidence Notebook to make a claim about this phenomenon. Your explanation should include a discussion of the following points:

Claim Make a claim to explain at the particle level why changing the temperature of a light stick affects the intensity of the light it emits.

Evidence Provide specific evidence to support your claim.

Reasoning How does the evidence support your claim? Explain how the breaking of bonds, particle collisions, and kinetic energy are related to this phenomenon.

Name Date

CHECKPOINTS

Check Your Understanding

1. Select the correct terms to complete the statement about reaction rates.

The rate of a chemical reaction depends on a number of different factors. At a higher concentration of reactants, the frequency of collisions decreases | increases | is not affected, so the reaction rate decreases | increases | remains the same. When temperature decreases, the kinetic energy of the particles decreases | increases | is not affected. As a result, particles collide less frequently and with less energy, so reaction rate decreases | increases | is not affected.

2. According to collision theory, which variables affect the rate of a chemical reaction? Select all correct answers.

- ☐ **a.** concentrations of dissolved reactants
- ☐ **b.** chemical properties of reactants
- ☐ **c.** size of crystals of solid reactants
- ☐ **d.** shape of the container holding reactants

3. Select the correct terms to complete the statement about particle collisions.

In order to form a new product, reactant particles must collide with sufficient kinetic | potential energy to break | form bonds in the reactant particles. This is why increasing temperature increases the rate of a chemical reaction.

4. Which of these are reasons that a collision between particles might not lead to the formation of a new product? Select all correct answers.

- ☐ **a.** The particles did not collide with sufficient energy to break bonds in the reactants.
- ☐ **b.** The particles had a very high mass, which prevents effective collisions.
- ☐ **c.** The particles do not have the correct shape to form new products.
- ☐ **d.** The orientation of the particles was not correct.

Use the table to answer Question 5.

Energy Values of a Chemical Reaction	
Chemical Species	**Energy (kJ/mol)**
Reactants	0
Products	−110
Activated complex	45

5. Complete the statement.

During the reaction described in the table, the overall energy of the reaction is −110 kJ/mol | 110 kJ/mol, indicating that the reaction is endothermic | exothermic. The energy required to cause effective collisions between particles is 45 kJ/mol | 110 kJ/mol.

Use the table to answer Questions 6 and 7.

Reaction Rates for A(*aq*) + B(*aq*) ⟶ C(*aq*)			
Experiment	**[A]**	**[B]**	**Rate (M/s)**
1	0.150 M	0.300 M	0.013
2	0.150 M	0.600 M	0.052
3	0.300 M	0.300 M	0.026

6. Complete the statement. Some terms may not be used or may be used more than once.

doubles | quadruples | remains unchanged

Based on the data in the table, when the concentration of reactant A doubles, the reaction rate ____________, and when the concentration of reactant B doubles, the reaction rate ____________.

7. What is the rate law for the reaction between A and B?

- ○ **a.** $R = k[A][B]$
- ○ **b.** $R = k[A]^2[B]$
- ○ **c.** $R = k[A][B]^2$
- ○ **d.** $R = k[A]^2[B]^2$

CHECKPOINTS (continued)

8. Describe two ways to make a chemical reaction proceed faster, and explain at the particle level why the rate increases.

9. Explain why a candle cannot start burning until a flame is brought to the wick, but it continues burning once started.

10. When vinegar and baking soda are mixed together in an aqueous solution, the solution becomes colder as the reaction proceeds. How does an endothermic reaction continue without the addition of energy from outside the solution system? What can you conclude about the activation energy of the reaction?

MAKE YOUR OWN STUDY GUIDE

In your Evidence Notebook, design a study guide that supports the main ideas from this lesson:

The rate of a chemical reaction can be measured, and it can vary depending on the nature of the reactants, surface area, temperature, concentration, and the presence of a catalyst.

According to collision theory, a reaction can occur when particles collide with sufficient energy and in a favorable orientation.

The rate law of a reaction describes the correlation between the concentration of each reactant and the reaction rate.

Remember to include the following information in your study guide:

- Use examples that model main ideas.
- Record explanations for the phenomena you investigated.
- Use evidence to support your explanations. Your support can include drawings, data, graphs, laboratory conclusions, and other evidence recorded throughout the lesson.

Consider how patterns in data obtained from experiments and simulations can be used to support explanations for how interactions at the particle level are related to changes in reaction rates.

5.2

Exploring Chemical Equilibrium

The water in public pools must be clear and clean to keep swimmers safe.

CAN YOU EXPLAIN THE PHENOMENON?

Public swimming pools are a great place to cool off on a hot day. Clean water in a pool makes swimming safer and more enjoyable. Depending on the size of the pool, there could be anywhere from thousands to millions of liters of water to keep clean. Larger materials, such as leaves, dirt, and hair, need to be removed from the pool. There also may be unseen microscopic contaminants, such as bacteria and algae, present in harmful concentrations in water that appears to be clean.

PLAN Brainstorm ideas for how to treat contaminants in pool water. Could you use the same solution for both larger debris and microscopic organisms? Which type of contaminant do you think is more dangerous to swimmers?

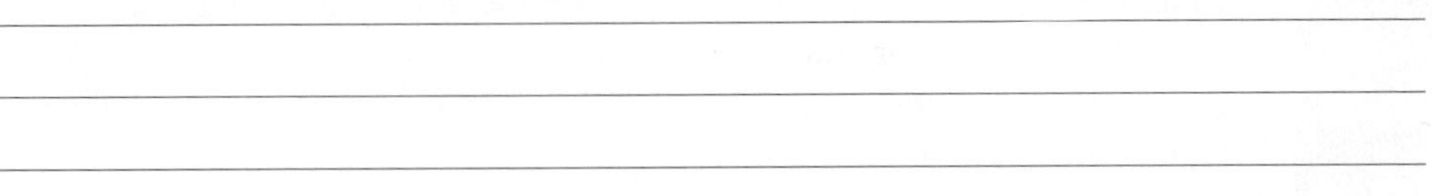

Evidence Notebook As you explore the lesson, gather evidence to explain how a chemical equilibrium system in swimming pools can be managed to provide safe water for swimmers.

Explaining Equilibrium

When wood burns in a fire, atoms in molecules such as cellulose are rearranged to form new products, such as carbon dioxide, water vapor, and ash. Burning wood is not a reversible process because wood cannot be remade from ash. However, some reactions are reversible and can proceed in both forward and reverse directions.

Reversible Reactions

A chemical reaction in which the products can react to reform the reactants is called a reversible reaction. An example of a reversible reaction is shown in Figure 1 and involves copper sulfate pentahydrate, a common fungicide and herbicide. The *hydrate* means water molecules are present in the copper sulfate crystal, and its formula is $CuSO_4 \cdot 5H_2O$.

FIGURE 1: Forward and reverse reactions involving copper sulfate pentahydrate

a Blue crystals of copper sulfate pentahydrate are placed over a hot flame.

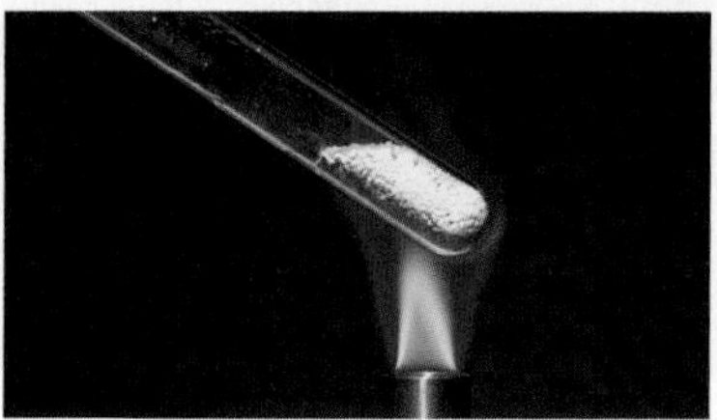

b Water is released from the compound, leaving white crystals of copper sulfate.

c Water is added back to the copper sulfate, and the crystals turn blue.

Stability and Change

FIGURE 2: The combustion of candle wax is effectively a one-way reaction.

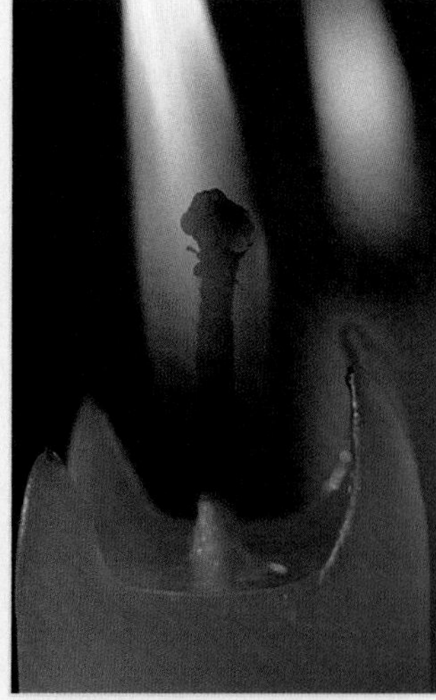

Reversible and Irreversible Reactions

It was once believed that all chemical reactions were irreversible, and once products formed they could not change back to reactants. For example, when a candle burns, wax cannot be rebuilt out of compounds in the air.

But some reactions are different. Solid ammonium chloride forms small white crystals. When ammonium chloride is placed in a test tube and held over a flame, the gases ammonia and hydrogen chloride are produced. As the reaction proceeds, some solid white crystals form on the cooler sides at the top of the glass test tube.

GATHER EVIDENCE What evidence is there that the reverse reaction is occurring in the ammonium chloride reaction?

- ○ **a.** The reactants are burned over a flame.
- ○ **b.** Crystals appear at the top of the test tube.
- ○ **c.** All reactants are consumed in the reaction.
- ○ **d.** Two different gases are released as products.

Data Analysis

Analyzing Concentrations of Reactants and Products

What evidence might indicate that a reaction can proceed in both directions? And, does this type of reaction ever come to a stop?

Consider nitrogen dioxide, NO_2, an orange-brown gas that is a common component of polluted air. Nitrogen dioxide interacts with oxygen, water, and other pollutants in the atmosphere and forms acid rain. It can also cause haze or smog that is yellowish-brown in color. Two molecules of NO_2 react to form dinitrogen tetroxide, N_2O_4. Dinitrogen tetroxide is a colorless gas that can be used as a rocket propellant because it is highly reactive. The molecular structures of NO_2 and N_2O_4 are shown in Figure 3.

The table shows the concentration of each compound over time as NO_2 reacts to form N_2O_4 in a closed system.

FIGURE 3: Molecular structures of NO_2 and N_2O_4

a Nitrogen dioxide, NO_2

b Dinitrogen tetroxide, N_2O_4

Concentration of NO_2 and N_2O_4 as Reaction Proceeds

NO_2 (mol/L)	N_2O_4 (mol/L)
0.0500	0.0000
0.0428	0.0036
0.0320	0.0090
0.0220	0.0140
0.0154	0.0173
0.0120	0.0190
0.0106	0.0197
0.0102	0.0199
0.0100	0.0200
0.0100	0.0200
0.0100	0.0200

MODEL Graph the data shown in the table as the concentration of each compound over time.

You can see based on the table data and your graph that the concentrations of nitrogen dioxide and dinitrogen tetroxide reach a steady state in which the concentrations do not change. A double arrow is used to show the reaction at a steady state, or equilibrium.

$$2NO_2(g) \rightleftharpoons N_2O_4(g)$$

ANALYZE Select the correct terms to complete the statement.

In this reaction, NO_2 molecules combine | break apart to form N_2O_4, and N_2O_4 molecules combine | break apart to form NO_2. The reaction reaches a stable state when the ratio of the two gases is 0.0100 | 0.0200 | 0.0500 mol/L NO_2 to 0.0000 | 0.0100 | 0.0200 mol/L N_2O_4. At this point, the gases are still | have stopped reacting. At a stable state, the rates of both reactions must be equal | unequal for the concentration of both compounds to remain steady.

Chemical Equilibrium

The NO_2/N_2O_4 system is an example of an equilibrium. As the reaction progresses, the concentrations of NO_2 and N_2O_4 present at specific conditions stabilize. At this point, called chemical equilibrium, the forward and reverse reactions occur at the same rate. In contrast, the concentrations of the reactants and products are often different.

Figure 4 shows changes in the concentrations of NO_2 and N_2O_4 as the reaction progresses.

$$2NO_2(g) \rightleftharpoons N_2O_4(g)$$

NO_2 and N_2O_4 Concentrations over Time

FIGURE 4: As the reaction progresses, chemical equilibrium is reached.

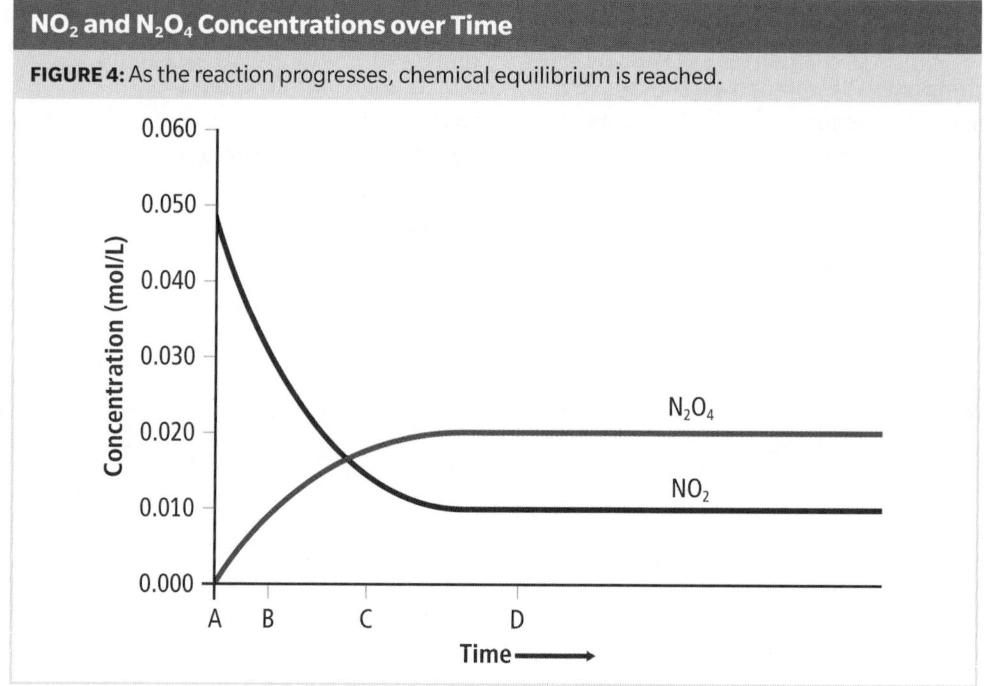

ANALYZE Which of the following statements about this reaction are true? Select all correct answers.

- ☐ **a.** At Time B, the reaction has not yet reached chemical equilibrium.
- ☐ **b.** Chemical equilibrium for this reaction occurs at Time C.
- ☐ **c.** At equilibrium, the concentrations of NO_2 and N_2O_4 are equal.
- ☐ **d.** At Time D, the reaction has reached chemical equilibrium.
- ☐ **e.** The concentrations of NO_2 and N_2O_4 differ when chemical equilibrium is reached.

Collaborate With a partner, discuss the limitations of models such as the Figure 4 graph in representing what occurs at chemical equilibrium. What kind of model could be used to represent the process more completely?

EVALUATE What is the relationship among reaction rate, effective particle collisions, and reactant concentration? How do these factors affect chemical equilibrium?

Consider this generalized reaction at equilibrium:

$$A + B \rightleftharpoons C + D$$

PREDICT If you start with only A and B, when will C and D be produced the fastest? How does this relate to concentration?

Modeling Chemical Equilibrium Develop a model of equilibrium using water and measuring cups.

The graph in Figure 5 shows the reaction rates as the system reaches equilibrium.

FIGURE 5: Change in reaction rates as a hypothetical chemical reaction reaches equilibrium

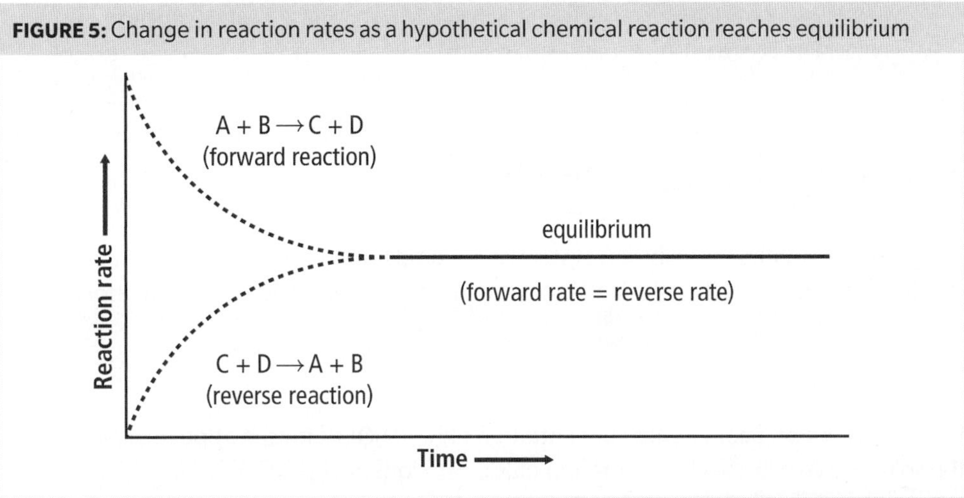

EXPLAIN Select the correct terms to complete the statement.

As the reaction proceeds, the rate of the forward reaction increases | decreases while the rate of the reverse reaction increases | decreases. This occurs because, as the concentrations of A and B increase | decrease, the concentrations of C and D increase | decrease. When the chemical reaction reaches equilibrium, the rate of the forward reaction is greater than | equal to | less than the rate of the reverse reaction.

This type of equilibrium is called a dynamic equilibrium because the system is in a constant, but balanced, state of change. Forward and reverse reactions continue, but no noticeable change in concentrations occurs because the reaction rates are the same.

Language Arts Connection Write an analogy that describes chemical equilibrium, including the relationship between the reaction at the molecular scale and the concentrations of the products and reactants measured at the macroscopic scale. Explain your analogy to a partner. How did different sources of information help you build your understanding?

Evidence Notebook Hypochlorous acid, HOCl, is used to treat pools. When HOCl is added to water, it breaks apart to form hydrogen ions, H^+, and hypochlorite ions, OCl^-. An equilibrium is established. Write the chemical equation for this equilibrium system. Describe how the concentration of each ion and HOCl changes when HOCl is added to water as a pool treatment.

Concentration Influences Equilibrium

As in the example of nitrogen dioxide and dinitrogen tetroxide, many chemical systems in nature and industrial chemistry involve chemical reactions in equilibrium. The equilibrium states can be shifted to form an increased or decreased amount of the products.

Collaborate With a group, develop a physical model for the reaction: $A + BC \rightleftharpoons BA + C$. One person should control the forward reaction and one person the reverse reaction. What happens when a classmate adds products or reactants? What happens when products or reactants are removed? Explain the changes in your model in terms of concentrations, collisions between particles, and reaction rates.

Adding Reactants or Products

Now consider another equilibrium system as a model for the principles of chemical equilibrium. The cobalt(II) chloride equilibrium system is modeled by the equation:

$$\underset{\textit{Pink}}{[Co(H_2O)_6]^{2+}(aq)} + 4Cl^-(aq) \rightleftharpoons \underset{\textit{Blue}}{[CoCl_4]^{2-}(aq)} + 6H_2O(l)$$

When the solution has a higher concentration of $[Co(H_2O)_6]^{2+}$ ions, it appears pink. When the solution has a higher concentration of $[CoCl_4]^{2-}$ ions, it appears blue. As with all chemical equilibria, the ions and molecules in solution are constantly reacting in forward and reverse reactions. Figure 6 shows the color changes when hydrochloric acid, HCl, and then water, H_2O, are added to the cobalt(II) chloride solution.

FIGURE 6: The cobalt(II) chloride solution changes color as the chemical equilibrium shifts.

Explore Online

a Initially, the solution is pinkish-orange.

b After HCl is added, the solution turns blue.

c After water is added, the solution begins to turn pink again.

GATHER EVIDENCE Using evidence from Figure 6, explain what happens to the product and reactant concentrations when hydrochloric acid or water is added to the system.

Adding HCl to the cobalt(II) chloride system effectively adds chloride ions, a reactant when the chemical equation is read from left to right. Adding water to the cobalt(II) chloride system adds more product. Either of these changes disrupts the equilibrium and causes it to shift.

EXPLAIN Select the correct terms to complete the statement.

Adding more reactant increases the frequency of collisions between product | reactant particles, which shifts the reaction to the left | right in favor of the products | reactants. Adding more product increases the frequency of collisions between product | reactant particles, which shifts the reaction to the left | right in favor of the products | reactants.

Figure 7 shows the cobalt(II) chloride system before and after the addition of Cl^- ions. The sharp increase in the Cl^- line indicates when HCl was added. Water is not shown on the graph because the concentration of water remains approximately constant.

$$[Co(H_2O)_6]^{2+}(aq) + 4Cl^-(aq) \rightleftharpoons [CoCl_4]^{2-}(aq) + 6H_2O(l)$$

Addition of HCl to the $CoCl_2$ System

FIGURE 7: The concentrations in the cobalt(II) chloride equilibrium system change with the addition of hydrochloric acid.

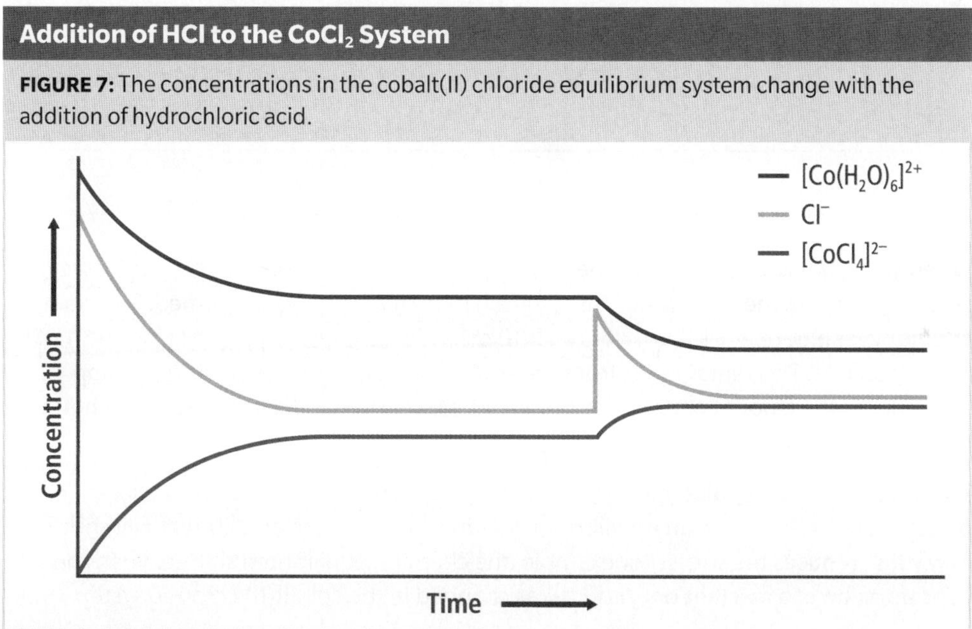

ANALYZE What keeps the concentrations in this reaction from reaching zero? Use evidence from the graph and reaction rates to support your claims.

During an equilibrium reaction, adding reactants disrupts the dynamic equilibrium. As more reactants are converted to products, the forward reaction will slow because there are fewer reactant particles colliding. At the same time, because the concentration of product particles increases, the rate of the reverse reaction will increase. Eventually, the rates will equalize at a new equilibrium position. The opposite shift occurs with the addition of a product.

Removing Reactants or Products

We saw that adding reactants or products can shift the equilibrium of a system. Now, what would happen if we removed a reactant or product from the cobalt(II) chloride system?

ANALYZE Complete the graph to illustrate the changes in reactant and product concentrations when chloride ions are removed from the system.

$$[Co(H_2O)_6]^{2+}(aq) + 4Cl^-(aq) \rightleftharpoons [CoCl_4]^{2-}(aq) + 6H_2O(l)$$

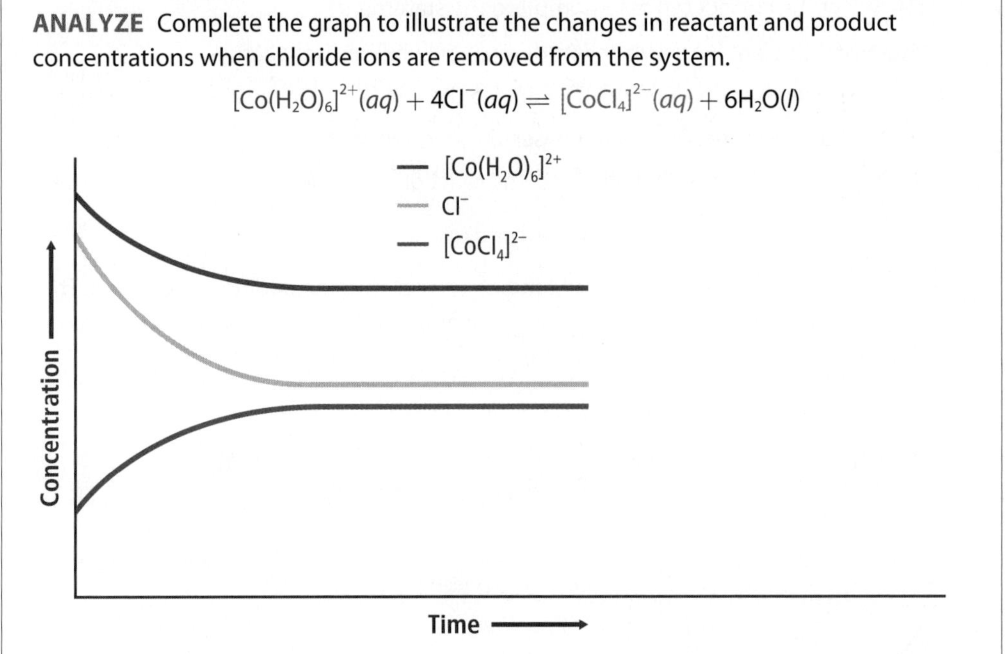

When a reactant is removed from the system, the forward reaction slows but the reverse reaction occurs at the same rate. This results in more reactants being formed. For example, adding silver nitrate, $AgNO_3$, to the cobalt(II) chloride solution forms silver chloride, AgCl, as a precipitate. This removes Cl^- from the system, which slows the forward reaction and reduces the amount of products produced. The opposite effect is observed when a product is removed.

The disruption of an equilibrium system places stress on the system. Le Châtelier's principle states that when an equilibrium system is stressed, the equilibrium will shift in a way that reduces the stress. For example, the chemical equilibrium shifted when the concentration of a reactant or product was changed in the cobalt(II) chloride system.

APPLY When HOCl is added to water, it dissociates to form hydrogen ions, H^+, and hypochlorite ions, OCl^-. HOCl is an effective pool treatment because the oxygen in the HOCl molecule destroys bacteria, algae, and other substances. This uses up the HOCl. Describe this stress at the molecular level, and explain the effect the stress has on the HOCl equilibrium in terms of Le Châtelier's principle.

Evidence Notebook Why does the concentration of HOCl in the water of public pools have to be regularly monitored?

Pressure and Temperature Influence Equilibrium

According to Le Châtelier's principle, an equilibrium system will change to reduce stress. Changing the concentration of reactants or products can add stress and shift an equilibrium system. Pressure can also influence equilibrium.

Shifting Equilibrium Use Le Châtelier's principle to predict changes in products and reactants as a chemical equilibrium system changes.

The pressure exerted by a gas on a surface depends on the frequency with which particles hit the surface. Increasing the pressure of a gas increases the number of collisions particles have with the surface and with each other. The gas molecules are in constant, random motion. The same number of moles of any gas occupies the same volume at a given pressure and temperature. Because volume and pressure are inversely related, decreasing the volume of a gas or gas mixture at constant temperature increases the pressure of the system.

Collaborate With a partner, discuss why pressure and volume affect a gaseous equilibrium system but do not affect liquid or solid equilibrium systems. Use real-world examples to support your claim.

Consider the differences between these two equilibria:

$$2NO_2(g) \rightleftharpoons N_2O_4(g) \qquad H_2(g) + Cl_2(g) \rightleftharpoons 2HCl(g)$$

EVALUATE Which chemical equilibrium system has an equal number of moles of reactants compared to products and which has an unequal number? How might this affect equilibrium if pressure increases?

Pressure and Equilibrium in a Gaseous System

When a molecule of NO_2 collides with another NO_2 molecule, a molecule of N_2O_4 may form. In the equilibrium system, N_2O_4 continuously decomposes into two molecules of NO_2. The number of effective collisions between reactant molecules determines the reaction rate. Increasing or decreasing the pressure on the system puts a stress on the system. Le Châtelier's principle predicts that the equilibrium will shift in a way that counteracts this stress.

Equilibrium shifts can be observed on the macroscopic scale when the reactants and products are different colors. For example, both tubes in Figure 8 contain a solution of NO_2/N_2O_4 at equilibrium. NO_2 is an orange-brown gas, and N_2O_4 is a colorless gas. Different concentrations of NO_2 give the tubes different colors. The tube on the left is a darker orange-brown color because it has a higher concentration of NO_2. The tube on the right is much lighter in color because it has a lower concentration of NO_2.

FIGURE 8: Two different NO_2/N_2O_4 equilibria

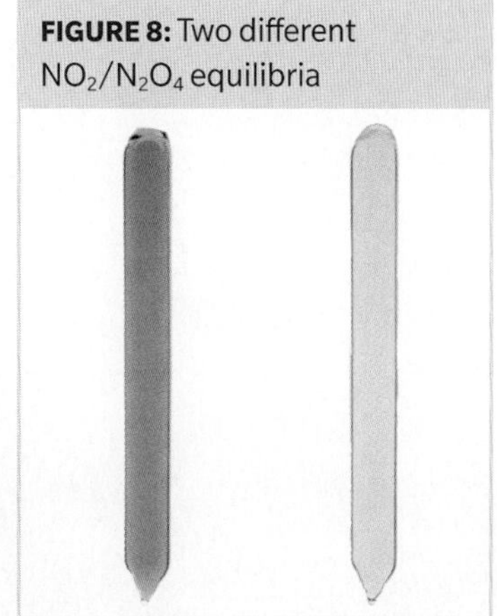

NO_2 and N_2O_4 form an equilibrium system that contains both gases. Figure 9a shows the system sealed in a syringe at room temperature and atmospheric pressure. The color of the gaseous solution in the syringe changes at each stage as stresses are applied to the system and the equilibrium shifts and is then reestablished at a different point.

FIGURE 9: The color of the NO_2/N_2O_4 gaseous equilibrium system changes as pressure changes.

Explore Online

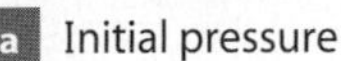

a Initial pressure

b Compressed—initial

c Compressed—final

d Return to initial pressure

MODEL Make a diagram that shows what is happening inside the syringe on a molecular scale. For each stage, show the relative rates for the forward and reverse reactions and whether the densities, volumes, and concentrations of the gases are increasing or decreasing from one stage to the next.

Collaborate Present your model of the NO_2/N_2O_4 system to a partner. Incorporate any feedback and discuss how changes at the molecular scale in this system affect what is observed at the macroscopic scale.

Pressure Affects Concentration

At the instant the pressure increased in the syringe, the concentrations of the gases also increased. The equilibrium shifted to reduce the stress by favoring the side with fewer particles. This decreased the particle collisions with the surfaces of the syringe, which decreased the pressure. Changing pressure affects the reactant and product concentrations. However, there must be a difference in moles between reactants and products for a pressure change to cause an equilibrium shift. The graph below shows the change in concentrations after a pressure increase.

$$2NO_2(g) \rightleftharpoons N_2O_4(g)$$

ANALYZE Label the point on the graph at which the pressure change occurs.

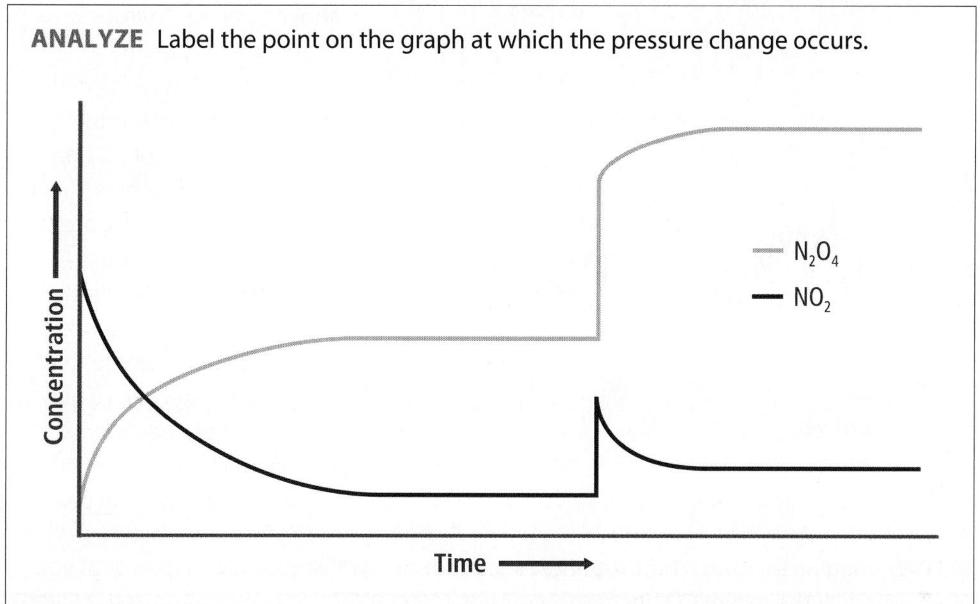

APPLY What can you conclude about the changes that occur in the nitrogen dioxide/dinitrogen tetroxide equilibrium system when the pressure on the system changes?

- ○ **a.** An increase in pressure results in a shift toward NO_2 because the reverse reaction increases the number of NO_2 particles in the container.
- ○ **b.** An increase in pressure does not change the ratio of NO_2 and N_2O_4 because the system remains in equilibrium when the number of particles is constant.
- ○ **c.** An increase in pressure results in a shift toward N_2O_4 because the product side of the forward reaction has fewer molecules and reduces the pressure.
- ○ **d.** An increase in pressure changes the ratio of NO_2 and N_2O_4 because the rate of both the forward and reverse reactions slowed down.

Nitrogen oxides, including nitrogen dioxide, are formed during any high temperature combustion reaction in internal combustion engines and are key components of photochemical smog. Nitrogen dioxide is responsible for the characteristic brown color of smog. Like many systems in nature, there are dynamic equilibria in smog systems.

Language Arts Connection With a partner, use multiple sources to research photochemical smog, a type of air pollution. Write an essay that analyzes how different conditions, such as air pressure and temperature, affect smog and how smog affects human health. Be sure to identify any gaps or inconsistencies in the data.

Equilibrium in the Earth System

Historical Carbon Dioxide Levels

FIGURE 10: Atmospheric carbon dioxide levels fluctuated in the past, but they increased significantly in recent years.

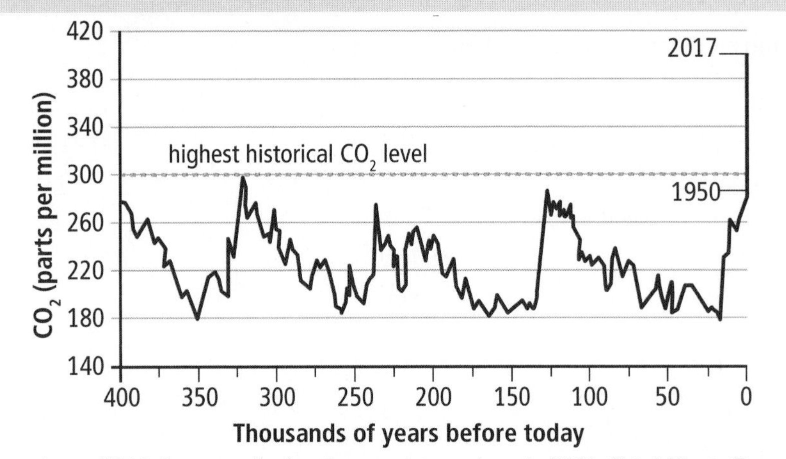

Source: NOAA, Reconstruction from ice cores data, as shown by NASA, Global Climate Change, Vital Signs of the Planet, Carbon Dioxide

Earth is a closed system. Although the total amount of matter on Earth does not change, it does cycle between various systems. Scientists are able to measure past levels of carbon dioxide in the atmosphere by determining the concentration of carbon dioxide, CO_2, in bubbles trapped in ice cores. Figure 10 shows that, over the past 400 000 years, CO_2 levels in Earth's atmosphere fluctuated within a relatively stable range. However, the amount of CO_2 in the atmosphere has increased significantly in recent years, outside of the historical pattern.

ARGUE Imagine the graph data went back an additional million years. What would you expect to see if the recent CO_2 increase is part of a longer CO_2 cycle over time in the Earth system? What would you expect to see if the recent CO_2 increase is not part of a longer CO_2 cycle over time?

Some CO_2 fluctuations over long periods of time could be the result of CO_2 levels in the ocean and atmosphere cycling as temperatures vary on the planet, changes in the biosphere, or massive volcanic eruptions. In the last century, however, CO_2 in the atmosphere increased significantly. The recent increase outside the historical range is due to human activities, including deforestation and burning fossil fuels.

EVALUATE A state of solution equilibrium exists in a closed soda bottle. Carbon dioxide gas is dissolved in both the liquid, making the drink fizzy, and in the gas above the liquid. CO_2 constantly moves between the liquid and the gas. Compare this small-scale system to how CO_2 moves on larger scales in the Earth system.

Endothermic and Exothermic Reactions

Adding or removing energy is another stress that can cause an equilibrium to shift. For example, the temperature on one side of the U-tube filled with cobalt(II) chloride solution in Figure 11 was increased using a Bunsen burner. The addition of energy caused the solution on that side to turn blue.

FIGURE 11: Energy in the form of heat is applied to the cobalt(II) chloride solution.

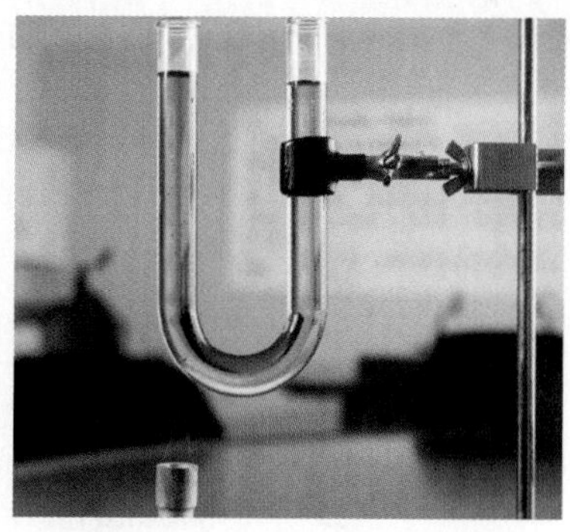

Collaborate With a partner, discuss what is happening on a molecular scale to cause the color on one side of the U-tube to change when the temperature increased.

ANALYZE Using the information in Figure 12, add the word *energy* to each equation as a product or reactant.

$$[Co(H_2O)_6]^{2+}(aq) + 4Cl^-(aq) \rightleftharpoons [CoCl_4]^{2-}(aq) + 6H_2O(l)$$

$$2NO_2(g) \rightleftharpoons N_2O_4(g)$$

APPLY Select the correct terms to describe how equilibrium shifts when energy is added.

For an endothermic reaction, adding energy in the form of heat shifts the reaction toward the products | reactants. In the cobalt(II) chloride system, adding energy formed more $[CoCl_4]^{2-}$ | $[Co(H_2O)_6]^{2+}$, causing the solution to turn blue. For an exothermic reaction, adding energy shifts the reaction toward the products | reactants. In the NO_2/N_2O_4 system, adding energy formed more NO_2 | N_2O_4.

The effect of adding or removing energy as heat from an equilibrium system can be predicted by considering energy as a product or reactant. For an endothermic reaction, energy can be modeled as a reactant. Adding energy has the same effect as increasing the concentration of a reactant, which shifts the equilibrium in favor of the products. Removing energy, like removing a reactant, shifts the reaction in favor of the reactants.

FIGURE 12: Equilibrium systems in an ice bath on the left and a warm temperature on the right

a Cobalt(II) chloride system—pink on the left and blue on the right

b Nitrogen dioxide/dinitrogen tetroxide system—light brown on the left and dark brown on the right

For an exothermic reaction, energy can be modeled as a product. Adding energy has the same effect as increasing the concentration of a product. The equilibrium shifts in favor of the reactants. Removing energy shifts the equilibrium in favor of the products.

Temperature and Equilibrium

Modifying the temperature of a system changes the average kinetic energy of the particles, which changes the number of effective collisions between molecules. For example, adding energy to the cobalt(II) chloride system increase the average kinetic energy of the particles and results in more effective collisions between reactants. This has the same effect as increasing the concentration of a reactant. The equilibrium will shift toward the products to relieve the stress. The reverse happens if energy is removed from the system. The equilibrium will shift toward the reactants.

$$\text{energy} + [Co(H_2O)_6]^{2+}(aq) + 4Cl^-(aq) \rightleftharpoons [CoCl_4]^{2-}(aq) + 6H_2O(l)$$

Changing the Temperature of a $CoCl_2$ Solution

FIGURE 13: The cobalt(II) chloride solution is initially at room temperature. Changing the temperature of the solution causes a change in the equilibrium concentrations.

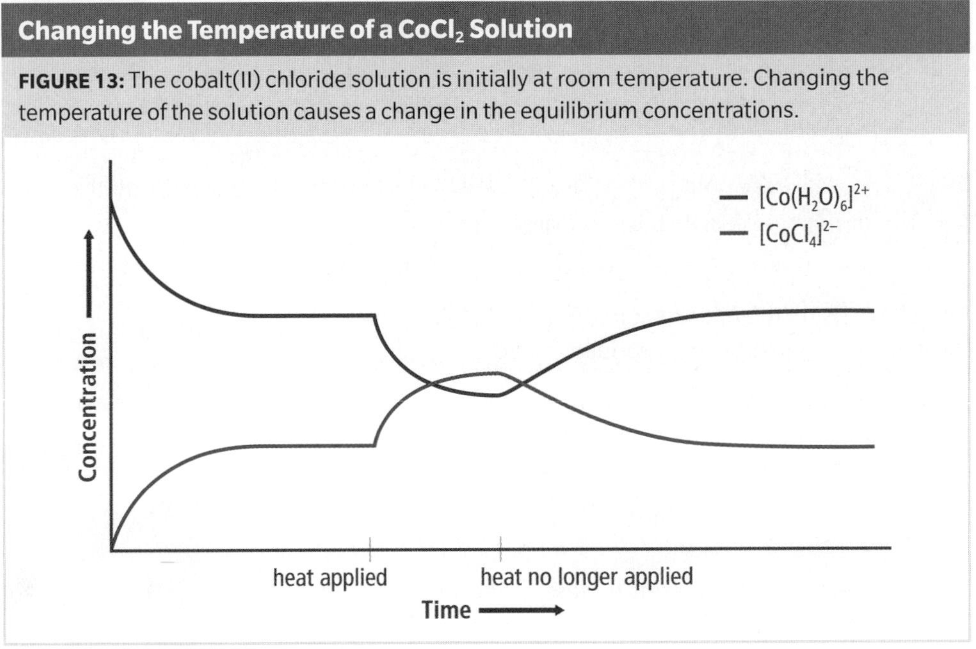

ANALYZE Based on Figure 13, which of the following statements are true? Select all correct answers.

- ☐ **a.** While heat is applied, a new equilibrium position is established.
- ☐ **b.** Increasing the temperature shifts the equilibrium toward $[CoCl_4]^{2-}$.
- ☐ **c.** When heat is no longer applied, the equilibrium returns to its original state.

Adding energy increases the concentration of $[CoCl_4]^{2-}$ in the solution, which changes the solution from pink to blue. This new equilibrium position can be maintained only as long as energy is added to the solution. When the solution is no longer heated, it changes from blue back to pink as the added energy dissipates and the equilibrium system shifts back to its original position.

Evidence Notebook What factors are used to control equilibrium in the Solvay process you are researching for your unit project?

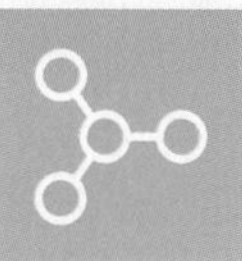

Temperature and Changing Oceans

Corals are marine invertebrates that mostly live in colonies consisting of many individual polyps. Coral reefs are formed from calcium carbonate, $CaCO_3$, that corals secrete in the process of forming their hard skeletons. Most corals display a range of colors, including brown, orange, red, yellow, and occasionally blue or green. The color comes not from the coral polyps, but from algae that live in the reef community. The corals provide habitat for the algae and, in exchange, corals receive food from the algae.

FIGURE 14: Bleached coral

Water temperatures in coral habitats are increasing due to climate change caused by human actions, most significantly the production of CO_2 through the burning of fossil fuels. As water temperatures increase, the corals become stressed and expel the algae. This is known as *coral bleaching* because the coral structure without the algae has a stark white color, shown in Figure 14. Bleached coral are still alive, but the bleaching increases the stress on the community even more. If they do not reincorporate the algae, the corals eventually die.

In 2005, the United States lost half of its coral reefs in the Caribbean in one year due to a massive bleaching event. And, coral bleaching is not the only consequence of rising ocean temperatures. Increasing temperatures also affect the amount of carbon dioxide that dissolves in the oceans. Concentration, pressure, and temperature have been discussed as stresses in a chemical system that can shift equilibria. In reality, all systems can be affected by stresses that change inputs, outputs, boundaries, and how parts interact.

EXPLAIN Discuss the relationship that exists among corals, algae, and water temperatures. Is this a chemical equilibrium? How does a stress on one component affect the rest of the system?

Evidence Notebook Warm temperatures allow bacteria in water to multiply quickly. Direct sunlight, which is common in warm climates, speeds up the release of chlorine gas from the water into the air because the OCl^- ions break down rapidly in sunlight. How would chlorine pool treatment need to change in a warmer climate?

Exploring Acids and Bases

Many substances can be classified as an acid or a base. When scientists first started using these terms, acids were described as things that tasted sour, such as vinegar or lime juice, and bases were things that tasted bitter or felt slippery, such as soap. As scientists learned more about the properties of acids and bases, they developed more exact definitions. Scientists now use these terms to describe substances based on how they chemically react with water and with other substances.

Collaborate Work with a partner or group to brainstorm questions you would like to investigate about acids and bases using the questions journalists ask: *Who? What? Where? When? Why? How?* Then share your questions with the class.

Properties of Acids and Bases

FIGURE 15: Many items that you use every day are acidic or basic.

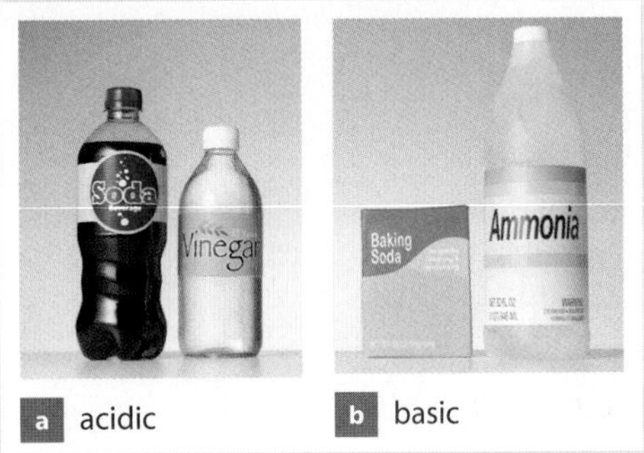

a acidic

b basic

Citric acid in limes and grapefruits gives these fruits their sour taste. Milk, yogurt, and sour cream contain lactic acid. Vinegar is dilute acetic acid. Acids react with bases and with some metals. Acid molecules generally contain one or more hydrogen atoms. When they are added to water, most acids form ions. If a substance does not exist as ions but forms ions in solution, the substance is said to *ionize*. If a substance exists as ions and these ions separate in solution, the substance is said to *dissociate*. The ionization of most acids leads to the release of hydrogen ions, H^+, into a solution. For example, nitric acid, HNO_3, forms the following ions in water:

$$HNO_3(l) \xrightarrow{H_2O} H^+(aq) + NO_3^-(aq)$$

When acids ionize, the solution has the capacity to conduct electric current. Therefore, an acid such as HNO_3 is an electrolyte. Strong acids ionize or dissociate completely in solution and are therefore strong electrolytes. Weak acids do not ionize or dissociate completely in solution and are therefore weak electrolytes. The strength of an acid is not related to its concentration. A strong acid can be dilute, and a weak acid can be concentrated. The strength of an acid is a measure of the degree to which it ionizes or dissociates.

Common bases include baking soda and sodium hydroxide, which is used in drain cleaner. Bases taste bitter and feel slick—the slick feel of some soaps is the result of the presence of a base. Bases react with acids, but usually not with metals. Some bases contain a hydroxide ion, OH^-. When added to water, these bases dissociate, releasing hydroxide ions into the solution. For example, sodium hydroxide, NaOH, dissociates in water to form sodium ions and hydroxide ions:

$$NaOH(s) \xrightarrow{H_2O} Na^+(aq) + OH^-(aq)$$

Similar to acids, bases can conduct electric current and may be described as strong or weak based on the degree to which they dissociate or ionize. The strength of an aqueous base depends on the number of hydroxide ions it produces in solution, not on the number of hydroxide ions in the base.

Acids Donate Protons

Hydrogen chloride, HCl, is a corrosive gas at room temperature. HCl is used for cleaning, pickling, and tanning, among other industrial applications. HCl initially ionizes in water to form H^+ and Cl^- ions in an aqueous solution. Almost immediately, the hydrogen ions released from the ionization of the HCl are attracted to negatively charged areas on water molecules, and form hydronium ions, H_3O^+.

$$H^+(aq) + Cl^-(aq) + H_2O(l) \rightarrow H_3O^+(aq) + Cl^-(aq)$$

Because a hydrogen atom is made up of one electron and one proton, a positive hydrogen ion is simply a proton. When HCl is in water, we say that a proton is transferred from the acid to the water, as shown in Figure 17. Thus, one way to define an acid is a substance that donates protons in solution.

FIGURE 16: Hydrochloric acid, sometimes called muriatic acid, is used to treat the water in swimming pools.

FIGURE 17: This molecular model shows that when hydrochloric acid is added to water, hydronium ions and chloride ions are formed.

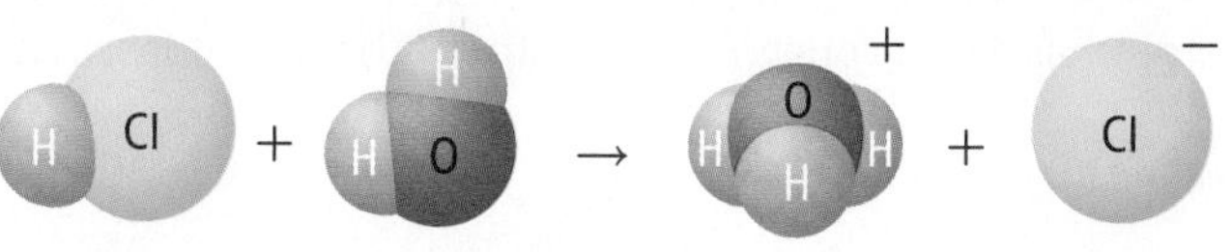

EXPLAIN Select the correct terms to complete the statement.

Sulfuric acid has the chemical formula H_2SO_4. When sulfuric acid interacts with water, protons are transferred to | from sulfuric acid to | from water, which produces hydroxide | hydronium ions.

Bases Accept Protons

The base ammonia, NH_3, is often found in household cleaners and is used in the production of fertilizer. Ammonia interacts with water to form ammonium ions and hydroxide ions:

$$NH_3(g) + H_2O(l) \rightarrow NH_4^+(aq) + OH^-(aq)$$

A base can be described as a substance that produces hydroxide ions in solution and accepts protons. Many bases, therefore, are metal hydroxides, such as sodium hydroxide, potassium hydroxide, and aluminum hydroxide. Ammonia is an example of a base that is a proton acceptor, as shown in Figure 18.

FIGURE 18: This molecular model shows that when ammonia is added to water, ammonium ions and hydroxide ions are formed.

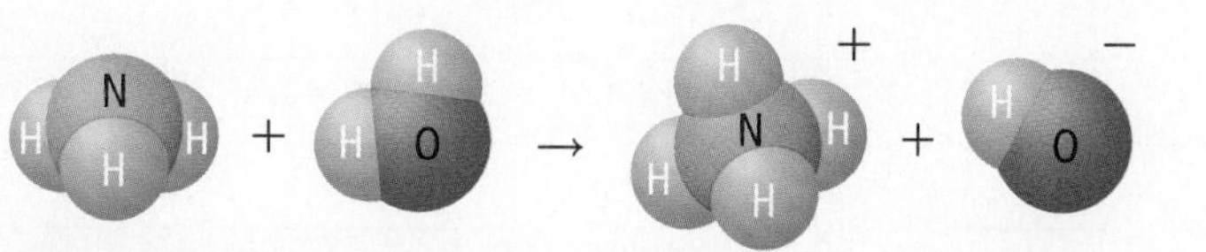

EXPLAIN Select the correct terms to complete the statement.

When ammonia is mixed with water, a proton is transferred to | from ammonia to | from water, which produces hydroxide | hydronium ions.

Engineering

The pH Scale

Acids form aqueous solutions with extra hydronium ions, and bases form solutions with extra hydroxide ions. A *neutral* solution contains equal amounts of both ions. Scientists can determine how acidic or basic a solution is by measuring the concentration of hydronium ions. Scientists use the pH scale for this measurement. The letters pH stand for the French *pouvoir hydrogène*, meaning "hydrogen power." pH is defined by the equation:

$$pH = -\log[H_3O^+]$$

The equation for pH is an example of a logarithmic function. The common logarithm, log, of a number is the power to which 10 must be raised to equal the number. When calculating pH, you take the negative of the log. So, if the hydronium ion concentration of a solution is 10^{-4} M, the log is −4. The pH is then −(−4), or 4. The pH scale allows scientists to model these large changes in concentration without the need for scientific notation.

FIGURE 19: The logarithmic pH scale

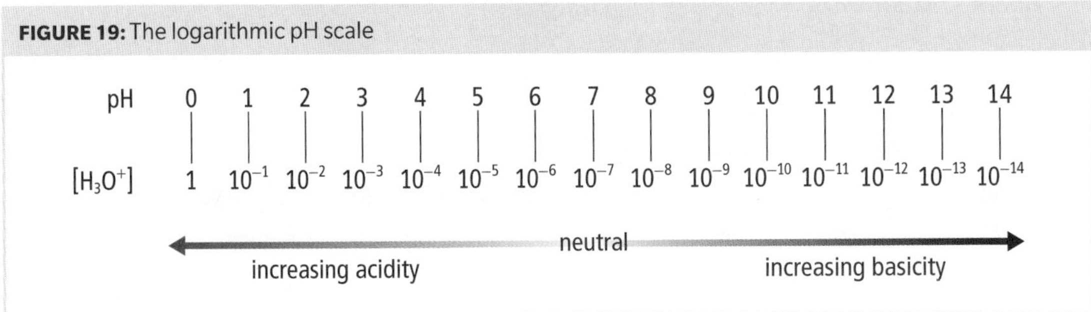

In treated pool water, an equilibrium exists between HOCl and H^+ and OCl^- ions. The pH scale is particularly useful for pool managers who have to decide how to adjust the chemicals in the pool water. The ideal pH of a swimming pool is 7.5. Above a pH of 7.8, the concentration of OCl^- ions in the water is too high. The OCl^- ions break down rapidly in sunlight and the chlorine is released as gas into the atmosphere. Therefore, having a high concentration of OCl^- ions at any given time can lead to losing too much chlorine from the system. Below a pH of 7.2, the concentration of HOCl becomes irritating to swimmers. Algae also flourish in this pH range. Pool managers test pool water using an acid-base indicator that changes color depending on the solution pH and the indicator being used.

IDENTIFY CONSTRAINTS What constraints guide the chemical treatment of a pool that an entire community uses? Think about the number one necessity for public pools, then consider other common constraints that may limit solutions. What happens to the water if the pool has to be drained?

Hands-On Lab

Analyzing Acids and Bases

Have you ever heard the term *acid* referenced in a movie or television show? If so, the acid was probably very strong and highly corrosive. It could have been powerful enough to eat through metal or dissolve evidence of a crime. Although these extreme applications of acids may be common storylines for entertainment, acids and bases are actually used in everyday household items. In this lab, you will design a procedure to determine whether several household substances are acidic or basic in solution based on the pH scale. Then, you will analyze what happens when you combine a strong acid and a strong base.

RESEARCH QUESTION Are there patterns to the way we use acids and bases in household products? Are acids better suited to certain tasks, and bases to other tasks?

MAKE A CLAIM

Predict whether each household substance will be acidic or basic. What do you think will happen when you combine a strong acid and a strong base?

MATERIALS

- indirectly vented chemical splash goggles, nonlatex apron, nitrile gloves
- chalk (contains calcium carbonate, $CaCO_3$)
- conductivity probe
- deionized water in wash bottle
- droppers
- HCl solution, 0.1 M, in dropper bottle
- NaOH solution, 0.1 M, in dropper bottle
- pH paper and pH probe
- well plate
- household substances in solution: baking soda, coffee, glass cleaner, lemon juice, milk of magnesia, seltzer water, soapy water, vinegar

SAFETY INFORMATION

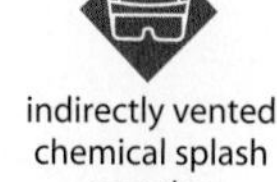

indirectly vented chemical splash goggles

- Wear indirectly vented chemical splash goggles, a nonlatex apron, and nitrile gloves during the setup, hands-on, and takedown segments of the activity.
- Never taste any substance or chemical in the lab. Tell your teacher immediately if you spill chemicals on yourself, the work surface, or floor.

PLAN THE INVESTIGATION

In your Evidence Notebook, develop procedures and safety plans for the following experiments. Have your teacher approve your plans before proceeding. If you need additional materials, discuss these with your teacher.

Part 1 Determine whether each household substance is acidic or basic. Consider properties such as pH, reactivity, and electrolytic behavior. Discuss the order in which you should make observations and how to best conserve time and materials. For example, if you placed 10 drops of lemon juice in a well plate, how could you most effectively perform multiple tests on the same 10 drops of this solution?

Part 2 Determine the pH of HCl, NaOH, and the solution produced when they are combined in equal parts. With your group, discuss appropriate procedures for safely making a solution composed of equal parts 0.1 M hydrochloric acid and 0.1 M sodium hydroxide. How will you make the solution, and how will you safely measure its pH?

COLLECT DATA

Make a data table in your Evidence Notebook in which to record your observations for both experiments. Decide on what you will measure, how many times you will take measurements, and the accuracy of measurements needed to produce quality data.

CONSTRUCT AN EXPLANATION

Answer the following questions in your Evidence Notebook.

1. What does the pH value tell you about each solution? What do the conductivity and reactivity tests tell you about each solution?
2. What did you notice about the pH of the solution made up of equal parts acid and base? What types of molecular-scale interactions might account for your observations?
3. What are the limitations of the data you collected during this lab? Describe how you could refine your procedure to improve the accuracy and precision of your data.

DRAW CONCLUSIONS

Claim Which solutions that you tested are acidic and which are basic? What happened when you combined a strong acid and a strong base?

Evidence Cite evidence from your data to support your claim. Include a chemical equation for the reaction in Part 2.

Reasoning Explain how the data you cited support your claim. What is the connection between the properties you observed and the acid-base reaction?

EXTEND

In Part 2, you combined a strong acid and a strong base. What would happen if HCl was instead combined with a weak base and NaOH was instead combined with a weak acid?

Evidence Notebook Explain why the concentration of HOCl in pool water would change if the pool pH was increased or decreased.

Analyzing Acid-Base Equilibrium Systems

When an acid and a base are combined, the products are water and a salt. A salt is formed from the cation of a base and the anion of an acid. The HCl and NaOH reaction you performed as part of your lab was an example of this type of acid-base reaction. The salt solution produced in an acid-base reaction may be acidic, basic, or neutral, depending on the strength of the reactants.

Collaborate With a partner, identify the salts that will form when nitric acid, HNO_3, and potassium hydroxide, KOH, are combined and when nitric acid and calcium hydroxide, $Ca(OH)_2$, are combined. What combinations of strong and weak acids and bases will produce an acidic, basic, or neutral solution? Which of these solutions will form an equilibrium?

Acids and Bases in Solution

Because not all acids and bases are the same, the equilibrium point of an acid-base reaction is determined by the properties of both the acid and the base. Figure 20 shows how strong acids, such as HCl, ionize in water. All of the HCl ionizes to form H_3O^+ ions and Cl^- ions. In weak acids, such as acetic acid, $HC_2H_3O_2$, hydrogen atoms are bound more tightly, so only some of the $HC_2H_3O_2$ molecules ionize.

FIGURE 20: Strong acids form more hydronium ions in solution than weak acids do.

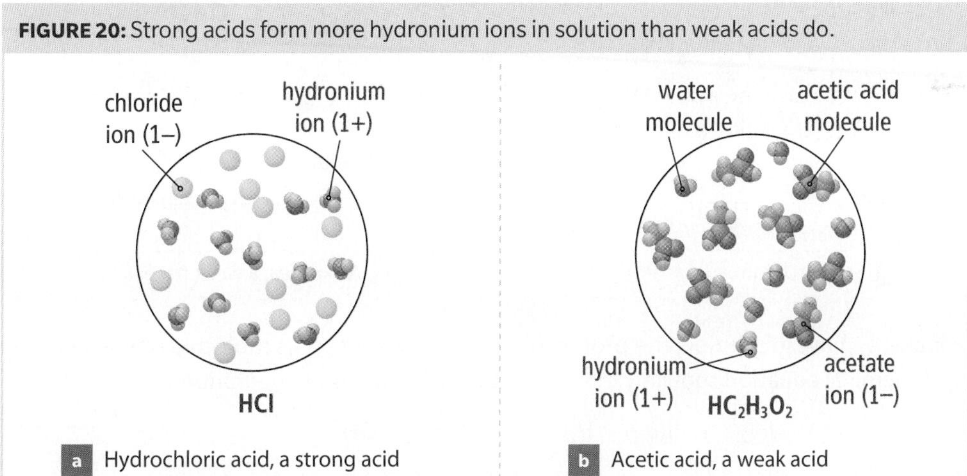

a Hydrochloric acid, a strong acid

b Acetic acid, a weak acid

EVALUATE Figure 21 shows solid calcium carbonate, $CaCO_3$, in hydrochloric acid in the left beaker, and in acetic acid, $HC_2H_3O_2$, in the right beaker. Make a claim for whether $CaCO_3$ reacts more vigorously with HCl than with $HC_2H_3O_2$. Use evidence from Figures 20 and 21 to support your claim, and explain your reasoning.

FIGURE 21: Reactions of $CaCO_3$ with HCl and $HC_2H_3O_2$ solutions

Strong acids ionize completely in water and no reactant molecules remain. Weak acids do not ionize completely. Thus, when a weak acid is combined with water, some amount of reactant is still present, and an equilibrium forms. The behavior of a weak acid can be written in the form of a chemical equilibrium equation. In this equation, HA represents a weak acid, such as acetic acid. The negative ion (A^-) formed in solution is known as that acid's *conjugate base*. In the reverse reaction, the conjugate base can accept a proton, like bases would.

$$HA(aq) + H_2O(l) \rightleftharpoons H_3O^+(aq) + A^-(aq)$$

ANALYZE How could you make more conjugate base in this equilibrium system? Select all correct answers.

☐ **a.** add more acid

☐ **b.** increase the pressure

☐ **c.** remove hydronium ions

☐ **d.** remove water molecules

Figure 22 shows how a strong base, such as sodium hydroxide, NaOH, dissociates completely in water, producing many hydroxide ions. A weak base, such as ammonia, NH_3, produces few hydroxide ions in solution.

FIGURE 22: Strong bases produce more hydroxide ions in solution than do weak bases do.

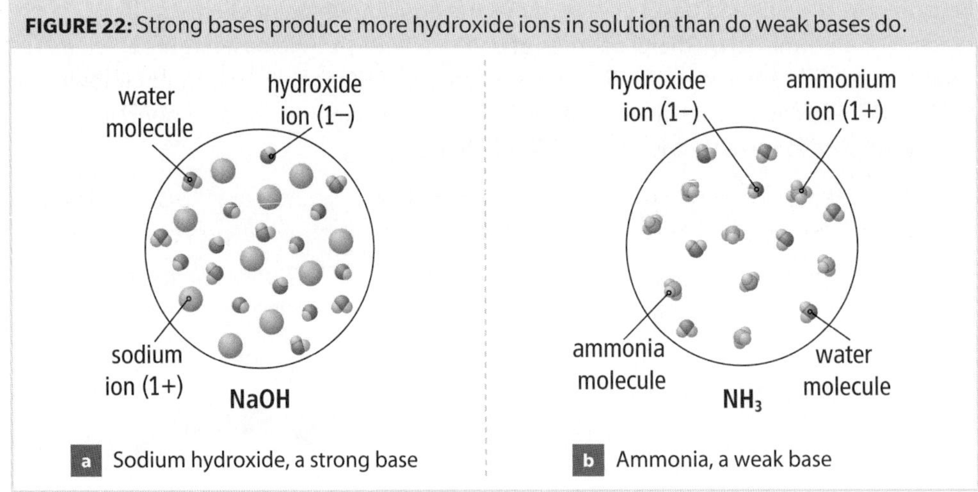

a Sodium hydroxide, a strong base

b Ammonia, a weak base

For a weak base in solution, the proton-transfer reaction of some molecules can be written as a chemical equation showing the reactants and products at equilibrium:

$$B(aq) + H_2O(l) \rightleftharpoons BH^+(aq) + OH^-(aq)$$

The positive ion, BH^+, is known as the weak base's *conjugate acid*. In the reverse reaction, the conjugate acid can donate a proton. Each pair of related molecules or ions forms a conjugate acid-base pair. Thus, HA, an acid, forms A^-, its conjugate base, and HA and A^- are a conjugate pair. Likewise, B, a base, forms BH^+, its conjugate acid, and together B and BH^+ are a conjugate pair.

Strong acids and strong bases are highly reactive, but their conjugates are only slightly reactive. In contrast, weak acids and weak bases are only slightly reactive, but their conjugates are more reactive.

Neutralization Reactions and Buffers

You have probably heard different forms of the term *neutralization* used in everyday life, such as neutralizing an odor or a country remaining neutral during a war. In chemistry, a *neutralization reaction* is one in which an acid and a base react to form a salt and water with a neutral pH. The individual properties of the acid and base are neutralized by the reaction between the two solutions.

EXPLAIN Select the correct terms to complete the statement.

HCl forms many | few hydronium ions in solution, and NH_3 produces many | few hydroxide ions in solution. When equal amounts of HCl and NH_3 are combined, there will be an excess of hydronium | hydroxide ions. The solution will be slightly acidic | basic. NaOH produces many | few hydroxide ions in solution, and $HC_2H_3O_2$ produces many | few hydronium ions. When equal amounts of NaOH and $HC_2H_3O_2$ are combined, there will be an excess of hydronium | hydroxide ions. The solution will be slightly acidic | basic.

A *buffer* is a solution of a weak acid and one of its salts, or a weak base and one of its salts. Buffers resist changes in pH. For example, a buffered solution can be made by combining equal concentrations of acetic acid and sodium acetate. If a strong base is added, the acetic acid neutralizes it. The equilibrium with the salt shifts, so there is little or no change in pH. If a strong acid is added, the conjugate base neutralizes it, and the equilibrium shifts, again maintaining the pH. Eventually, enough base may be added to completely neutralize the acid, and a large pH change occurs.

MODEL With a group, construct a mathematical model or graph that shows how the acid-base equilibrium changes and the hydronium ion concentration changes in a buffered solution as a strong acid or base is added

FIGURE 23: Aspirin is acidic and is buffered to prevent large changes in pH within the body.

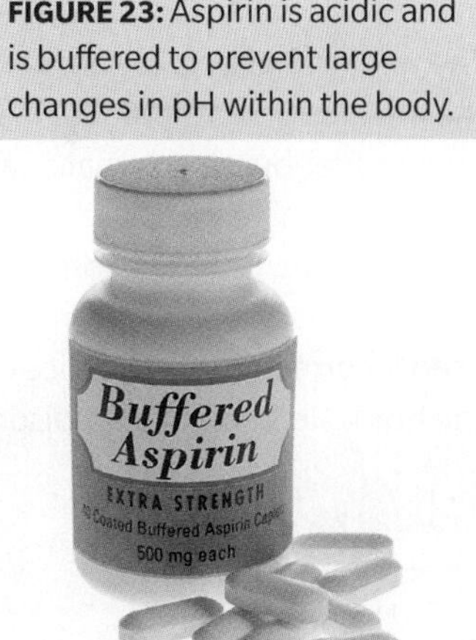

Buffer action has many important applications in chemistry and physiology. Human blood is naturally buffered to maintain a pH of between 7.3 and 7.5. This is essential because large changes in pH would lead to serious disturbances of normal body functions. Figure 23 shows an example of one of the many medicines that are buffered to prevent large and potentially damaging changes in pH when medication is taken orally or intravenously.

Evidence Notebook The ideal equilibrium for pool water is equal concentrations of HOCl and OCl^- ions. This occurs at a pH of 7.5. Explain how you would treat a pool that has a pH of 6.5 and a pool that has a pH of 8.5 in order to restore the ideal equilibrium.

Language Arts

Carbon Monoxide Poisoning

Every year, more than 400 people in the U.S. die from carbon monoxide, CO, poisoning, and approximately 50 000 more people require hospital treatment for CO exposure. What causes carbon monoxide's harmful effects on human health and the environment?

Carbon monoxide is a product of the incomplete combustion of carbon-containing fuels, including coal, petroleum products, and natural gas. When these fuels burn in pure oxygen, most carbon atoms are converted to CO_2. However, when O_2 is a limiting factor, CO may form as one of the combustion products.

The majority of CO in the atmosphere comes from automobile emissions. Atmospheric CO reacts with hydroxyl radicals, OH, to form CO_2, a greenhouse gas. This reaction also affects climate change by reducing the concentration of hydroxyl radicals in the atmosphere. These radicals are able to break down methane and other pollutants in the atmosphere.

The negative effects of carbon monoxide extend from the environment to human health. For example, inside homes, fuel-burning furnaces are designed to vent the CO-containing exhaust gases into the atmosphere. During power outages, some people use portable fuel-fired heaters and generators that are not vented. When used incorrectly, these devices can release exhaust into the home, leading to CO poisoning.

APPLY How can you minimize exposure to carbon monoxide when burning carbon-containing fuel?

- ○ **a.** Burn fuel in areas with low oxygen.
- ○ **b.** Burn fuel in enclosed spaces with ventilation.
- ○ **c.** Burn fuel in enclosed spaces without ventilation.

In addition to ensuring that fuel-burning devices are operated properly, carbon monoxide detectors may be used in the home to alert people when CO levels become dangerous. Incidents of CO poisoning increase during events that cause disruption of electrical or natural gas service, such as natural disasters.

What is the mechanism of CO poisoning? In the human body, O_2 is absorbed by blood as it passes through the lungs. The O_2 moves through the body bound to hemoglobin molecules in the blood. Each hemoglobin molecule can bind up to four O_2 molecules in a reversible reaction, forming oxyhemoglobin $Hb(O_2)_4$. Hb represents hemoglobin.

$$Hb(aq) + 4O_2(g) \rightleftharpoons Hb(O_2)_4(aq)$$

When carbon monoxide is inhaled, CO molecules bind to hemoglobin in place of O_2 and form carboxyhemoglobin. CO binds to hemoglobin more tightly than O_2 does, and so the product is favored.

$$Hb(aq) + 4CO(g) \rightleftharpoons Hb(CO)_4(aq)$$

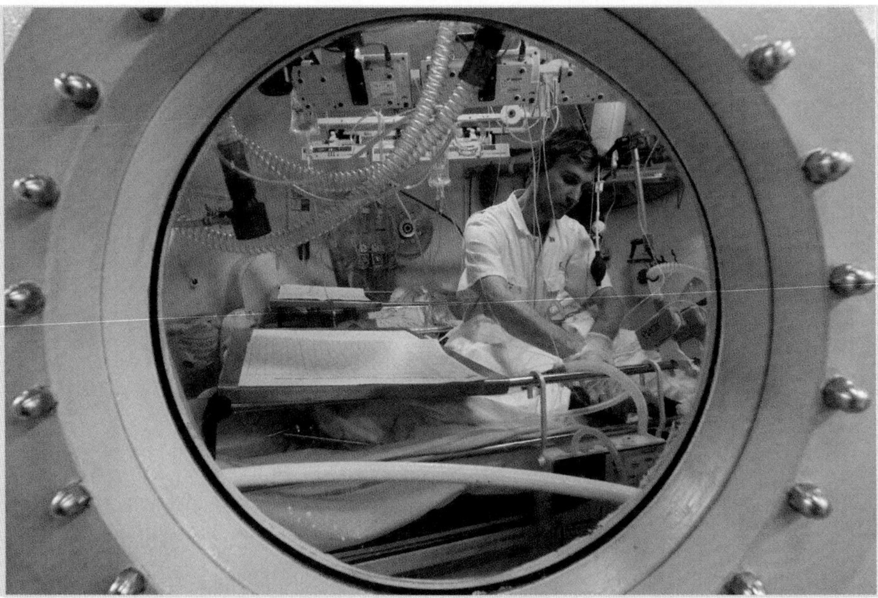

FIGURE 24: A hyperbaric oxygen chamber can be used to treat carbon monoxide poisoning.

Because of the binding power of CO, some of the hemoglobin in a person who has been breathing CO cannot bind with oxygen. O_2 is blocked from reaching the cells, and cells cannot carry out vital processes. The most effective way of treating CO poisoning is to replace the CO with O_2 using this equilibrium reaction:

$$Hb(CO)_4(aq) + 4O_2(g) \rightleftharpoons Hb(O_2)_4(aq) + 4CO(g)$$

ANALYZE In which direction would you force this equilibrium to make a person with CO poisoning better sooner? What conditions would you change to shift the equilibrium? Use evidence to support your claim.

In mild cases of carbon monoxide poisoning, breathing pure oxygen is sufficient treatment to remove CO from the hemoglobin. Periodically, CO is exhaled and leaves the equilibrium system, allowing oxygen to be bound by hemoglobin. In more severe cases, it may be preferable to use a hyperbaric chamber, shown in Figure 24, for treatment. The patient is placed in a chamber where the air pressure is increased by two or three times that of normal air pressure. These conditions increase the concentration of O_2 present in the blood as well as the rate of the reaction in which CO is replaced by O_2, so the patient recovers faster.

Language Arts Connection Create a pamphlet that helps people recognize the risks of carbon monoxide emissions and poisoning. Explain why CO is dangerous in terms that someone who has not studied chemistry could understand. Use multiple sources to research devices that release CO, how the levels of released CO are measured, and how these devices have changed over time to be safer. How could these devices be improved to reduce the amount of CO released? What are the costs and benefits associated with improving these devices?

MODEL Diagram at the molecular level the equilibrium shift that occurs in the hemoglobin, oxygen gas, and carbon monoxide gas equilibrium system in a person recovering from carbon monoxide poisoning.

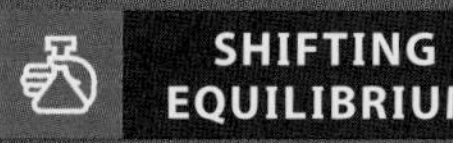
SHIFTING EQUILIBRIUM | EQUILIBRIUM IN THE HUMAN BODY | PRACTICE WITH THE EQUILIBRIUM CONSTANT

Go online to choose one of these other paths.

Lesson Self-Check

CAN YOU EXPLAIN THE PHENOMENON?

FIGURE 25: Swimming pool water is treated to protect the health of the swimmers.

Keeping swimming pool water clean and free of harmful bacteria is important for the health of the people swimming in the pool. Large debris is removed from pools by physical filters. Smaller pollutants are commonly treated with chemicals. Hypochlorous acid, HOCl, is used to treat pools because it destroys harmful bacteria and other microscopic contaminants.

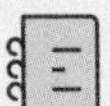

Evidence Notebook Refer to your notes in your Evidence Notebook to make a claim about how a chemical equilibrium system is used to treat pool water. Your explanation should include a discussion of the following points:

Claim How can an equilibrium system in swimming pools be managed to provide safe water for swimmers?

Evidence What evidence supports the idea that reactions at equilibrium produce chemicals that are harmful to bacteria? How does the pH of the swimming pool water affect the equilibrium?

Reasoning How does the evidence you provided support your claim about the chemical equilibrium used to treat pool water?

Name Date

CHECKPOINTS

Check Your Understanding

1. Select the correct terms to complete the statement about the pH scale.

The pH of a solution is a measure of the concentration of the hydroxide | hydronium ions it contains. The pH can be calculated by finding $\log[H_3O^+]$ | $\log[OH^-]$ | $-\log[H_3O^+]$ | $-\log[OH^-]$. The pH of milk is about 6.6, so milk is acidic | basic | neutral. The pH of soapy water is about 12, so soapy water is acidic | basic | neutral.

2. Which of the following are true of a chemical reaction at equilibrium? Select all correct answers.

- ☐ **a.** The forward and reverse reactions proceed at the same rate.
- ☐ **b.** The concentrations of the reactants and the products are the same.
- ☐ **c.** The rate of the forward reaction is greater than the rate of the reverse reaction.
- ☐ **d.** The concentrations of the reactants may differ from those of the products.

3. Which of these shows an acid followed by its conjugate base?

- ○ **a.** HSO_4^-, H_2SO_4
- ○ **b.** HCl, NaCl
- ○ **c.** HCO_3^-, CO_3^{2-}
- ○ **d.** H_2O, H_3O^+

4. Increasing the concentration of a reactant in an equilibrium system

- ○ **a.** shifts the equilibrium toward the products.
- ○ **b.** shifts the equilibrium toward the reactants.
- ○ **c.** does not shift the equilibrium.

5. Decreasing the temperature of an endothermic equilibrium system

- ○ **a.** shifts the equilibrium toward the products.
- ○ **b.** shifts the equilibrium toward the reactants.
- ○ **c.** does not shift the equilibrium.

Use the following information to answer Question 6.

Historically, sulfur dioxide, SO_2, generated from the burning of coal has been a major precursor to acid precipitation by way of its conversion to sulfur trioxide, SO_3, and its subsequent reaction with water.

Imagine you have a sealed vessel containing the following equilibrium system:

$$2SO_3(g) \rightleftharpoons 2SO_2(g) + O_2(g)$$

6. Select the correct terms to complete the statement about how the equilibrium will shift under the following conditions.

Decreasing the pressure of the container will produce more SO_3 | SO_2 | O_2 | SO_2 and O_2. Decreasing the volume of the container will produce more SO_3 | SO_2.

7. Under what conditions will increasing the pressure on a gaseous equilibrium system shift the equilibrium? Select all correct answers.

- ☐ **a.** A shift will further increase the pressure on a system.
- ☐ **b.** A shift will decrease the pressure on a system.
- ☐ **c.** A shift will increase the number of molecules in the system.
- ☐ **d.** A shift will decrease the number of molecules in the system.
- ☐ **e.** There are an unequal number of moles in the reactants and the products.
- ☐ **f.** There are an equal number of moles in the reactants and the products.

8. Which of the following examples involve an acid-base equilibrium system? Select all correct answers.

- ☐ **a.** a weak base reacting with water
- ☐ **b.** a strong acid reacting with water
- ☐ **c.** a strong acid reacting with a weak base dissolved in water
- ☐ **d.** a strong base reacting with a strong acid dissolved in water

CHECKPOINTS (continued)

9. Consider the generic reaction: $A + B \rightleftharpoons C + D$. If you start with only A and B, how do the rates of the forward and reverse reactions change as the reaction progresses? What can be predicted about the concentrations once the reaction reaches equilibrium? Does the reaction ever stop completely?

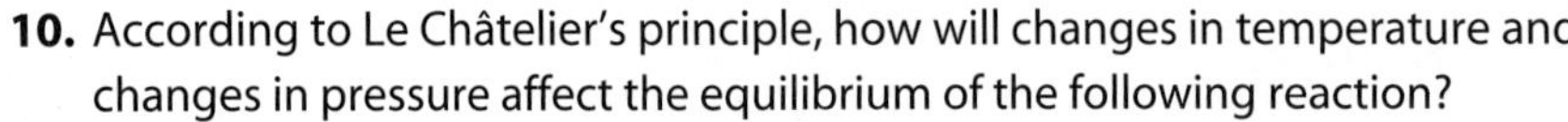

10. According to Le Châtelier's principle, how will changes in temperature and changes in pressure affect the equilibrium of the following reaction?

$$CO(g) + 3H_2(g) \rightleftharpoons CH_4(g) + H_2O(g) + \text{energy}$$

11. Phosphoric acid, H_3PO_4, is a weak acid and is found in many soft drinks. Hydrochloric acid, HCl, is a strong acid that is toxic if ingested. Explain how the degree of ionization differs for these two acids and how this difference affects their properties at the larger scale.

MAKE YOUR OWN STUDY GUIDE

In your Evidence Notebook, design a study guide that supports the main ideas from this lesson:

Reversible reaction systems form a state of equilibrium when the forward and reverse reactions occur at the same rate.

Le Châtelier's principle states that an equilibrium system responds to a stress, such as changing pressure, temperature, or concentration of reactants or products, by shifting the equilibrium in order to relieve that stress.

Remember to include the following information in your study guide:

- Use examples that model main ideas.
- Record explanations for the phenomena you investigated.
- Use evidence to support your explanations. Your support can include drawings, data, graphs, laboratory conclusions, and other evidence recorded throughout the lesson.

Consider how the microscale models for macroscale equilibrium you have developed in this lesson can be used to analyze the stability and change of many different types of systems.

5.3

Analyzing Chemical Systems

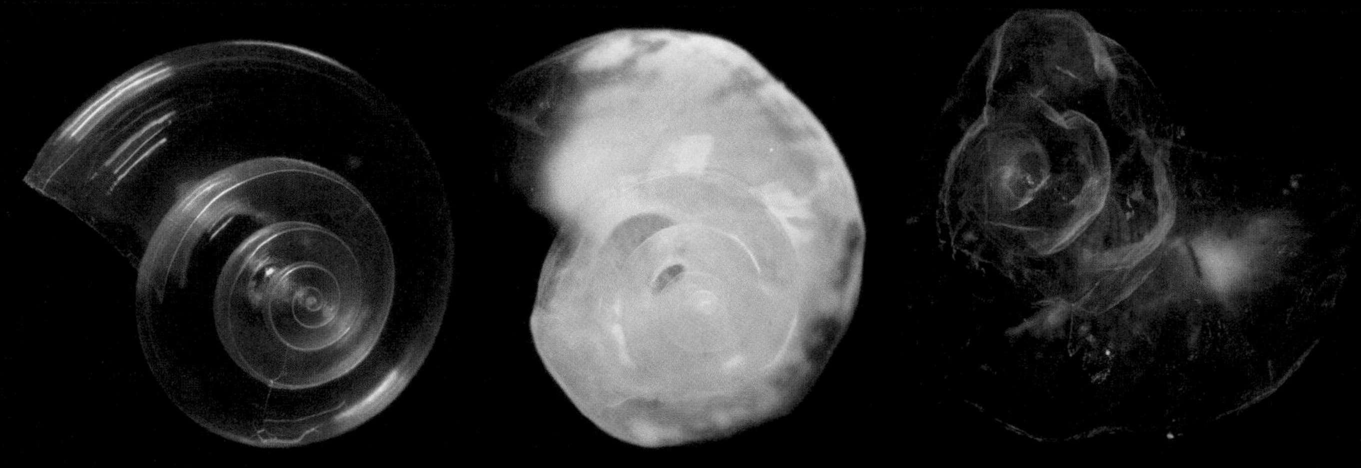

Pteropod shells degrade when ocean carbon dioxide levels increase.

CAN YOU EXPLAIN THE PHENOMENON?

Scientists and engineers must find ways to understand complex questions and problems in order to reach conclusions and develop solutions. In this lesson, you will investigate ways to explain the complex relationship between carbon dioxide, which is a product of respiration and of fossil fuel combustion, and the ability of some marine organisms to grow shells. These seemingly unrelated processes are linked by a series of equilibrium reactions, which in turn are linked to the cycling of matter and energy in the Earth system.

Some pteropods, also known as sea snails, and other marine organisms have shells and skeletons made of calcium carbonate, $CaCO_3$. These structures are built from calcium and carbonate ions in ocean water. The concentration of carbonate ions in the water depends on the amount of carbon dioxide, CO_2, dissolved in the ocean. Human activity has dramatically increased the concentration of atmospheric CO_2 over the past 50–100 years. This means that the amount of CO_2 dissolved in the ocean has also increased. The calcium carbonate structures of some marine organisms are degrading in response to this shift.

ANALYZE How might Le Châtelier's principle be related to the degradation of calcium carbonate structures in marine animals?

Evidence Notebook As you explore the lesson, gather evidence to help you explain the link between carbon dioxide emissions and shell degradation. How can you develop and use models to explain shell degradation at the atomic scale and at the macroscopic scale?

Defining Chemical Systems

As you have seen, chemistry involves the study of matter and its interactions at many different scales. Whether studying a nuclear reaction or optimizing a heat pack, chemists and engineers must first identify the scope and relevant components of the question or problem they are addressing. Often, they do this by defining the system or set of systems involved in the question or problem. How can chemical systems be defined, modeled, and refined to help study phenomena or solve problems?

Collaborate Discuss with a partner how a chemical reaction can be viewed as a system. What parts of the system are described when the reaction is modeled with a chemical equation? Are there parts of the system that are not included in this type of model?

A Chemical System in the Natural World

The Earth system is a dynamic, complex set of interacting chemical, physical, and biological components, processes, and cycles, all involving a variety of systems and subsystems. The carbon cycle, shown in Figure 1, is one of the ways Earth's subsystems are interconnected. Some of the most pressing problems facing scientists and engineers—such as energy production and climate change—involve the carbon cycle. Plants, algae, and other photosynthetic organisms require carbon dioxide to produce glucose for energy and release carbon dioxide as a product of respiration. Humans also release large amounts of carbon dioxide into the atmosphere by extracting and burning fossil fuels.

FIGURE 1: The carbon cycle involves interactions among all of Earth's subsystems.

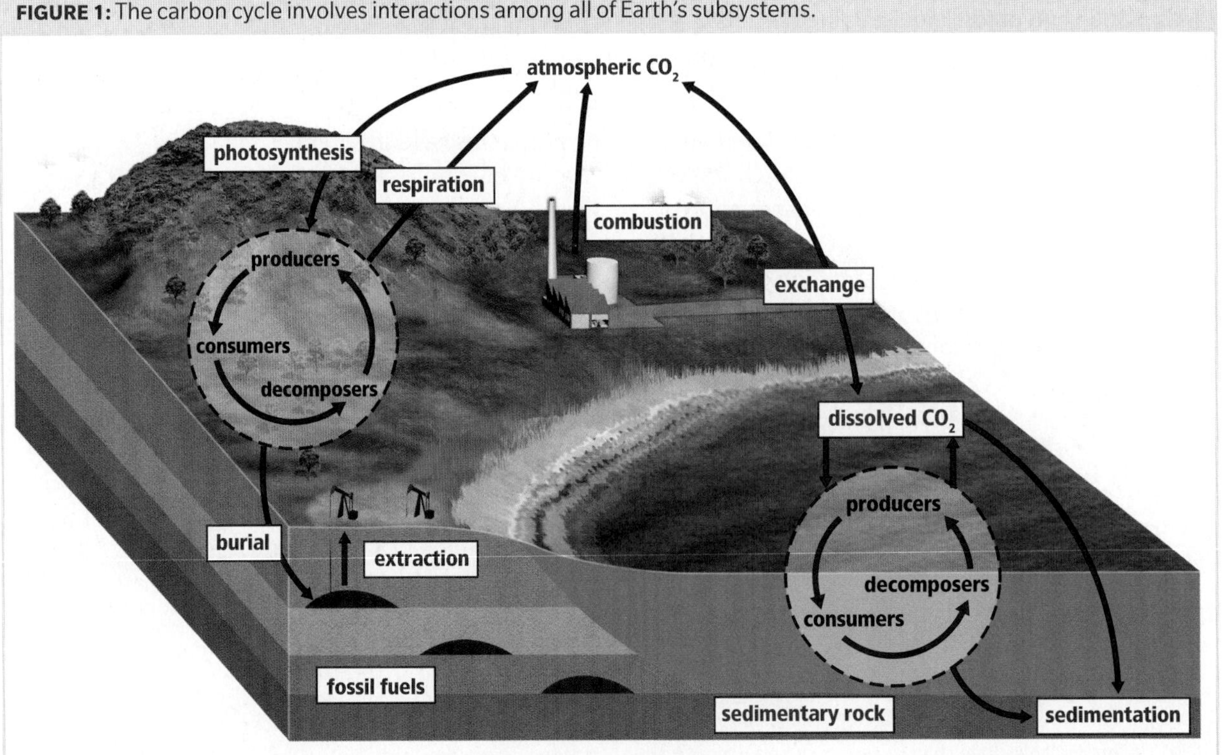

APPLY How might a global decrease in use of fossil fuels, such as coal to generate electrical energy, affect the system shown in Figure 1? Select all correct answers.

- ☐ **a.** Photosynthesis would happen more often.
- ☐ **b.** Atmospheric carbon dioxide concentrations would decrease.
- ☐ **c.** Cellular respiration would increase.
- ☐ **d.** Less carbon dioxide would dissolve in the oceans.

As Figure 1 shows, the matter in fossil fuels does not disappear when extracted and burned for energy. Rather, like all matter in a closed system, the carbon released during the combustion of fossil fuels moves to another part of the system in a different form.

A Chemical System in the Designed World

Reactions and processes occurring in natural systems can be difficult, and sometimes impossible, to control. For example, solar energy may produce an excess of electrical energy on a sunny day, but very little electrical energy on a rainy day. Scientists and engineers use their understanding of chemical systems and of Earth's systems to find ways to capture and store this energy, including by recharging electrochemical batteries.

DEFINE What are three criteria for a designed system that stores electrical energy?

Most batteries work by converting chemical energy into electrical energy. This is done via an oxidation-reduction reaction, in which electrons are transferred from one substance to another. In some oxidation-reduction reactions, energy is released as heat. But batteries use this reaction in a system called an electrochemical cell, which generates electrical energy instead of energy as heat.

Consider a strip of zinc metal in a copper(II) sulfate solution. In this reaction, zinc loses electrons and has been oxidized. Copper(II) gains electrons and is said to have been reduced, because its charge has been reduced. When the copper(II) ions are reduced, they fall out of solution as copper atoms. This can be seen as a layer of copper on the zinc bar in the beaker on the right in Figure 2.

Explore Online

YOU SOLVE IT

How Can You Design a Battery? Optimize the voltage and energy storage in an electric vehicle battery by changing the composition of the electrodes.

FIGURE 2: The blue color of the copper sulfate solution is due to the presence of the copper(II) ions. The solution becomes lighter in color as copper ions in the solution are replaced by zinc ions. The copper atoms replace zinc atoms on the zinc bar.

We can model the changes in the zinc and copper species as:

$$Zn(s) + Cu^{2+}(aq) \rightarrow Cu(s) + Zn^{2+}(aq)$$

If the substance that is being oxidized is separated from the substance that is being reduced, as shown in Figure 3, the electron transfer is accompanied by a transfer of electrical energy instead of energy as heat. This is how an electrochemical cell operates. This name comes from the transformation from chemical energy to electrical energy that occurs in the cell. Inside an electrochemical cell are two electrodes—the negative anode and the positive cathode. Each electrode is in contact with an electrolyte, in what is called a half-cell.

One means of separating oxidation and reduction reactions is by separating them with a porous barrier, or salt bridge. The salt bridge permits the flow of ions, but not metal atoms, between the solutions. Ions in the two solutions can move across the salt bridge, which keeps a precipitate from building up on the electrodes, as you saw in Figure 2. Electrons can be transferred from the anode to the cathode through an external connecting wire.

In the electrochemical cell shown in Figure 3, the half-cell on the left is composed of a zinc anode submerged in a solution of zinc sulfate, $ZnSO_4$. The half-cell on the right is composed of a copper cathode submerged in a solution of copper sulfate, $CuSO_4$.

FIGURE 3: The reactions in this electrochemical cell cause electrons to build up on the zinc electrode (left). When the circuit is completed, electrons flow through the circuit to the copper electrode (right).

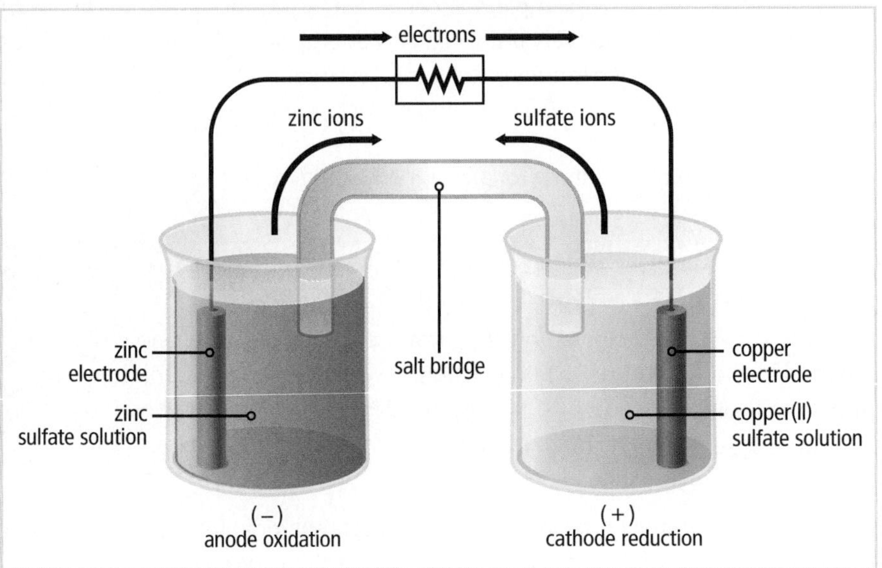

EXPLAIN Select the correct terms to complete the statement explaining how electrons and ions move in an electrochemical cell.

Electrons | Ions spontaneously flow through the connecting wire from the anode to the cathode. The anode loses | gains electrons, and the cathode loses | gains electrons. Electrons | Ions in the solution move across the salt bridge. If the half-cells were not separated, current would continue to flow | stop flowing.

The electrochemical cell in Figure 3 is called a wet cell battery, because the electrolyte solutions are liquid. However, everyday electronics are usually powered by dry cell batteries, which use a paste electrolyte. Batteries may also have one or more electrochemical cells. The batteries in a flashlight contain only one cell. Other batteries, such as small 9-volt batteries and most 12-volt car batteries, contain several cells in series.

Evidence Notebook The chemical equation for the Zn and Cu^{2+} reaction and the diagram of an electrochemical cell are both models of electrochemical reactions. How could you use these two types of models to explain the link between carbon dioxide emissions and shell degradation?

Engineering Lab

Storing a Charge

You are probably familiar with the batteries used to power devices such as calculators, watches, and toys. These batteries are most likely zinc-carbon batteries, alkaline batteries, or lithium ion batteries. All of these batteries convert chemical energy to electrical energy. Electrical energy is converted into chemical energy when rechargeable batteries are in a recharge cycle. In this investigation, you will design a system that uses common household items to generate electrical energy to power a small LED bulb. With your classmates, you will investigate how different combinations of these materials affect the design's performance.

The items that you will use for this investigation act as an electrochemical cell. Recall that in an electrochemical cell, electrons are lost during a chemical reaction at the *anode*. Electrons are gained in a chemical reaction at the *cathode*. The flow of electrons from the anode to the cathode makes up the electrical current.

DESIGN CHALLENGE The class has been tasked with figuring out which combination of food item and metals will produce the highest voltage and current. Groups will test either lemons or potatoes with different combinations of metal electrodes. All possible combinations should be tested, no materials other than those listed may be used, and groups must complete their work within the available time frame. Groups will combine their data to determine which design performs best.

POSSIBLE MATERIALS

- indirectly vented chemical splash goggles, nonlatex apron, nonlatex gloves
- aluminum foil
- copper strip, 1 mm × 1 cm × 5 cm
- copper wire
- LED bulb
- lemon
- magnesium strip, 1 mm × 1 cm × 5 cm
- multimeter
- potato
- scalpel
- zinc strip, 1 mm × 1 cm × 5 cm

SAFETY INFORMATION

- Wear indirectly vented chemical splash goggles, a nonlatex apron, and nonlatex gloves during the setup, hands-on, and takedown segments of the activity.
- Never taste any substance or chemical in the lab.
- Use caution when using sharp tools, which can cut or puncture skin.
- Wash your hands with soap and water immediately after completing this activity.

indirectly vented chemical splash goggles

DEFINE THE PROBLEM

How will you determine which design is best? List at least three criteria and two constraints for the battery system design. Rank the criteria from most to least important.

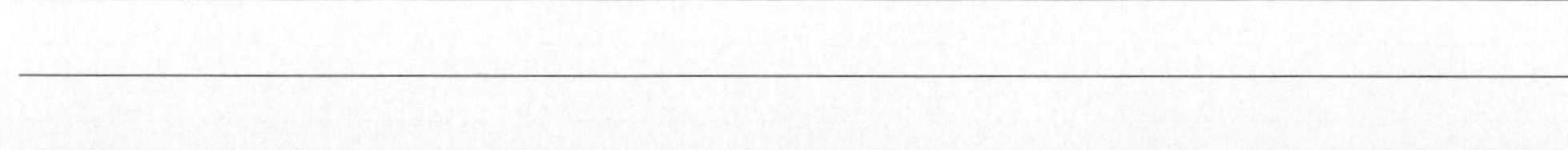

DESIGN SOLUTIONS

1. With your group, write a procedure in your Evidence Notebook to safely determine which combination of materials best meets the criteria and constraints for the design. As you plan the procedure, consider the following questions:
   - How will you conduct tests on each combination?
   - What variables will you measure in each test?
   - What will your control be?
   - How can you divide the work in your group so that it is completed within the allotted time frame?
2. Make a data table in your Evidence Notebook in which to record your measurements.
3. Make sure your teacher approves your procedure and safety plan before proceeding. If necessary, adjust your plans based on your teacher's suggestions.

TEST

1. Obtain your materials and set up any equipment you will need. Take appropriate safety precautions.
2. Perform your tests and record your measurements.
3. Organize the data into tables and graphs. Make sure the tables and graphs are logically constructed and clearly labeled.
4. Compare each design's performance to the criteria you listed and choose the one that best meets the criteria.
5. Make a labeled diagram of the best design, including any measurements and the flow of electric current.
6. Clean all equipment and your lab station. Return equipment to its proper place. Follow your teacher's instructions for discarding materials. Wash your hands thoroughly after all work is finished and before you leave the lab.

ANALYZE

1. Which combination of materials performed best, and which performed the worst? Do you notice any patterns in your data? Explain.

2. Combine all the data gathered by the class into a table. Which system had the highest voltage overall? Which system had the highest current overall? Were any patterns evident in the data? Describe the results.

OPTIMIZE

Answer the following questions in your Evidence Notebook.

1. Based on the data and observations your class made, what changes might you make to increase the maximum current obtained? What changes might you make to increase the maximum voltage?
2. What additional data or research would be helpful if you were to repeat your experiment?

DRAW CONCLUSIONS

Write a conclusion that addresses each of the points below.

Claim Which combination of materials resulted in the best battery?

Evidence Cite evidence from the results of your group and your classmates to support your claim.

Reasoning Explain how the evidence you gave supports your claim. Describe, in detail, the connections between the evidence you cited and the argument you are making.

EXTEND

Imagine you are asked to test which design in this experiment has the longest battery life, but you have only one sample of each food with which to conduct your test. In your Evidence Notebook, describe how you would approach the problem.

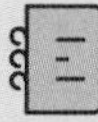

Evidence Notebook Think about the diagram you made for your battery investigation. Were the scale and type of model useful for your investigation? Why or why not? How can your answer help you construct your models of the effect of carbon dioxide on marine shell degradation?

Case Study: Optimizing an Industrial Reaction

Nitrogen compounds are an essential part of fertilizer for agriculture because nitrogen atoms are a key component of plant DNA, proteins, and chlorophyll molecules. Nitrogen is abundant in the atmosphere in the form of nitrogen gas, N_2, but few organisms are able to metabolize it in this form. Nitrogen fixation, the conversion of atmospheric nitrogen into a form that is usable for plants, is therefore crucial for agriculture and plant health.

In the early 1900s, scientists and engineers began looking for ways to fix nitrogen industrially. One process used an electric arc to convert atmospheric nitrogen into nitric oxide. Because of the large amount of electrical energy needed for this process, it was abandoned in favor of a second process. This second method used calcium carbide, CaC_2, which reacts with N_2 at 1000 °C to form calcium cyanamide, $CaCN_2$, and carbon. But this process also required high inputs of electrical energy to produce calcium carbide.

PREDICT Which criteria or constraints would a new nitrogen-fixation process have to meet in order to be considered an improvement over the two methods discussed above? Select all correct answers.

☐ **a.** a higher amount of product per unit of energy put into the system

☐ **b.** a process that uses lower reaction temperature

☐ **c.** a process that does not cause air pollution

☐ **d.** a process that uses more electrical energy

Harnessing an Equilibrium Reaction

Around 1905, German chemist Fritz Haber began work on a nitrogen-fixation method based on the equilibrium reaction between atmospheric nitrogen and hydrogen:

$$N_2(g) + 3H_2(g) \rightleftharpoons 2NH_3(g)$$

Under normal conditions, this reaction proceeds so slowly that the amount of ammonia it produces is too small to be useful in agriculture. Haber needed to refine the process to maximize the amount of ammonia produced.

FIGURE 4: Chemical plants worldwide produce over 140 million metric tons of ammonia per year.

ANALYZE What stresses could engineers apply to increase the amount of ammonia obtained from this equilibrium reaction?

The mechanism of a reaction can also be altered by adding a *catalyst*, a substance that changes the rate of the reaction without being consumed or changed significantly. The addition of a catalyst speeds up the overall rate of a reaction for both the forward and the reverse reactions in an equilibrium system.

MODEL Draw two additional lines showing how the equilibrium reaction will proceed when a more efficient catalyst is present.

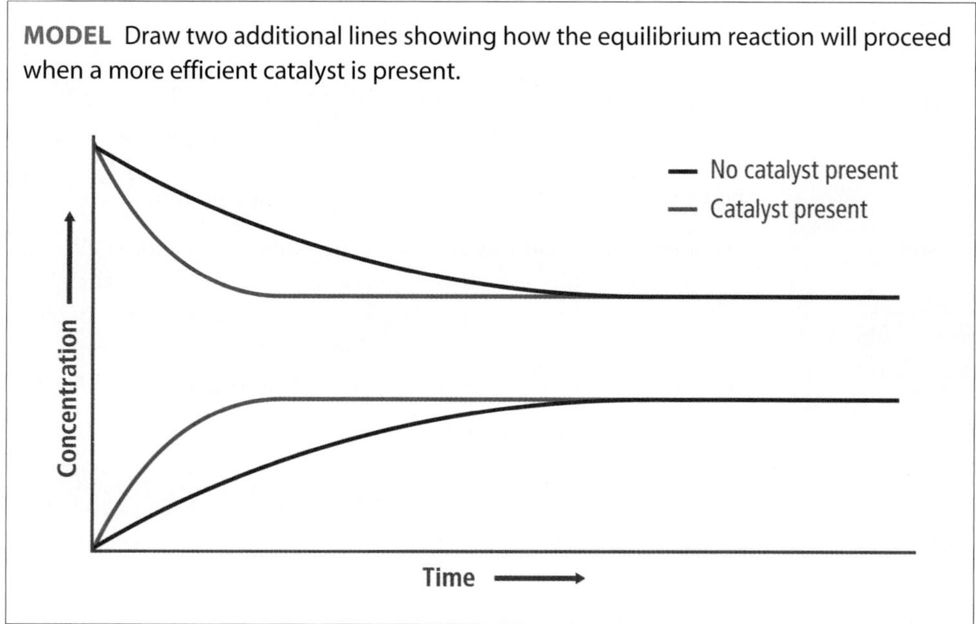

Haber developed a method to produce ammonia from nitrogen and hydrogen using a combination of high temperature, high pressure, and a catalyst. In 1909, another German chemist named Carl Bosch began developing a way to use Haber's method to produce ammonia at an industrial scale. By 1929, the Haber-Bosch process had become the world's main source of nitrogen for synthetic fertilizers.

Explore Online

YOU SOLVE IT

How Can You Increase Ammonia Production?

Adjust reaction conditions to increase the amount of ammonia produced.

Collaborate With a partner, find a simulation that will allow you to test the effects of temperature and the presence of a catalyst on a chemical equilibrium system. Make a claim about how you can change the conditions of the system to produce more product at equilibrium. Run several tests with the simulation and collect data that either support or refute your claim.

EXPLAIN Removal of ammonia from the system as the reaction proceeds is another important component of the Haber-Bosch process. How does removing ammonia affect the equilibrium reaction?

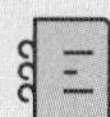

Evidence Notebook In your unit project, you are investigating the Solvay process. Similarly to the Haber-Bosch process, the Solvay process involves manipulating the inputs and outputs of an equilibrium reaction to maximize the amount of product obtained. How is equilibrium controlled in the Haber-Bosch process? How is it controlled in the Solvay process?

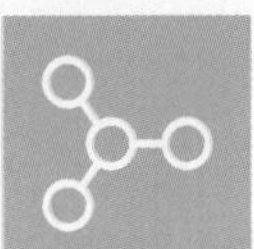

Influence of Engineering, Technology, and Science on the Natural World

The Green Revolution

FIGURE 5: Ammonia is used to make fertilizer for crops.

Beginning around 1945, many areas of the world saw rapid increases in agricultural production. Developing countries such as Mexico, India, and Pakistan underwent massive increases in farm productivity and land use in what is now called the Green Revolution.

The Green Revolution was due to the development of high-yield crop varieties, improved pesticides, and a large increase in the availability of nitrogen fertilizers, driven in large part by the Haber-Bosch process. Figure 6 shows the changes in world population and the changes in the amount of fertilizer used (in kilograms of nitrogen per hectare per year) in the latter half of the 20th century.

Impacts of the Haber-Bosch Process on Population and Fertilizer Use

FIGURE 6: These graphs show world population and estimated population growth without the influence of the Haber-Bosch process (left), and use of nitrogen fertilizers since 1900 (right).

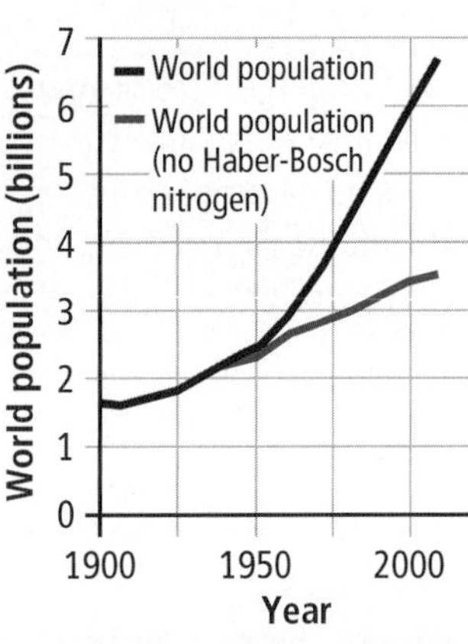

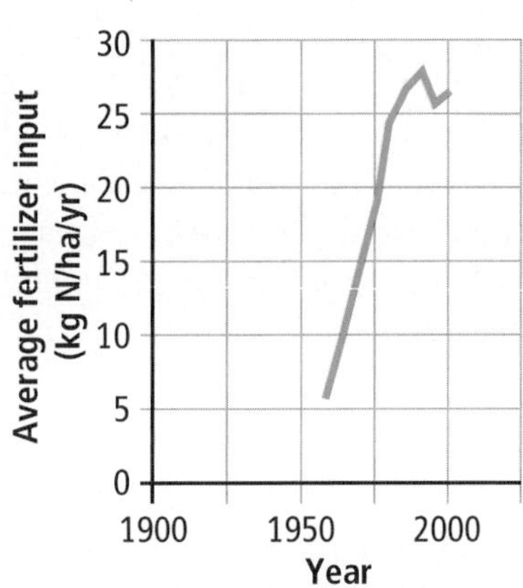

Credit: Adapted from "How a century of ammonia synthesis changed the world" by Jan Willem Erisman et al., from *Nature Geoscience*, September 28, 2008. Copyright © 2008 by Springer Nature. Used with permission of Copyright Clearance Center.

ANALYZE What conclusion can you draw from Figure 6 about the relationship between nitrogen fertilizer use and population growth?

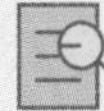

Language Arts Connection Fritz Haber received a Nobel Prize in Chemistry for his work on the Haber-Bosch process. The award was controversial because of Haber's role in the development of chemical weapons in World War I. Using multiple sources, including scientific texts, develop an argument for or against awarding the Nobel Prize in Chemistry to Haber. Write a letter to the prize committee explaining your position. Support your argument with data from your research and include a list of sources.

New technologies, such as the Haber-Bosch process, involve tradeoffs. Societies need to weigh the immediate benefits against longer-term ecological and economic costs. For example, the increased use of fertilizer as a result of the Haber-Bosch process led to increased chemical runoff from farms. Excess nitrogen in oceans leads to overgrowth of algae, which leads to oxygen depletion as the algae die and decompose. Figure 7 shows how runoff from farms along the Mississippi River watershed affects the Gulf of Mexico.

Effects of Industrial Fertilizer Use on the Environment

FIGURE 7: The Gulf of Mexico dead zone is an area of about 15 000 square kilometers that is polluted by agricultural runoff. The concentration of oxygen in this area is too low for many fish and marine species to survive there.

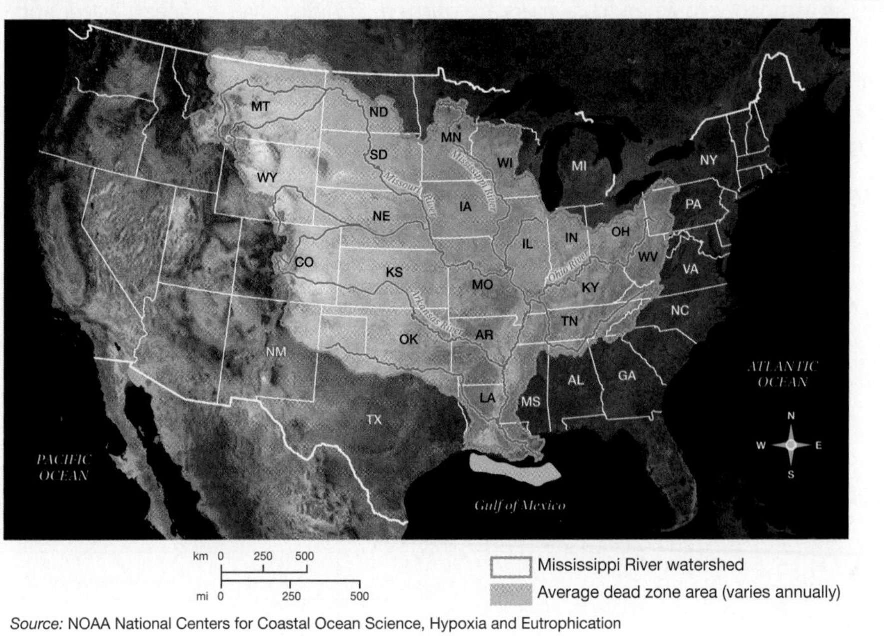

Source: NOAA National Centers for Coastal Ocean Science, Hypoxia and Eutrophication

ARGUE Do you think the development of industrial fertilizers was an overall positive or negative development? Use evidence from the text to support your argument.

Predicting the impacts of new technologies is difficult, which is one reason the engineering design process includes iterative steps of evaluating and refining solutions. Problems caused by the new technology may be corrected, or other solutions may be developed.

Collaborate Work with a partner to think of potential solutions to fertilizer pollution in water systems. List and prioritize criteria and constraints, brainstorm solutions, and choose which ideas seem most likely to meet the criteria and constraints.

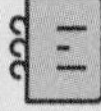

Evidence Notebook You have seen several ways to model an equilibrium reaction and the effects of that reaction on the Earth system. What types of graphs or other models could you use to model the series of equilibrium reactions that affect shell degradation? What additional information would you need to develop these models?

Hands-On Lab

Exploring the Effects of Carbon Dioxide and pH

The production of industrial fertilizer addressed an important need by helping to boost agricultural production, but its use had unanticipated impacts on the health of aquatic ecosystems. In this lab, you will investigate potential impacts of another technological solution—the burning of fossil fuels to obtain energy. Carbon dioxide, CO_2, is released into the atmosphere when fossil fuels are burned. CO_2 dissolves in ocean water and is part of a system of equilibrium reactions that take place in the ocean. At the macroscopic level, this system appears stable, but the forward and reverse reactions taking place occur constantly and adjust in response when stress, such as an increased input, is added. In this investigation, you will model two parts of this process at the macroscopic scale.

RESEARCH QUESTION What is the relationship between carbon dioxide in water and the integrity of marine animals' shells?

MAKE A CLAIM

Why do you think structures made of calcium carbonate, $CaCO_3$, deteriorate with increased levels of atmospheric carbon dioxide? What is the role of pH?

Part I: Modeling the Effects of Carbon Dioxide on Water pH

As cells oxidize glucose to release energy, they produce carbon dioxide, which is removed from the body mainly through the circulatory and respiratory systems. So, when you breathe out, you emit carbon dioxide. In Part I of this investigation, you will use your breath and a pH indicator called bromothymol blue to investigate the relationship between carbon dioxide and the pH of water. Bromothymol blue looks blue at pH values higher than 7. When the pH is acidic, the color changes.

MATERIALS

- indirectly vented chemical splash goggles, nonlatex apron, nitrile gloves
- beaker, 200 mL
- bromothymol blue indicator solution (100 mL)
- drinking straw

indirectly vented chemical splash goggles

SAFETY INFORMATION

- Wear indirectly vented chemical splash goggles, a nonlatex apron, and nitrile gloves during the setup, hands-on, and takedown segments of the activity.
- Only exhale through the straw in this investigation. Do not inhale or ingest the bromothymol blue solution. Do not share your straw with anyone else.
- Wash your hands with soap and water when you are finished handling chemicals.

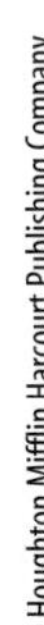

CARRY OUT THE INVESTIGATION

1. Pour 50 mL of indicator solution into a beaker. Observe and record the color of the indicator in your Evidence Notebook.
2. Place the end of the straw in the indicator solution and start a timer. Exhale gently through the straw for 8–10 seconds. You should see bubbles. Observe and record the color of the solution as you exhale, and the time it took for the color to change.
3. After the color has changed, stop exhaling into the solution.
4. If you have time, exercise in place for 1 minute, then repeat steps 1–3.

ANALYZE

Answer the following questions in your Evidence Notebook.

1. What did you observe when you exhaled into the water? What do your results tell you about the relationship between carbon dioxide and water pH?

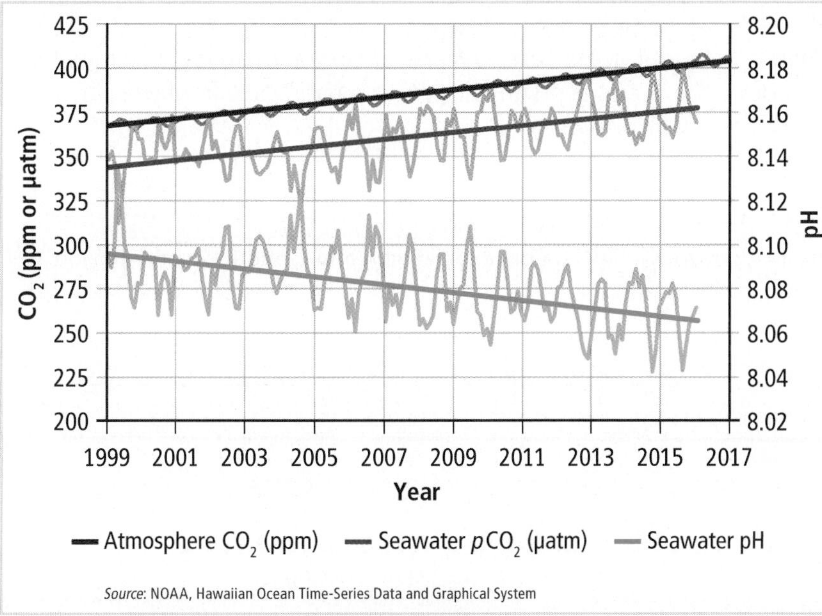

Carbon Dioxide and pH

FIGURE 8: Data collected between 1999 and 2017 show a correlation between carbon dioxide concentrations in the atmosphere and the pH of ocean water.

2. Based on your results, how would the graph in Figure 8 look if carbon dioxide concentrations in the atmosphere began to decrease? Explain your answer using evidence from the investigation.

Part II: Modeling the Effects of pH Changes

In Part II, you will model how the pH of water affects structures made of calcium carbonate, such as chalk and seashells. Because this change is relatively slow, you will use vinegar, which is much more acidic than seawater.

POSSIBLE MATERIALS

- indirectly vented chemical splash goggles, nonlatex apron, nitrile gloves
- beaker, 250 mL (2)
- chalk
- distilled vinegar
- hand lens
- pH indicator or probe
- seashells
- water

indirectly vented chemical splash goggles

SAFETY INFORMATION

- Wear indirectly vented chemical splash goggles, a nonlatex apron, and nitrile gloves during the setup, hands-on, and takedown segments of the activity.
- Immediately wipe up spilled water on the floor so it does not become a slip/fall hazard.

PLAN THE INVESTIGATION

Design your own investigation that safely models the effects of pH change on the shells of marine organisms. Think about what would indicate a change in calcium carbonate. In your Evidence Notebook, write a procedure, develop a data collection plan, write a safety plan, and list the materials you will need. Identify your control, variables, and how you will measure change in your investigation. Make sure your teacher approves your procedure and safety plan before proceeding. Once you have approval, carry out the investigation.

ANALYZE

In your Evidence Notebook, summarize your results. Do you think your investigation accurately modeled the effects of pH on calcium carbonate? Explain why or why not, citing evidence from your investigation.

CONSTRUCT AN EXPLANATION

Using evidence from your investigation, explain how atmospheric carbon dioxide, pH, and calcium carbonate are related.

DRAW CONCLUSIONS

Write a conclusion that addresses each of the points below.

Claim Make a claim explaining why the calcium carbonate shells and skeletons of marine organisms deteriorate with increased levels of atmospheric carbon dioxide.

Evidence Use evidence from the two parts of this investigation to support your claim.

Reasoning Describe how the evidence you gave supports your claim.

Evidence Notebook What data from this lab would be helpful in constructing your models of how atmospheric carbon dioxide is related to marine organisms' shells?

Case Study: Ocean Acidification

Since the Industrial Revolution, the increase in the release of sequestered carbon by burning fossil fuels has changed the equilibrium between carbon dioxide in the atmosphere and carbon dioxide in the ocean, as shown in Figure 9. This change in equilibrium results in an increase in H^+ ions, which corresponds to a decrease in pH, in the world's oceans. This decrease in pH is known as ocean acidification.

Ocean systems cover approximately 71% of Earth's surface and are Earth's single largest reservoir for human-generated carbon dioxide. When carbon dioxide dissolves, it reacts with water to form carbonic acid, H_2CO_3, which ionizes to form hydrogen, H^+, and bicarbonate, HCO_3^-, ions, as shown in the equilibrium equation:

$$CO_2 + H_2O \rightleftharpoons H_2CO_3 \rightleftharpoons H^+ + HCO_3^-$$

Bicarbonate ions then ionize to form hydrogen and carbonate ions:

$$HCO_3^- \rightleftharpoons H^+ + CO_3^{2-}$$

EXPLAIN Recall that when a stress is applied to an equilibrium reaction, the rate of the reaction shifts. What shift would you expect to see in the above equilibrium reactions if carbon dioxide concentration increases? What would you expect if it decreases?

FIGURE 9: The equilibrium system of carbon dioxide, water, carbonic acid, bicarbonate ions, hydrogen ions, and carbonate ions is affected by changes in the concentration of atmospheric carbon dioxide.

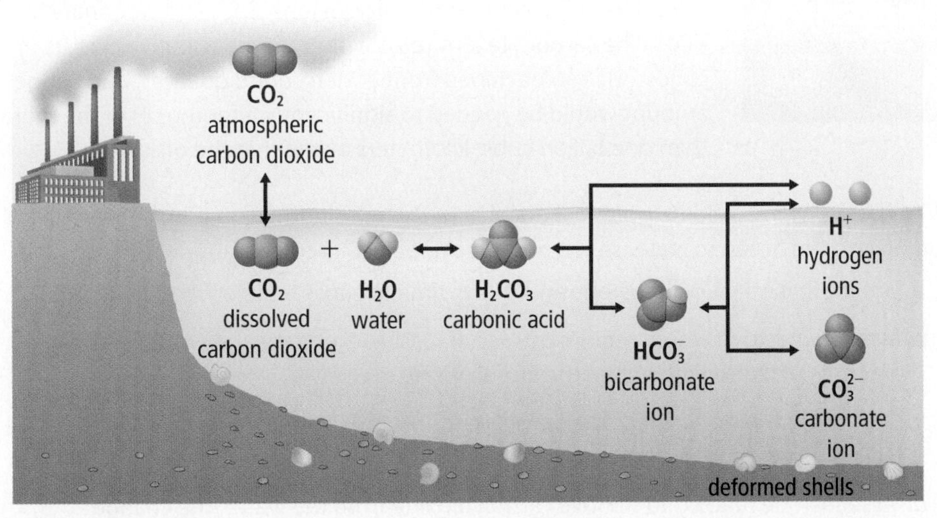

When the CO_2 concentration increases, the first equilibrium reaction shifts in favor of producing more H^+. These these additional H^+ ions shift the second reaction towards producing more bicarbonate ions. This means there are fewer carbonate ions in the water for pteropods and other marine organisms to use to build shells.

Mitigating Ocean Acidification

Ocean acidification occurs because of the increase in atmospheric carbon dioxide, primarily released by the burning of fossil fuels. Acidification does not mean that the world's oceans are acidic. Recall that 7 is neutral on the pH scale. Numbers higher than 7 are basic, and numbers lower than 7 are acidic. Until a few hundred years ago, the pH of the oceans was about 8.2. Today the ocean pH is about 8.1, but because the pH scale is logarithmic rather than linear, that 0.1 difference represents a 25% increase in acidity. This change in pH can have devastating effects on aquatic ecosystems by harming populations of shelled organisms.

EXPLAIN What negative impacts might the loss of shelled marine animal populations have on other parts of the marine ecosystems they live in?

____

____

____

FIGURE 10: Kelp can reduce acidification by using carbon dioxide for photosynthesis.

Local Approaches

Solutions to ocean acidification have been proposed on different scales. At the local scale, such as in coastal communities, some proposed solutions rely on technologies. Others rely on organisms, like the kelp shown in Figure 10, that remove carbon dioxide from water and convert it into oxygen and glucose via photosynthesis.

Growing new or reestablishing beds of kelp or eelgrass can have relatively quick, positive effects on ocean acidification and marine ecology. Even though this solution has benefits, it has some limitations, and even risks. Aquatic organisms must be carefully selected to enhance, and not disrupt, the local ecosystems.

Other communities have proposed adding limestone, or calcium carbonate, to ocean water to increase its pH. $CaCO_3$ is a base, and it dissociates in water to form calcium ions, Ca^{2+}, and carbonate ions, CO_3^{2-}. The carbonate ions react with H^+ in the water, raising its pH. Limestone can be mined from underground quarries, but a huge amount would be needed to significantly alter the pH of the more than one billion cubic kilometers of water in the ocean.

EVALUATE What are some potential drawbacks to the solution of mining limestone and adding it to the ocean to increase the ocean's pH? Select all correct answers.

- ☐ **a.** It would take a lot of limestone and a long time to cause a major change in pH.
- ☐ **b.** Mining limestone would require the use of fossil fuel energy and would add large amounts of carbon dioxide to the atmosphere.
- ☐ **c.** The constant movement of the ocean's currents means that chemicals added in one location to change pH would quickly disperse over a very large area.
- ☐ **d.** As limestone reacted to remove carbon dioxide from the water, the change would cause surface water to take in more carbon dioxide from the air.

Evidence Notebook How would the addition of CO_3^{2-} from limestone affect the equilibrium reactions in the system in Figure 9?

Global Considerations

Ocean acidification is a global, system-level problem that involves the interaction of Earth's systems and human activities. Ocean water around the world is affected because it interacts with the atmosphere and circulates. Although local solutions to acidification play an important role in protecting or restoring specific ecosystems, engineers must consider the greater problem of pH in the entire ocean in order to design a truly effective solution.

FIGURE 11: This model shows current oceanic pH levels and predicted pH levels if people reduce or do not reduce atmospheric CO_2 levels.

Explore Online

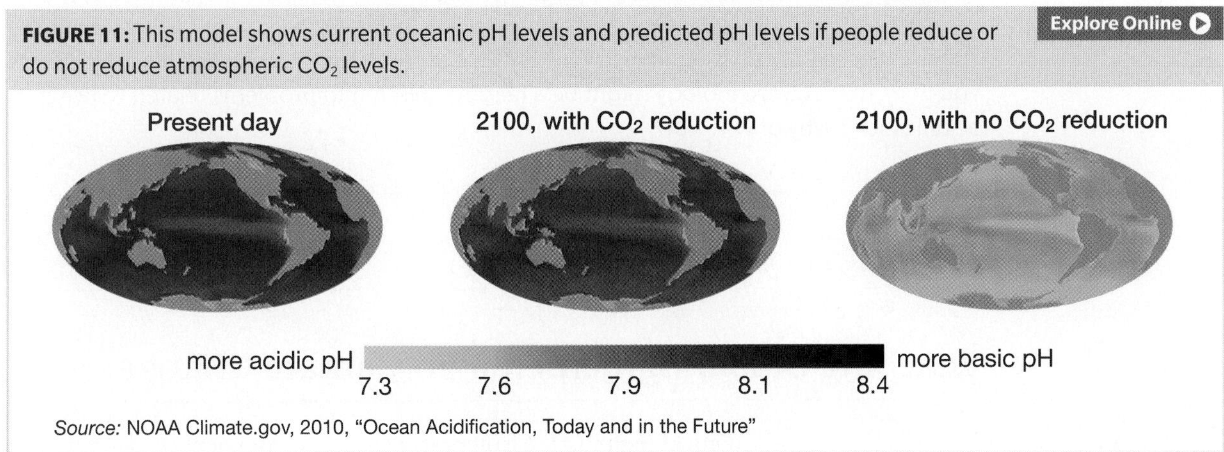

Source: NOAA Climate.gov, 2010, "Ocean Acidification, Today and in the Future"

Scientists use known and expected levels of carbon dioxide in the atmosphere to make computer models that project these changes over time. From these and other data, they can determine the pH levels of the ocean. Figure 11 shows a projection of how pH in the ocean might change if humans reduce carbon dioxide emissions significantly, and if emissions continue at the current rate. Because the pH scale is logarithmic, the third map indicates a change in acidity to a level that is three times the current level.

INFER Based on Figure 11, what are some likely constraints on any global solution to ocean acidification?

____

____

____

Reducing carbon dioxide emissions is an important part of mitigating ocean acidification. Societies can greatly reduce carbon dioxide production by conserving energy and relying more on alternative energies such as wind, solar, and geothermal energy. Even so, we will continue to use some fossil fuels for many years. Thus, one method engineers have developed to lower carbon dioxide emissions is through carbon capture and storage (CCS). In this process, carbon dioxide emitted during fossil fuel combustion is captured and moved through a pipeline into rock several kilometers below the ground.

Good locations for carbon dioxide storage include oil and gas fields, where underground pipes already exist; saline formations, where the gas can be absorbed by saltwater; and porous rock formations, such as basalt. Basalt is volcanic rock that includes a number of different minerals. Over time, the carbon dioxide reacts with other molecules in the basalt, forming calcite, dolomite, and other materials. These reactions keep carbon "stored" underground and out of the atmosphere. However, they have only been tested on relatively small scales and short time frames. We do not yet know the long-term economic and ecological costs and benefits of geoengineering solutions such as this one.

CCS is one potentially effective way to keep carbon dioxide from being emitted into the atmosphere, and it is already in use in a small number of power plants. There are, however, disadvantages to using CCS. Carbon dioxide is just one of the harmful products of combustion of fossil fuels. Sulfur and nitrogen oxides, heavy metals, and other contaminants are also released into the environment. CCS can be very expensive, which limits its application. Another concern is that carbon dioxide stored underground might cause earthquakes, releasing the stored carbon dioxide.

ARGUE Based on your list of constraints on a global solution to ocean acidification, do you think that CCS technology might be a feasible solution to problems related to ocean acidification? Why or why not?

Reaching Global Agreements on Climate Change

FIGURE 12: Involved citizens can urge governments to find solutions.

One of the most difficult parts of addressing global challenges, such as climate change or ocean acidification, is reconciling the interests, resources, and cultural values of different countries. Solutions to these problems require nations to work together.

The Kyoto Protocol is an international agreement that sets internationally binding emission reduction targets. During the first commitment period, 2008–2012, a total of 37 countries and what was then called the European Community committed to reduce greenhouse gas emissions by an average of 5% compared to 1990 levels. During the second period, 2013–2020, parties committed to reduce emissions to at least 18% below 1990 levels. The Protocol established a credit trading system that allows countries that exceed these goals to sell credits to countries that do not. The Kyoto Protocol is seen as an important first step towards emission reduction. However, some of the countries responsible for the most greenhouse gas emissions, including the United States, have not agreed to the treaty.

The Paris Agreement is another example of an international agreement that aims to reduce greenhouse gas emissions as a way of strengthening the global response to climate change. The central aim of the treaty is to limit the amount of greenhouse gases emitted by human activity to levels that trees, soil, and oceans can absorb, beginning at some point between 2050 and 2100. The agreement went into effect in 2016. By 2019, 184 parties had ratified the agreement.

Language Arts Connection Research the Kyoto Protocol and the Paris Agreement. Prepare a report that explains what they are trying to do, and how countries are trying to achieve the goals. How are countries held accountable and how are emission levels monitored? What is the history of the participation of the United States in these treaties?

Evidence Notebook As you have seen, ocean acidification is a global problem that stems from atomic-level interactions. Now that you have learned more about the process at the macroscopic and atomic scales, define the system boundaries, inputs, outputs, and scale you will use for each model.

Careers in Science

Environmental Chemist

Human activities and resource use are causing changes in Earth's systems. Environmental chemists study the causes and effects of these changes at both the molecular and societal scales, and recommend solutions when those changes are detrimental. They study the effects of human pollution on systems as small as the area around a manufacturing plant and as large as the atmosphere and oceans. Environmental chemists work with other scientists and engineers to identify and solve environmental problems.

FIGURE 13: Environmental chemists help clean up oil spills.

Environmental chemists study the impact of pollution on plants, animals, and ecosystems. They are often called upon during environmental emergencies to test water, air, or soil samples and determine the extent of the damage. This information helps contain emergencies such as a ship leaking oil in the ocean or a spill of industrial or agricultural chemicals. Environmental chemists also help determine the procedure for containing an emergency and neutralizing or minimizing the damage.

Projects involving environmental chemistry extend beyond the response to a single event. Over the last few decades, the air quality in many large cities in the United States has improved significantly. An understanding of the chemistry of the atmosphere and of the interactions between the atmosphere and contaminants from burning fossil fuels led to many laws and technologies that reduced pollution. Environmental chemists played a large role in developing that understanding.

Chemists play a key role in marine environmental studies as well. The complex chemical interactions within and between the atmosphere and the hydrosphere are only partially understood, and there is still much more to learn. Environmental chemists work to understand the natural processes within these environmental systems and they try to determine how to mitigate the effect of human activities on Earth's systems.

While some environmental chemists may spend a lot of time in the field or at sea collecting samples, they also work in laboratories analyzing data and drawing conclusions from their findings. For a given project, problem, or even large-scale environmental disaster, environmental chemists use a scientific approach to find an explanation.

Environmental chemistry focuses not only on responding to existing environmental pollution, but also on preventing future problems. Environmental chemists seek to develop sustainable methods to reduce, reuse, and recycle matter, conserve energy, and reduce pollution by aligning human-engineered systems with natural systems.

Chemistry in Your Community Research an environmental chemist who studies issues that affect your community. If possible, conduct a personal interview with the chemist. Learn about the chemist's background and what experiences influenced his or her decision to work in environmental chemistry. Make a video or podcast about the chemist and their work.

CARBON RESERVOIRS | USING SHELLS TO TREAT WATER | MEASURING OCEAN pH | Go online to choose one of these other paths.

Lesson Self-Check

CAN YOU EXPLAIN THE PHENOMENON?

FIGURE 14: The shells of some pteropods and other marine organisms deteriorate with increasing atmospheric carbon dioxide levels.

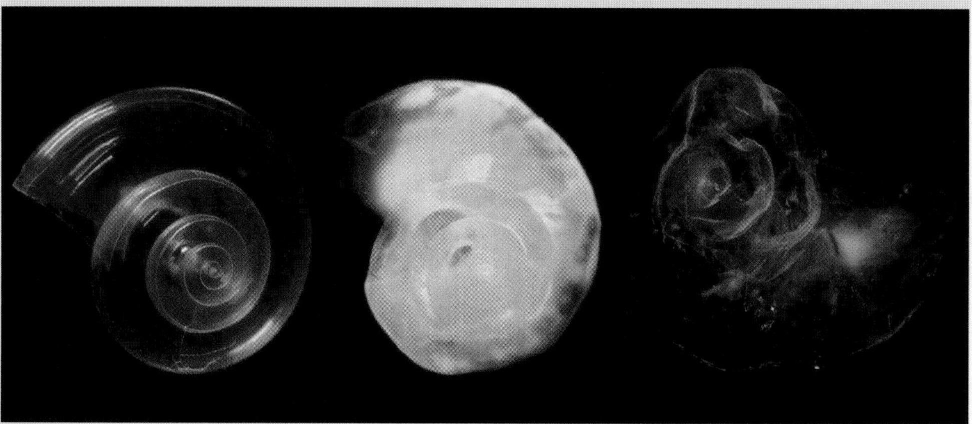

Dramatic changes can occur to marine organisms when they are not able to build or maintain their calcium carbonate shells or skeletons. This phenomenon has been observed in many species of marine organisms around the world. The deterioration of shells has increased dramatically as the concentration of carbon dioxide in the atmosphere has increased over time, and it appears to be accelerating.

There is a strong correlation between the increase in atmospheric carbon dioxide and the damage to coral colonies. Coral reefs are made from thin layers of calcium carbonate, and scientists have established that there is a clear cause-and-effect relationship between the human production of carbon dioxide and the decline of coral reefs around the world. When carbon dioxide levels increase, marine organisms are not able to add to their carbonate shells. These organisms are also losing the carbonate ions that are in their shells, causing the deterioration shown in Figure 14. Such changes have effects that ripple through entire ocean ecosystems.

Evidence Notebook Refer to the notes in your Evidence Notebook to help you explain the link between carbon dioxide emissions and shell degradation and model the process at the atomic scale and at the macroscopic scale. Be sure to address the following points:

Claim How do your models show the relationship between carbon dioxide in the atmosphere and marine organism shell degradation?

Evidence What evidence supports this claim?

Reasoning How does this evidence support your claim?

Name Date

CHECKPOINTS

Check Your Understanding

1. Why does adding a catalyst to an equilibrium system not change the concentration of reactants or products? Select all correct answers.

- ☐ **a.** The forward and reverse reaction rates stay the same.
- ☐ **b.** The forward reaction rate increases.
- ☐ **c.** The reverse reaction rate increases.
- ☐ **d.** The forward reaction rate decreases.
- ☐ **e.** The reverse reaction rate decreases.

2. Which factors made the Haber-Bosch process a good solution for producing synthetic nitrogen fertilizers more efficiently than previous methods? Select all correct answers.

- ☐ **a.** the use of a catalyst
- ☐ **b.** the use of high pressure
- ☐ **c.** the use of electrical energy
- ☐ **d.** the use of an equilibrium reaction

3. Adding limestone to ocean water has been proposed as a solution to ocean acidification. Which constraint below is not met by this solution?

- ○ **a.** The solution should be safe.
- ○ **b.** The solution should have global effects.
- ○ **c.** The solution should have local effects.

4. What are some possible outcomes of ongoing ocean acidification? Select all correct answers.

- ☐ **a.** decreases in coral or pteropod populations
- ☐ **b.** increase in ocean pH
- ☐ **c.** changes in coral reef ecosystems
- ☐ **d.** loss of carbon dioxide from the atmosphere

5. Why is the development of a battery system essential for the effective use of wind power?

- ○ **a.** Windmills require batteries to turn them.
- ○ **b.** Batteries supply power for transporting electricity from one place to another.
- ○ **c.** Batteries store excess power for use when the wind does not blow.

6. The reaction between hemoglobin, Hb, and oxygen, O_2, in red blood cells is responsible for transporting O_2 to body tissues. This process can be represented by the equilibrium reaction

$$Hb(aq) + O_2(g) \rightleftharpoons HbO_2(aq)$$

Many people experience shortness of breath at high altitudes, where the pressure of O_2 is lower than it is at sea level. What would help increase a person's blood oxygen levels at high altitudes?

- ○ **a.** increasing the concentration of O_2 in the air the person inhales
- ○ **b.** increasing the person's blood pressure
- ○ **c.** removing CO_2 from the air the person exhales

7. Match each step in designing a battery to the corresponding step in the engineering design process.

Step in designing a battery	Engineering design step
evaluating battery designs against established criteria	optimizing
listing the features of a successful design	modeling
adjusting design based on test results	defining the problem
making a sketch that shows the flow of current in the design	testing

8. Reducing carbon emissions could help mitigate ocean acidification. What are some possible barriers to implementing such a solution? Select all correct answers.

- ☐ **a.** Governments may be reluctant to spend money on a solution if other countries do not also agree to do so.
- ☐ **b.** Scientists and engineers do not know how carbon emissions affect oceans.
- ☐ **c.** Updating facilities to reduce carbon emissions could be costly.
- ☐ **d.** Employees of fossil-fuel companies might fear that they will lose their jobs.

CHECKPOINTS (continued)

9. What are the strengths and weaknesses of current approaches to using industrial fertilizer? Give examples to support your answer.

10. An industrial facility uses the equilibrium reaction $A + B \rightleftharpoons C + D$ to produce C, an important chemical in manufacturing processes. The facility wants to increase production of C without increasing energy use or adding to the production time. What would you recommend, and why?

11. What is the chemical basis of the idea to add calcium carbonate to the ocean to reverse ocean acidification? Why is this approach unlikely to solve the issue?

MAKE YOUR OWN STUDY GUIDE

In your Evidence Notebook, design a study guide that supports the main ideas from this lesson:

Scientists and engineers define systems to help study phenomena or solve problems. Chemical systems can be designed or harnessed to meet various needs, including storing electrical energy.

Technologies and innovations, such as the use of fossil fuels for energy and the Haber-Bosch process for nitrogen fixation, can address needs while having unforeseen economic, social, and environmental impacts.

Remember to include the following information in your study guide:

- Use examples that model main ideas.
- Record explanations for the phenomena you investigated.
- Use evidence to support your explanations. Your support can include drawings, data, graphs, laboratory conclusions, and other evidence recorded throughout the lesson.

Consider how the models for equilibrium you developed in this lesson can be used to analyze the stability and change in the systems you modeled.

Life Science Connection

Explore Online

Enzymes An enzyme is a biological catalyst that increases the rate of a chemical reaction. Enzymes are critical for maintaining cellular functions in the body. The enzyme glucose oxidase is used in biosensors to monitor blood glucose levels of people with diabetes. Glucose is a reactant in the reaction catalyzed by glucose oxidase and hydrogen peroxide is a product. Although glucose is difficult to measure, hydrogen peroxide is not. A higher glucose level in the blood causes more hydrogen peroxide to be produced, and the hydrogen peroxide can be measured in biosensors.

Make a multimedia presentation that explains how enzymes work and describe the function of several enzymes in the human body. Integrate and evaluate multiple sources in your presentation.

FIGURE 1: Glucose oxidase is used in biosensors to monitor blood glucose levels.

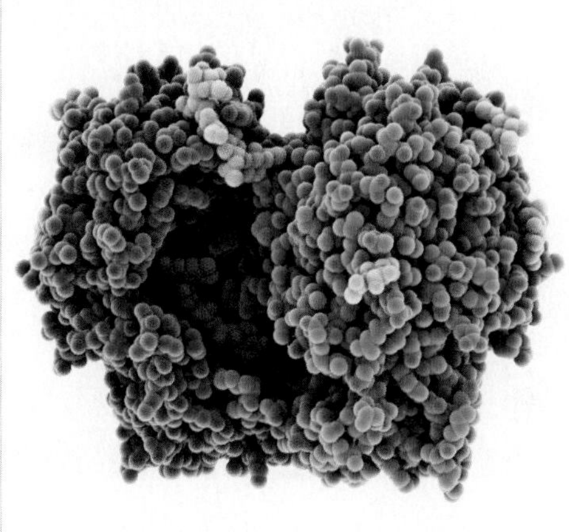

Health Connection

Time Release Pharmacokinetics is the study of interactions between medications and chemicals inside the human body. Understanding how a medication affects a person is important for determining correct dosages. Given the many differences between individuals, scientists are developing medications that are more individualized. Researchers can decide whether to allow a slow, steady release, or immediate exposure to the full dose.

Write a medical pamphlet that explains why different timed releases are important for medical treatment. Also discuss how differences between individuals can affect how medication interacts with body processes. Cite specific text evidence to support your claim.

FIGURE 2: Pharmacokinetics helps scientists develop medications that interact with the body at different rates.

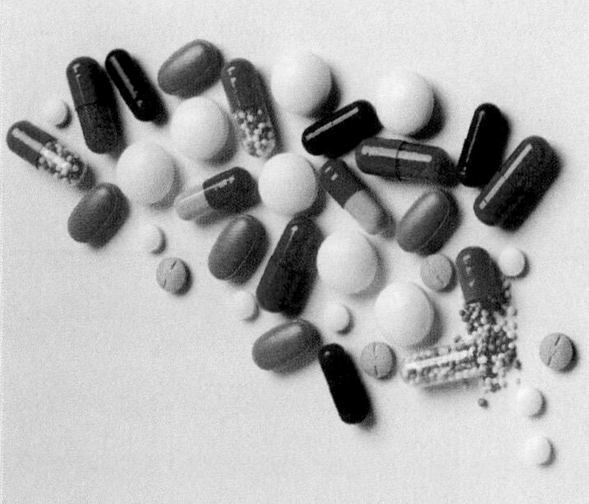

Social Studies Connection

Human Population The human population of an area may change at a predictable rate, or it may be stable for a long time. Many factors can affect this equilibrium state, such as changes in birth or death rates, a large employer moving in or away, or many people moving in or out. These factors may cause shortages or oversupply of some resources. Over time, a new equilibrium is reached.

Build a timeline of the history of your community and label significant events that affected the population. What events caused sudden or long-term changes to its size or makeup? Include text and media comparing the changes to the concept of dynamic chemical equilibrium. How is this a good or poor analogy for chemical equilibrium?

FIGURE 3: Changes in human populations lead to changes in the need for resources.

POWER BOXES

Making power from different metals

You've learned that batteries generate power through electrochemical reactions. Here's a look at their insides.

THE STORY OF HOW POWER BOXES WORK

IT'S HARD TO UNDERSTAND HOW POWER BOXES WORK, BECAUSE THEY'RE FULL OF WATER AND METAL DOING THINGS THAT ARE TOO SMALL TO SEE. IDEAS FROM OUR NORMAL LIVES DON'T REALLY HELP US TO THINK ABOUT WHAT THEY'RE DOING.

TO TRY TO EXPLAIN HOW THEY WORK, WE HAVE TO MAKE UP NEW IDEAS. THESE IDEAS AREN'T REAL—WE CAN'T SEE THE "REAL" THINGS—BUT THE IDEAS CAN EXPLAIN AN IMPORTANT IDEA ABOUT HOW THEY WORK.

A LOT OF LEARNING WE DO WORKS THIS WAY. THE IDEAS ON THIS PAGE ARE PRETTY FAR AWAY FROM "REAL," BUT THEY SHOULD HELP EXPLAIN PART OF HOW POWER BOXES WORK.

IDEAS FOR THINKING ABOUT POWER BOXES

A power box has two sides, one holding a carrier wanter and the other holding a carrier maker. Between them is a wall that lets carriers through. The carrier maker would make carriers that cover the carrier wanter. But eating carriers puts pieces of power in the carrier wanter, and you can't have too many pieces of power together, because they push each other away. This stops the carrier wanter from eating too many carriers.

● **PIECE OF POWER**

◯ **POWER CARRIER**

⦿ **POWER** (in power carrier)

CARRIER MAKER

This metal wants to get rid of carriers. If it gets a piece of power inside it, it will send it away in a carrier made from its surface.

CARRIER WANTER

This metal wants to be covered in carriers. It will grab them if they come near and stick them to its surface, and the power from the carrier will go inside them.

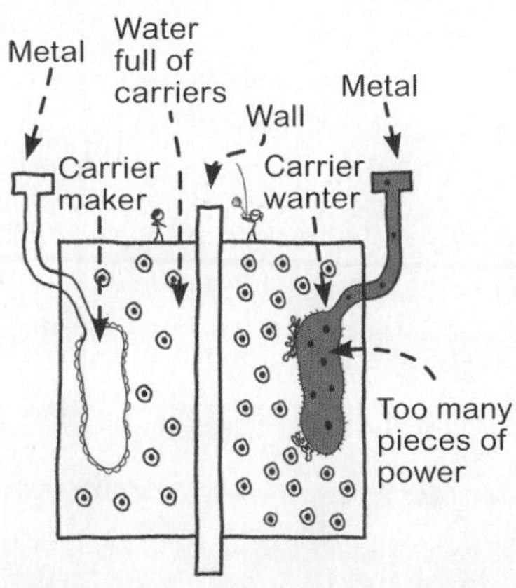
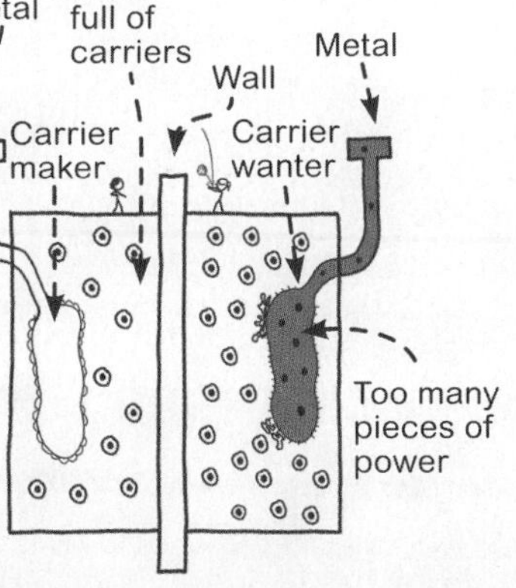

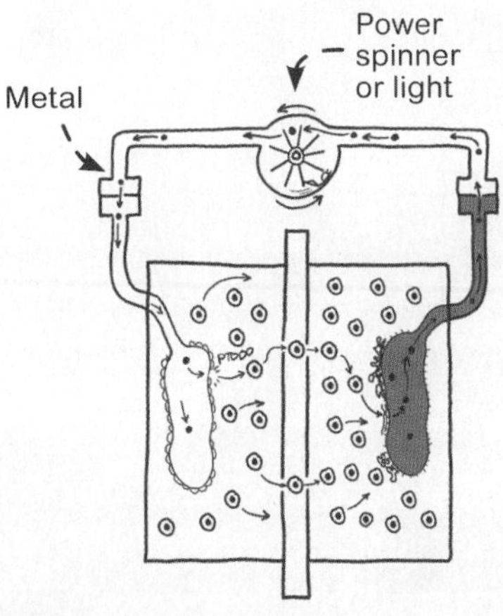

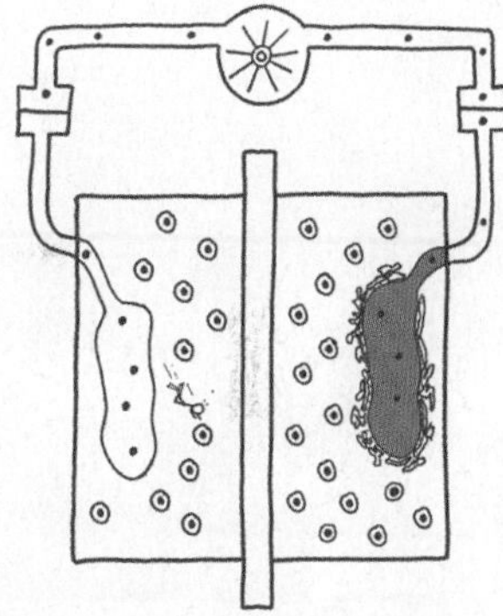

FULL

The two sides of a power box have a wall between them. This wall lets carriers through, but not pieces of power. It also stops the carrier wanter and carrier maker from touching, which would make the carriers all move to the carrier wanter without sending any power anywhere.

Extra pieces of power gather in the carrier wanter, but they can't go anywhere at first.

RUNNING

When you join the two sides with a stick of metal, the pieces of power can get from the carrier wanter to the carrier maker.

If you put a machine in their way—like a light or a power spinner—they can push on it and make it run, just like water pushing on a water wheel.

When the pieces of power get to the carrier maker, it uses them to make new carriers.

EMPTY

After a while, the carrier wanter gets covered in empty carriers, and the carrier maker gets used up. There's nothing left to push the power pieces through the metal path; the power box is dead.

With some power boxes, you can turn the wheel and push power back into the power box. This fills the power box back up.

POWER BOXES

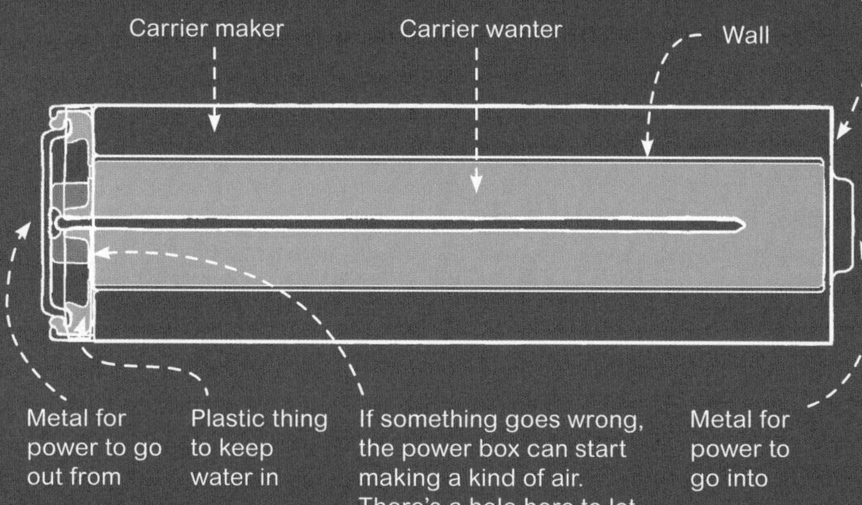

SMALL POWER BOX

This kind of power box is used in a lot of places. It powers hand lights, face hair cutters, and things kids play with.

In this kind of power box, the carrier wanter and carrier maker are made from different kinds of metal. The stuff in between is water with a kind of white stuff in it which lets the carriers move across. If the power box breaks, that stuff can come out. Don't worry, it's safe to clean up; it won't hurt your skin.

All power boxes run out of power after a while. With some kinds, you can put power back in and use them again and again, but you can't really do that with the kind shown here.

YOU CAN DROP THESE TO SEE IF THEY'RE DEAD

The carrier wanter in these boxes is made from metal dust. When it gets covered in carriers, it becomes stronger and sticks together, so the dust can't move around. This makes dead power boxes fly back up when you drop them, but full ones just hit the ground and stop.

CAR POWER BOX

These power boxes are used in cars. They use two kinds of heavy metal as the carrier wanter and the carrier maker, which is why they're so heavy.

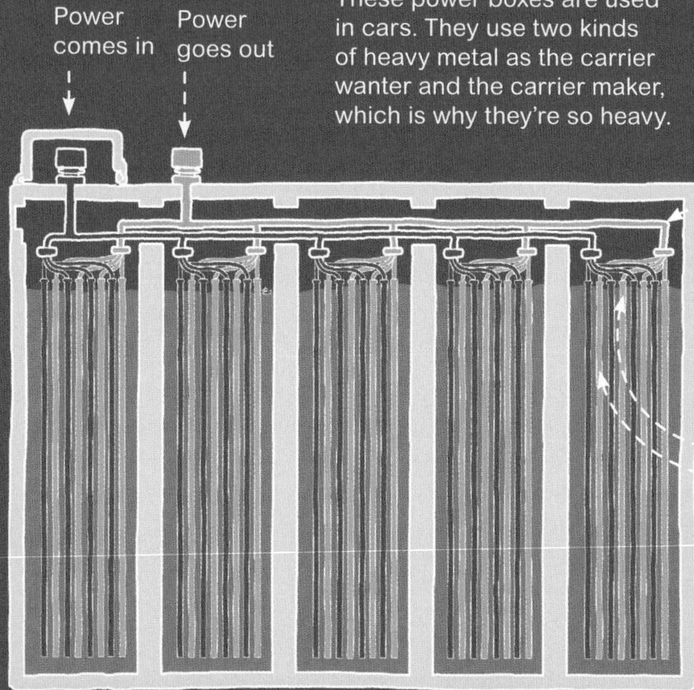

Go online for more about *Thing Explainer.*

HAND COMPUTER POWER BOX

These power boxes hold more power for their size than any other. We first made them to power helper machines in people's chests. Those machines need to hold a lot of power, since people don't like it if you take them out too often.

When we started making lots of hand computers, we got better at making these power boxes, since lots of people wanted their computers to work all day without having to get power from the wall.

Of course, people also wanted their hearts to work, but more people have hand computers than heart boxes.

If you cut one of these open, it would look like this—but never cut these open. They can blow up.

LIGHT METAL

In these power boxes, the carrier wanter and carrier maker are both made of very light metals. To make this kind of carrier maker and wanter work together, they're laid down in sheets almost touching each other, like two long sheets of paper laid flat and then rolled up.

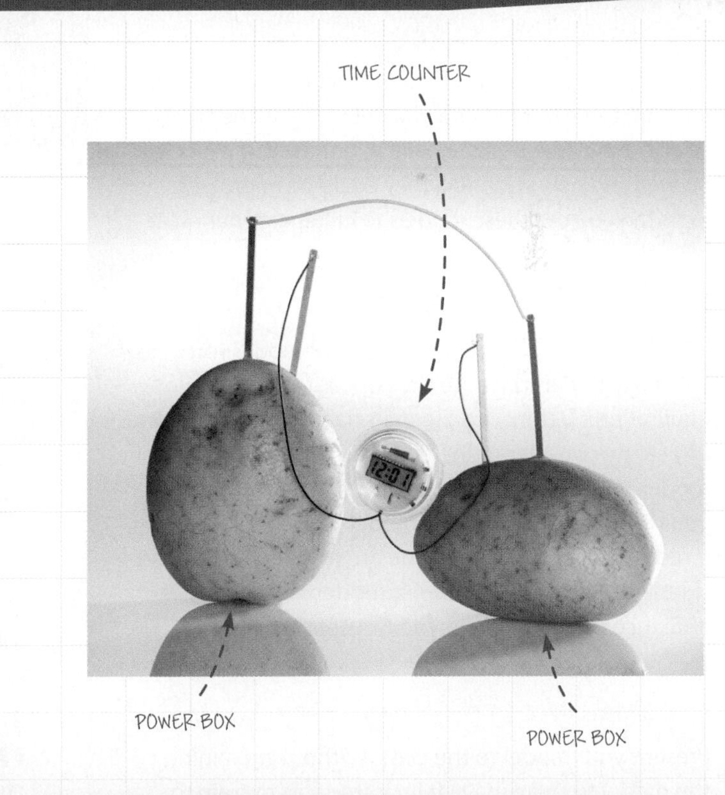

Modeling Chemical Equilibrium

A reaction at equilibrium has not stopped. Reactants are still forming products, and products are still forming reactants, but at a constant rate. Therefore, the relative concentrations of reactants and products do not change once the reaction reaches equilibrium. How could you model this idea for someone who does not understand how concentrations could stay the same, but the reactions still continue? How could you show them that equilibrium is a dynamic system?

FIGURE 4: These students are modeling equilibrium using pompoms.

1. DEFINE THE PROBLEM

Describe what types of information a model needs to demonstrate about an equilibrium system. Could you make a model that demonstrates equilibrium when the concentration of reactants is greater than products, as well as when the concentration of products is greater than reactants?

2. CONDUCT RESEARCH

Research a chemical equilibrium reaction that interests you. Are there models and analogies of this chemical equilibrium system? Note what you think these models do well and how you think they could be improved. How can you use these models to influence your own?

3. DEVELOP A MODEL

With your team, decide on the type of model you will make to demonstrate the concept of chemical equilibrium. Determine the materials you will need and any safety considerations. If you are making a physical model, you should consider how many participants you will need to make your model work and whether it requires a lot of space. If you are making a computer simulation or video animation model, consider audience participation in your presentation.

4. COMMUNICATE

Present your model to the class. Without explaining the model to them, have fellow students explain to you how it is showing the dynamic nature of chemical equilibrium. Have them suggest ways in which the model could be improved to either model your reaction more clearly, or to model the concept of equilibrium more clearly.

Once you have completed this task, you should have the following:

- a clearly defined problem statement with questions that you answer in the presentation
- information on the chemical reaction you chose and typical conditions under which it operates
- a model of the process that shows how a change in the reaction can disrupt the equilibrium and how equilibrium is restored after the change
- a presentation that shows an understanding of the process and how equilibrium is restored
- a list of references cited

Name Date

SYNTHESIZE THE UNIT

In your Evidence Notebook, make a concept map, other graphic organizer, or outline using the Study Guides you made for each lesson in this unit. Be sure to use evidence to support your claims.

When synthesizing individual information, remember to follow these general steps:

- Find the central idea of each piece of information.
- Think about the relationships among the central ideas.
- Combine the ideas to come up with a new understanding.

DRIVING QUESTIONS

Look back to the Driving Questions from the opening section of this unit. In your Evidence Notebook, review and revise your previous answers to those questions. Use the evidence you gathered and other observations you made throughout the unit to support your claims.

PRACTICE AND REVIEW

1. According to collision theory, which variables affect the rate of a chemical reaction? Select all correct answers.

- ☐ **a.** concentration of reactants
- ☐ **b.** temperature of reaction mixture
- ☐ **c.** volume of reaction vessel
- ☐ **d.** chemical structure of the reactants
- ☐ **e.** surface area of a solid reactant

2. Complete the statement about acids and bases.

Acids form aqueous solutions containing excess hydronium | hydroxide ions, and bases form solutions containing excess hydronium | hydroxide ions. A neutral solution has a pH that is equal to 0 | 1 | 7 | 10. When crushed limestone is added to a lake that has become acidic, the limestone causes a decrease | an increase in pH as acid is neutralized.

3. Consider the equilibrium reaction:

$$CO(g) + 3H_2(g) \rightleftharpoons CH_4(g) + H_2O(g) + \text{energy}$$

How will increasing the temperature affect the equilibrium of the reaction?

- ○ **a.** There is more energy available, so the equilibrium shifts toward the products.
- ○ **b.** The rate of collisions increases, so the equilibrium shifts toward the products.
- ○ **c.** There are fewer molecules on the left, so the equilibrium shifts toward the reactants.
- ○ **d.** The rate of the reverse reaction increases, so the equilibrium shifts toward the reactants.

4. Phosphorus pentachloride decomposes into phosphorus trichloride and chlorine. In a closed system, the reaction reaches equilibrium:

$$PCl_5(g) \rightleftharpoons PCl_3(g) + Cl_2(g)$$

Complete the statement about the reaction.

If a sample of pure PCl_5 could be isolated and placed in a closed container, the forward | reverse reaction would begin immediately. Once the system reaches equilibrium, the amount of chlorine gas in the system would remain constant | steadily increase. At equilibrium, the forward and reverse reactions stop completely | continue to occur. In order to produce more PCl_3, the concentration of PCl_5 | Cl_2 could then be increased.

5. An enzyme is a catalyst that is used by an organism to control the reaction rate of biological reactions. Which of these could be a function of an enzyme in a cell? Select all correct answers.

- ☐ **a.** to cause a reaction to occur at a lower temperature than outside the cell
- ☐ **b.** to increase the reaction rate of a reaction that would otherwise be too slow for the cell to function
- ☐ **c.** to shift a reversible reaction in the direction of the products
- ☐ **d.** to reduce the concentration of reactants needed to form a given amount of products

6. Explain how the activation energy and the energy of the activated complex of an endothermic reaction compare to the activation energy and the energy of the activated complex of an exothermic reaction.

7. Explain why there is a danger of explosion in places—such as coal mines, sawmills, and grain elevators—where large amounts of dry, powdered, combustible materials are present.

8. In a reversible reaction, the forward and reverse reactions both occur. Why does the forward reaction in an equilibrium system never go to completion? Explain in terms of reactants and products.

9. In a manufacturing process, the product of the forward reaction is continually removed. A catalyst is added, increasing the rates of both the forward and reverse reaction. How will adding a catalyst affect production during the process?

UNIT PROJECT

Return to your unit project. Prepare a presentation using your research and materials, and share it with the class. In your final presentation, evaluate the strength of your original claim, data, analysis, and conclusions.

Remember these tips while presenting:

- Include a clear statement explaining how equilibrium is controlled in the Solvay process.
- Use graphics or multimedia tools to explain how the Solvay process can be optimized to increase the amount of sodium carbonate produced.
- Include criteria and constraints that drive process decisions about optimizing the amount of product produced.
- Incorporate the concepts of stability and change in your explanation of processes.

The Interactive Glossary for *Chemistry* is provided on *Ed: Your Friend in Learning*.

Index

Page numbers for definitions are printed in **boldface type**.
Page numbers for illustrations, maps, and charts are printed in *italics*.

F

G

H

N

R

S

T

U

V

W

X

Y

6 **C** Carbon 12.01	
6	Atomic number
C	Chemical symbol
Carbon	Element name
12.01	Average atomic mass

Values appearing in parentheses do not represent average atomic mass but instead represent the mass number of that element's most stable or most common isotope.

Period	1	2	3	4	5	6	7	8	9
1	1 **H** Hydrogen 1.008								
2	3 **Li** Lithium 6.94	4 **Be** Beryllium 9.012							
3	11 **Na** Sodium 22.99	12 **Mg** Magnesium 24.31							
4	19 **K** Potassium 39.10	20 **Ca** Calcium 40.08	21 **Sc** Scandium 44.96	22 **Ti** Titanium 47.87	23 **V** Vanadium 50.94	24 **Cr** Chromium 52.00	25 **Mn** Manganese 54.94	26 **Fe** Iron 55.85	27 **Co** Cobalt 58.93
5	37 **Rb** Rubidium 85.47	38 **Sr** Strontium 87.62	39 **Y** Yttrium 88.91	40 **Zr** Zirconium 91.22	41 **Nb** Niobium 92.91	42 **Mo** Molybdenum 95.95	43 **Tc** Technetium (97)	44 **Ru** Ruthenium 101.1	45 **Rh** Rhodium 102.9
6	55 **Cs** Cesium 132.9	56 **Ba** Barium 137.3	57–71	72 **Hf** Hafnium 178.5	73 **Ta** Tantalum 181.0	74 **W** Tungsten 183.8	75 **Re** Rhenium 186.2	76 **Os** Osmium 190.2	77 **Ir** Iridium 192.2
7	87 **Fr** Francium (223)	88 **Ra** Radium (226)	89–103	104 **Rf** Rutherfordium (267)	105 **Db** Dubnium (270)	106 **Sg** Seaborgium (269)	107 **Bh** Bohrium (270)	108 **Hs** Hassium (270)	109 **Mt** Meitnerium (278)

Lanthanide Series	57 **La** Lanthanum 138.91	58 **Ce** Cerium 140.1	59 **Pr** Praseodymium 140.9	60 **Nd** Neodymium 144.2	61 **Pm** Promethium (145)	62 **Sm** Samarium 150.4	63 **Eu** Europium 152.0
Actinide Series	89 **Ac** Actinium (227)	90 **Th** Thorium 232.0	91 **Pa** Protactinium 231.0	92 **U** Uranium 238.0	93 **Np** Neptunium (237)	94 **Pu** Plutonium (244)	95 **Am** Americium (243)

Metals | Metalloids | Nonmetals

State of Element at STP

Solid | Liquid | Gas | Not yet known

10	11	12	13	14	15	16	17	18
								2 **He** Helium 4.003
			5 **B** Boron 10.81	6 **C** Carbon 12.01	7 **N** Nitrogen 14.007	8 **O** Oxygen 15.999	9 **F** Fluorine 19.00	10 **Ne** Neon 20.18
			13 **Al** Aluminum 26.98	14 **Si** Silicon 28.085	15 **P** Phosphorus 30.97	16 **S** Sulfur 32.06	17 **Cl** Chlorine 35.45	18 **Ar** Argon 39.95
28 **Ni** Nickel 58.69	29 **Cu** Copper 63.55	30 **Zn** Zinc 65.38	31 **Ga** Gallium 69.72	32 **Ge** Germanium 72.63	33 **As** Arsenic 74.92	34 **Se** Selenium 79.0	35 **Br** Bromine 79.90	36 **Kr** Krypton 83.80
46 **Pd** Palladium 106.4	47 **Ag** Silver 107.9	48 **Cd** Cadmium 112.4	49 **In** Indium 114.8	50 **Sn** Tin 118.7	51 **Sb** Antimony 121.8	52 **Te** Tellurium 127.6	53 **I** Iodine 126.9	54 **Xe** Xenon 131.3
78 **Pt** Platinum 195.1	79 **Au** Gold 197.0	80 **Hg** Mercury 200.6	81 **Tl** Thallium 204.38	82 **Pb** Lead 207.2	83 **Bi** Bismuth 209.0	84 **Po** Polonium (209)	85 **At** Astatine (210)	86 **Rn** Radon (222)
110 **Ds** Darmstadtium (281)	111 **Rg** Roentgenium (281)	112 **Cn** Copernicium (285)	113 **Nh** Nihonium (286)	114 **Fl** Flerovium (289)	115 **Mc** Moscovium (289)	116 **Lv** Livermorium (293)	117 **Ts** Tennessine (293)	118 **Og** Oganesson (294)

64 **Gd** Gadolinium 157.3	65 **Tb** Terbium 158.9	66 **Dy** Dysprosium 162.5	67 **Ho** Holmium 164.9	68 **Er** Erbium 167.3	69 **Tm** Thulium 168.9	70 **Yb** Ytterbium 173.1	71 **Lu** Lutetium 175.0
96 **Cm** Curium (247)	97 **Bk** Berkelium (247)	98 **Cf** Californium (251)	99 **Es** Einsteinium (252)	100 **Fm** Fermium (257)	101 **Md** Mendelevium (258)	102 **No** Nobelium (259)	103 **Lr** Lawrencium (262)

Elements with atomic numbers of 95 and above are not known to occur naturally, even in trace amounts. They have only been synthesized in the lab. The physical and chemical properties of elements with atomic numbers 100 and above cannot be predicted with certainty.